YACHT INTERIOR

游艇室内设计

高迪国际出版有限公司 编

赵波 段佳燕 田育婧 译

大连理工大学出版社

Dalian University of Technology Press

图书在版编目(CIP)数据

游艇室内设计 / 高迪国际出版有限公司编；赵波，
段佳燕，田育婧译. — 大连：大连理工大学出版社，
2012.5

　ISBN 978-7-5611-6826-4

　Ⅰ. ①游… Ⅱ. ①高… ②赵… ③段… ④田… Ⅲ.
①游艇—室内装饰设计 Ⅳ. ①U674.91

　　中国版本图书馆CIP数据核字（2012）第053689号

出版发行：大连理工大学出版社
　　　　　（地址：大连市软件园路80号　邮编：116023）
印　　刷：利丰雅高印刷（深圳）有限公司
幅面尺寸：240mm×320mm
印　　张：23
插　　页：4
出版时间：2012年5月第1版
印刷时间：2012年5月第1次印刷
责任编辑：刘　蓉
责任校对：李　雪
封面设计：屈舒丽

ISBN 978-7-5611-6826-4
定　　价：348.00元

电　话：0411-84708842
传　真：0411-84701466
邮　购：0411-84703636
E-mail：designbooks_dutp@yahoo.cn
URL：http://www.dutp.cn

如有质量问题请联系出版中心：（0411）84709246　84709043

PREFACE 序言

HOT LAB: YACHT & DESIGN

There is a reason why maybe just 200 studios all over the world are involved in this particular field of the design. It's not architectural, it's not simply interior design and it's not transportation as well, yacht design contains all these areas together. The description "architecture in movement" maybe could explain this "art". There are walls and spaces to plan, crew and guest areas to design with different stairs and ways, functional areas such as convivial too, bedrooms and exterior spaces...

Is not only a matter of beauty and design, a yacht has to be first of all safe and practical. It is important to remember that we're talking of an "object" that is always in the middle of the sea.

The criteria for good design haven't really changed over the years: man-made objects with one or more functions are given an emotionally appealing form.

Talking about "custom interior design" for yachts up to 30m, the designers become also a psychologist (and sometimes best friend) of the final client. Houses do not all look the same, why should yachts?

The interior yacht design has to understand the request of the client, analyze his/her tastes and way of living.

A good yacht design has to collect all these important information, adding his own taste and knowledge to create something unique such as a good tailor does. Each yacht design project is conceived, using a combination of carefully hand-drawn sketches and detailed computer renderings, ensuring, down to the very last detail, that the client's requirements are matched and their dreams fulfilled.

Architect's role has changed during the last decades. He was used to act only on the structural part, while the interior decorator was responsible for the style of all the furnishings. Today these features have blended together and the designer is now the expert of beauty and function.

When we talk about "Architecture in Movement", we refer to one of the most challenging project in the design world. The yacht industry represents the state of the art of this concept because it's the best balance of dynamism and a combination of technics, technologies, and engineering studies, proportions of volumes, architecture, style and materials. The interior designer is one actor of this scene.

In last 10 years, we have assisted to a real revolution in the yacht design, that means not only a new way to think about the living conditions, but also a new interpretation of the hull and the upper structure, more focused on seductive and charming shapes.

This takes its origins from the constant contamination of different fields such as industrial design, transportation and architecture in general. When we look at the exterior of our yacht we can see a car. We live our house when we get in, and it reminds us of the industrial design when we seat on a chair in the main area.

These multiple inputs have a strong impact also regarding the way we can customize a boat. This very fertile environment opens a lot of opportunities which are not only about the style but also about the space itself.

If we want to focus on yacht interiors, we can satisfy the client's requests with new materials (and combination between them), adding correct lights, colors and shapes, create new fashion language like a tailor who designs a unique suit.

But this "just style" way is not the only one to let the client express his/her own personality, there is a second chance for the designer to make it happen: the organization of space.

As Le Corbusier did in the 20ties, defining new types of urban plans in "Contemporary City for three million inhabitants", the interior designer must take in to consideration the position and the separation of spaces.

A yacht could be similar to another from an aesthetic perspective, but what makes the real difference is the experience that the guests can live inside. Playing with the layout of interior spaces the owner can communicate a different message and show his/her own way of being and living the boat. The position of the living space, the master as well as the guest or the crew cabins, the entertainment or the relaxing areas etc. together with the equilibrium between public and private spaces can give a different soul to entire yacht. This is all about the "social dimension" of customized interior design.

ANTONIO ROMANO AND LAURA RIZZO

全世界从事游艇设计这一特殊领域的工作室只有大约200家，这其中是有原因的。游艇设计并不是单纯的建筑行业，不是简单的内部设计，也并非仅仅与交通运输有关，而是囊括了以上所有领域。或许可以用"移动中的建筑"来解释游艇的建造与设计这门"艺术"。具体地讲，设计建造一艘游艇，不仅要计划诸多端壁和空间的分配，又要有区别地设计船员工作区和会客厅的不同通道与楼梯的设计；同时还要考虑各个功能区，比如娱乐区、卧室以及大量外部空间的构造。

游艇建造不仅仅是一个关乎美感和设计的问题，一艘游艇首先应该安全实用。务必牢记至关重要的一点，我们所谈论的，是一个日夜漂浮在海上的"物品"。

多年来，出色的游艇设计标准并没有发生实质性的变化：物件采用纯手工制作，并具备一项或多项功能，同时兼具令人赏心悦目的外观。

从长达30米以上的游艇："定制内部设计"，设计师同时也承担作为终极客户心理咨询师的角色（有时甚至是会成为客户的好朋友）。即使是房屋，其设计也会因主人的不同而各有特色，更何况是个性化的游艇。

游艇内部设计团队一定要了解客户的要求，并做一步分析客户的品位和生活方式。

一个优秀的游艇设计方案一定要收集以上所有重要信息，并能融入设计师自己的品位和知识技能，以创造出与众不同的产品，这个过程正如一位出色的裁缝为顾客量体裁衣一样。每一个游艇设计项目的构想，是一系列工作的综合——精准细致的手工绘图，配合计算机的辅助，对细节的不断修正，直到完成最后一个细节，以做到与客户的要求完全一致，实现他们的理想。

在过去的几十年里，设计师的角色已经发生了改变。以前，设计师只负责建筑结构，室内装修师才负责整体的家居风格。然而现在，这些工作已融合在一起，由设计师全权负责，兼顾设计的美观与功能。

我们所提及的"移动中的建筑"是建筑界中最富有挑战的领域。游艇业代表了这种理念的顶尖水平，因为它达到了动态的最佳平衡，是工艺、科技、工程学、体积比、建筑、风格与材料的完美结合。室内设计师则成了上演这场戏的主角。

在过去的10年里，我们经历了游艇设计的一场革命，我们不仅努力提高游艇的舒适度，而且重新诠释了船体和上层结构，更加注重游艇美丽诱人的外观。

工业设计、交通运输和普通的建筑等多种领域的设计也对游艇设计产生了持续的影响。游艇的外观有时候看上去就像一辆小汽车，走进里面又有了家居的感觉，坐到主厅的椅子上，又容易让我们想到工业设计。

计。

这些多元的影响因素对我们定制船只的方式产生了较大的影响，在风格和空间的设计上，为我们提供了多种选择。

如果我们只是关注游艇的内部设计，我们完全可以像裁缝设计出独特的套装一样，通过使用新材料（和新材料的组合），增加合适的照明灯、选用恰当的色调和外观，创造新的流行风，来满足客户的需求。

但这种"恰当的风格"并不是表达客户个性的唯一选择，设计师还有另外一招：空间的组合。

正如著名建筑设计大师勒·柯布西耶在20世纪20年代所实践的，把新型城市规划定义为"为了300万居民的现代都市"，室内设计师必须考虑各个空间的位置和隔断。

从美学角度看，很多游艇可能看着挺相似的。但是让游艇具有个性的地方在于：客人在游艇内部的生活体验。通过内部空间的不同布局，船主能传递出不同的信息，显示出其与众不同的生活方式。起居空间、船主舱、客舱、船员舱、娱乐区和休闲区的不同位置，以及公共区域和私人区域的互相平衡，都会赋予整个游艇完全不同的性格，这就是定制室内设计的"社会维度"。

安东尼奥·罗马诺和劳拉里佐
HOT LAB 游艇设计公司

CONTENTS 目录

SEA FORCE ONE

>	DESIGN	Luca Dini Design
>	NAVAL ARCHITECT	Admiral Techhnical Department
>	BUILDER	Admiral
>	LENGTH	53.80m
>	BEAM	10.50m
>	MAX SPEED	17kn
>	CRUISING SPEED	14kn
>	PHOTOGRAPHER	Maurizio Paradisi

How many ways are there to arrange and rearrange the 308 bones that make up the human skeleton? When the time came for Captain Magic, the mysterious owner of Sea Force One, the arrange Kiki Smith's perfect replica of the male human skeleton – painted an irreverent gold, of course – he didn't hesitate before making them into the shape of a Jolly Roger, the flag that has been the symbol of the pirate ship since the times of Edward England. And there is a strong whiff of the pirate ship about the 54-metre Admiral launched last year by the Amy yard, itself a joint venture between the Cantieri Navali Lavagna and Cantieri Mariotti.

"I consider that work of art to be the heart of my boat," explained Captain Magic. It's not hard to believe. Even the most cursory of glances reveals that this is no ordinary yacht. The lines are striking. Not only do they beautifully meld a sense of gentleness and aggressiveness, but the hull is black while the superstructure is a military grey. Two balconies are integrated into the sides and are the brainchild of Luca Dini. The balconies slightly roung the imposing lines bringing an unexpected gracefulness to such an aggressive-looking yacht. Some have even gone so far as to describe the result as "sexy". However, Sea Force One is at her most impressive inside rather than out. Her interiors really do toss the whole yacht concept up in the air and reassemble it in quite a fantastic and post-modernist way.

The official entrance is on the starboard side where a positively regal staircase leads to a foyer that leaves no doubt as to what the rest of the vessel holds. The first thing you meet is the transparent Plexigls staircase with its waterfall-effect illuminated stairs which links all three of the yachts' decks. However, the main deck is the owner's private territory and, as a result, it's better to make your entrance through the stern cockpit. You will be amazed. You walk into the saloon on the main deck where your eye will immediately be caught by an extraordinary work of art, the Virtual Sea, a video–sculpture by Venetian artist Fabrizio Plessi. Twelve overturned stainless steel cones representing champagne corks with monitors displaying video images of water. But Plessi's is just one of the many works of art in the main saloon. Alongside the sober grey sofa that separates this area from the entrance corridor is Mai-Thu Perret's Big Golden Rock. Moving through the foyer, you'll find the owner's office and then suite where the dominant colours are black and white. The bed and its marine-themed papier-mache headrest are white while the stained walnut flooring (similar to the main deck) and velvet walls are black. The latter walls by the way have been treated with a blue fluorescent paint which creates a night-sky effect in the dark.

Back in the foyer, we move to the lower deck where there are four double guest staterooms, each one with its own name and décor. The upper deck is reserved for partying. Thanks to the wonderful natural light flooding it, the dark tones used on the lower deck vanish up here. The whole area is designed like a disco. The walls are white while the ceilings are partly barrisol and partly woven wall, a fabric wall particularly suited to plays of light. There's a big bar, a DJ booth and lots of low seating – perfect to stretch out on with drink in hand. These include Zanotta bean bags, a sofa/mattress upholstered in Missoni fabric and a white leather chaise lounge on steel cables.

Moving aft, just in front of the glass door leading into the external cockpit, is a huge 20-seater table which can be lowered to floor level to create an authentic private space. On this deck the art is all on the walls. There are pieces by Cordero, Lombardini and even Philip Guston which Captain Magic took down from the walls of his London apartment.

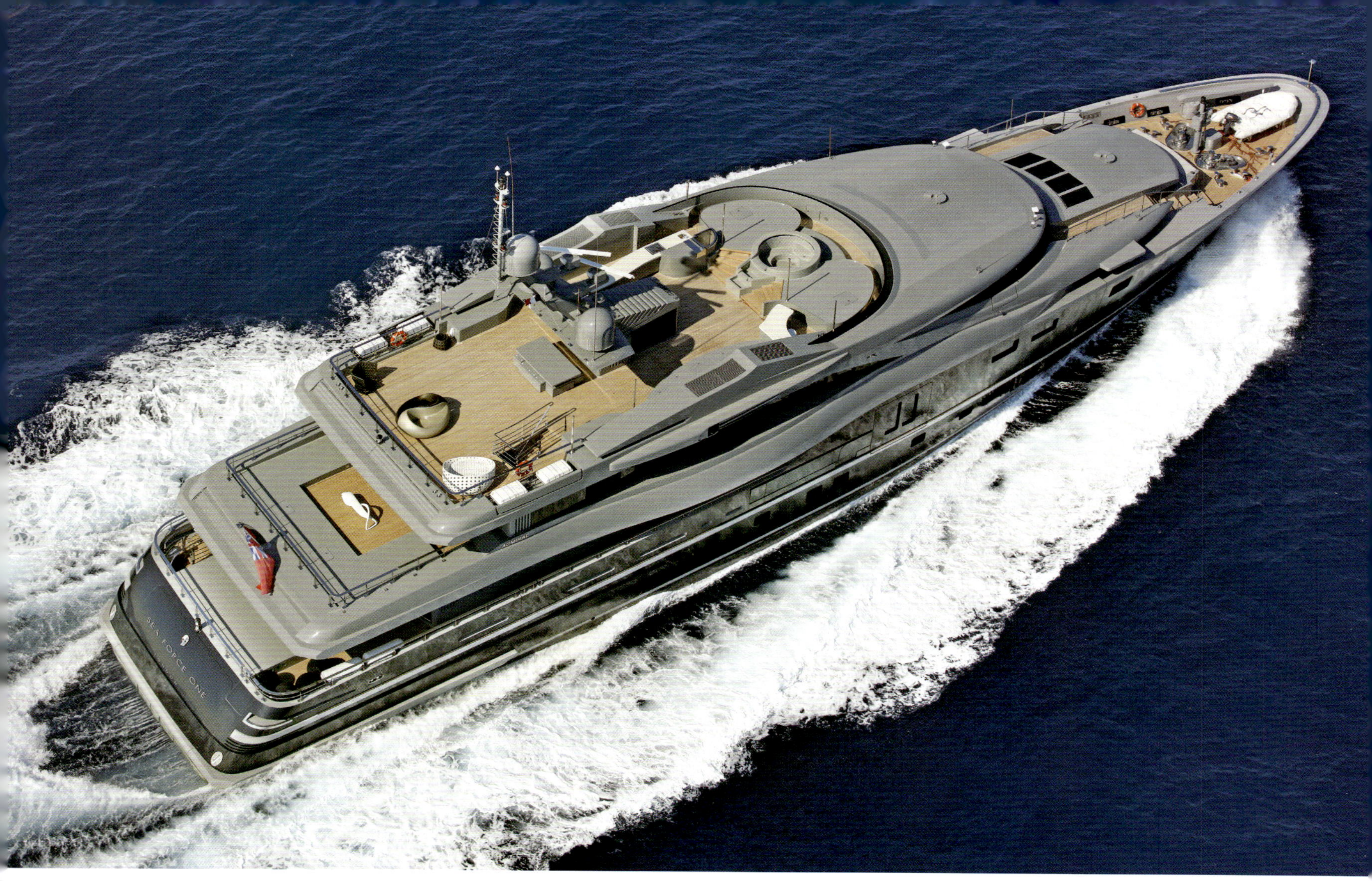

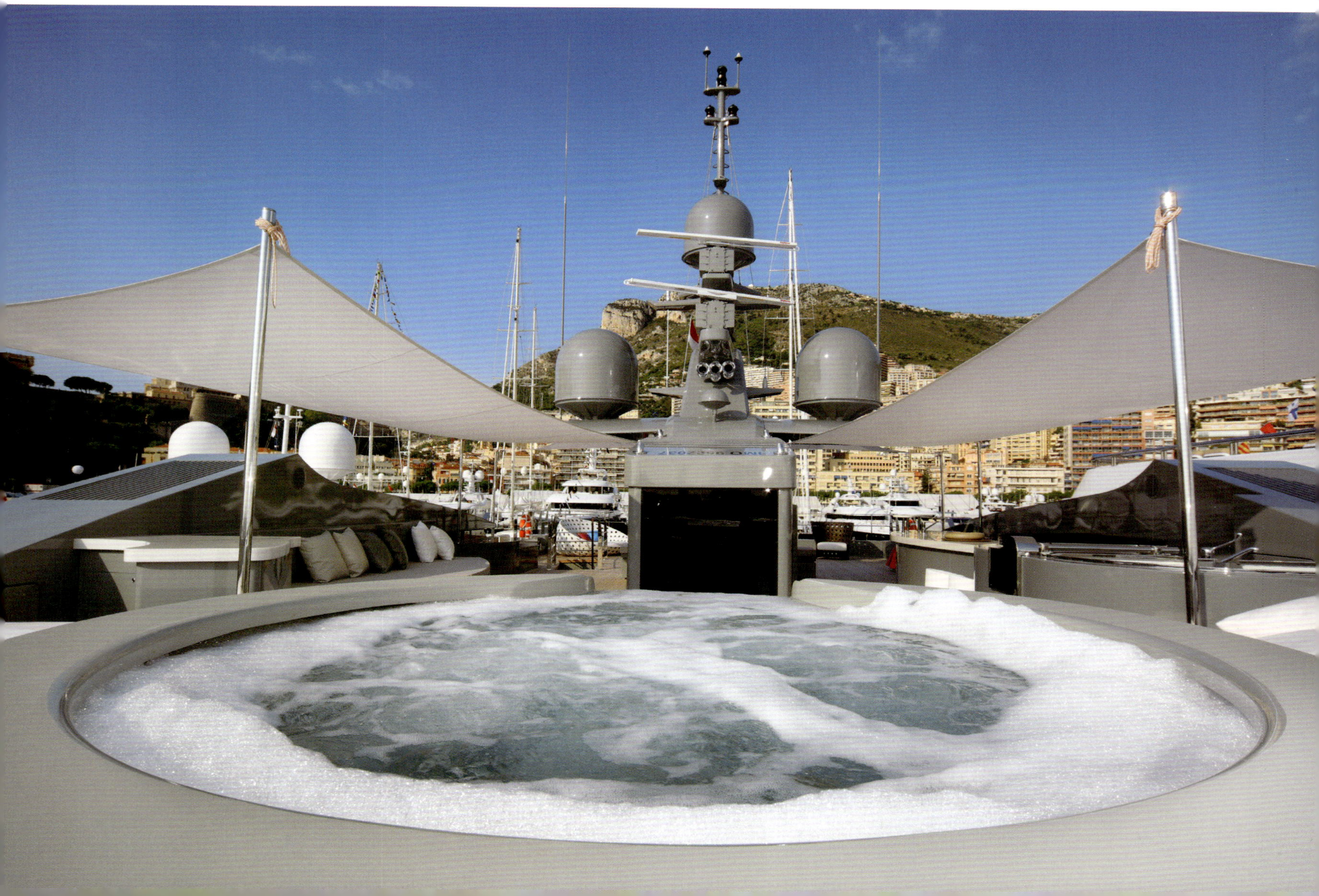

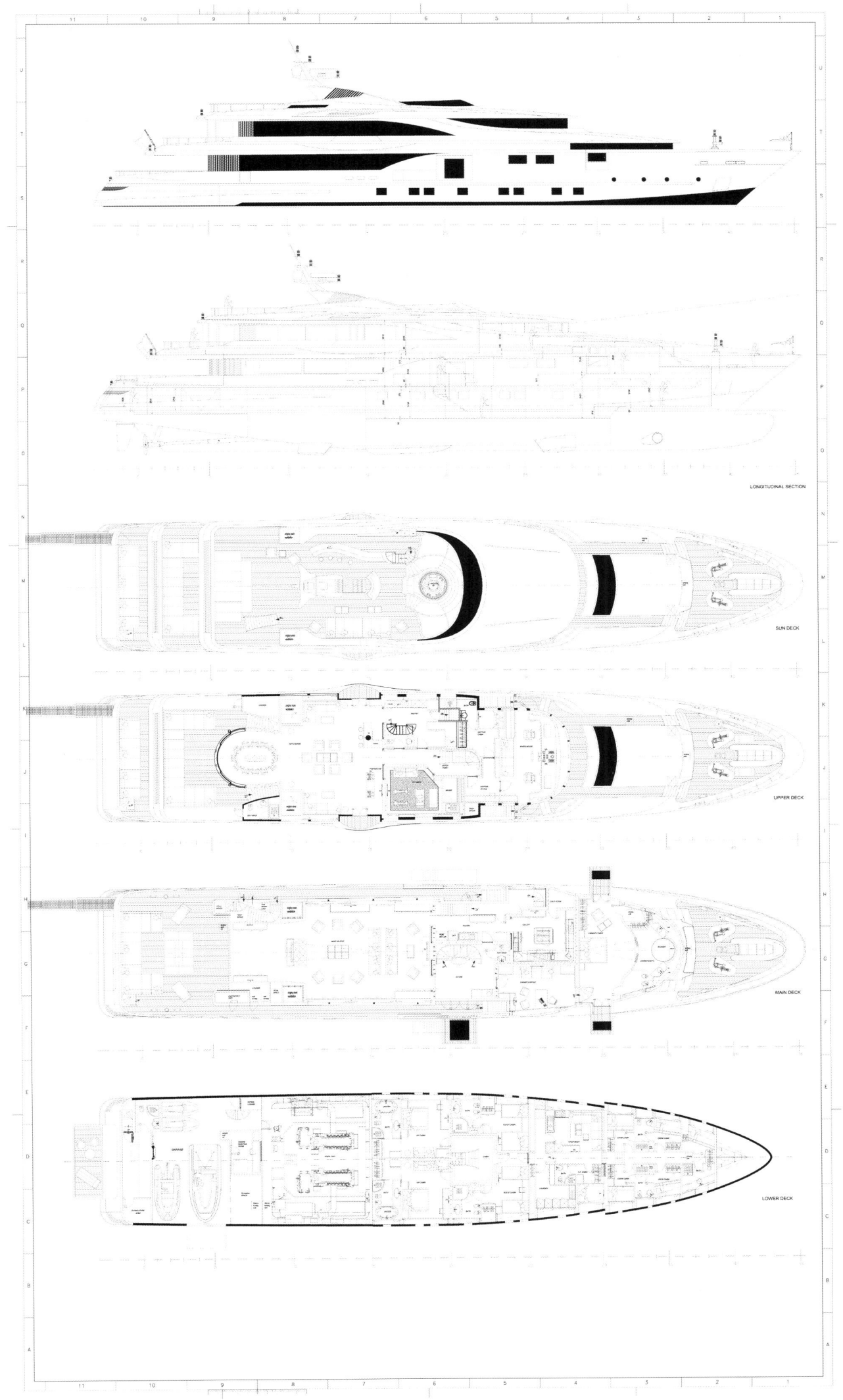

LONGITUDINAL SECTION

SUN DECK

UPPER DECK

MAIN DECK

LOWER DECK

9

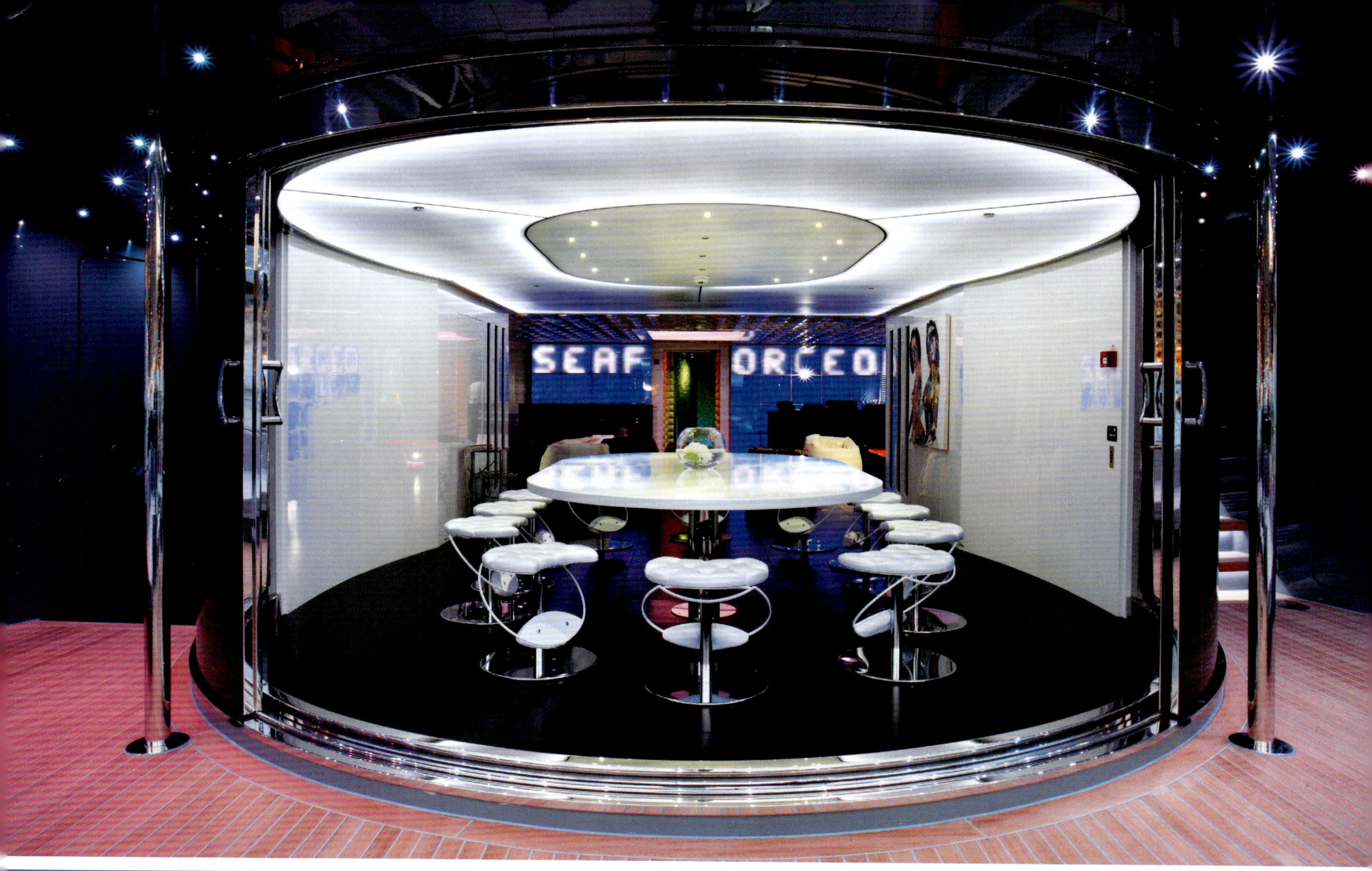

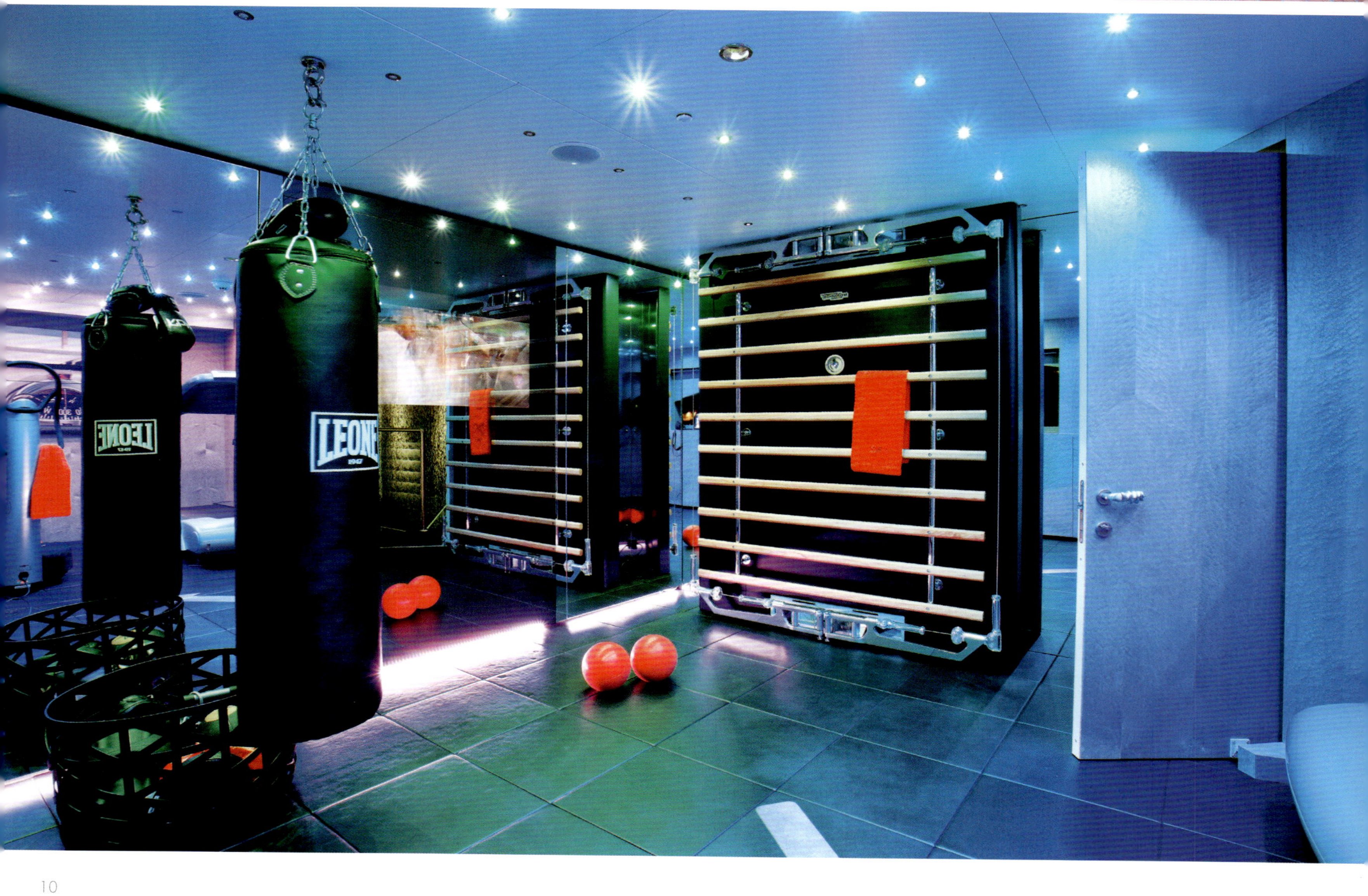
LEONE
1947

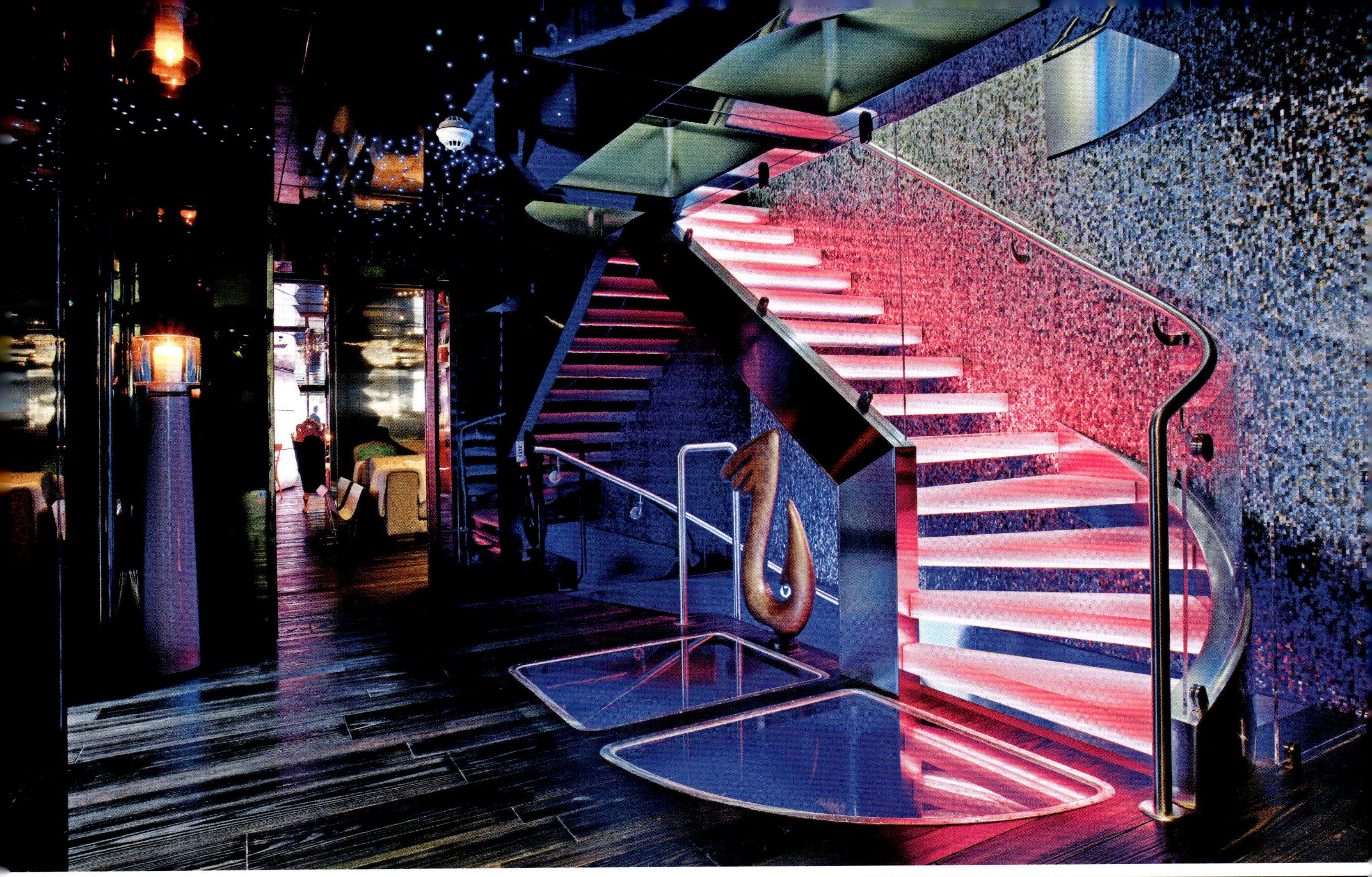

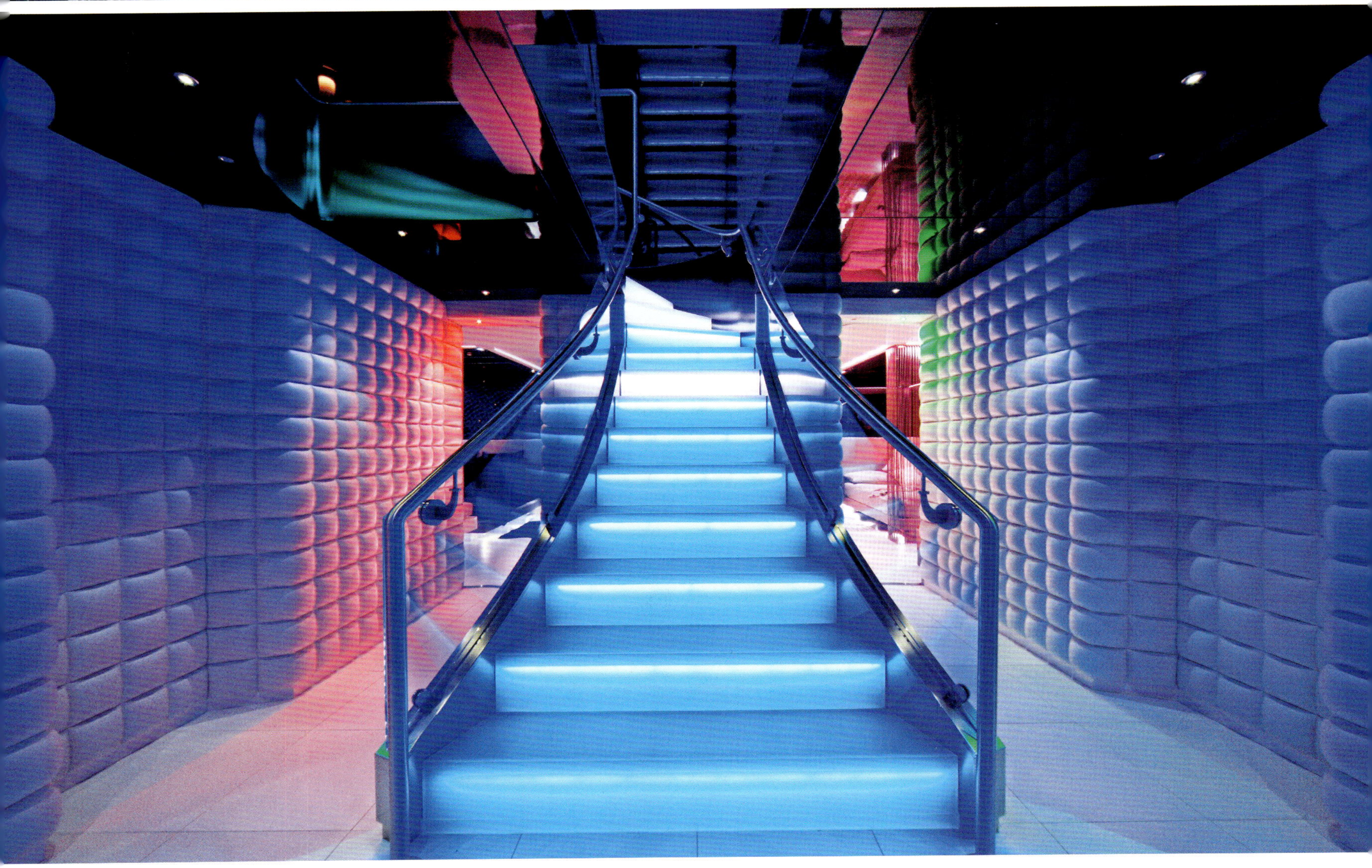

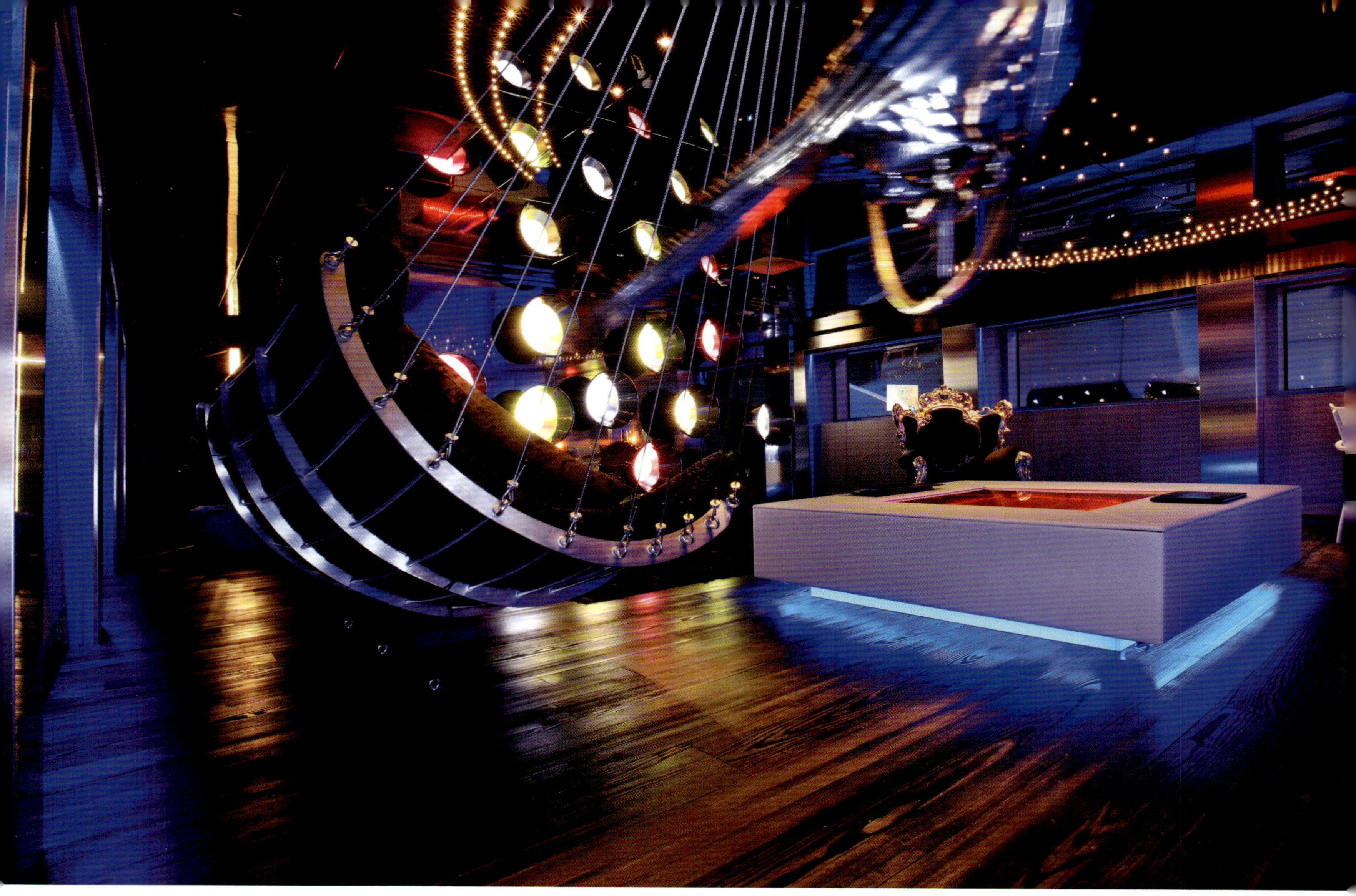

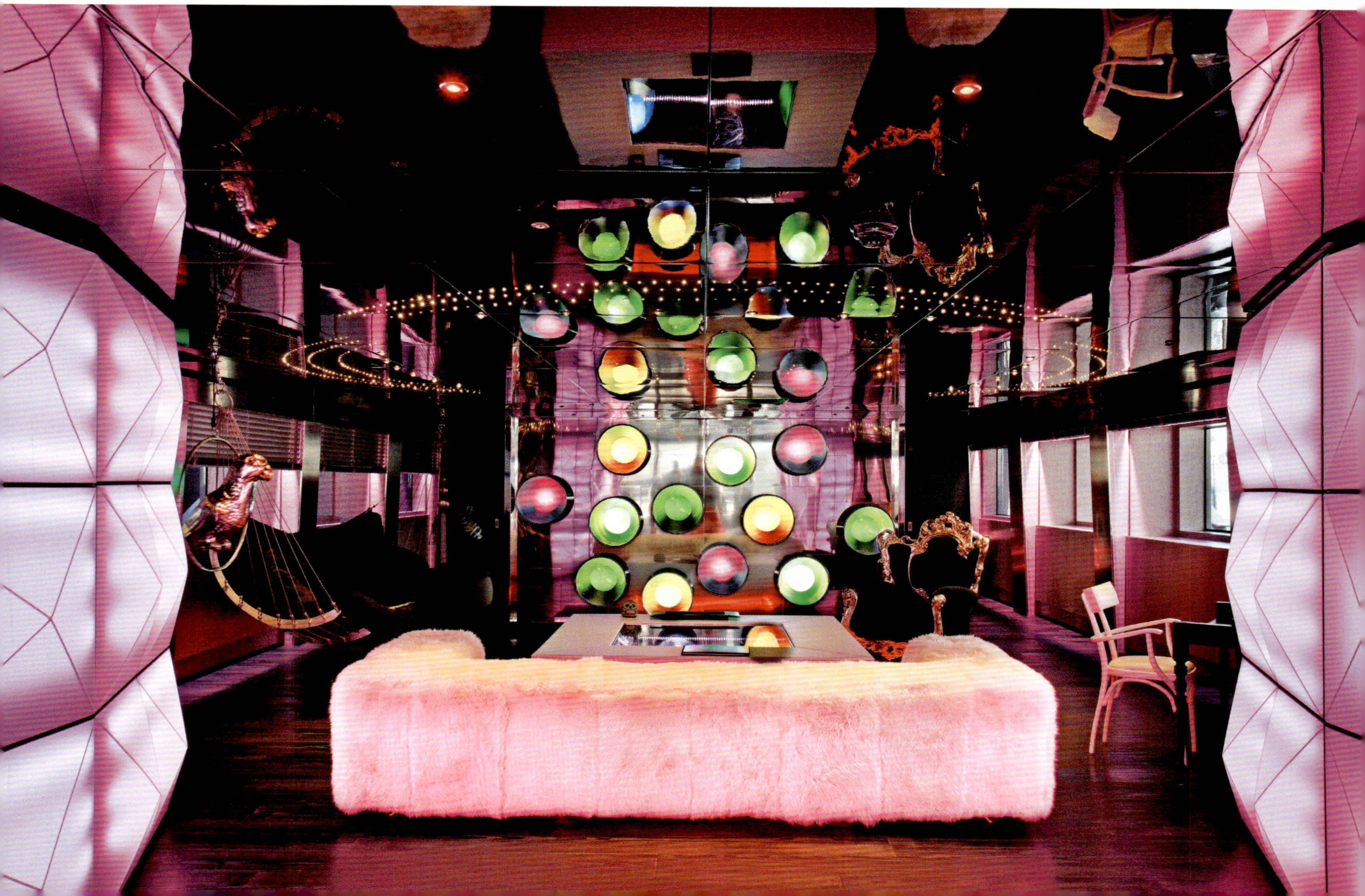

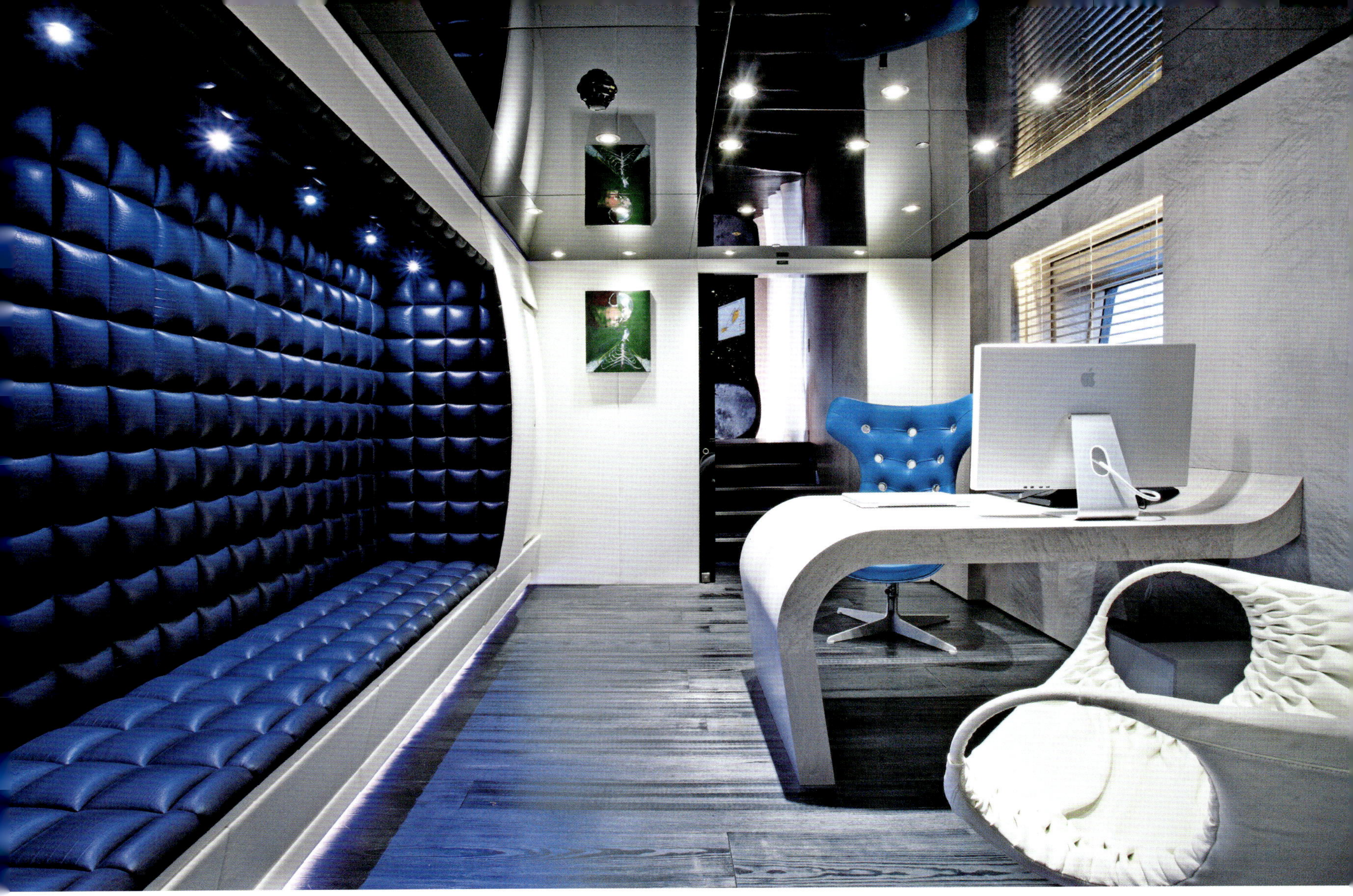

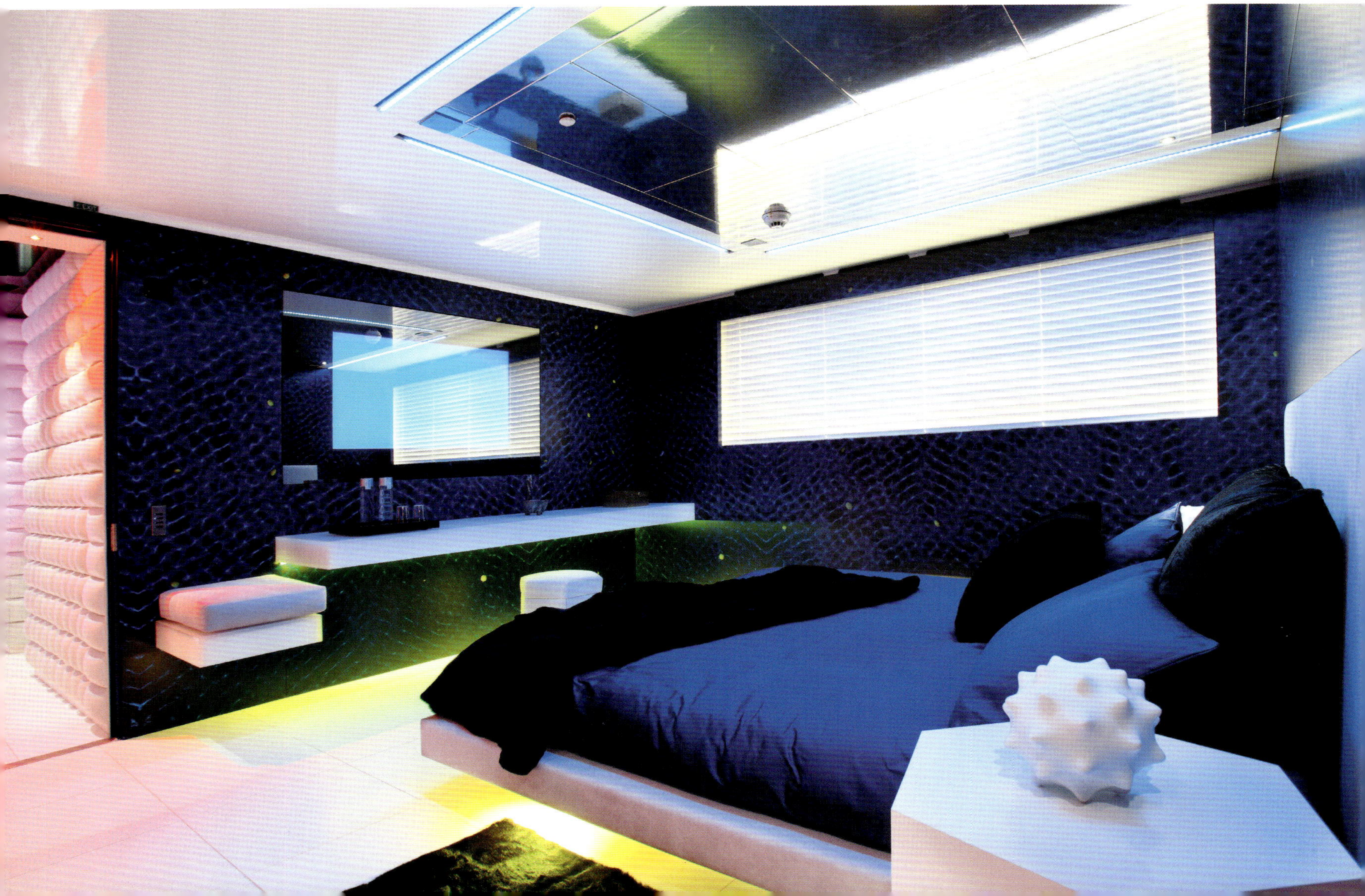

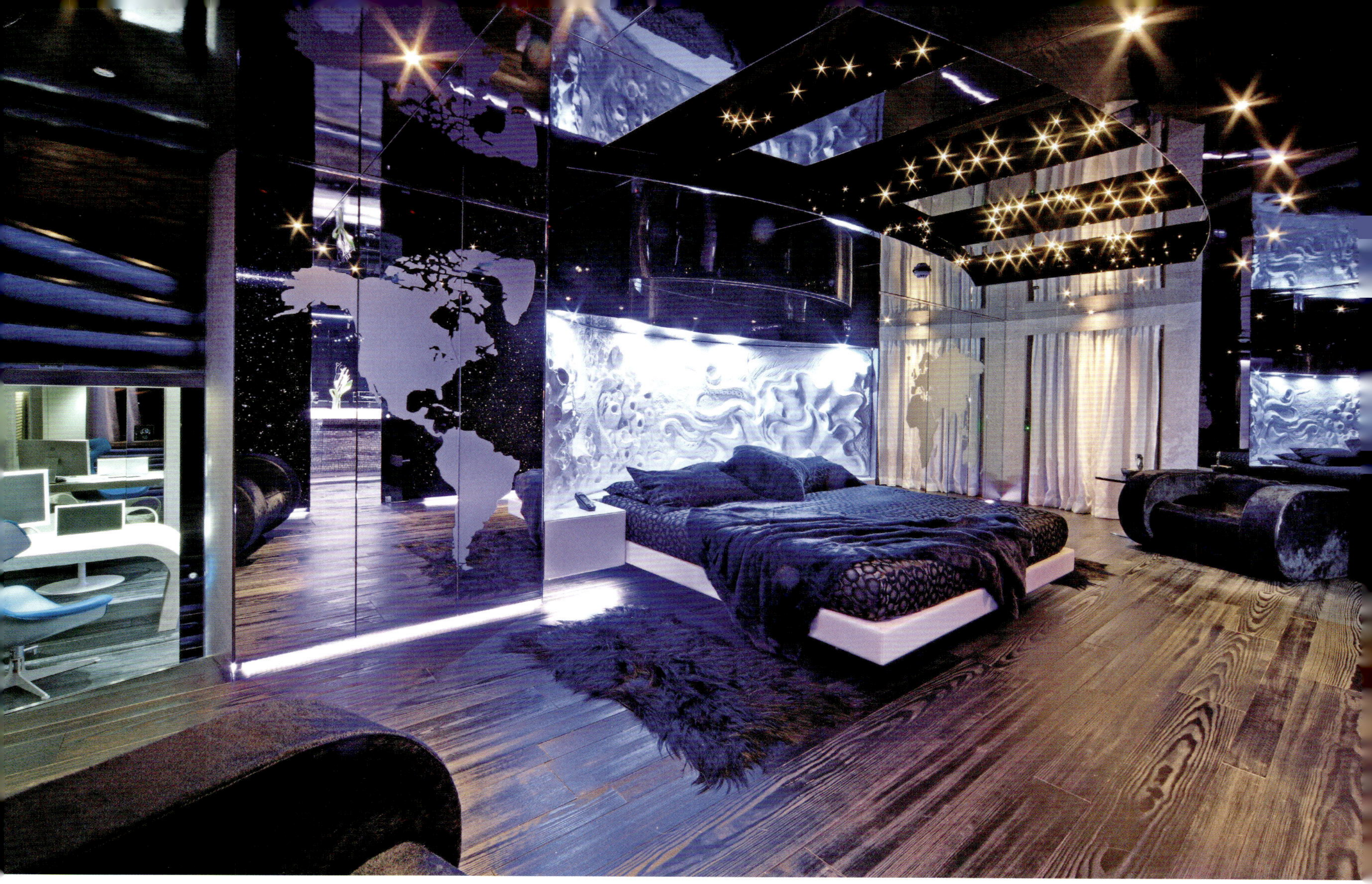

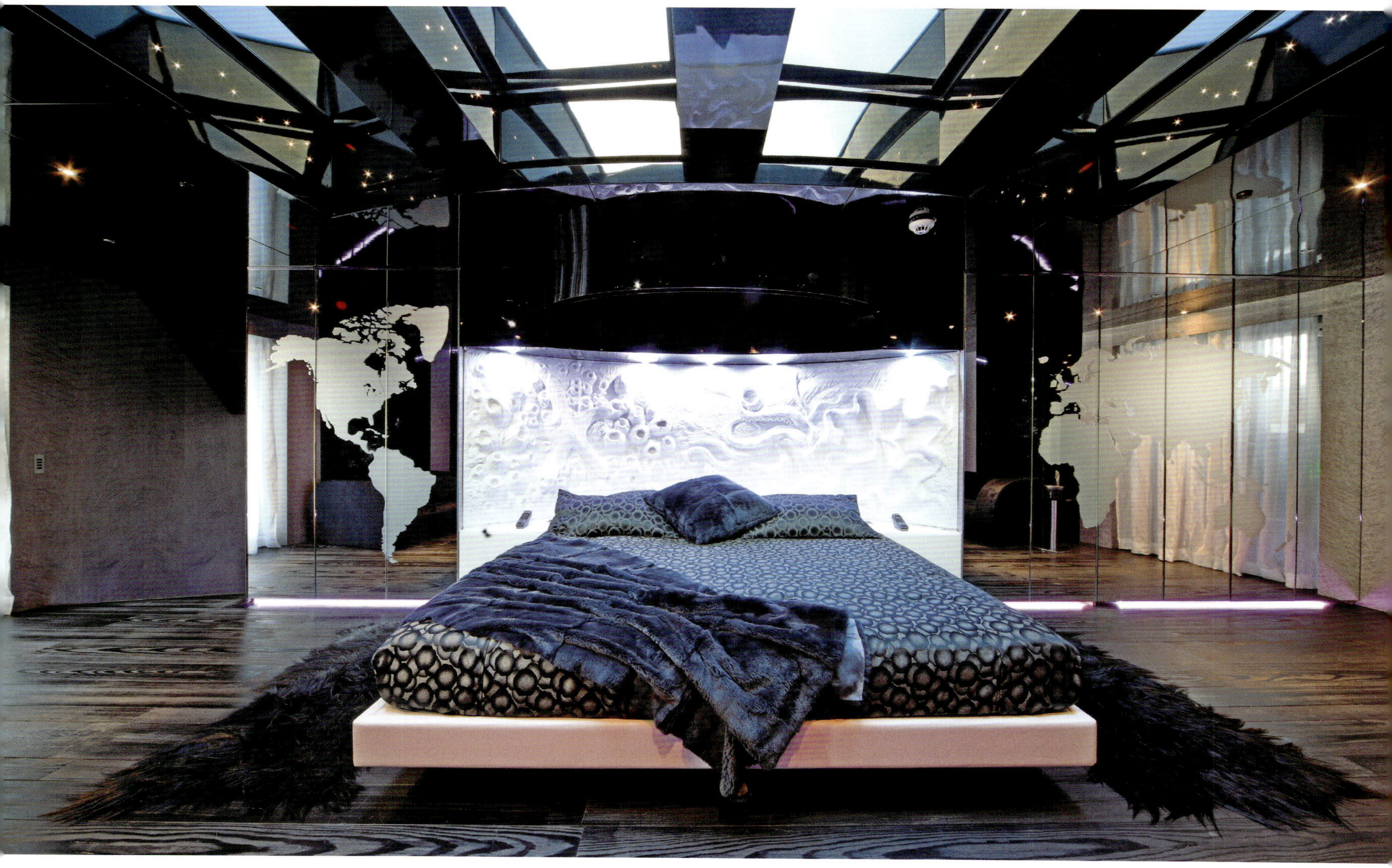

　　设想，有多少种方法可以把308块骨头重新组合成人类骨架子？当这样的工程摆在玛吉克船长，这位"海上力量一号"神秘船主面前的时候，他的杰作与艺术家奇奇·史密斯对男性骨架的组合杰作同出一辙——玛吉克船长貌似"不敬地"将船体漆成金黄色，当然，在决定将其形状建造成"海盗旗"，这一自英格兰爱德华时代就作为海盗船象征的时候，船主并没有丝毫犹豫。与"艾美"造船厂（艾美是意大利公司 Cantieri Navali Lavagna 和 Cantieri Mariotti 的合作项目）去年推出的长达54米的舰艇类似，这艘"海上力量一号"也与海盗船的结构设计有很多相似之处。

　　玛吉克船长解释说："我把艺术之作看作我游艇的核心"。这并不难以置信，因为即便是草草地瞥一眼这艘船，都可以看出它的非凡之处。线条如此引人入胜，这些线条融合了柔和雅致与刚性好胜的特点。同时，色彩上，船身的黑色与主结构的军灰色相呼应。两个阳台的设计出自设计师卢卡迪尼之手，巧妙地与周围空间融为一体。阳台的线条格局使得这艘外表刚性的游艇增加了几分优雅和柔美。有人竟然夸张地称其为"性感之舰"。然而，"海上力量一号"的宏伟之处却在其内部而非外部。其内部结构的设计真正意义上颠覆了传统的游艇设计理念，是将传统理念重组后创造出的后现代主义的佳作。

　　游艇正门设在船的右侧，这里建有一座富丽堂皇的楼梯，通向一间前厅；在大厅里，可以对游艇各个部分一览无余。首先映入眼帘的是透明的树脂玻璃楼梯，台阶照明采用瀑布效果设计，光亮瞩目，引人入胜，这里可以通往游艇所有的三个甲板。不过，主甲板是船主的私人领地，他人最好绕道船尾的驾驶室进入。走进主甲板的客舱，你的眼睛立刻会为这不同寻常的艺术作品所吸引：威尼斯艺术家法布里齐奥·普莱西的作品——

虚拟海洋（虚拟大海和视频动画雕像）。普莱西巧妙地设计了十二个倒置的不锈钢圆锥体呈现出香槟瓶塞的形状，作为托盘，支撑着动态的视频画面，画面里是虚拟的海水。当然，普莱西的艺术作品只是主舱中众多杰作之一。沿着素淡的灰色沙发所陈列的，把主舱的艺术展览区与入口走廊分隔的是艺术家麦-浮·佩雷特的"金色大岩石"作品。一直穿过前厅，就来到了船主的办公室和套房，这里的主色调是黑色和白色。床和以海为主题而设计的靠头枕均为白色，地板用不纯色的核桃木制作，与主甲板色调相似；壁为黑天鹅绒色，漆墙壁的材料采用蓝色荧光涂料，因而在夜晚的黑暗中呈现出夜空般的效果。

　　再回到前厅，我们便来到下层的甲板上，这里有四间双人客舱，每一间都有各自的名字和独特的布置。上层的甲板预留供举办聚会时使用。这里享受着充足的自然光照射，弥补了下层甲板因缺乏足够的阳光而略显昏暗的不足。整个区域的设计犹如一个迪斯科舞厅。墙壁为白色，天花板好似由各种颜色浑然拼接而成的，这样的墙壁和天花板组合尤其适合于对光的灵活运用。游艇上还有一个大型的酒吧，一个专供主持人的包间和众多舒适的座位——客人可以手里拿着饮料随心所欲地调整姿势，座位的种类很多，有按摩效果的豆枕，各种编制精美的沙发坐垫和钢结构的白色皮沙发。

　　继续向船尾走去，穿过玻璃门，前面便是外部的驾驶室，这里有一张可以容纳20人围坐的桌子，需要时还可以降低到地面的高度，以营造完全的私人空间。在这个甲板上，所有的艺术品都挂于墙上。其中有科德罗、罗姆巴蒂尼，还有菲利普·古斯顿的作品，全部是玛吉克船长从他在伦敦的公寓中取下来陈列于此的。

LADY TRUDY

>	**INTERIOR DESIGN**	Zuccon International Project + Centro Stile CRN
>	**EXTERIOR DESIGN**	Zuccon International Project
>	**NAVAL ARCHITECT**	CRN Engineering
>	**ENGINES**	2 x Caterpillar C32-C 1044 Kw@2300rpm
>	**GUEST**	N° 10 (n. 1 owner suite + n. 4 VIP cabins)
>	**CREW**	N° 9
>	**LENGTH**	43m
>	**BEAM**	8.6m
>	**MAX SPEED**	15.5kn
>	**CRUSING SPEED**	13kn

> Among the peculiarities of this mega yacht are certainly the interiors, which are finely furnished, representing a plunge into the American colonial sphere, with a touch of the romantic "Hampton style".

The main features of the guest cabins are made of white ash wood while the construction details and the decorations are made of mahogany. Same wood is used for the crew quarters (dinette and cabins).

Each of the four guest cabins, is characterized by a dominant colour that is purposely linked to an American locality of the North Atlantic coast: cabin "Newport" for the VIP cabin at the bow where yellow is the predominant colour, cabin "Cape Cod" on the right towards the stern where green is predominant, the guest cabin "Mystic" on the left towards the stern with twin beds and a foldaway bed, where everything is in red and the after cabin "Nantucket" on the left which is blue.

Each cabin has its own bathroom with white ash slats and a shower covered with natural teak. The basin unit has a top made of charcoal grey natural porous "San Gaudenzio" stone.

Extreme aft lower deck, there is also a wide fitness area, overlooking the beach platform at sea level and it has a bathroom made of natural teak. The gym equipment is branded Techno gym.

The master cabin is situated on the main deck. Its main characteristics, besides great luminosity, is the large four-poster bed made of dark mahogany with mocha-coloured leather headboards. The tones are beige for the carpet and the bed cover, as well as grey and brown.

There are two bathrooms, both covered in white ash and teak slats. The basins are made of San Gaudenzio stone while the taps are antique bronze colour, with a hammered effect.

A distinctive feature of this boat and the entire CRN fleet is the terrace in the master cabin, furnished like a balcony with a coffee table and armchairs where one can have breakfast, enjoyable even while sailing.

In the study, lies a large desk by the wall, made of mahogany with a top covered in brown leather. The large windows offer greater luminosity to the rooms. On the opposite side of the bulkhead there is a library and a built-in sofa bench, all made of white ash to contrast the rest of the room. The patterned fabrics of the cushions have the same cream and beige tones of the master cabin.

Another feature of this boat's interiors are the Persian sliding bay windows found in the dining room, in the lobby upper deck and in the master cabin creating a warm and intimate atmosphere, creating a pleasant "home" effect.

The main hall of the main deck has an armchair made of natural wicker with white linen cushions and custom-made sofas in white linen keeping to the Colonial style, and a coffee table made of dark mahogany.

A central custom-made unit is found towards the stern of the living room and contains a built-in 46 inch TV.

Two libraries, predominantly in teal colour, furnish and separate the living room from the dining room with an electrical sliding door that has a "Venetian" pattern in white ash.

The dining room, with a designed idea for the dining table that stands on two pedestals and columns and on top which is a hole filled with sand and shells all covered by a glass top.

The bow bulkhead is furnished with wooden frames with black and white photos of scenes from everyday life in the United States of the fifties.

Further on, immediately after the main lobby, on the left, is galley in white ash wood entirely designed on the American model including all the appliances.

Moreover, the boat is supported by an innovative, integrated entertainment system.

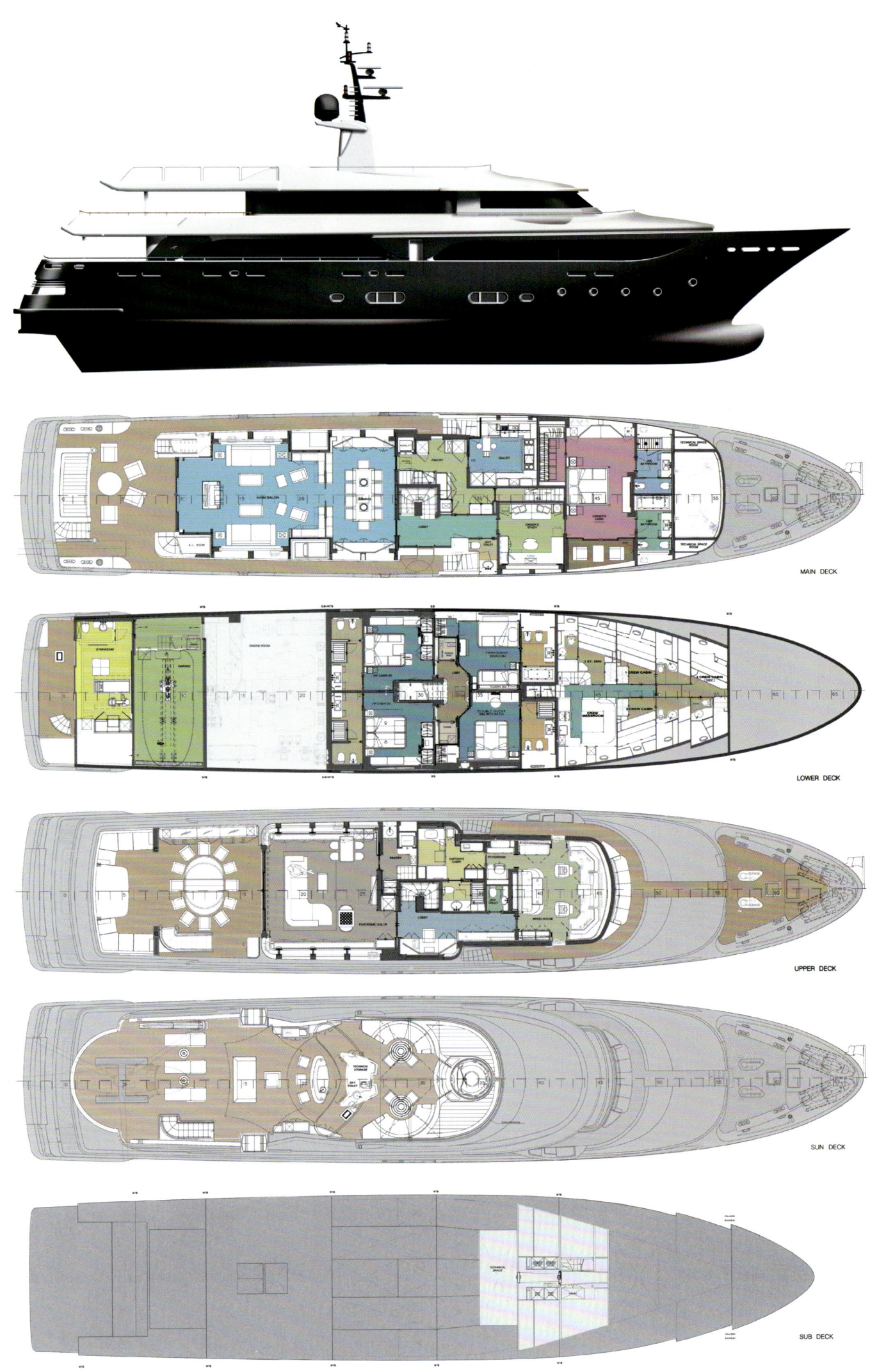

MAIN DECK

LOWER DECK

UPPER DECK

SUN DECK

SUB DECK

21

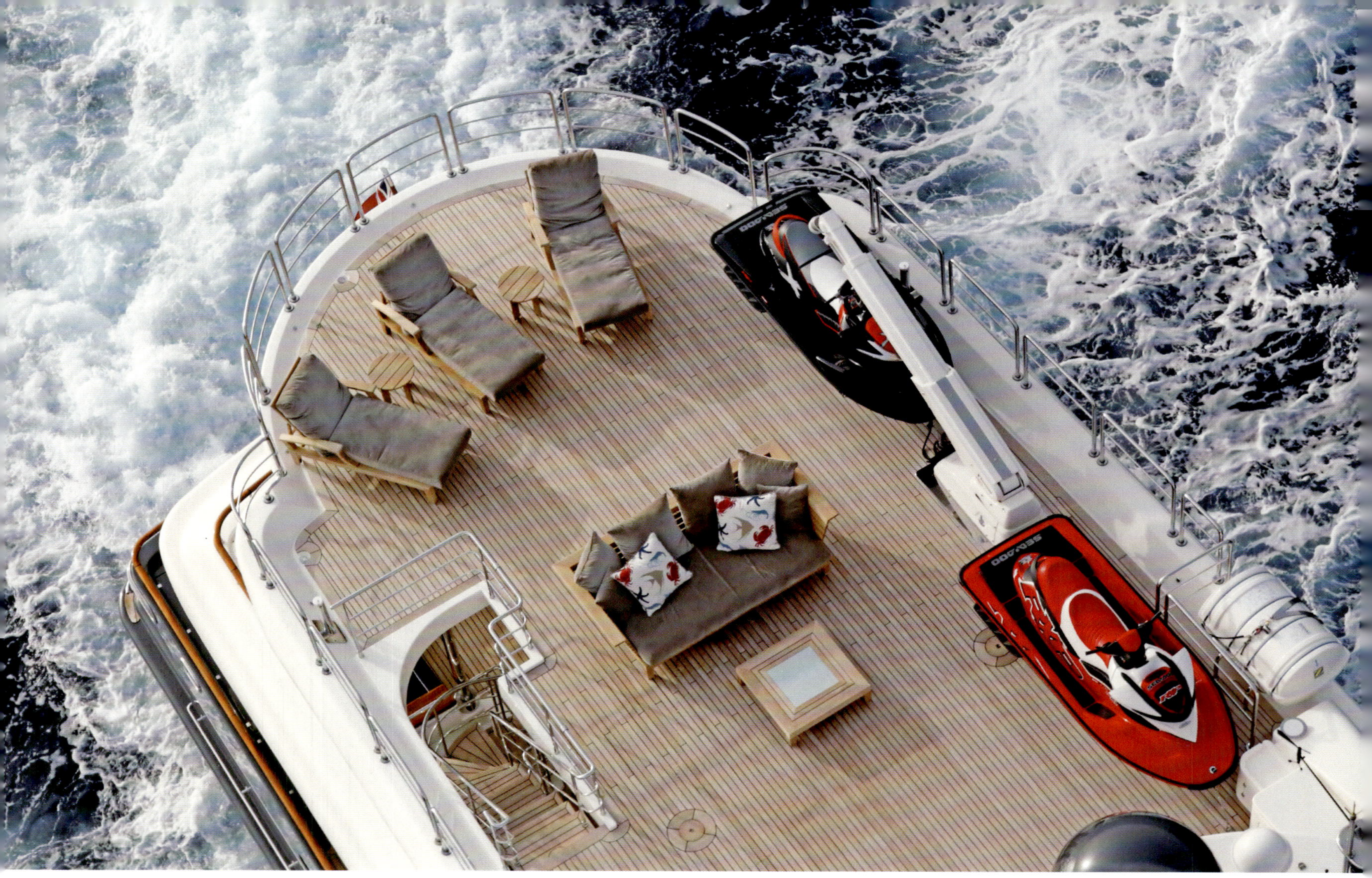

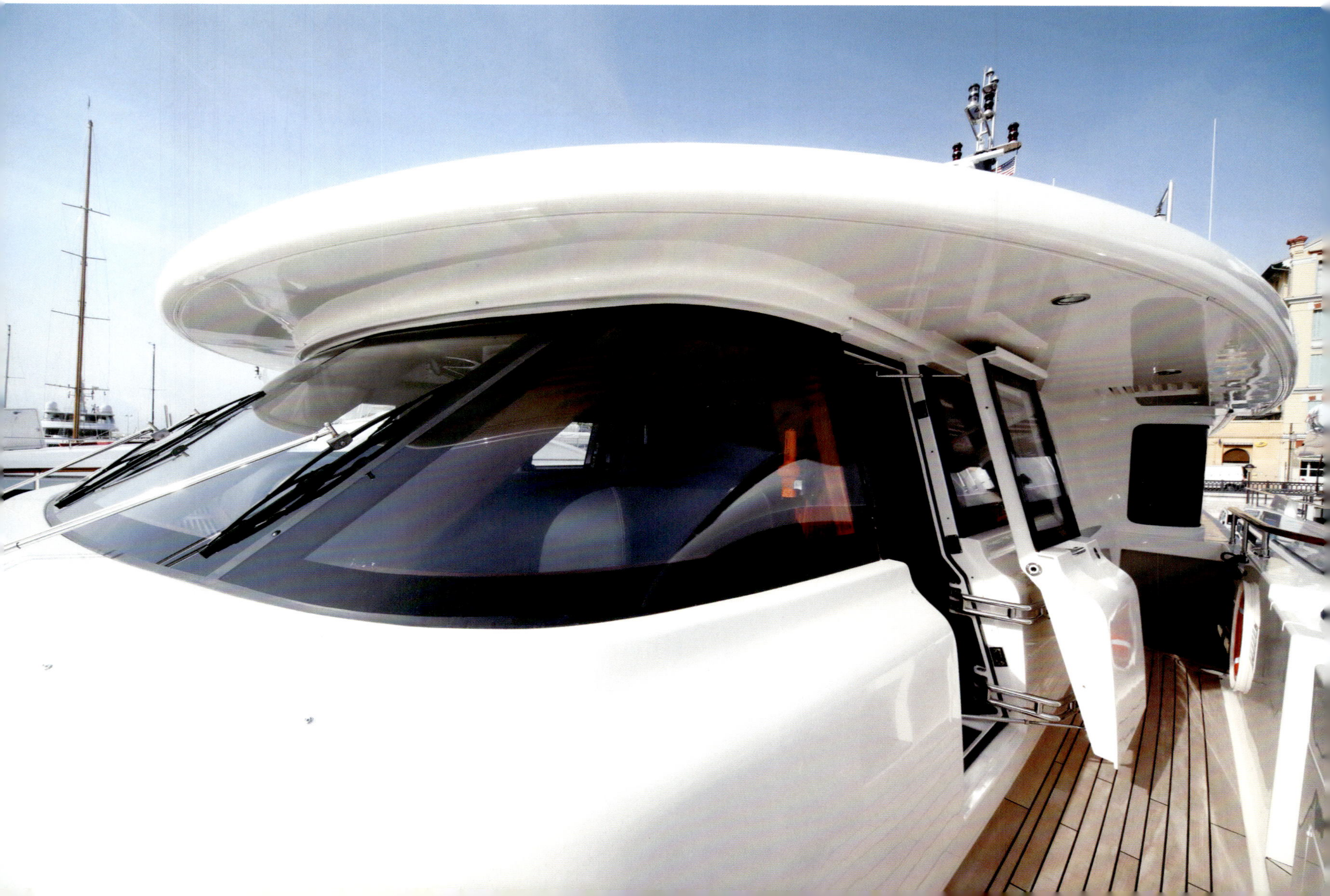

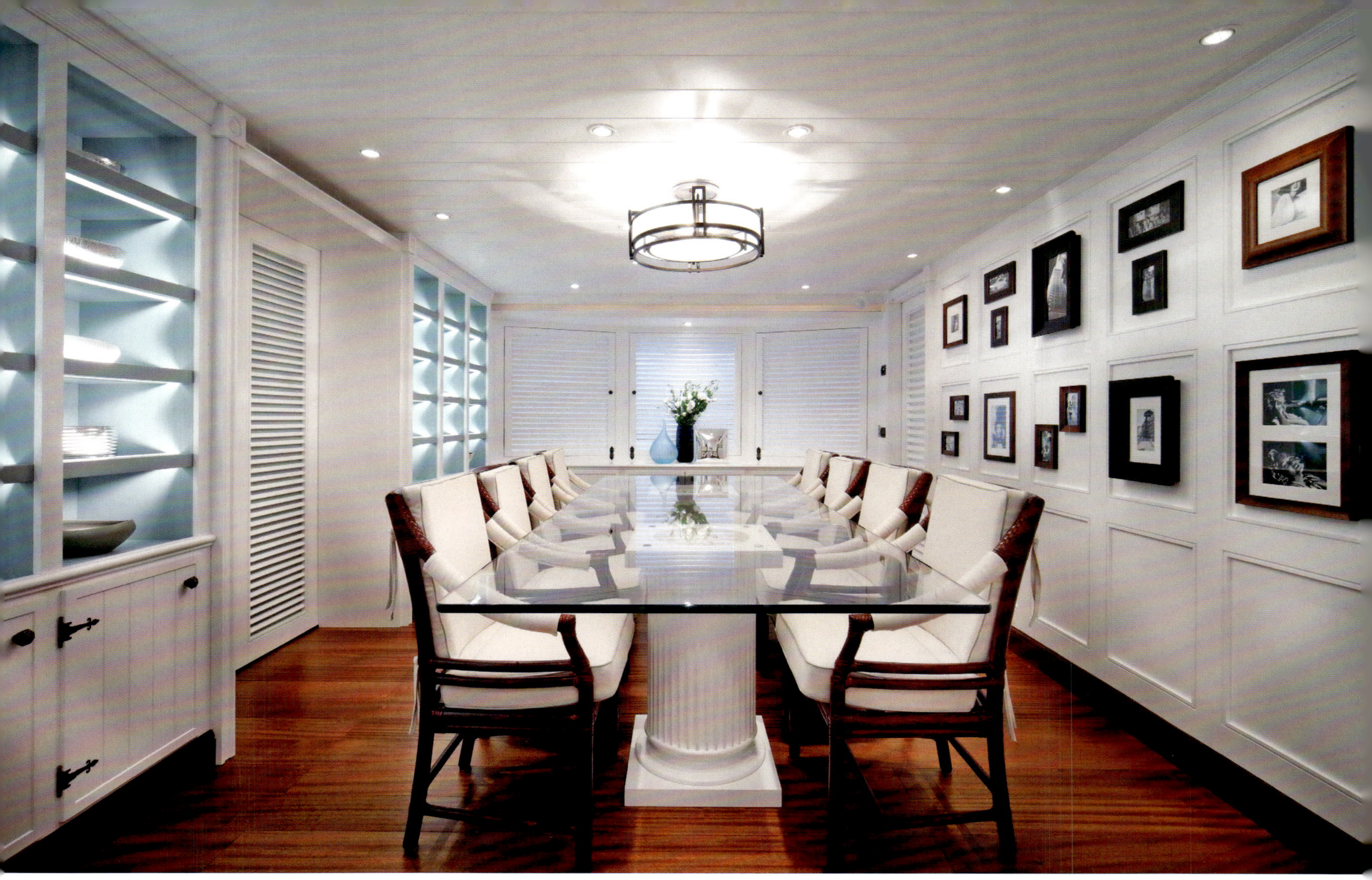

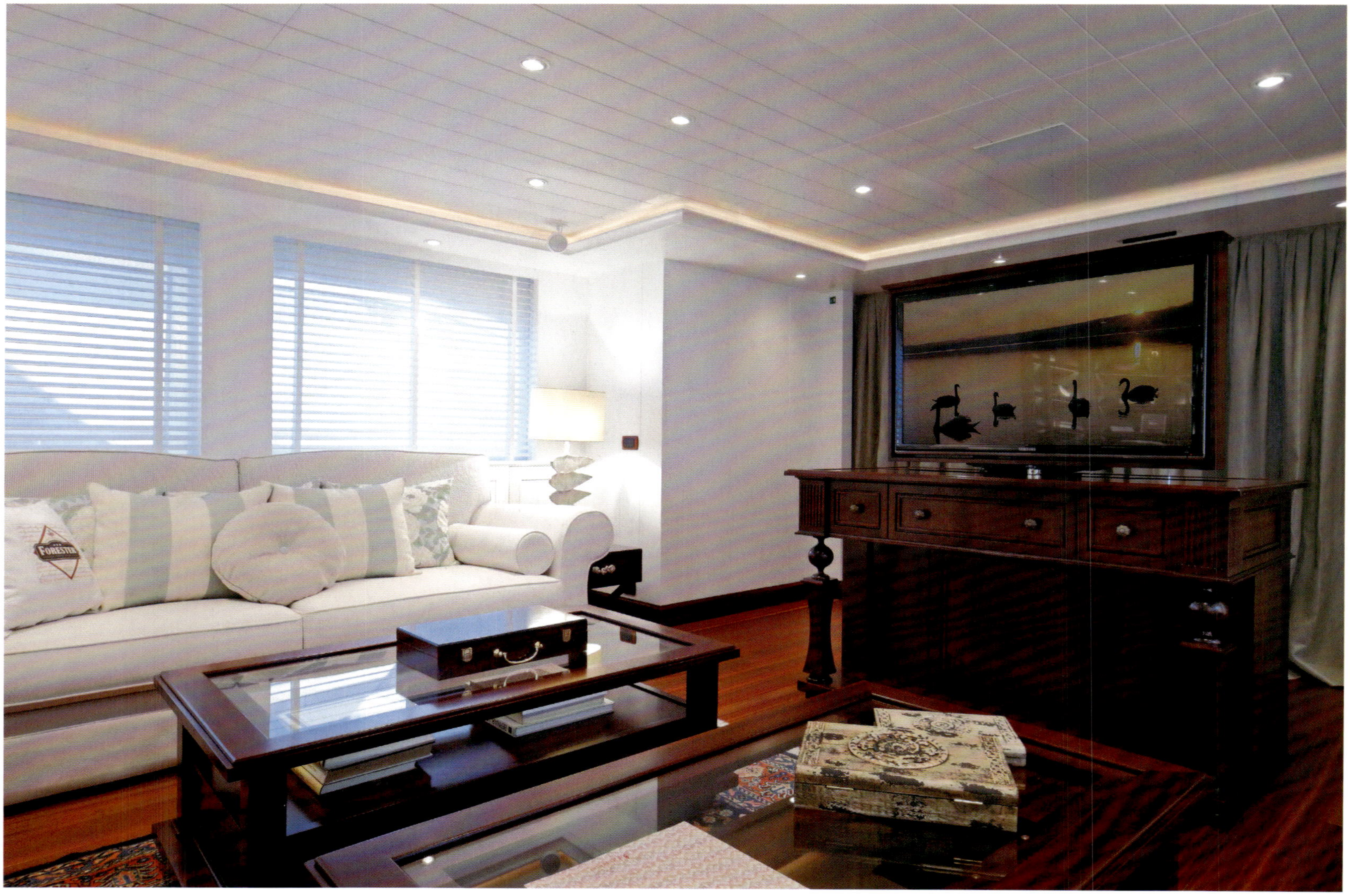
FORESTER

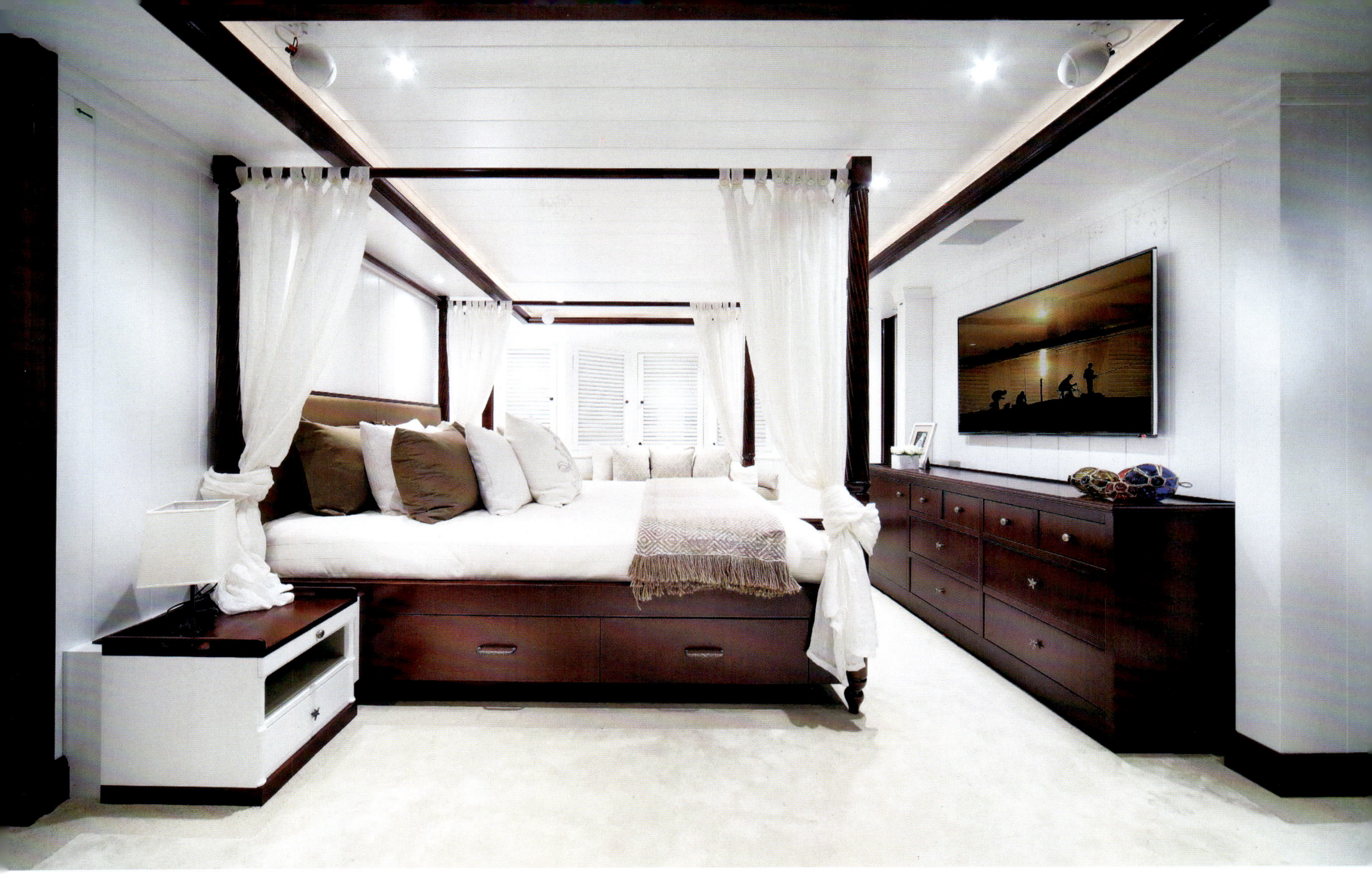

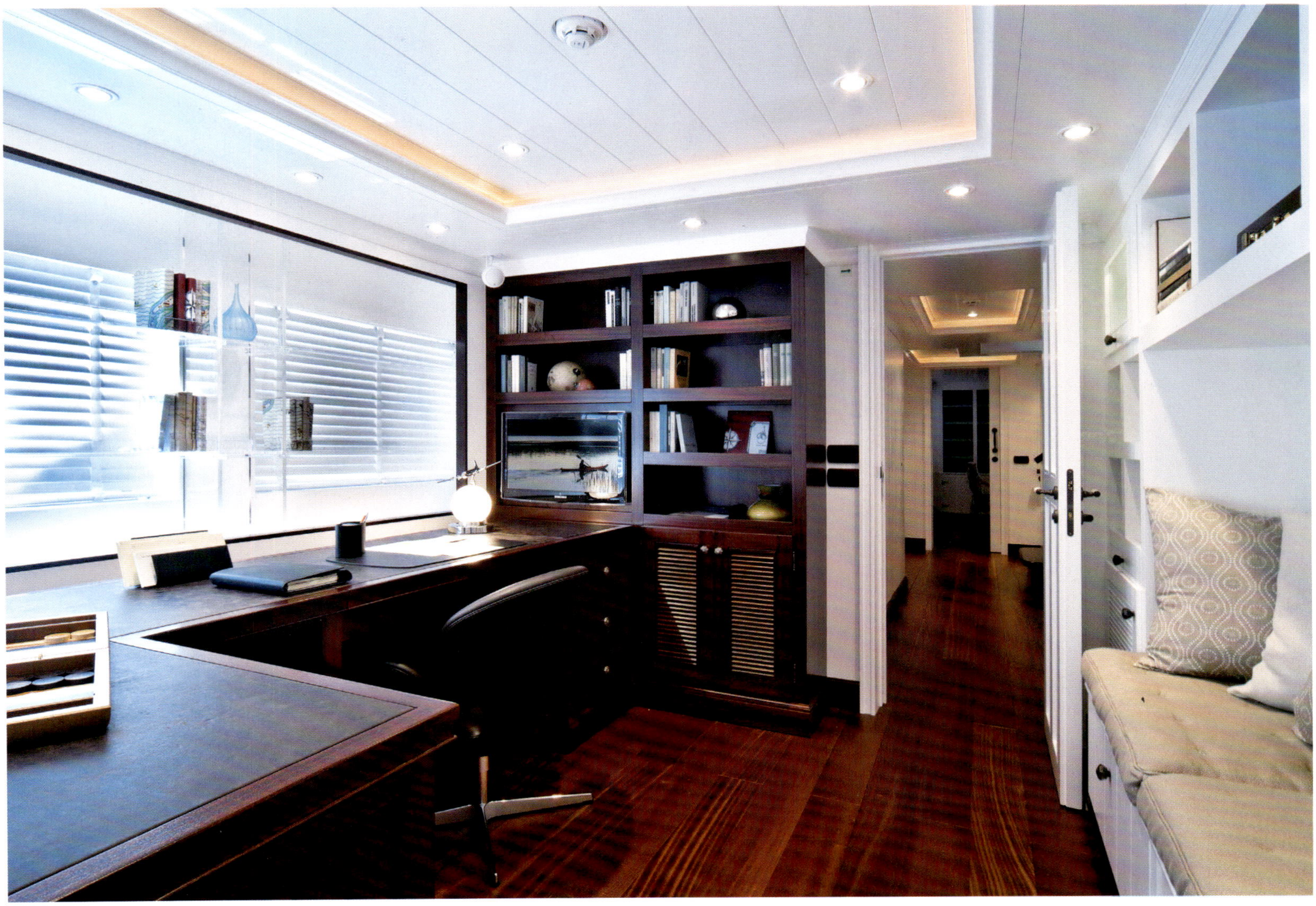

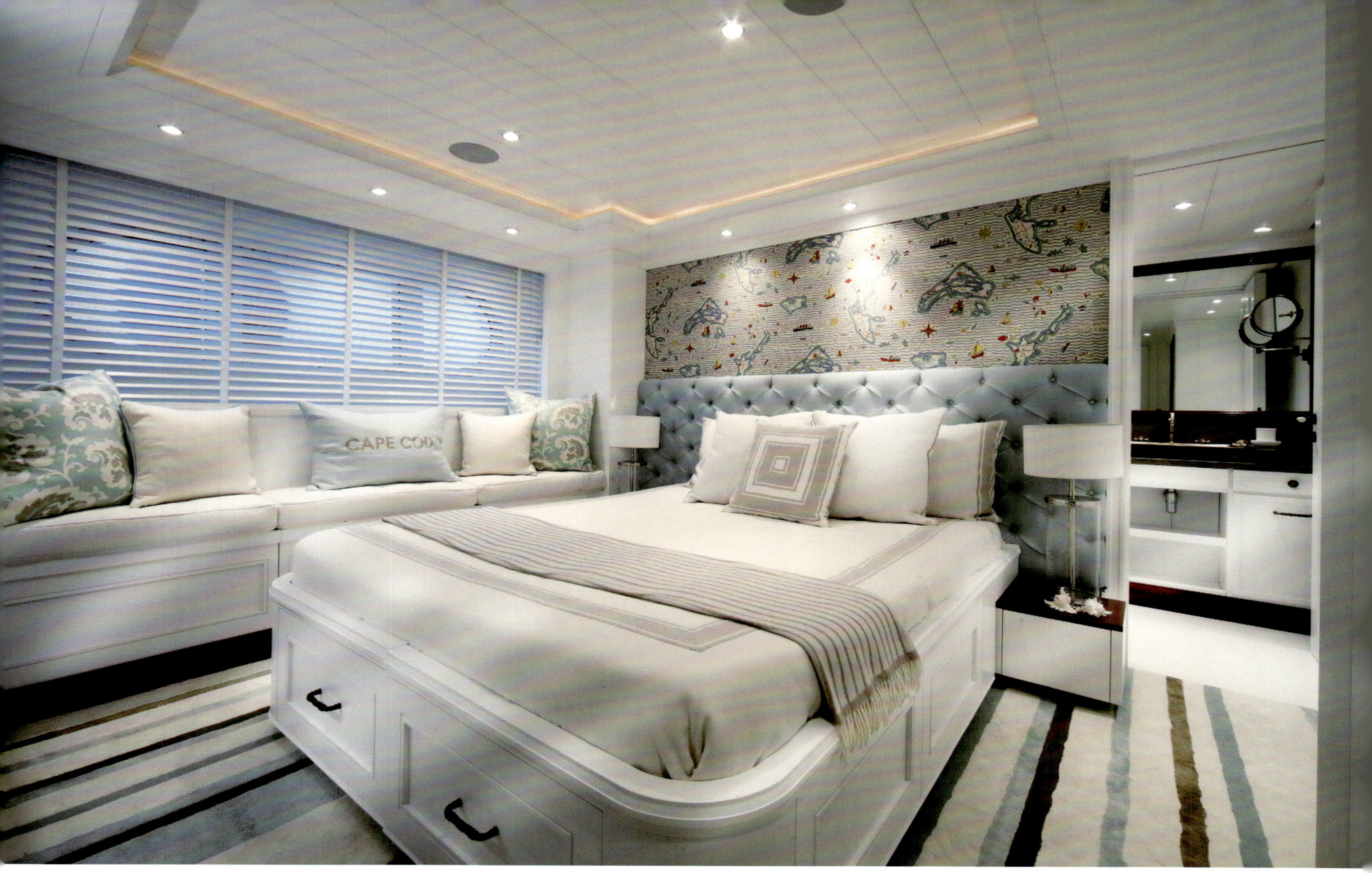
CAPE COD

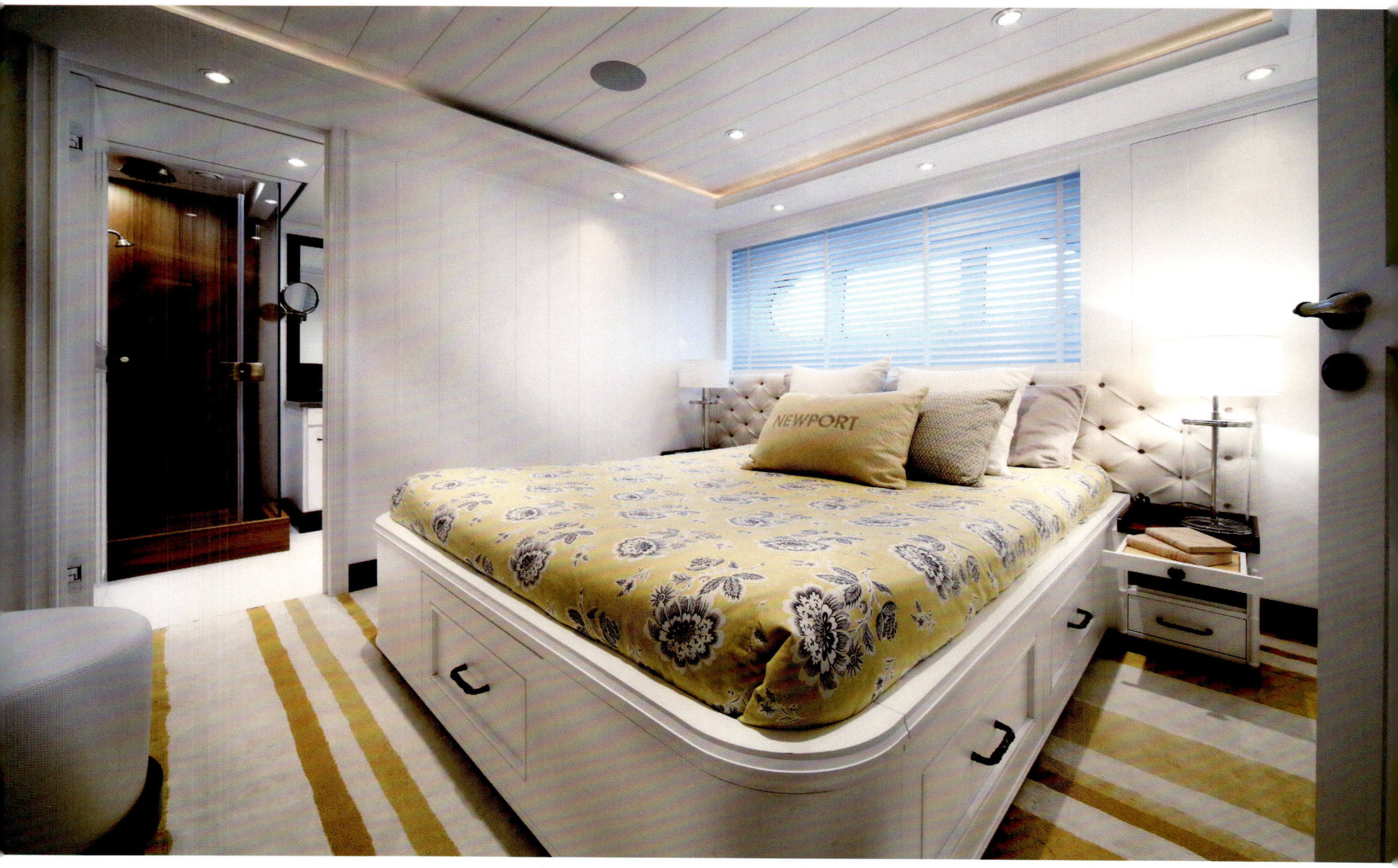
NEWPORT

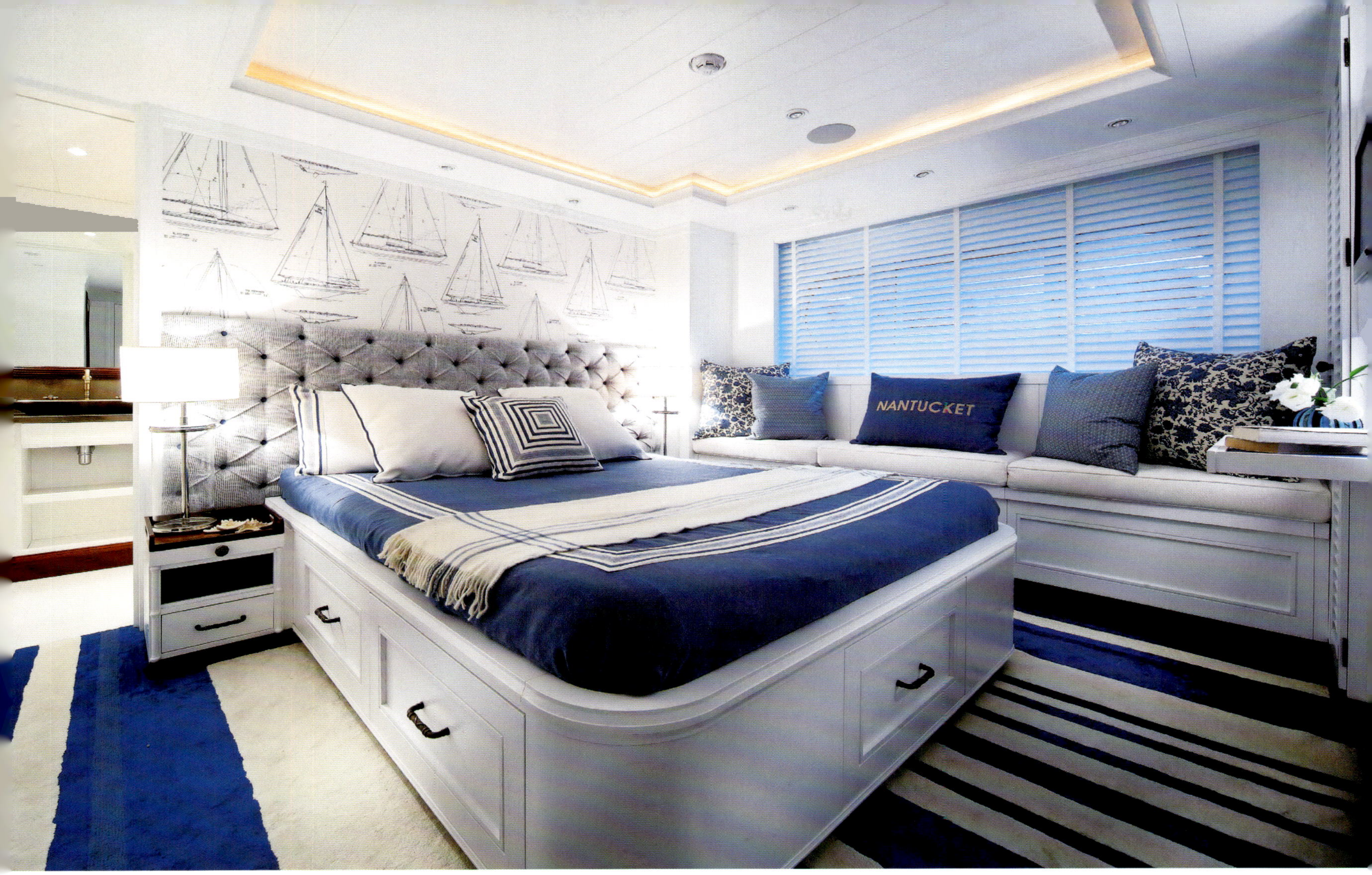
NANTUCKET

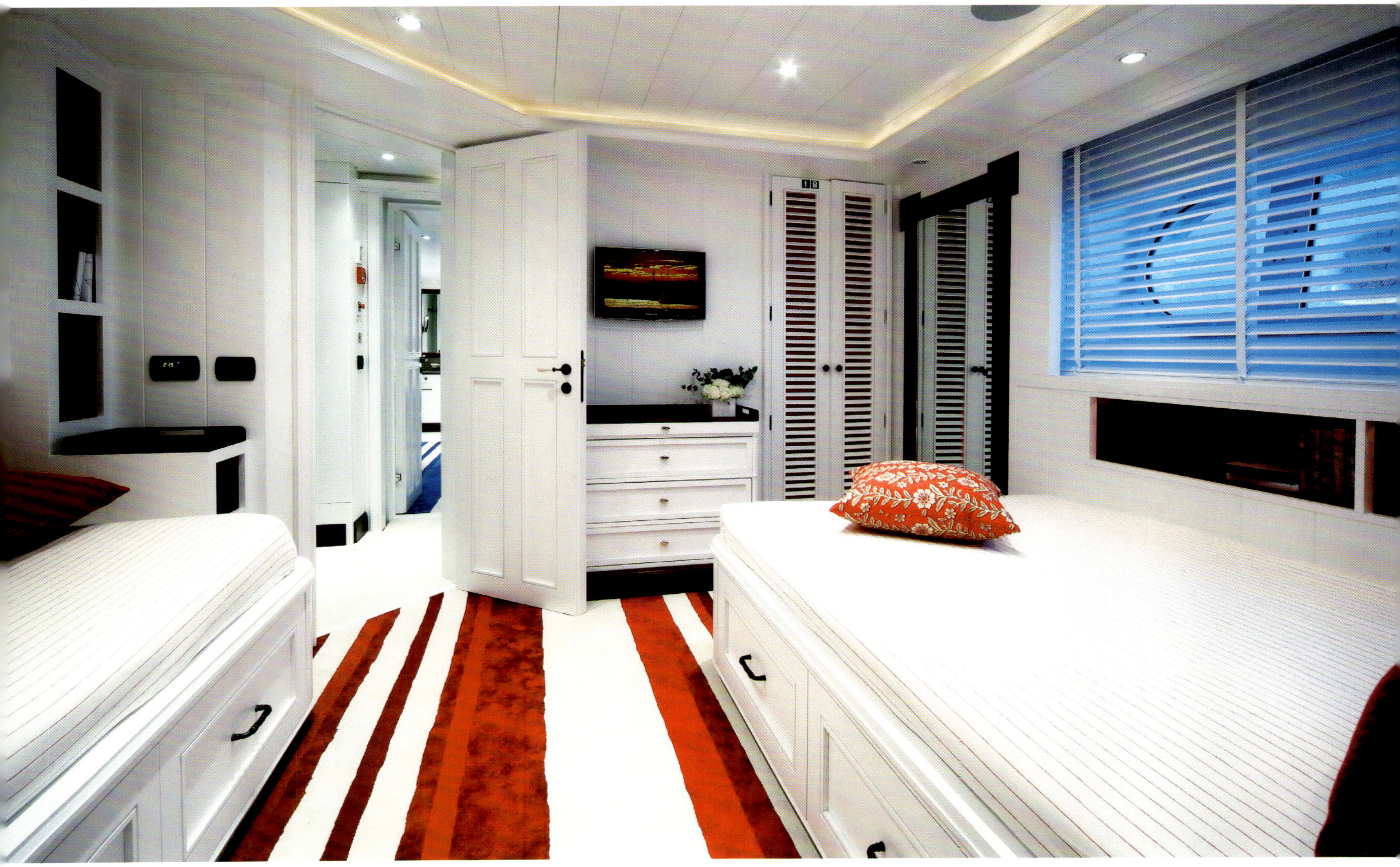

这艘巨型游艇的特点之一当然是它精致的内部设计，给人一种走进了美国殖民地的感觉，带有一种浪漫的"汉普顿风格"。

客舱的主要材料是白蜡木，而在细节和装饰方面则主要使用红木。船员区（包括餐室和舱室）均使用同样的木材。

在四个客舱中，均使用了不同的主色调，分别代表北大西洋沿岸的四个不同的美国城市。在船头的"新港"号贵宾舱主打黄色；船尾靠右的"科德角"号客舱则主打绿色；"米斯蒂克"号客舱位于船尾左侧，主打红色，内设一张双人床和一张折叠床；而左侧更靠船尾的"南土克特"号客舱则主打蓝色调。

每一个舱室都有独立的卫生间，采用白橡木板条。淋浴间则使用了天然柚木。水池上端是由一种炭灰色的天然多孔"圣高登扎奥"石头制造而成。

在船尾底层甲板也有一个宽敞的健身区，可以俯瞰与海平面平齐的沙滩平台。那里也有一个用天然柚木建成的洗浴间。健身器材全部采用意大利"泰诺健"品牌。

船主舱位于主甲板，不仅宽敞明亮，而且四柱床的床体采用深色红木，床头采用咖啡色皮革。地毯和床罩的色调是米黄色或灰色或褐色。

两个卫生间均采用白橡木板与柚木板。水池采用"圣高登扎奥"石材，水龙头采用石铜色，有一种复古效果。

这艘船和所有 CRN 公司设计的船舰均有一个特点，那就是船主舱中的平台。装饰后的平台很像一个阳台，一张咖啡桌，几张靠椅，人们可以坐下来吃早点，即便航行时也可享受美好时光。

书房靠墙的位置有一张红木材质的大书桌，表面包有棕色皮革，巨大的窗户确保了书房的良好采光。在墙的另一面是一个图书室和一个嵌入式沙发长椅，由白橡木制成，与房间的其他色彩形成鲜明的对照。床垫的织物图案的色调与船主舱一样，都是乳白色和米黄色。

游艇内部设计的另外一个特点是：你可以在餐厅、上层甲板大厅、船主舱发现一扇扇波斯风格的滑动凸窗，给人一种温馨亲切的氛围，创造了一种怡人的"宾至如归"的感觉。

主甲板的主厅有一张用天然柳条制成的扶手椅，白色亚麻坐垫；定制的白色亚麻沙发，继续散发出殖民地风格；一张咖啡桌，深色红木材质。

船尾的起居室中部有一个定制的装置，里面是一台嵌入式 46 英寸电视机。

两个图书室以蓝绿为装饰的主色调，把起居室与餐厅隔绝开来。餐厅采用电动滑动门，白橡木门上有 "威尼斯"图案。

餐厅的餐桌经过了特别的设计。桌面下是两个底座和支柱，支柱顶端开了一个洞，填满了沙子和贝壳，然后用玻璃盖封上。

船头的防水墙上装饰了木制相框，里面摆放了美国 50 年代日常生活的黑白照片。

继续往前，在主厅的后面，左侧是一个白橡木搭建的厨房，包括电器在内，全部采用美国模式。

另外，游艇还拥有一个颇具新意的完整的娱乐系统。

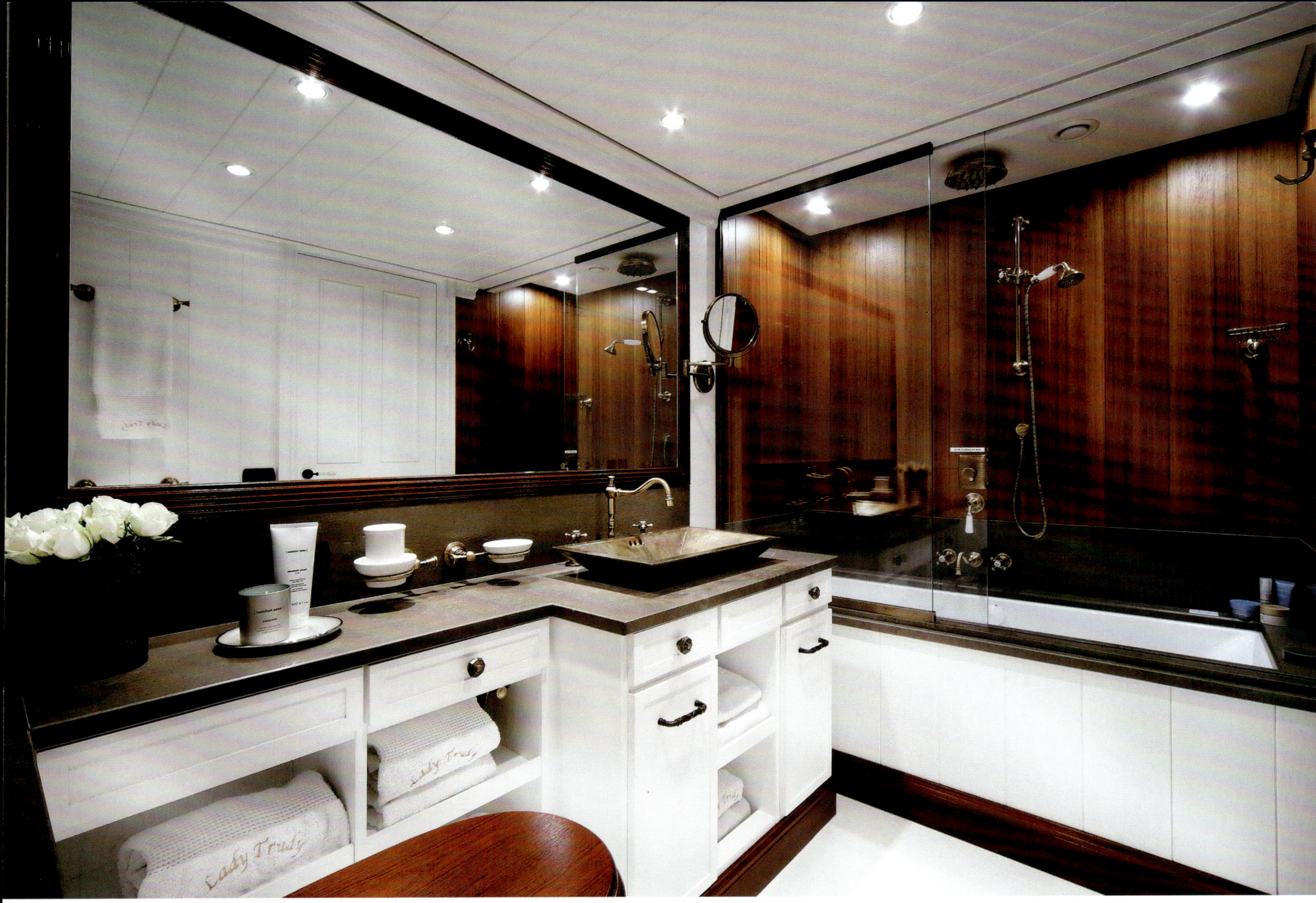
Lady Trudy

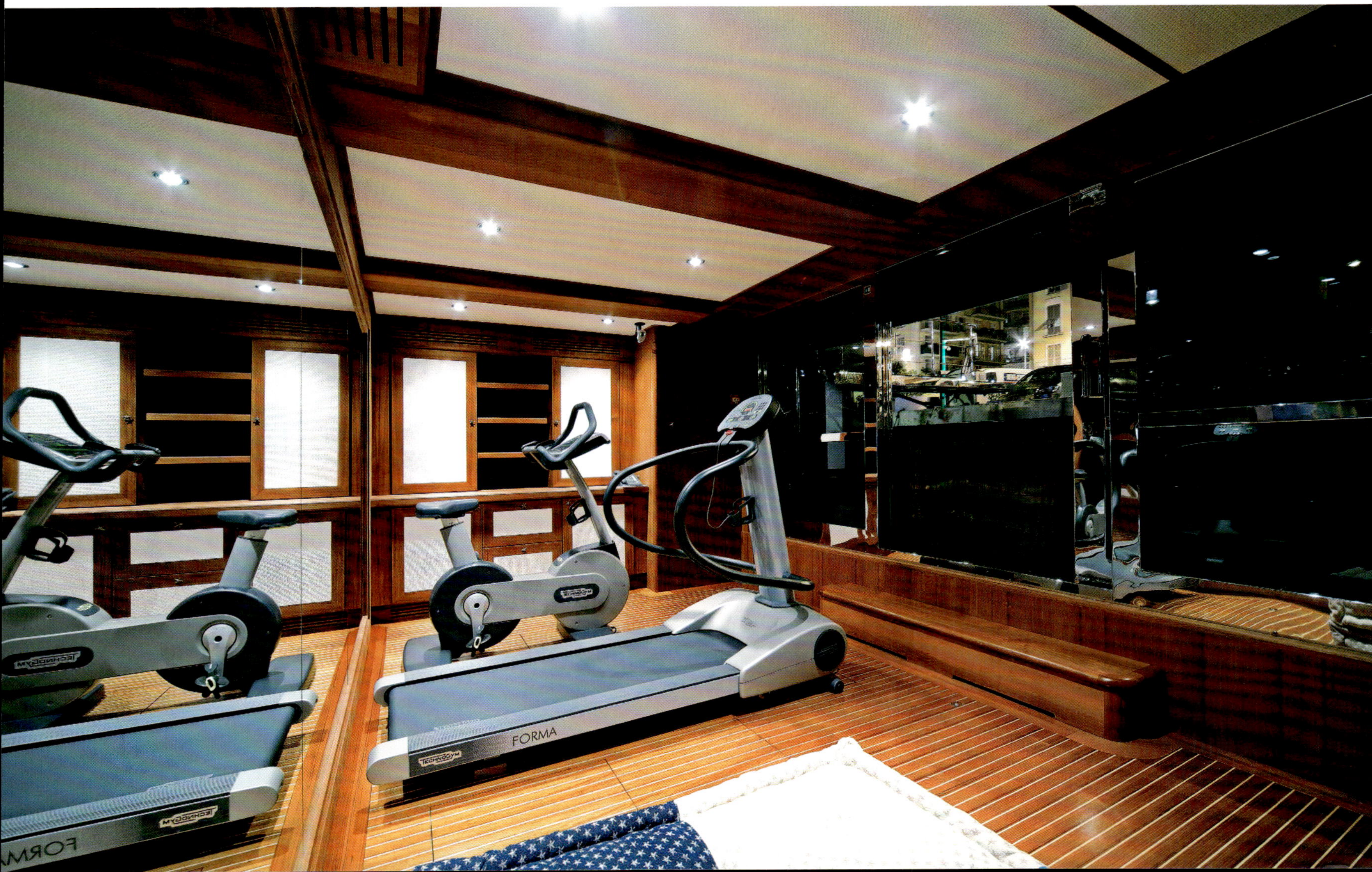
FORMA

ANCORA

> DESIGNER	Marilyn Bos- de Vaal, Frank L. Pieterse
> DESIGN COMPANY	Art-line Interiors B.V.
> SHIPYARD	Baglietto Shipyards
> LENGTH	42.75m
> BEAM	8.9m
> CRUISING SPEED	15.5kn
> PHOTOGRAPHER	Dick Holthuis

> A dream of a journey,

The movement of the water,

Its reflection in the roughly cut iced floes

The light sprinkles from everywhere.

The dining table carries its delicious burden on silver wires.

The spaces are defined and designed,

Furniture is blended in the peaceful landscape

Surface structures mark out the functional areas

Day loungers like safe cradles

Individual-and-social area's carefully mixed.

Architectural sculptures and sculptural architecure

Life should be the biggest party on earth.

SALON
301
302
303
304
WHEEL HOUSE
CAPTAIN'S CAB.
WHEELHOUSE DECK

MAIN SALON
201
202
203
204
GALLEY
OWNER'S CABIN
MAIN DECK

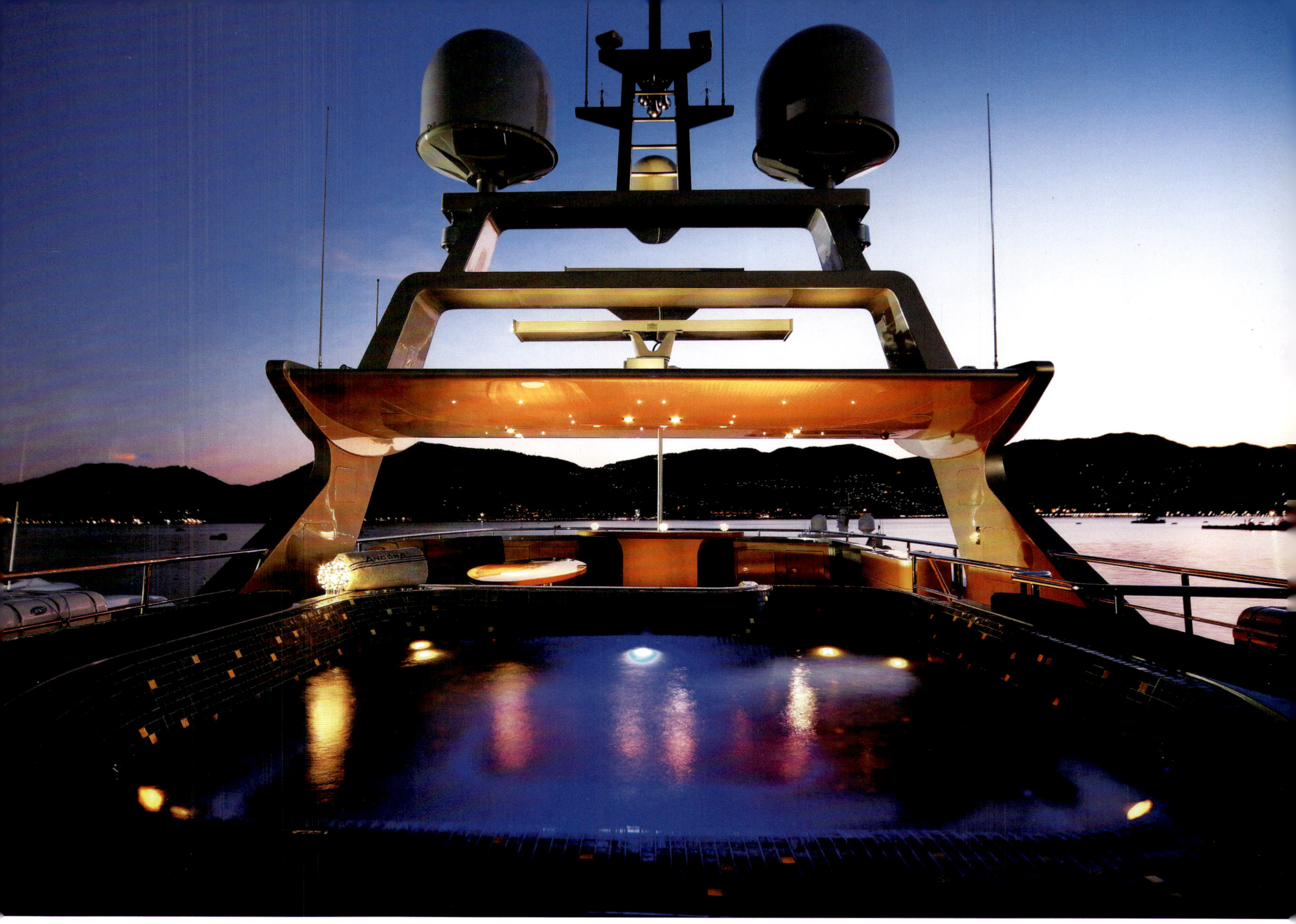

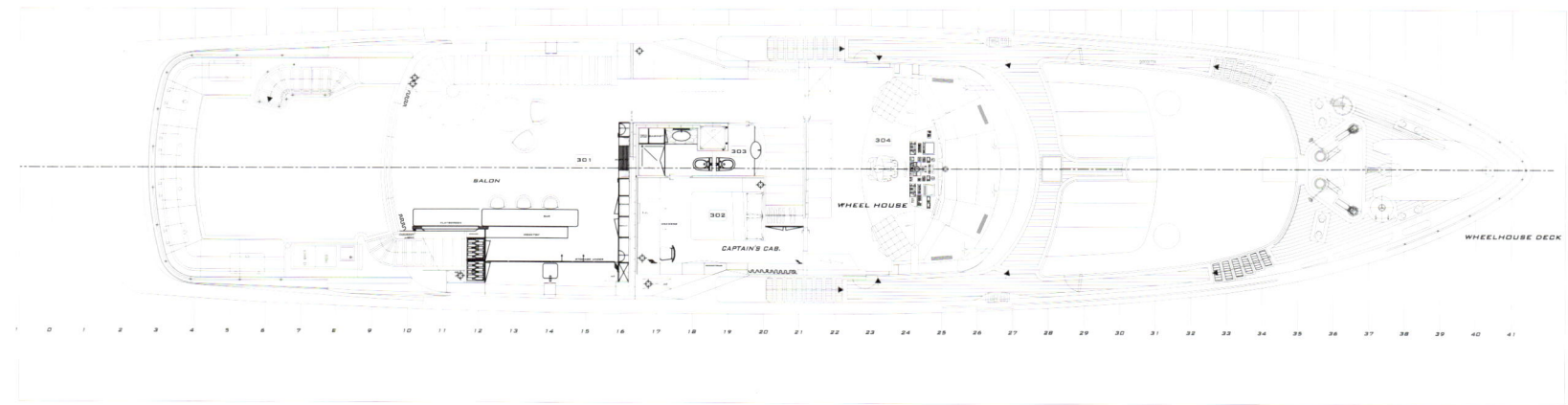

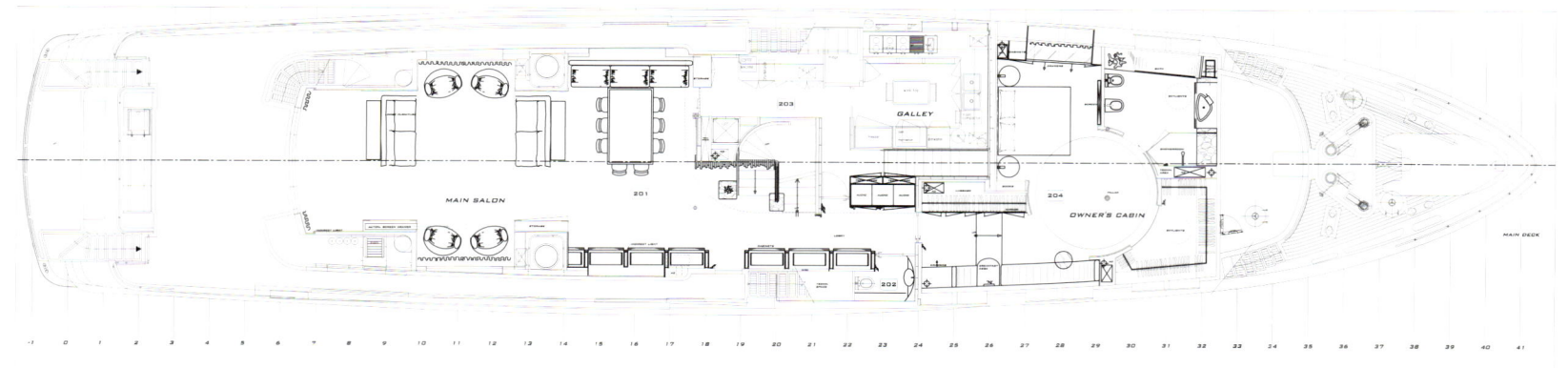

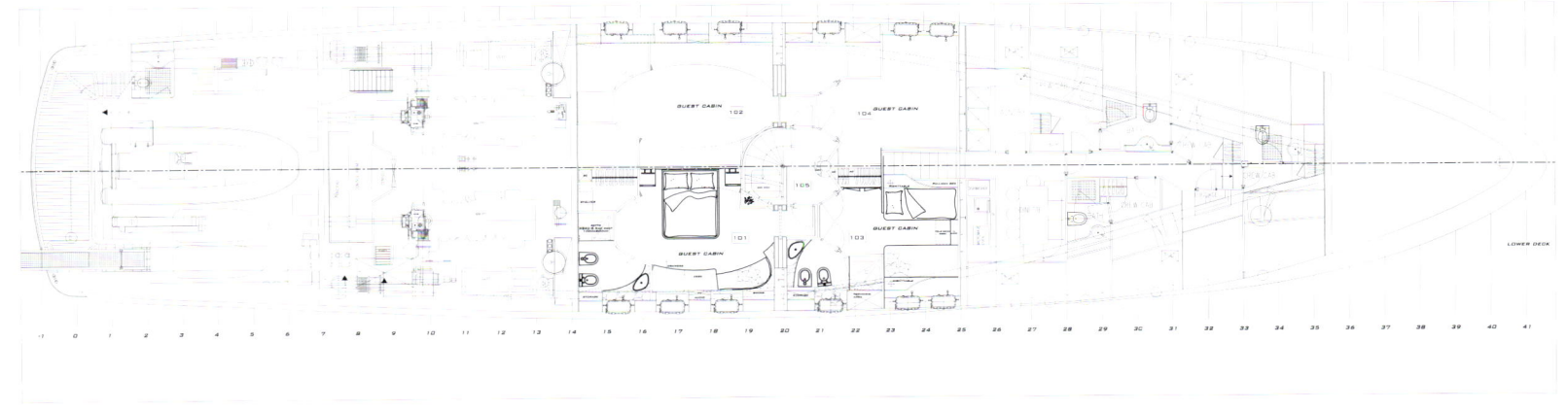

这是一艘梦幻之舟，
水波荡漾，
破开浮冰
晶莹闪烁。
餐桌银器，美味佳肴。
格局分明，设计精美，
大小家具，一应俱全，
景观和谐，生活便捷，
卧室隐蔽，随时可寝，
公私空间，相互交错，
是雕塑，亦是建筑，
世间最欢愉的生活，尽在其中。

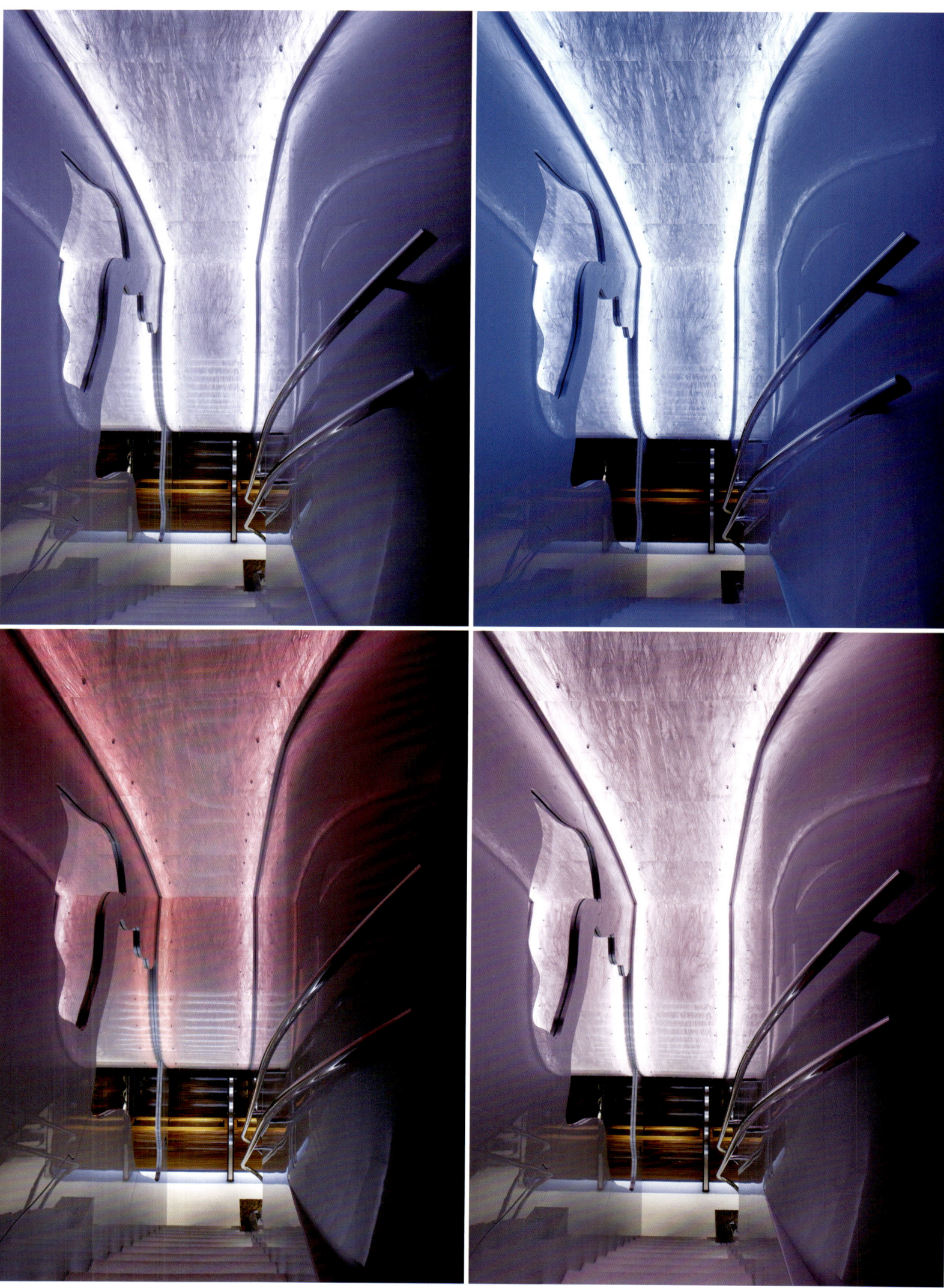

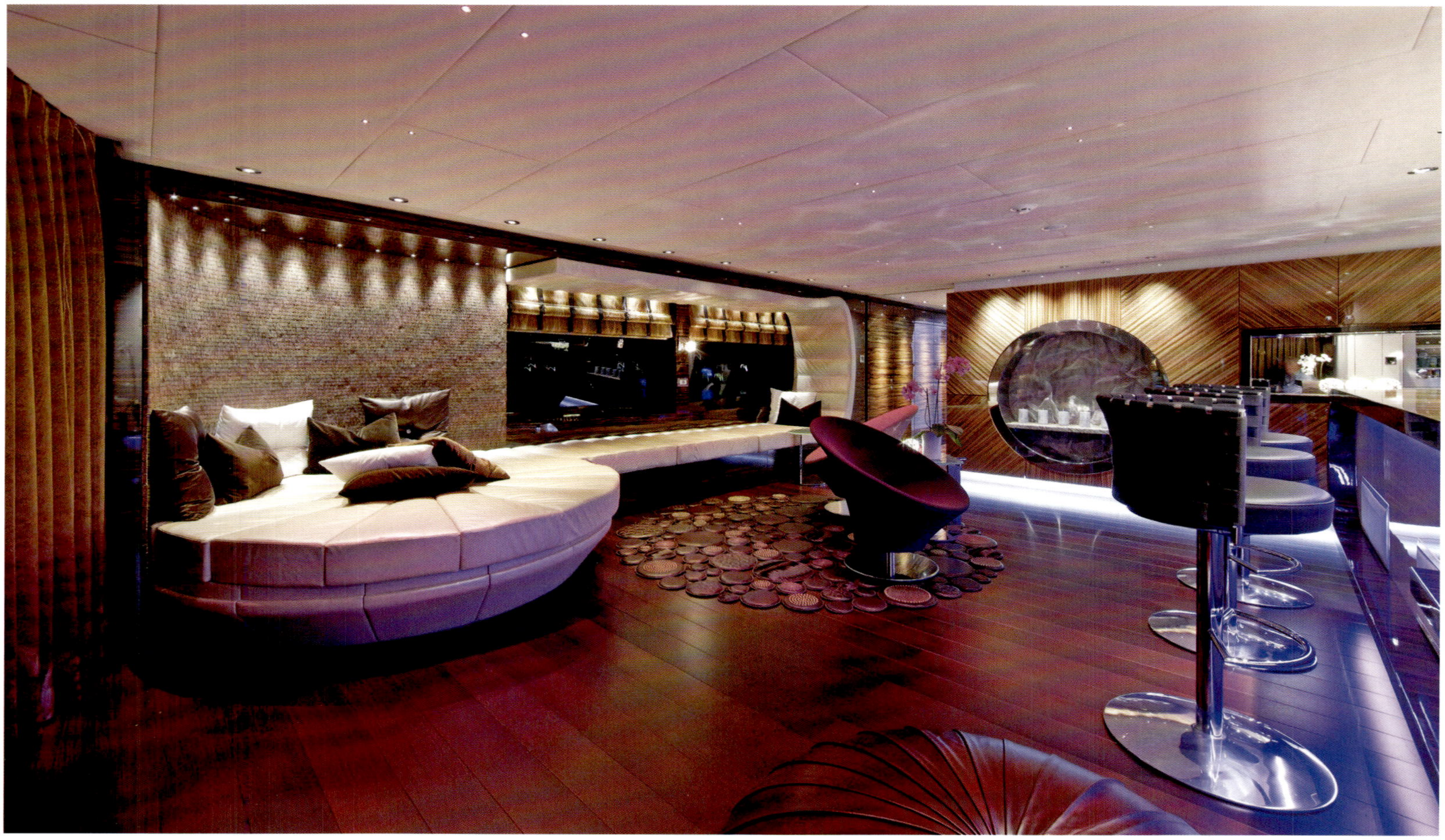

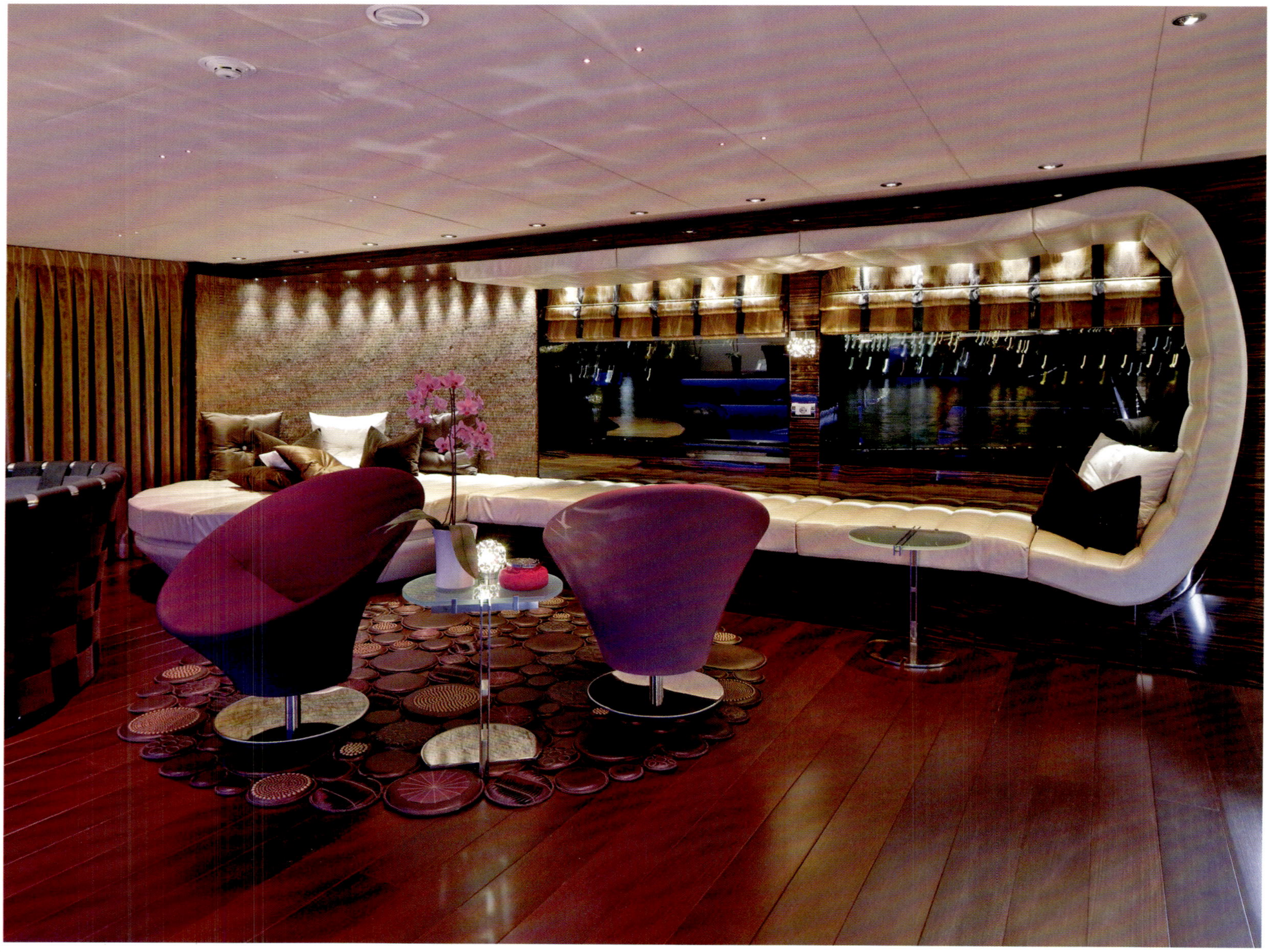

HELIX

> INTERIOR DESIGN Sinot Yacht Design
> EXTERIOR STYLING Feadship / Sinot Yacht Design
> NAVAL ARCHITECT Feadship
> SHIPYARD Feadship
> LENGTH 44.65m
> BEAM 9.20m
> MAX SPEED 14.5kn

Helix offers the maximum space possible in a 45-metre boat thanks in no small part to its centralised air conditioning. This system works with ducted air and dispenses with the need for separate fan coil units in each room. This innovative solution is not only quieter; it requires less maintenance and enhances layout flexibility. Moreover, with no cabinets required around the edges of the rooms to house airco units, the windows are much larger.

Social hub: The social life onboard Helix is usually the bridge deck lounge, the flexible layout of which offers you countless options for private pleasures. Thanks to an inventive system of sliding doors and windows, this is the place where you can truly bask in an indoor-out lifestyle. Enjoying the luxury in the lounge itself.

An equally refined treat for the senses await when dining on the vast aft deck or lounging on the fabulous sun pads. Enjoy…

The beach side of life: Helix contains a veritable treasure trove of watersport toys in all shapes and sizes, ensuring that there is never a dull moment onboard your beach-house on the water. Launch the tender,

fold out the platform and a lovely secluded private beach is created. This extends the yacht's length by almost four metres and serves as an ideal place for swimming, diving, snorkelling or playing with the waverunners, wakeboards and sailboats.

Fast forward: While the bulk of the crew are pampering to the needs of the onboard party, the skipper and his team enjoy the fruits of Feadship's technical expertise in the wheelhouse. The dashboard consists of a completely flush panel, amalgamating the bowthruster and engine controls. With the very latest equipment at the captain's fingertips, your safety and comfort is assured at all times.

Power packed: All the machinery (F45 Vantage) is easily accessible for service and - from pipe runs to pump placement - the entire layout has been considered to the finest degree. There is a reason that chief engineers love to work on a Feadship, and it's not just because the crew beds are the best.

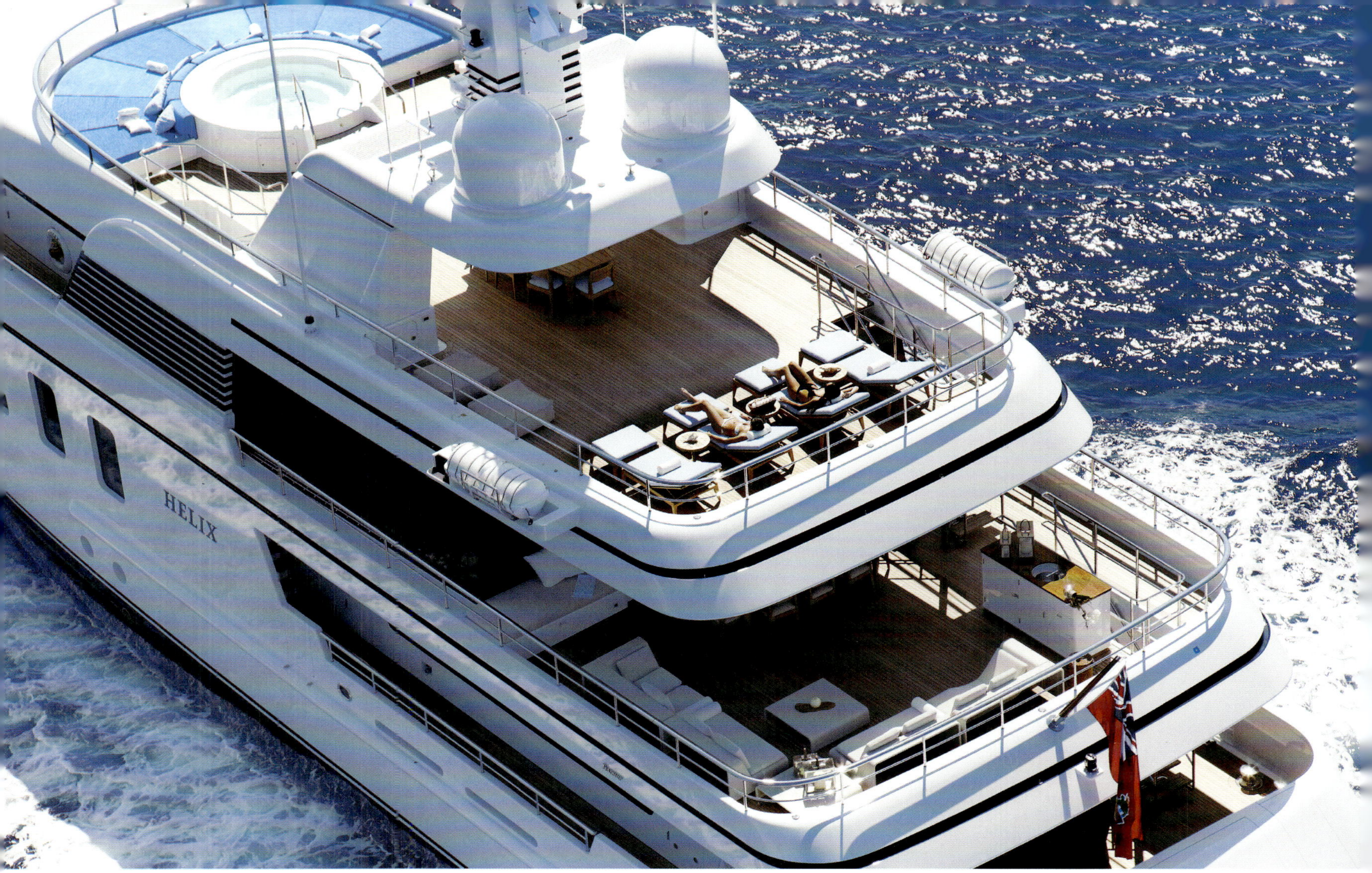
HELIX

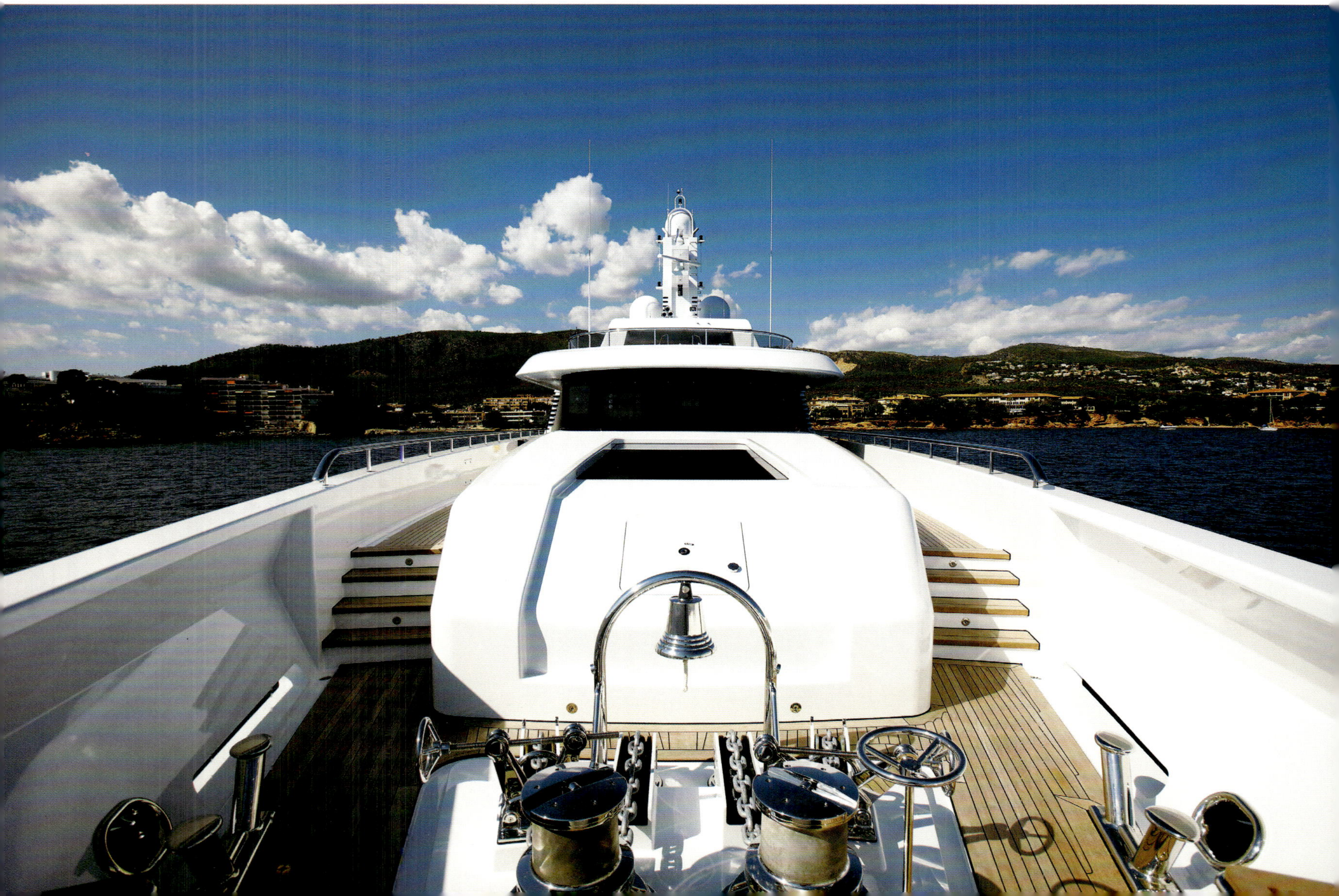

SUN DECK

1. Sun deck aft
2. Jacuzzi

BRIDGE DECK

3. Bridge deck aft
4. Bridge deck lounge
5. Hall
6. Pantry
7. Bathroom
8. Multi-purpose room
9. Wheelhouse

MAIN DECK

10. Main deck aft
11. Main deck lounge
12. Day head
13. Hall
14. Pantry
15. Guest bathroom 1
16. Guest bedroom 1
17. Guest bathroom 2
18. Guest bedroom 2
19. Guest bathroom 3
20. Guest bedroom 3
21. Guest bathroom 4
22. Guest bedroom 4
23. Owners' stateroom
24. Owners' bathroom

LOWER DECK

25. Beach platform
26. Lazarette
27. Steam bath / day head
28. Engine room
29. Galley
30. Captain's cabin
31. Crew mess
32. Laundry room
33. Crew quarters

GENERAL

OWNER

GUEST

CREW

TECHNICAL

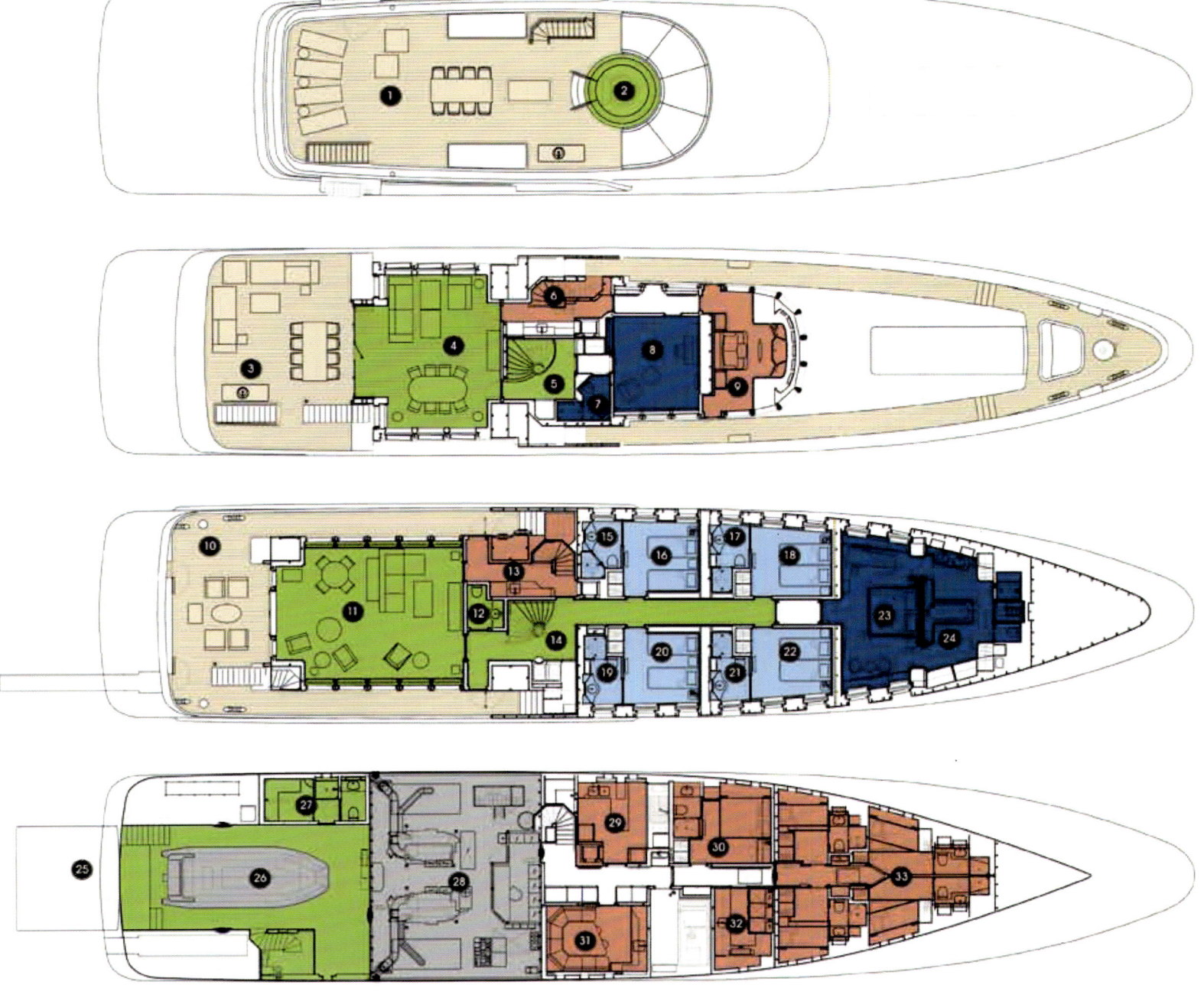

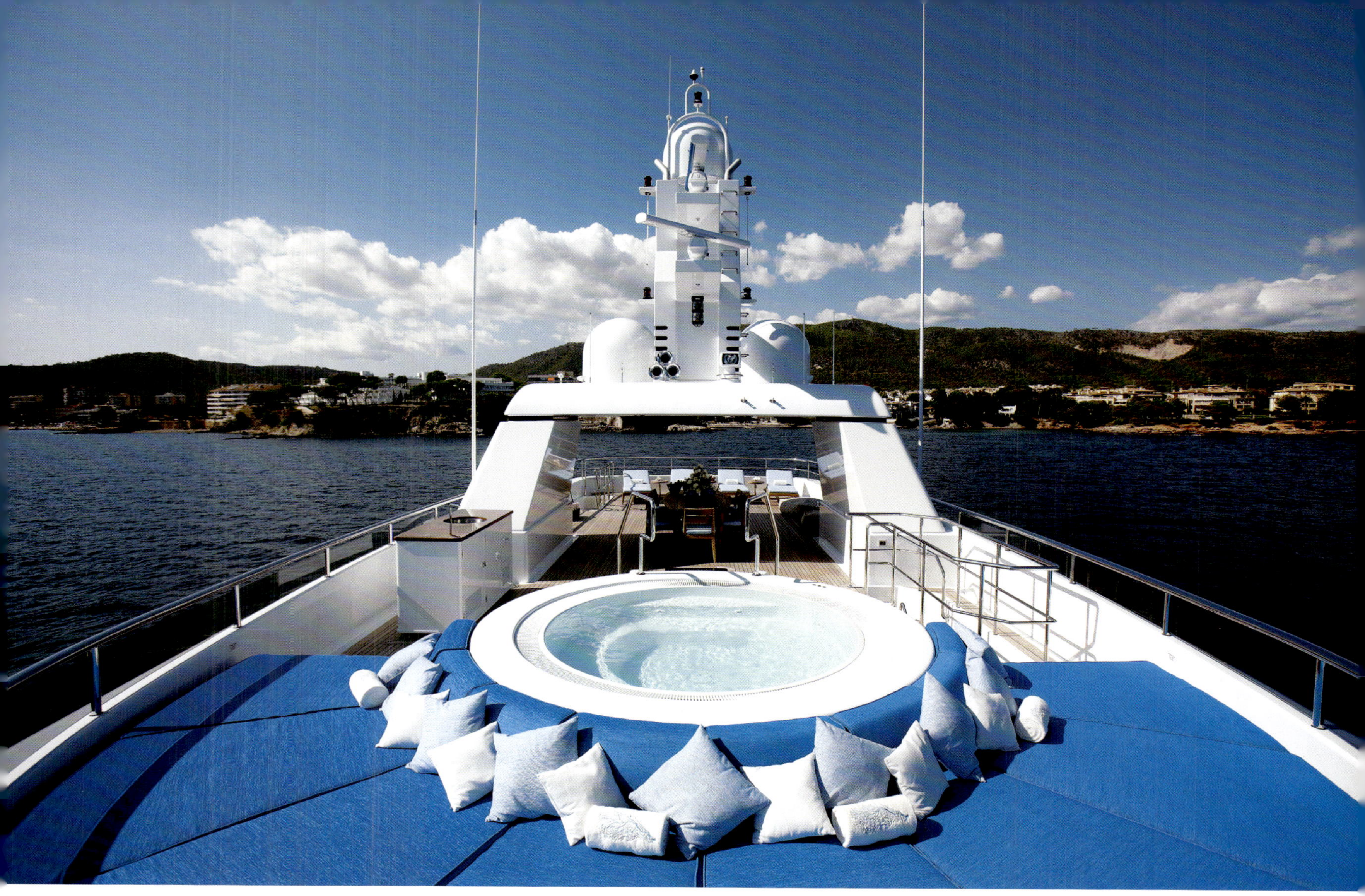

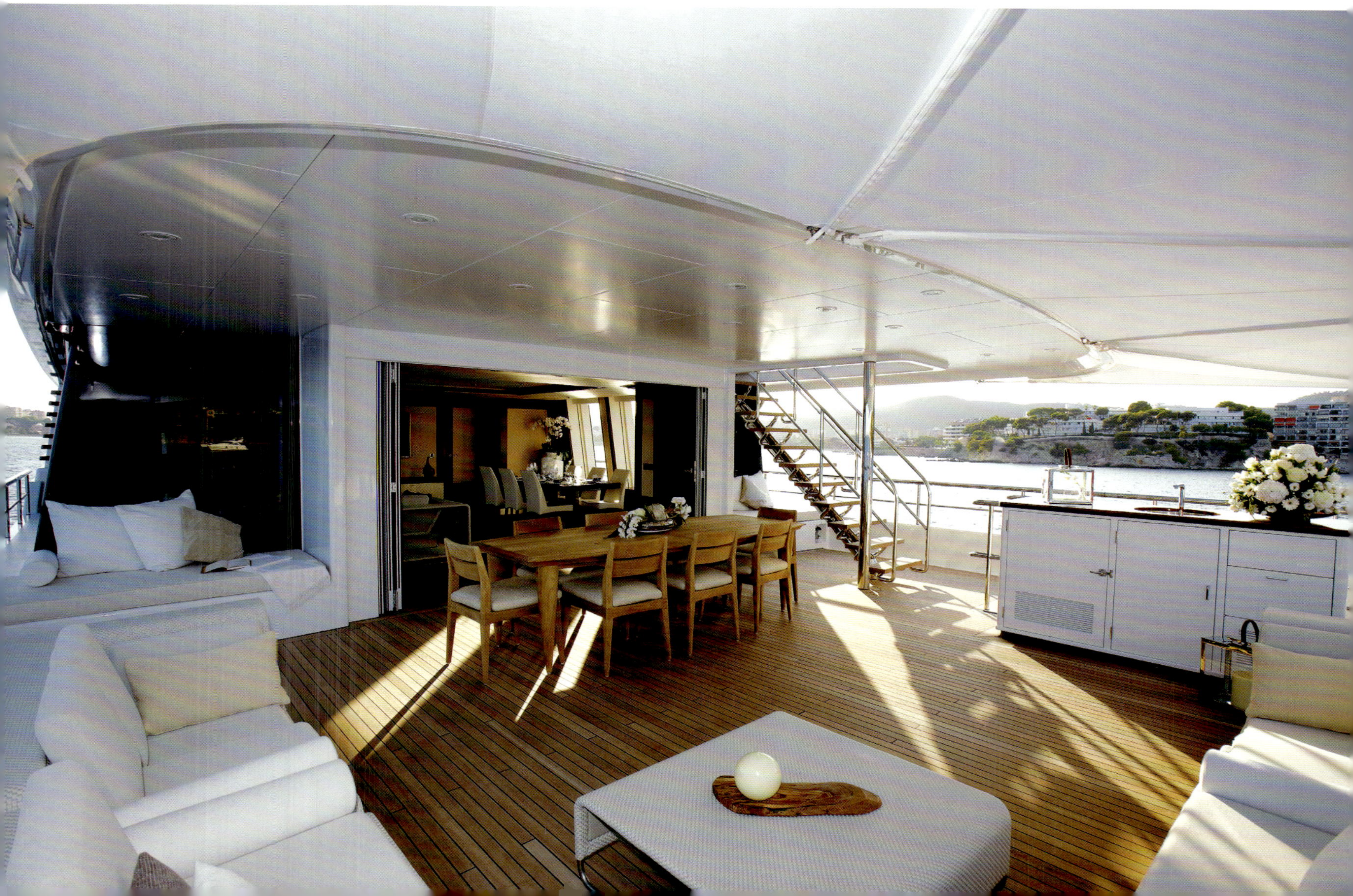

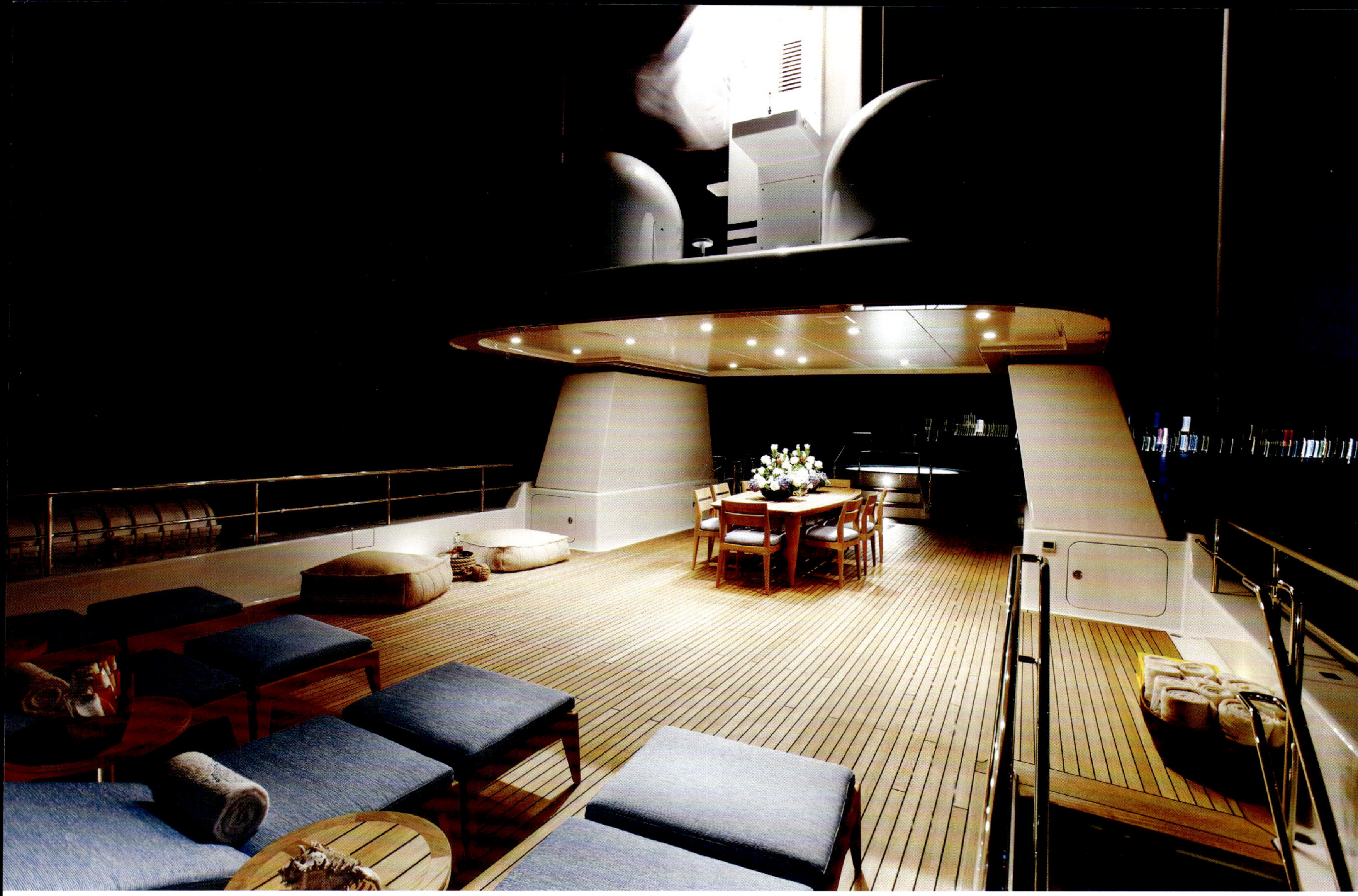
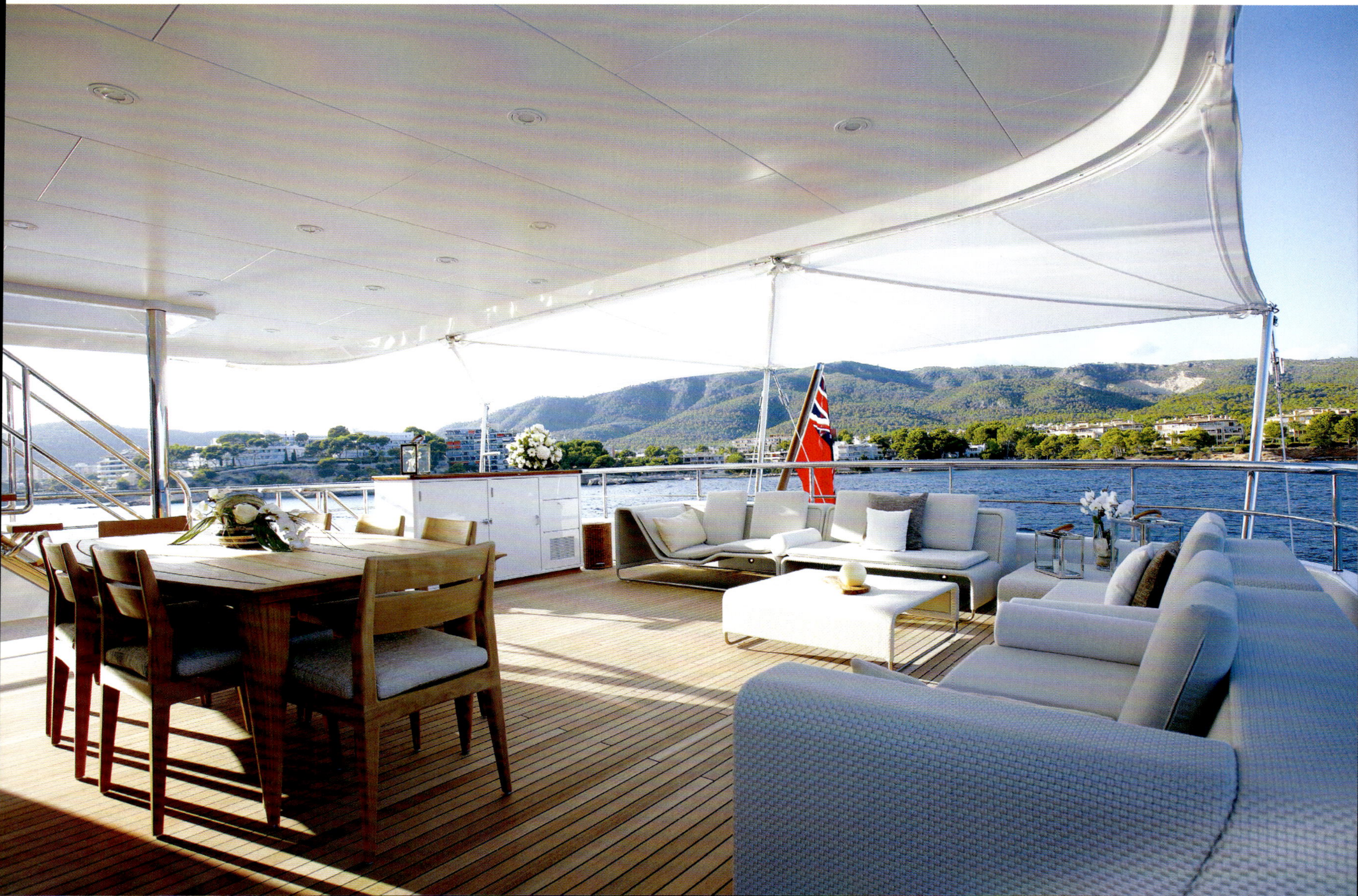

Helix游艇长约45米、结构布局为整艘船提供了宽敞的空间，还设有中央空调。整个空调设备由管道输送气体，然后按需分配到每个房间独立的风扇线圈组件。这一创新方案不仅更安静，而且维护起来更容易，又增加了布局的灵活性。同时，不需要在各个房间内壁周围另设箱柜安装空调设备组件，这就为窗户的布局提供了更大的空间。

丰富的社交娱乐场地： Helix游艇上的休闲社交生活通常在桥面甲板的娱乐区，灵活的布局为乘客提供了丰富多样的私人娱乐选择。锦上添花的是，独特的滑动门窗系统为乘客提供了能够真正在室内享受阳光浴的休闲生活情调。尽情享受游艇娱乐休息厅的奢华吧！

同样令人倍感惬意的还有，乘客可以坐在宽敞的船尾甲板上或是在仙境般的太阳浴垫上，享受味觉的盛宴。尽情享用吧！

安逸的海边生活： Helix游艇是一艘真正的水上运动游乐场，船上汇集了各种

形状和大小的水上运动设备及器械，确保乘客在水上的海景房里不会在任何时候感到沉闷与寂寞。搭起敞篷，折起站台，便是一个僻静的私人海滩。这样可以使游艇的长度延伸将近4米，为游泳、跳水、通气潜水以及冲浪、划水和帆船运动等提供了绝佳的场地。

先进的操作设备： 当游艇工作人员竭尽全力满足船上乘客的娱乐需求的同时，船长和他的团队也正在操舵室享受着Feadship（斐帝星）游艇品牌的先进技术专长的成果。仪表盘由一个平镶板配合船首推进器和发动机控制。船长指尖所操作的都是最新最前沿的机器设备，因此在任何时候都可以保证乘客的安全和舒适。

强有力的机械装备： Feadship推出的所有 F45 Vantage系列游艇的机械配置，从管道运行到水泵安装，操作起来简单方便。整个船的布局都被业界公认为达到最高配置。操舵手们酷爱在Feadship品牌的游艇上工作，不只是因为游艇提供了最好的船员卧铺，更重要的原因在于其机械装备。

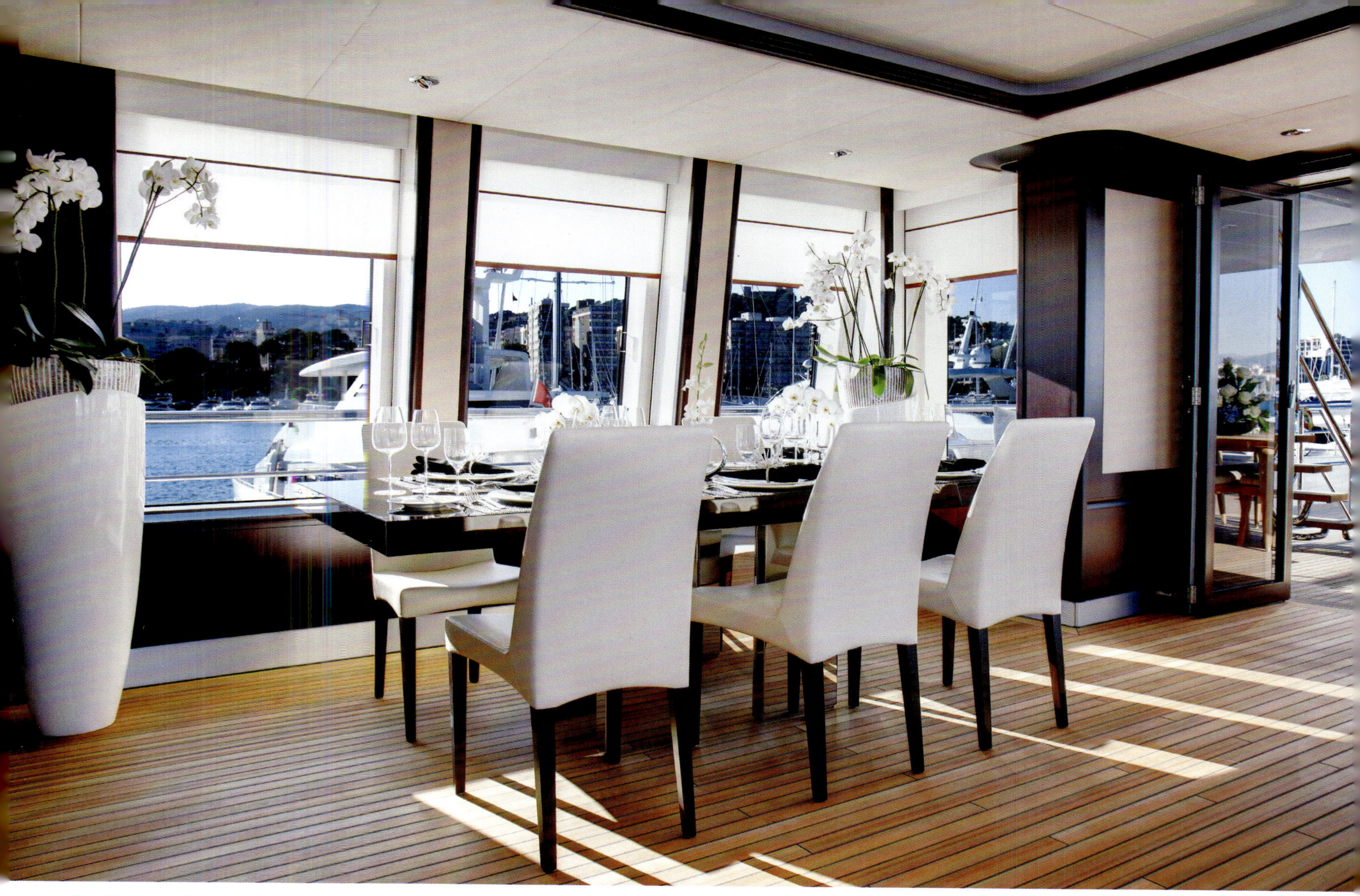

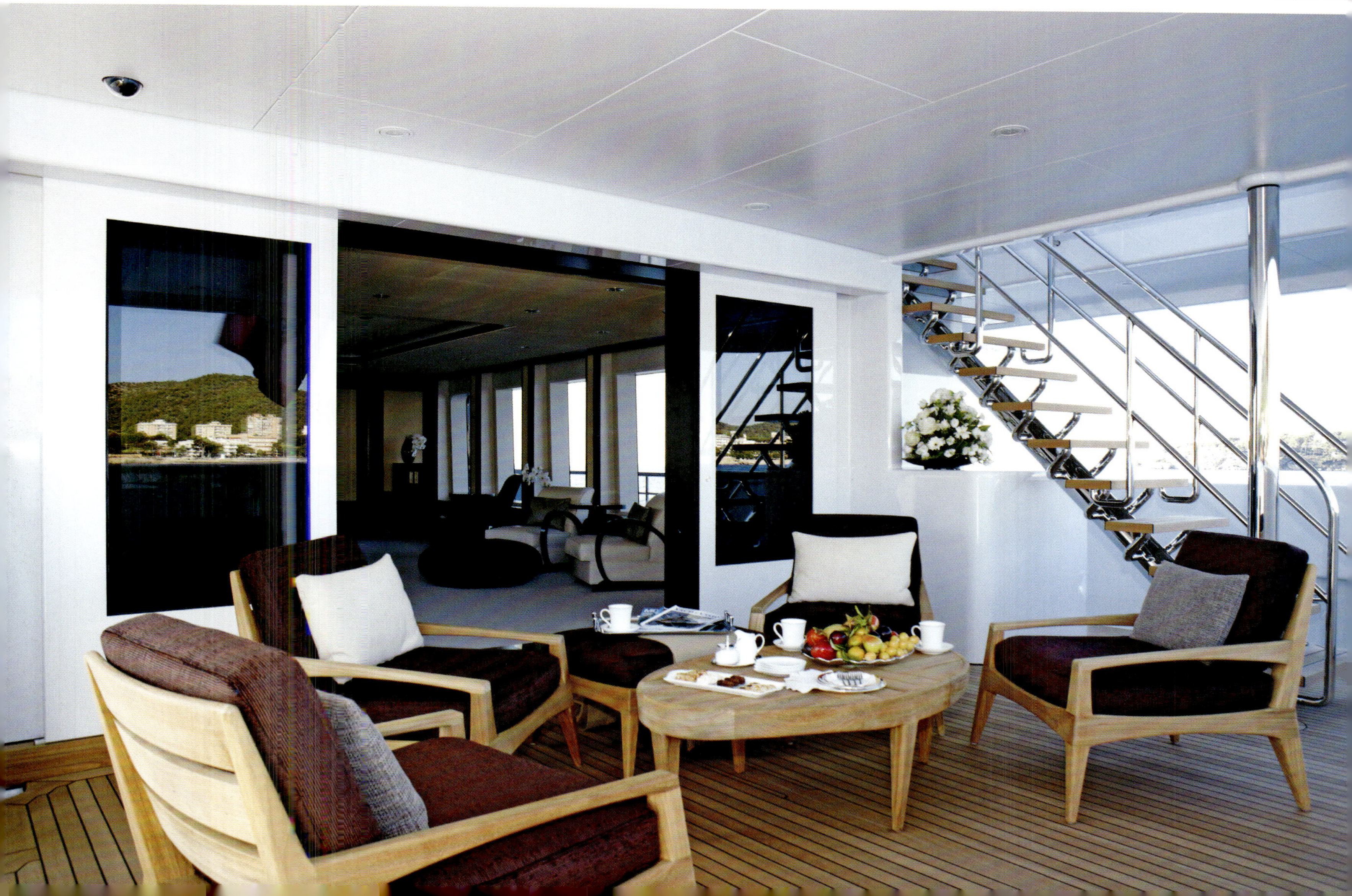

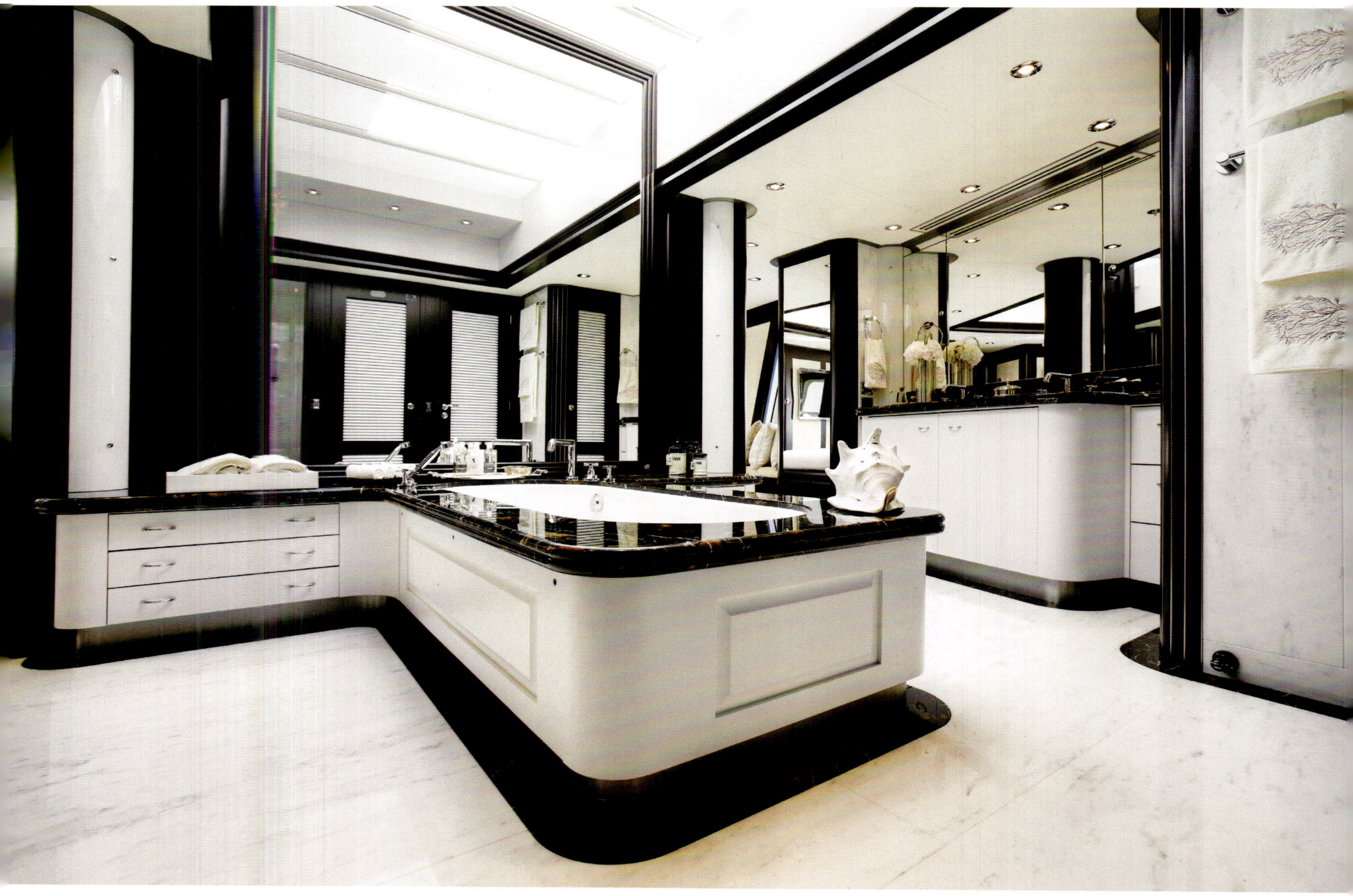

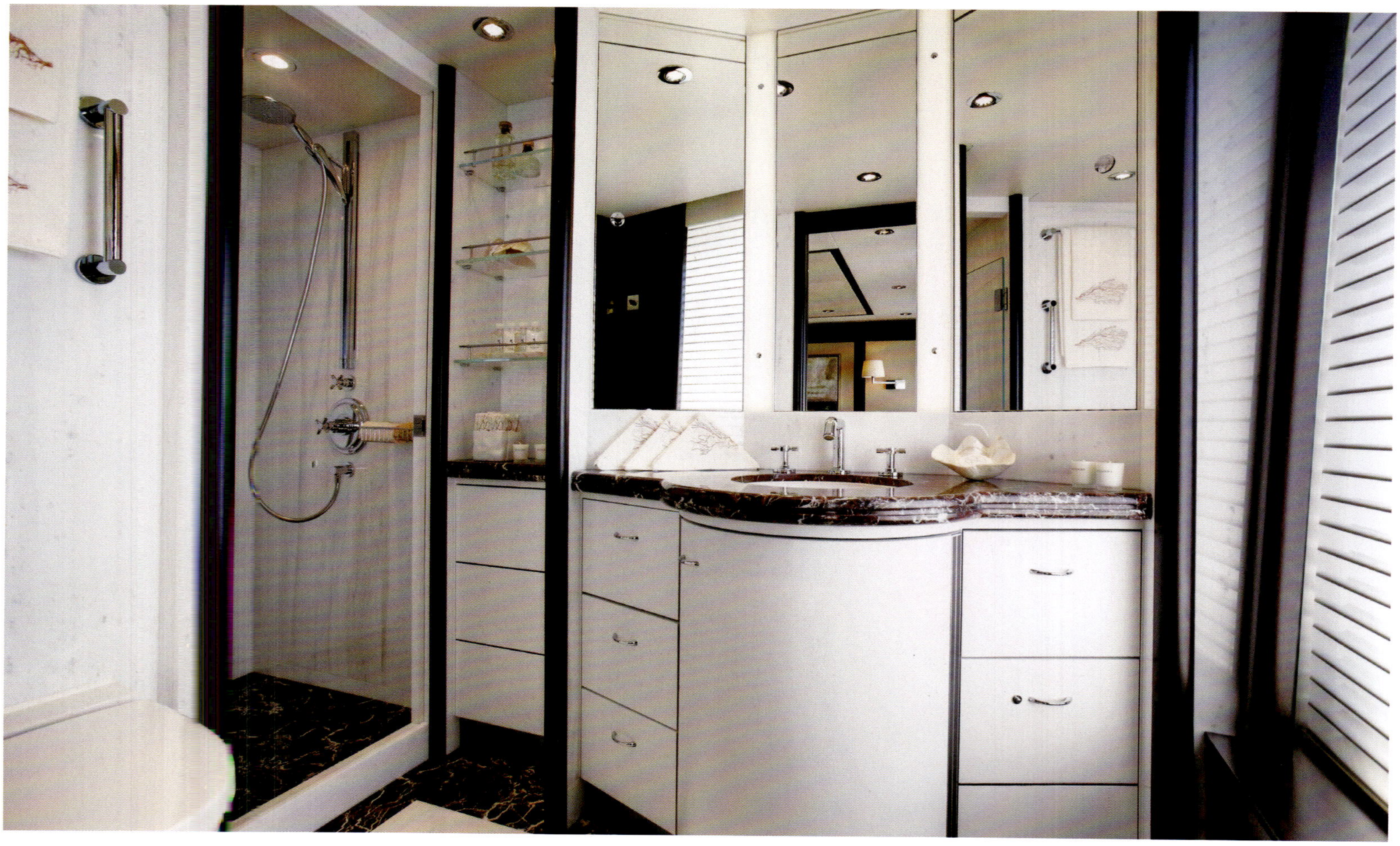

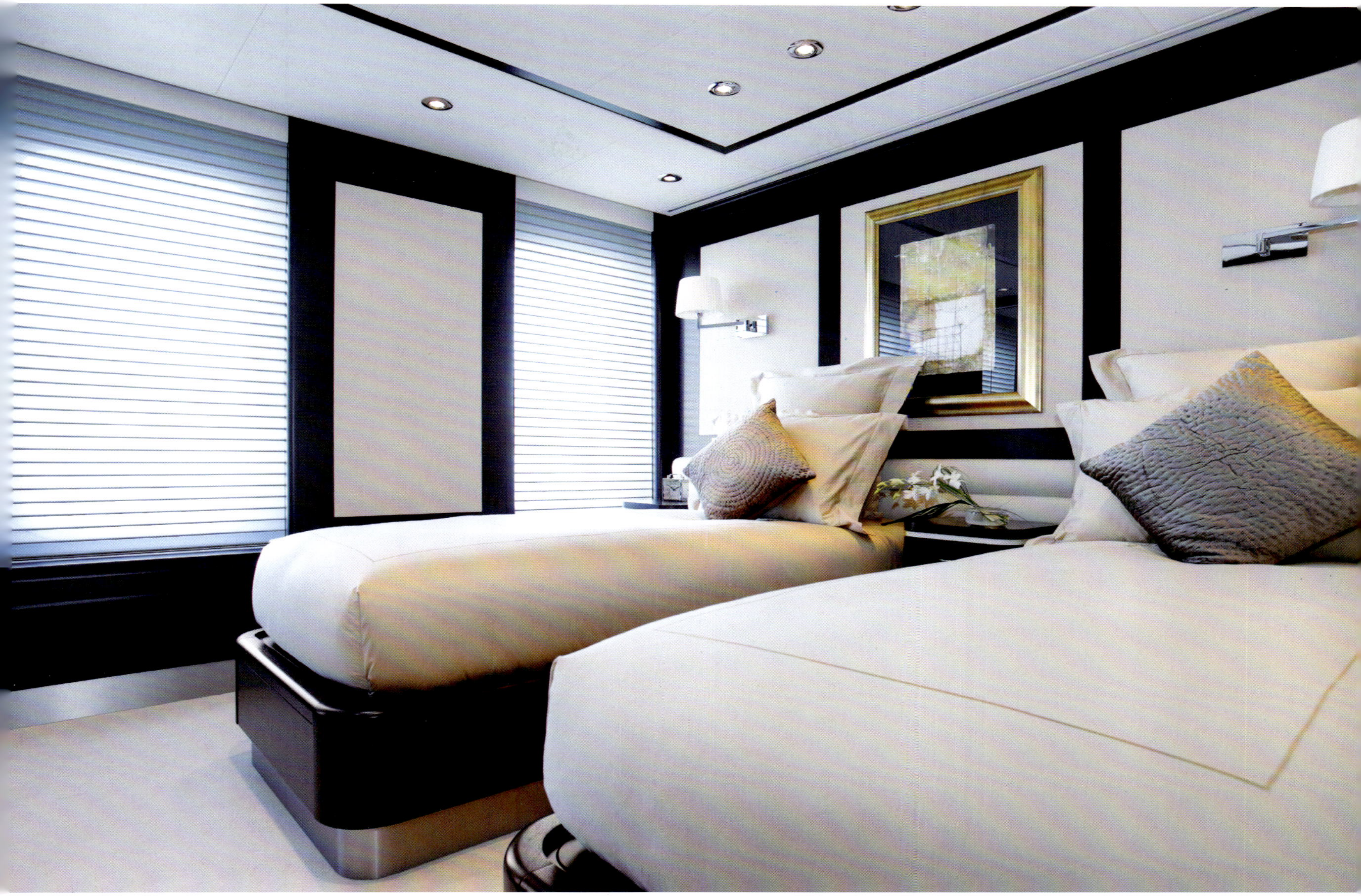

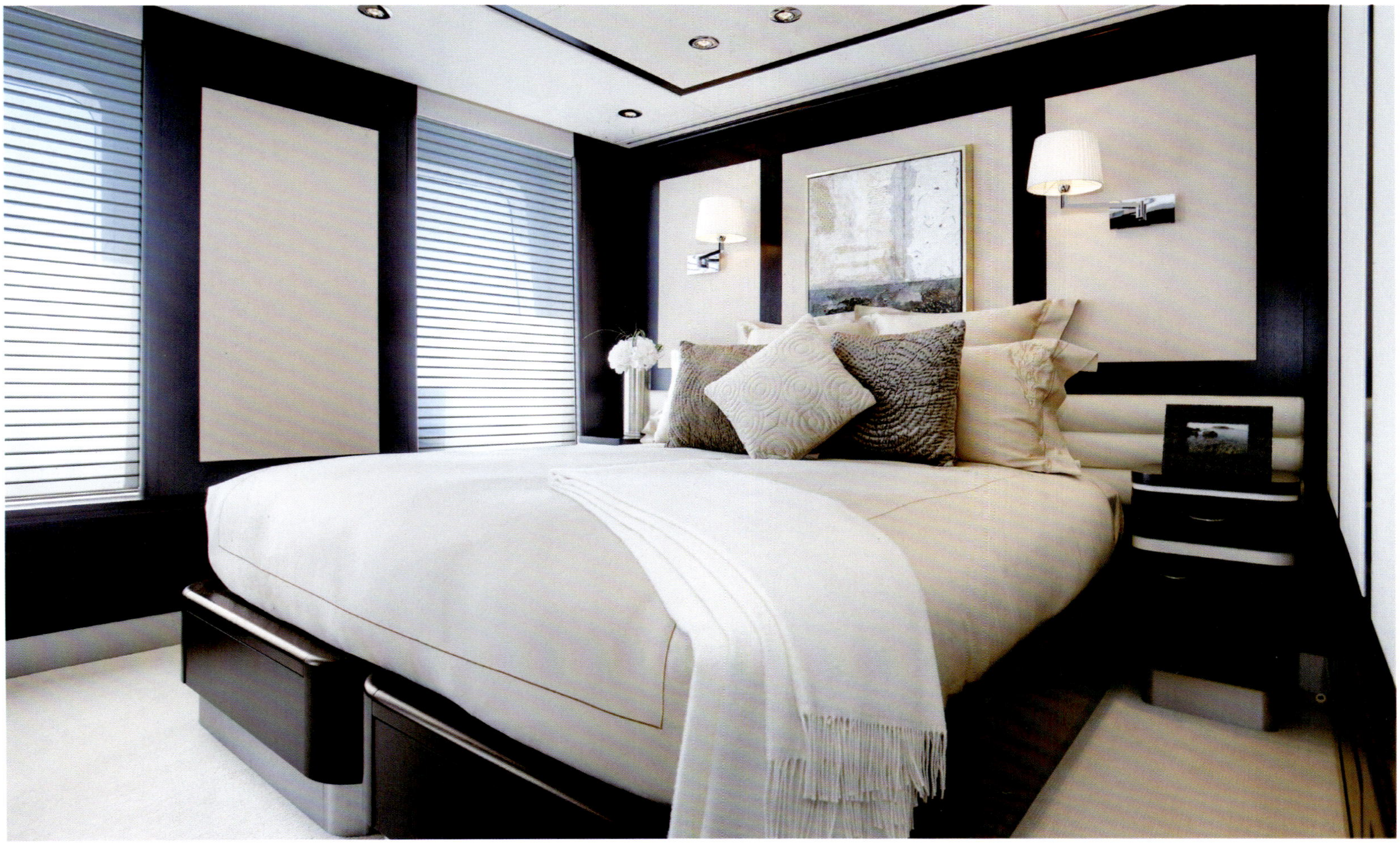

MANIFIQ

› INTERIOR DESIGN	Luca Dini Design
› EXTERIOR DESIGN	Cor D. Rover
› NAVAL ARCHITECTURE	Mondo Marine Engineering
› LENGTH	40.50m
› BEAM	8.40m
› MAXIMUM SPEED	19kn
› CRUISING SPEED	17kn

> Decoration aboard is entrusted to the elegance of polished ebony, used in a contrasting pattern between lighter and darker wood, strongly ruled, and the elegant use of precious marble. The use of leather on panelling makes the environment comfortable and rigorous at the same time.

Furniture is partly made in Macassar ebony, chrome steel and glossy black lacquered wood, with large parts covered with leather decorated with a recurrent lozenge pattern.

Great care has been taken over lighting aboard: daylight is ensured by the presence of large windows. The sophisticated artificial lighting aboard has been obtained thanks to a clever mix of ceiling low energy LEDs, giving an indirect light, and diffused and recessed lighting, running around the perimeter of the rooms and furnishings and accentuating the environment evocative power, accompanied by light sources given by design lamps.

Particular attention has been paid to the distribution and use of volumes.

The outfit includes also a large hall in the main deck, which consists of two parts: a convivial area and a dining area. Further on is a spectacular staircase connecting the lower and the upper deck.

On the yacht left side is the kitchen, while on the right side it is possible to reach the large owner's area consisting of a relax area equipped with a comfortable sofa and a large wardrobe for the owner, running along the entire port side, and of a large stateroom with a wardrobe for the owner's wife and a bathroom characterized by the presence of precious marble.

The entire lower deck is for guests. Below deck are 4 cabins, two full-width vips with a bathroom and a separate wardrobe area and two guests, one with a double bed and the other with two single beds and a pullman bed.

Everywhere it is possible to admire the ebony and leather of vertical surfaces arranged in alternate horizontal bands with the addition of chrome fillets, precious marble, rich fabrics and specially designed pieces of furniture.

In the upper deck is a home cinema with 10 Art Deco style seats equipped with small specially designed steel tables. The home cinema can be completely blacked out and is fully automated; a film projector with a screen, both sliding away into the ceiling, and a 65' TV ensure picture quality.

In order to enlarge and integrate internal and external spaces, it has been decided to use rich decorative cushions and ebony also in the dining area of the upper deck.

A buffet bar, the convivial extensible round table with a precious ebony finish and the fine black chairs make it a space suitable not only for fast snacks and meals but also for more formal and elegant full-dress dinners.

The Fly deck layout includes the small stern swimming pool, a central cocktail cabinet with stools and the forward relax area. The swimming pool is embedded into a raised sundeck and decorated with a teak edge. The composition of seats and tables can be modified in order to change it from a large lounge into a comfortable sun lounge.

While sailing, Manifiq goes beyond 19 knots and has a range of 4,828 kilometers at the cruising speed of 12 knots. The absence of vibrations, the search for advanced solutions in the field of soundproofing, the reliability and comfort enhance the quality level of life aboard and represent the values which make MONDO MARINE an excellence of Made in Italy in the seas of all over the world.

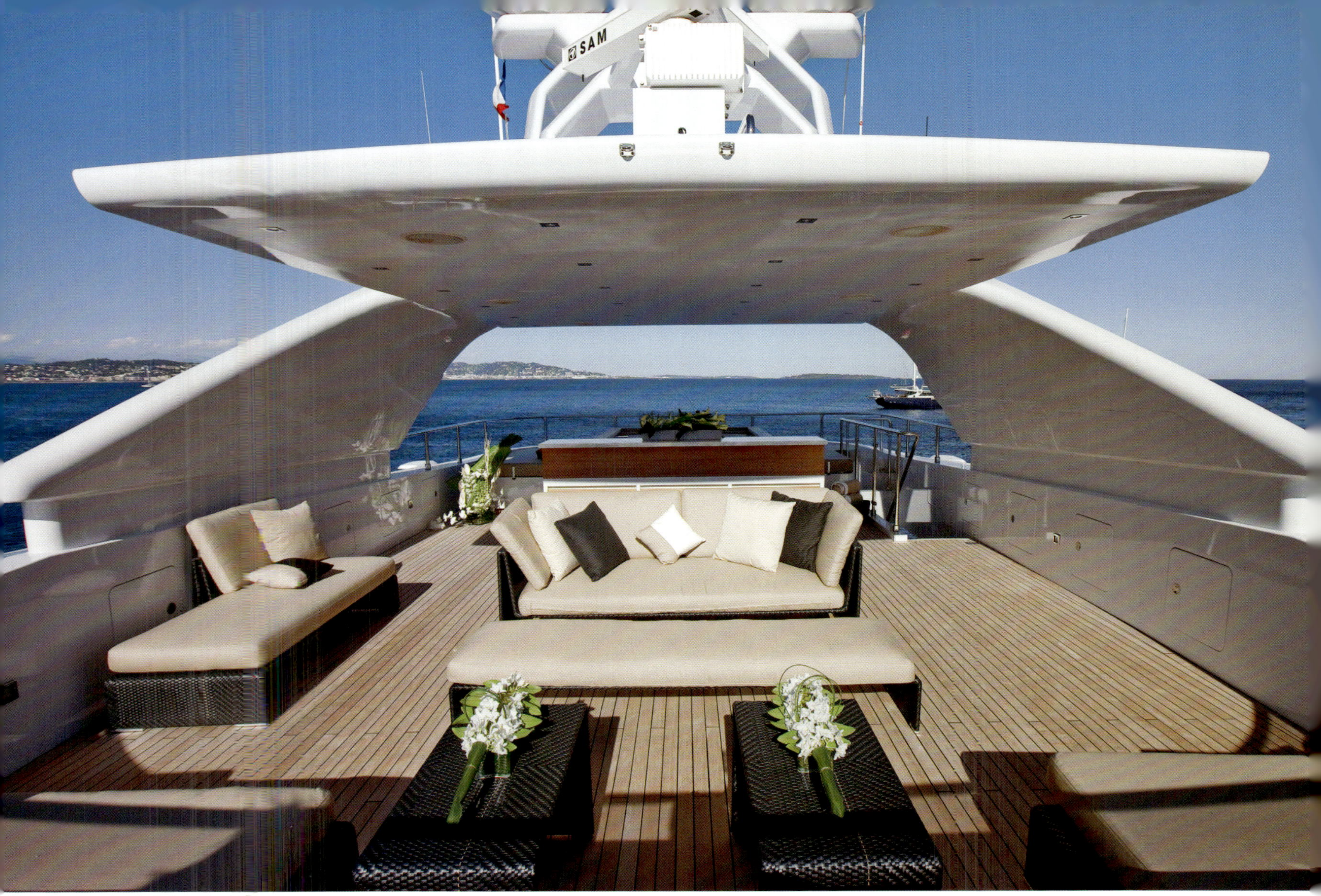
SAM

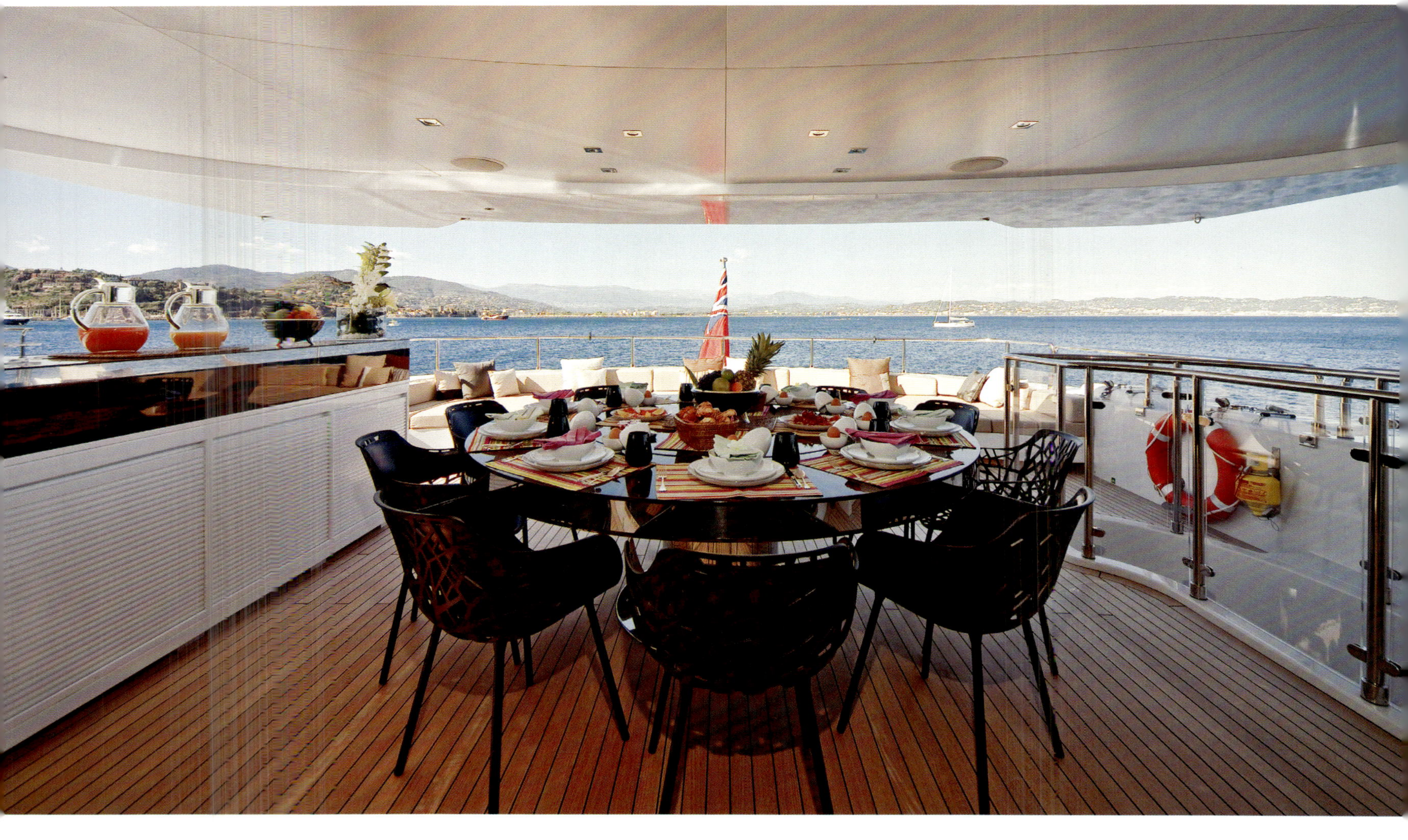

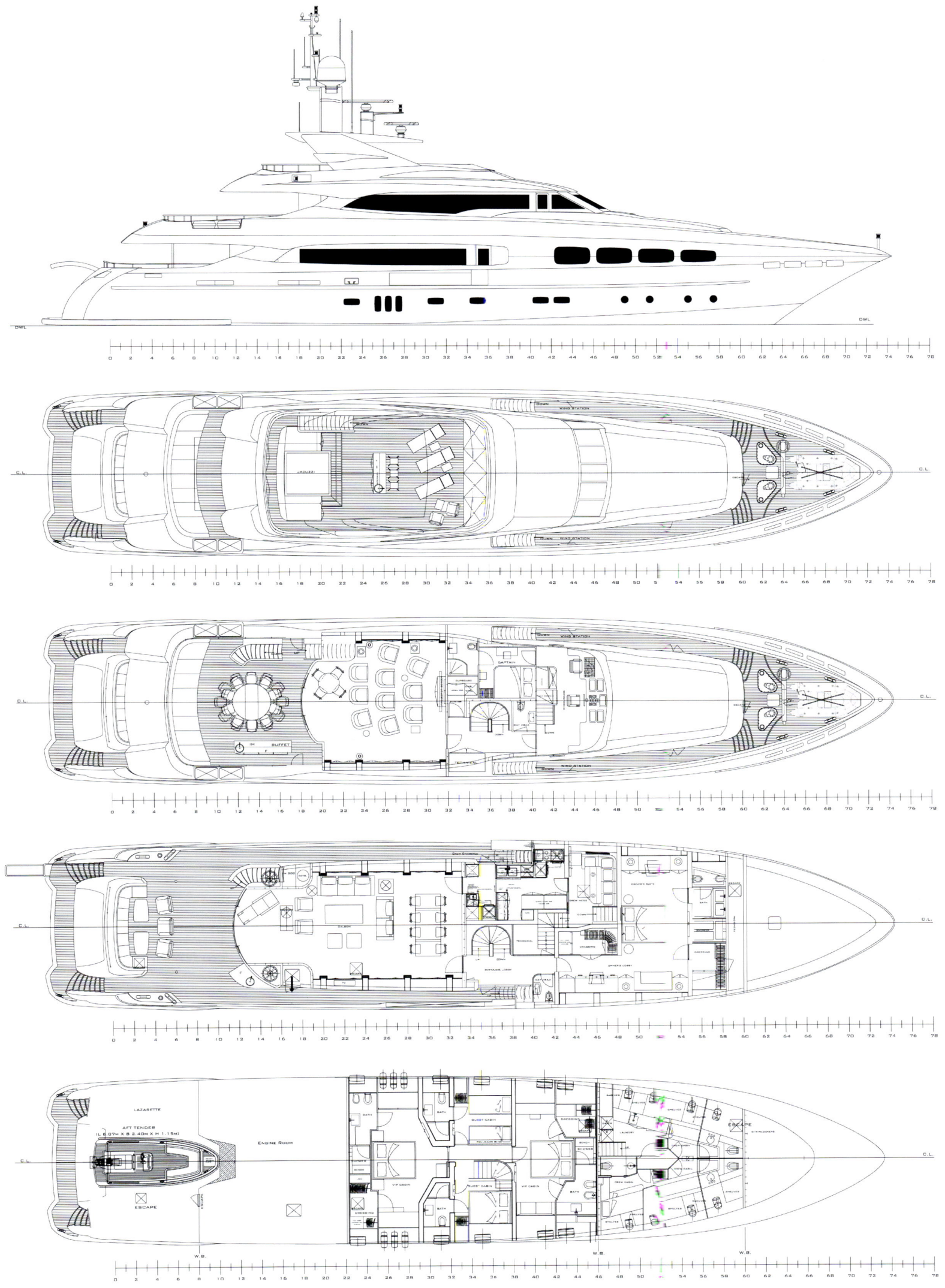

　　游艇室装修使用精致打磨的黑檀木料，让深色和浅色木料平行交错搭配，形成鲜明的对比，恰如其分地运用大理石，体现出一种高贵雅致。面板上使用皮革，使环境既显得轻松舒适，又不失严谨。

　　音分家具采用了望加锡黑檀木、铬钢和光滑的黑漆木，主体部分使用皮革装饰，形成一环环菱形图纹。

　　船体的照明设计也是颇具匠心：大窗设计确保了白天的日照。精密的人工照明系统也巧妙地使用了天花板节能LED灯，呈现出柔和的光照效果。房屋、家具的四周的散射与凹式光照，辅以景观饰灯的弱光，更突显出环境的怀旧气息。

　　同时，柱子的分布与使用也十分考究。

　　主甲板还有一个大厅，包括两个区域：一个活动区，一个用餐区。再往前就是一个楼梯，连接底层甲板和顶层甲板。

　　游艇的左侧是厨房，而在右侧则可以到达船主的区域。船主区沿着左舷有一个休闲区，内设一个舒适的沙发和一个大的私人衣柜。船主区还有一个大的梳妆间，里面的衣柜供船主的妻子专用，而这里的卫生间也装饰着豪华的大理石。

　　整个底层甲板是供宾客使用的，甲板下有四个客舱。其中两个是与船同宽的贵宾舱，内设独立卫生间和衣橱。第三个是双人客舱，最后一个客舱放置了两长单人床和一个折叠床。

  游艇每一处的垂直墙面上，都能看到檀木与皮革呈水平交替排列。还能看到铬钢条、大理石、纺织物和特别设计的家具物件。

  上层甲板是一个家庭影院，10张艺术装饰派风格的座椅，每张座椅都配有特别制造的小钢桌。这个家庭影院采用一键控制电源和全自动化操作系统。电影放映机和屏幕都可以收缩到天花板内，65英寸的电视确保了画面的质量。

  为了扩展空间，将室内外空间融合，游艇上层甲板的用餐区还采用了大量的装饰垫和黑檀木料。

  还有餐饮吧台和折叠式圆形餐桌，配上珍贵的黑檀抛光面板和优质的黑色座椅，使这个空间不又适合简单的小吃与快餐，更适合正式典雅的高级聚餐。

  驾驶甲板上有一个小型的船尾泳池，中间是一个鸡尾酒柜，前面摆着一排小凳子，再往前是一个休闲区。泳池嵌在高起一截的太阳甲板上，用柚木包边。桌椅的大小都可以微调，以便于在大的休闲厅与小的日光浴区来回搬动。

  该游艇的最大航行速度可以超过19海里/小时。以12海里/小时长速度可以穿越4828千米的距离。在船上感受不到震动，隔音技术先进，可靠舒适，确保了高质量的游艇生活。这也意味着"梦都海洋"公司在世界造船业成为"意大利制造"卓越品牌。

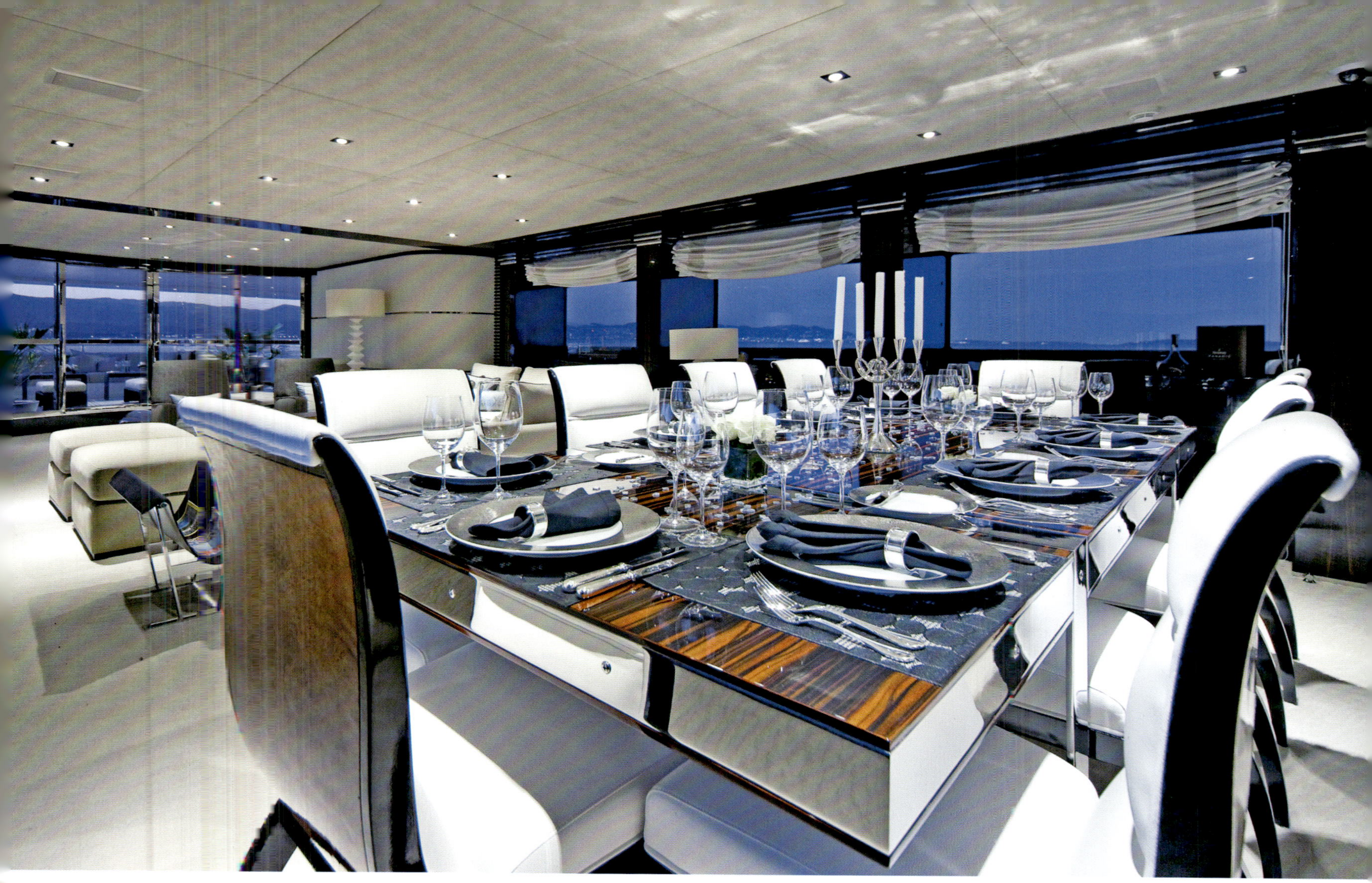

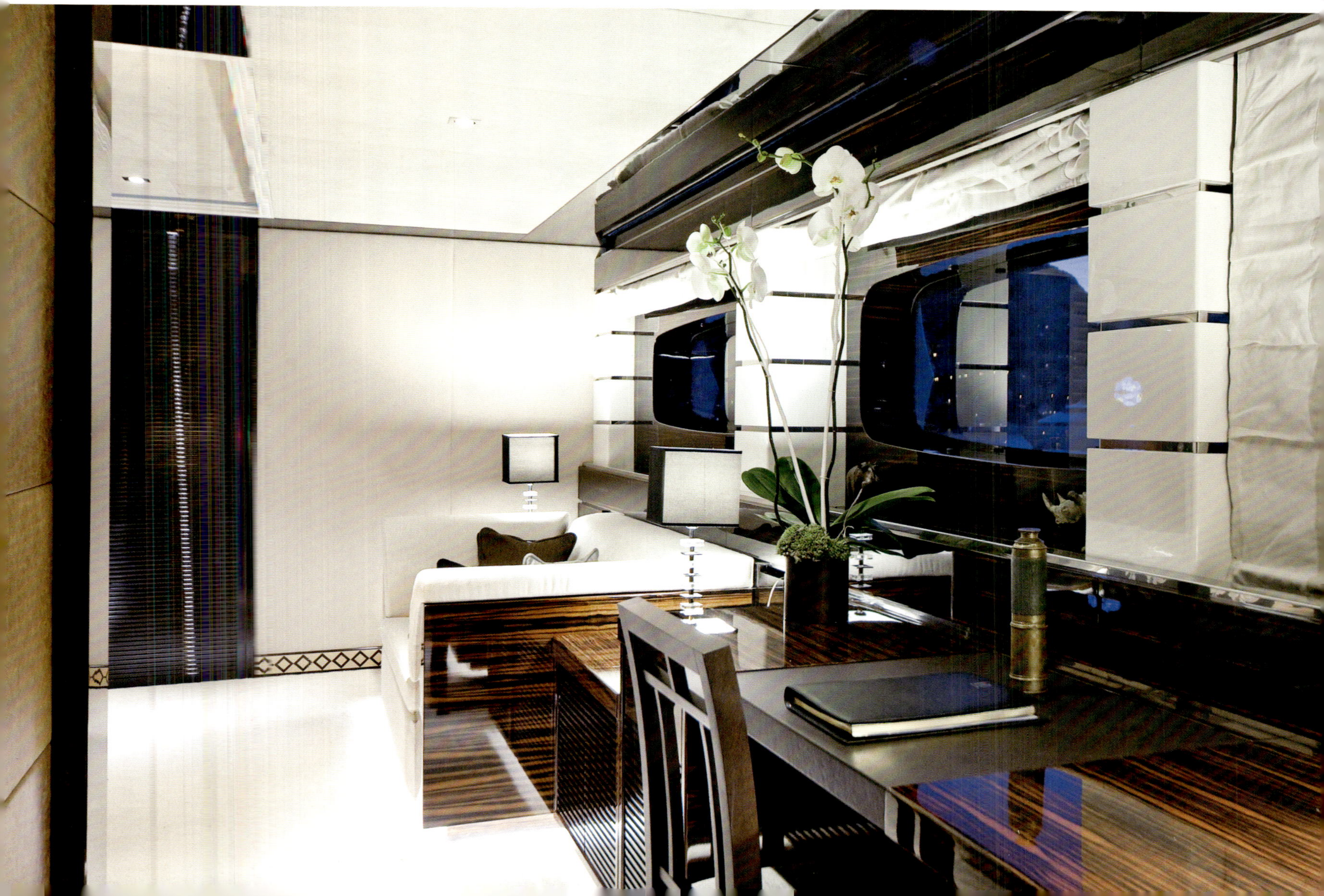

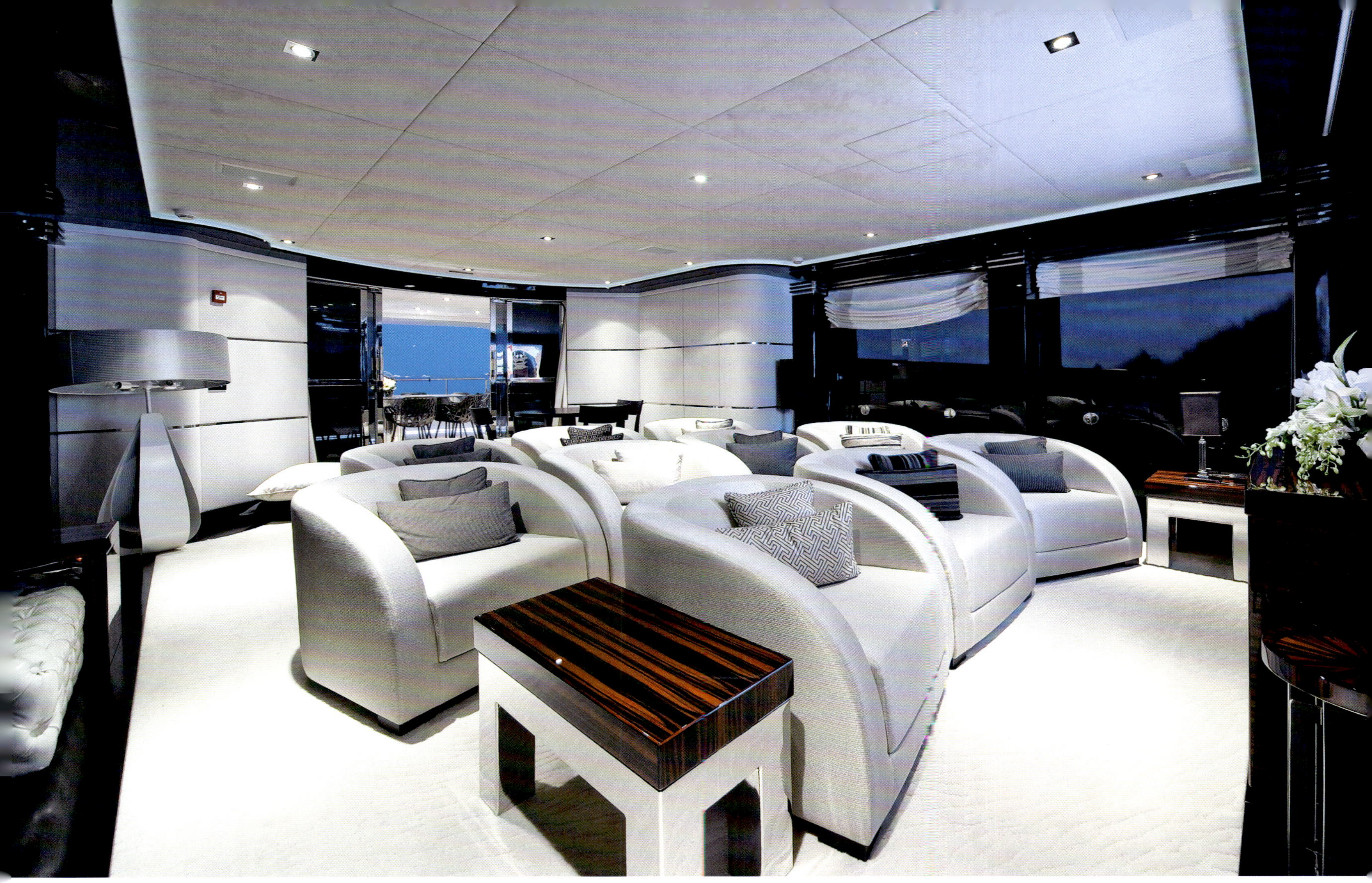

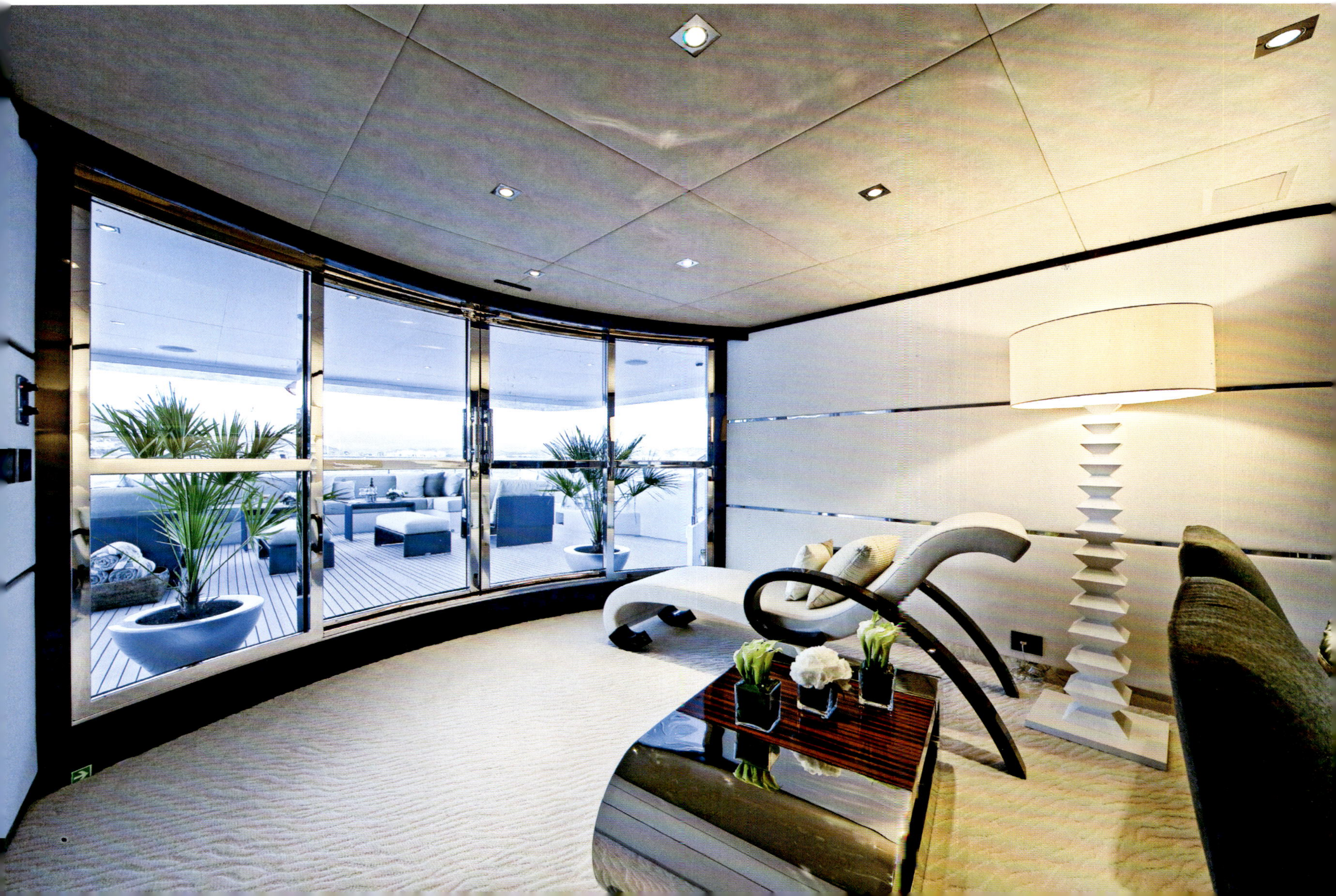

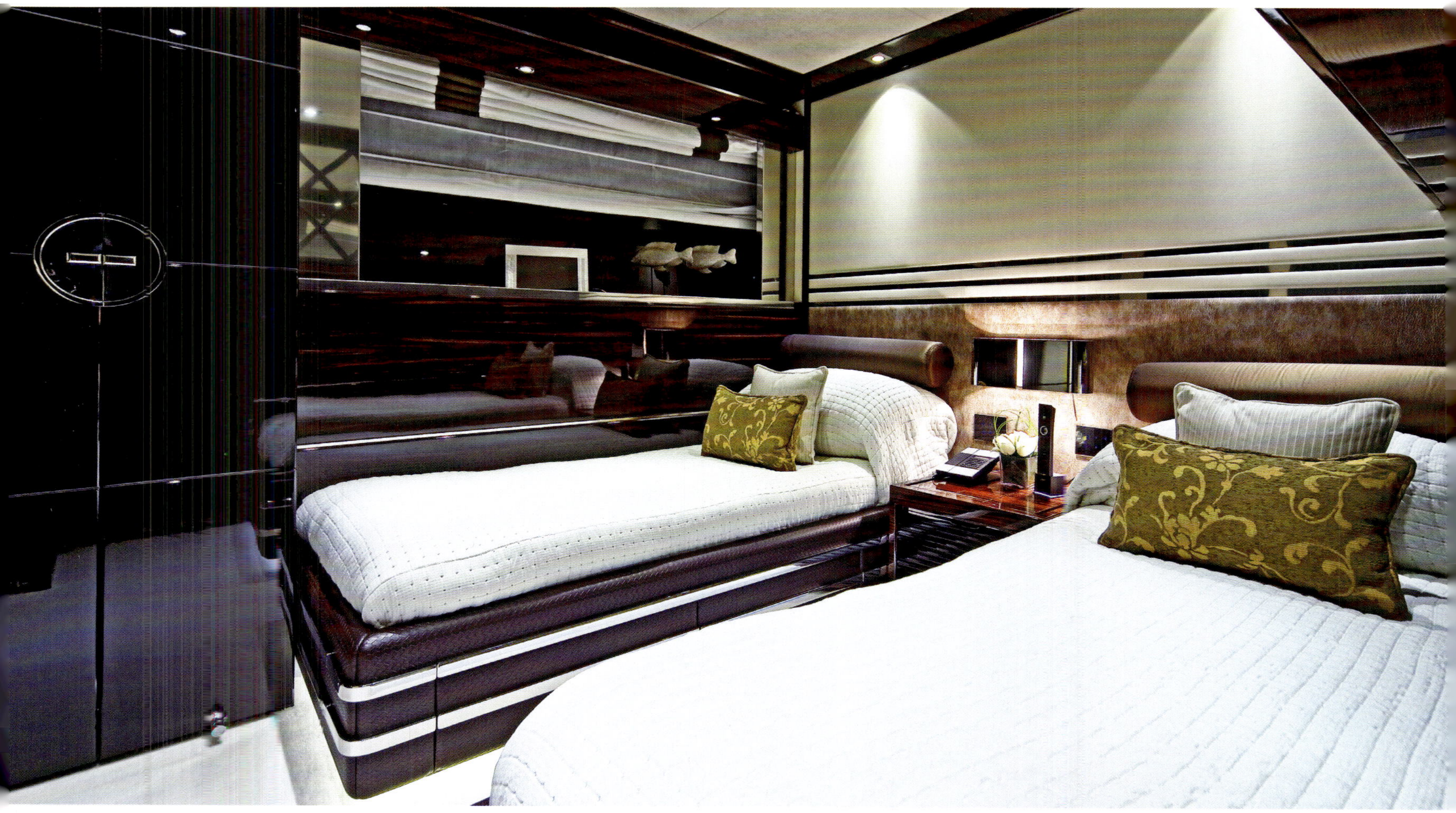

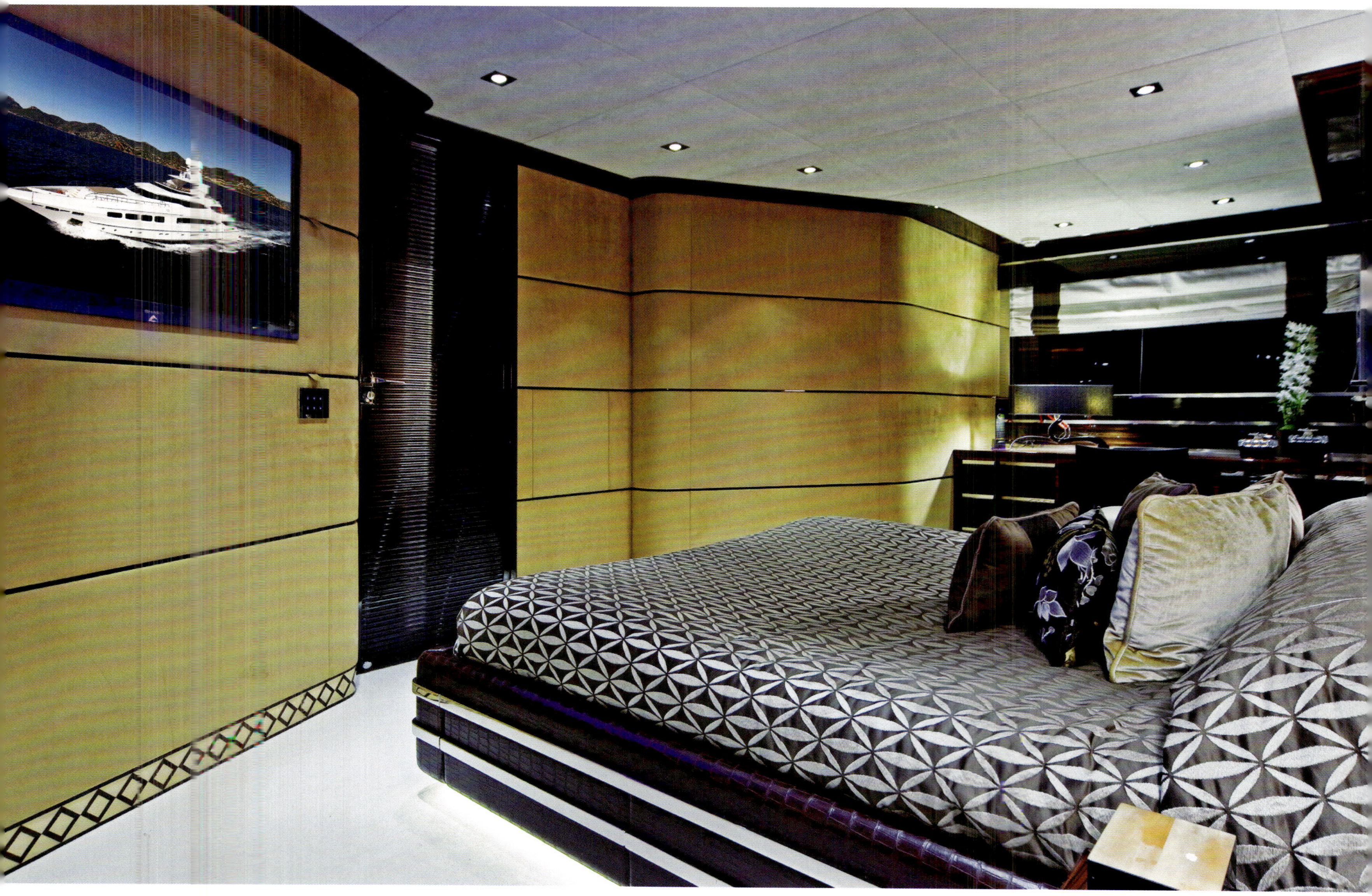

NORTHERN STAR

> INTERIOR DESIGN	Pauline Nunns
> EXTERIOR DESIGN	Espen Øino Naval Architects
> SHIPYARD	Lürssen Yachts
> LENGTH	75.40m
> BEAM	13.50m
> CRUISING SPEED	17.00kn

> Northern Star has a length of 75 metres and is designed for extensive and extended cruising in both northern and southern hemispheres. She features large outdoor spaces and provides ample seating for open air dining, lounging and sun bathing. In cooler weather conditions a heater in the overhead as well as glass panels for wind protection ensure that guests feel comfortable at all times.

The interior, designed by Pauline Nunns, can best be described as a grand country home, which is executed in every single detail and dominated by light airy and comfortable traditional interiors.

When entering Northern Star through the main entrance into the marble floored hallway you instantly get the feeling of a classic rather than a flashy yacht. The hallway provides a very impressive cylindrical glass elevator which accesses all decks and is encircled by the main staircase.

The main deck hosts the main salon and dining area, which are executed in a warm red tone. Comfortable couches and chairs are placed around a real working fireplace and a self-playing Steinway piano offers musical entertainment.

The 5 guest suites are also situated on the main deck and offer generous accommodations and very large windows. The decoration of each cabin is different but all is held in light colours. The beauty and massage room next to the guest cabins is a much sought-after spot onboard.

Most of the upper deck is dedicated to the owner's suite which includes a cosy lounge with library as well as private study. The suite offers most spectacular panoramic views and two side doors offer the possibility to walk outside to a cosy seating area. The sky lounge on the same deck is a masterpiece in its own right and has the same light-blue and white colours as the owner's suite.

Northern Star is a yacht built for pleasure, but above all other considerations she is a yacht intended to be self-sufficient during extended voyages on the high seas and well equipped for whatever she may face.

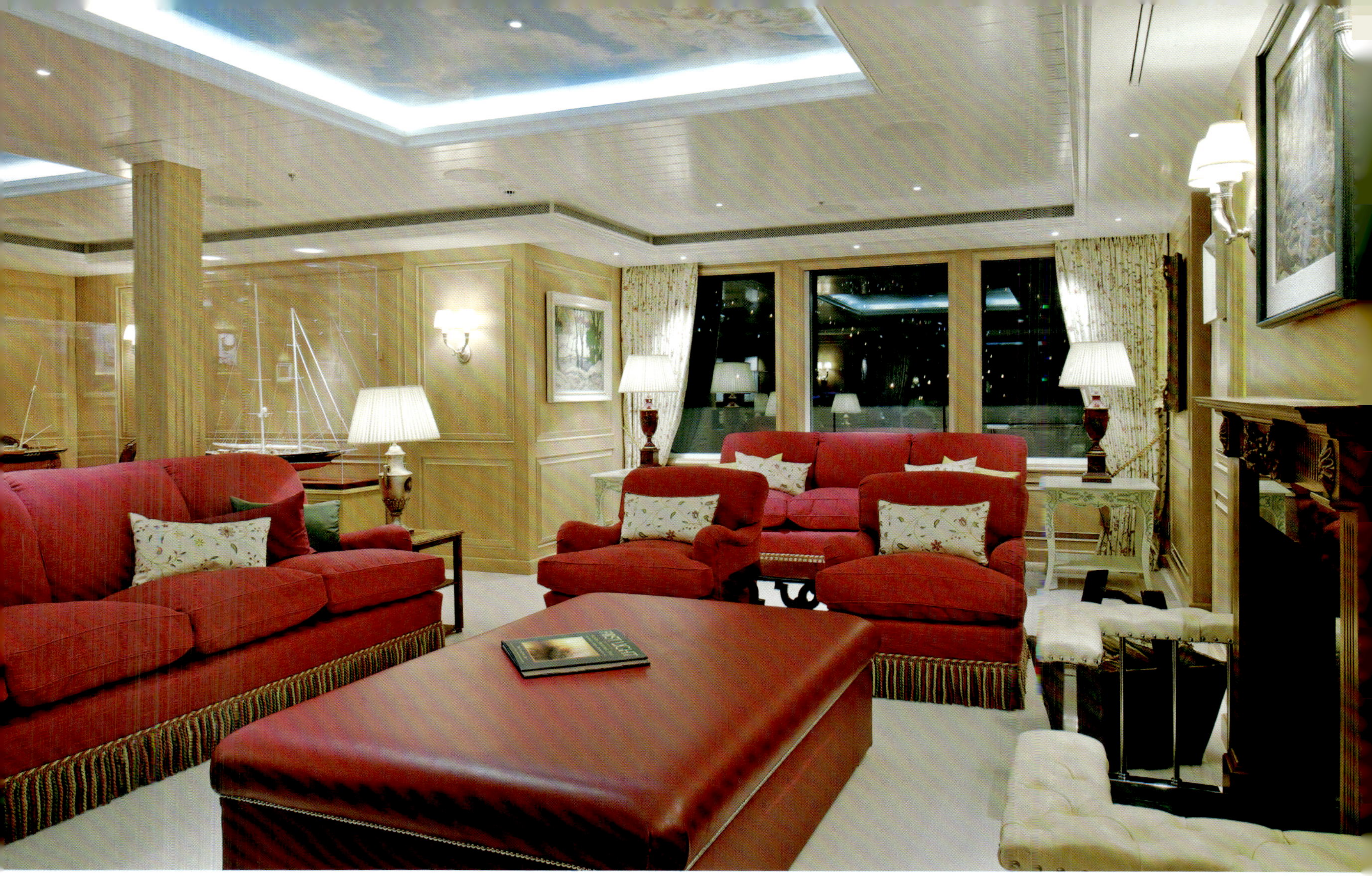

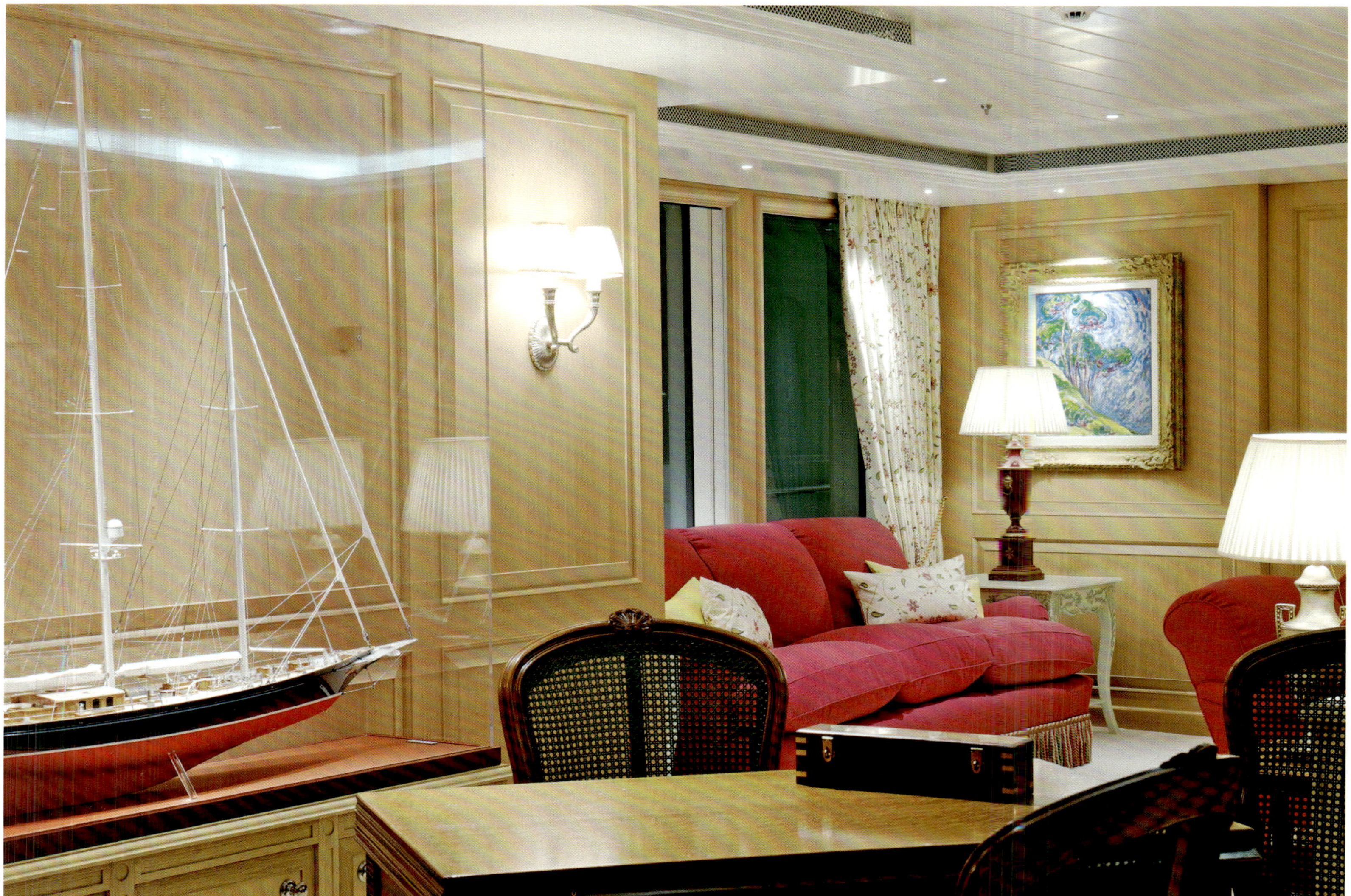

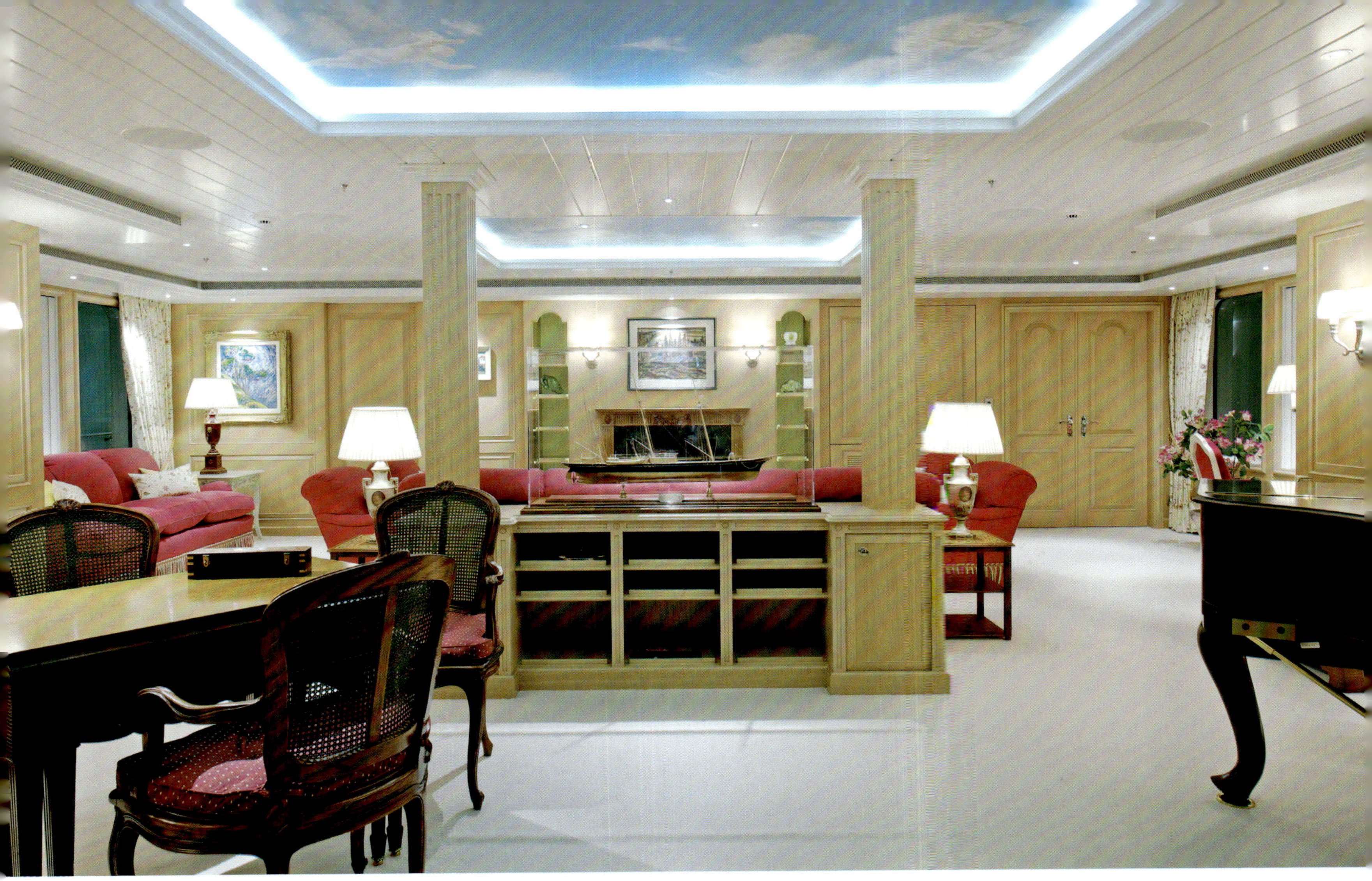

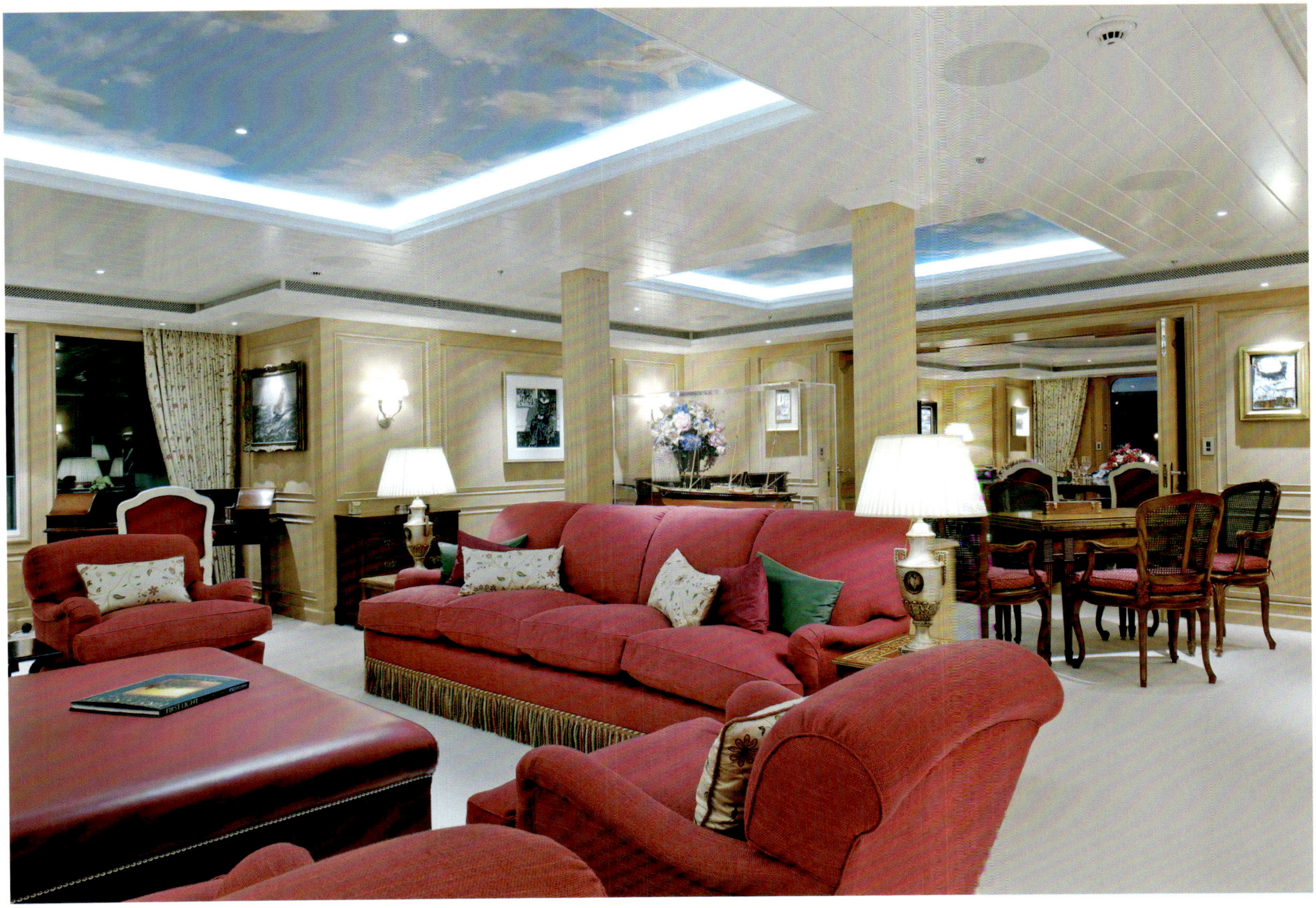

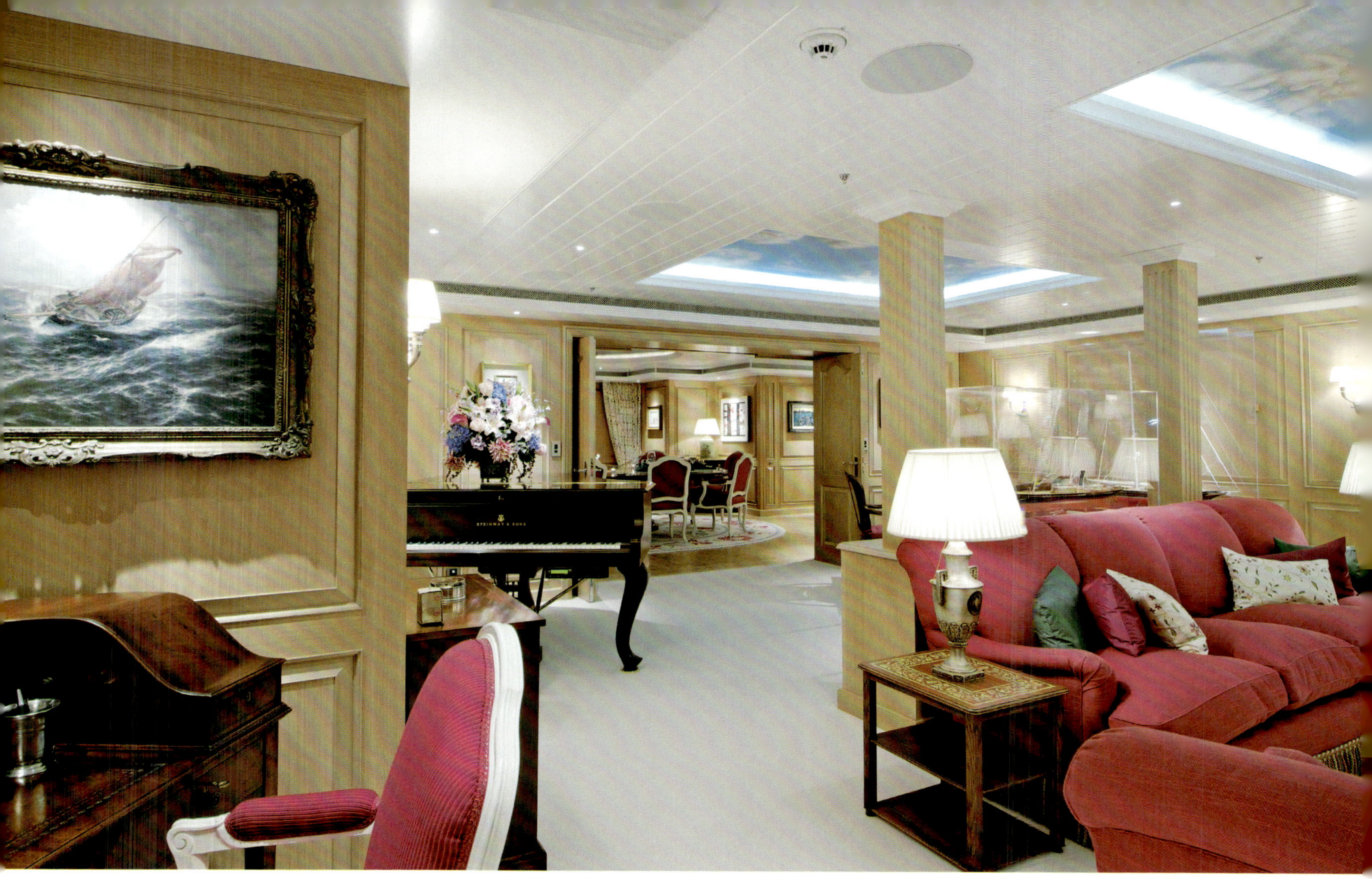

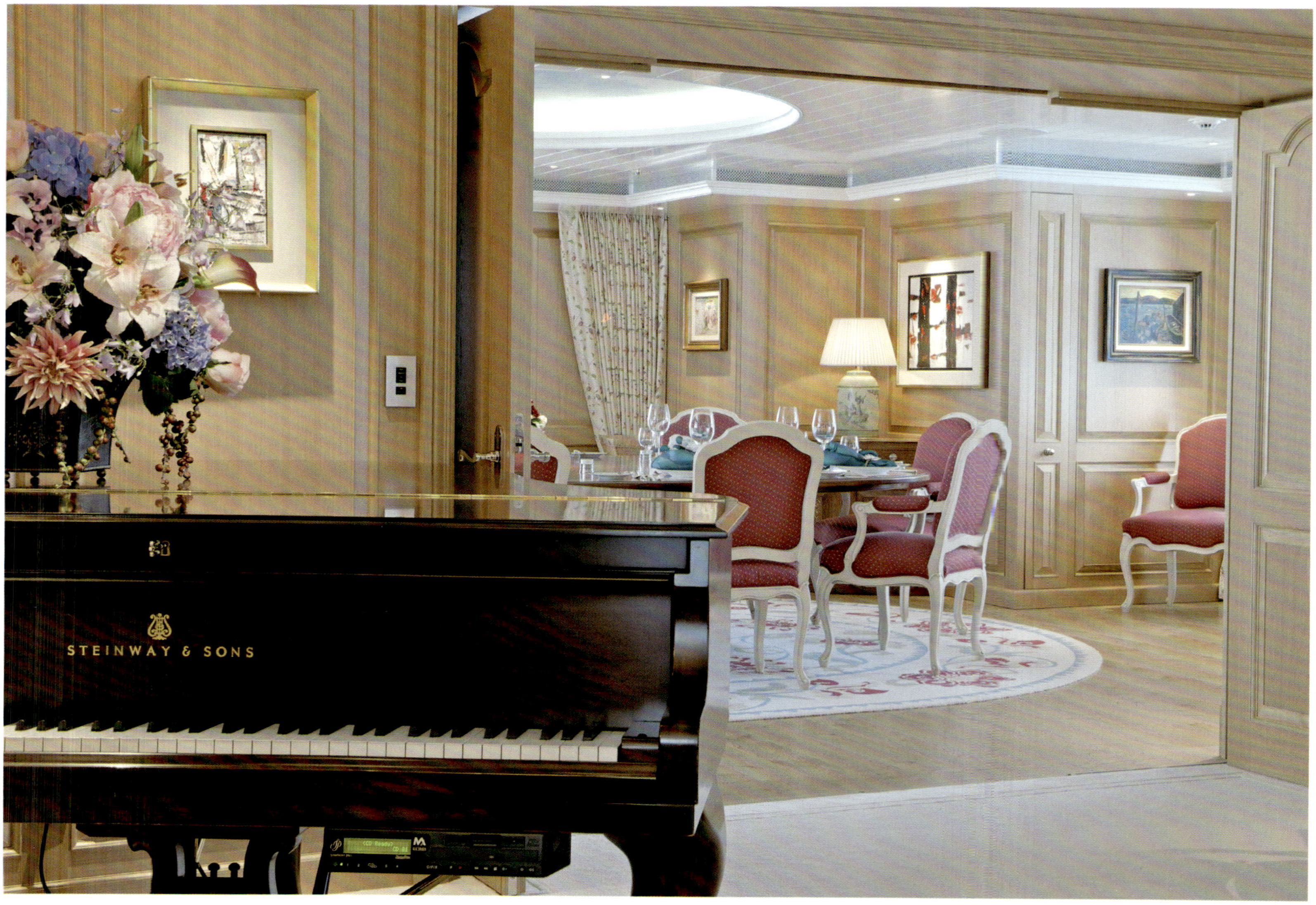
STEINWAY & SONS

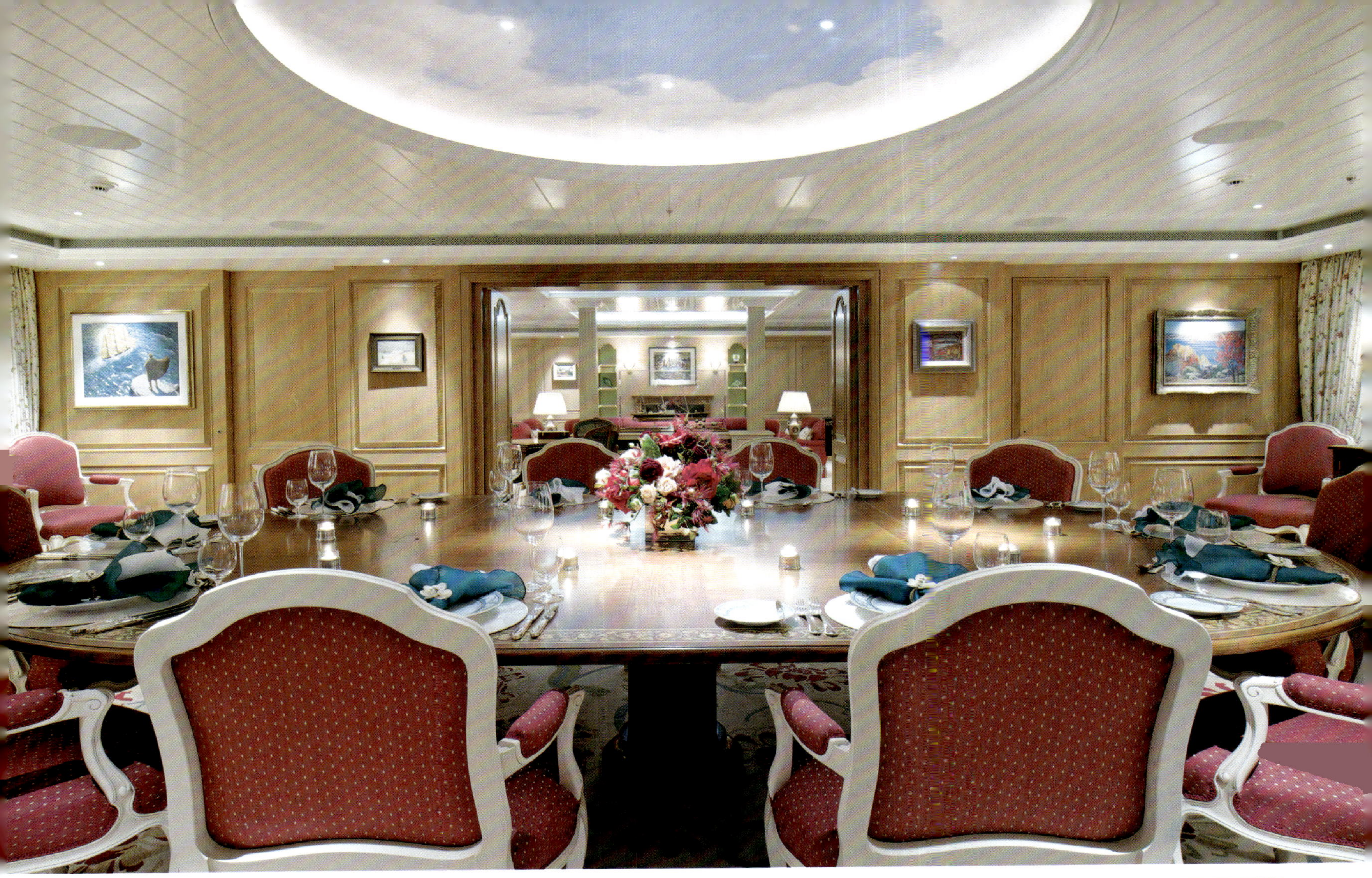

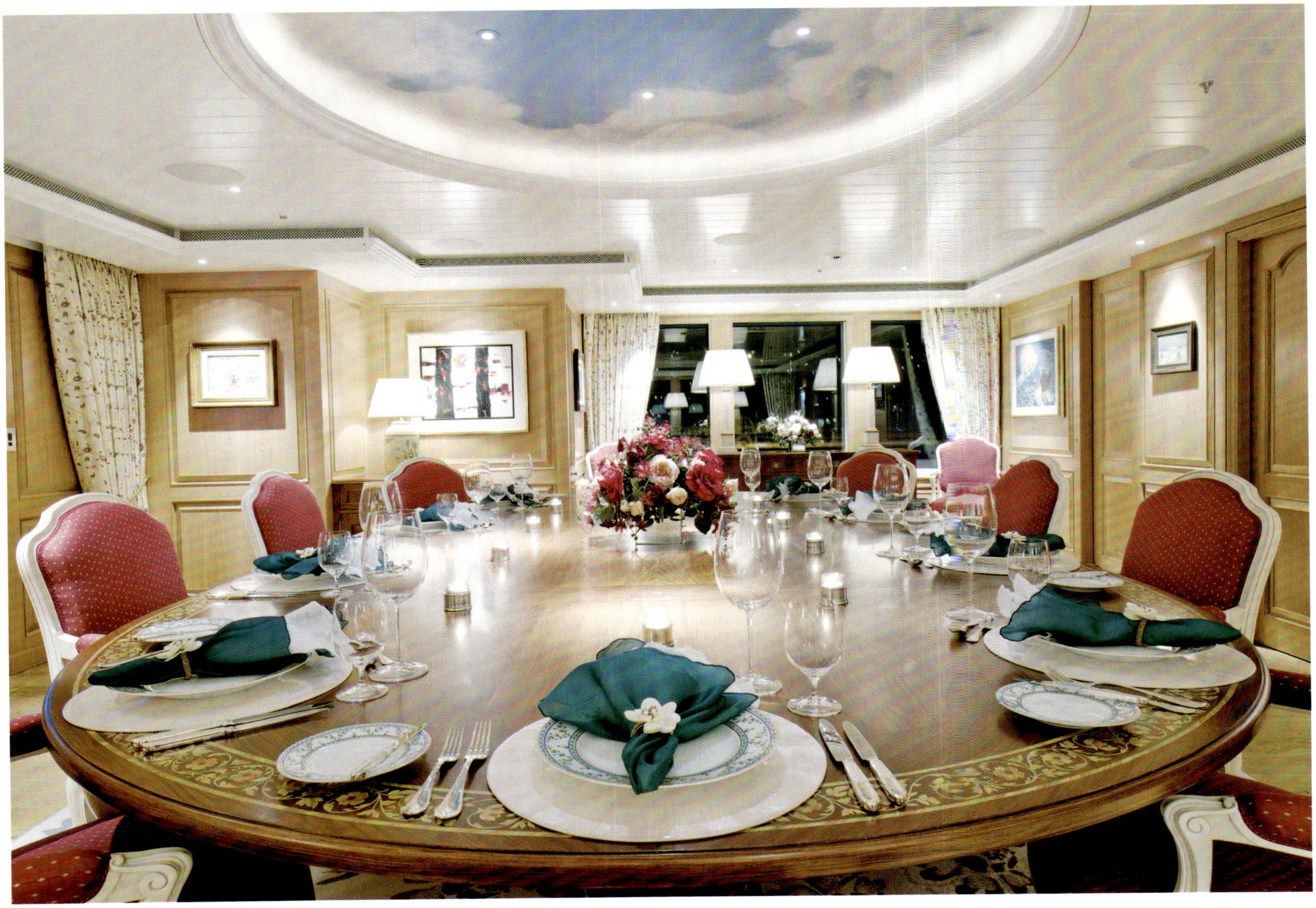

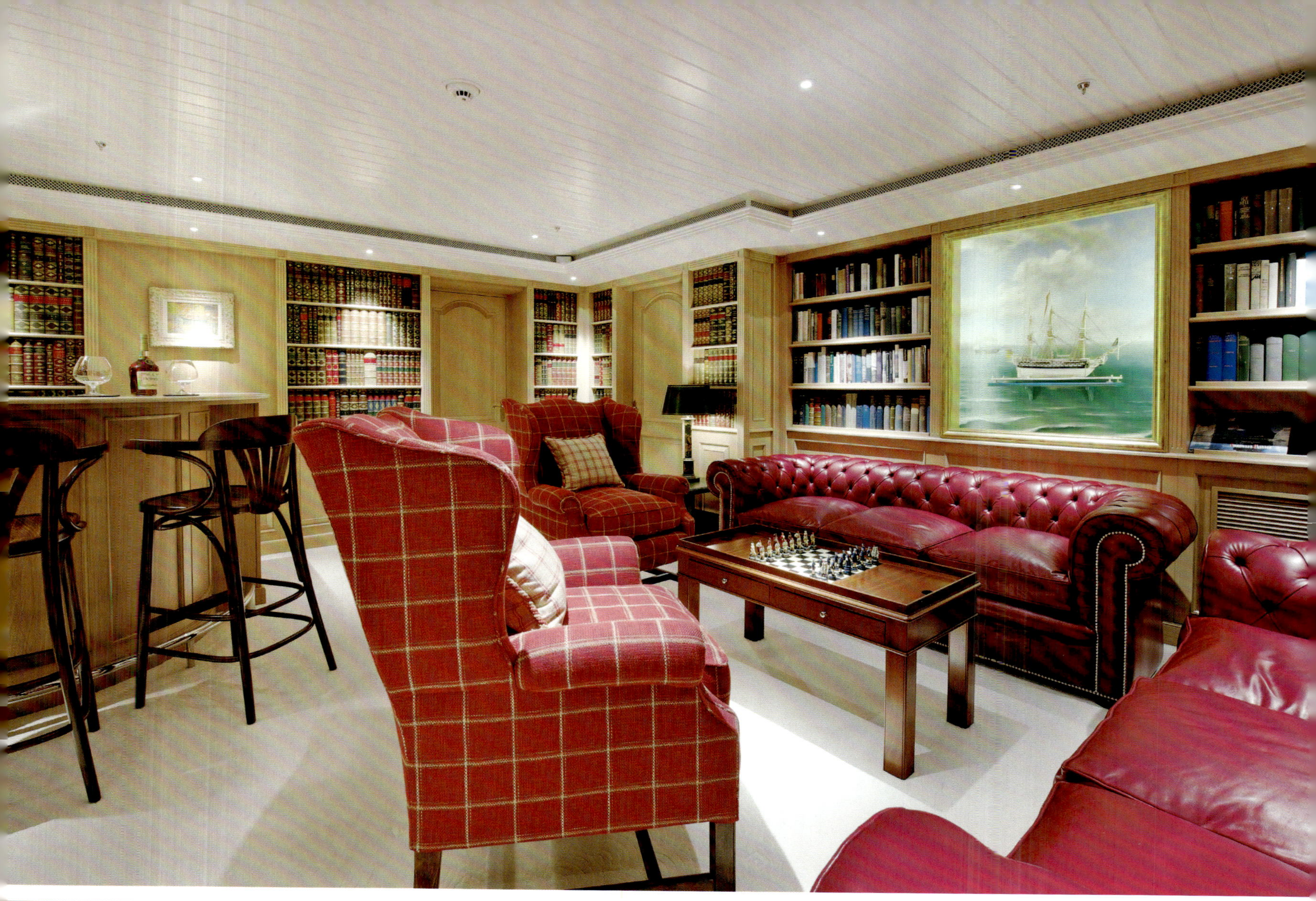
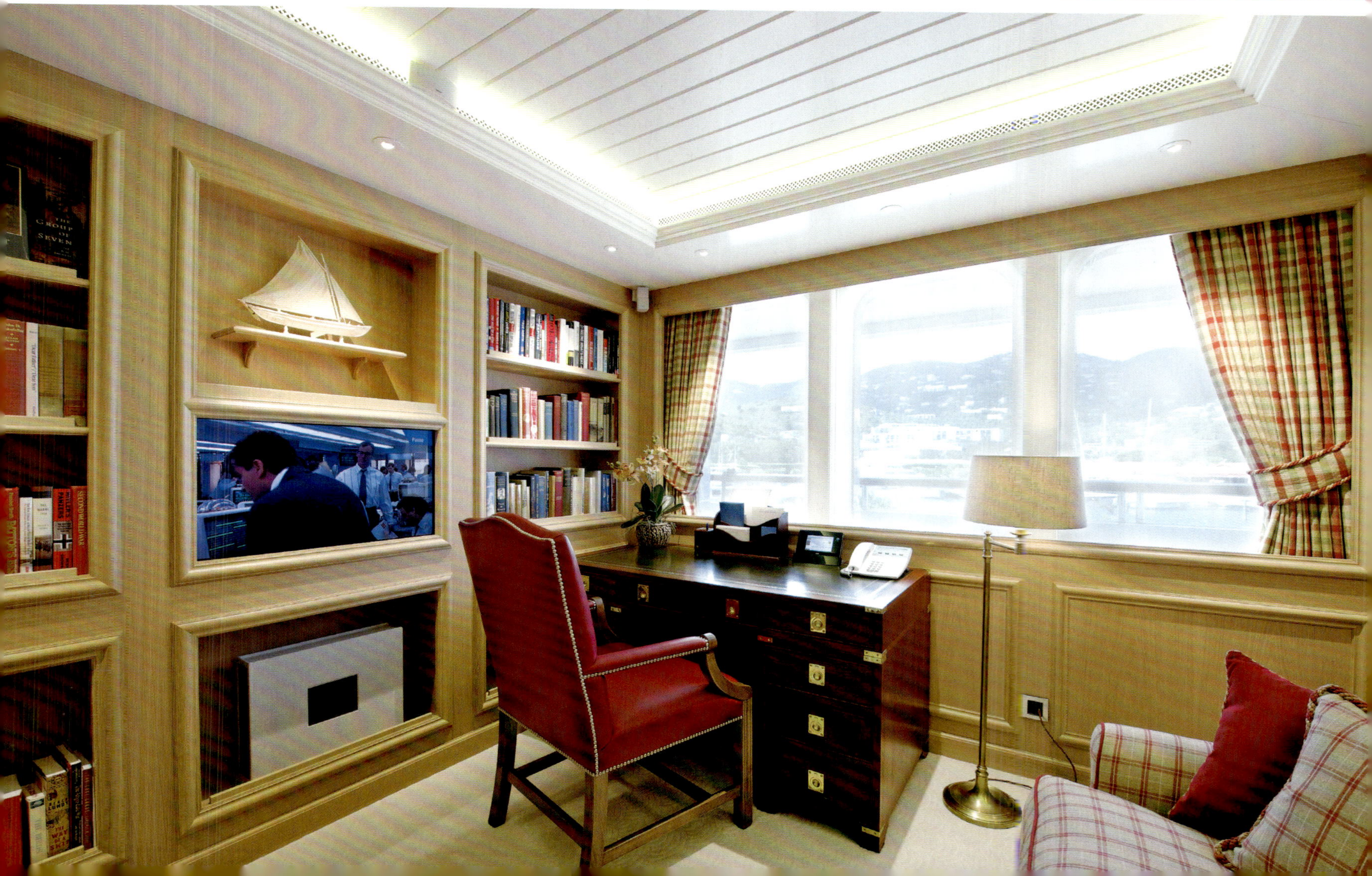

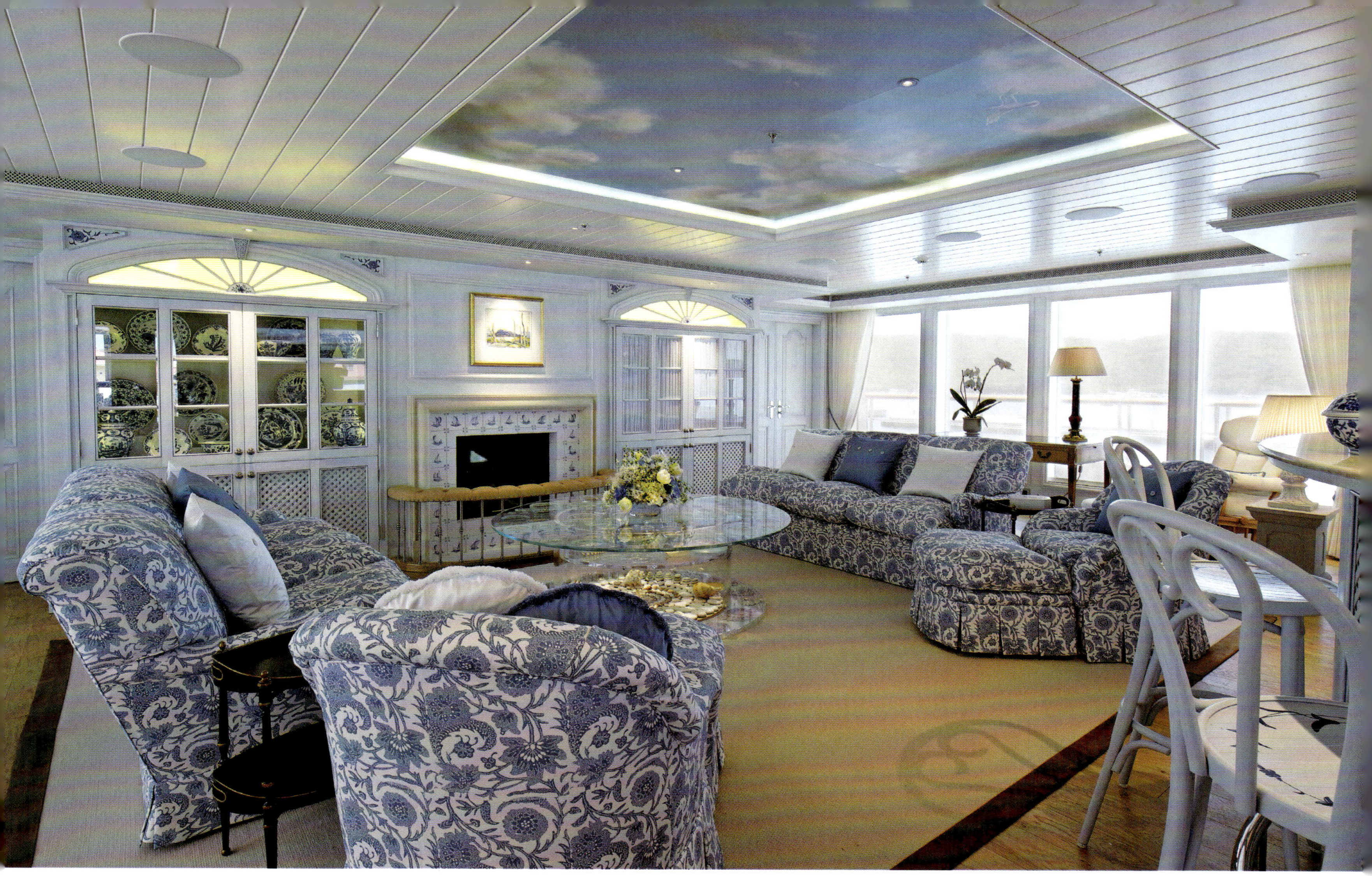

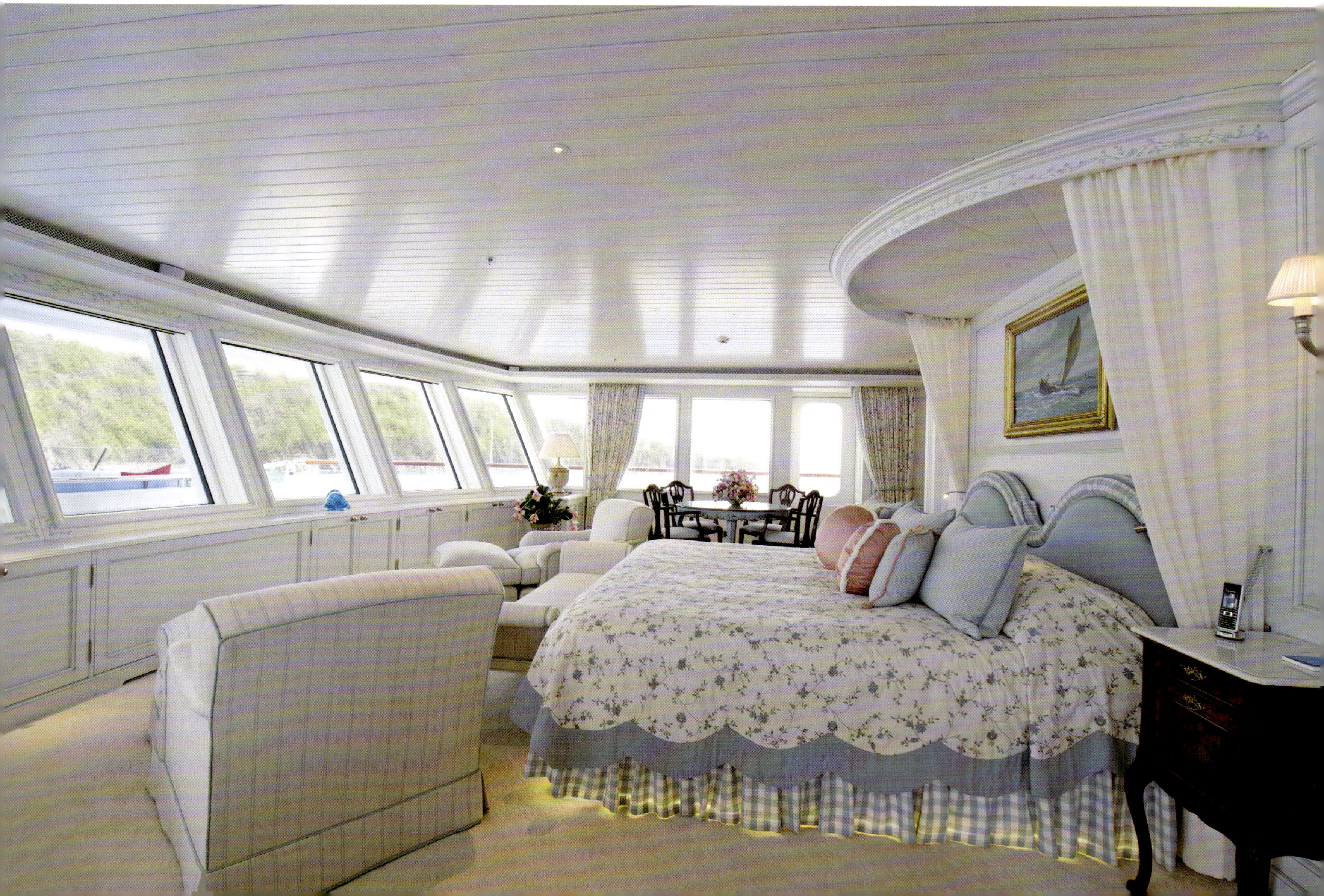

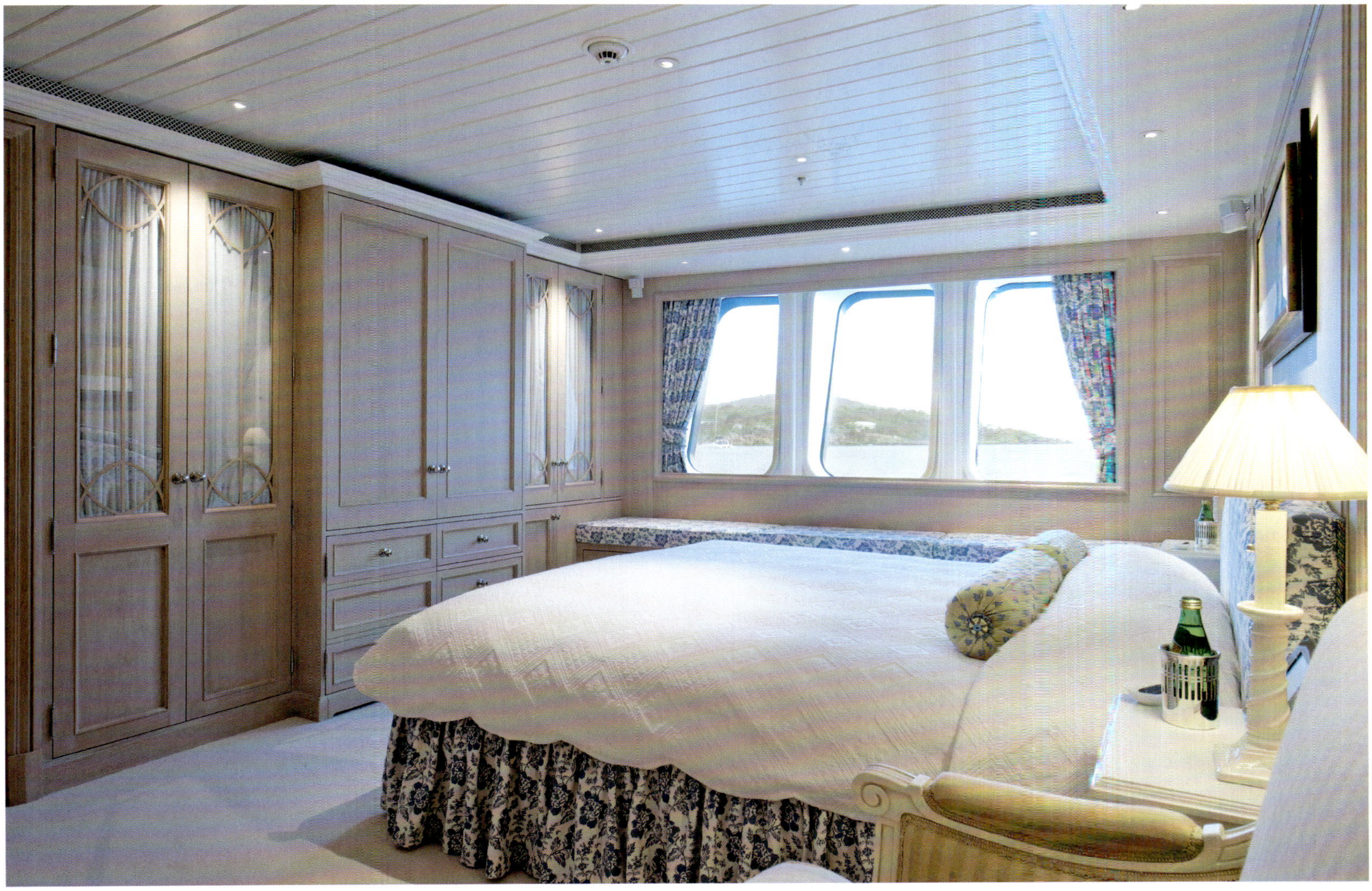

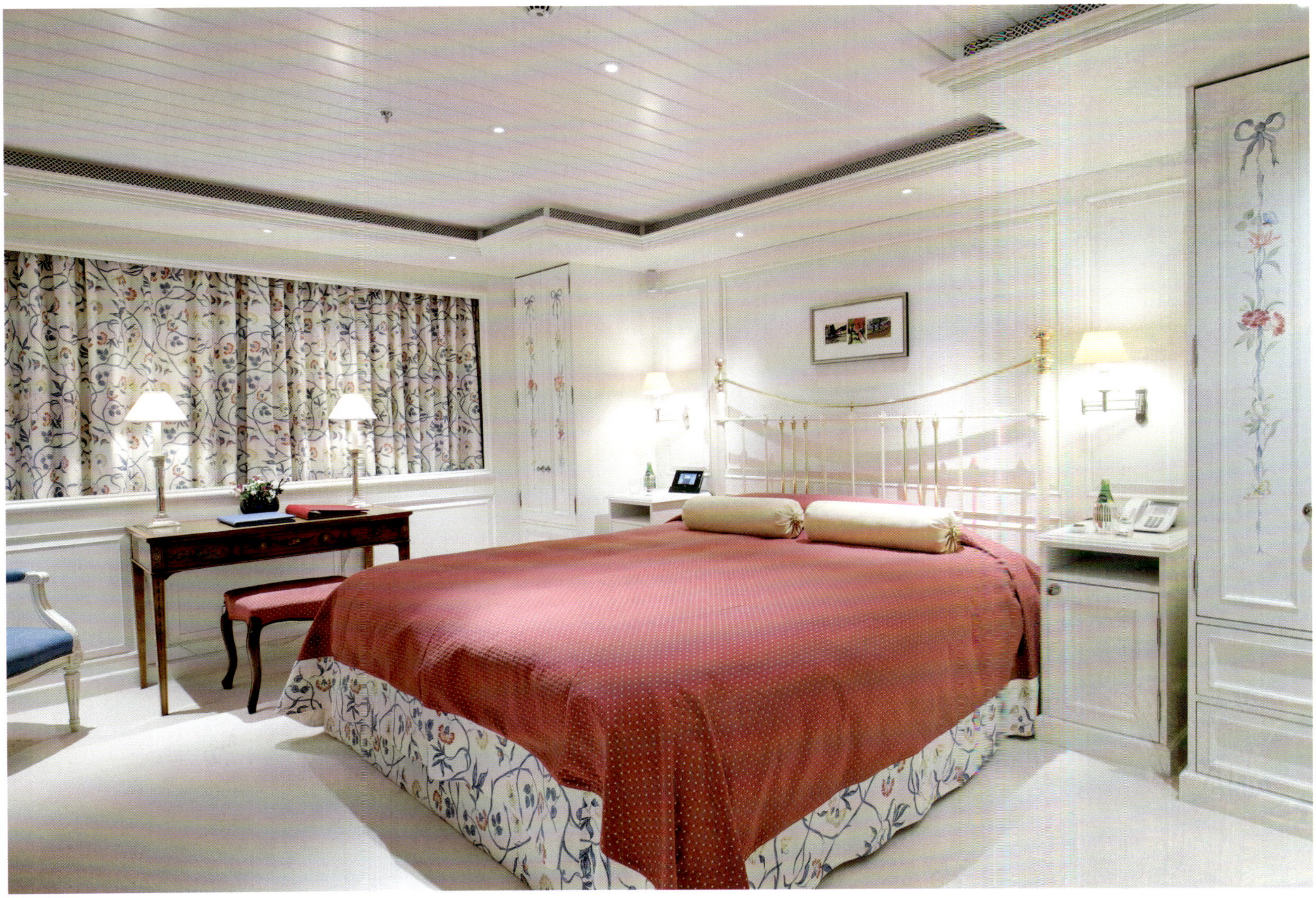

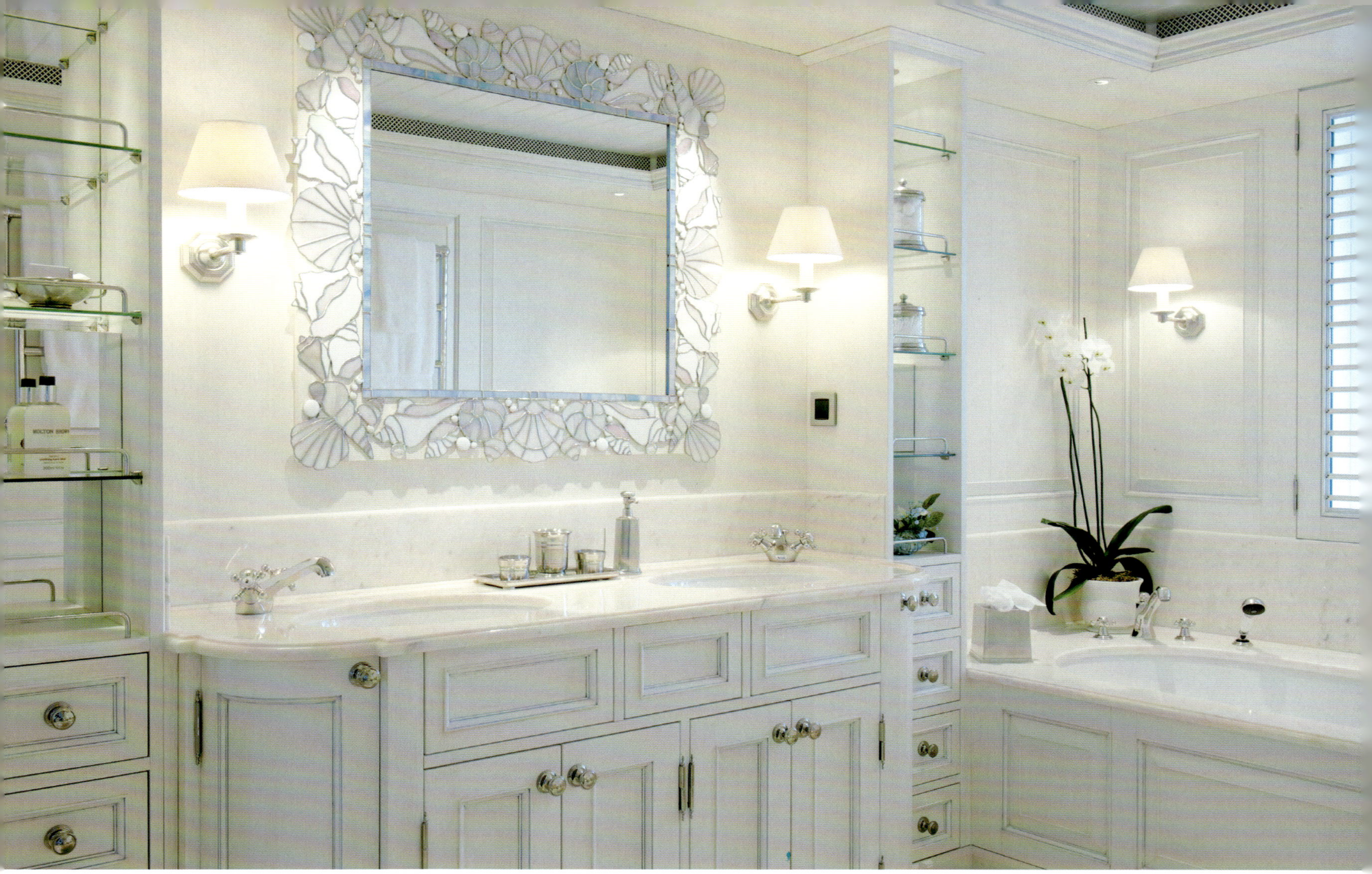

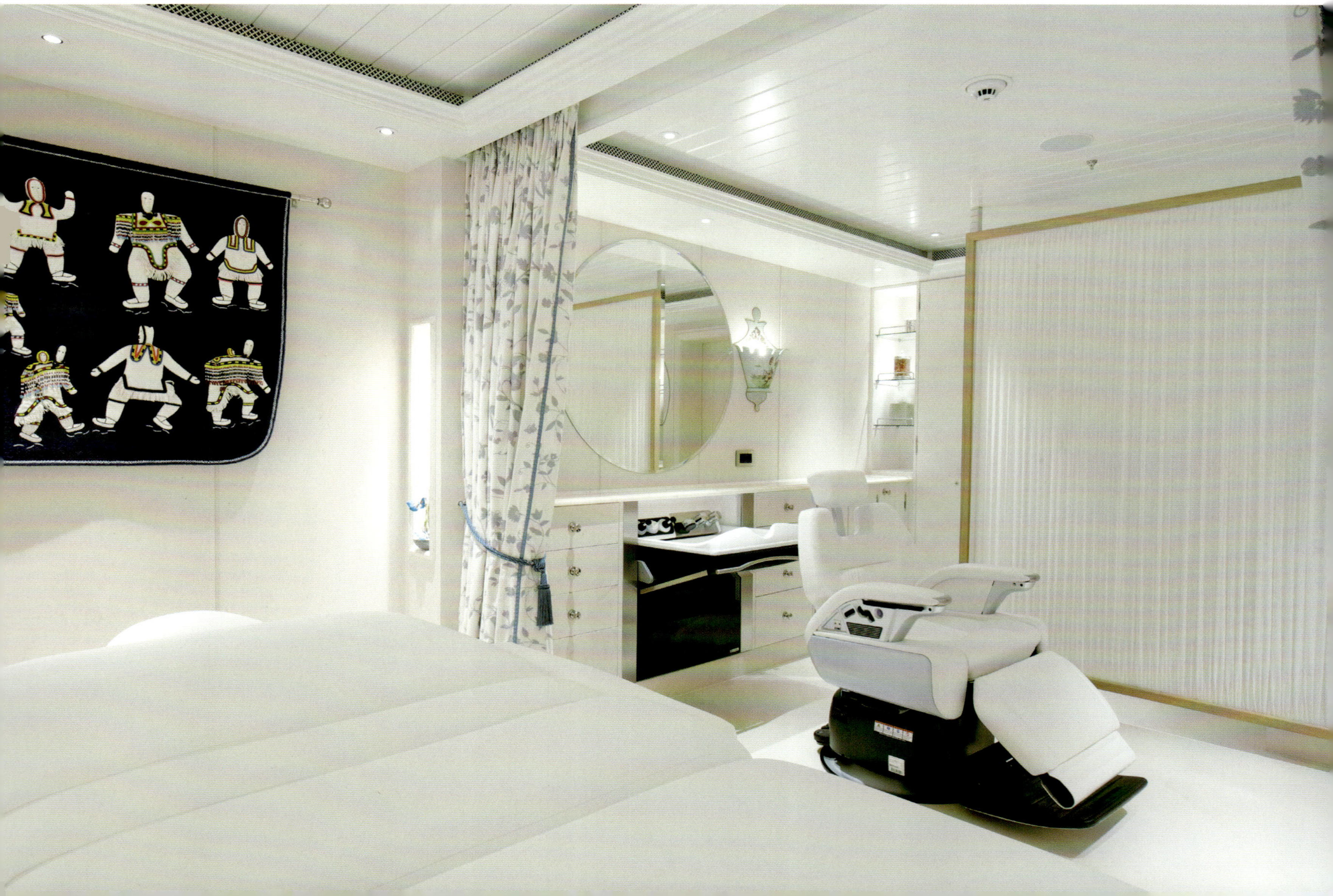

　　"北方之星"游艇身长75米，是为了能在南北半球进行远途航行而专门设计的。它有广阔的户外空间，为室外就餐、室外休息和太阳浴提供了充足的场所。天气转冷时，游艇上方还有温度调节器可以调节室温，玻璃顶可以遮风挡雨，为客人带来始终如一的舒适之感。

　　游艇内部设计由设计师保罗·纳恩斯操刀，将游艇打造成了一个宏伟的海上村庄，他注重每一个细节，设计了一个采光通风良好、居住舒适的传统的室内环境。

　　当通过主通道进入大理石地面的门厅时，你马上能感觉到：这是一艘经典不俗的游艇。走廊中有一架圆柱形玻璃电梯，直达所有的甲板，电梯周围环绕着主楼梯。

　　主甲板上有主沙龙区和用餐区，采用了红色的暖色调。舒适的沙发椅和座椅围绕一个壁炉铺开。一架自动弹奏的斯坦威钢琴奏出怡人的音乐。

　　主甲板上还有五个客房套间，有很大的窗户、宽敞的住宿空间。各套间的装饰设计各不相同，但都采用浅色色调。美容沙龙和按摩室位于客房旁边，在游艇上是最受人们欢迎的地方。

　　上层甲板主要是船主套间，包含一个舒适的客厅、一个藏书室和一个私人书房。在套间可以领略到壮观的全景式海景，两个侧门还可以通往座椅区。同层甲板上的露天休息室本身就是设计精品，与船主套间有着同样的浅蓝色和白色色调。

　　"北方之星"游艇为休闲而建，但最重要的是，它可以在海上长时间巡航，并且自给自足，配备的设施能够应对可能遇到的一切挑战。

VIVE LA VIE

> **DESIGNER** Marilyn Bos- de Vaal, Frank L. Pieterse
> **DESIGN COMPANY** Art-line Interiors B.V.
> **LENGTH** 60m
> **BEAM** 11.1m
> **PHOTOGRAPHER** Dick Holthuis, Klaus Jordan

> An interior that celebrates life, rejoices in existence.

The grand staircase resembles the movement of her motion-giving propellers, connected by bridges, like translucent frozen glaciers. The elevator tower, with colourful lighted floes of acrylic "ice," surrounds a fur-enveloped elevator, with softness like a moving chamois. Sunlight filters through layers of hand-woven copper.

The cold night outside is haughtily ignored by leather window shutters within. All is a warm embrace of gentle materials, secure blankets, soft guards that make rest come easily.

A circle with a view, rotating with the light of day and night, as a happy childhood merry-go-round. Bathing in palpable affluence, warm in never-ending wellness. A crow's nest for those without fear of heights... those who dare.

Breakfast in an embracing leather-covered retreat, observing the nautical valley from an indoor veranda, or a lazy afternoon snack. Dancing, dining, dancing more in a panoramic tower, abducted by a gourmet chef. Gazing at stars around an aft deck "campfire," light-headed, light-hearted, raking in gold of a moonlit world.

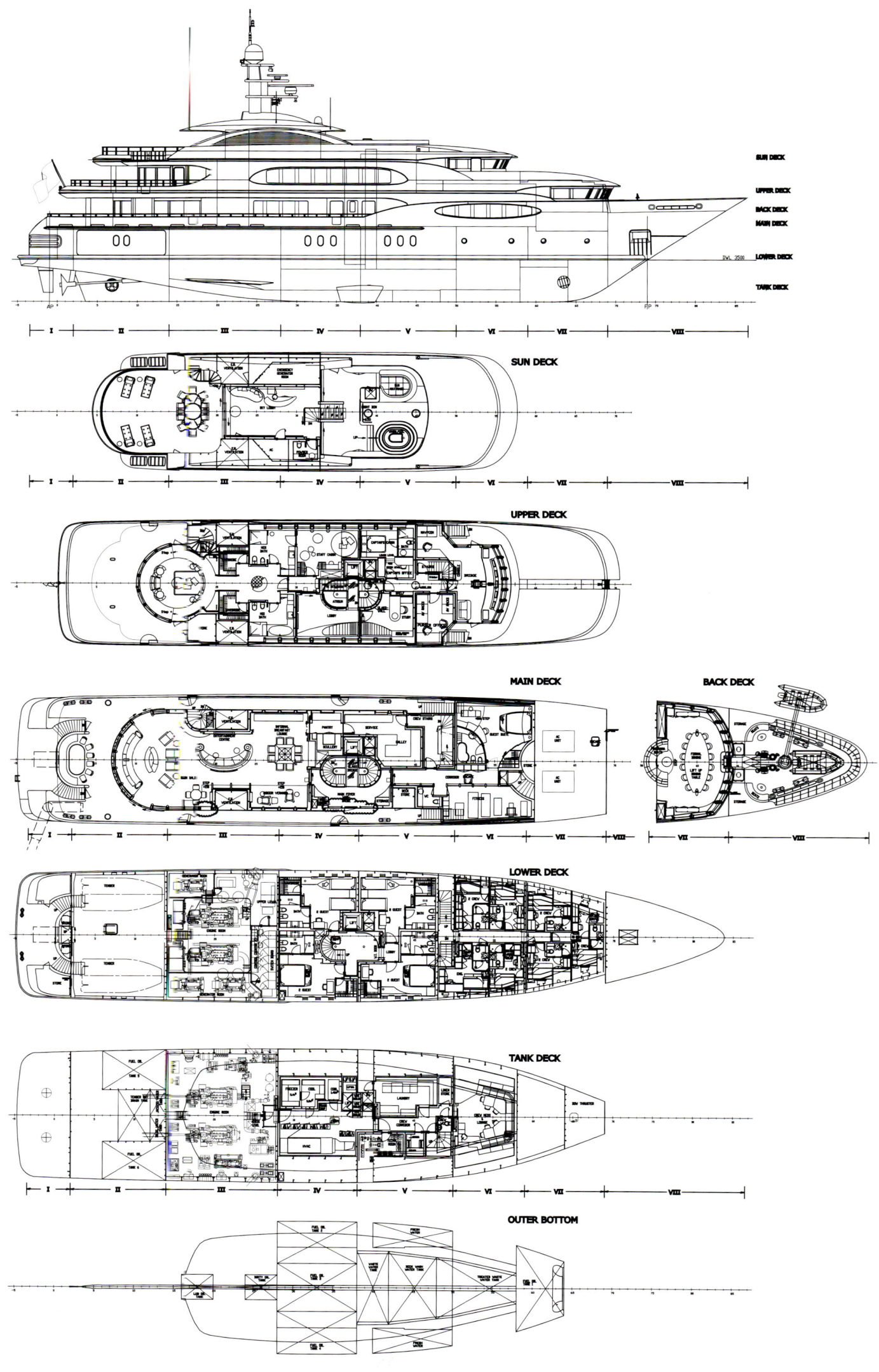

SUN DECK

UPPER DECK

MAIN DECK

BACK DECK

LOWER DECK

TANK DECK

OUTER BOTTOM

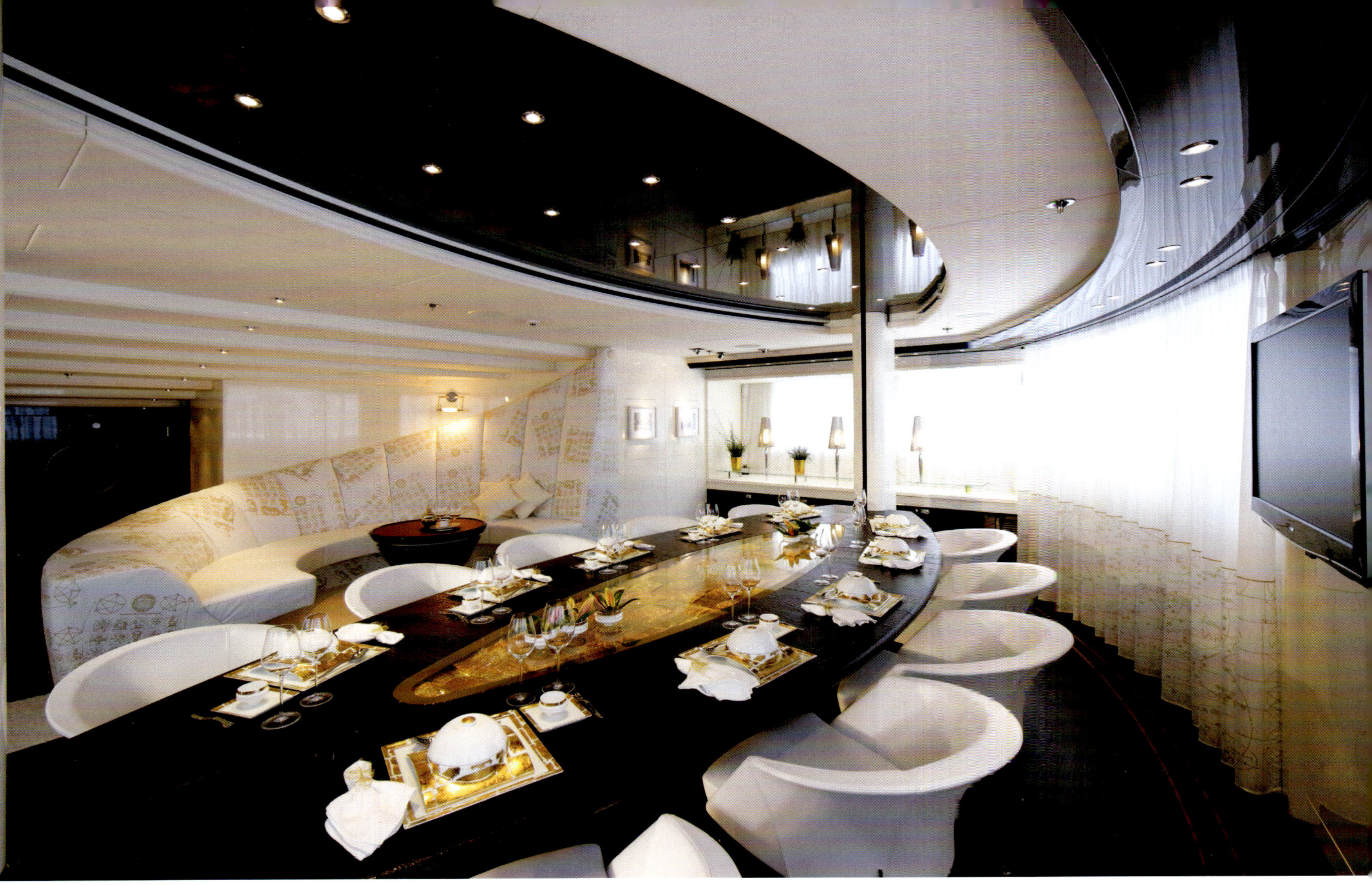
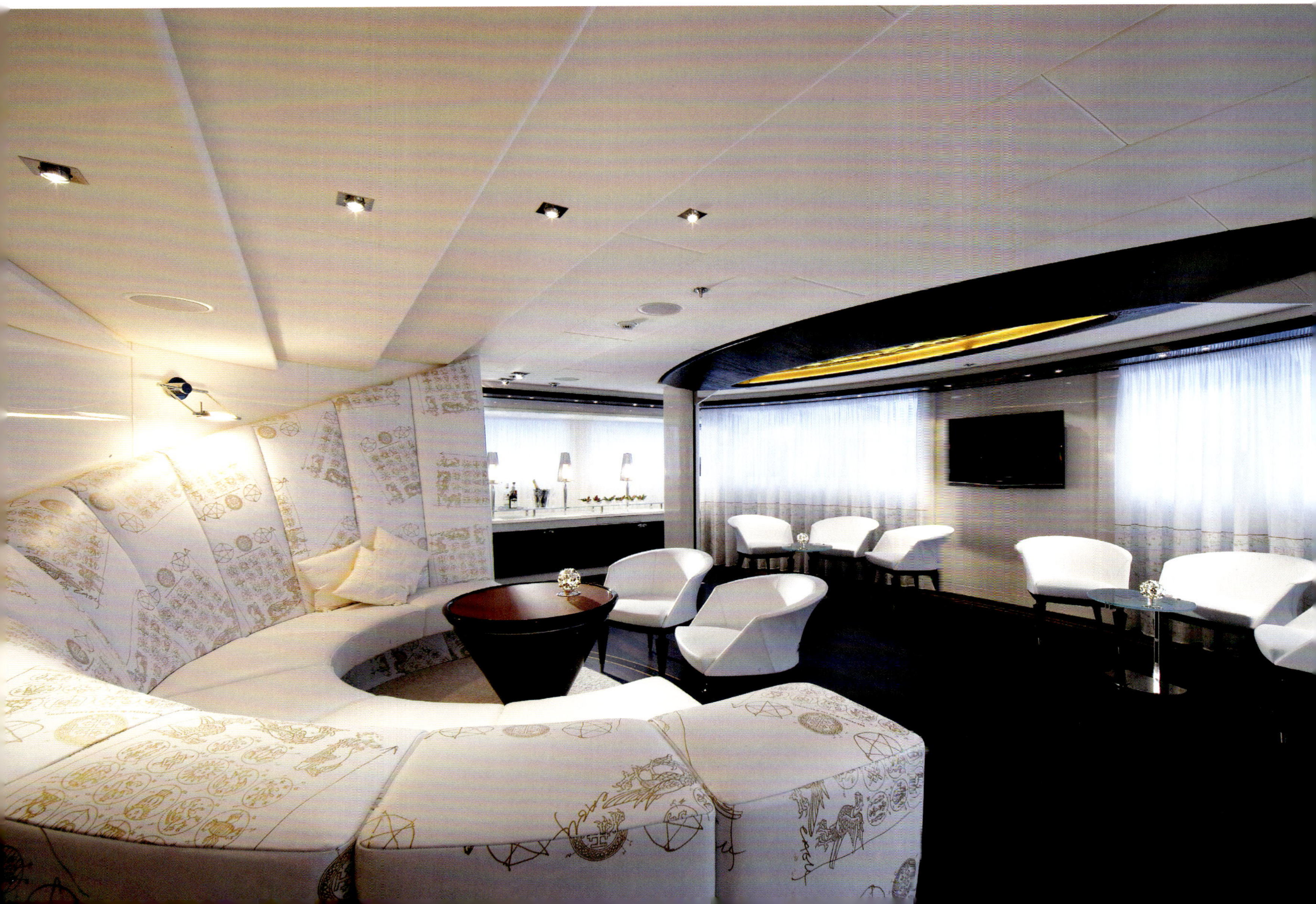

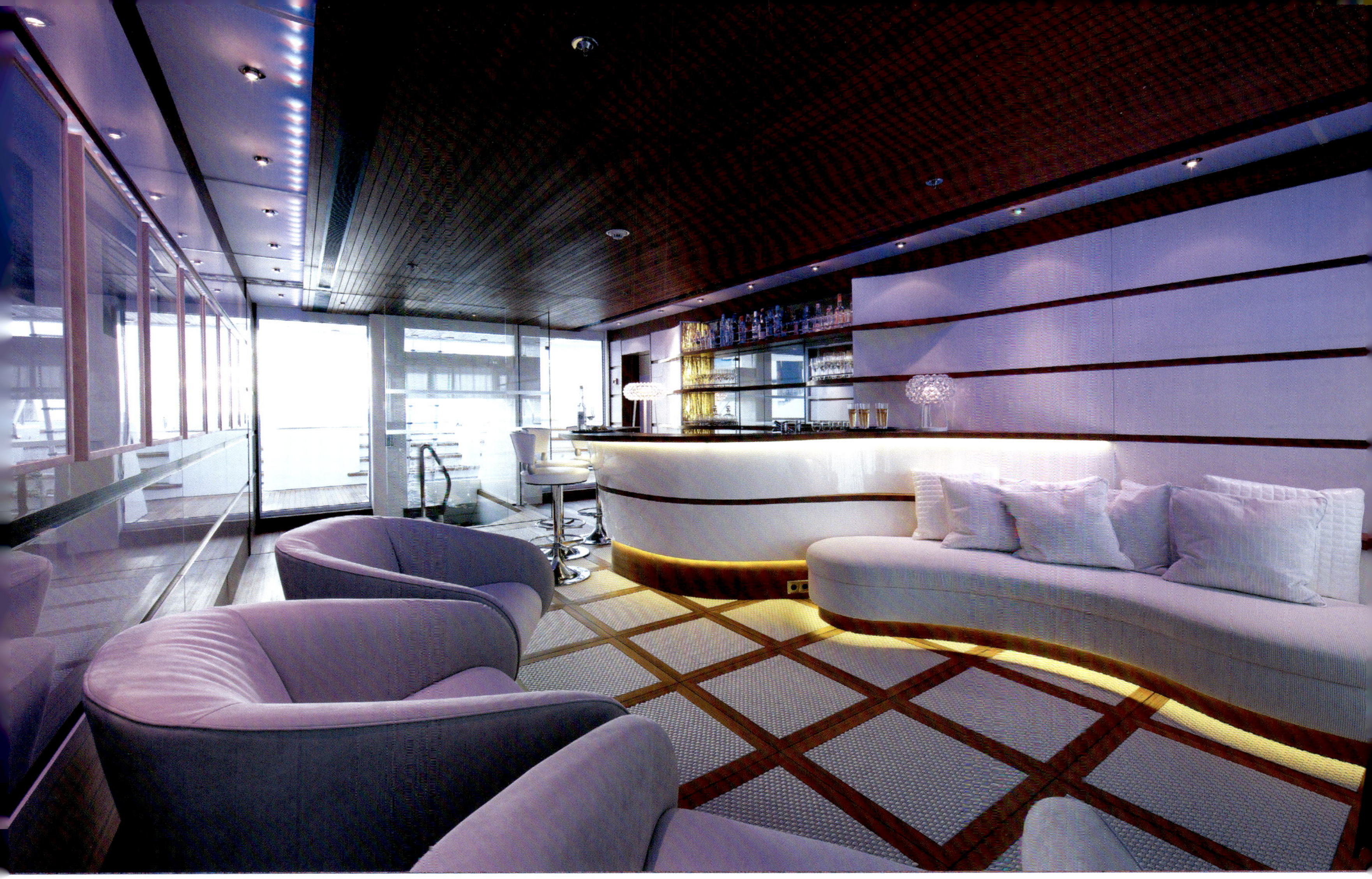

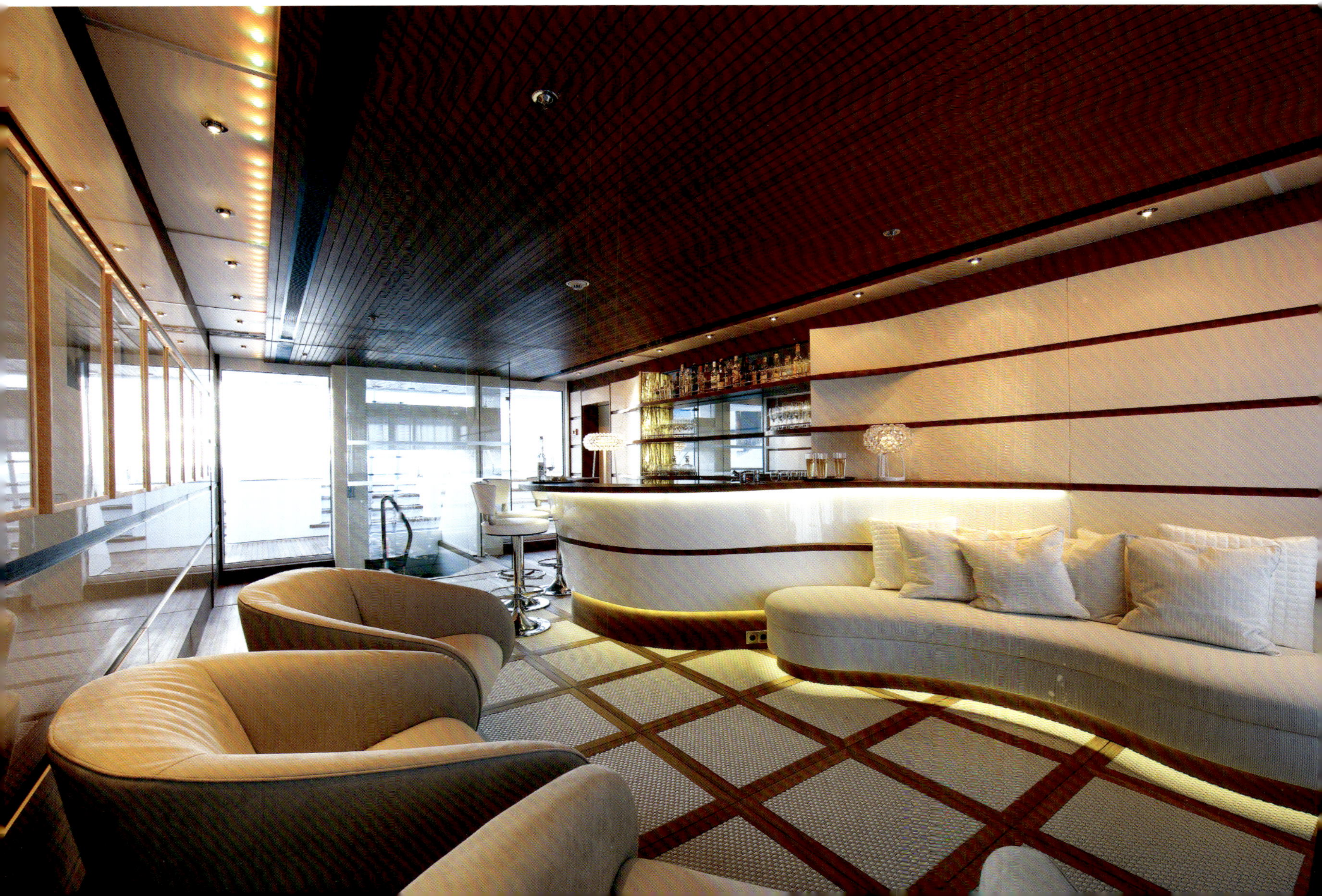

游艇内部充满了生机和欢愉。

雄伟的楼梯很像运动的螺旋桨，由桥梁连接，整体如同晶莹剔透的冰川。电梯间镶有五颜六色的"冰块"，电梯由毛皮包围，柔软细腻，运行时像一个跳动的羚羊。阳光透过手工编织的铜网。

皮革窗户将夜晚的寒冷拒之门外。拥抱温暖，感受细腻的材质，舒适的毛毯，给您带来安全的休息场所。

欣赏着周围的美景，感受着日夜的更替，犹如儿时的旋转木马。浴室豪华，温暖舒适。高高的**瞭望台**专为那些不惧高的勇士而建。

在皮质的桌椅上用早餐，在室内的阳台观赏海上风景，或者在一个慵懒的下午品尝点小点心。在**瞭望台**上尽情起舞，品尝着由高级厨师提供的美味佳肴。躺在船尾甲板的"篝火"旁边，凝望着星空，怀着愉悦轻松的心情，沉醉在迷人的月色中。

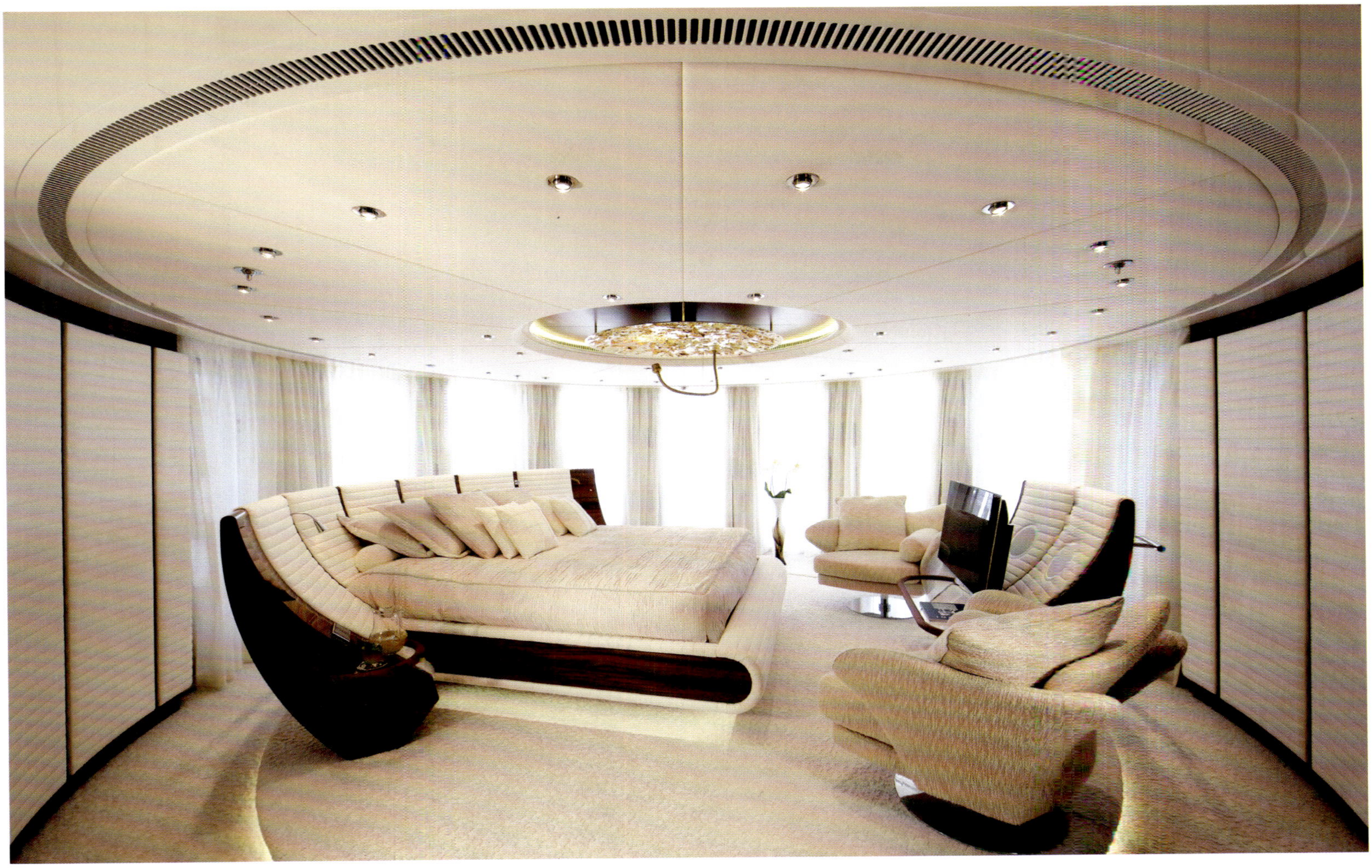

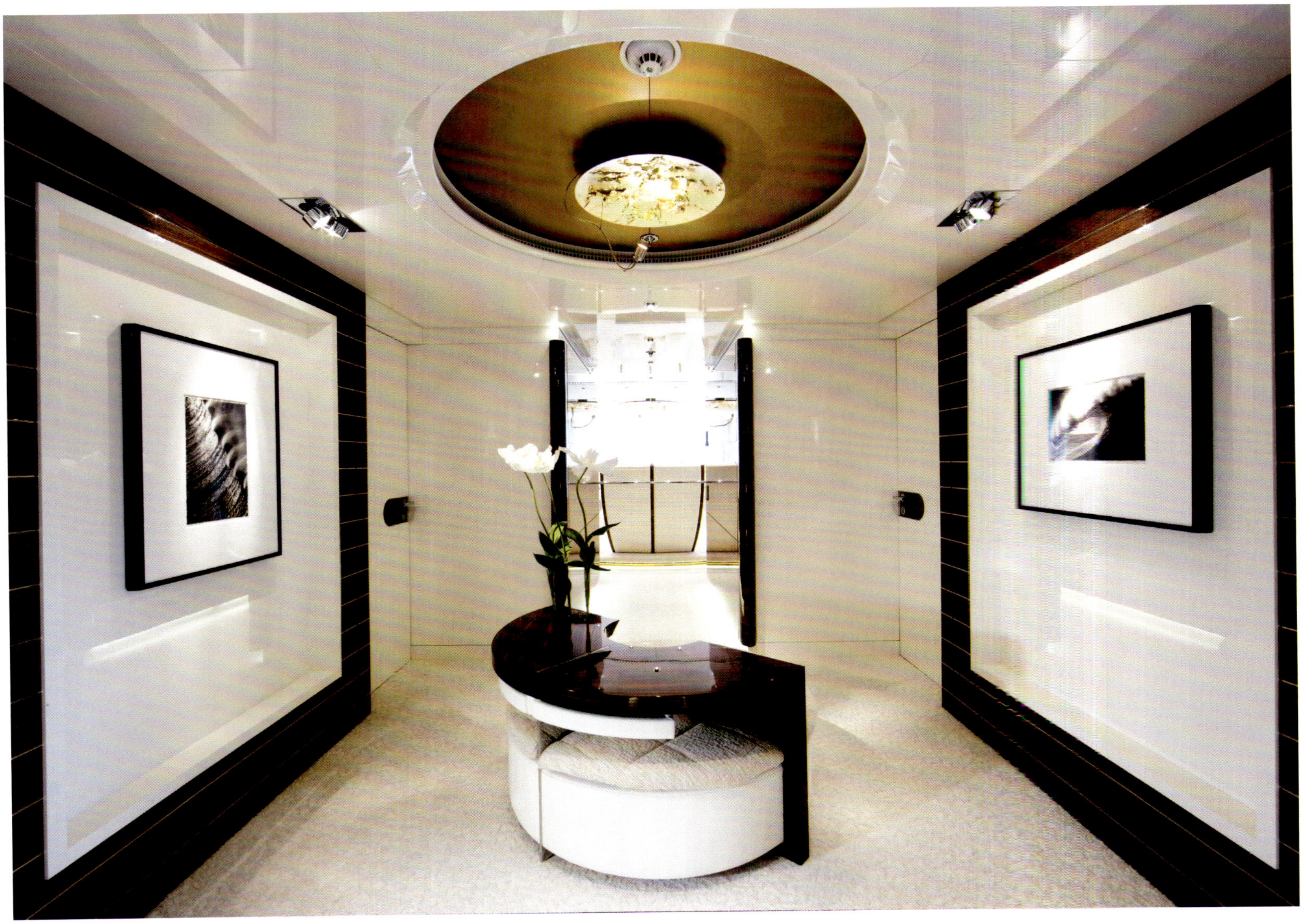

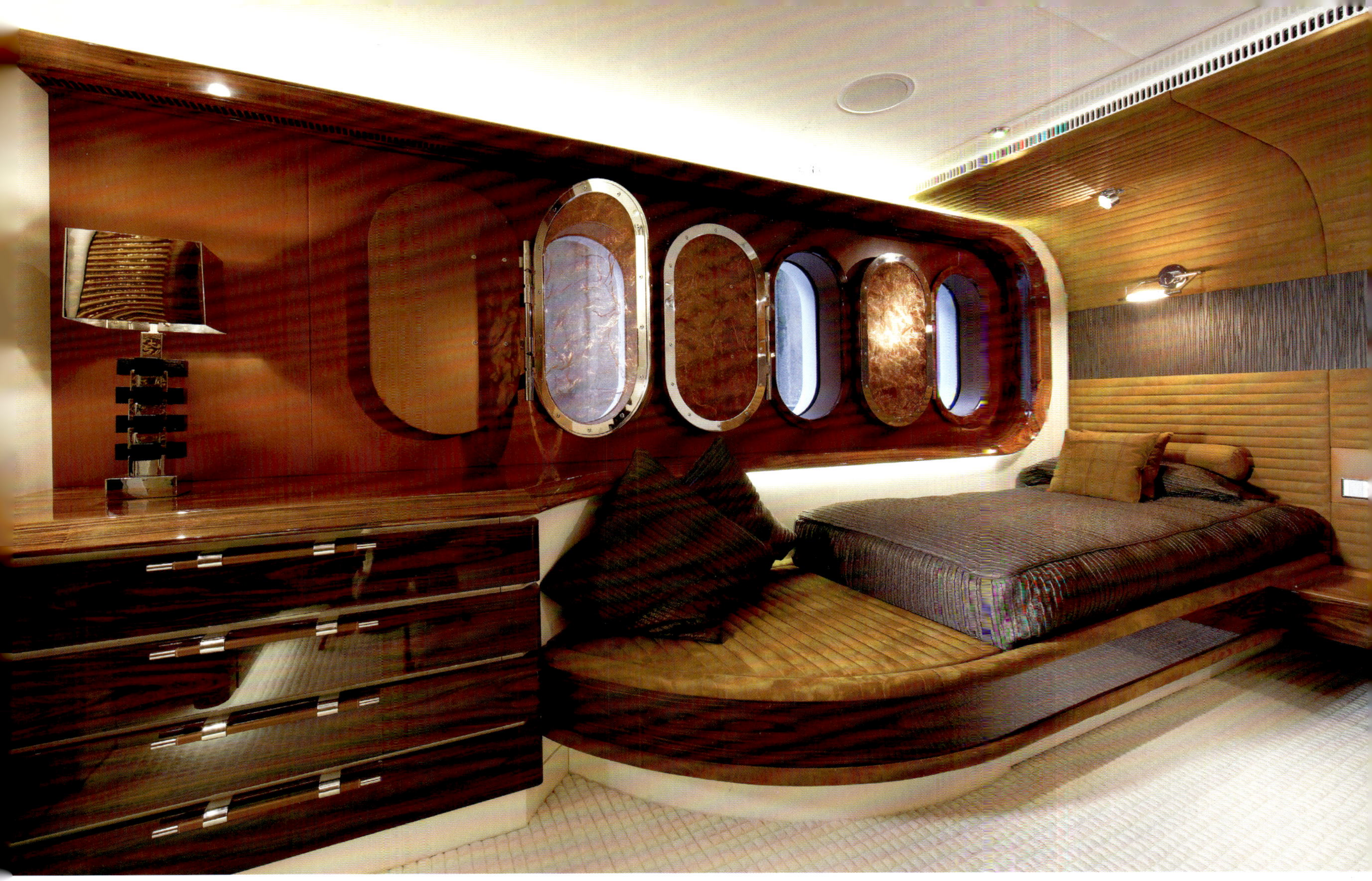

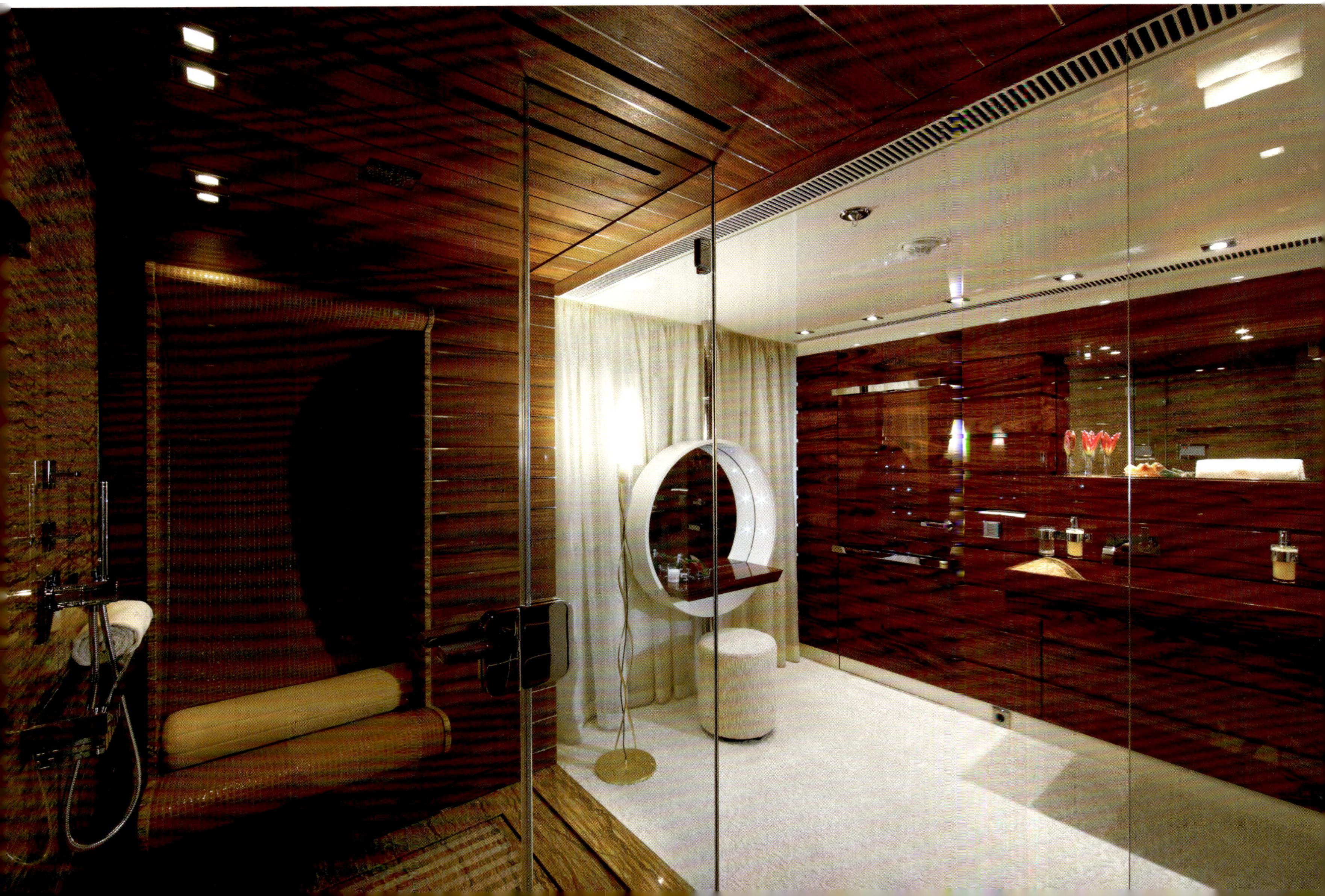

LADY BRITT

> **INTERIOR DESIGN**	Redman Whiteley Dixon
> **NAVAL ARCHITECT**	De Voogt
> **SHIPYARD**	De Vries Shipyard
> **LENGTH**	63m
> **TEXT**	Toby, Ecuyer

> "Inspired by the Scandinavian background of her owner, RWD have created an interior that weaves together a combination of woods and freshness. The palette of veneers have a relaxed level of polish, giving a informality to the timbers and allowing the varying grain to be appreciated, naturally patterned textiles abound and work with the spaces to give a lively and colourful feel to the yacht. Differing themes to saloons, master and guest cabins are given foundation by the careful detailing of the joinery with architecture and furnishings changing to suit the mood. Unique spaces such as the sensational sauna opening up onto its own private sea terrace express the personality are the beautifully constructed de Vries Feadship."

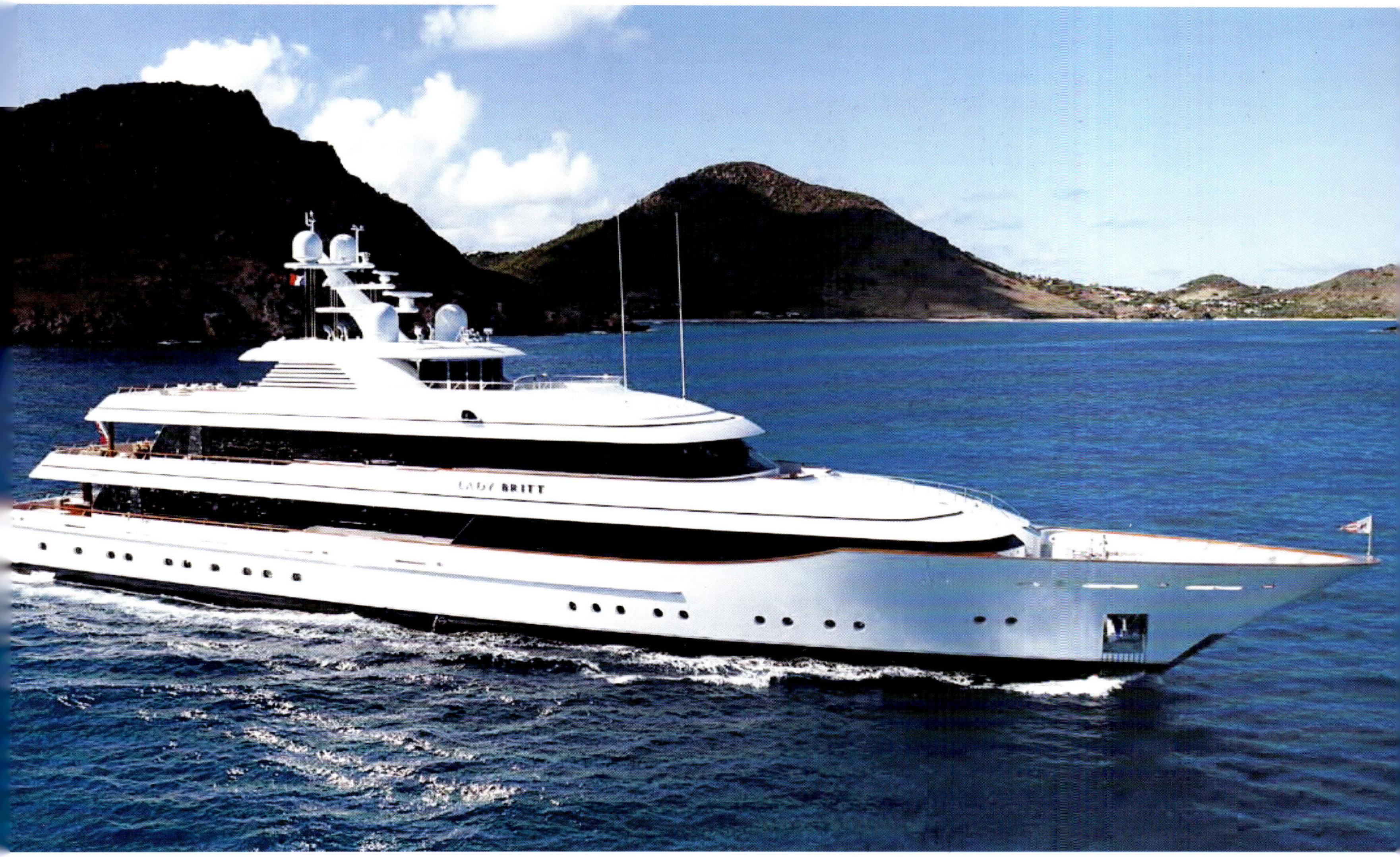

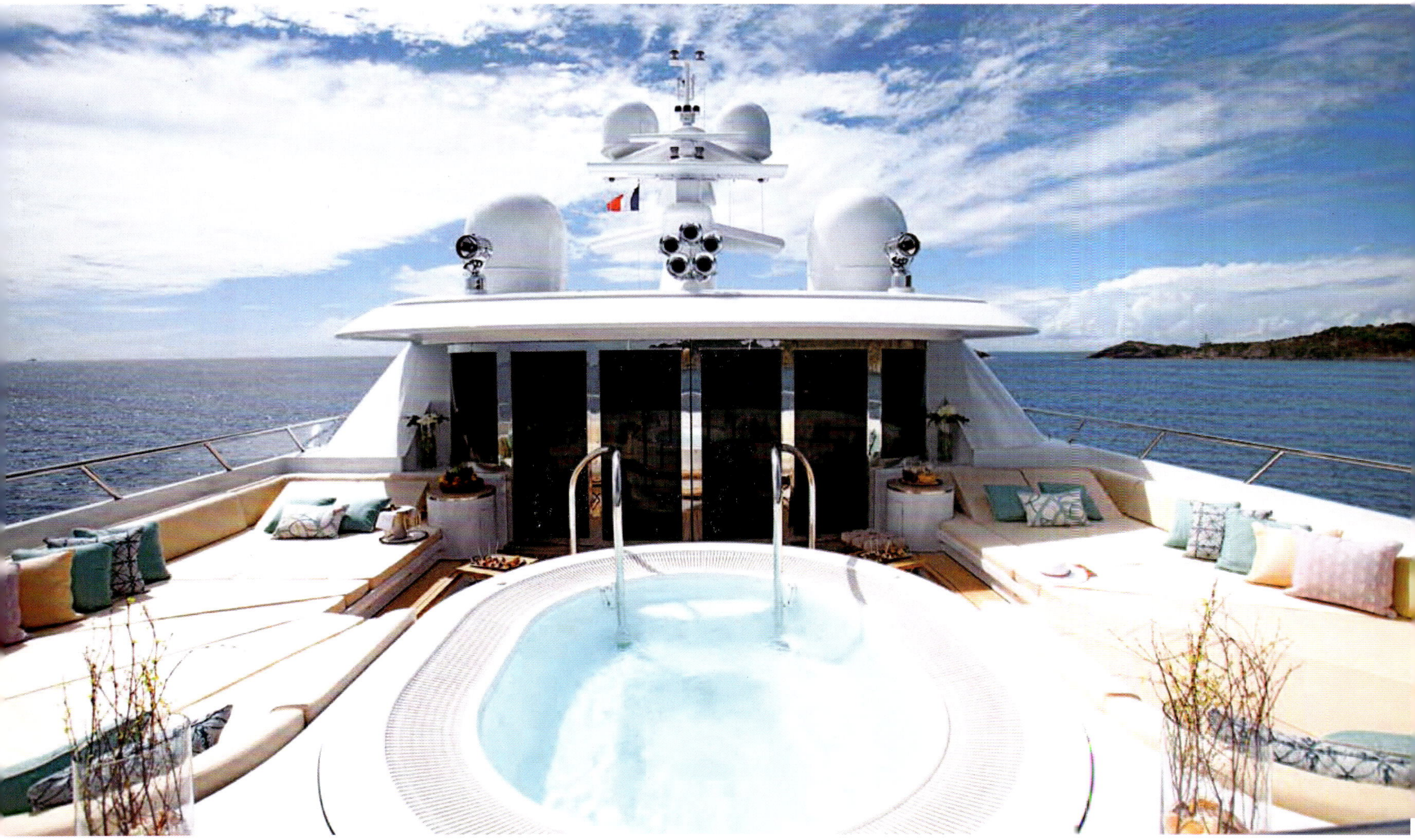

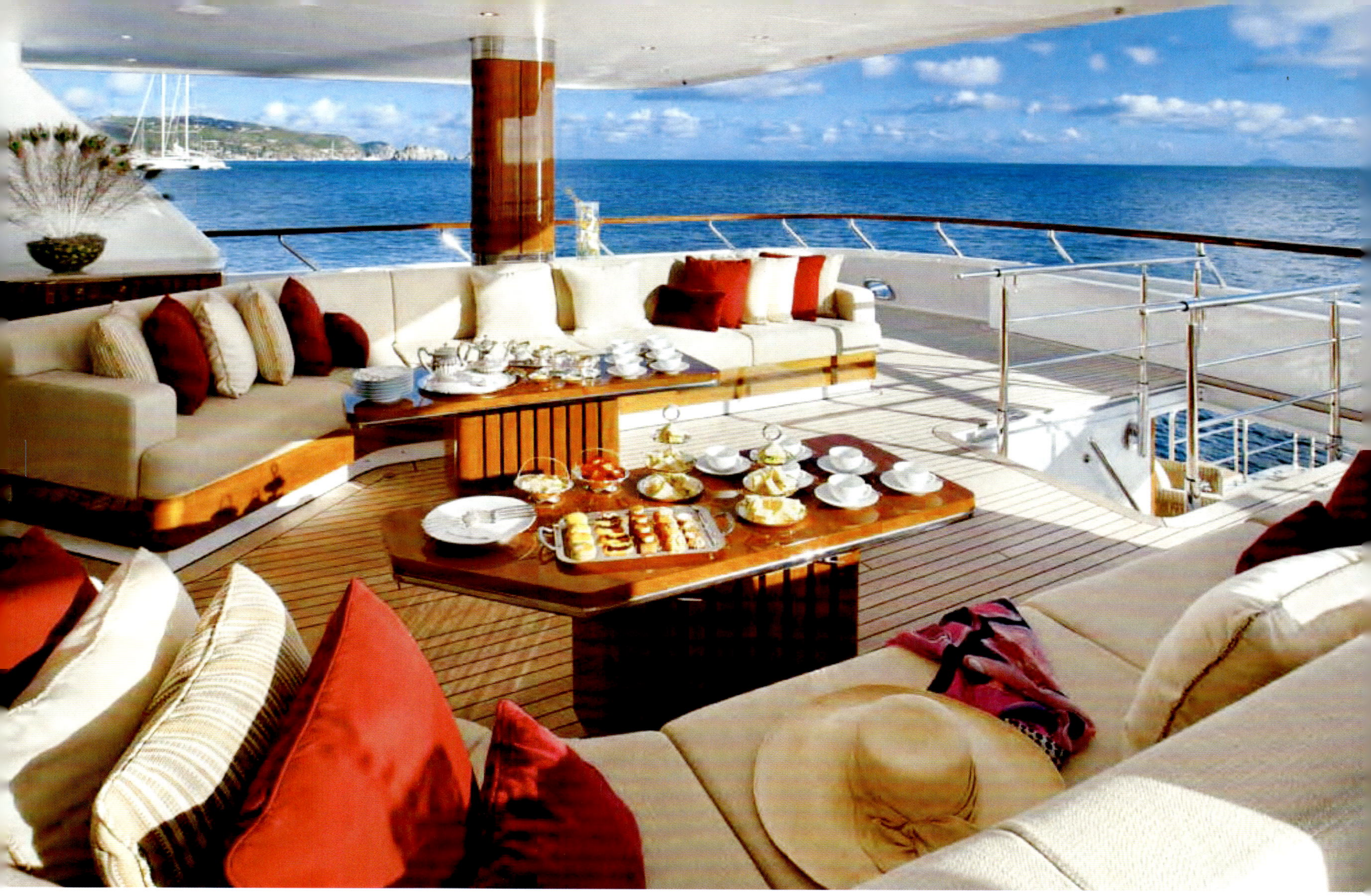

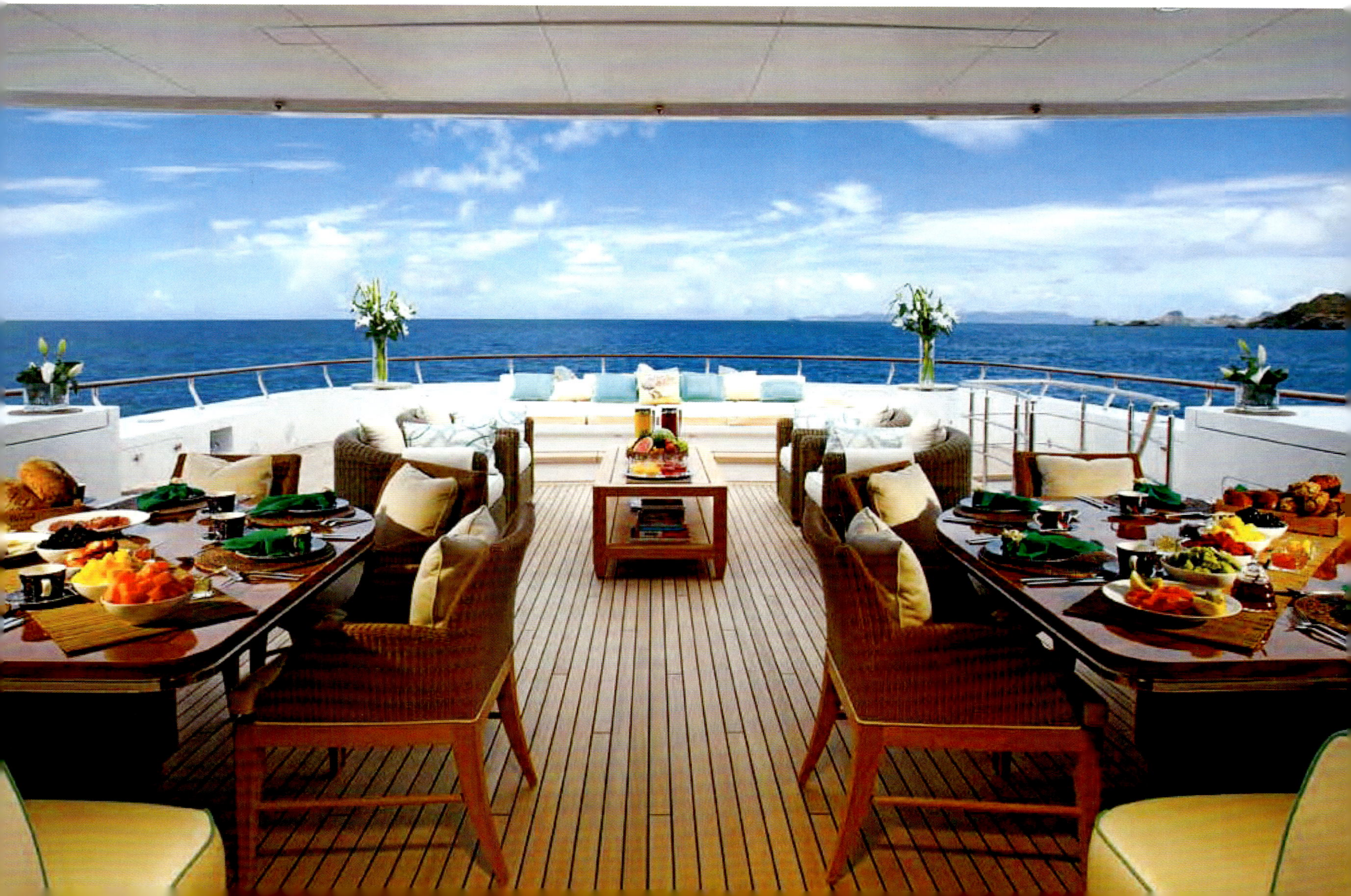

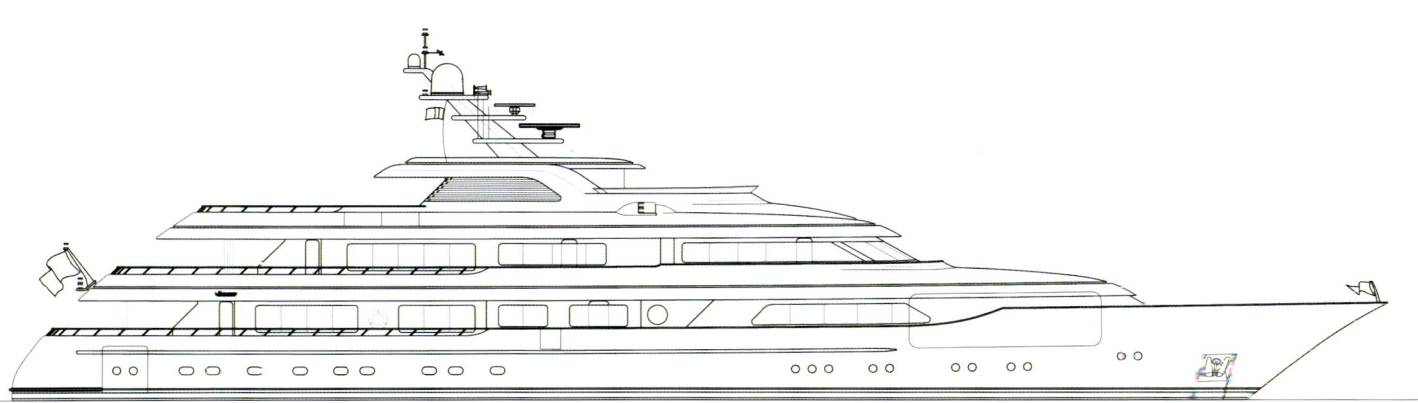

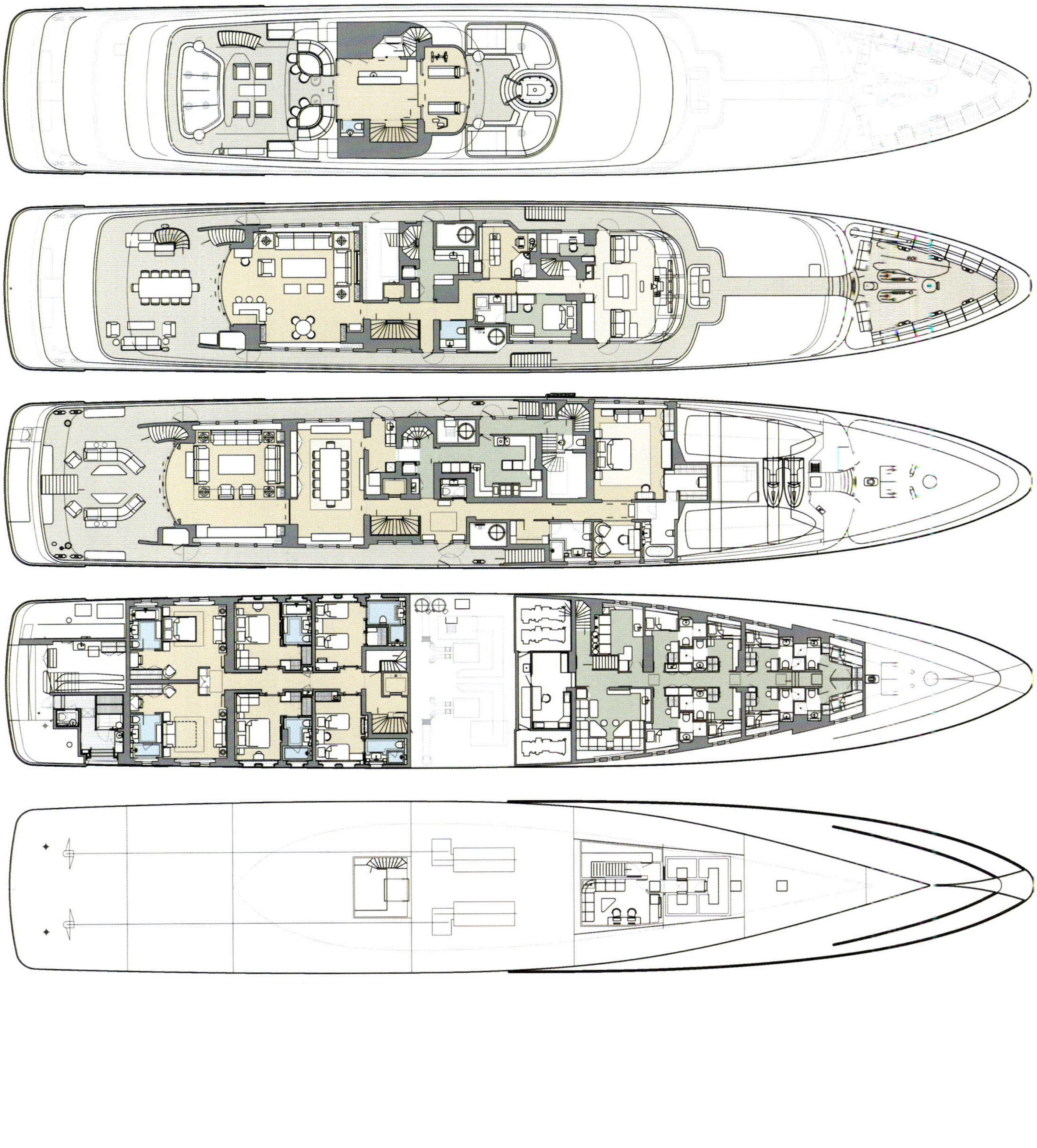

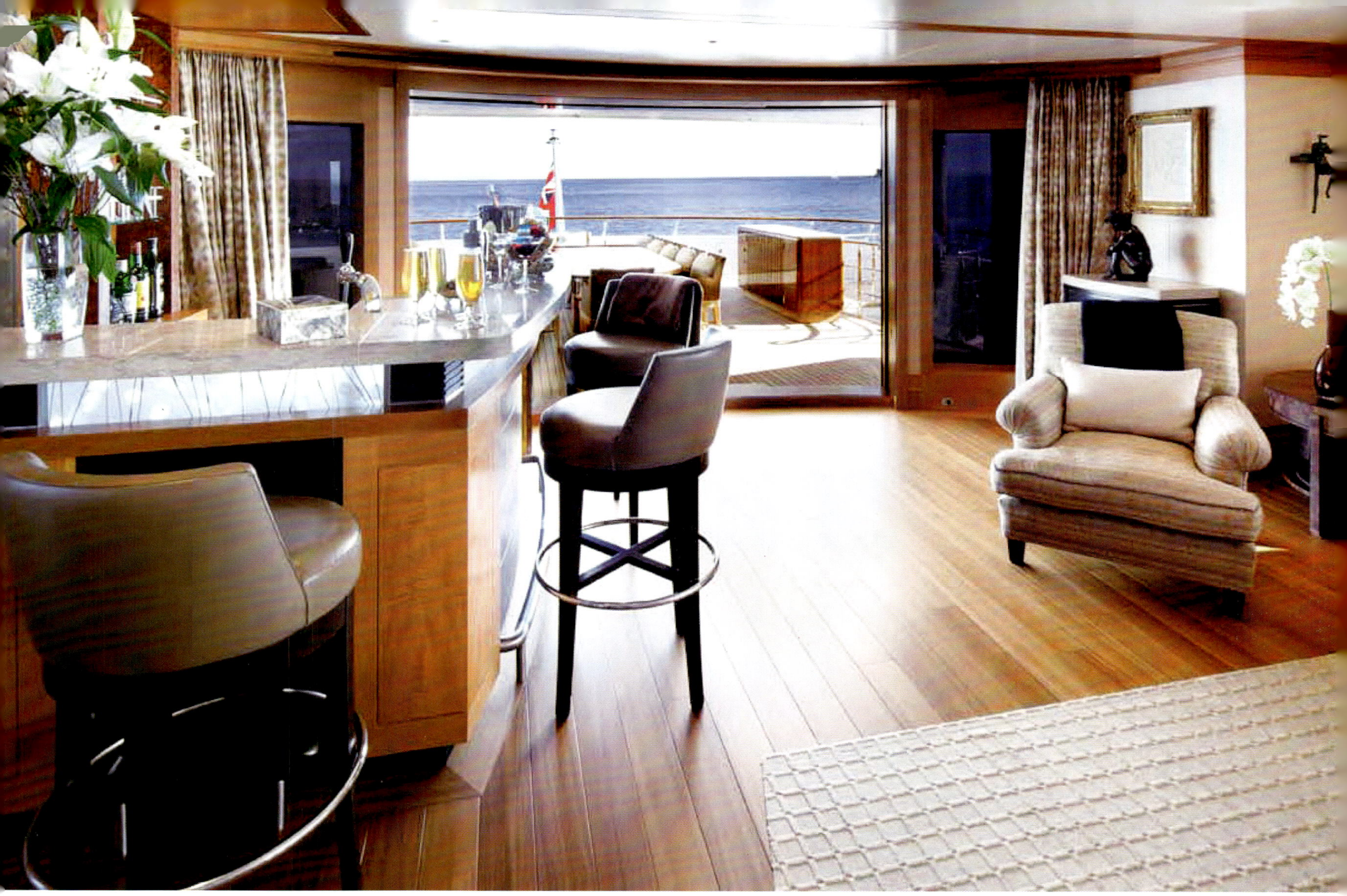

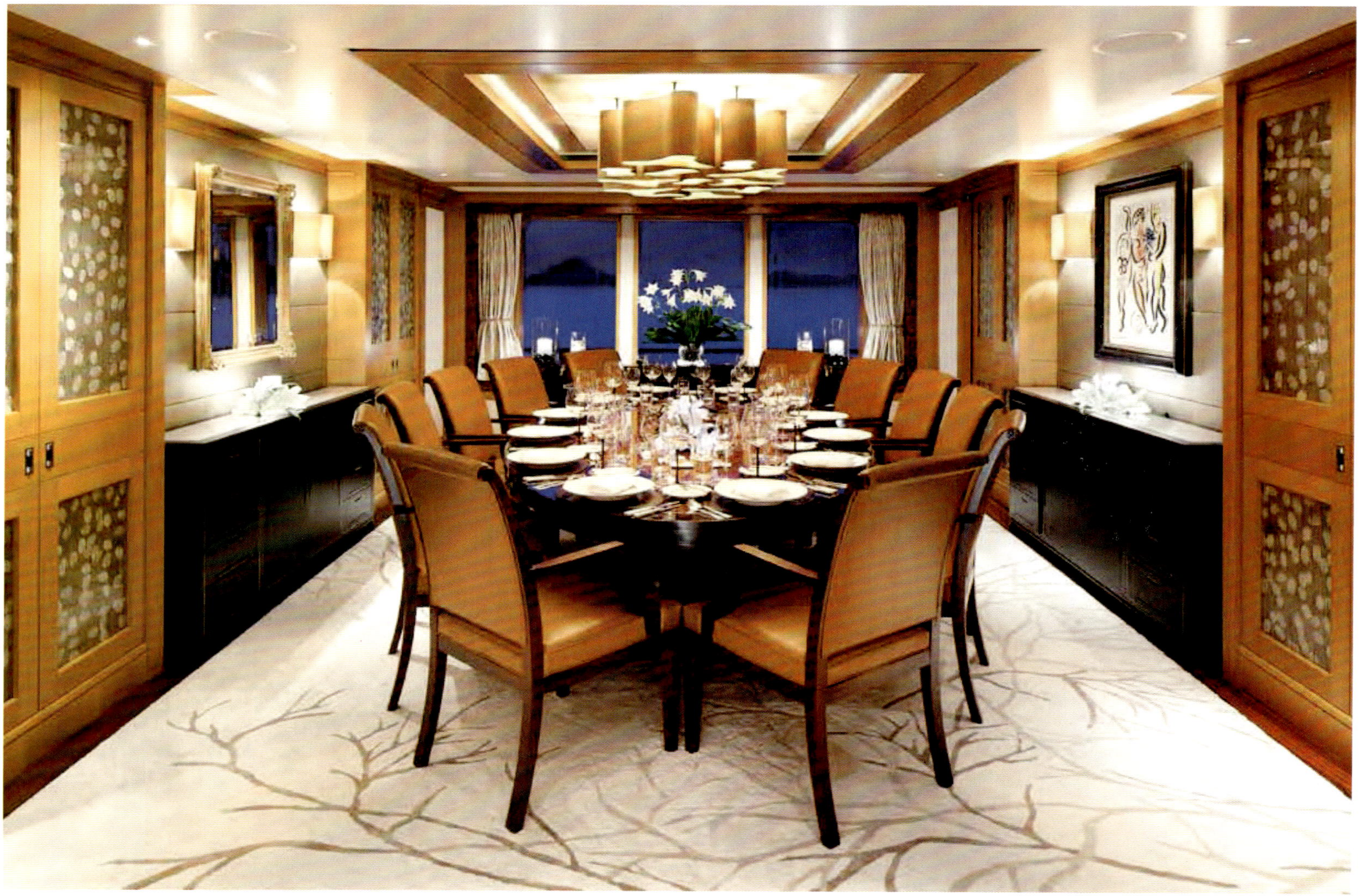

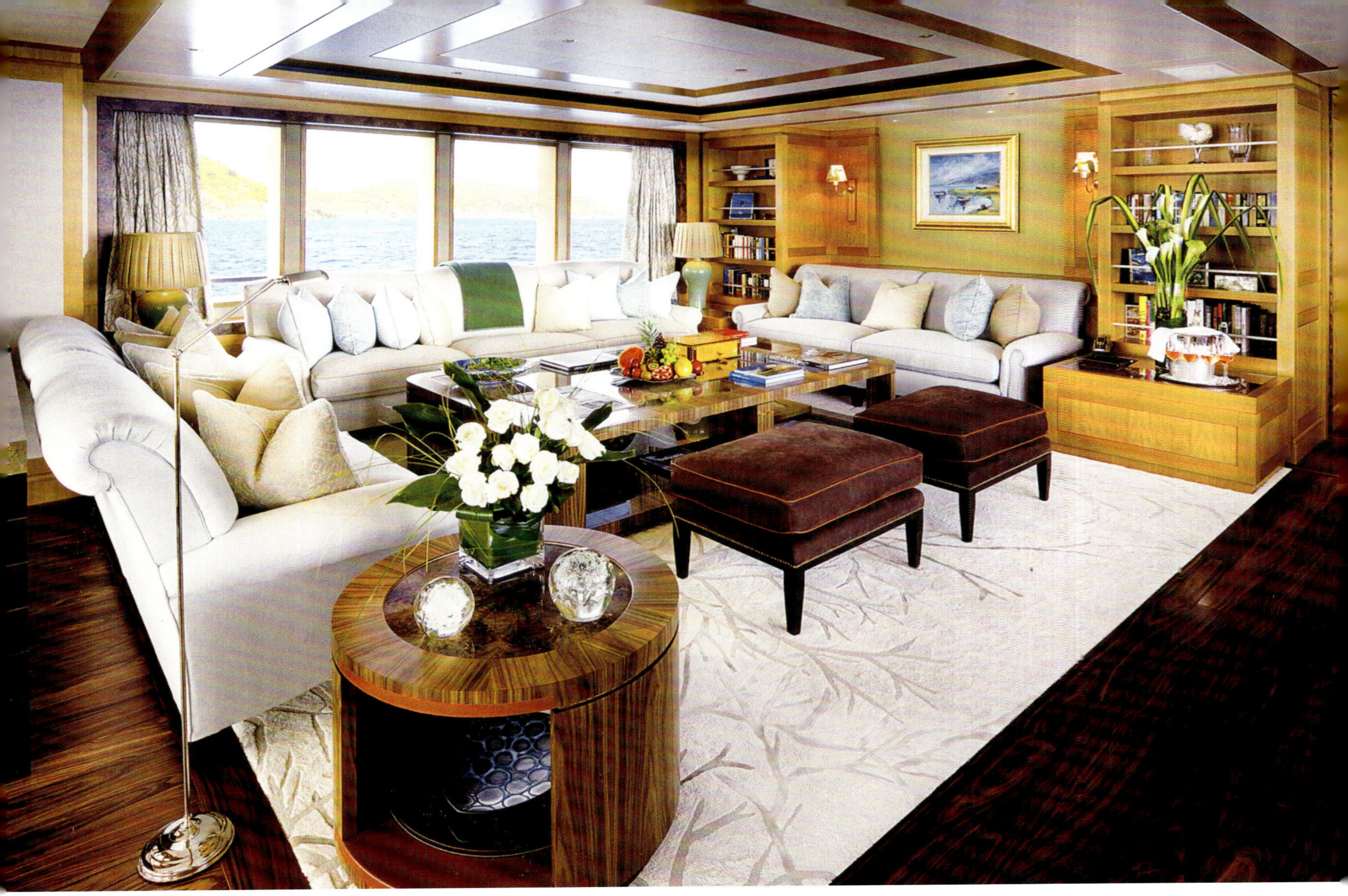

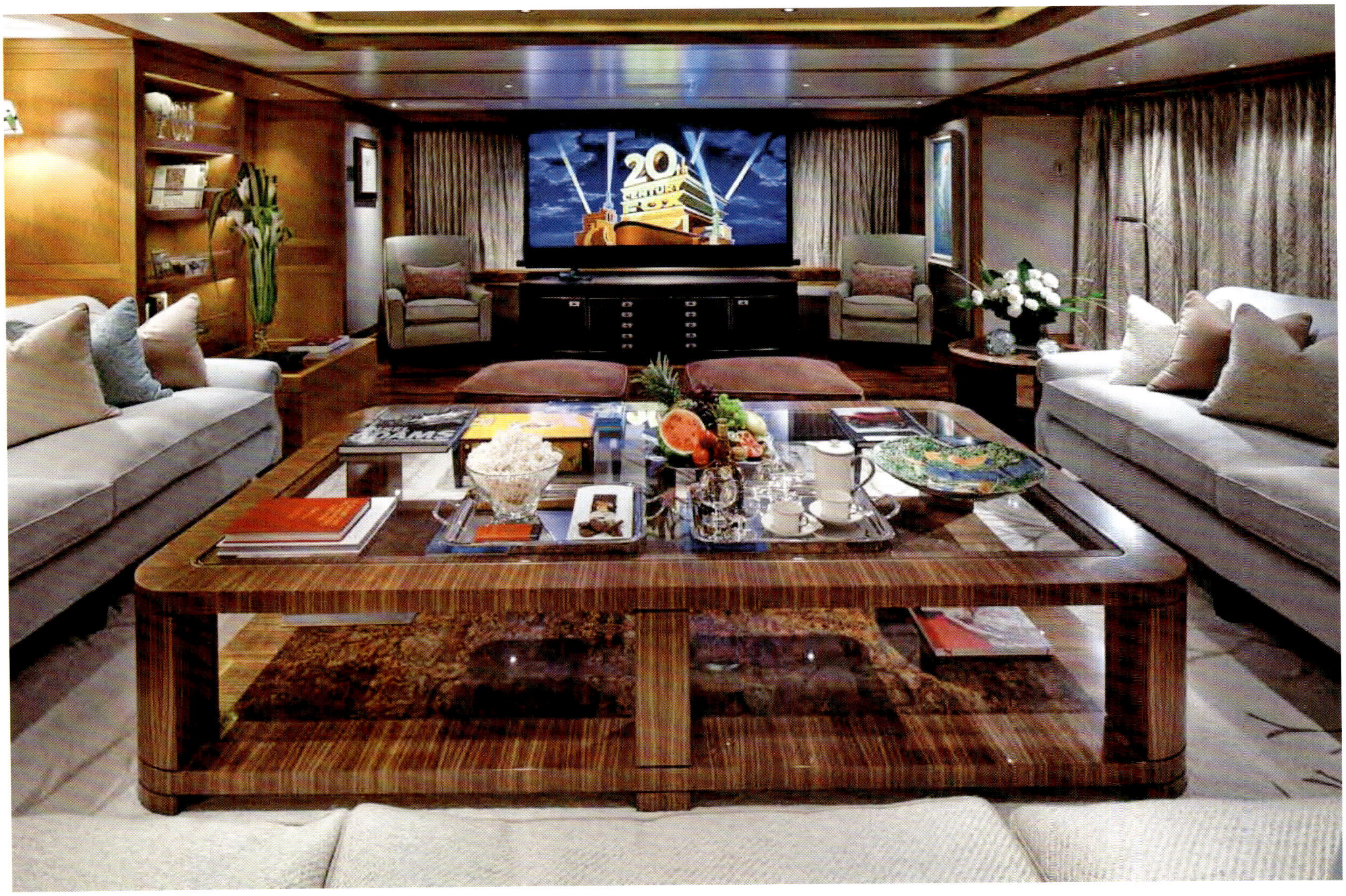
ADAMS

　　船主来自斯堪的纳维亚半岛，受其背景影响，负责设计的 RWD 团队在内部装修上将木质和新鲜感巧妙地结合。木质表面自然的抛光处理，给人一种轻松愉悦的感觉；同时，原木自然多变的纹理使人倍感亲切自然，另有图案搭配自然的织物衬托，使游艇的空间多了几分活泼和丰富之感。每间舱室主题各异，在木器的建构和布置上都经过了细致斟酌，以配合主舱和客舱的不同情调。游艇上设计有独特的区域，比如美轮美奂的桑拿区设计在私人海域台面上，体现个性的同时也体现了德弗里造船厂一直以来的建造精美游艇的声誉。

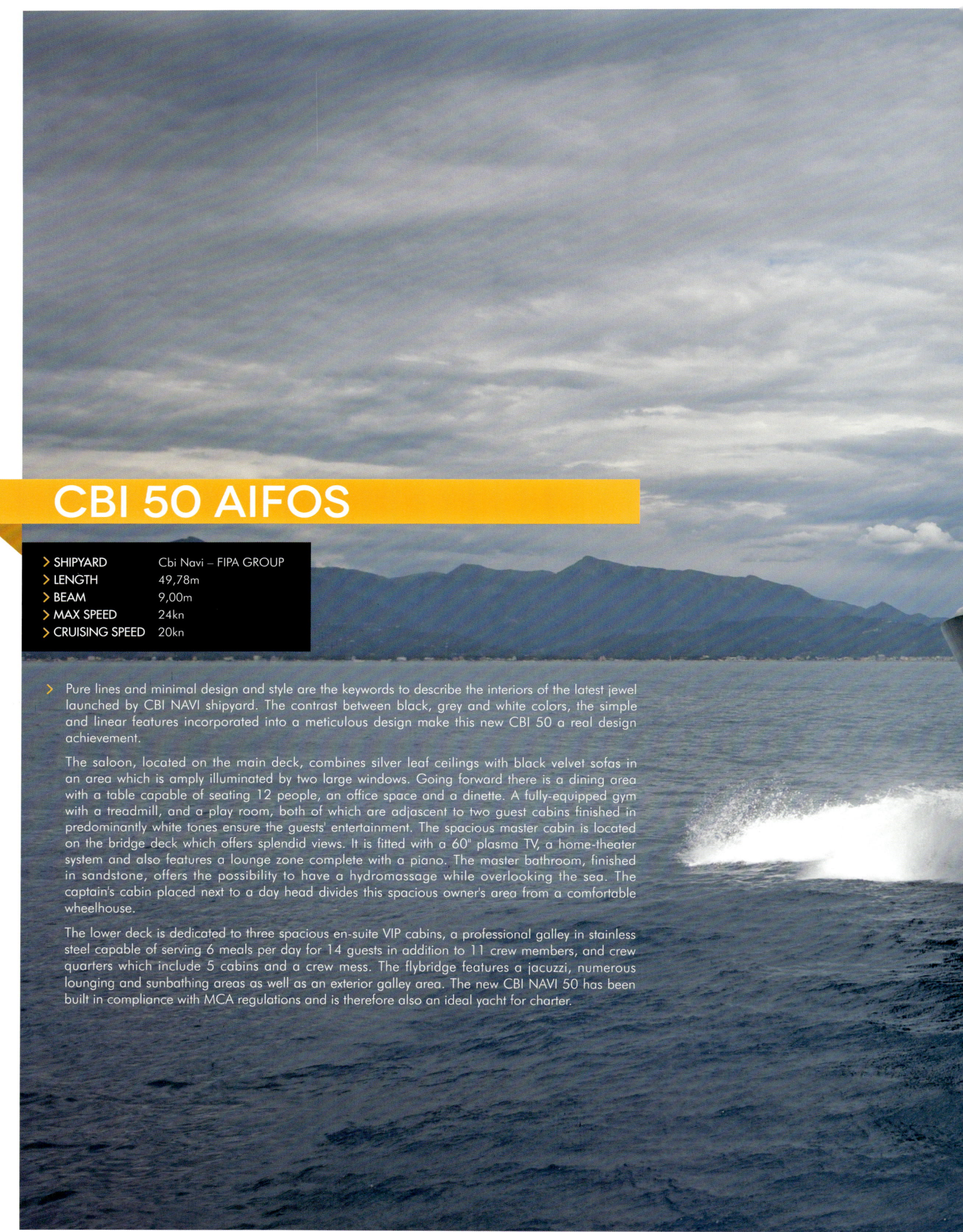

CBI 50 AIFOS

>	SHIPYARD	Cbi Navi – FIPA GROUP
>	LENGTH	49,78m
>	BEAM	9,00m
>	MAX SPEED	24kn
>	CRUISING SPEED	20kn

> Pure lines and minimal design and style are the keywords to describe the interiors of the latest jewel launched by CBI NAVI shipyard. The contrast between black, grey and white colors, the simple and linear features incorporated into a meticulous design make this new CBI 50 a real design achievement.

The saloon, located on the main deck, combines silver leaf ceilings with black velvet sofas in an area which is amply illuminated by two large windows. Going forward there is a dining area with a table capable of seating 12 people, an office space and a dinette. A fully-equipped gym with a treadmill, and a play room, both of which are adjacent to two guest cabins finished in predominantly white tones ensure the guests' entertainment. The spacious master cabin is located on the bridge deck which offers splendid views. It is fitted with a 60" plasma TV, a home-theater system and also features a lounge zone complete with a piano. The master bathroom, finished in sandstone, offers the possibility to have a hydromassage while overlooking the sea. The captain's cabin placed next to a day head divides this spacious owner's area from a comfortable wheelhouse.

The lower deck is dedicated to three spacious en-suite VIP cabins, a professional galley in stainless steel capable of serving 6 meals per day for 14 guests in addition to 11 crew members, and crew quarters which include 5 cabins and a crew mess. The flybridge features a jacuzzi, numerous lounging and sunbathing areas as well as an exterior galley area. The new CBI NAVI 50 has been built in compliance with MCA regulations and is therefore also an ideal yacht for charter.

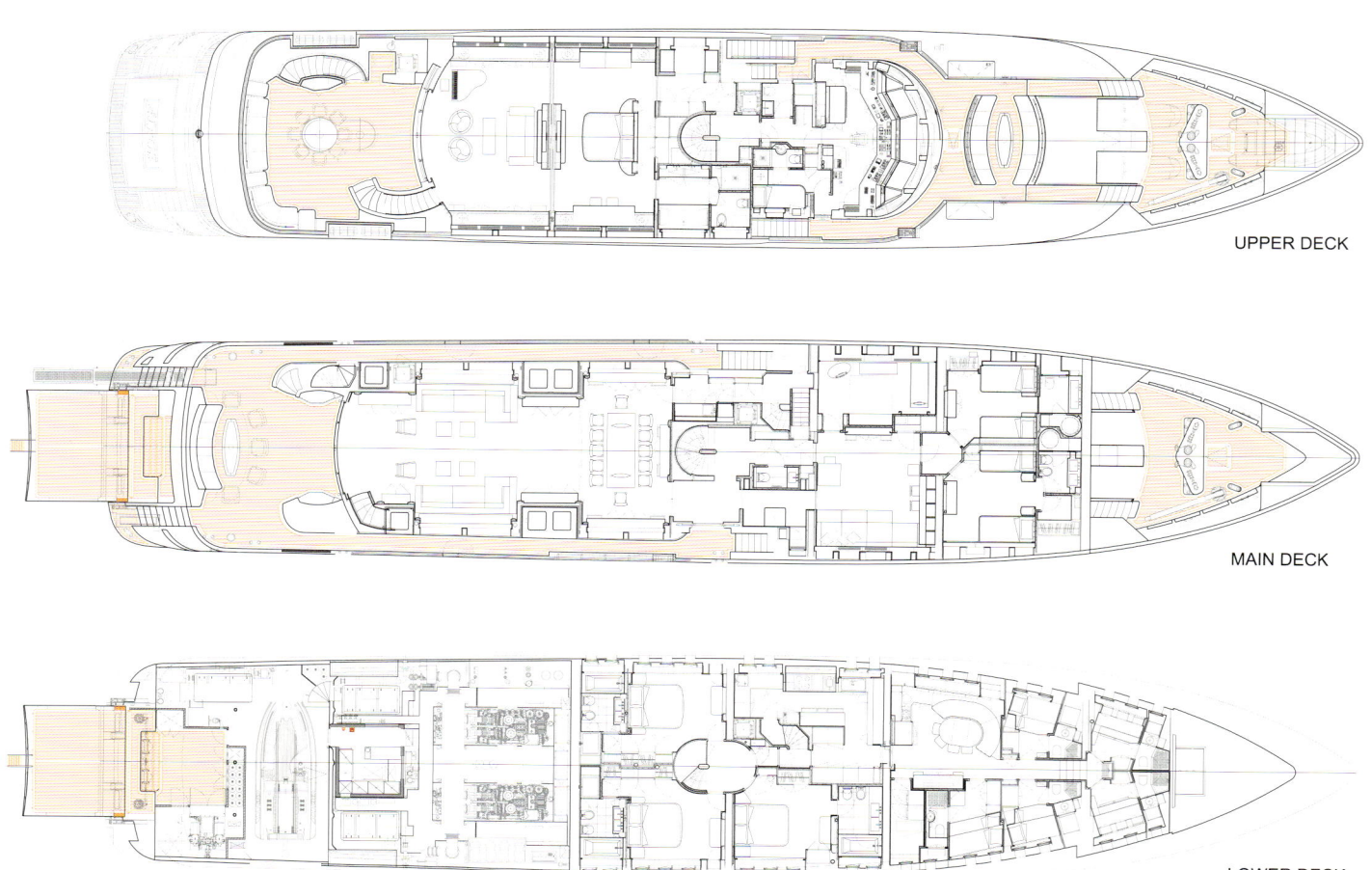

UPPER DECK

MAIN DECK

LOWER DECK

PROFILE

SUN DECK

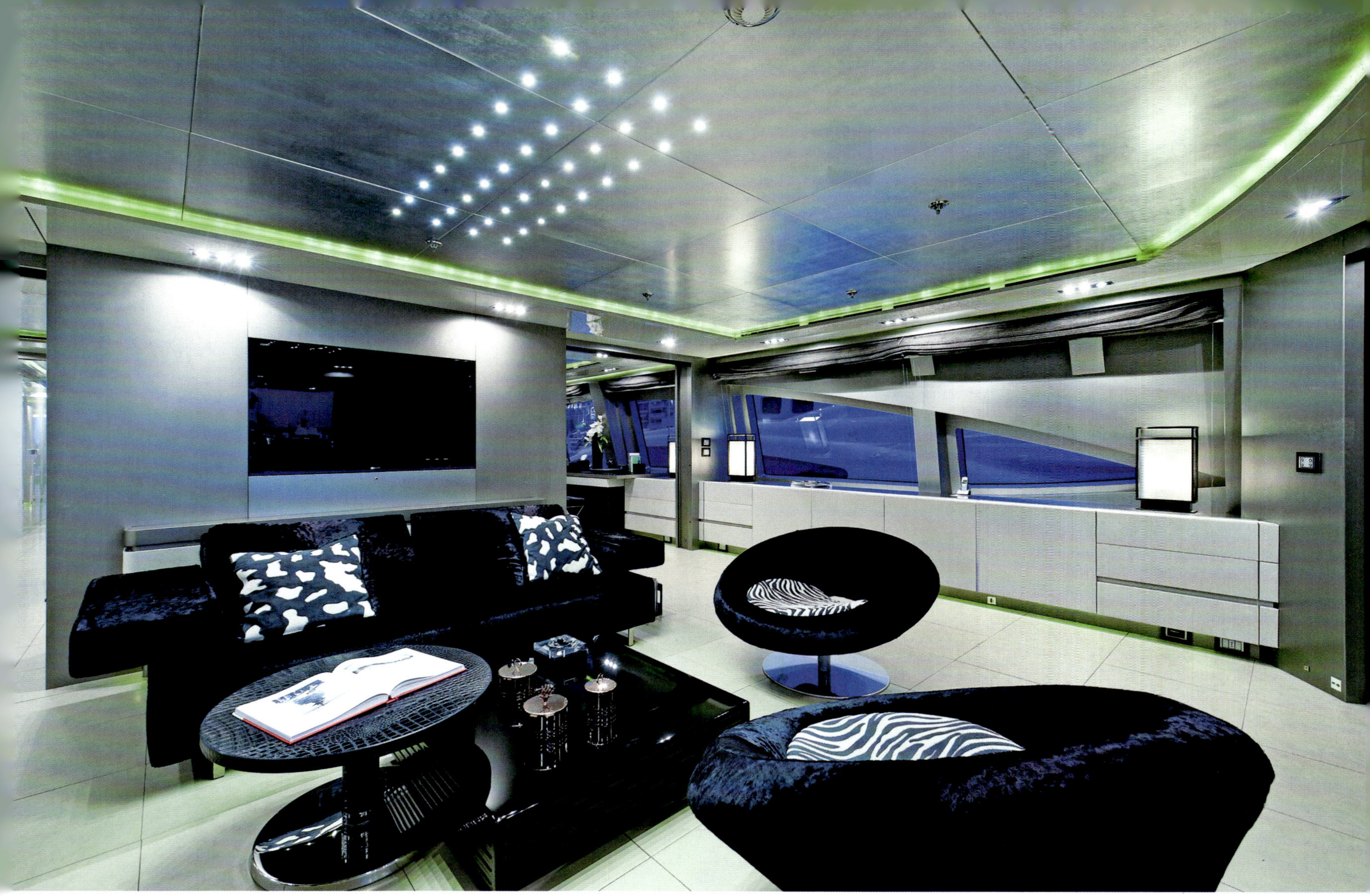

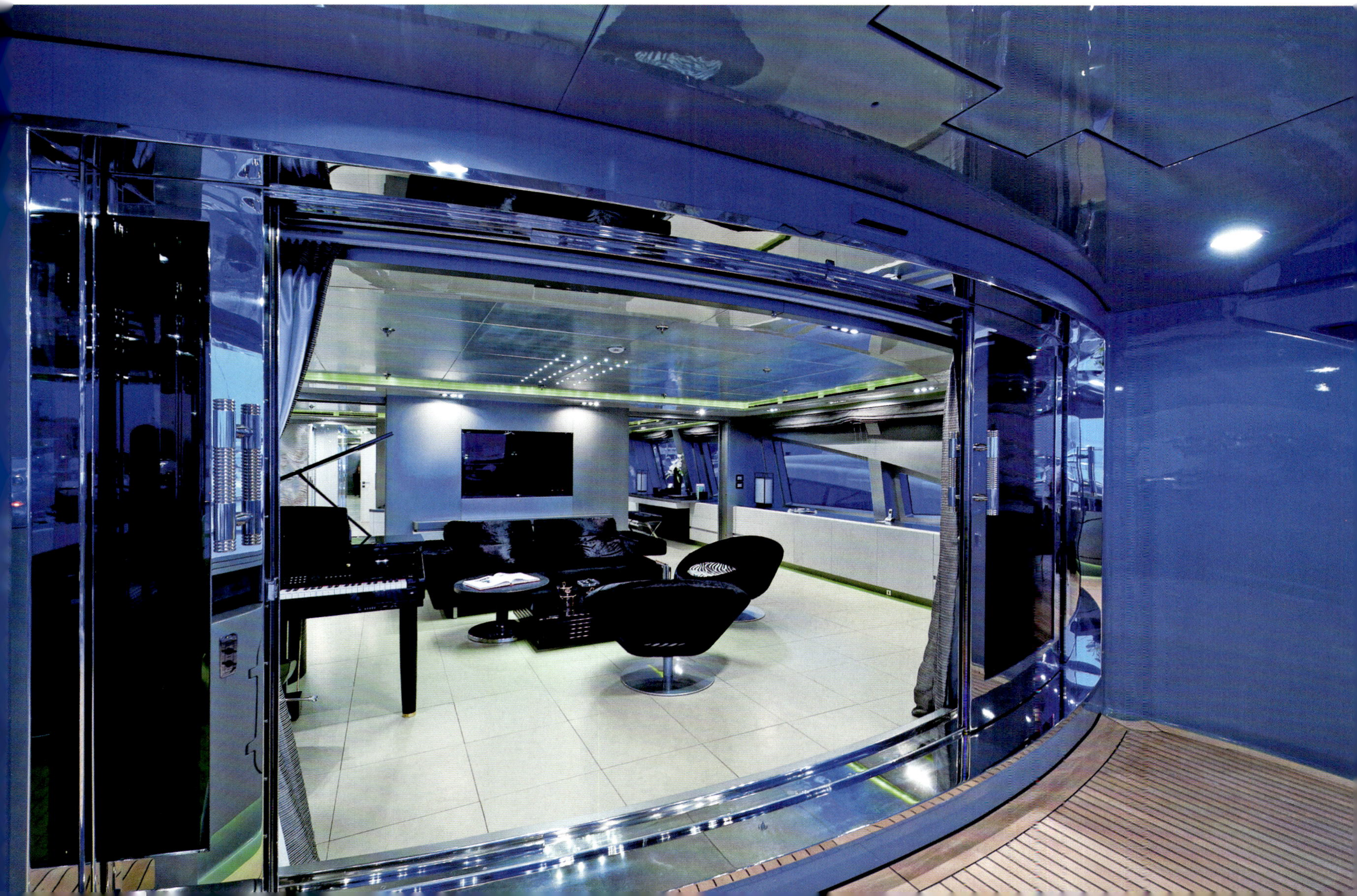

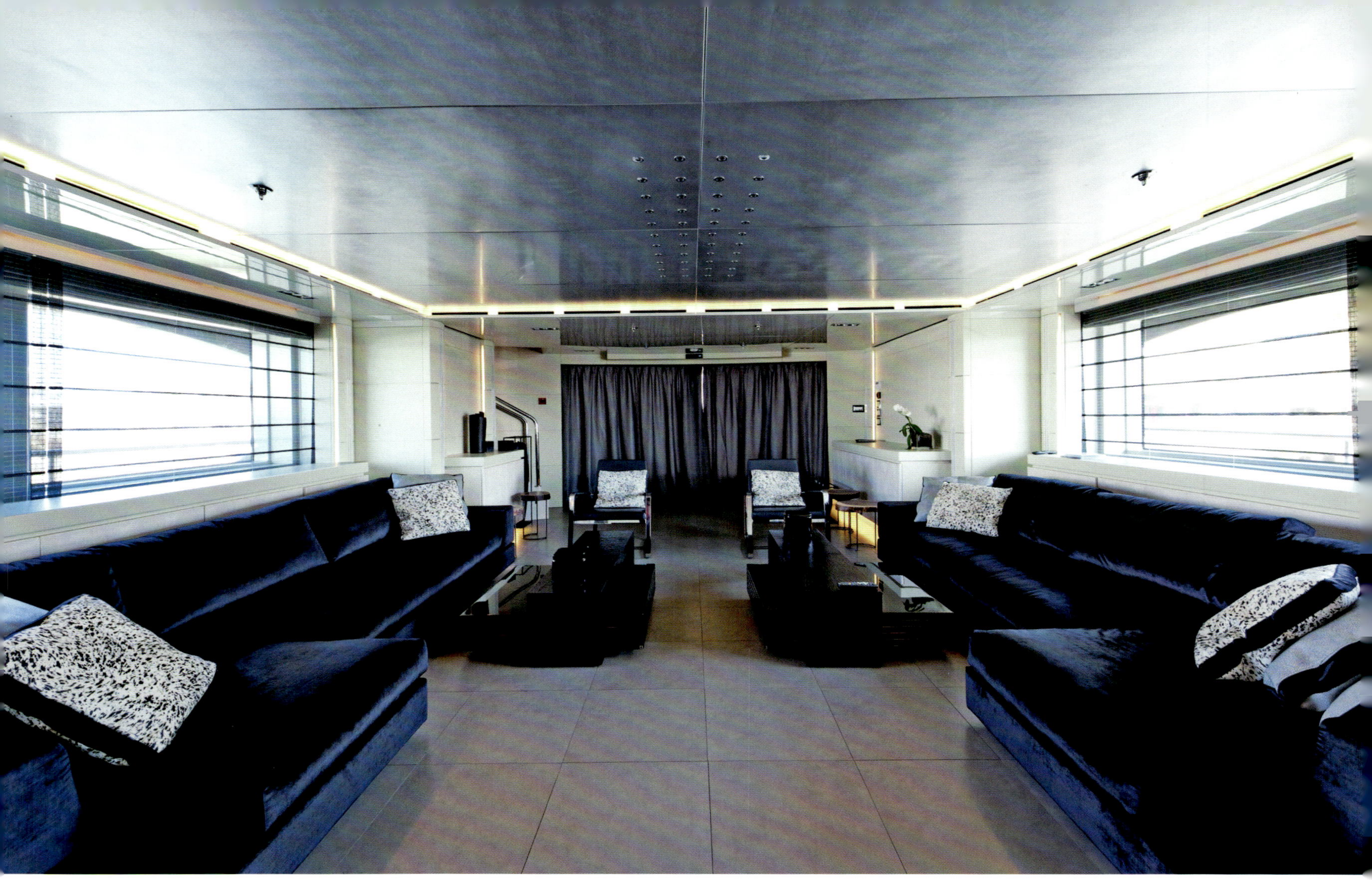

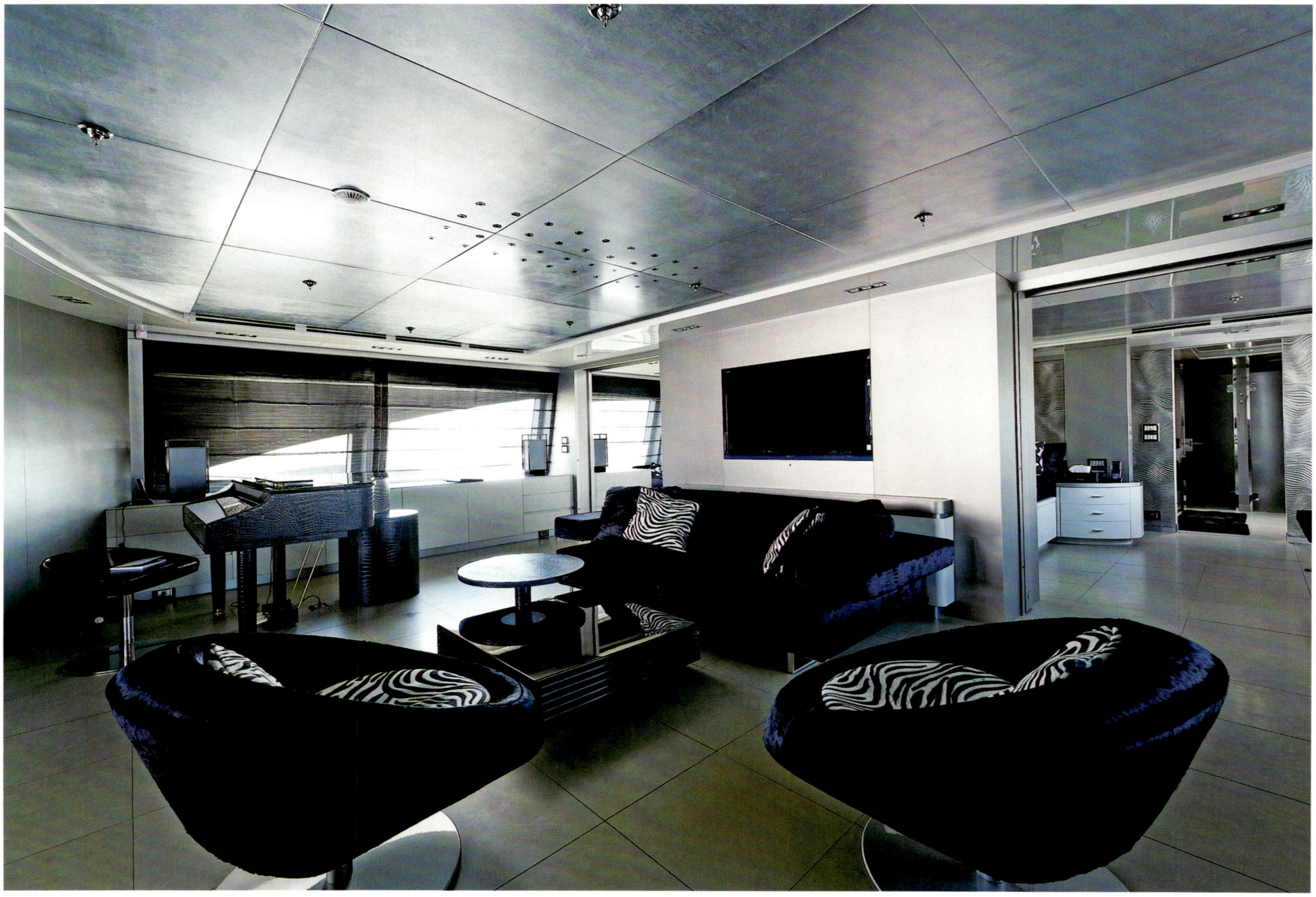

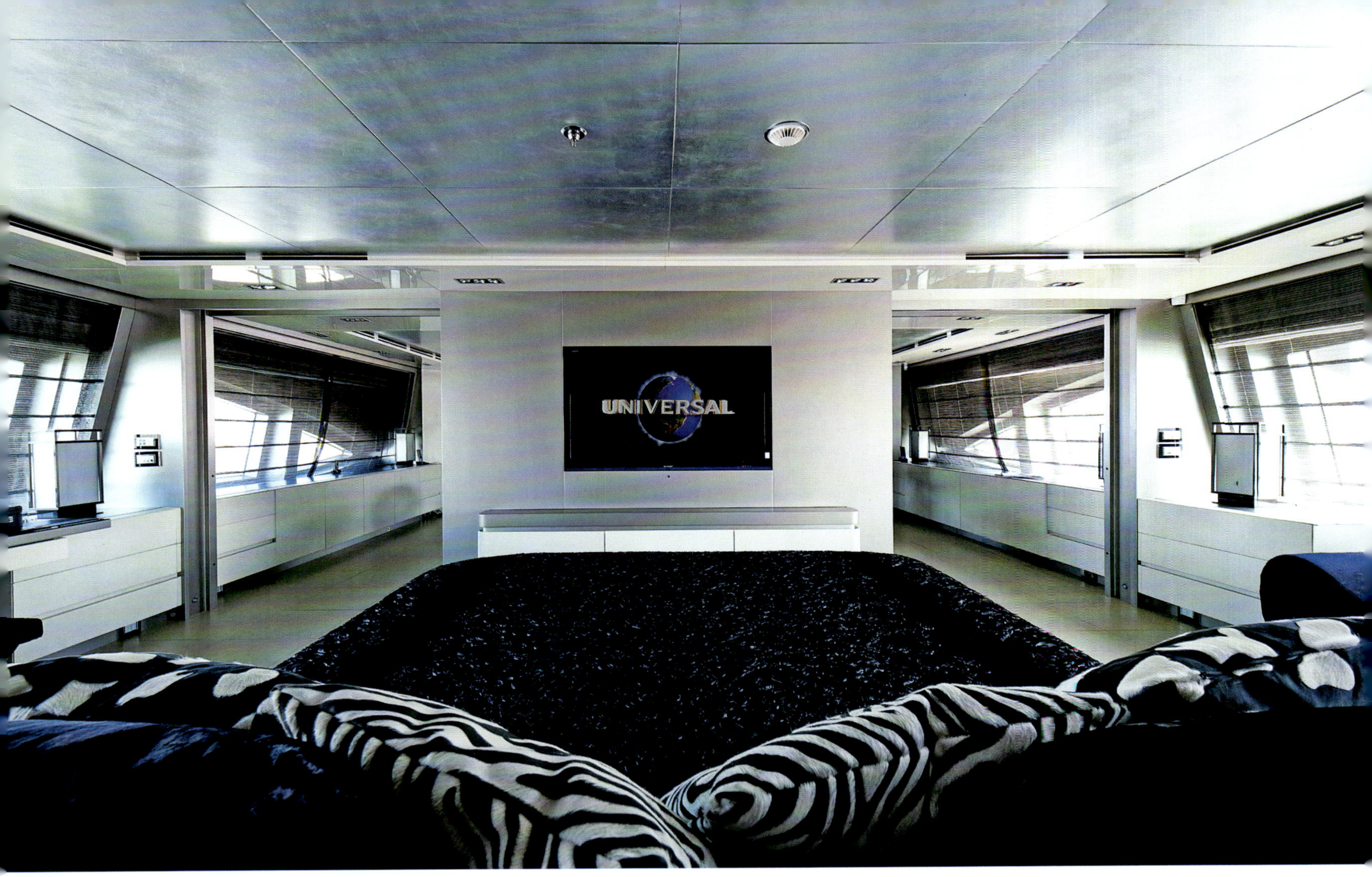
UNIVERSAL

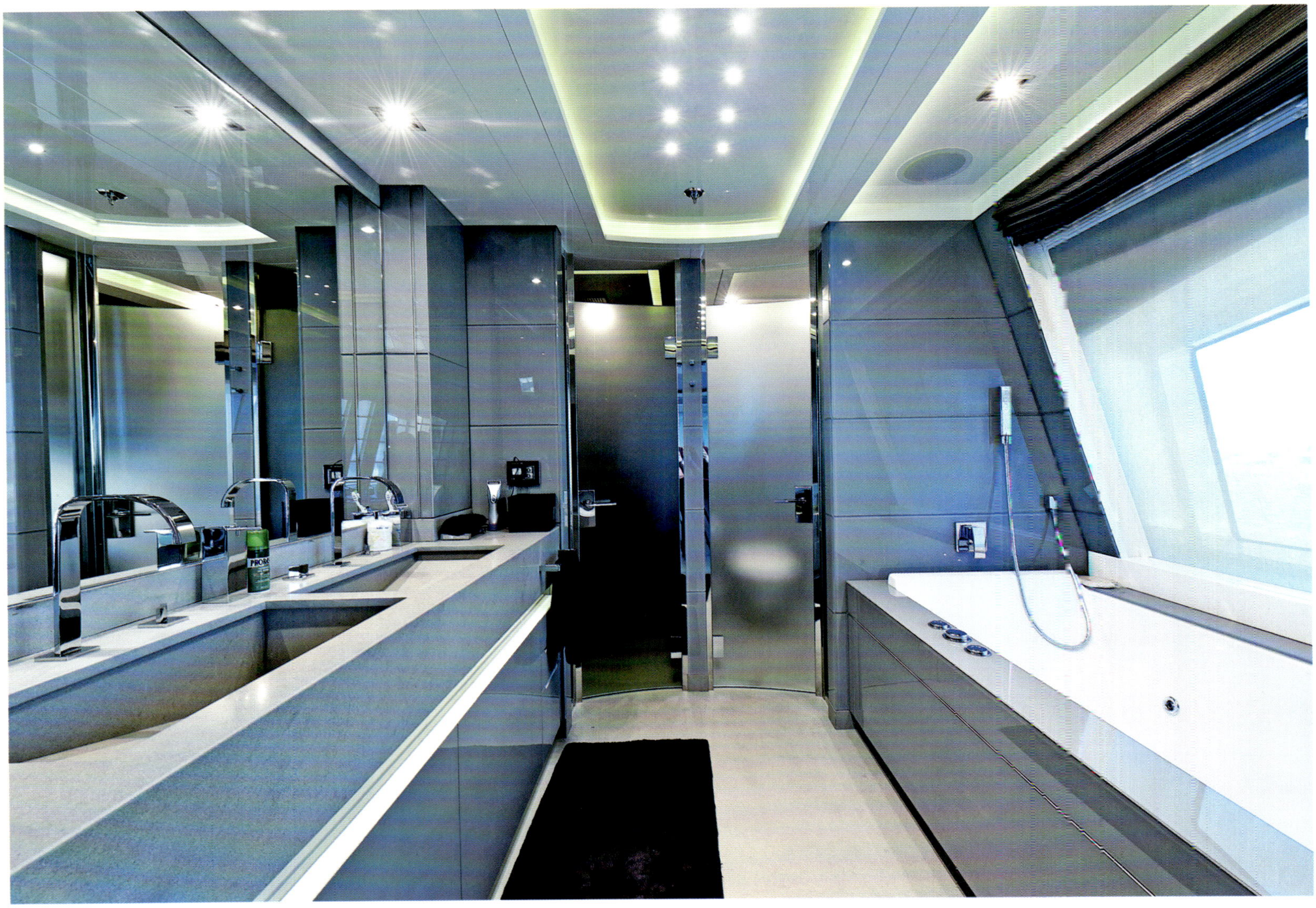

　　由 CBI NAVI 造船厂最新推出的游艇可以用以下关键词来形容其内部设计：整洁的线条、简约的设计和风格。黑、白、灰三色的运用，简约和流线型的设计中又不乏精致，使这艘新款 CBI 50 游艇真正成为设计史上的突破之作。

　　位于主甲板的大厅有着银箔天花板，内设黑色丝绒沙发，两扇大窗让整个空间明亮无比。再往前是用餐区，餐桌可容纳 12 人，还有一个办公区和一个小餐室。此外，健身设施齐全，有跑步机和游戏室，旁边的两个客舱主打白色调，让游客充分享受娱乐氛围。位于船桥甲板的船主舱空间宽敞，视野开阔，内设 60 英寸等离子电视、家庭影院，客厅还放着一架钢琴；船主舱的卫生司采用砂岩石材，可以一边享受旋水按摩，一边欣赏大海的风景。船长舱旁的蒸汽室将宽敞的船主区与舒适的舵手室分隔开来。

　　底层甲板主要有三个宽敞的独立贵宾客舱，还有一个不锈钢制成的专业厨房，每天可为 14 名客人和 11 名船员提供 6 次用餐。船员区包括 5 个舱室和 1 个船员食堂。驾驶桥楼设有浴缸，大量的休息区和日光浴区以及一个室外厨房。这艘新款 CBI NAVI 50 游艇是按照 MCA 标准建造而成的，因此也是包租的理想游艇。

AB 116

> DESIGN	AB Yachts – Fipa Group
> LENGTH	36.2m
> BEAM	7.5m
> MAX SPEED	50kn
> CRUISING SPEED	44kn
> ENGINES	3xMTU 16V2000 M94
> WATERJETS	2xMJP 550 CSU+1xMJP 550 Booster

> The new AB 116 perfectly showcases the recognizable AB Yachts style with her streamlined and aggressive hull lines. Like every jewel in this line, she is based on the idea of navigating at high speed in any sea condition without having to compromise comfort thanks to ample and generous interior spaces. The construction techniques used are those AB Yachts have become renowned for, with the use of lightweight materials, advanced composites and special bonding methods which have become the point of reference in the yachting industry.

The contrasting colors of interiors, where white, black and grey predominate, create an elegant harmony with the exterior for which the new "Silver Gold" color was chosen. Pure and sober lines are combined with precious marbles to give the interiors a unique and elaborate look. The main saloon was conceived with guest comfort and entertainment in mind with a spacious U-shaped lounge area, a TV concealing system and a large dining table capable of seating up to twelve people.

Another main characteristic of this AB 116 is undoubtedly her second saloon located on the lower deck where the windshield in front of the main helm acts as a light well and bathes this area in natural light thereby ensuring a complete relaxation under open skies for its occupants. Located aft of this lower deck saloon is the guest accommodation which features 2 twin and 1 double VIP cabins, each en-suite with their own bathroom, and a grand full-beam master cabin with large portholes which give the impression of being in contact with the sea. This master cabin is itself divided in several distinct areas: a lounge, a gym with a shower, main bathroom and the sleeping area with its king-size bed.

AB 116 was created following the idea of the yacht able to navigate at high speed with any sea conditions. The constructions technologies are the AB yachts standard ones that represent the point of reference in the yachting world. The result of this incredible mixture of technology and hydrodynamic merge is that thanks to its three engines of 2600 HP accurately coupled to three waterjets can give you the sensation to fly over the water.

STARBOARD

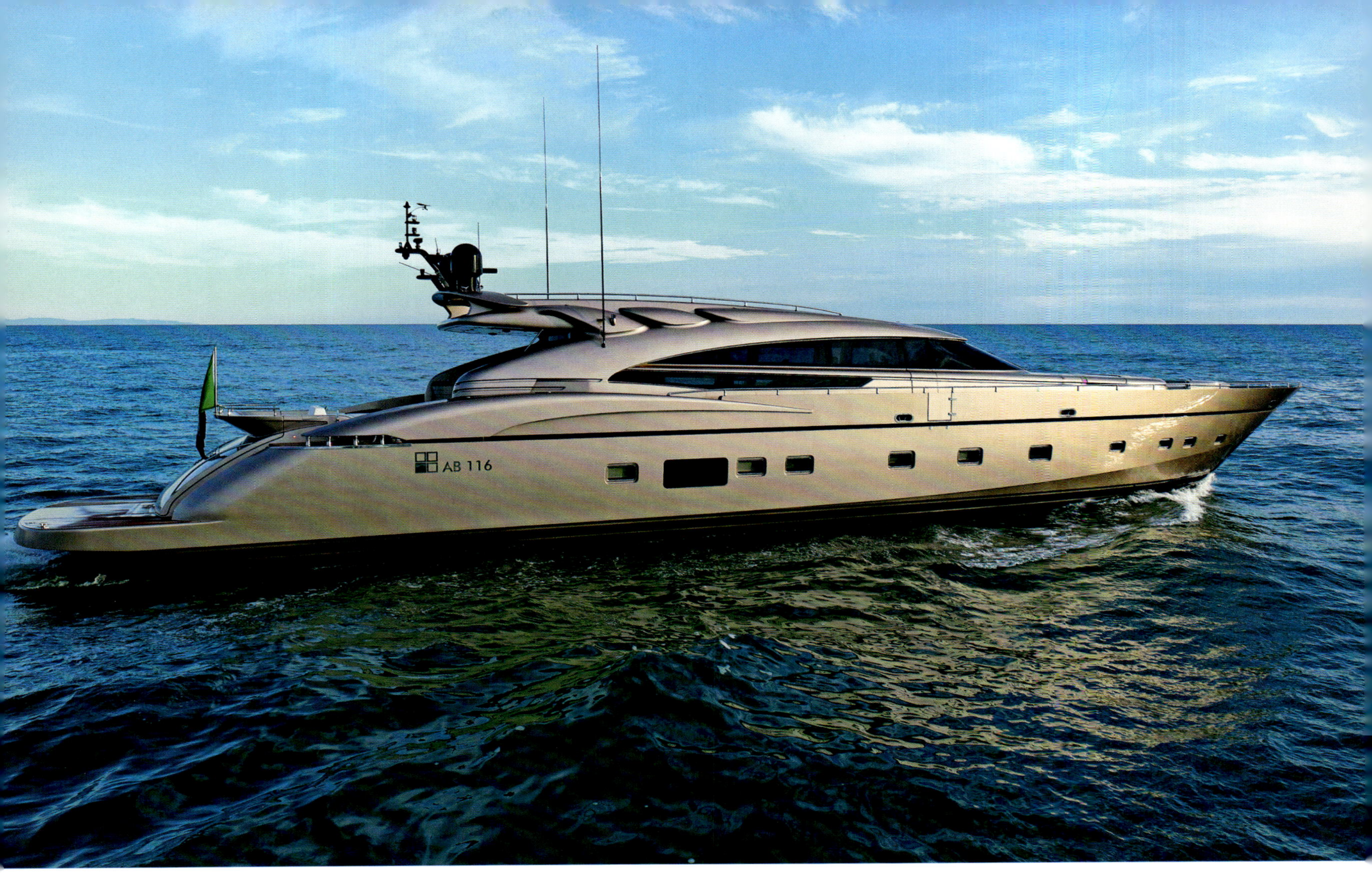

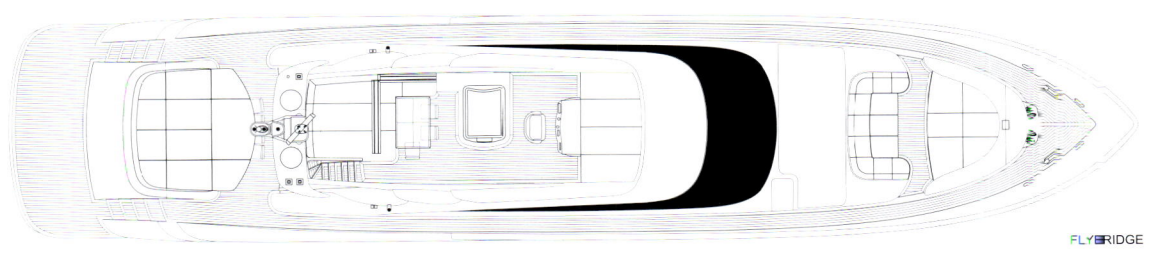

FLYBRIDGE

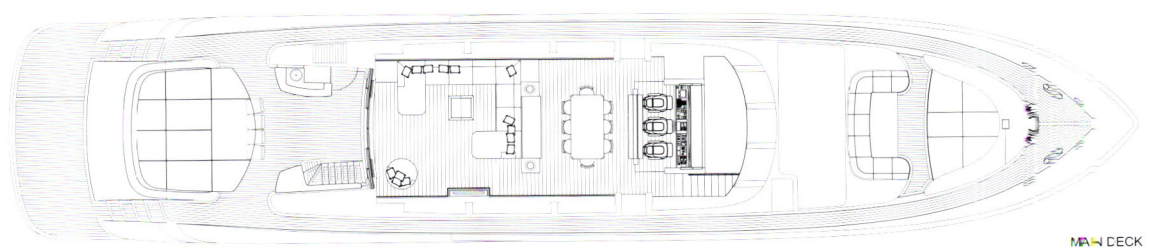

MAIN DECK

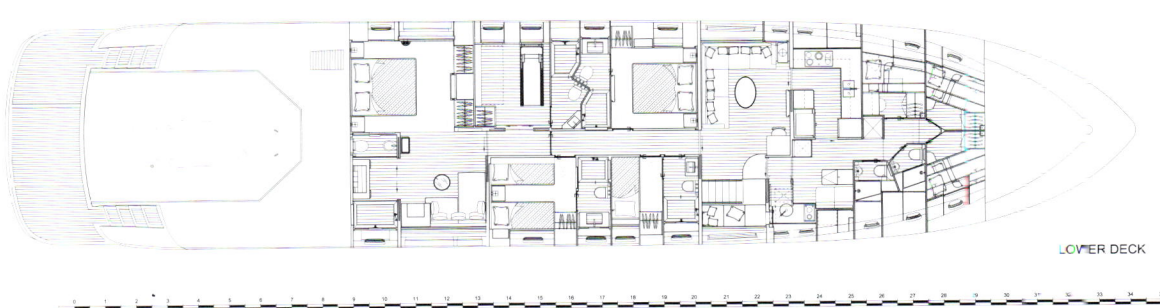

LOWER DECK

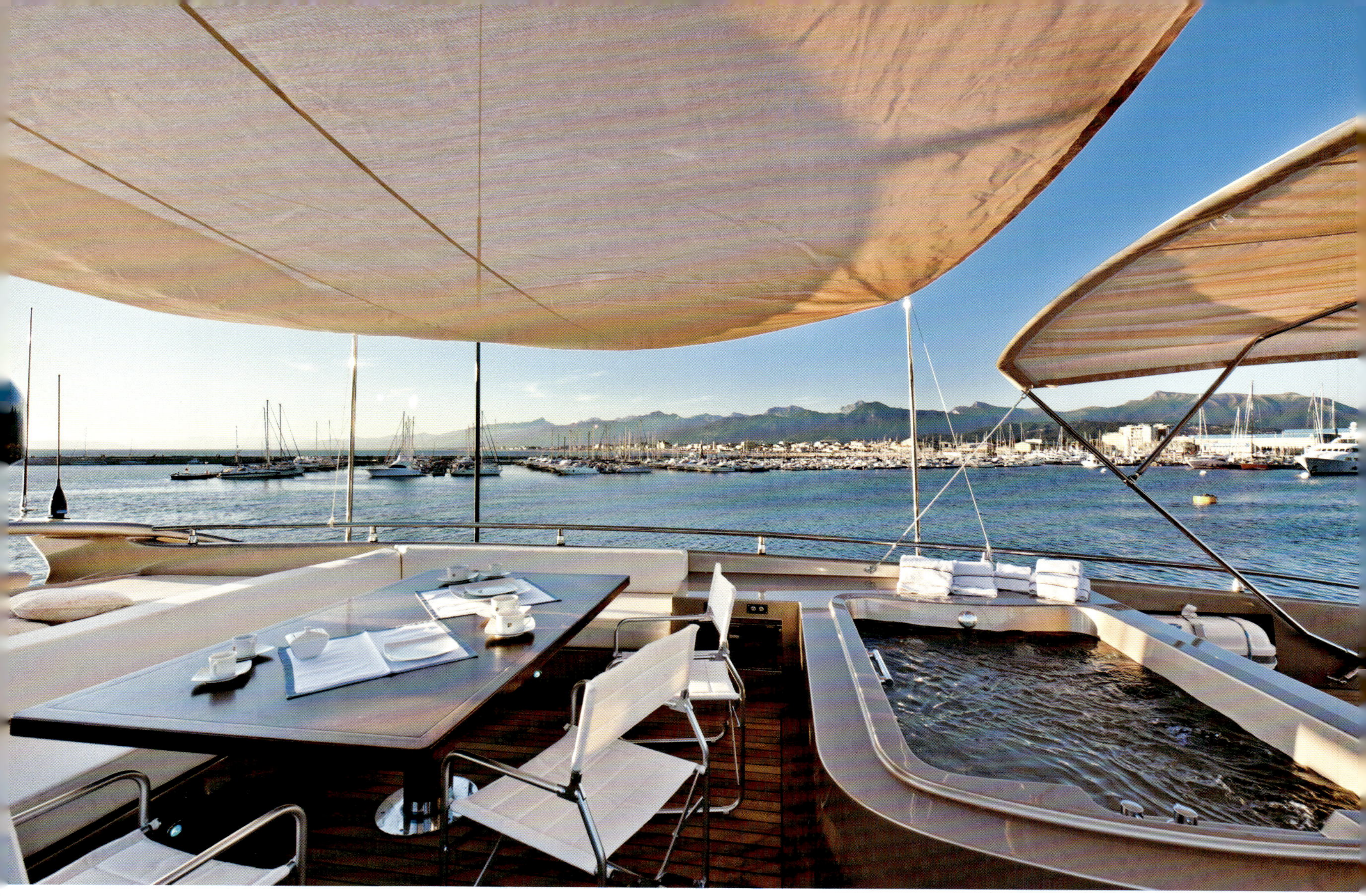

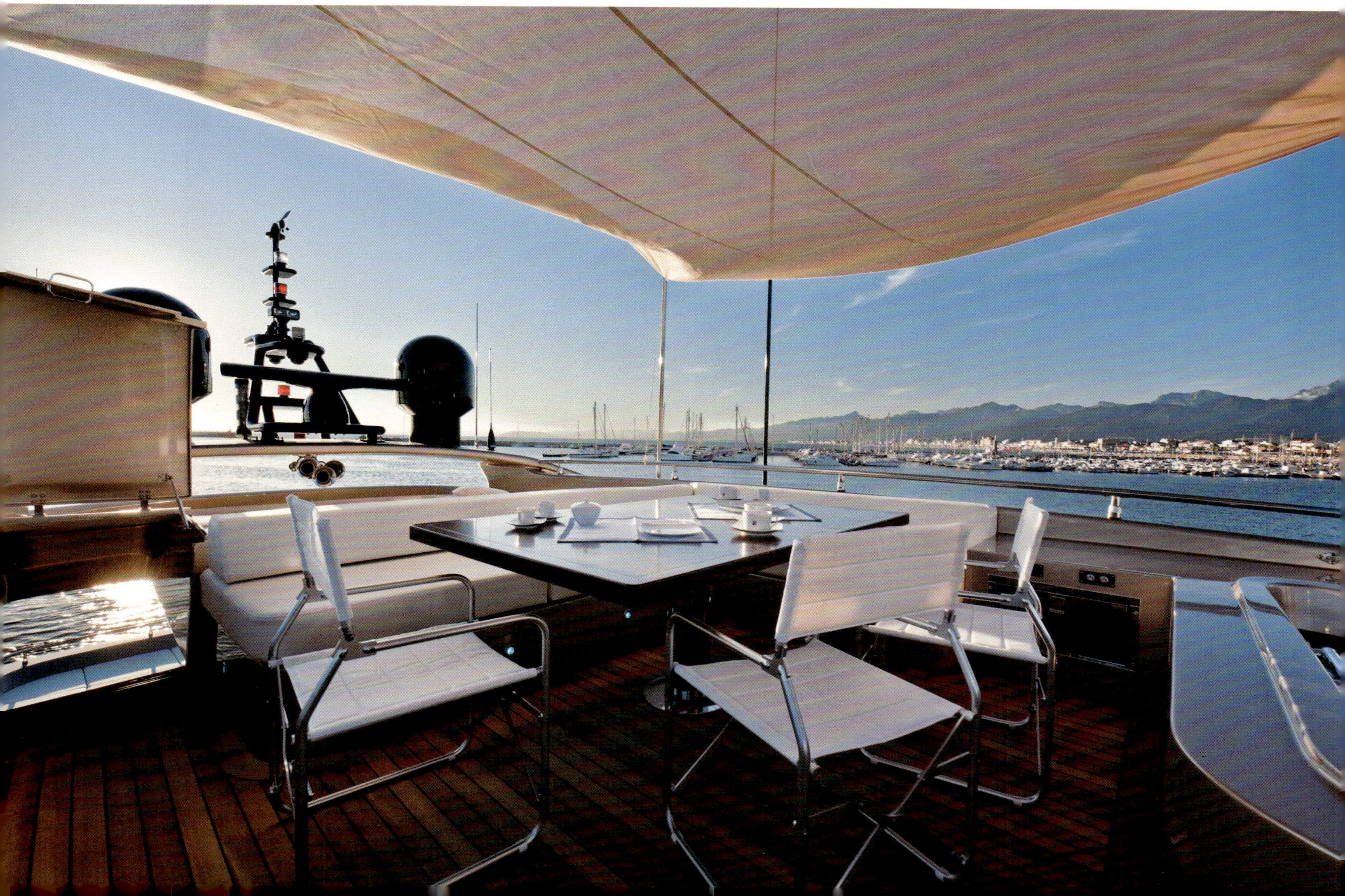

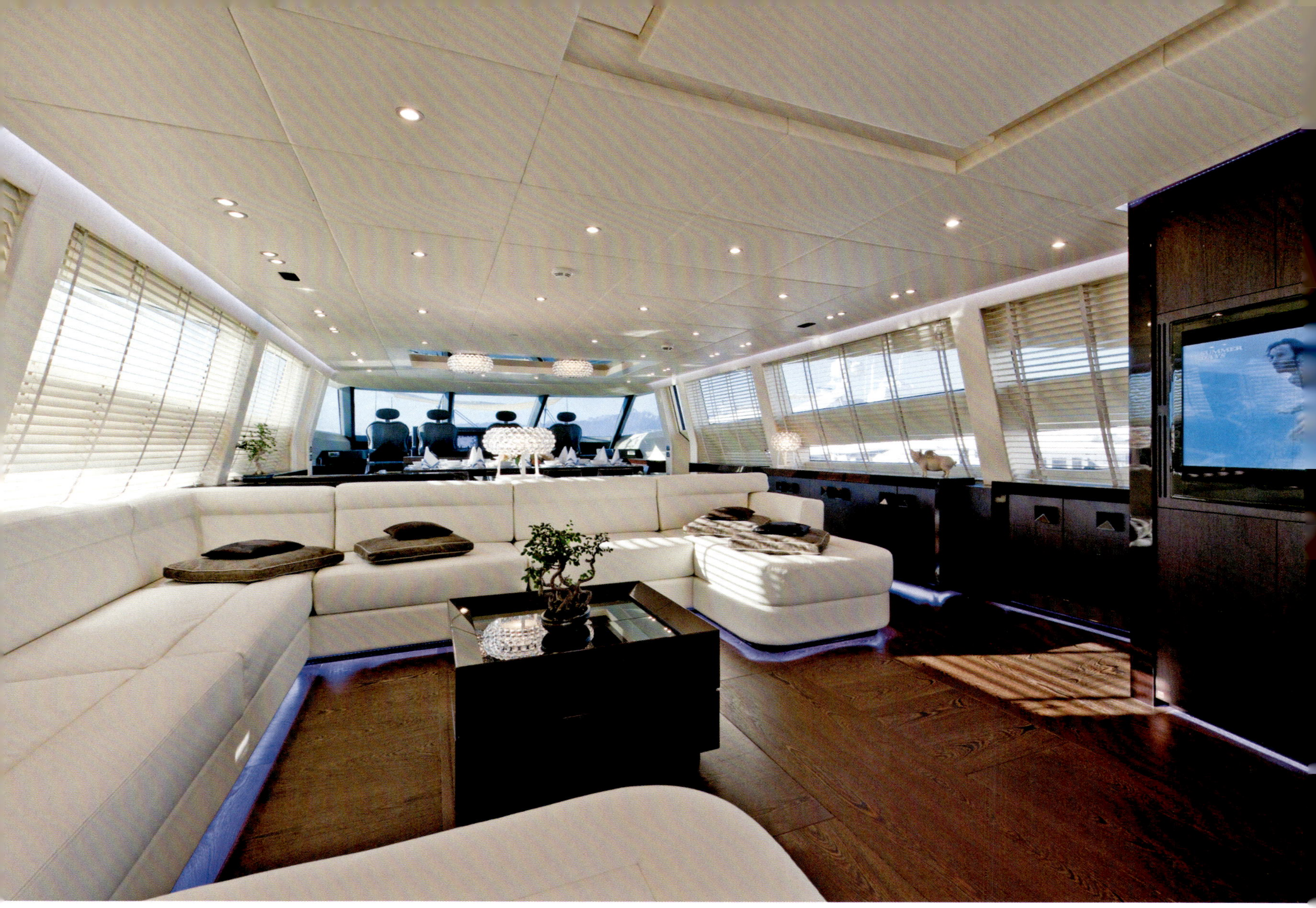

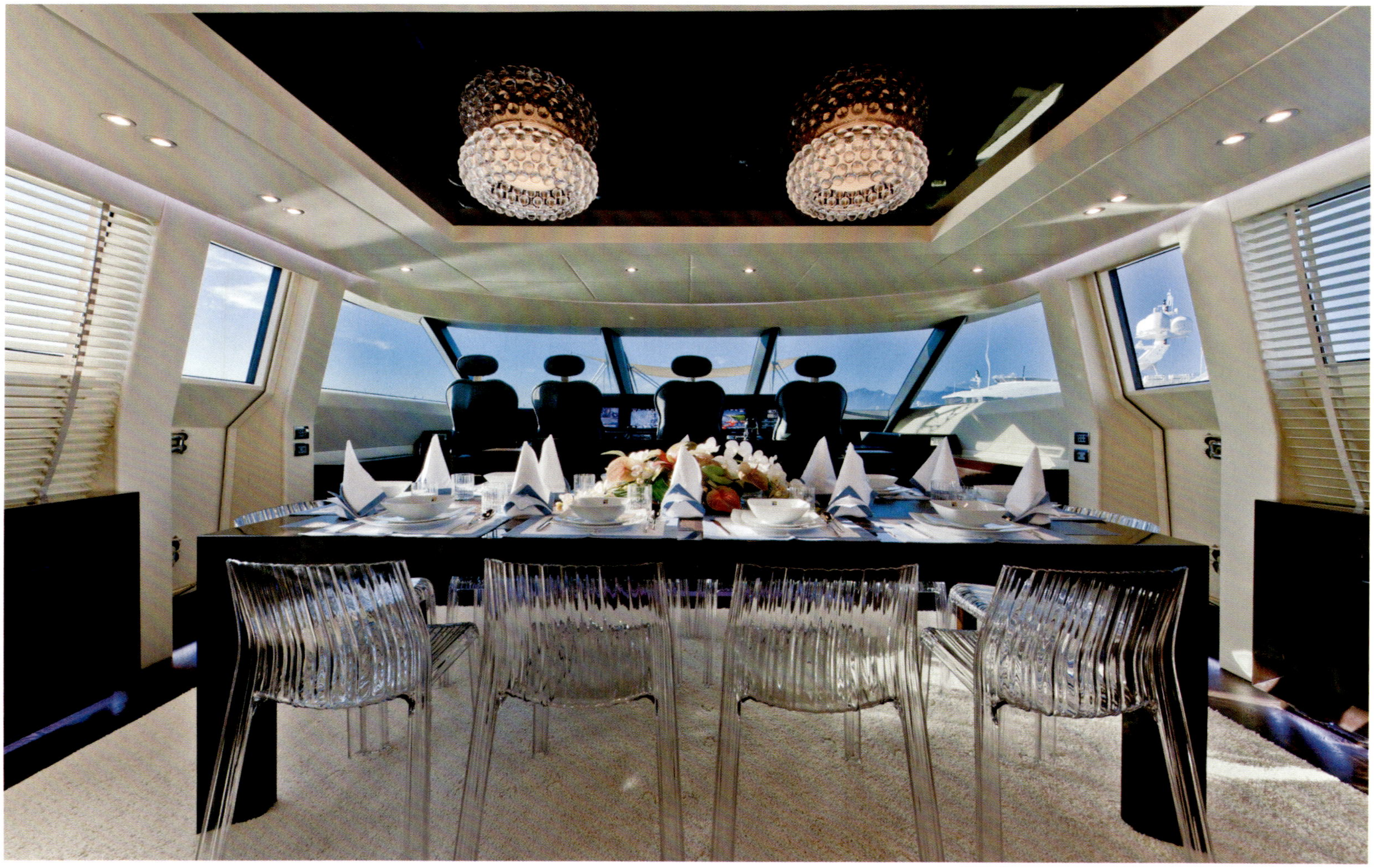

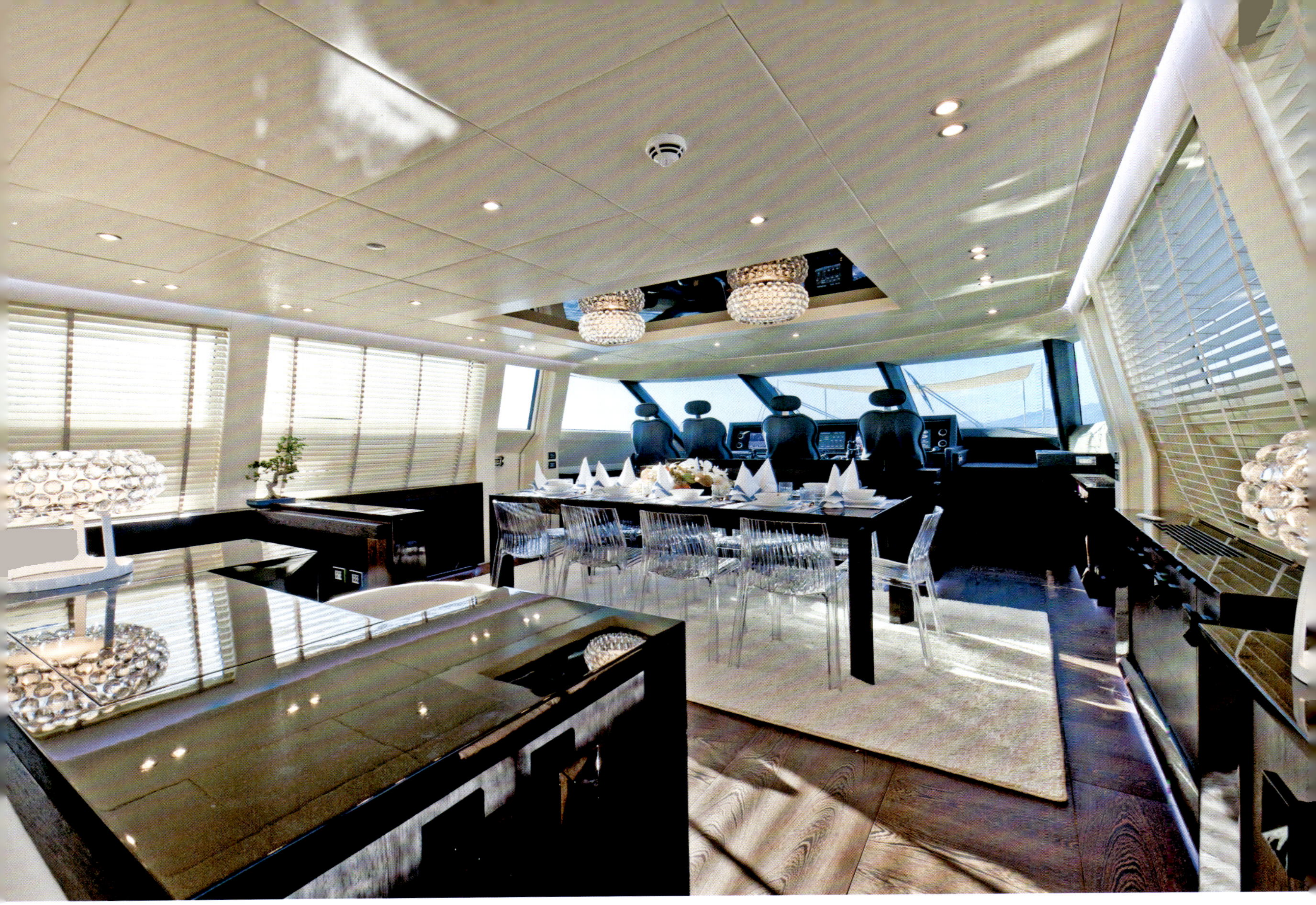

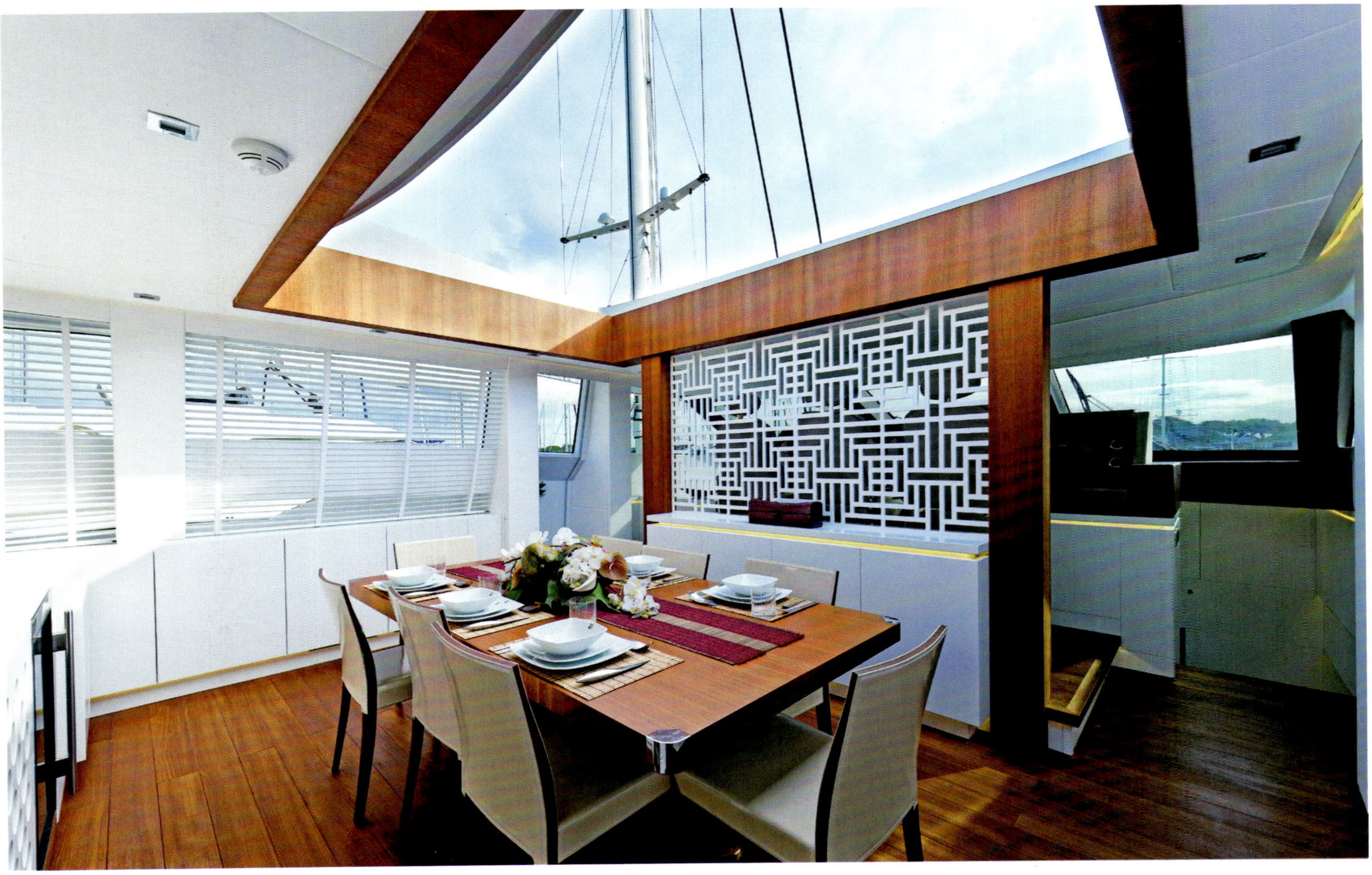

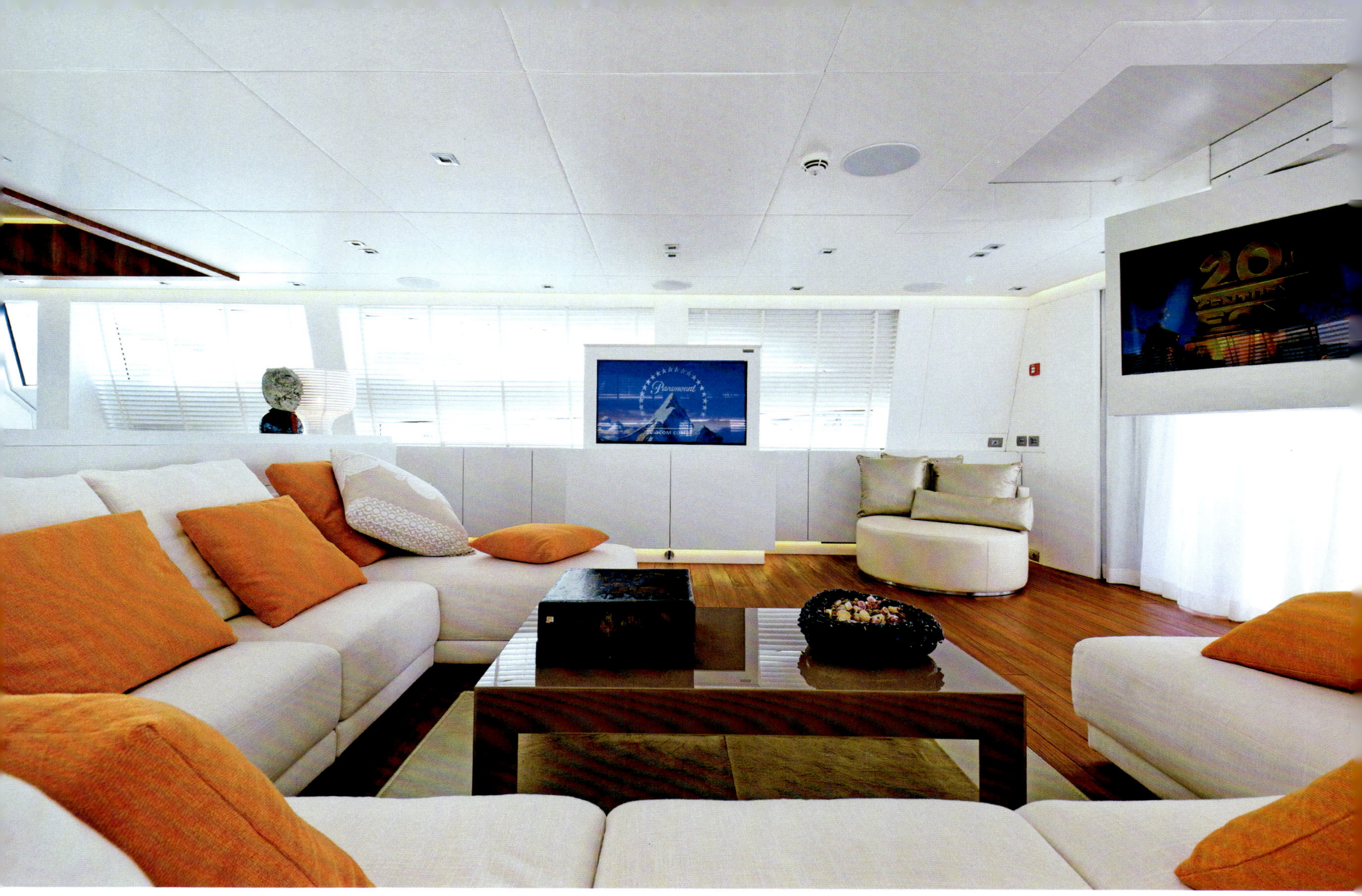

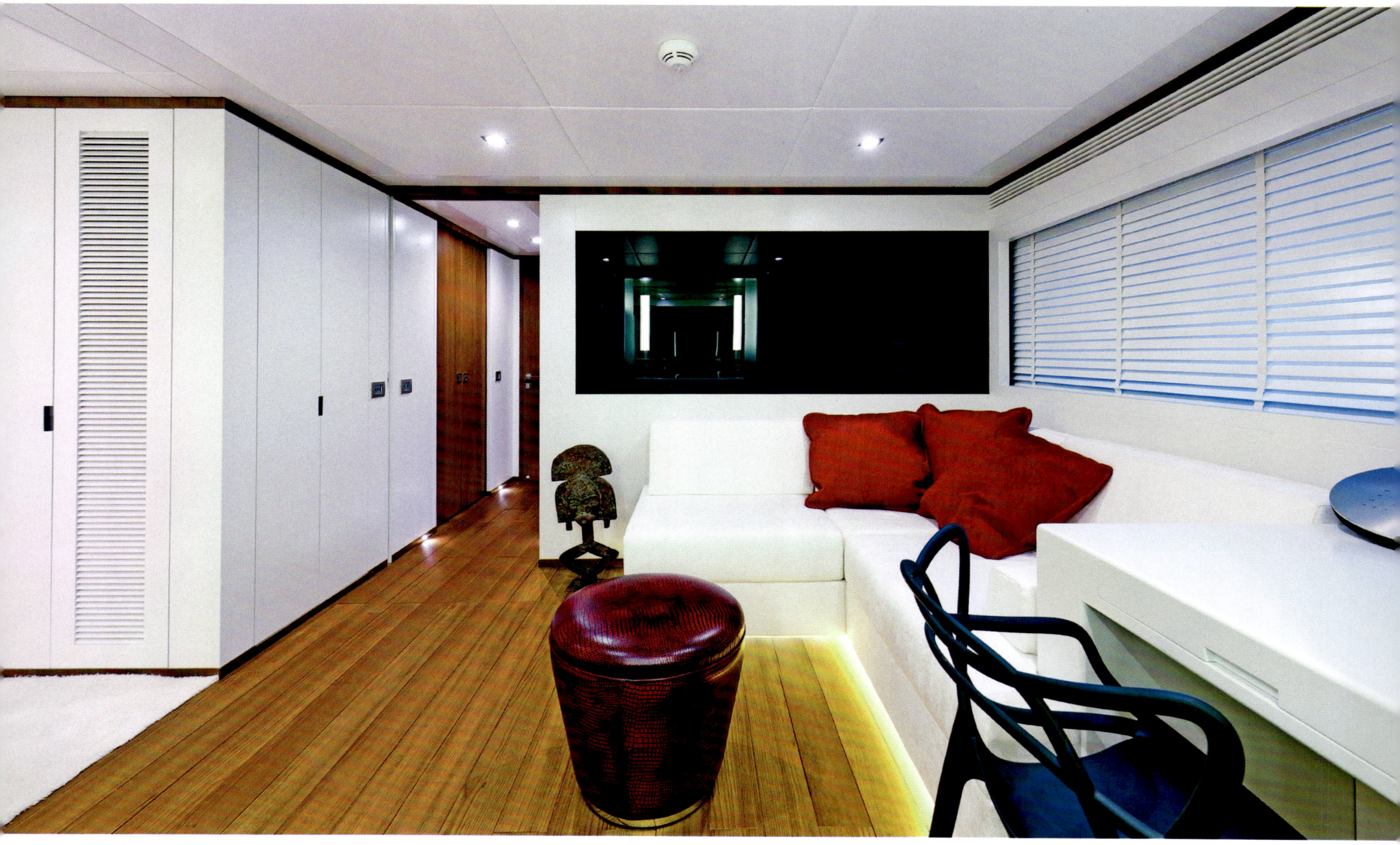

　　新款的 AB 116 游艇完美演绎了 AB 系列游艇的独特风格：那就是它的流线型和极具动感的船体线条。和这一个系列的每个游艇一样，该游艇的主要特色在于可以在各种海况下高速行驶，而丝毫不降低其舒适程度，这主要归功于其宽敞宏大的内部空间。游艇的建筑技术也是这些 AB 系列游艇引以为豪的地方，使用了轻体材料和先进的复合材料以及独特的焊接技艺，成为整个游艇业的典范。

　　游艇内部主要采用黑、白、灰作为主色调，与游艇外部的银金色形成鲜明的反差，创造出一种高雅的和谐之美。纯洁冷静的线条、高贵的大理石让游艇的内部空间渗透出独特、精美的气质。大厅注重满足客人的舒适与娱乐需求，设计了一个 U 形的休息区，嵌入式的电视系统，以及一个能容纳 12 人就餐的大餐桌。

　　AB 116 游艇的另一个主要特点毫无疑问就是底层甲板的小厅，主舱前面的挡风玻璃充当了采光井的作用，让整个小厅沐浴在自然光照下，确保船上的人可以在此看到广阔的蓝天，获得完全的放松。底层甲板靠近船尾的地方是客舱。有两个双人客舱和一个双人贵宾客舱，每个房间都配有独立卫生间。还有一个超大的船主舱，巨大的舷窗给人一种亲密接触大海的感觉。船主舱内还分为若干功能区：休息区、健身区（设淋浴区）、卫生间、卧室（配有豪华大床）。

　　AB 116 游艇的设计理念在于，能够让游艇在各种海况下保持高速行驶。船体的建筑技术采用了 AB 系列方面的标准，代表了游艇业的最高水准。这艘游艇完美融合了技术与水动力学，三个 2600 马力的发动机以及三个喷水式推进器功不可没，给人一种"在海面上飞行"的奇妙感受。

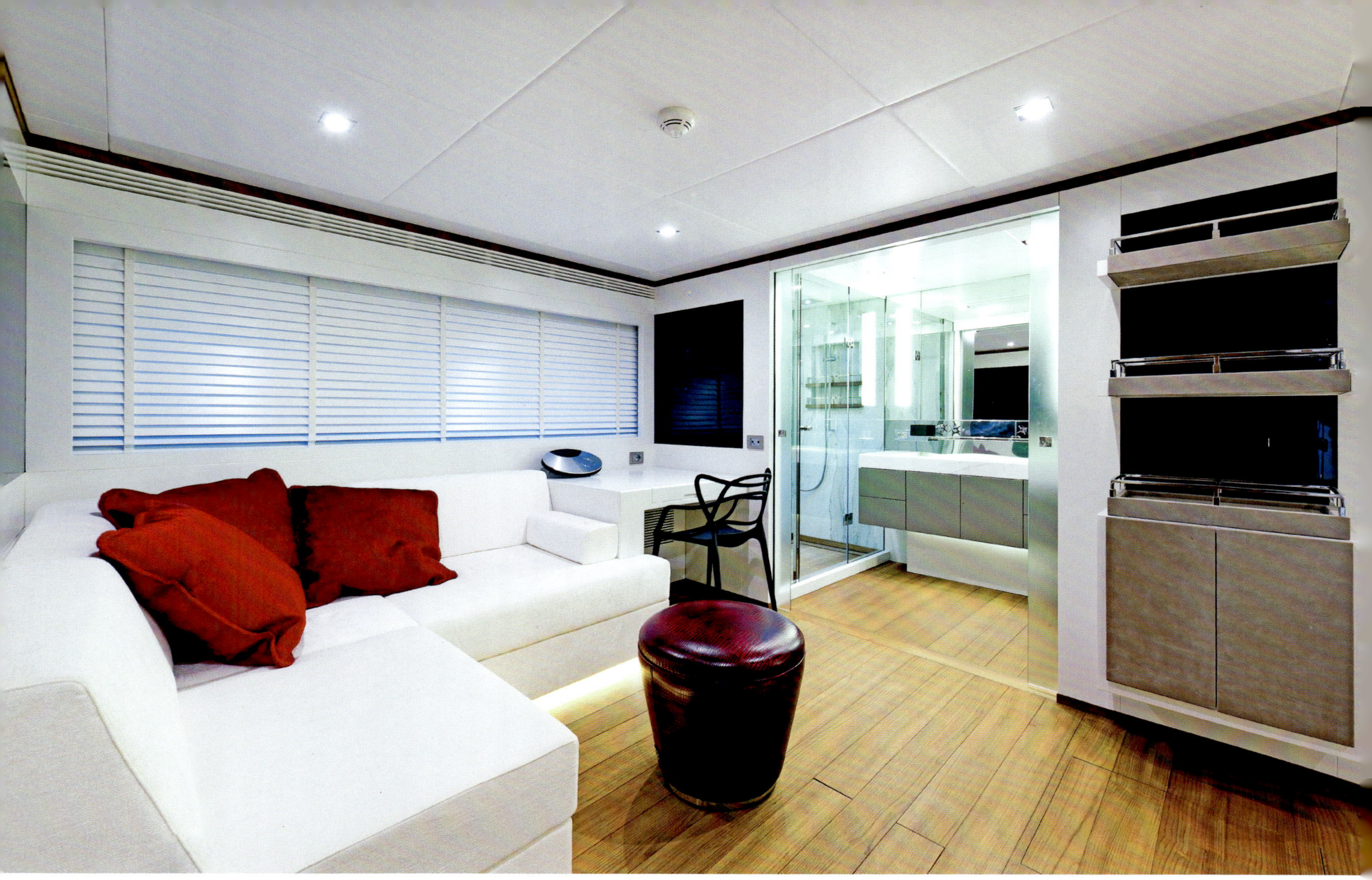

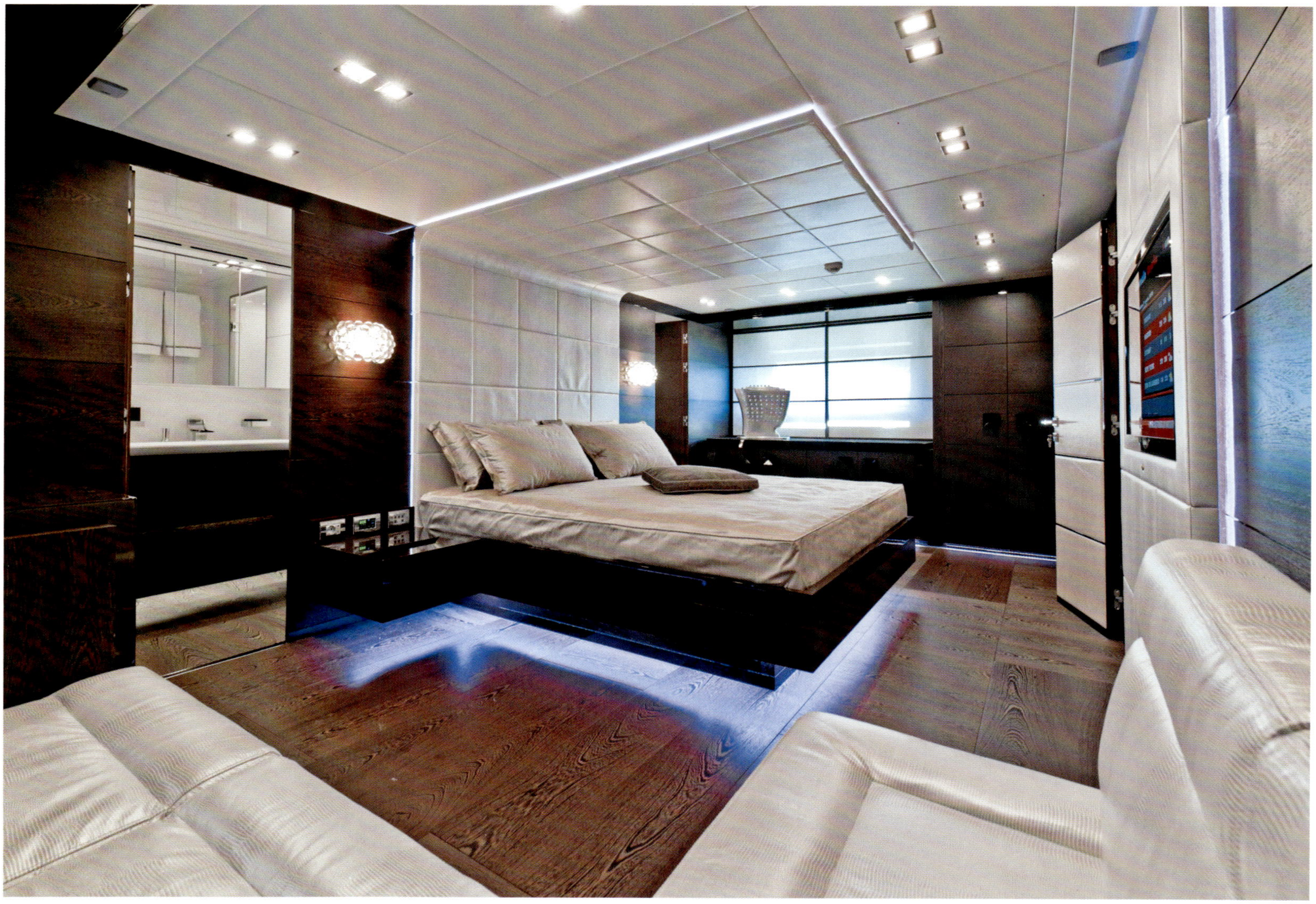

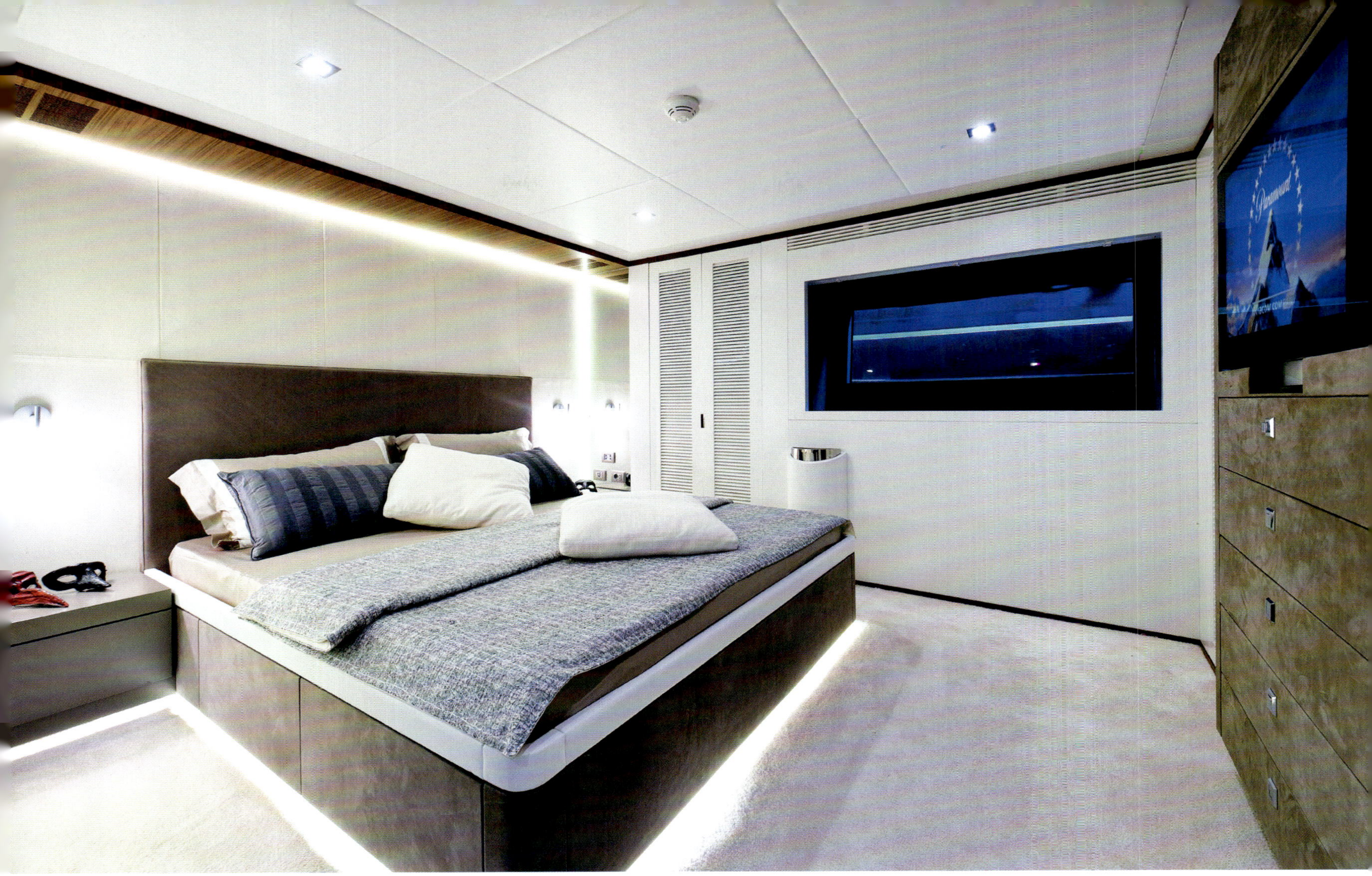

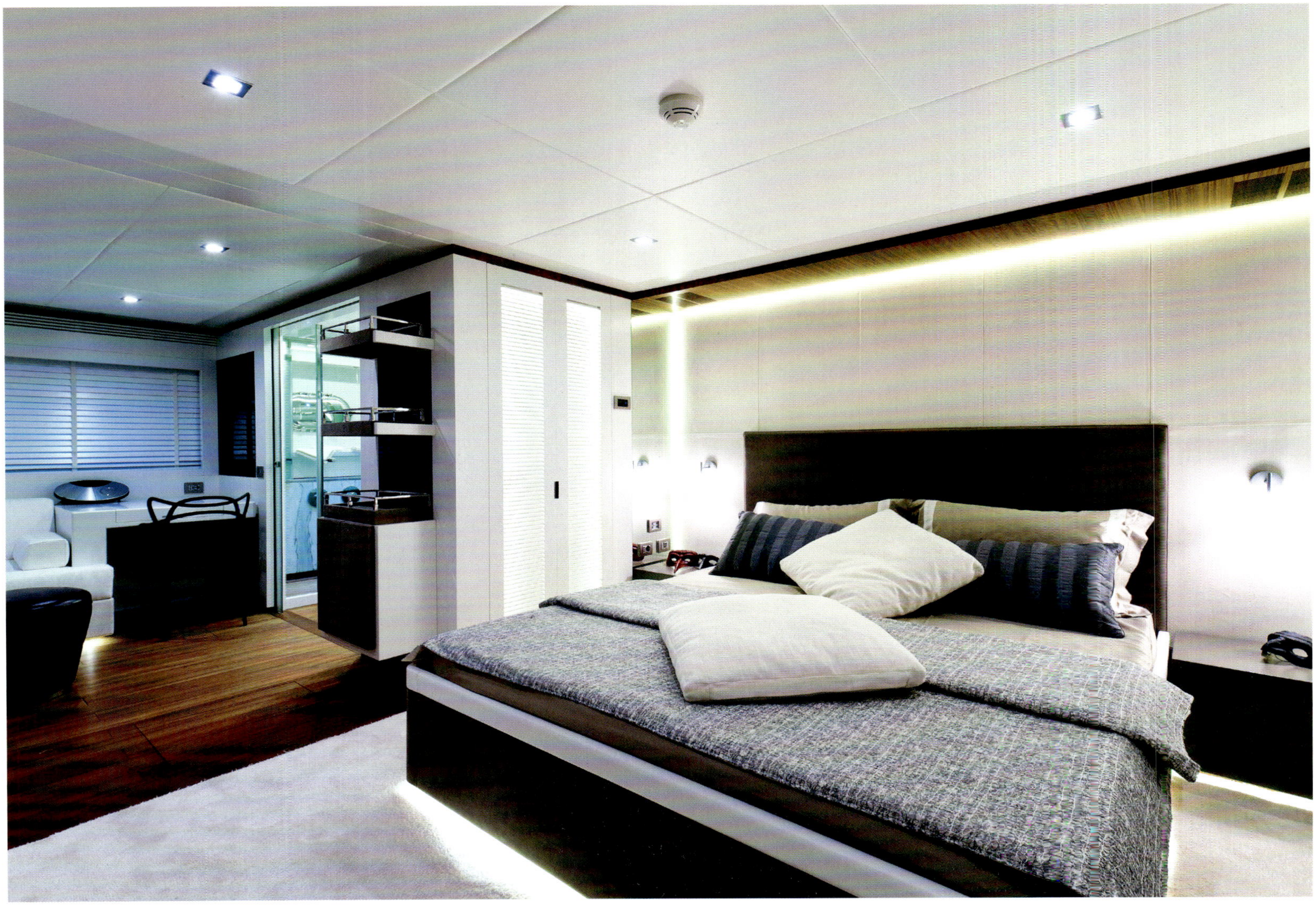

MY 45M AFRICA

> INTERIOR DESIGN   Franck Darnet Design
> NAVAL ARCHITECT   Studio Scanu
> SHIPYARD   Sunrise Yachting Ltd

The client is truly passionate for Africa. He has the African continent in his blood. It has been obvious every time the designers met him.

So for the designers, the concept is naturally based on both a classical approach and an ethnical one.

The main idea is to obtain strong contrasts between materials and also between colours. Thus, the interior design is classical based on an Edwardian English style but the decoration is influenced by an ethnical touch.

The mix matches so well together and brings a serene but powerful atmosphere.

From an aesthetical point of view, the designers have tried to draw a quite contrasted decoration based on dark wood, white fabric and polished stainless steel. Much like the wonderful Africa which is a contrasted continent...

The goal is as well to obtain a mild (light) decoration in order to highlight the amazing pictures and the great Art pieces that the owner wanted to get onboard.

From a technical point of view, the designers wished to get the latest technology in term of Hi-Fi, video and yacht automation. In this field, Sunrise Yachts company is an expert.

Most of storage spaces in the salon are hidden in the wood walls.

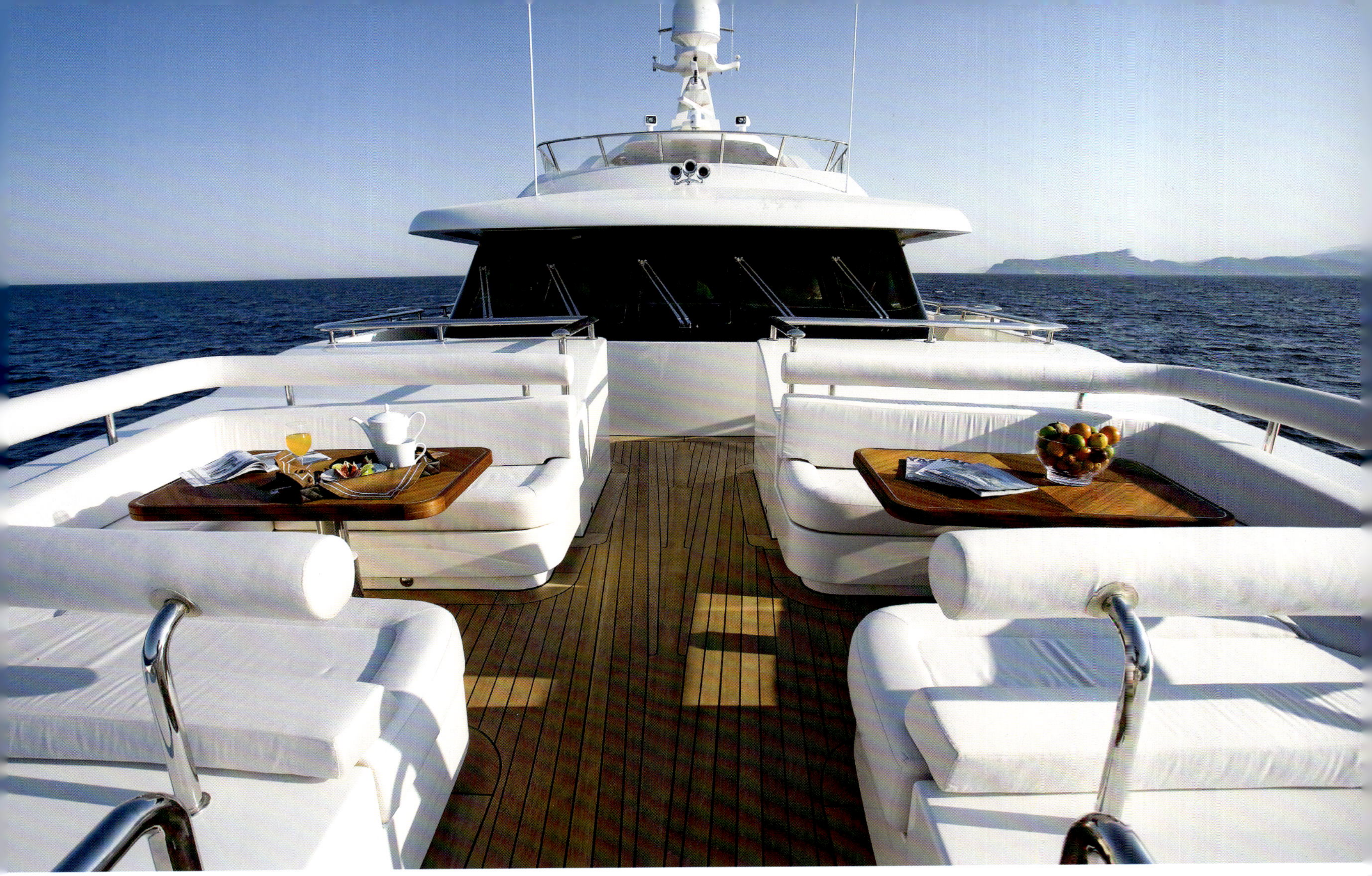

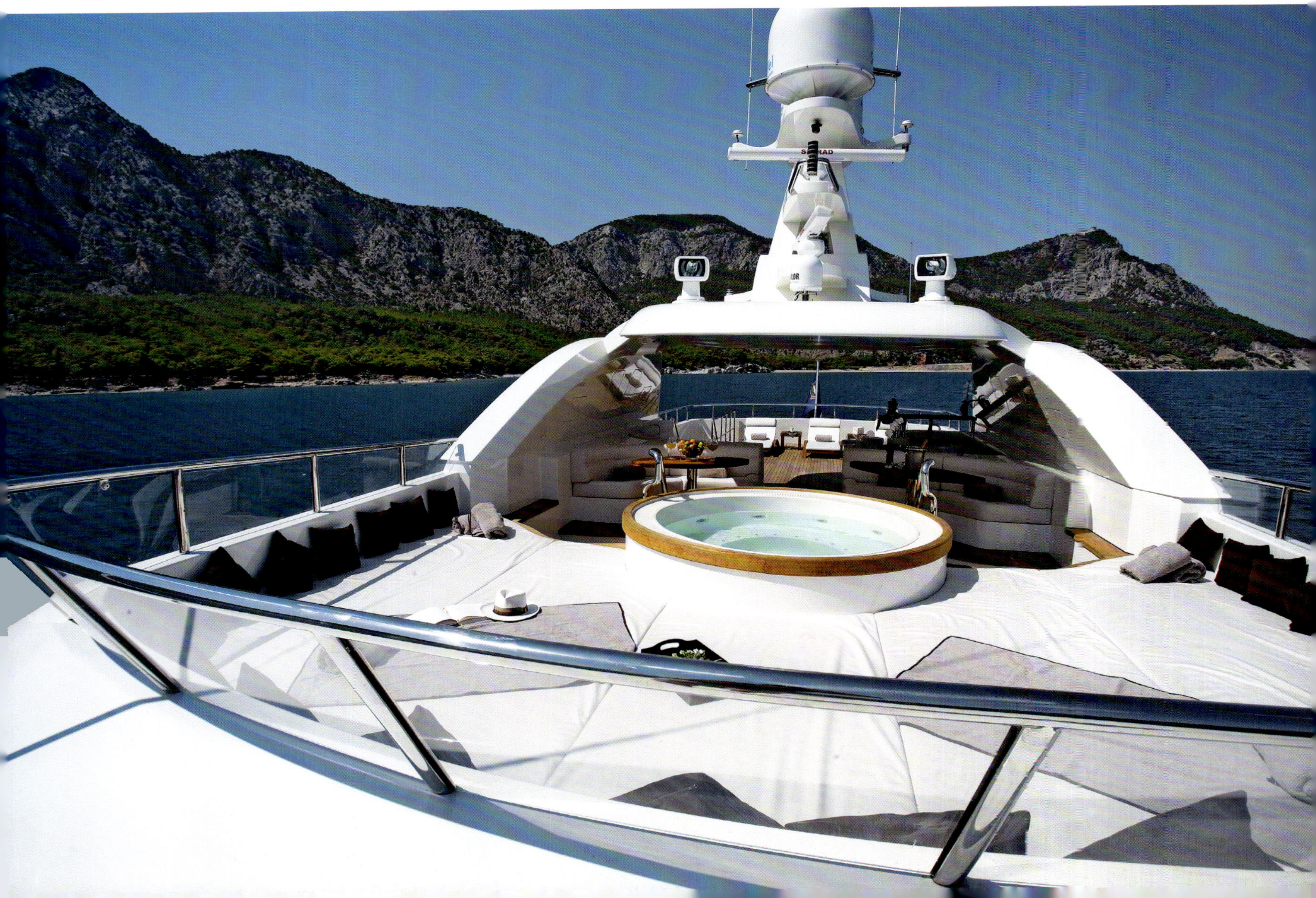

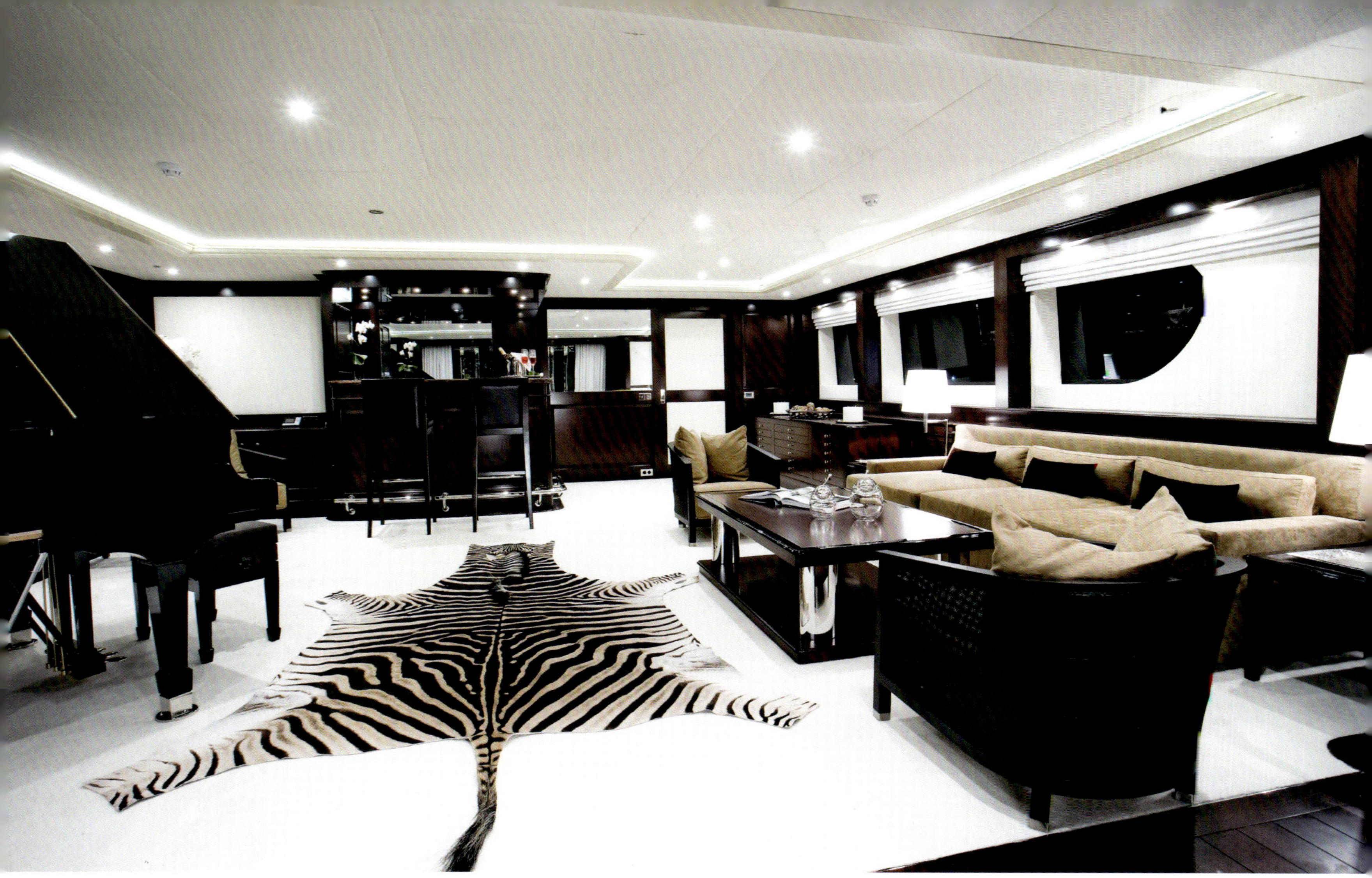

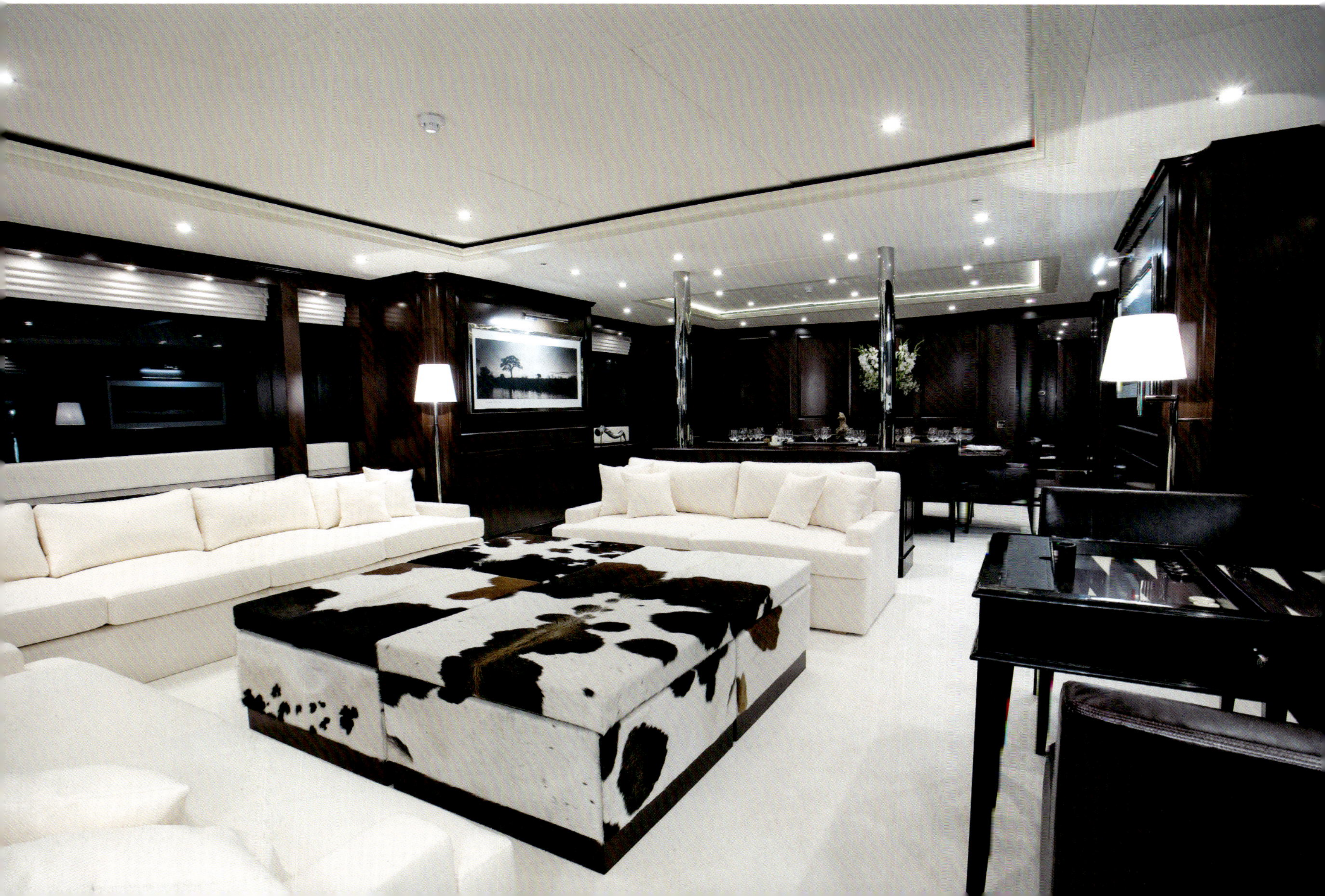

委托人非常热爱非洲，这种热爱已经与他的血液融为一体。每次设计师和他见面时都能深深地体会到这一点。

所以，对于设计师来说，游艇的设计理念自然而然就离不开经典与民族性。

设计的主要思路是形成材料间的反差，同样，颜色上也要形成强烈的反差。因此，内部设计采用英国爱德华七世时的经典风格，同时在装饰上突出了民族特征。

这样的混搭非常的和谐，营造出一种宁静却震撼的效果。

从美学角度来看，设计师使用黑木、白布和光滑的不锈钢来努力营造装饰上的一种强烈反差，像极了那个反差强烈、多彩多样的非洲大陆。

设计的另一个目标是要创造一种柔和的（轻）装饰效果，以便于凸显出船主随船携带的各种画作和艺术作品。

从技术的角度来看，设计师希望在高保真音响、录像机和游艇自动化方面采用最先进的技术。在这方面，升洋游艇公司可是专家。

大厅的很多储物空间都隐藏在木质墙体中。

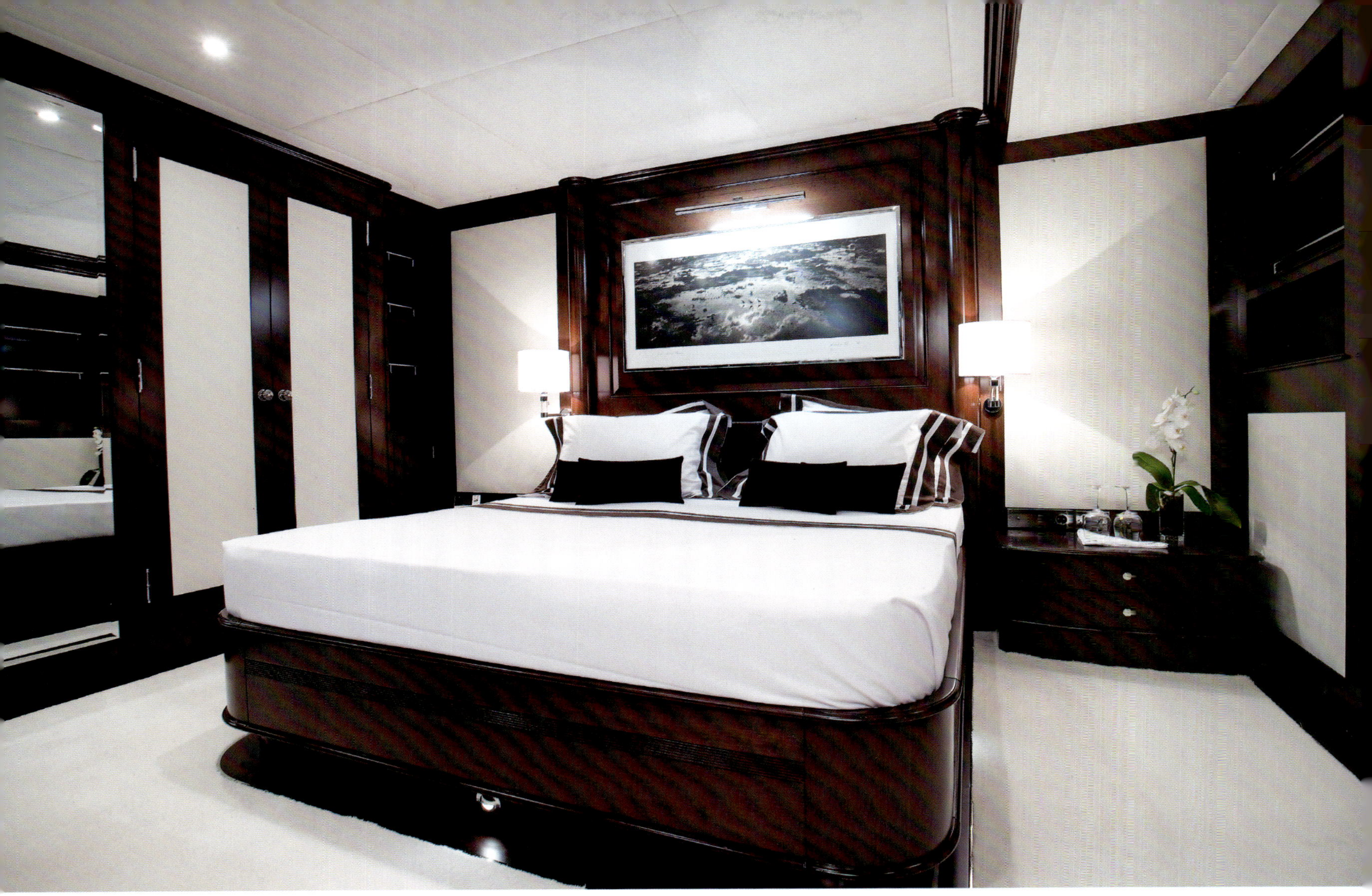

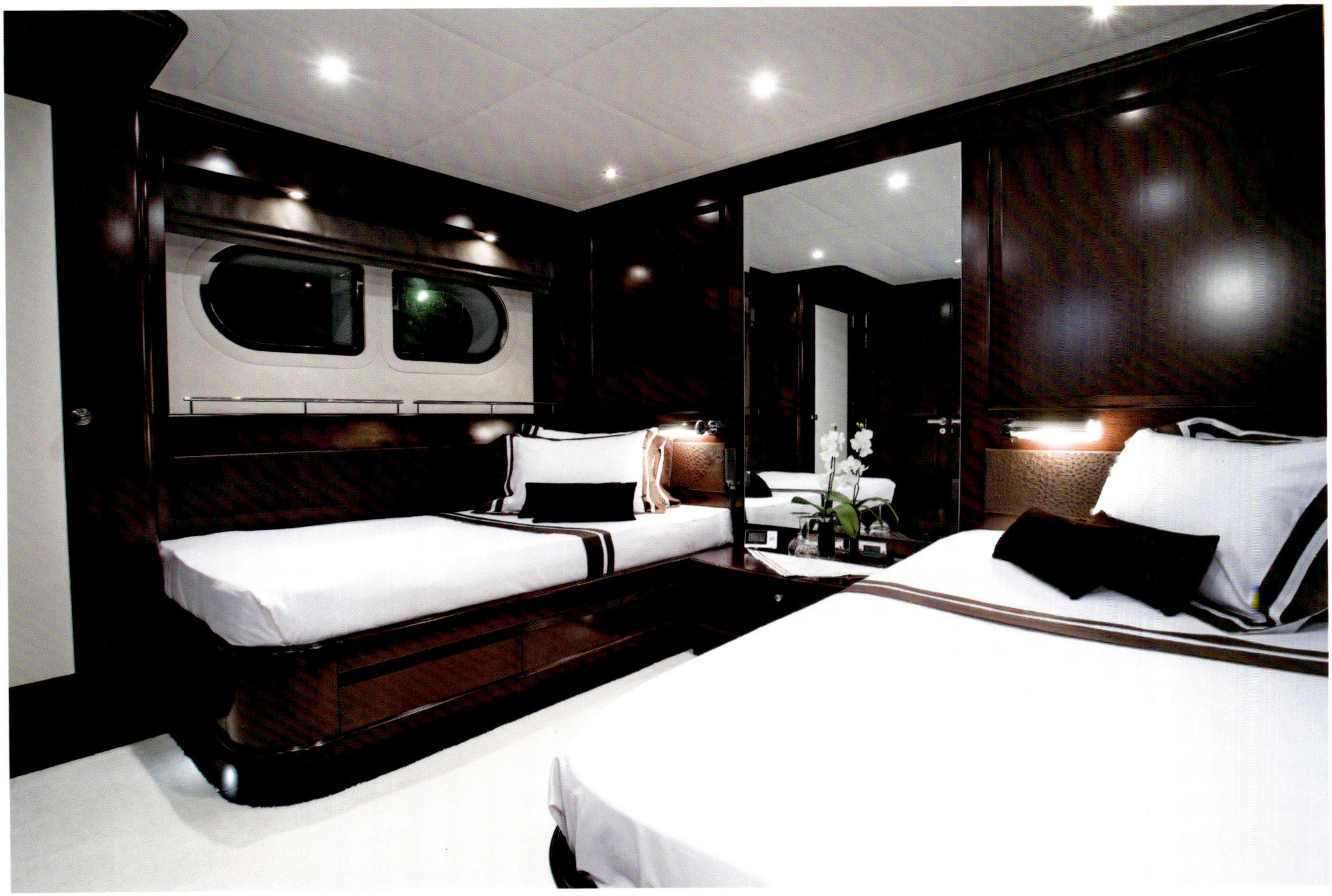

BISCUIT

> **INTERIOR DESIGN** Hot Lab : yacht & design
> **SHIPYARD** Filippetti Yacht

> The project stems from two factors: the interior styling bearing the signature of Hot Lab Studio and the thirty-year experience of Filippetti family, now driving a new shipyard that builds unique and high quality craftsmanship boats.

For the interior design the owner has chosen the elegant and refined touch of Hot Lab Studio.

Hot Lab worked not just on the interior design but also on the décor of the yacht. From the finest linen by Frette to the flatware by Christofle and to the painting in the living room, done by the emergent Artist Paola Di Iusto, everything on board has been chosen by Hot Lab with the kind collaboration of the owners.

The construction of "Biscuit 95", first assigned to a shipyard in Calabria - Italy, was then entrusted to Filippetti Yacht in Mondolfo (PU), where the yacht was delivered to be refitted and completed. Filippetti Yacht was involved in building the superstructure, painting and assembling all components of the boat: from engines to steels up to the whole furniture.

"Biscuit 95" has two decks and a sunbathing area. On the lower deck there are two twin staterooms, the VIP and the master cabin, each fully equipped. Also on the lower deck, the crew area has been designed to comfortably house four crew members. A stunning full-beam master stateroom matches a mix of dark woods with fair leather and steel. A precious leather floor completes the décor.

On the main deck the brightness of the various area is highlighted by fair colors on walls and ceilings. The living area is spacious and comfortable, with a bar and an office corner.

A big L-shaped sofa by Moroso, with in front a coffee table in leather and ebony from Poltrona Frau, and a funny sofa from Futura are the main elements of the living area. Two armchairs by Moroso and colored custom made pouf are also present in the layout.

The dining area is detached and composed by a ten-person table designed by Saarinen, with small armchairs by Moroso. A wine cellar is also present. The galley and the crew living area are juxtaposed.

The galley is a synthesis of pragmatic use of space and elegance. Gaggenau components are fully included in the interior layout of the galley: two refrigerator- freezers, 90-mm induction hobs, microwave and 90-cm electric fridge, icemaker, washing machine and coffee machine. A crew mess equipped with TV and housing up to four members, is also present.

The flying bridge has been conceived for relax and outdoor leisure: wet bar, wash basin, grill and refrigerators.

At starboard there are two sofas. Each sofa has been studied for a different use: the former can be used as dining area and includes a teak table for twelve people designed by Hot Lab; the latter, "L" shaped, can be converted in a spacious sunbathing area.

A second cockpit and two chaises longues are the final touch to the furniture on the sun deck.

SIDE VIEW

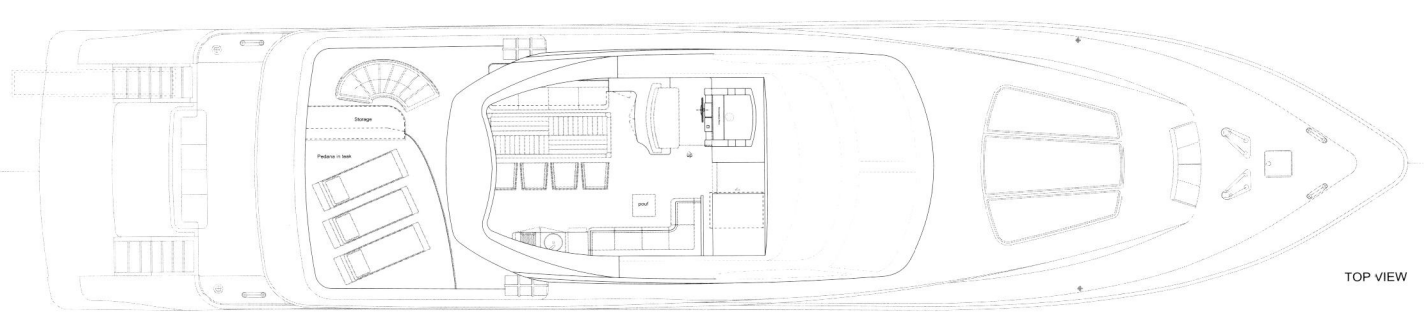

TOP VIEW

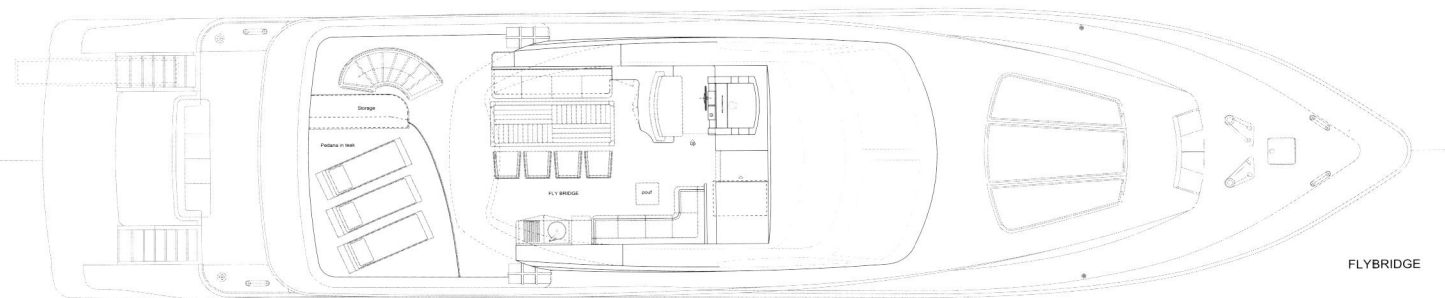

FLYBRIDGE

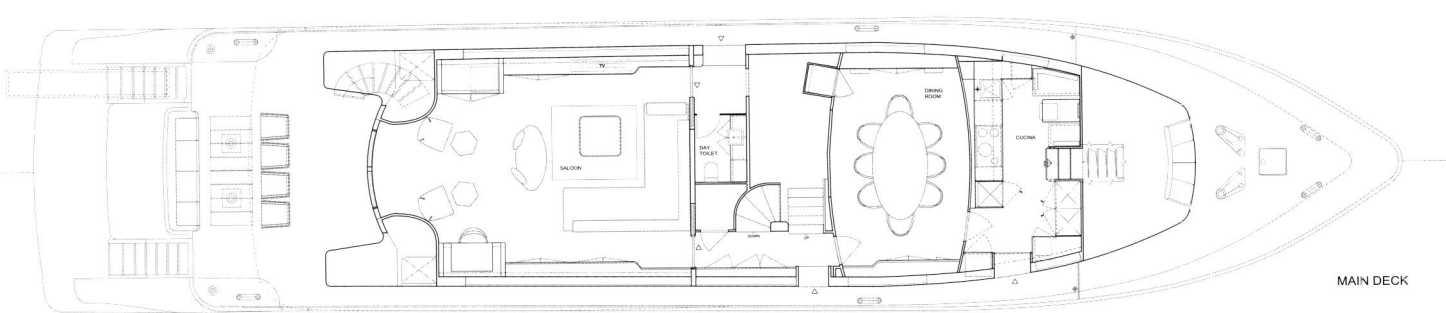

MAIN DECK

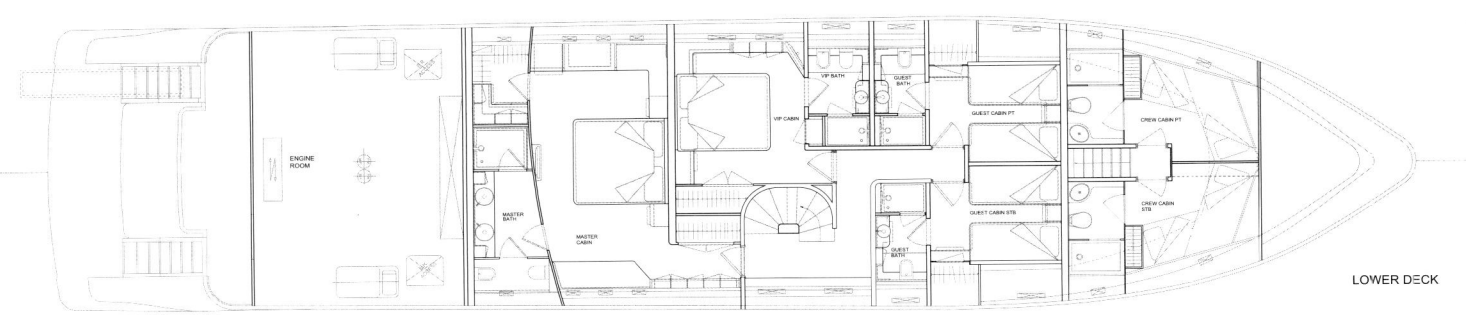

LOWER DECK

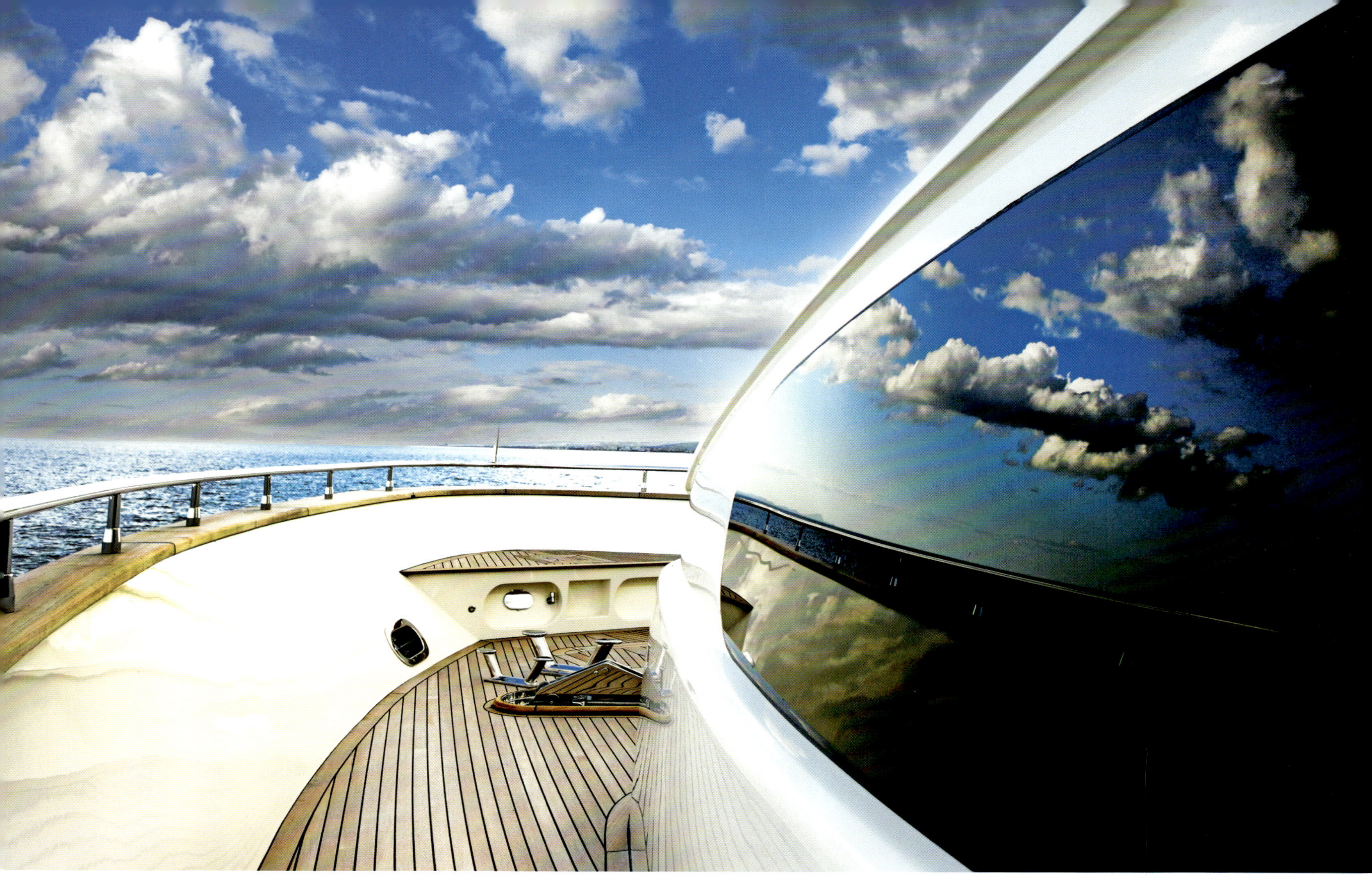

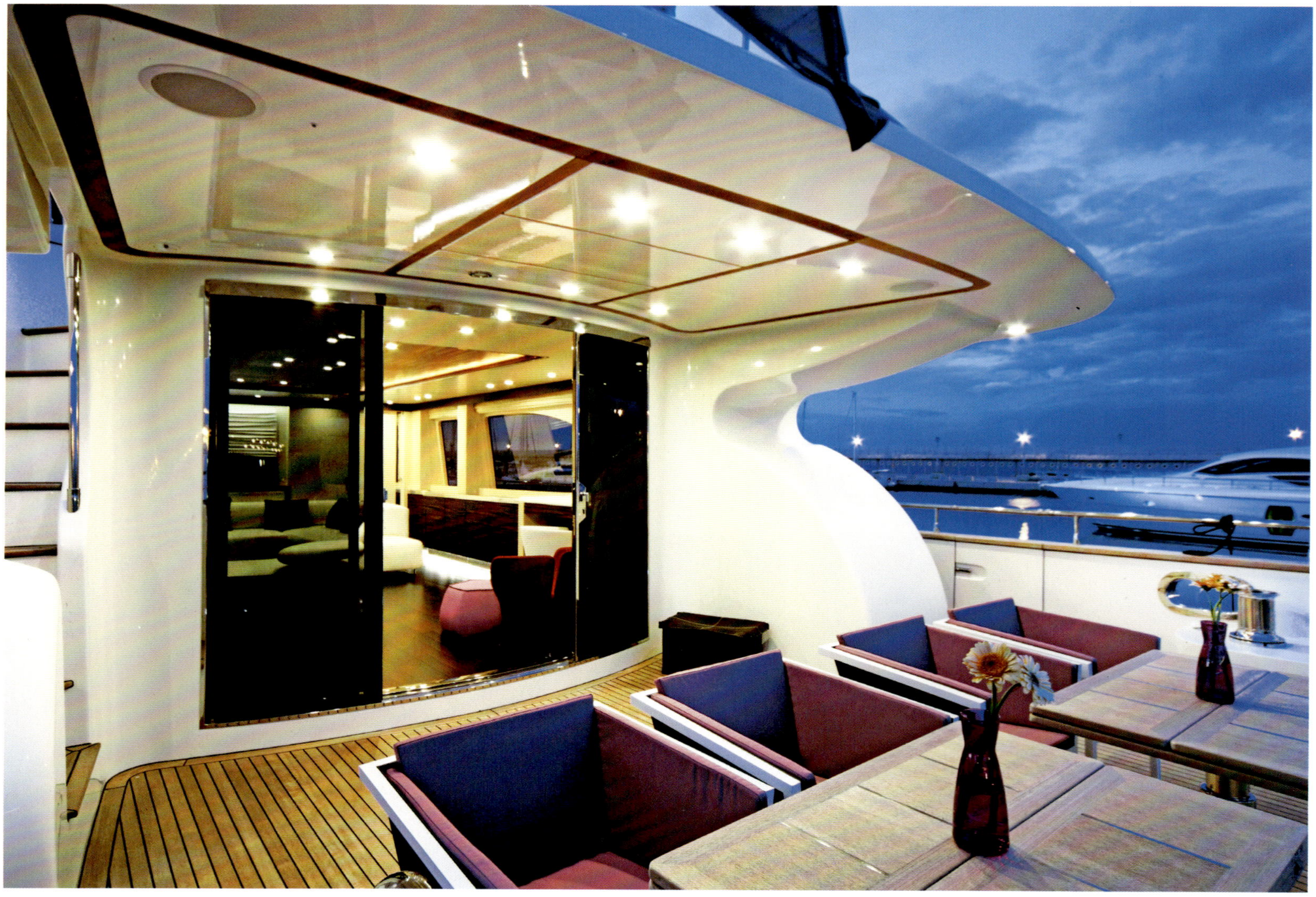

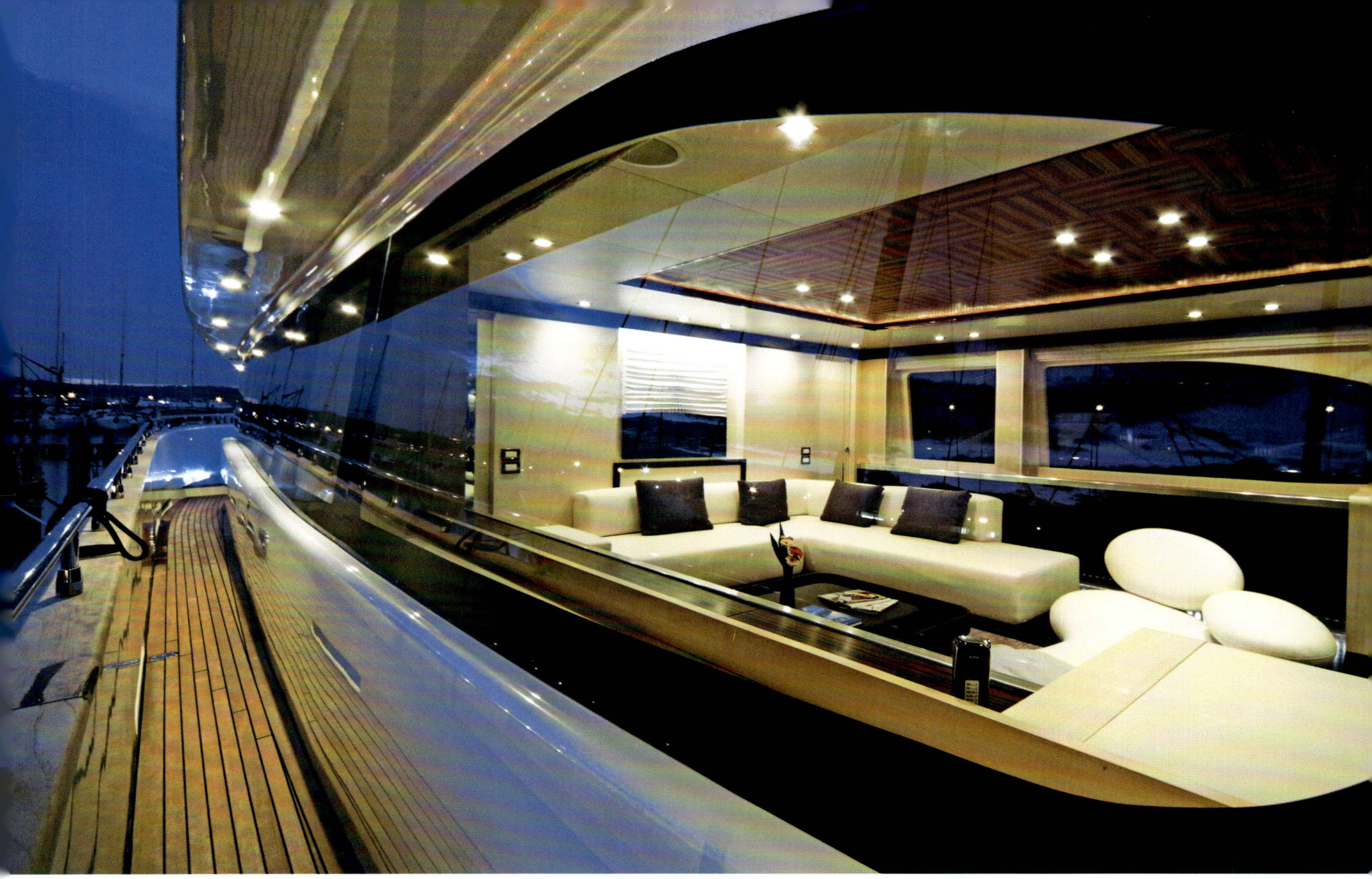

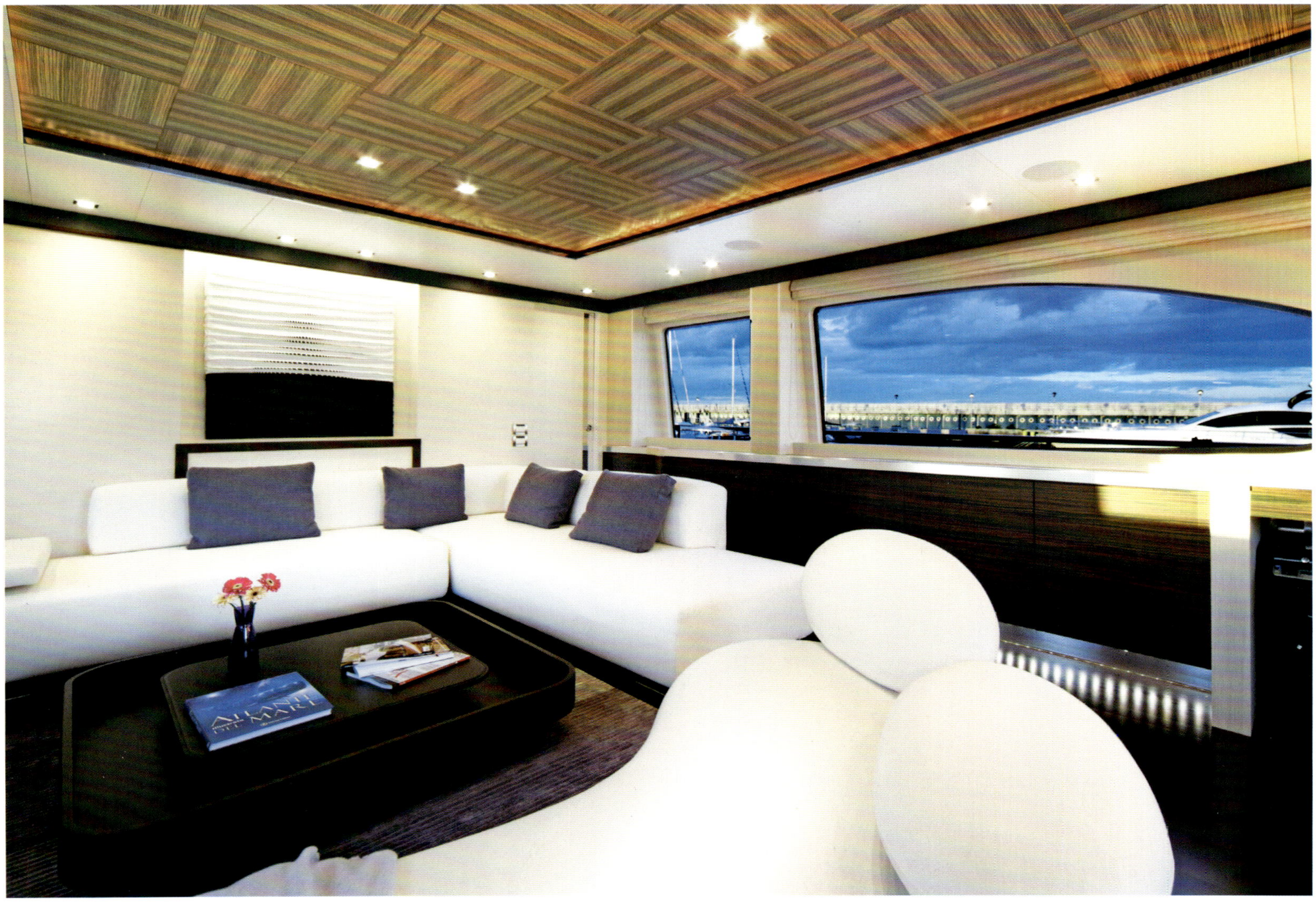

　　游艇的设计源于以下两点：内部造型具有"好来宝"（Hot Lab）工作室的标志；弗利皮特家族三十年丰富的造船经验。弗利皮特家族现经营一个新船厂，专门生产独特、高质量的船只。

　　室内设计上，船主选用了设计雅致，注重细节的"好来宝"工作室。

　　该工作室不仅负责内部设计，而且还为游艇进行了装潢。从豪华纺织品制造商芙蕾特的亚麻布到欧洲顶级银器商生产的餐具，到客厅里装饰的著名艺术家保拉·迪·罗斯托（Paola Di lusto）的油画，船上每处细节的设计都是"好来宝"工作室与船主通力合作的成果。

　　"毕思奇95号"游艇最初由意大利卡拉布里亚区的一个船厂负责建造，之后则移交给蒙多尔福地区的弗利皮特造船厂，进行改装和完善。弗利皮特造船厂对甲板结构进行建造和涂漆，并且对艇身所有的零部件，包括引擎、钢结构组件和艇内设备进行了组装。

　　该游艇有两层甲板和一个日光浴区。下层甲板有两间一模一样的特别舱房、贵宾舱和主人舱，设备都很齐全。另外，该层的船员室很宽敞，可容纳四人。主人舱采用全灯光设计，黑色的木质装饰，加上自然色彩的真皮家具与不锈钢饰物，使得整个房间浪漫温馨。特殊的真皮地板使装修趋于完美。

　　主甲板上墙体和天花板的颜色搭配合理，使各区域都通透明亮。客厅宽敞舒适，有一个吧台和办公区。

客厅中有一组来自意大利名牌"莫罗斯"（Moroso）的L形沙发和一张"波尔托那·弗劳"（Poltrona Frau）的真皮包裹黑檀木的咖啡桌，还有一个设计独特的意大利"福多乐"（Futura）品牌沙发。旁边有两个"莫罗斯"扶手椅与特别定制的颜色鲜艳的矮凳相映衬。

分隔出来的用餐区中放置了一个可容纳10人的餐桌，餐桌是由沙里宁设计的，还搭配了"莫罗斯"的小扶手椅。此外，还设置了一个酒窖。厨房和船员室相邻。

厨房的设计既考虑了空间的合理使用，又顾及了整体的美感。室内有全套的嘉格纳厨具，其中包括两个冷藏柜、一个90毫米电磁炉、90厘米电冰箱、微波炉、制冰机、洗衣机和咖啡机。船员餐厅配备电视，可容纳4人用餐。

该船的飞桥设计目标明确，主要是为了让客人放松身心，因此设置了酒吧、盥洗池、烧烤区和冰箱。

船的右舷上有两组沙发，每组沙发都有独立的功能。其中一组配有一张柚木材质的桌子可以用来就餐，可容纳12人。它们由"好来宝"公司设计。另外一组呈L形，为客人提供晒日光浴的完美场地。

在日光浴甲板上可以看到另外一个驾驶舱和两个躺椅。

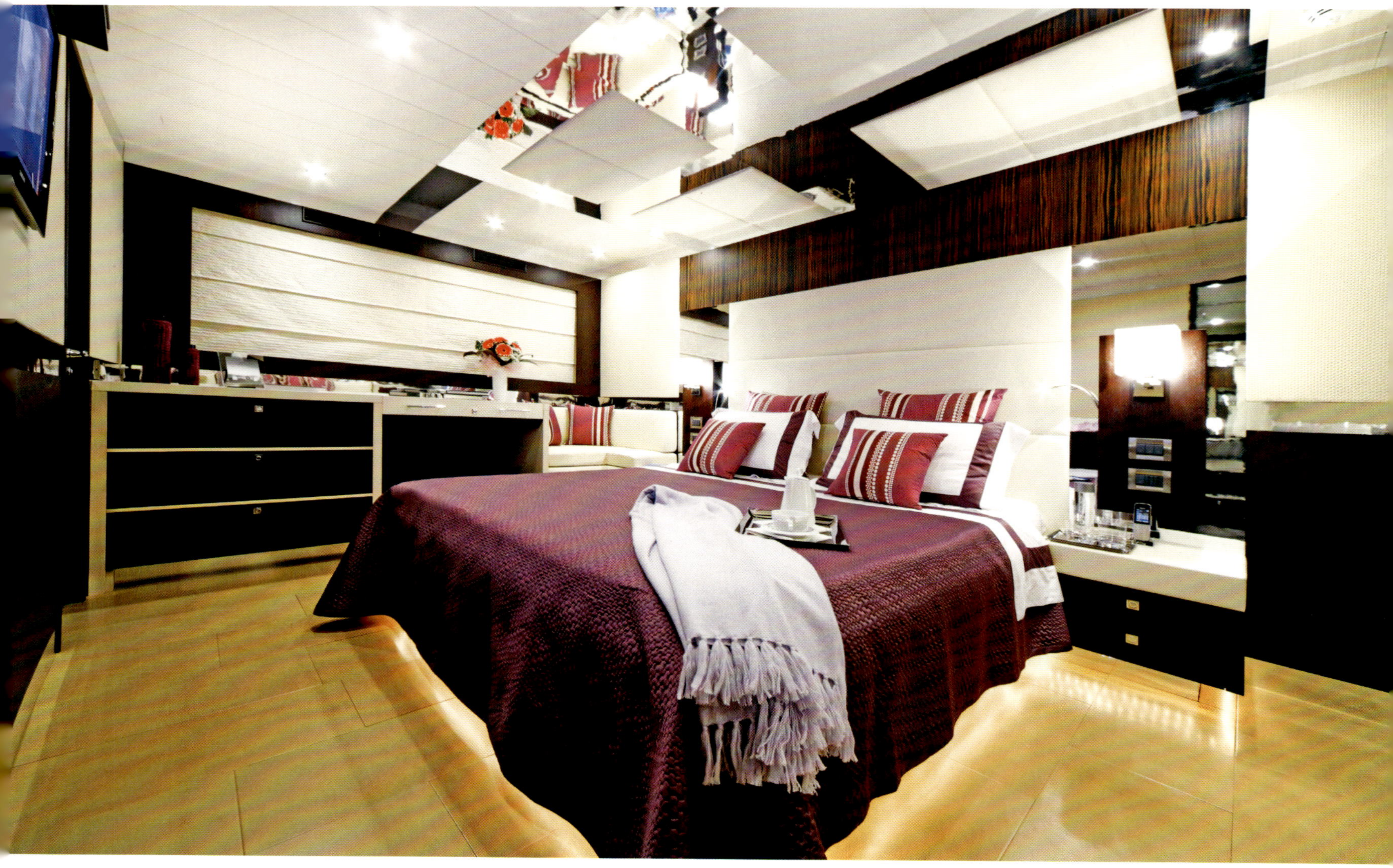

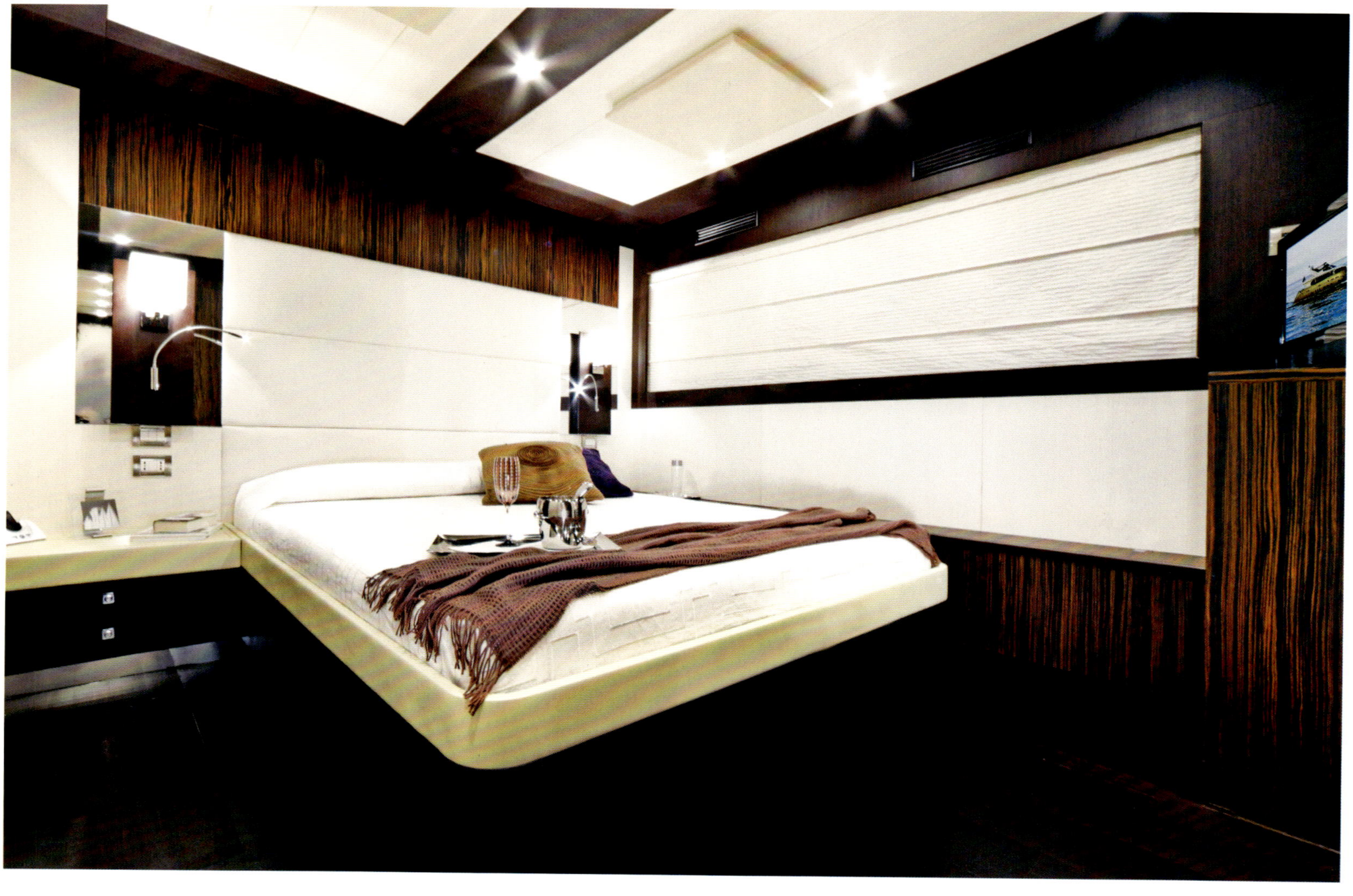

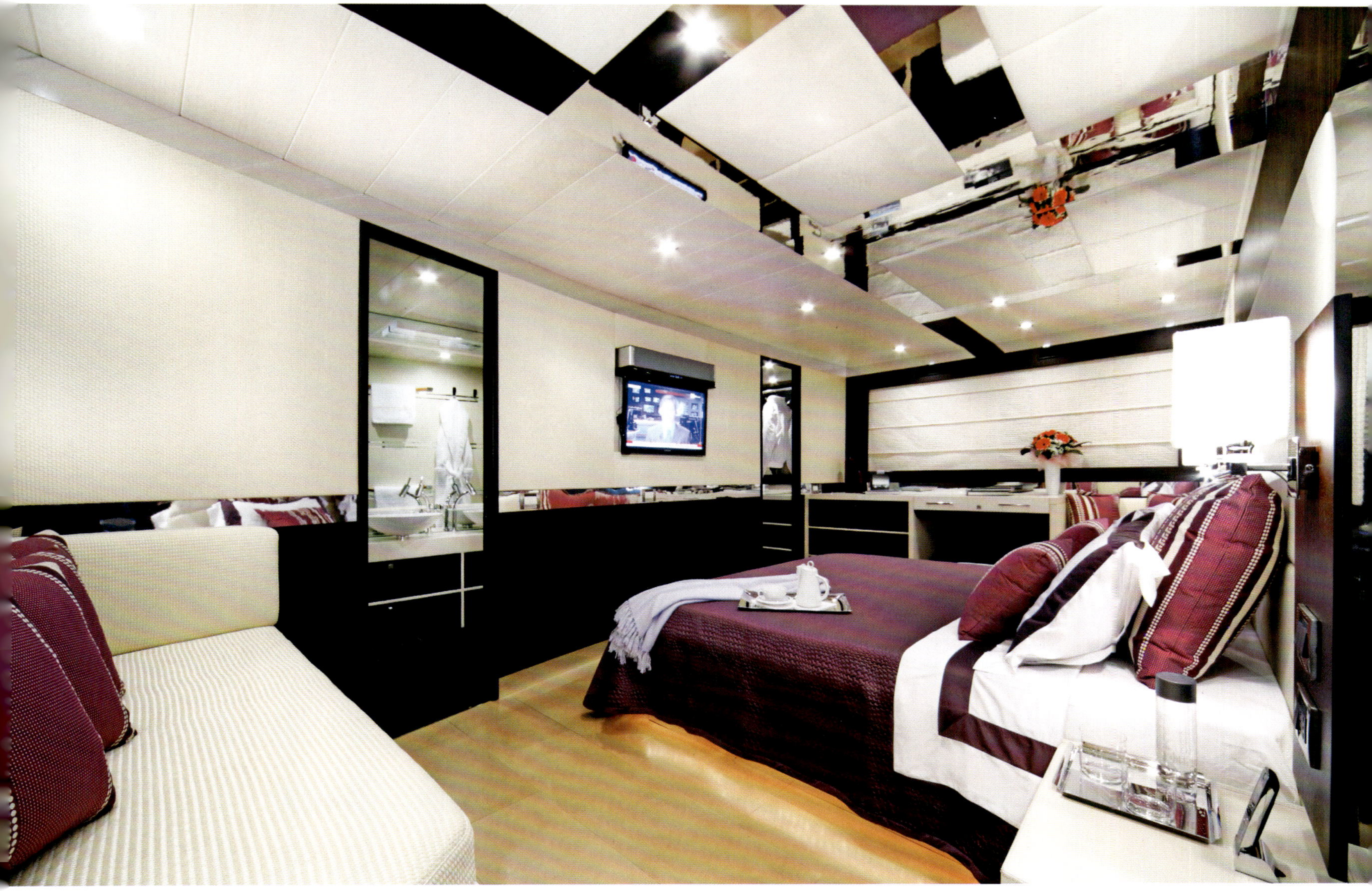

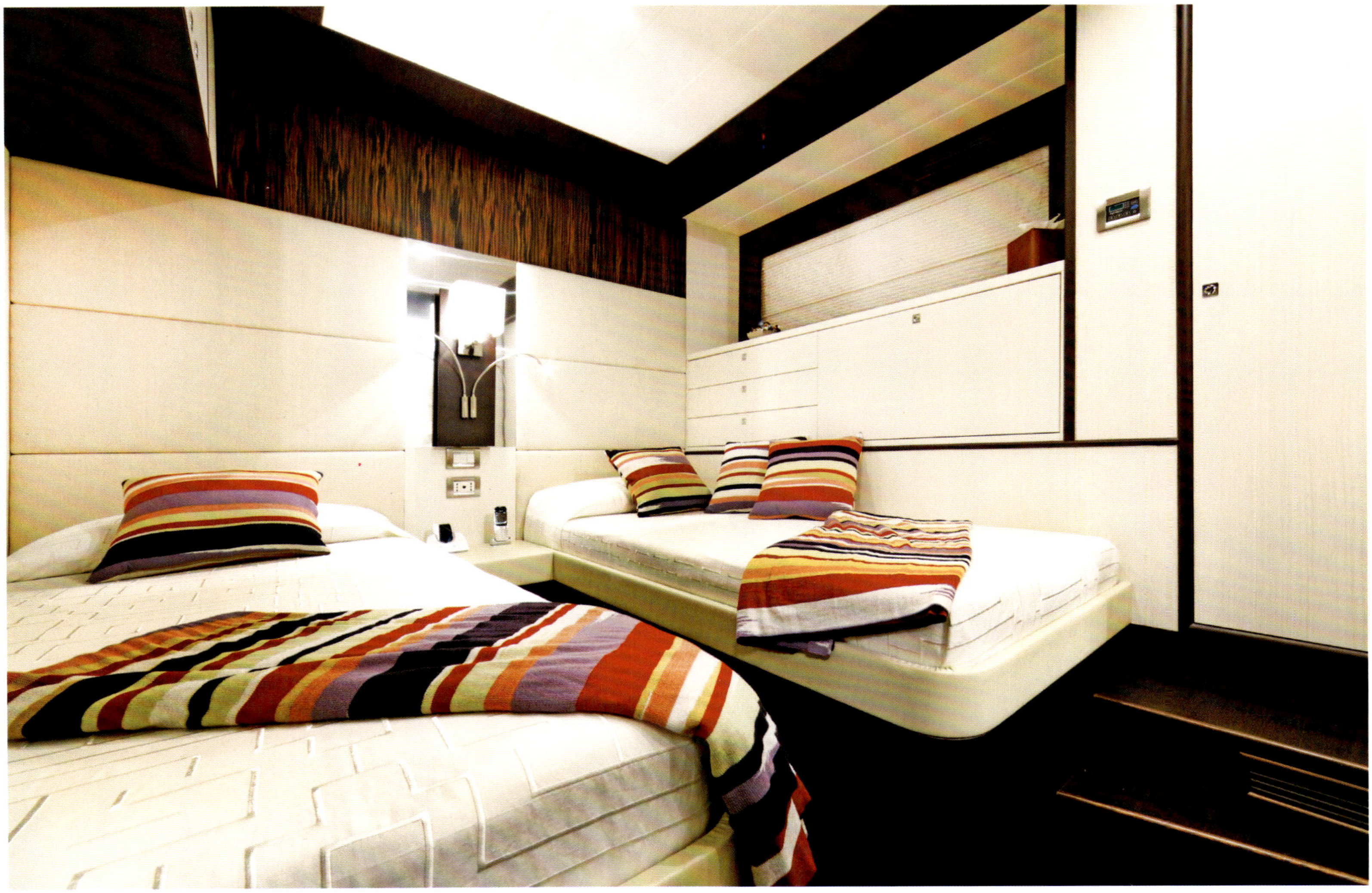

JOYME YACHT

> DESIGN	Stand By
> SHIPYARD	Philip Zepter Yachts
> LENGTH	49.9m
> BEAM	9.1m
> MAX SPEED	15kn
> CRUISING SPEED	14kn
> PHOTOGRAPHER	Ivan Bura

> This challenge was addressed by creating an interior universe with many different dimensions as each unit of space has been treated as a separate entity with its own story, philosophy and atmosphere. Each area therefore communicates different emotions and feelings to suit the mood of every occupant without alienating anybody and this is the true notion of user-friendliness. Rather than creating an interior with one uniform atmosphere, the client wanted a space with enough flexibility to suit his every mood. However, all the individual spaces within the yacht's interior are connected by a common thread, which is to create a young and dynamic, yet comfortable and functional interior with an emphasis on good communication between different areas so as to make it supremely user-friendly.

Another design characteristic of the interior is the emphasis on the notion of open space, where different areas for different moods were created within the same space by avoiding compartmentalization. The premise is that a space can stand on its own as a tangibly different entity without necessarily being physically separated from others, as demonstrated by the layout and design of the main saloon.

Main saloon with a lounge area, relax zone, bar, and dining is left as an open space with no separation walls but at the same time distinctly different and separated areas are created.

"joyMe" Fitness and Beach club is situated at the aft part of the cabin deck close to the sea and offers views which virtually unify this area with the surface of the sea in one continuous sight line. Fitness has been designed around the "fish" theme and features a "rainforest storm" shower and a sauna. Sundeck lounge consists of a large pool and a bar which reprise the yacht's characteristic paint scheme.

It is also worth noting the importance that was given to natural light, while the carefully studied concealed lighting system that takes over during the night maintains the elegance of this modern yet warm interior.

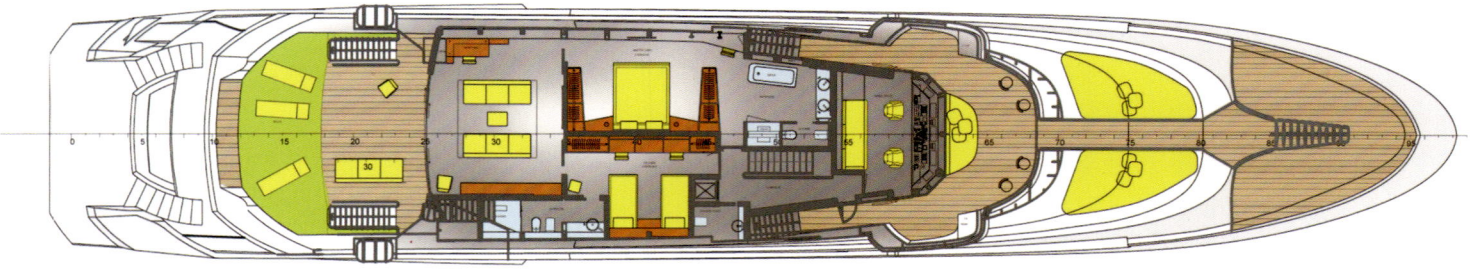

SUN DECK

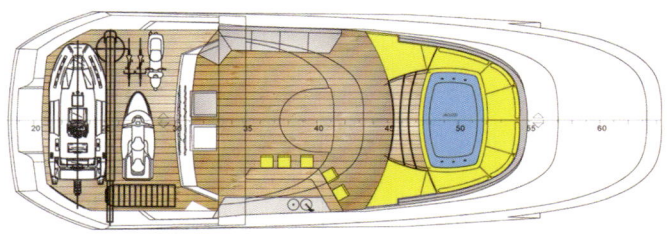

VIP DECK

MAIN DECK

CABIN DECK

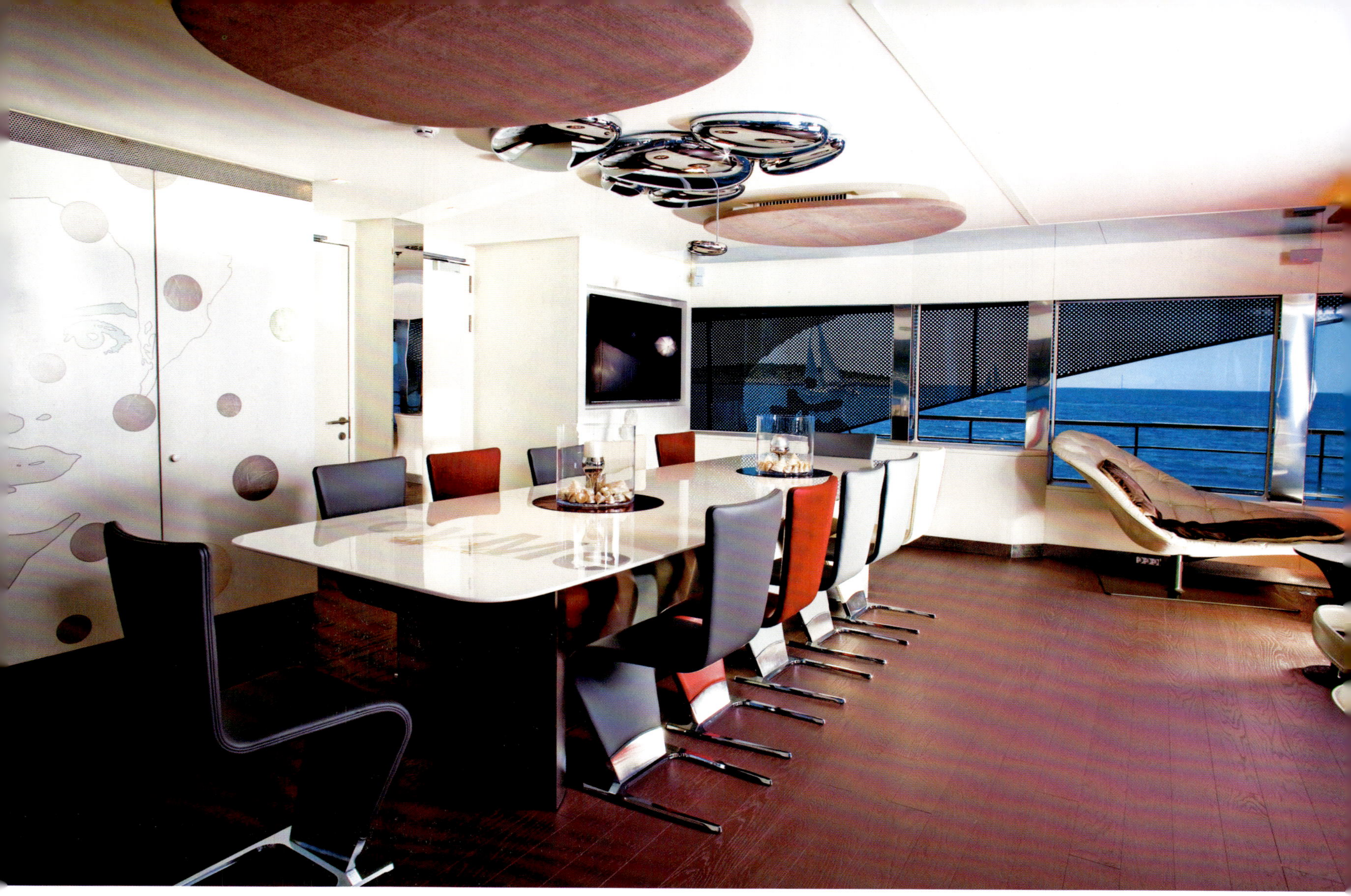

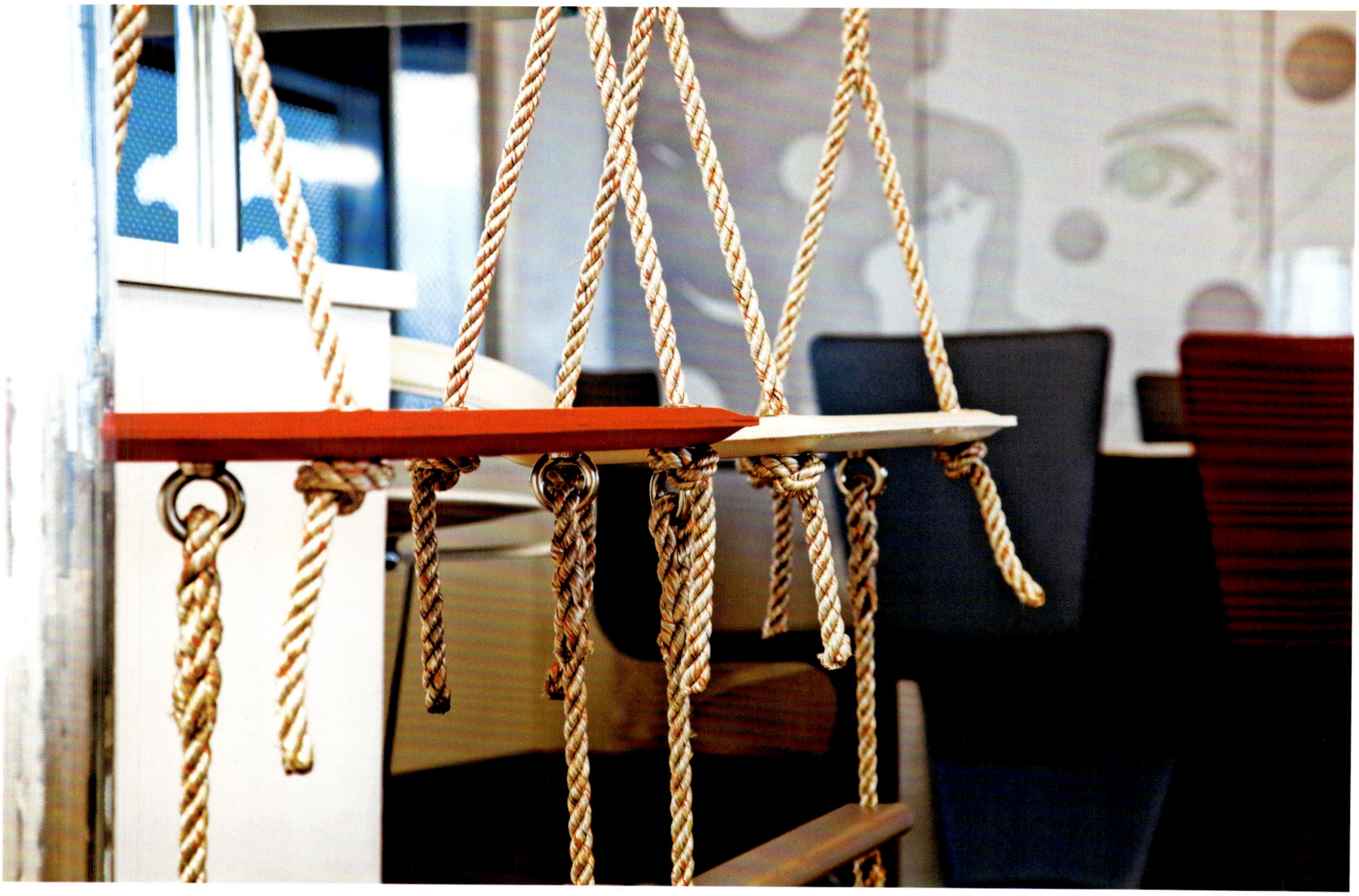

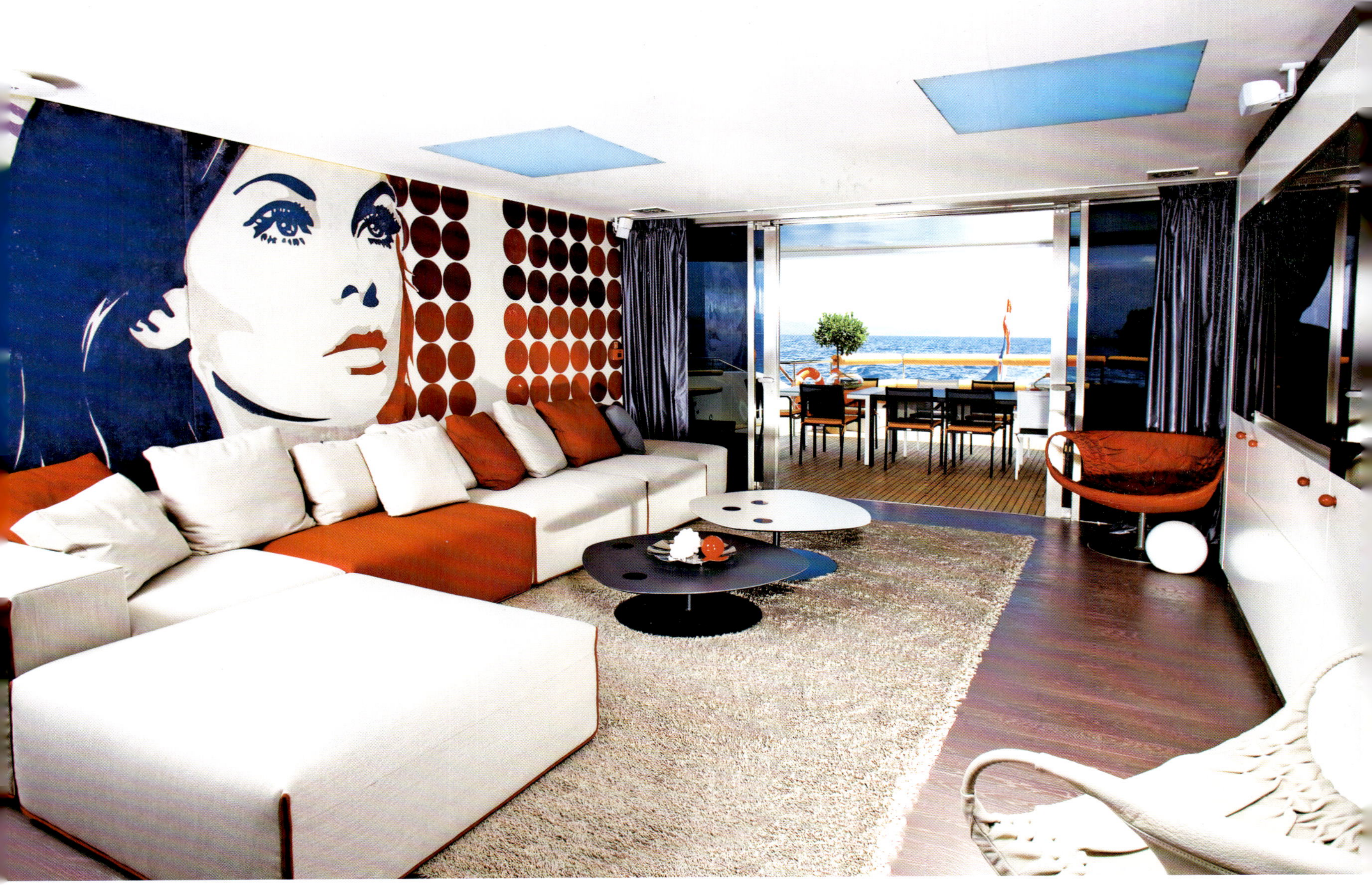

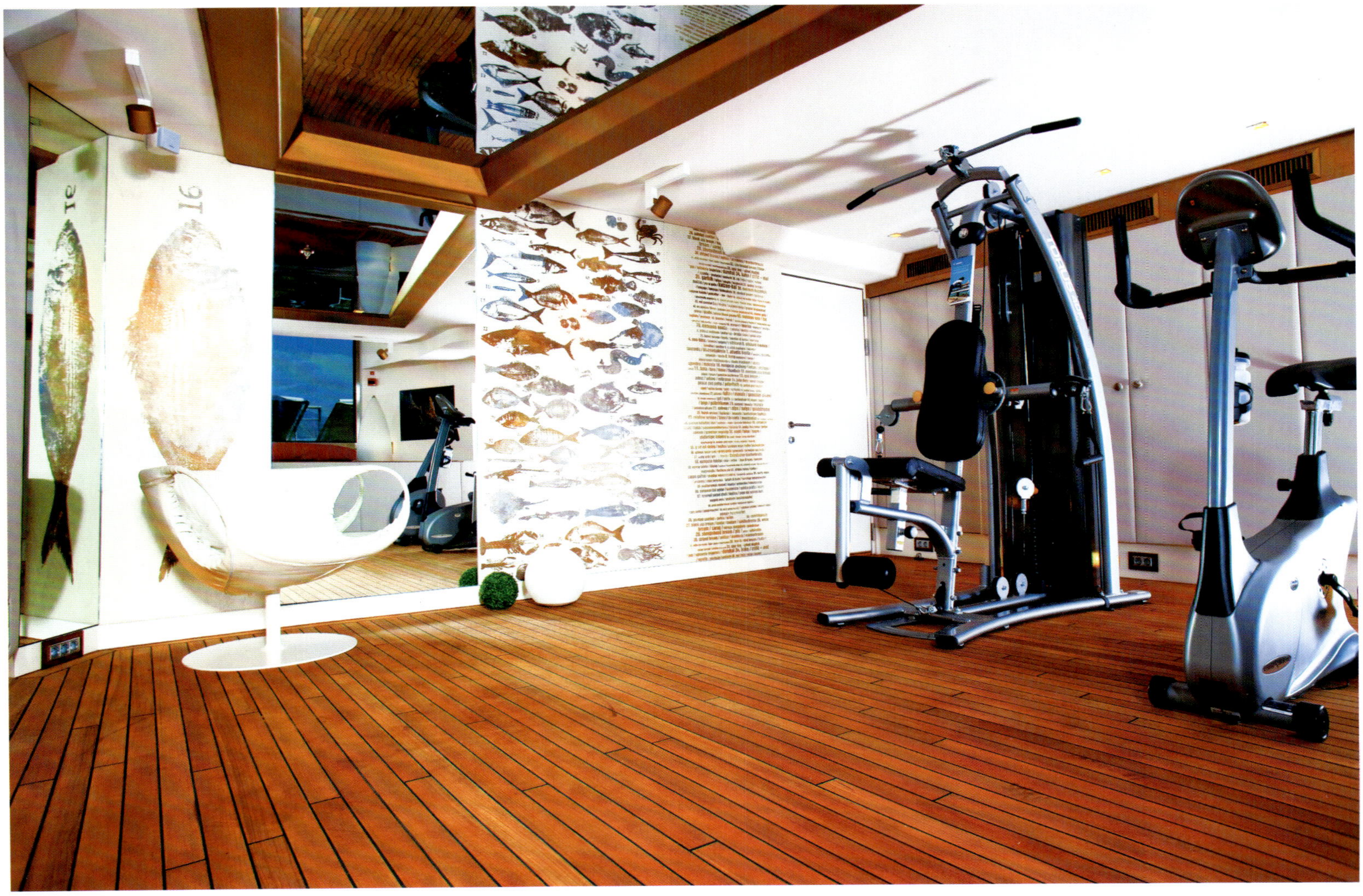

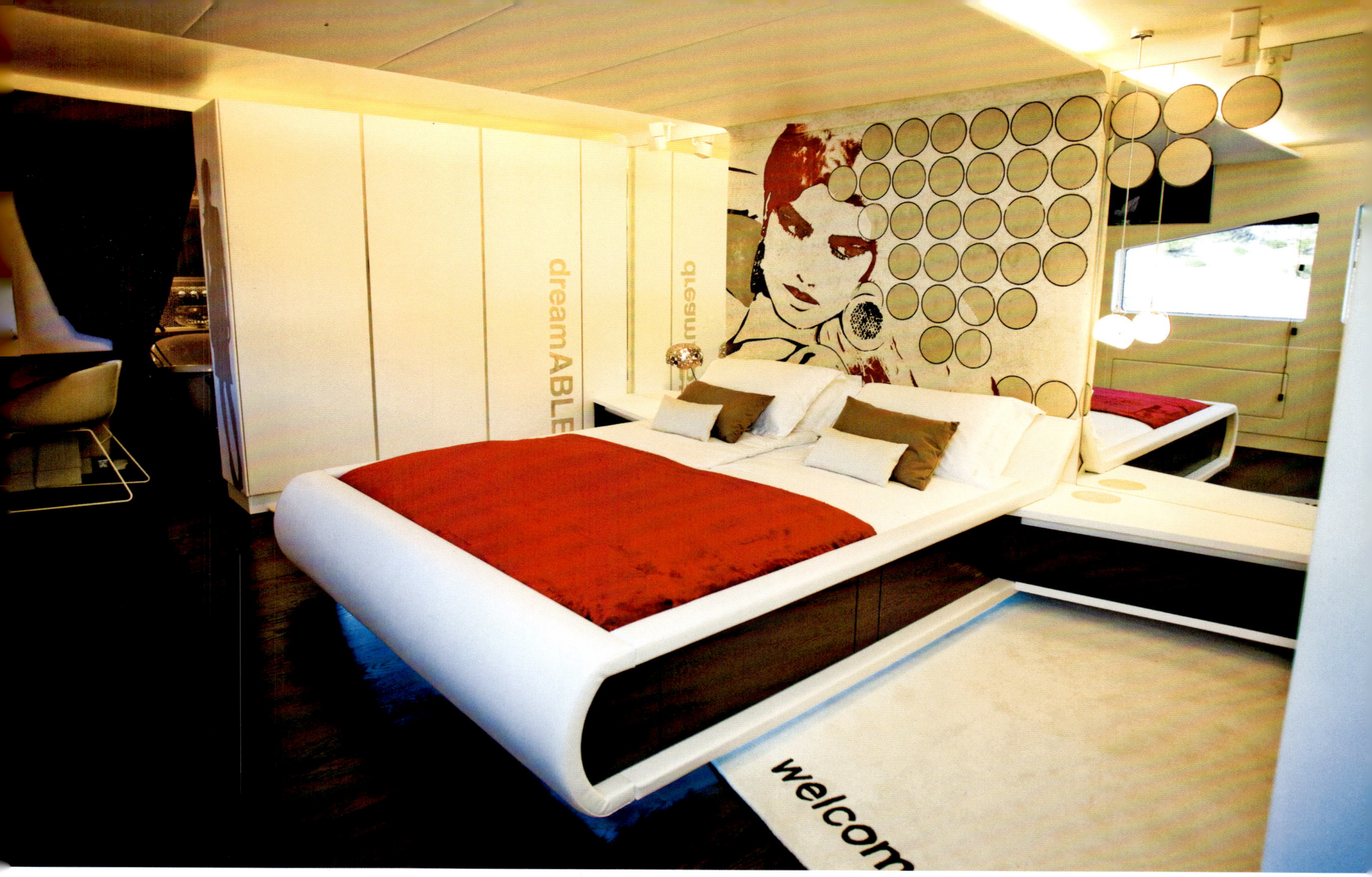
dreamABLE
welcom

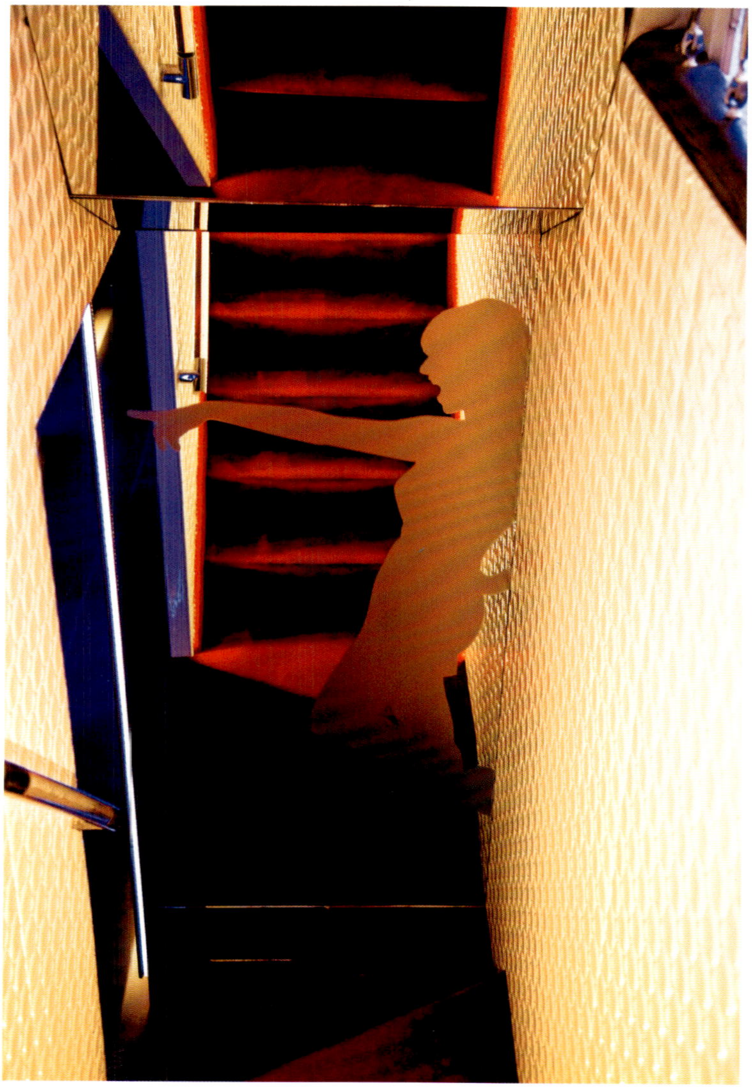

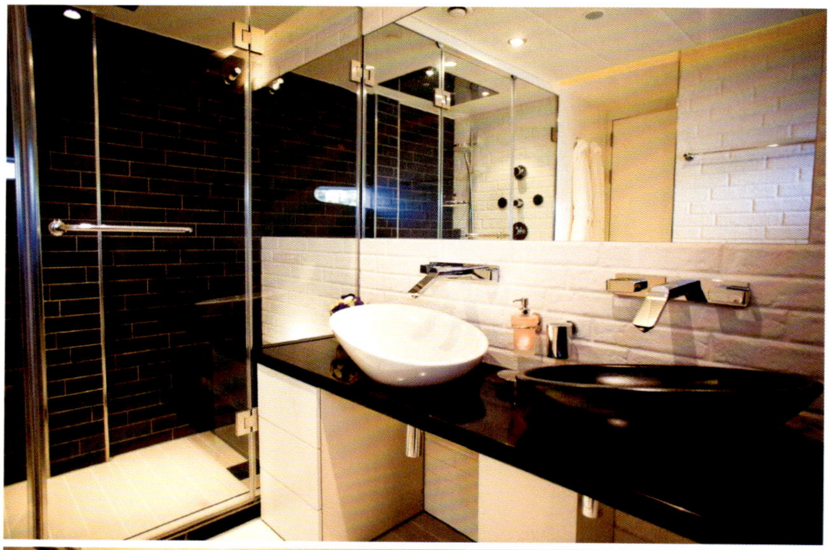

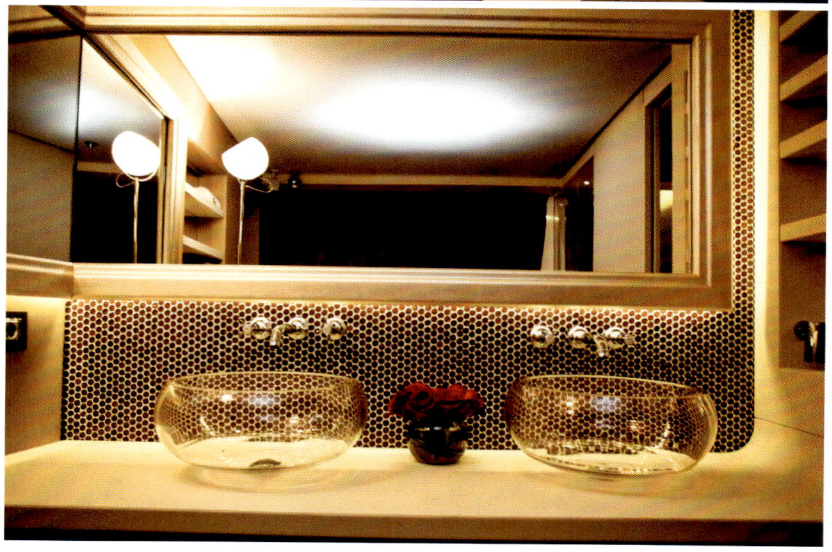

挑战在于创造一种多维度的内部环境，每个空间单元都要有独立的个性，有自己的故事、理念和氛围。因此，每个区域都表现出一种不同的情绪和感情，以适应使用者不同的心情，不会给任何人陌生的感觉，这也正是"用户至上"的真正内涵。委托人不喜欢单一的风格，而是希望能有一个足够多元的空间来满足他不同的心情。但是，游艇内部所有的个性空间都通过一个主线串联了起来，因而创造了一种青春动感、轻松舒适、功能多样的内部设计，并强调了各部分间的互动与交流，从而达到"用户至上"的极致。

内部设计的另外一个特点是强调了它的开放空间：在同一个空间内，没有使用隔断，就实现了不同区域体现出不同的心情。当然，前提是这个空间本身就个性鲜明，没必要非得使用隔断来把它与其他空间区别开来。主厅的布局与设计所展示的正是这样的特点。

主厅包括休息区、休闲区、吧台、餐台，全部都处于一个大空间下，没有使用隔断墙，但同时却达到了泾渭分明、区域独立。

"着迷"健身沙滩俱乐部就位于船舱甲板尾部靠近大海的区域，那里，你可以体验到船海相融的壮观景色。健身区的设计以"鱼"为主题，并有一个"雨林风暴"的淋浴间和桑拿间。日光浴甲板上巨大的泳池和吧台，体现了游艇与众不同的喷涂设计。

同样值得指出的是，设计特别重视对自然光照的利用。到了晚上，巧妙设计的隐藏式照明系统接替了自然光照，让这艘游艇现代而又温馨的内部设计散发出夺目的光辉。

MY LADY LARA

> **INTERIOR DESIGN**	Studio Massari
> **SHIPYARD**	Benetti Shipyard
> **LENGTH**	59.30m
> **BEAM**	10.4m

> The realization of Lady Lara comes from a successful collaboration between a very present and Determinate Client and an experienced design team, from the Studio Massari.

Working on this project has been a challenging task – says Alessandro Massari – the client had a clear idea of what she wanted and how she wished to use her yacht, therefore we had to follow a very specific decoration's request to create a tailor made design concept. Clearly Yacht Design can't be treated like a residential or a retail project, there are certain limits to consider and our first approach to this work was to make the owner understand what life on board is and how the design has to accord to that. Consequently a blend of client's desire, our direct experience in the marine field, together with quality of build, were the key point to complete Lady Lara and delivering a winning final solution. The paramount owner's request we had to meet was to introduce on board the Fendi Style, from the accessories, leathers, lighting to loose furniture. We – A. Massari affirms – with our design discipline and skills, have worked on producing a design scheme that conforms as much as possible to the charm of the note Fendi label.

According thus to the Fendi Style, the overall design idea that stands behind the final product is a pleasing fusion of a classic and contemporary style. Such a principle will reflect in all the ambient on board; indeed a unique sumptuous layout that combines perfectly with practical and effective. The shades of colors present on Lady Lara are nuance of gold and silver, which create a harmonious and very balanced atmosphere, yet very luxurious.

Starting our tour on board atop from the Sun Deck we will found a central glazed area, where the Gymnasium is located, this area allows doing workouts and enjoy the view at the same time whilst cruising, thanks to the glazed walls and doors structure. The Forward part features large sun-pads leading to a swimming pool provided with a Jacuzzi; two umbrellas shelter the area. Positioned at the Aft is a twelve-seater round table, ideal for Al Fresco dining, a bar and a seating area on the starboard side. On the Helideck we find a very cozy padded seating zone, parts of this area will also be used to practice yoga classes. The all Aft is sheltered by a cleverly studied jigsaw puzzle of white veils.

Down to the Upper Deck we pause on to one of the most dramatic Lady Lara's feature: the lift. The accurate choices of leathers: gold Iguana on its main structure, gold Croco on its handrail and Galuchat skins on the surrounding walls, are surely a right combination to deliver a sleek and striking result. On the lift's floor and on the lobby's the logo "LL" is featured, to note that not by a chance both Lady Lara and Fendi's Luxury Living logo, use the same double "L's" as trademark.

Lady Lara（"海上名媛"）号游艇的成功建造是两方通力合作的结果，一方是有着丰富经验的 Massari 设计工作室专家团队，另一方是有主见和决心的客户。

建造这艘游艇是一项极富挑战性的工程——设计方 Alessandro Massari 指出：客户清楚她自己想要什么样的游艇，也对游艇建成后如何使用有自己的计划，所以设计方必须遵照客户的特殊要求拿出一套为船量身定做的设计理念。游艇的设计当然不同于住宅或是零售项目，不同之处首先在于，设计游艇需要考虑特定的局限性。鉴于此，Massari 设计团队的首要任务是引导船主理解游艇上的生活将是什么样子，以及如何使设计方案与船主所期待的船上生活相符合。最终，结合客户的意愿、设计团队在海洋领域的直接经验以及造船厂的建造质量等众多关键因素，成功建造了 Lady Lara（"海上名媛"）号，并提出了一项实用的解决方案。船主提出，希望把 Fendi（斐迪）风格（Fendi 是意大利奢侈生活用品品牌）运用到游艇上，这一点要求，设计团队自然须严格遵循。从室内配件、皮革、照明设备到各种散装家具的设计都必须符合这样的风格。Massari 设计团队声明：秉承公司一贯的设计作风和技能，我们提出了一套尽可能展现斐迪风格魅力的设计方案。

依照斐迪风格，整个游艇设计完成之后给人一种这样的感觉：在古典与现代风格的融合中，使人沉浸于惬意的氛围。这样的风格在船上处处可见；事实上，这一独特的奢华布局是实用性和有效性的完美结合。Lady Lara（"海上名媛"）号的色彩设计整体呈金银色调，为整个游艇创造出了和谐、平衡的气氛，同时又极显奢华。

从游艇上层甲板顺势走到船上，会看到一处中间上过釉的地方，这里是船上的体育馆、馆内墙和门窗结构都经过釉面处理，这样方便船上的乘客可以边训练、边在航行中欣赏海景。船前部是游泳池，配备有水流式按摩浴缸，还有大垫子，供乘客舒适地享受太阳浴；同时，还配有两把支起的太阳伞供乘凉用。船尾处有一张可容纳 12 人的大圆桌，是露天月餐的理想场所；在右舷一侧还有一间酒吧和休息区。在直升机降落甲板，还有一个舒适惬意的坐卧区，这里有一部分留出专供乘客练习瑜伽。整个船尾上方都使用精心研究的白色拼接图案的帐幕来遮阳。

从阳光沐浴的顶部甲板下到上层甲板，就看到了"海上名媛"号游艇最引人注目的设计之一：电梯。精心挑选的皮革：主体结构上金色的鬣鳞蜥、扶手上金色鳄鱼的雕塑和四周墙上带有装饰的粗革皮革的绝妙组合创造了个性而又婉约的氛围。电梯内和大厅的地板上醒目的"LL"标志正说明了，Lady Lara（"海上名媛"）号和 Fendi（斐迪）奢侈生活用品的商标都使用双"L"做标志，并非纯属巧合。

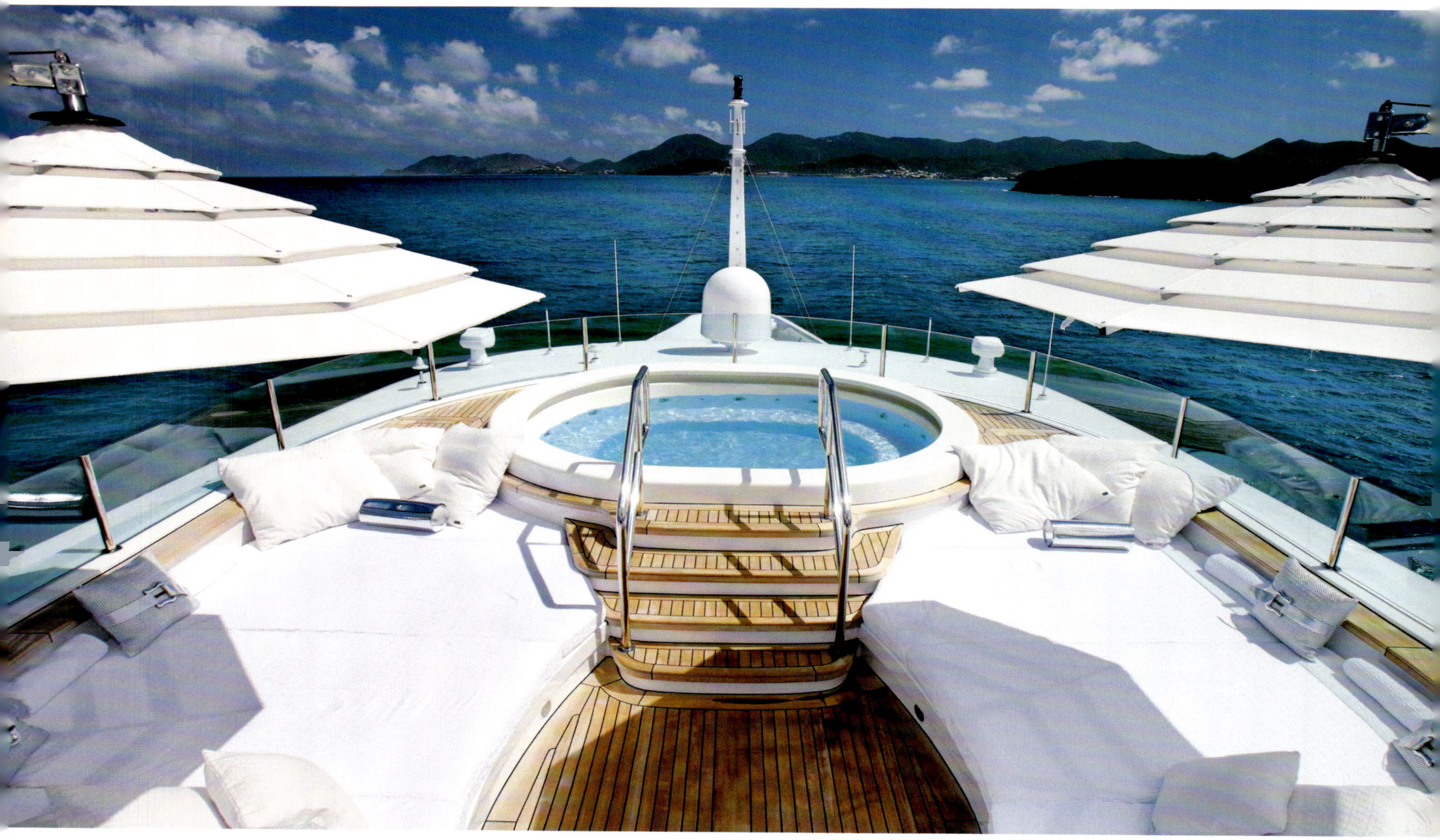

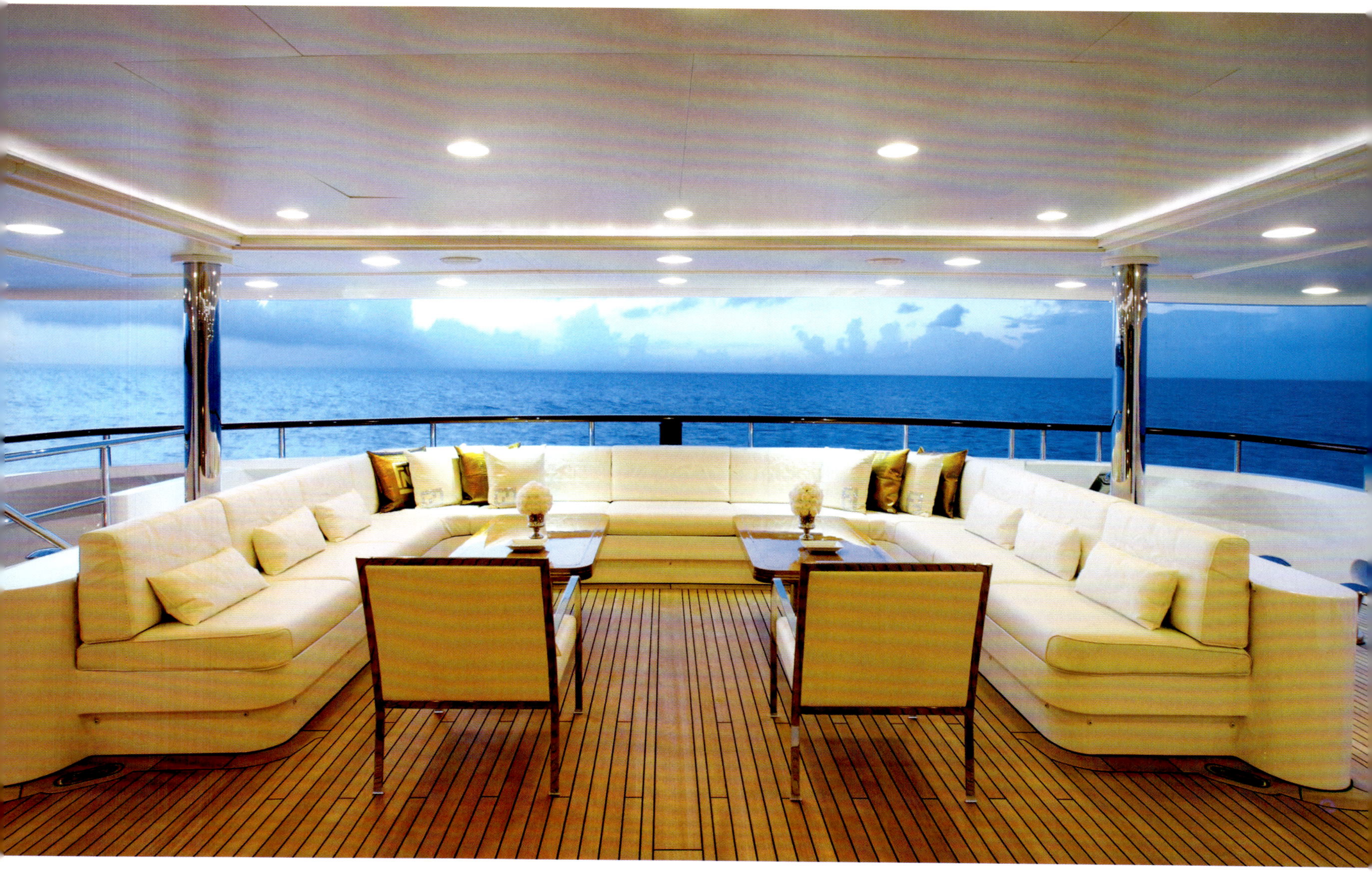

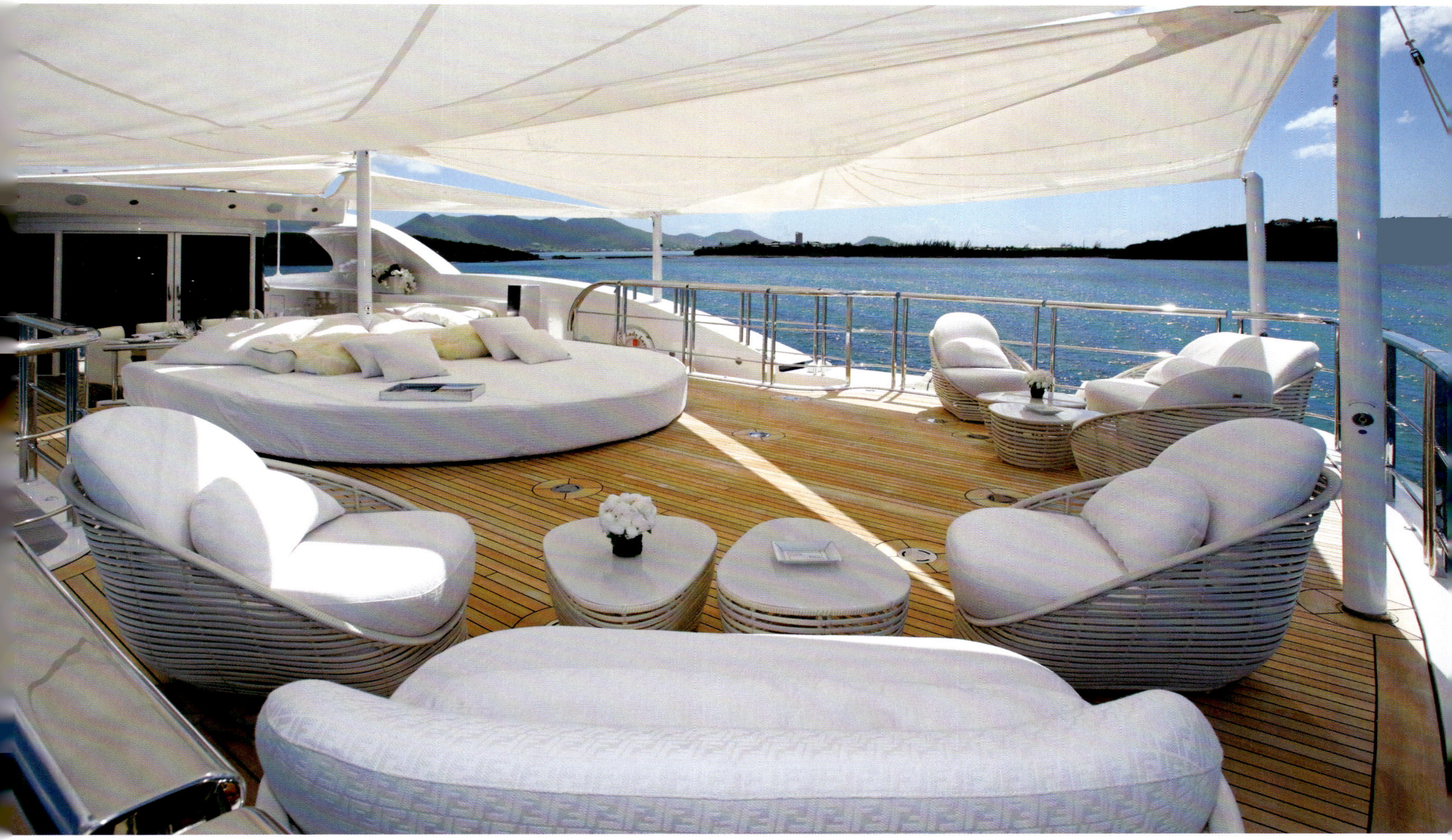

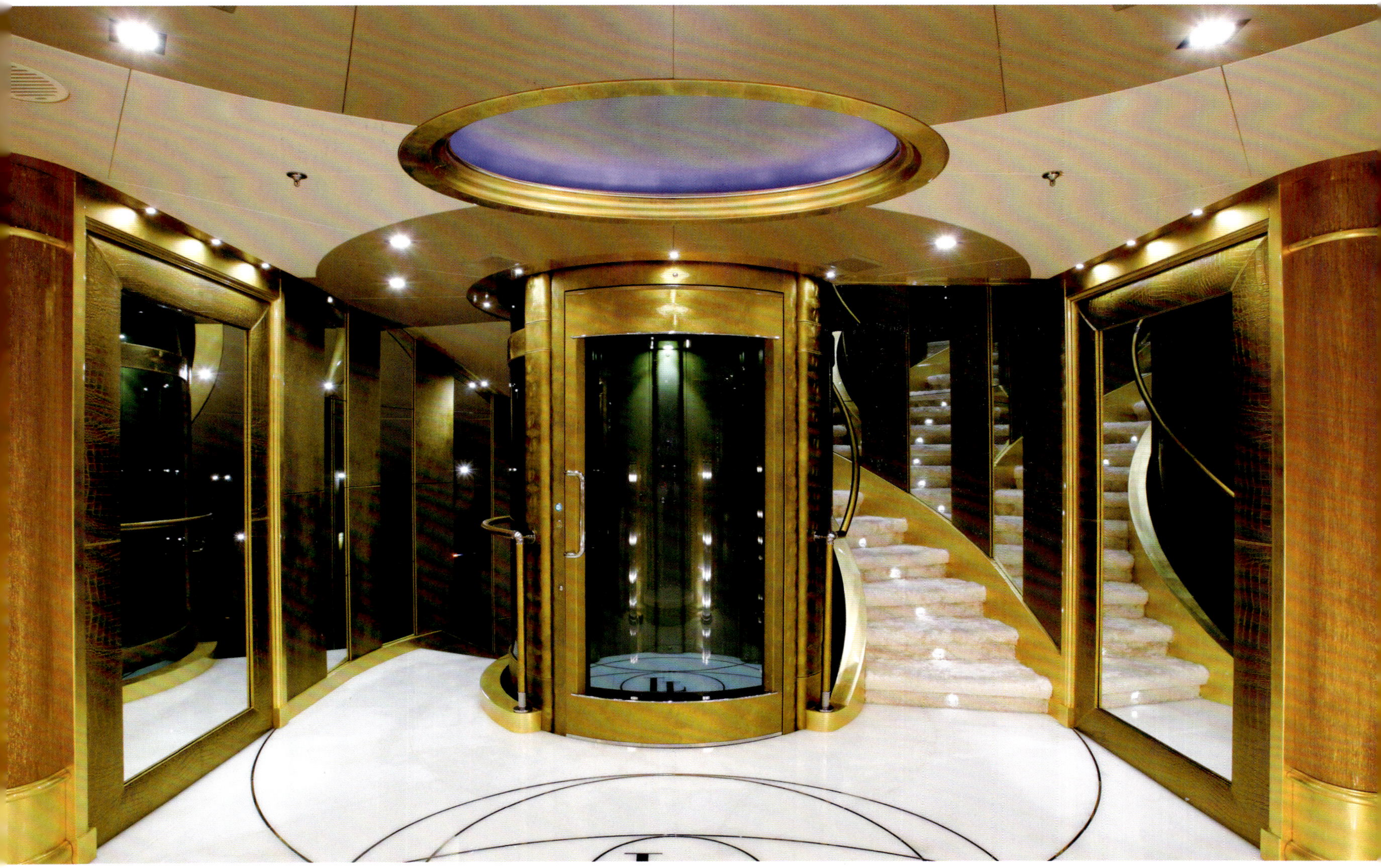

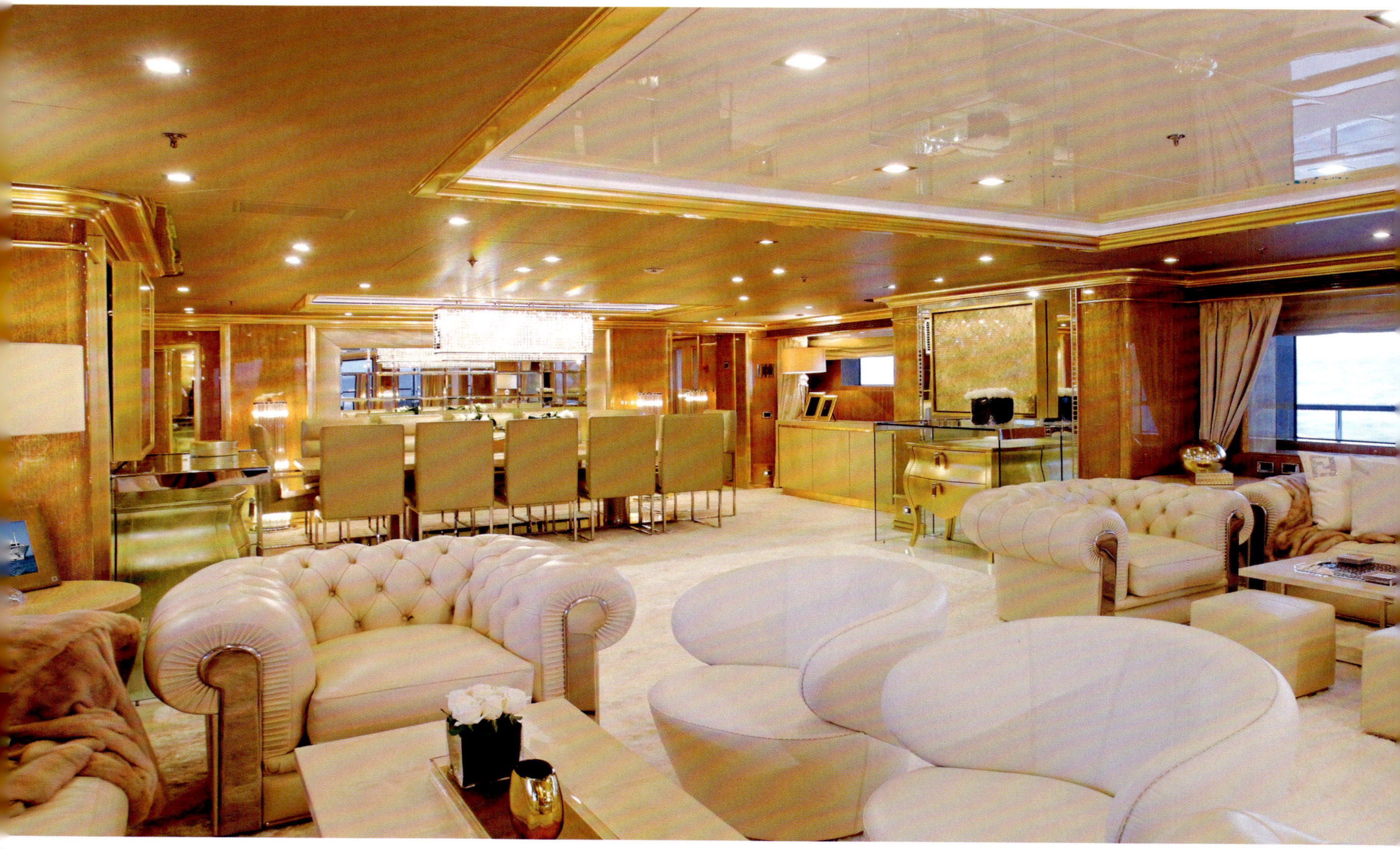

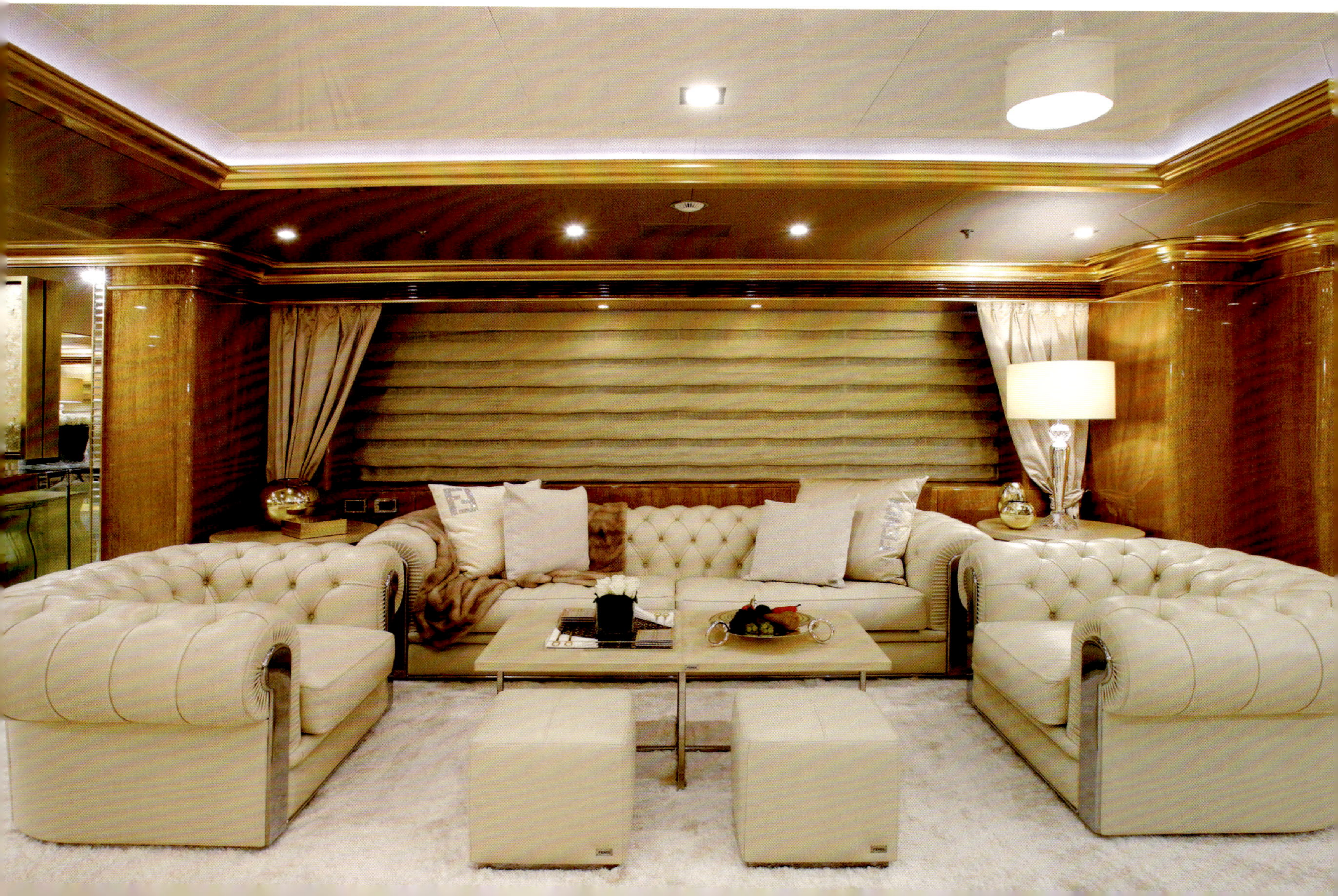

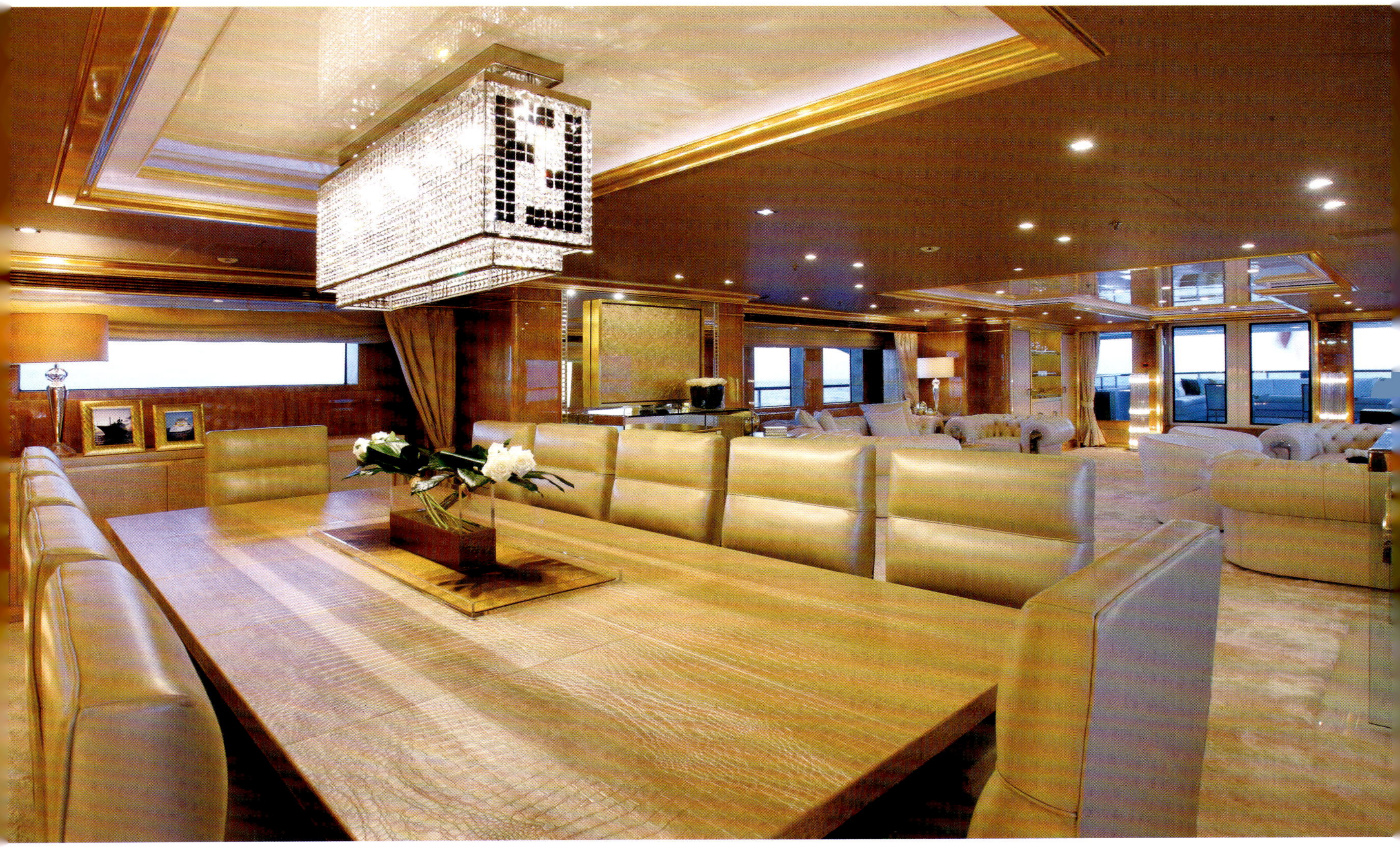

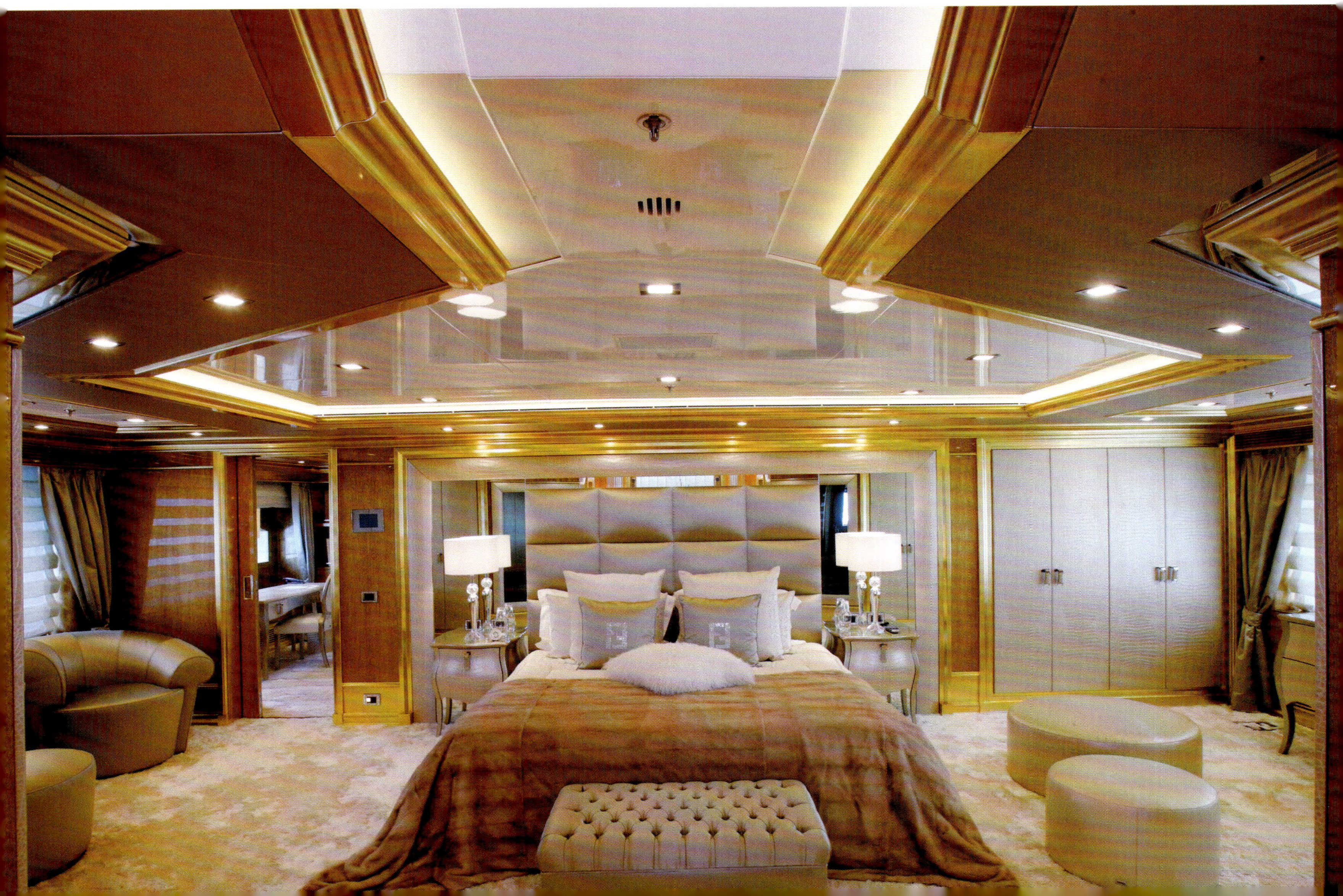

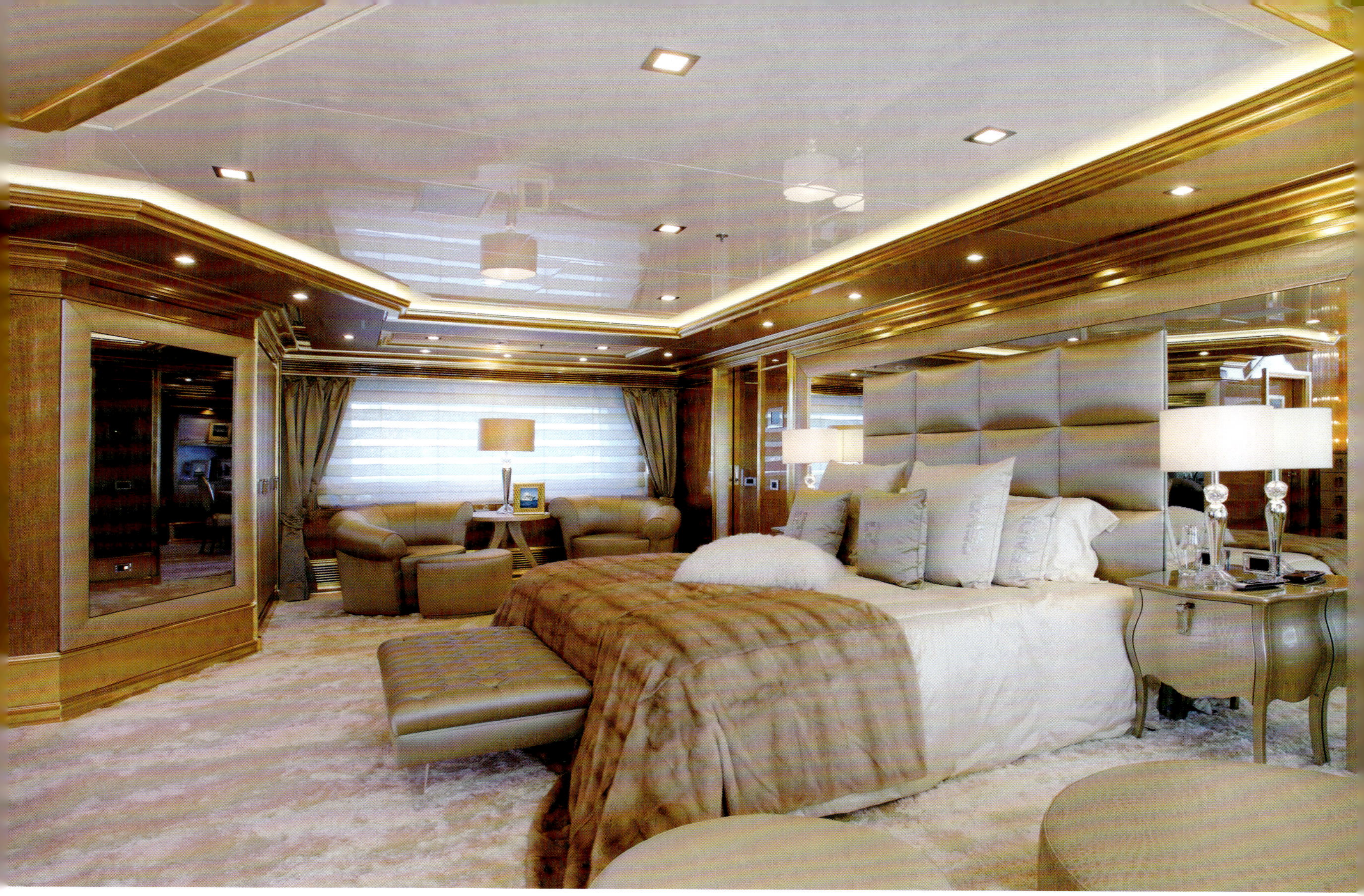

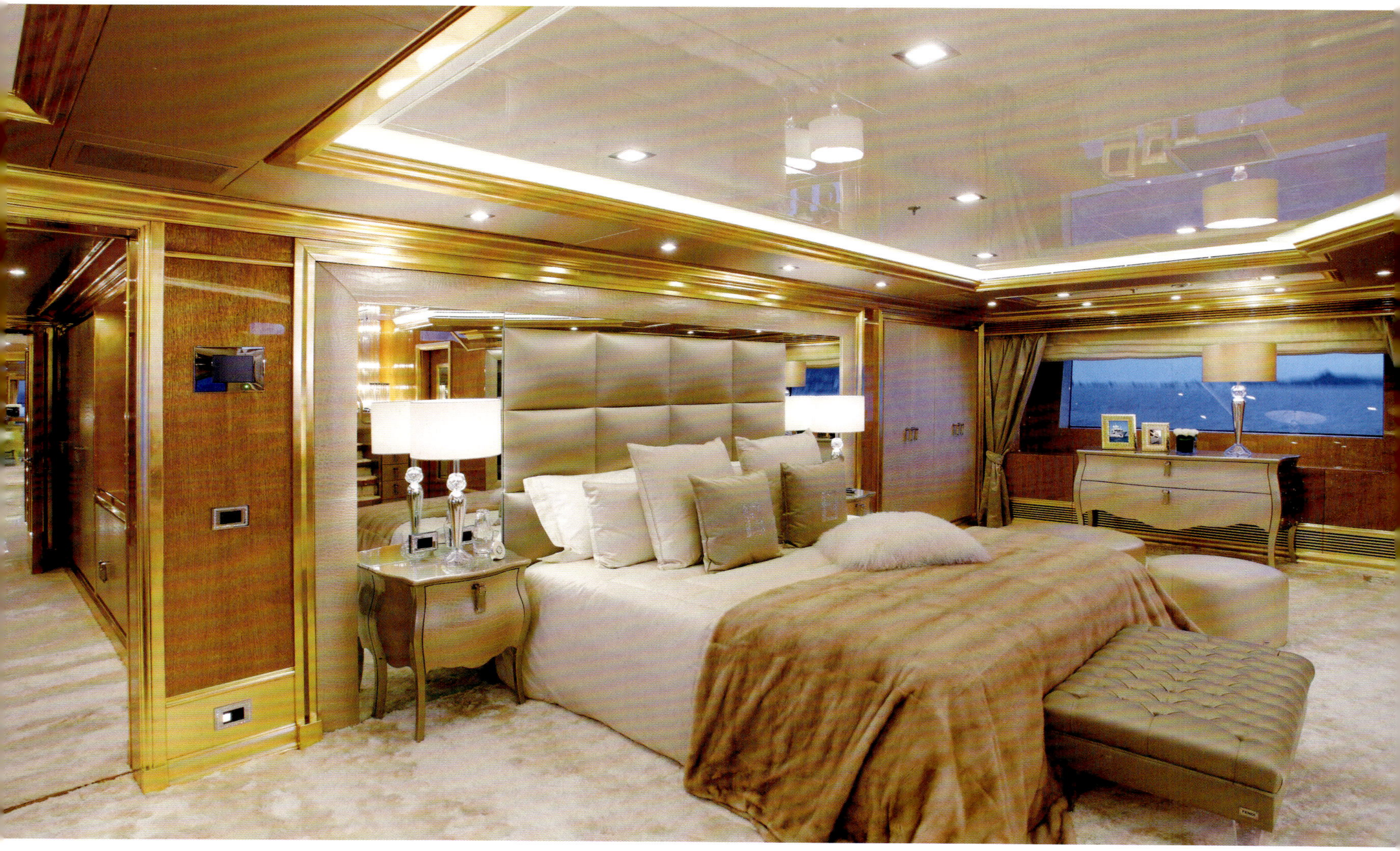

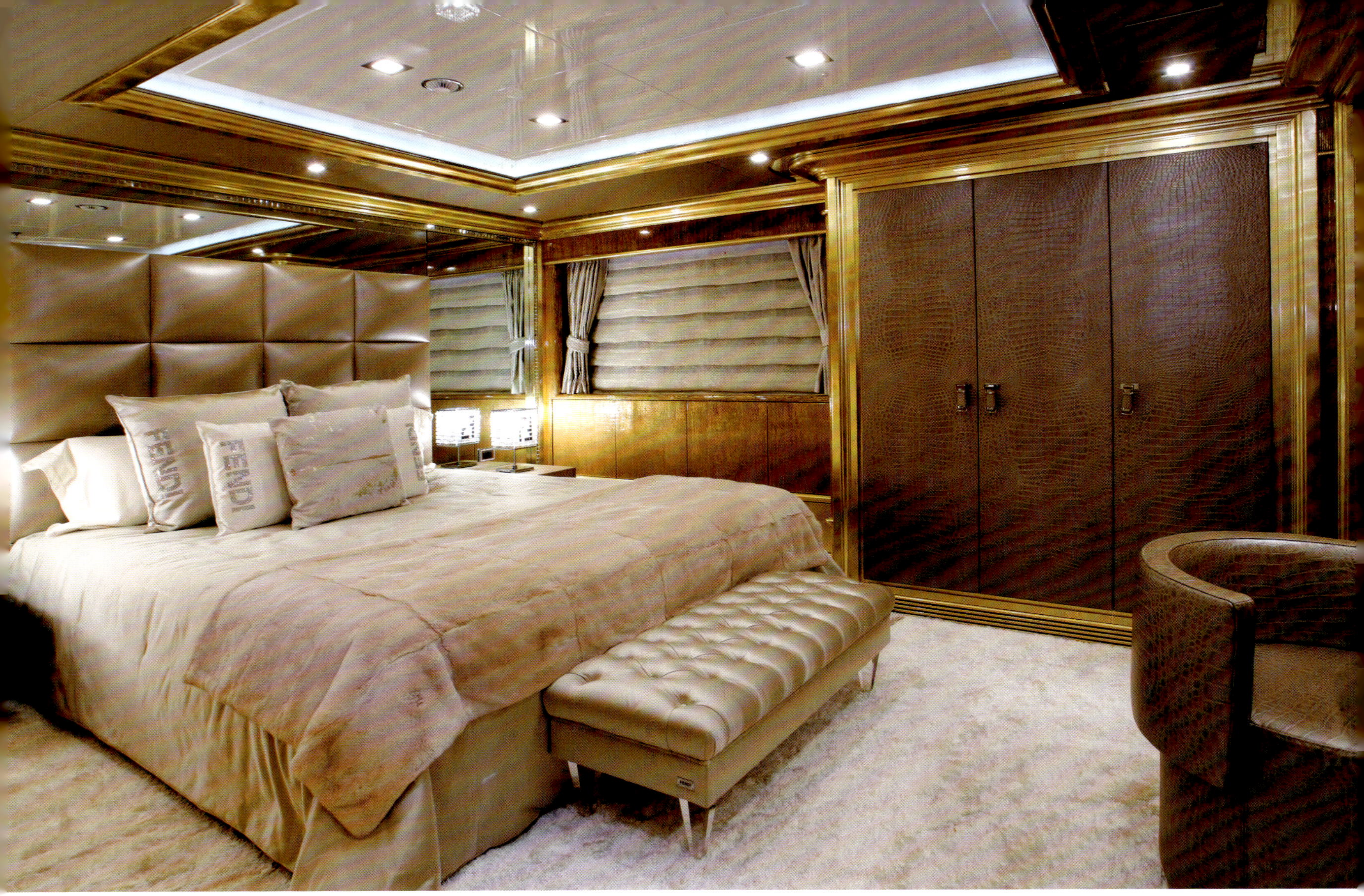
FENDI
FENDI

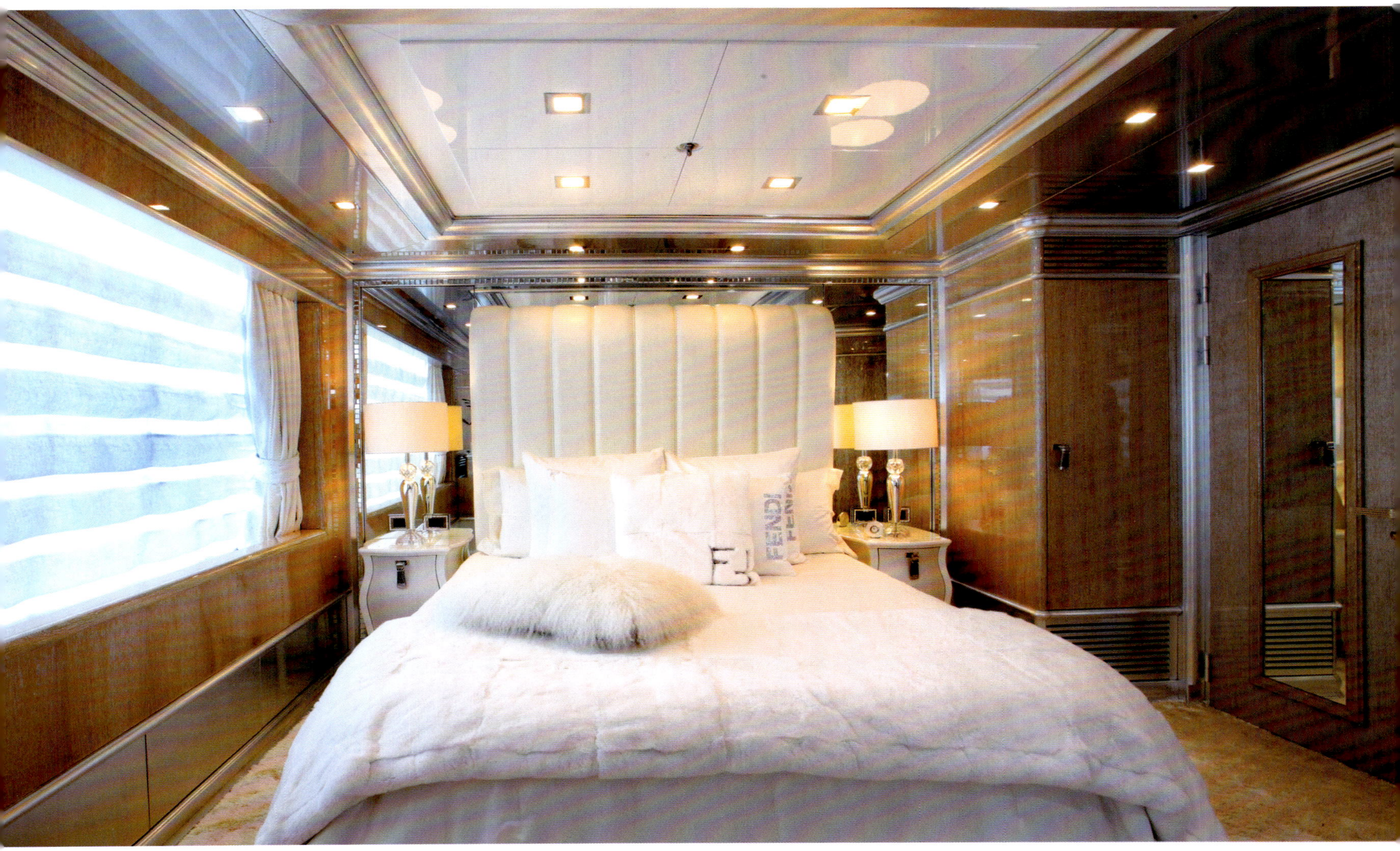
FENDI

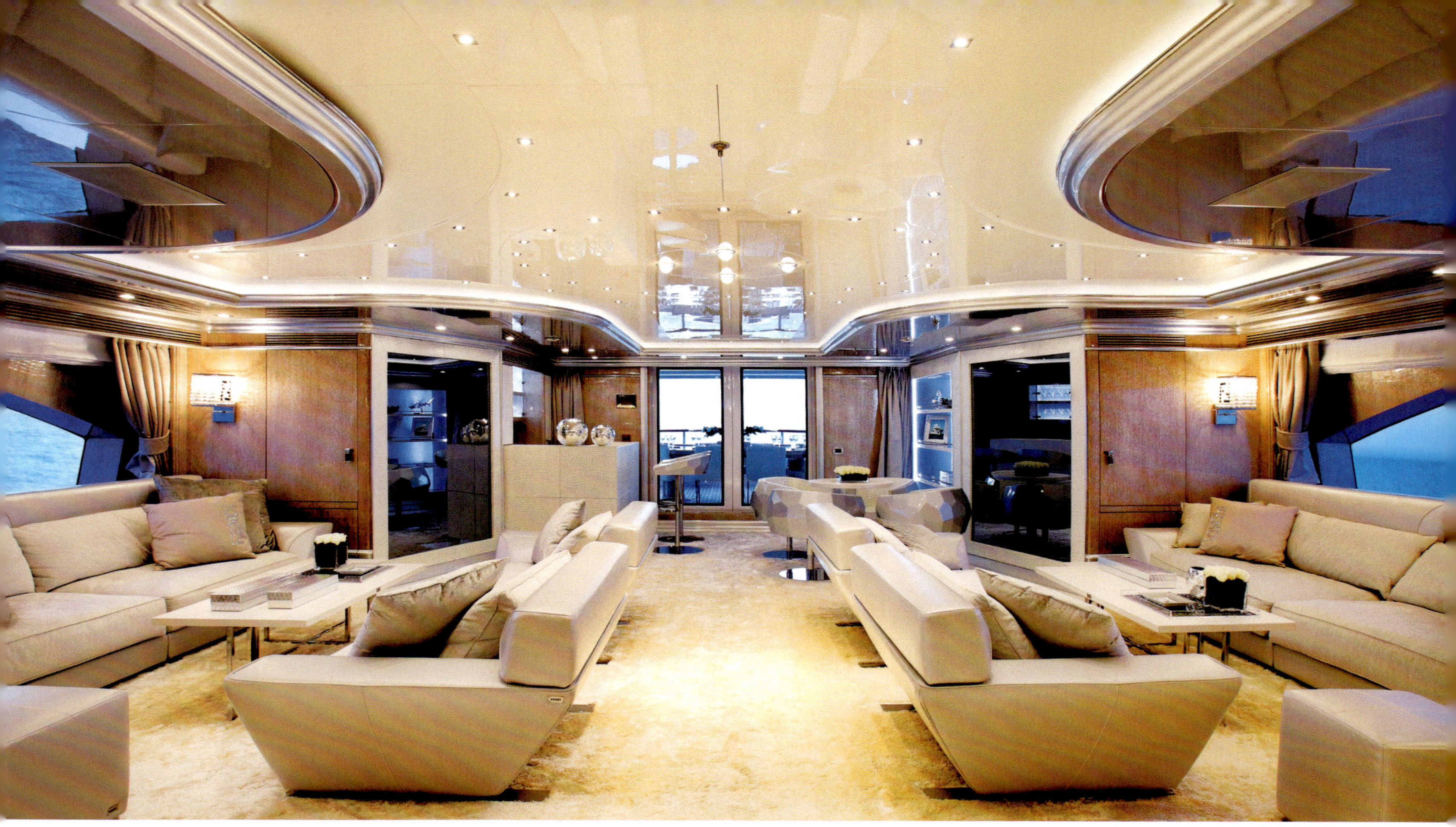

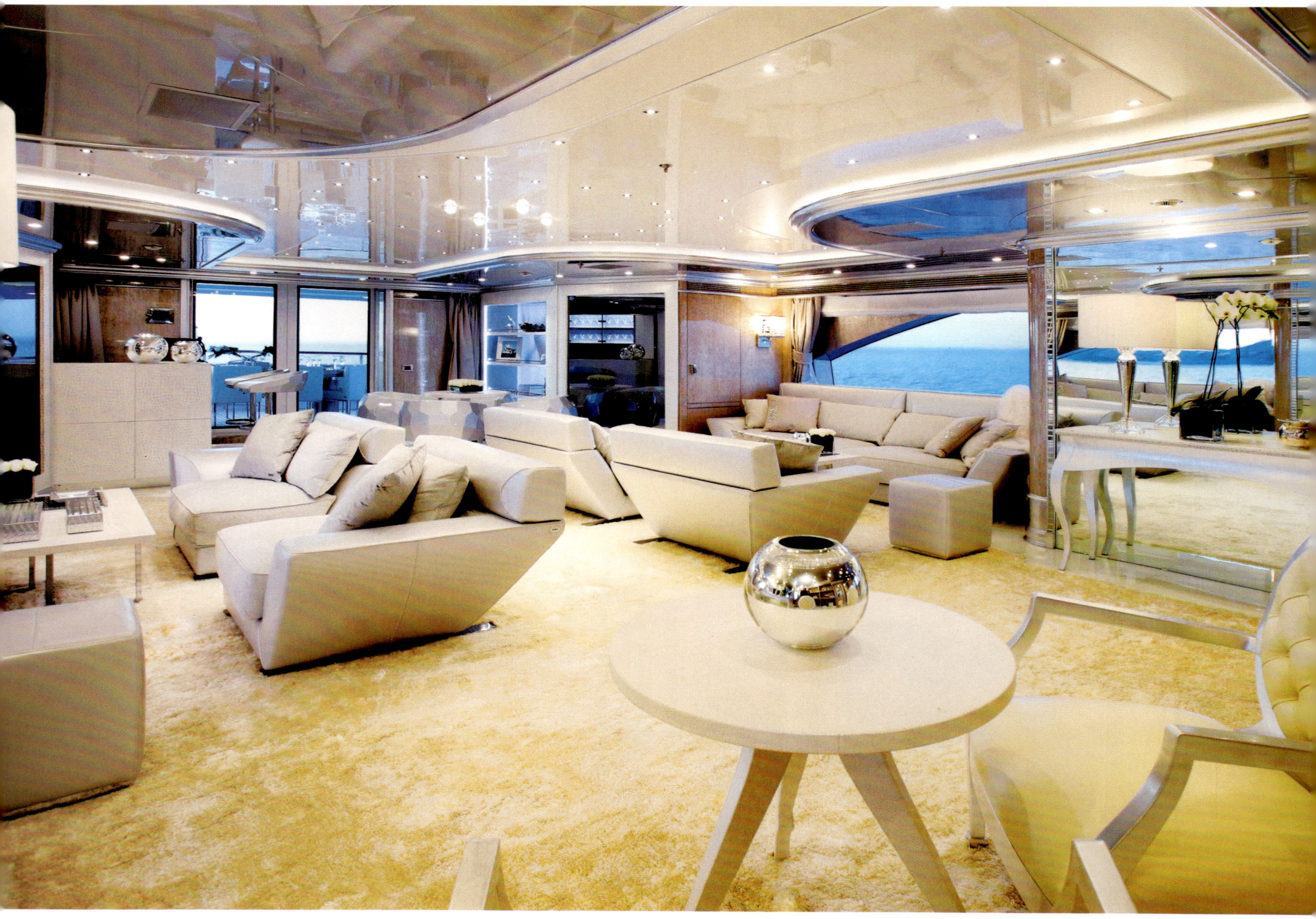

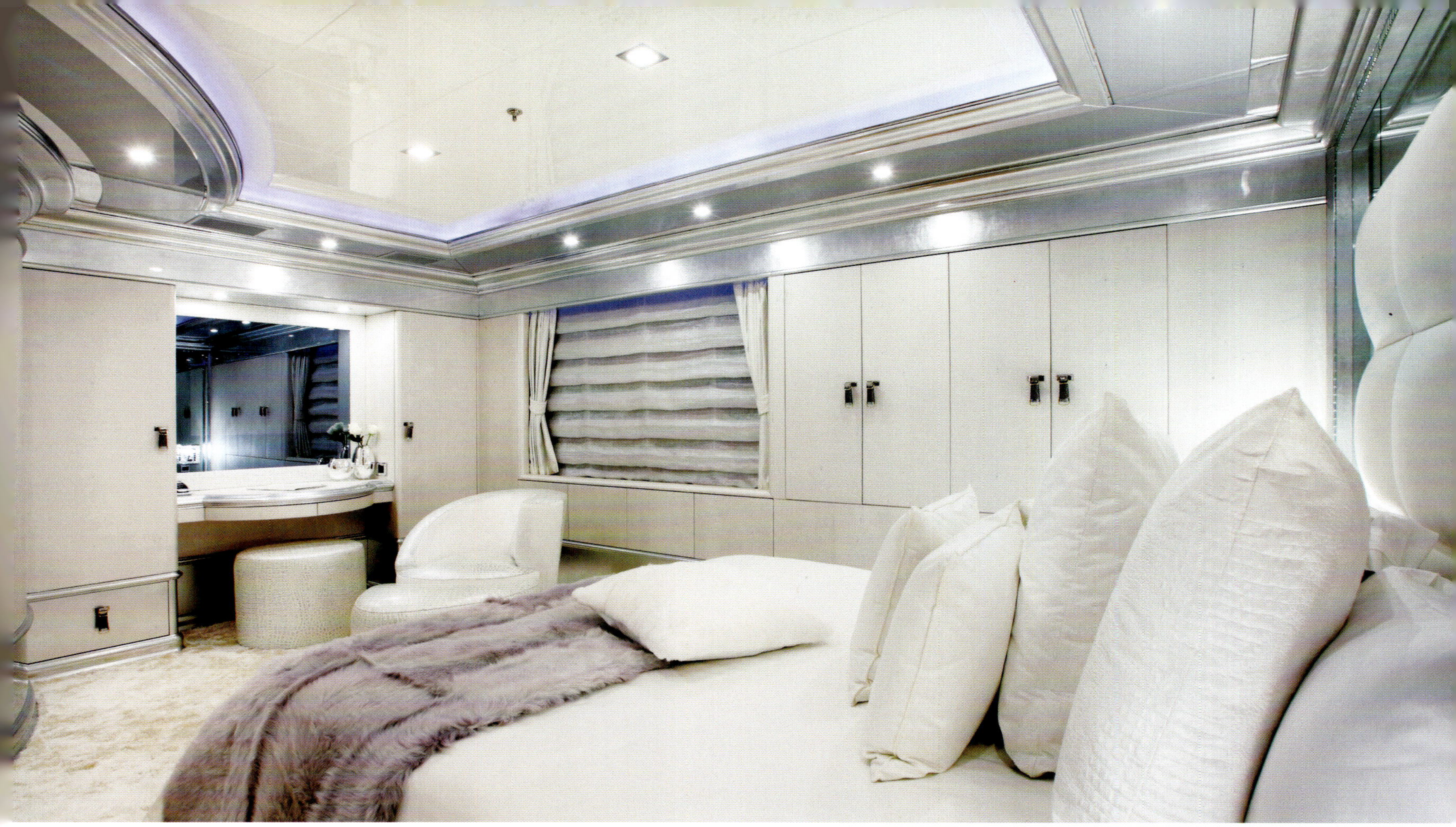

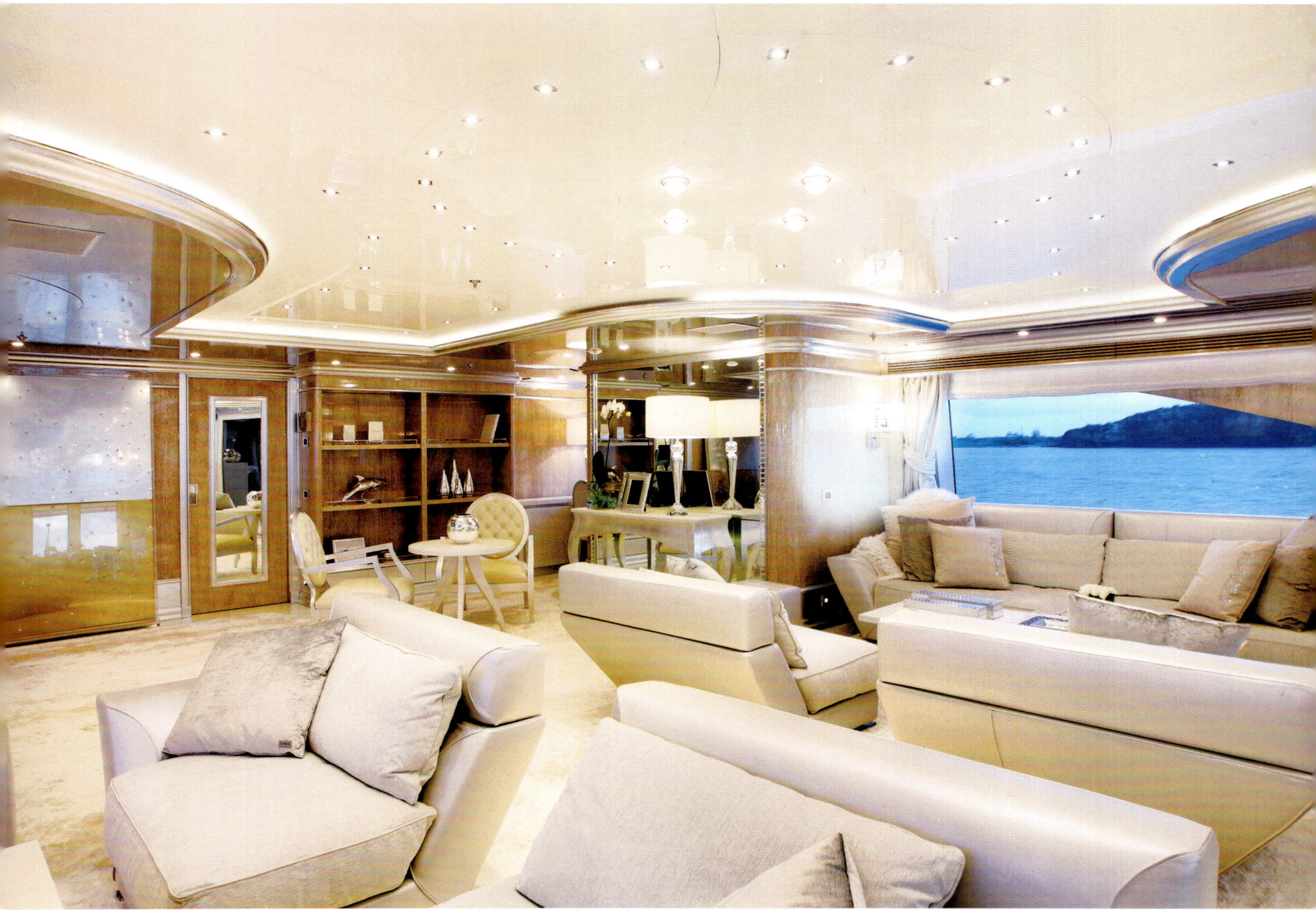

SAPPHIRE

> DESIGN	NEWCRUISE - Yacht Projects & Design
> SHIPYARD	Nobiskrug
> BEAM	12.5m
> MAX SPEED	17kn
> CRUISING SPEED	15kn

> Completed in time for the busy superyacht summer, comes the stunning new 73.5 m/ 242 ft SAPPHIRE delivered to her new owners in April of this year. A masterpiece that combines the talents of designers and naval architects Frank E. H. Neubelt and Roland Krueger with the interior architecture of Katharina Raczek, all from the German design – house NEWCRUISE.

A great deal of attention has been taken in the design of the exceptional outdoor illumination. SAPPHIRE excites with an exquisite and stunning "Night-Time Look" highlighting her lines and her furniture while she literally floats on a bed of light courtesy of her underwater array.

NEWCRUISE -follows their in-house design philosophy of well balanced inside-outside design themes which reflect a real masterpiece full of character in all aspects from the Interior to the Exterior and back.

The very carefully created arrangement plan offers a full-width owners apartment plus four amazing guest cabins, a beach club, an upper deck superior cabin, a sky lounge and a cinema.

Modernism inspired by Art Deco describes the interior styling which displays clean and pure lines underlined by very strong light and dark contrasts and very elaborate details refect in all aspects of the interior, furnishing and accessories. The muted schemes reflect the palette of clear and mellowed blue tones, which are a tribute to the name of the yacht.

Special attention was given to the development of her hull lines and naval architecture and the careful matching of equipment to give her a comfortable cruise speed of 15 knots and maximum speed of 17 knots powered by twin 2,360hp MTU diesel engines with a range of over 5,000 nautical miles. She is equipped with zero speed stabilisers and contains large tender garages on port and starboard.

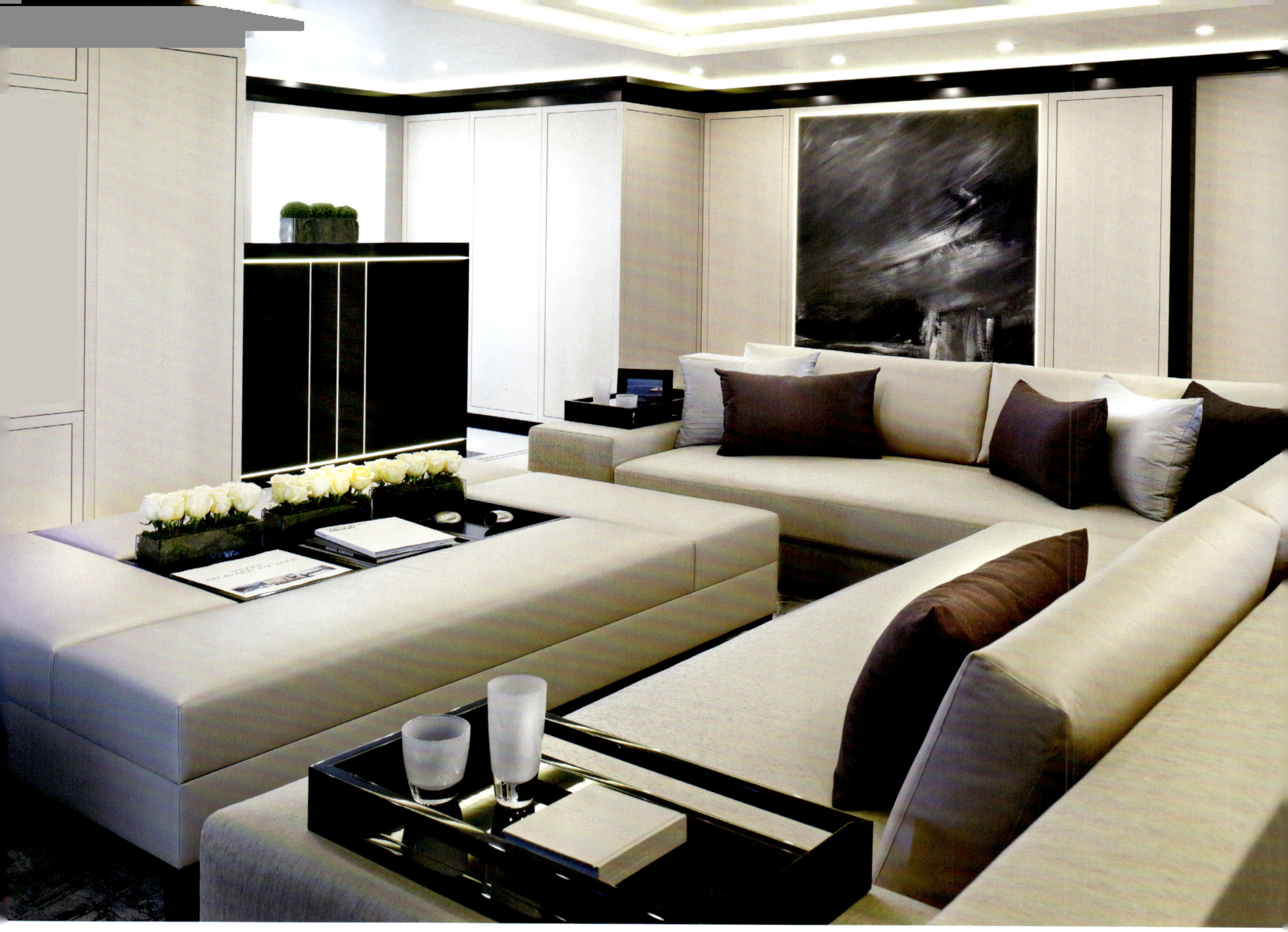

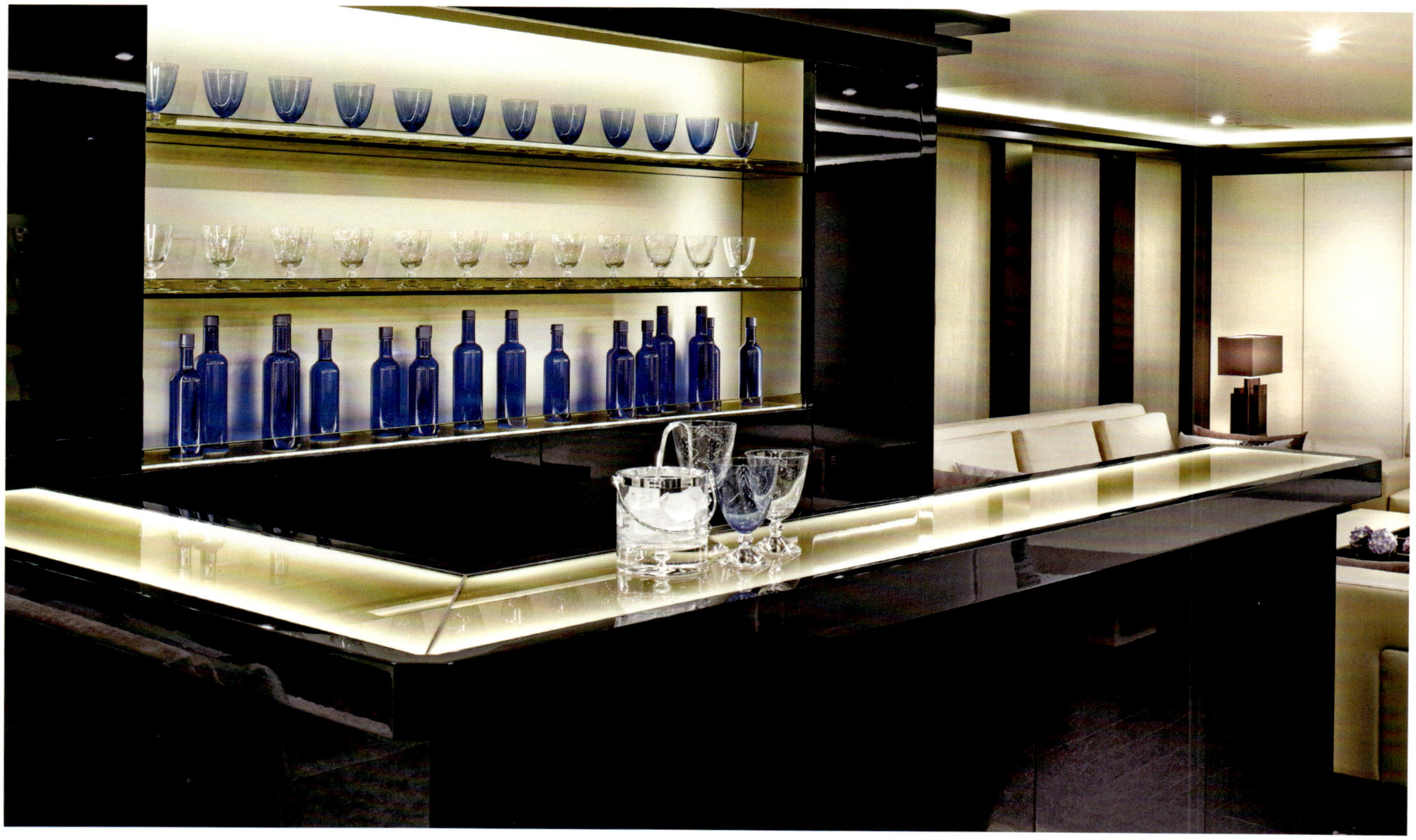

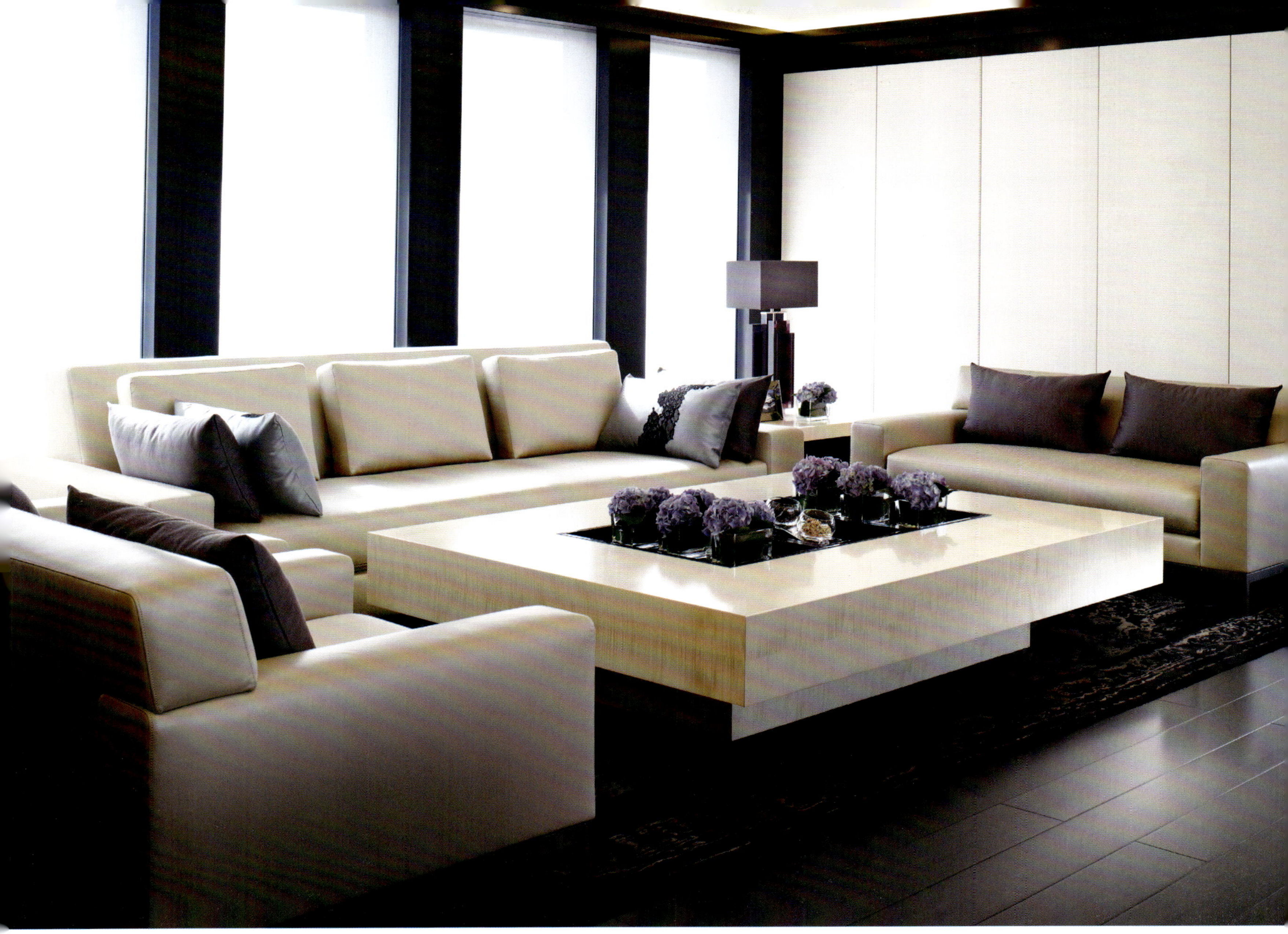

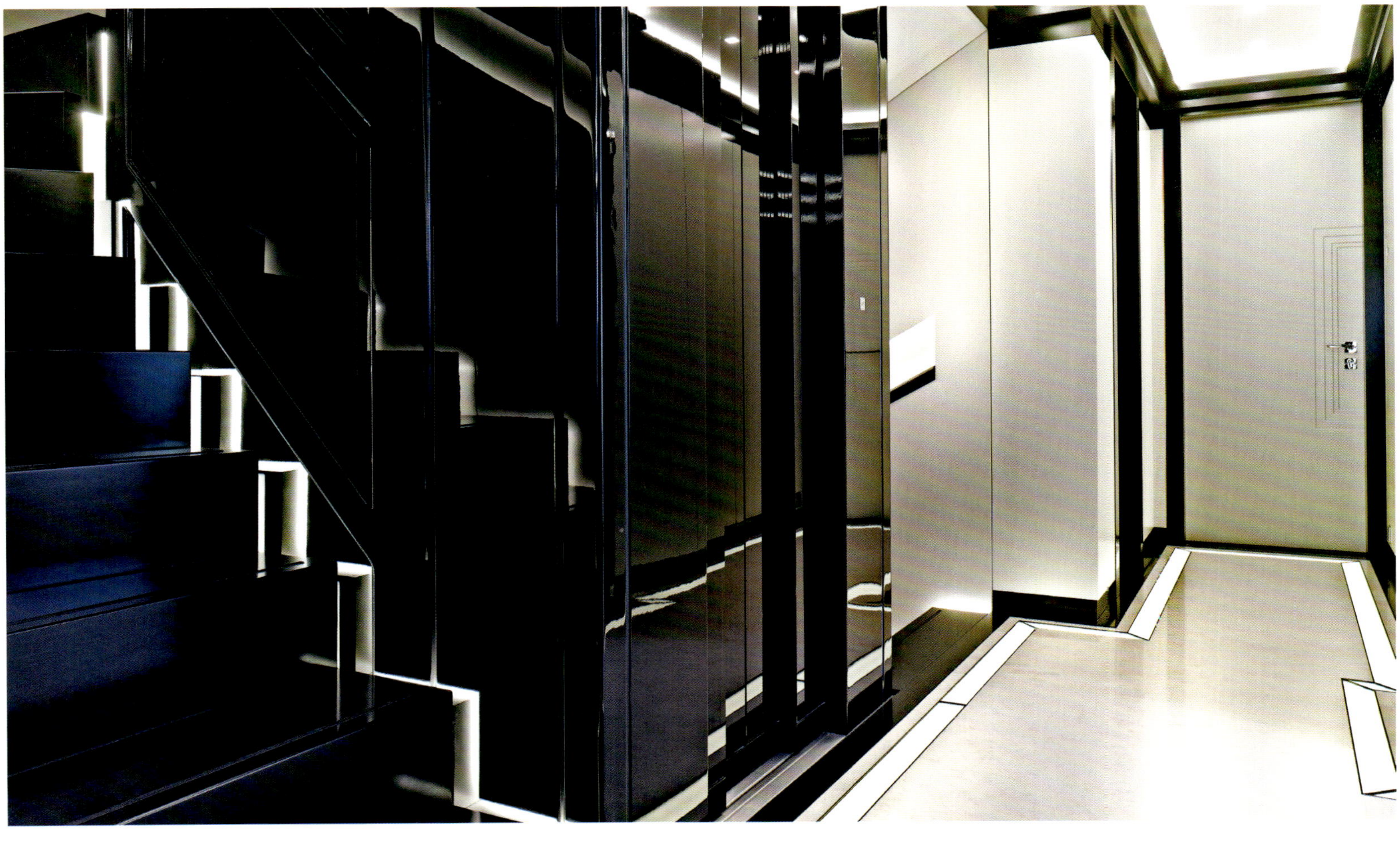

　　"蓝宝石"号游艇于今年四月交付使用，正好赶上了豪华游艇的需求旺季。它身长73.5米，这艘杰出的游艇融合了设计师和舰艇制造师弗莱克·E·H·纽贝和罗兰·克鲁格的才华，以及内部设计师凯瑟琳·莱扎克的通力合作。所有的设计全部来自德国"新航"建筑设计公司。

　　游艇非常重视室外照明的独创设计。它的夜景照明美轮美奂，烘托了游艇的线条和家具美感，而游艇水下的镶嵌式排灯更让"蓝宝石"释放出"船在灯上游"的意境。

　　"新航"设计公司秉承了自己一贯的设计理念——室内外设计和谐相融的主题，这艘杰出游艇从内部到外观，从前到后都体现了自己独特的风格。

　　精心设计的布局为我们展现了一个宽敞明亮的船主公寓，四个精美绝伦的客房，一个水景房，一个上层甲板高级舱，一个露天大厅和一个电影院。

　　受装饰派艺术的启发，现代风成为内部设计的主题，明与暗的对比，展现了整洁而又纯粹的线条；所有的内部设计、家具和装饰都体现了细节上的精致入微。蓝色主调的使用，体现出一种清澈柔美的宁静，也与游艇的名字"蓝宝石"交相呼应。

　　游艇设计还特别关注了船体线条和舰艇制造的技术革新以及游艇设备的精心装配，以确保游艇能以15海里/小时的速度稳定行驶。在两个2360马力的MTU柴油机驱动下，最高时速可达17海里/小时，可航行5000多海里，游艇仍能保持稳定。游艇的左舷和右舷都安装了零速稳定器和大型的防滑车库。

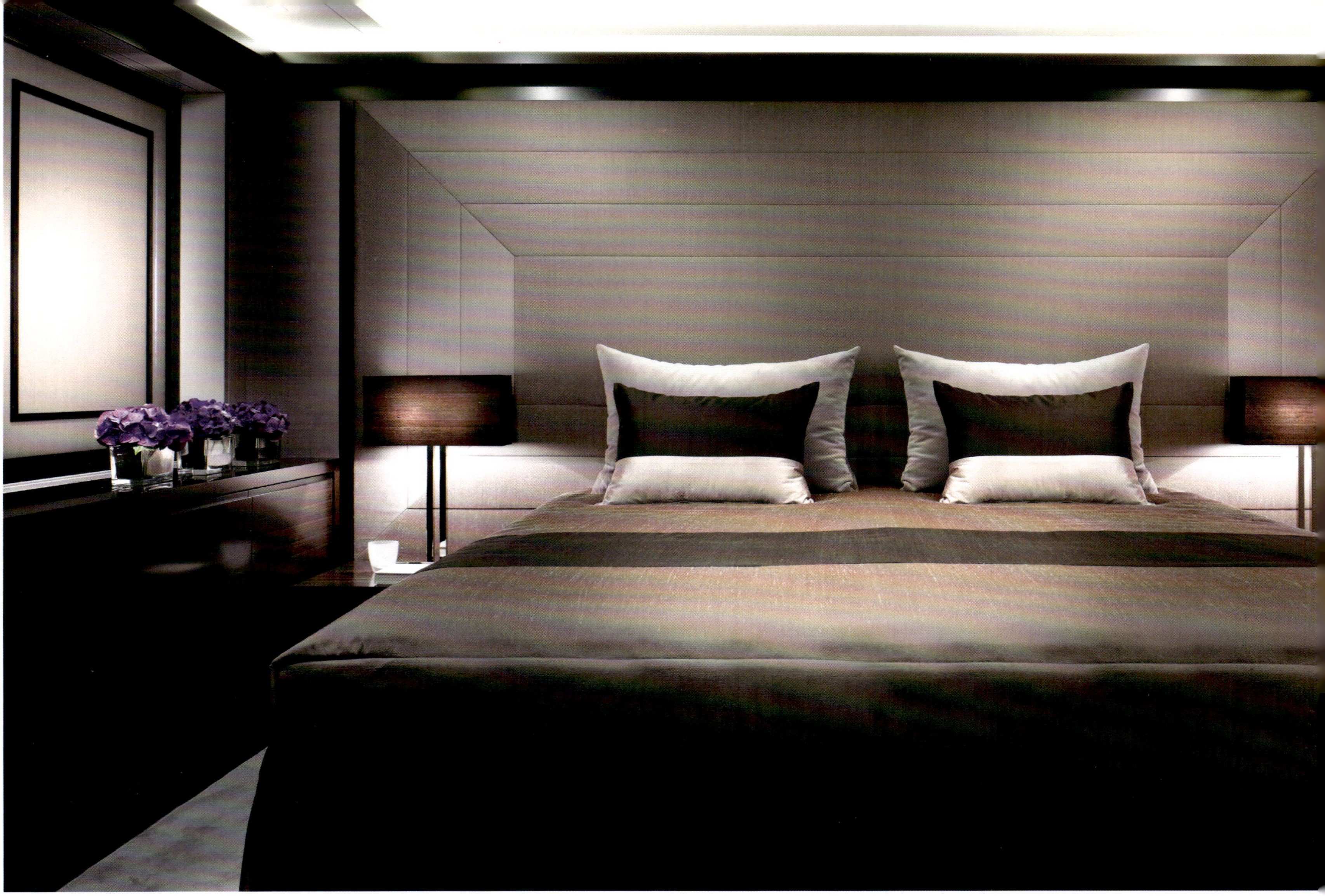

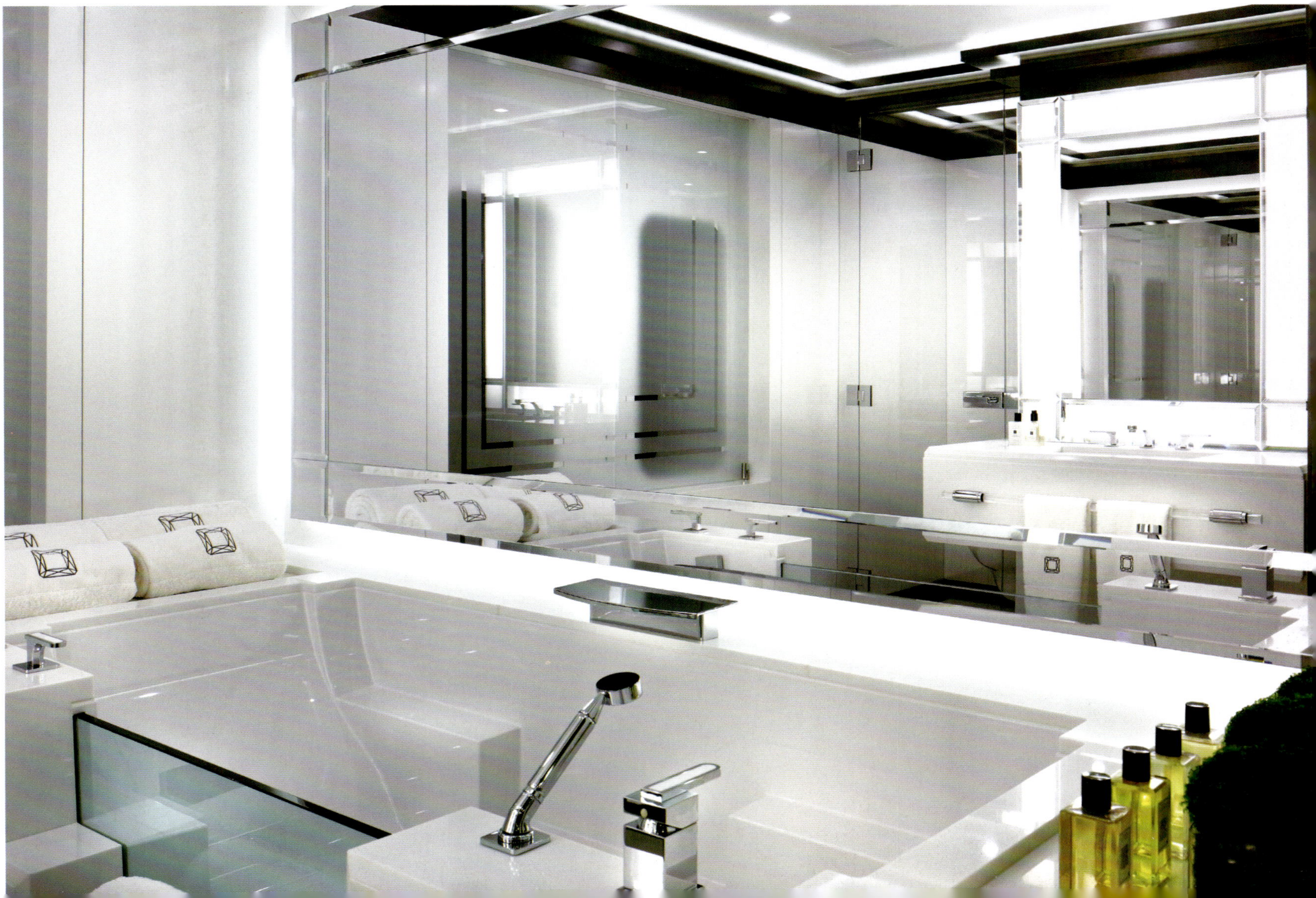

AB 140

> DESIGN	AB Yachts – Fipa Group
> LENGTH	42m
> BEAM	8m
> MAX SPEED	46kn
> CRUISING SPEED	43kn
> ENGINES	3 x MTU 16V2000 M93
> WATERJETS	MJP650 CSU + 1xMJP 650

> The new AB 140 was entirely built in Massa. The interior design is elaborate and luxurious, without any compromises with regards to comfort aboard. The black and gold colors are dominant and combined with rare and very special materials indicate a deep style and design research which makes this vessel truly unique. This is also evident in the interior paneling where canaletto walnut and the olive wood create a relaxing and soothing environment. The entertainment aboard is guaranteed by the most advanced equipment the market can offer today which puts out a total of 30,000 watts and transforms this AB 140 into a true open-air nightclub on water. The same attention went into the design and installation of navigation offer the very attention of navigation systems which are "state of the art" and offer the very best in terms of safety even in adverse weather conditions.

AB 140 is the outcome of an ingenious hydrodynamic and technological study whose aim was to obtain extraordinary performances with modest power, yet ensuring an excellent comfort of navigation also in rough seas. It reaches 46 knots of max speed and 43 knots of cruising speed thanks to the three engines of 2600hp coupled with 3 waterjet, which give extraordinary results.

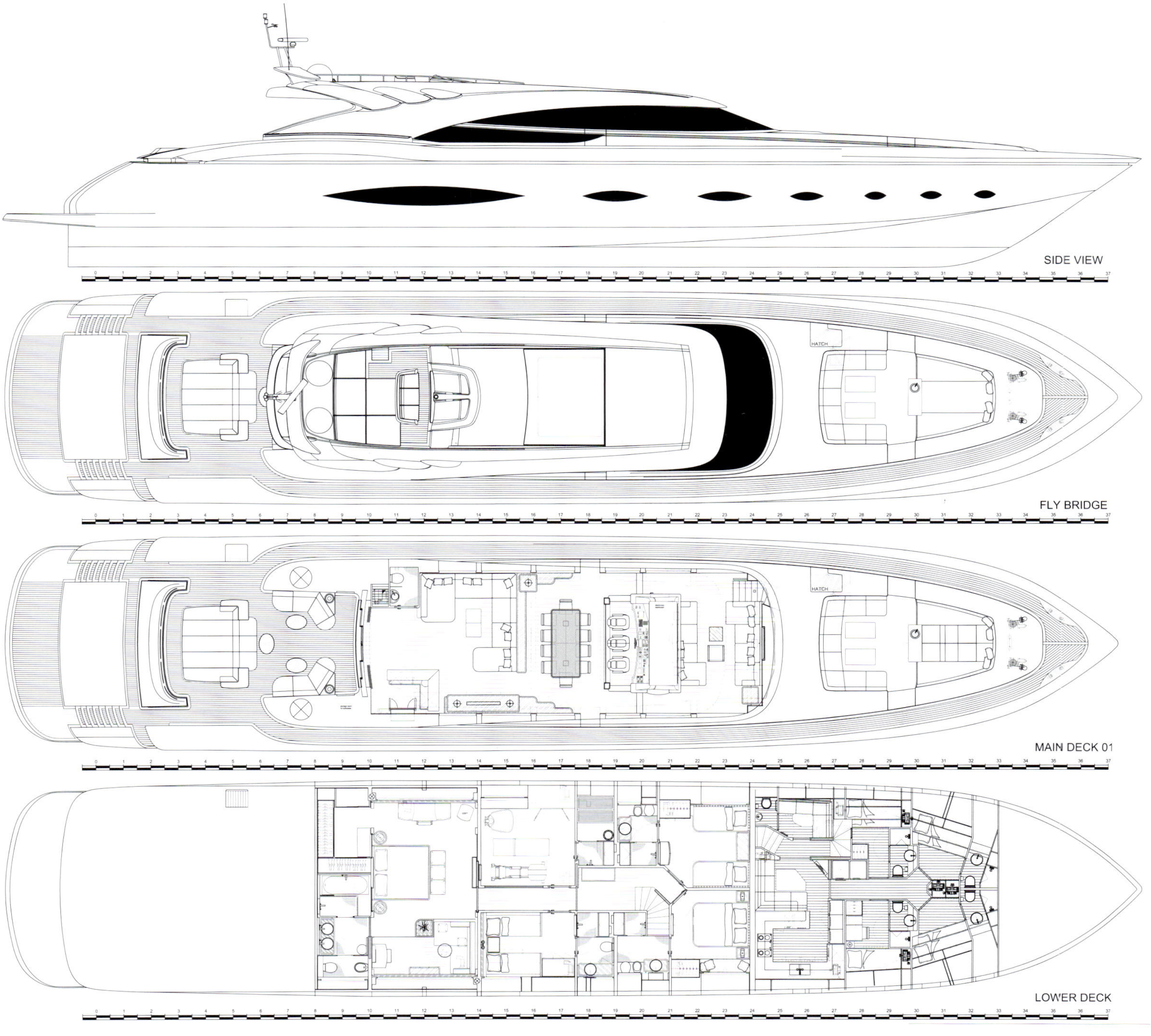

SIDE VIEW

FLY BRIDGE

MAIN DECK 01

LOWER DECK

HATCH

HATCH

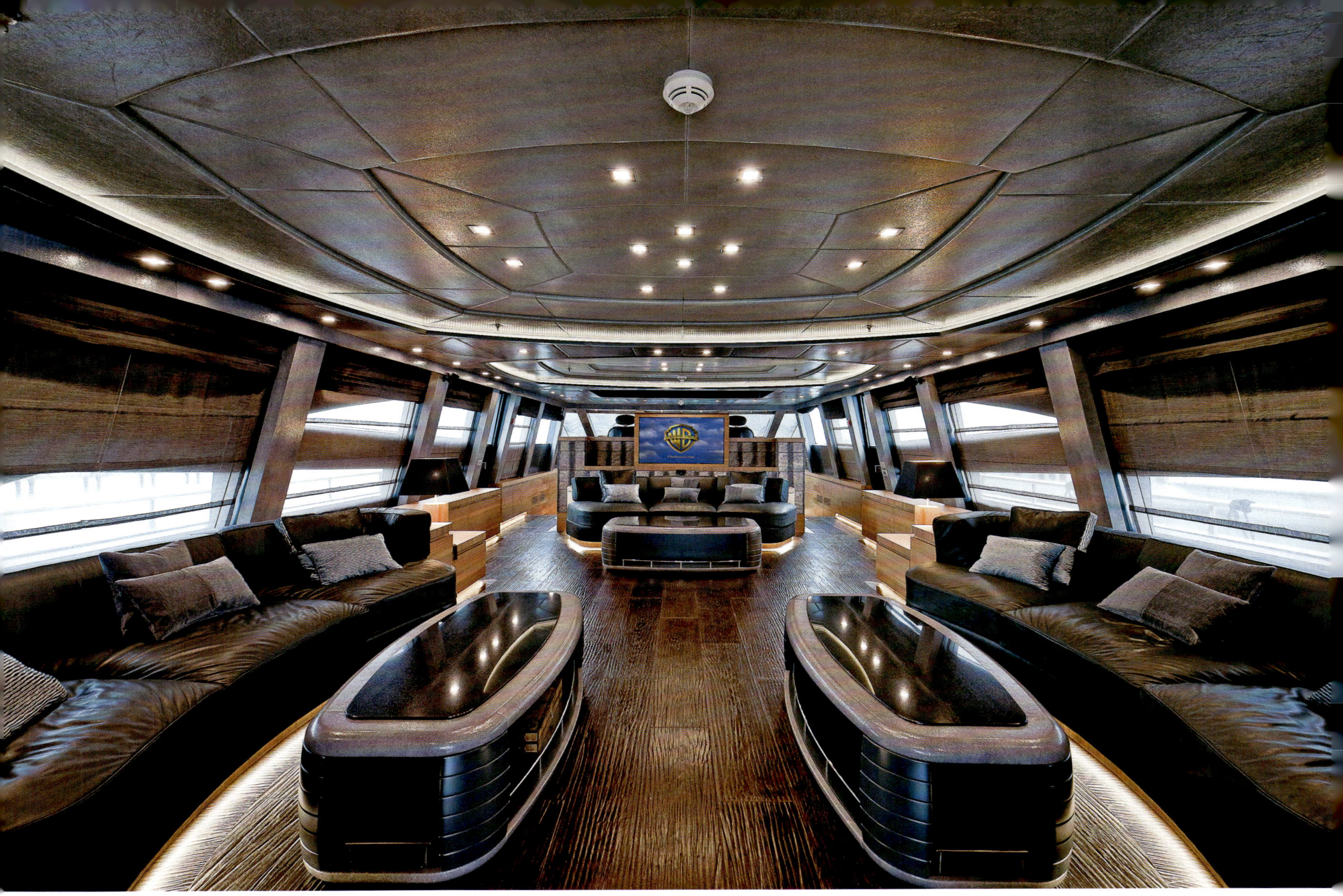

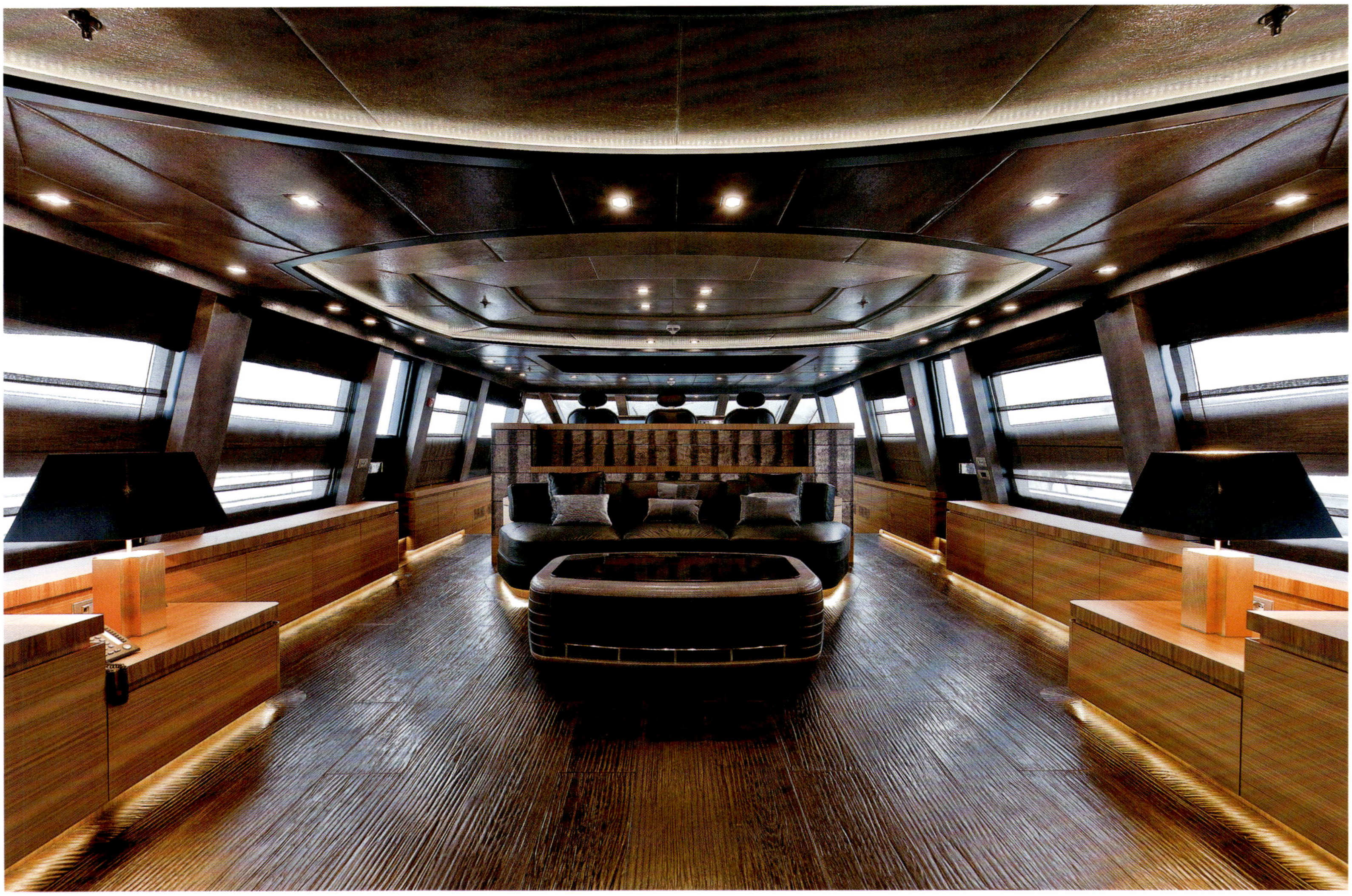

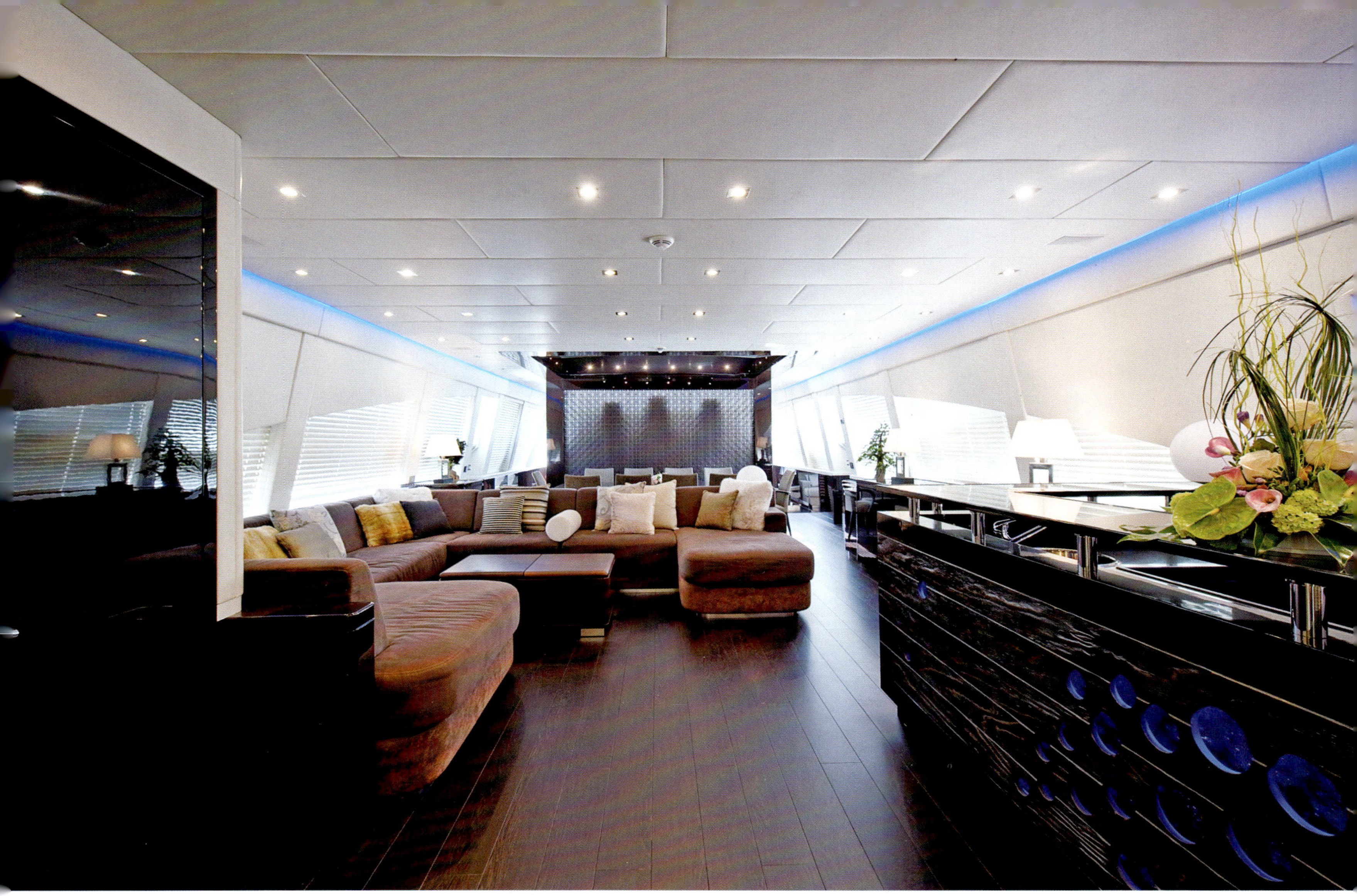

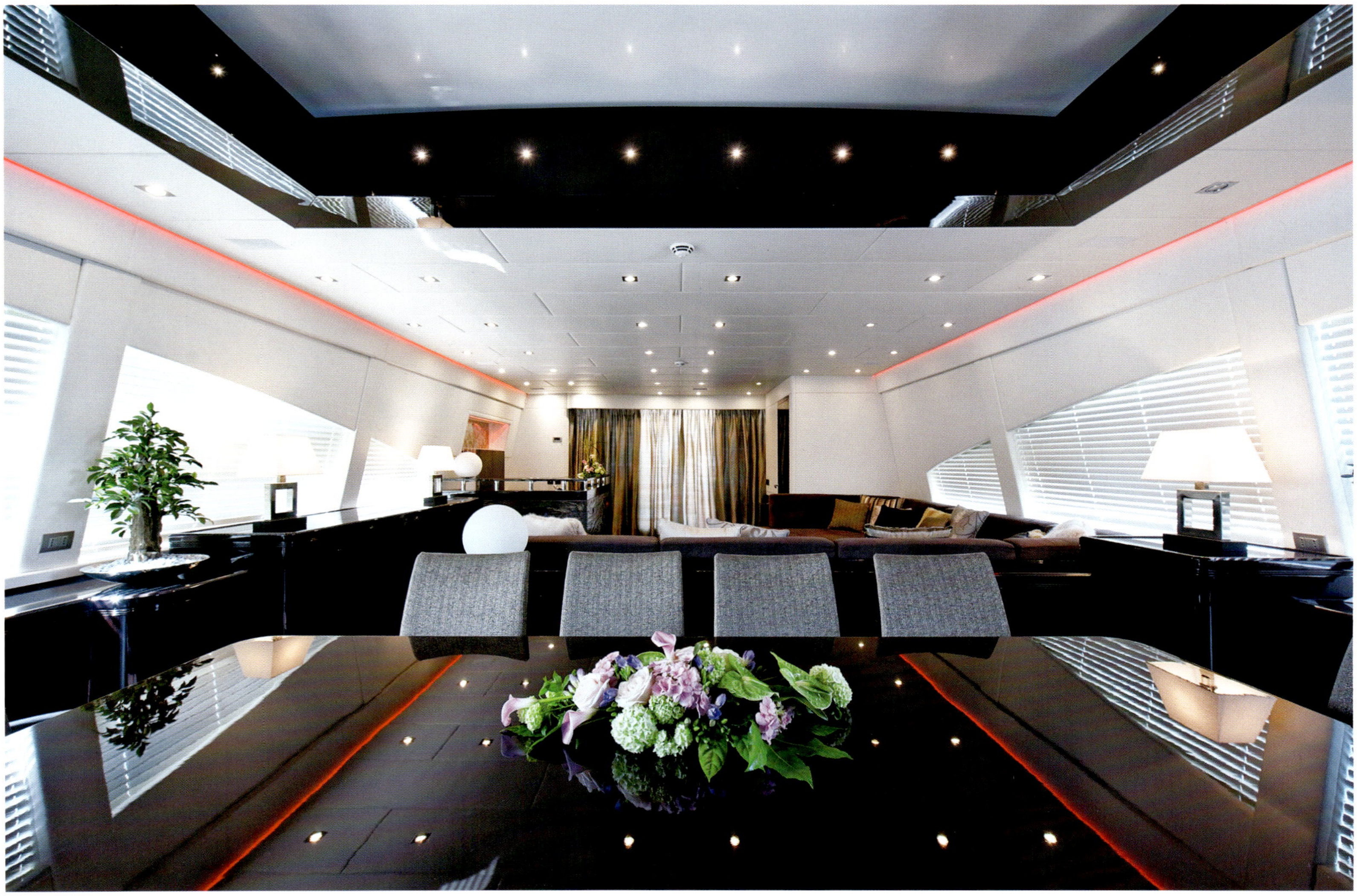

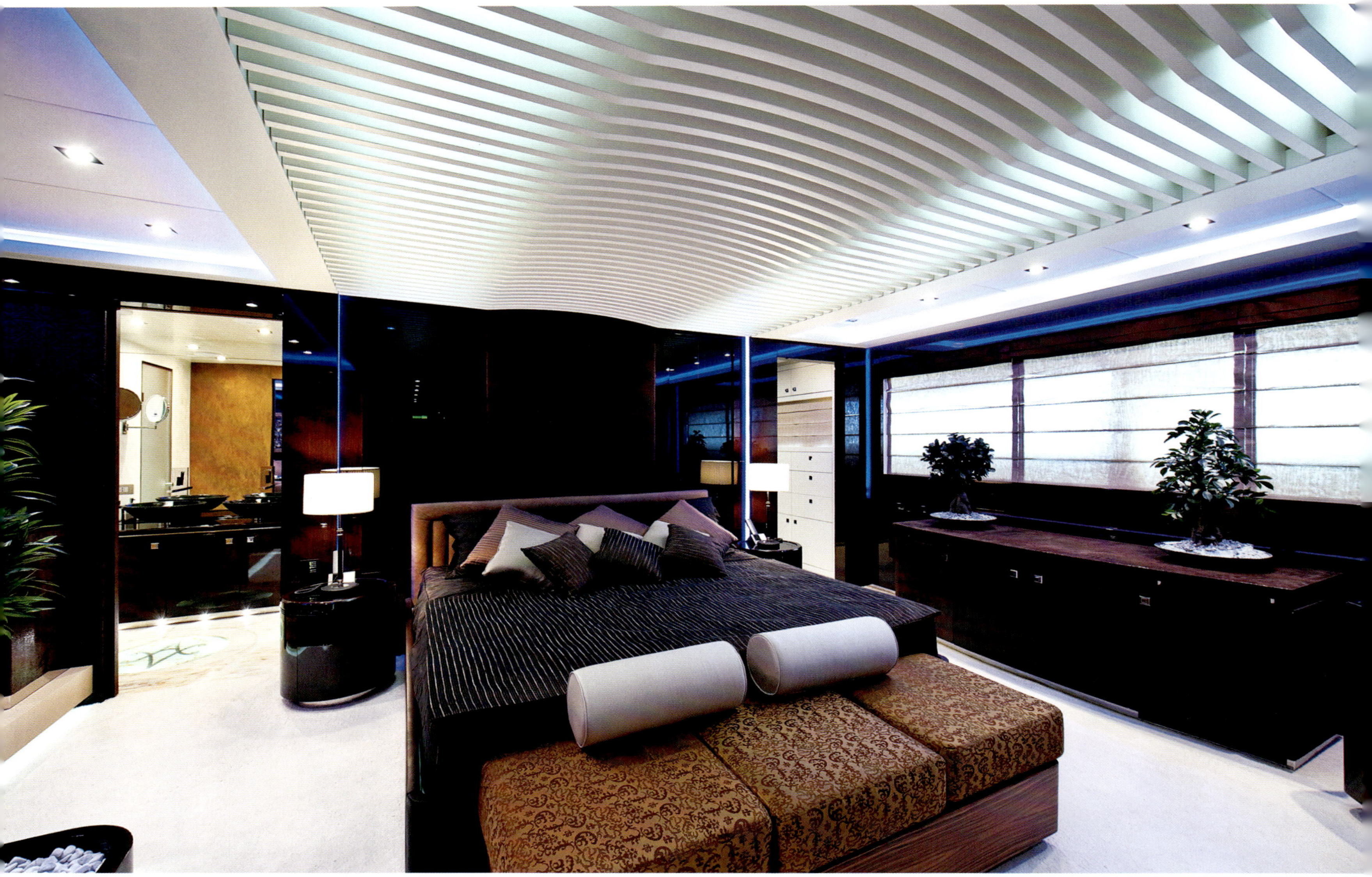

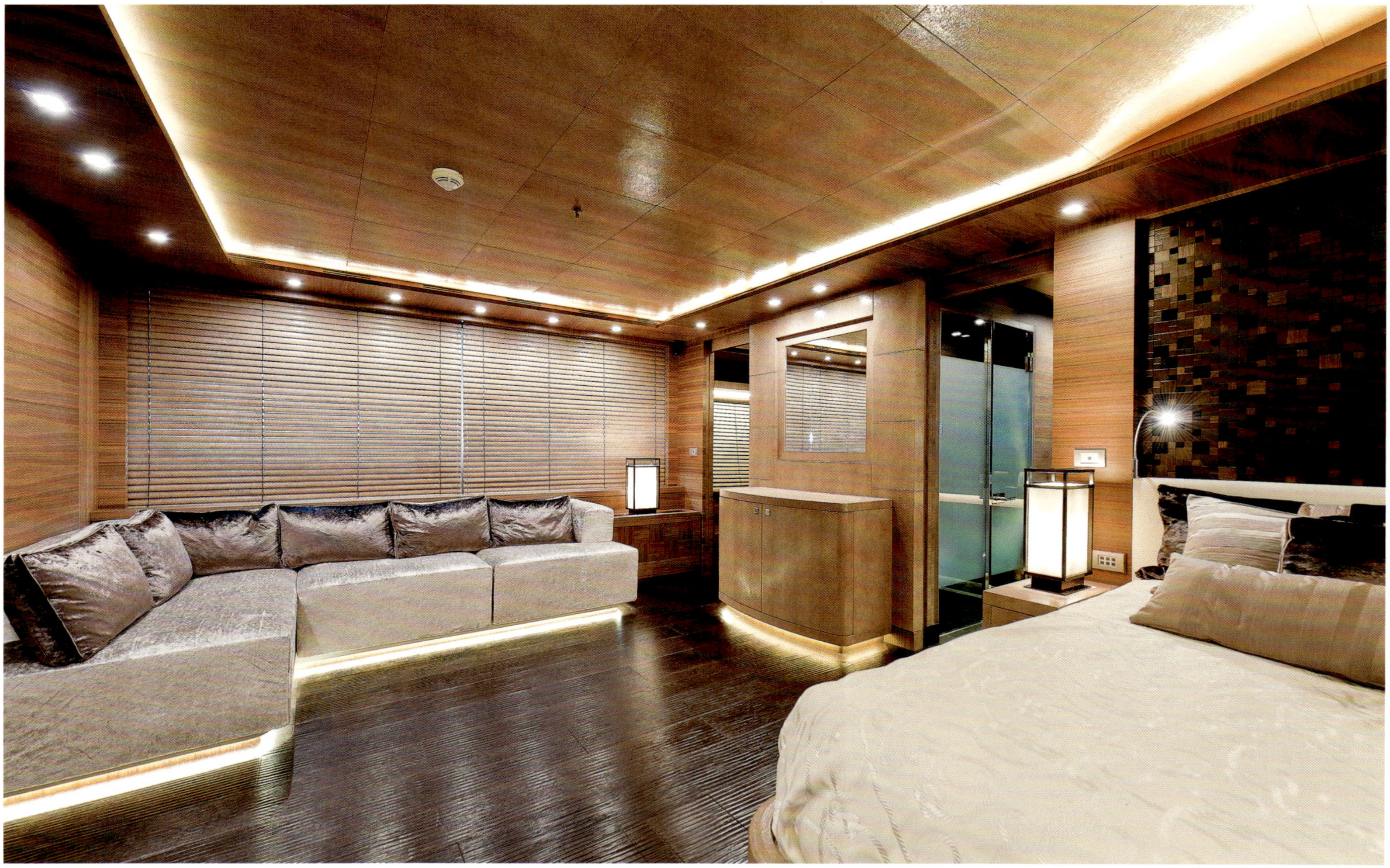

　　新型的游艇AB 140全部在意大利马萨市建造。内部设计精致豪华，丝毫没有降低游艇的舒适程度。游艇主要采用黑色和金色，并结合使用了一些特别的罕见的材料，体现出一种厚重感，让这艘游艇真正与众不同。这一点在内部的嵌板工艺上也体现得非常明显：卡纳莱托胡桃木与橄榄木的使用，创造出一种轻松、宁静的氛围。游艇上的娱乐设施采用了当今市场上最先进的设备，总耗电量30000瓦，让这艘AB 140游艇成为一个真正的水上露天夜总会。同样值得关注的是，游艇上的导航系统的设计和安装也完全是顶尖级的，在安全方面最有保障，特别是在不利的天气状况下。

　　游艇AB 140采用了最先进的水动力技术研究成果，致力于用最少的动力打造出最出色的游艇，同时确保游艇在波涛汹涌的大海上航行时的舒适感。游艇的最高时速达到46海里/小时，巡航航速达到43海里/小时。这一切都要归功于三个2600马力的发动机引擎和三个喷水式推进器，它们合力创造出非凡的效果。

32M SAILING YACHT AKALAM

> **INTERIOR**   Barracuda Yacht Design, Javier Munoz
> **NAVAL ARCHITECT**   Iñigo Toledo, Barracuda Yacht Design
> **SHIPYARD**   Pendennis Shipyard
> **LENGTH**   32m
> **BEAM**   7.6m
> **CRUISING SPEED**   13.5kn
> **PHOTOGRAPHER**   Lloyd Images

32m sailing yacht which has been designed to maximize outdoors living and create a "home from home" feeling. This unique design makes best use of natural lighting as a result of 24x large, panoramic windows set within the hull.

The owner wanted an interior that was fairly simple and easy to live with and not "over-decorated" with too much ornate detail. The intention was to create an "apartment-style" look and feel, in fact, completely unlike something that you would normally expect to find on a fairly traditional looking hull design such as this.

The final look is sharp, sophisticated and very contemporary and incorporates a typically Spanish architectural feel by showing a dramatic contrast between light Sycamore woods interspersed with dark tinted Zebrano.

The twin shower-rooms are also very contemporary and use marble sinks, decorated wall tiles and plenty of shiny stainless steel and chrome fittings to great effect, once again, the effect of the large windows in the shower-rooms is amazing.

The emphasis on the layout was for a large pilothouse area with large open doors to the aft-deck, so that the owner could wander in and spread out in comfort with friends and family around the large TV screen, or listen to some music from the sophisticated sound system. Very similar, in fact, as if it were an apartment building on dry land.

The accommodation deck is dominated by an extremely large owner's cabin, which is much larger than you would normally expect to find on a yacht of 32m. This has meant that the two twin berth guest cabins are perfectly adequate in size, but they are not what you could call large. Same applies to the captain and crew areas, which are adequate but not overly spacious.

41
40
39
38
37
36
35
34
33
32
31
30
29
28
27
26
25
24
23
22
21
20
19
18
17
16
15
14
13
12
11
10
9
8
7
6
5
4
3
2
1
0

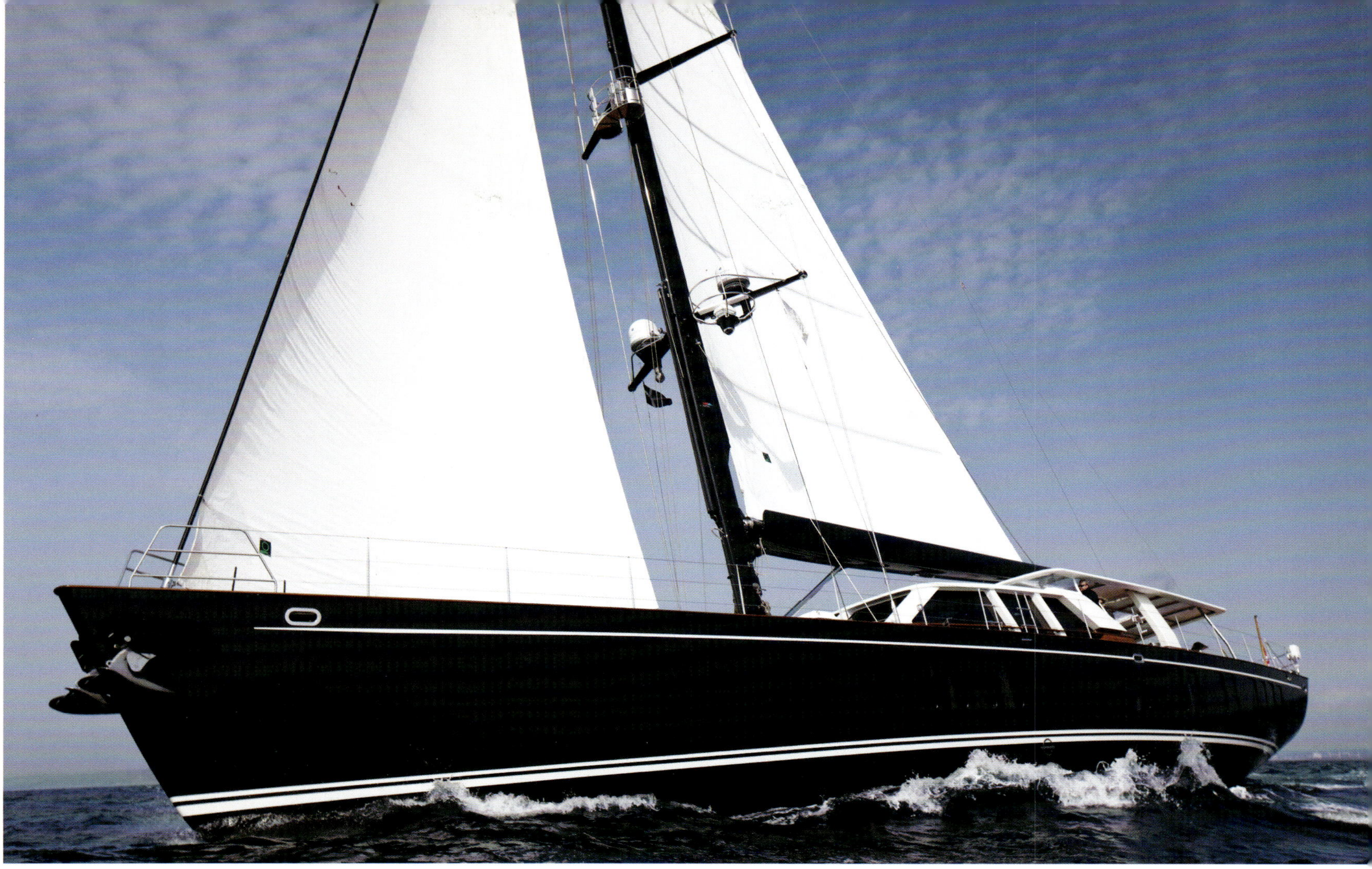

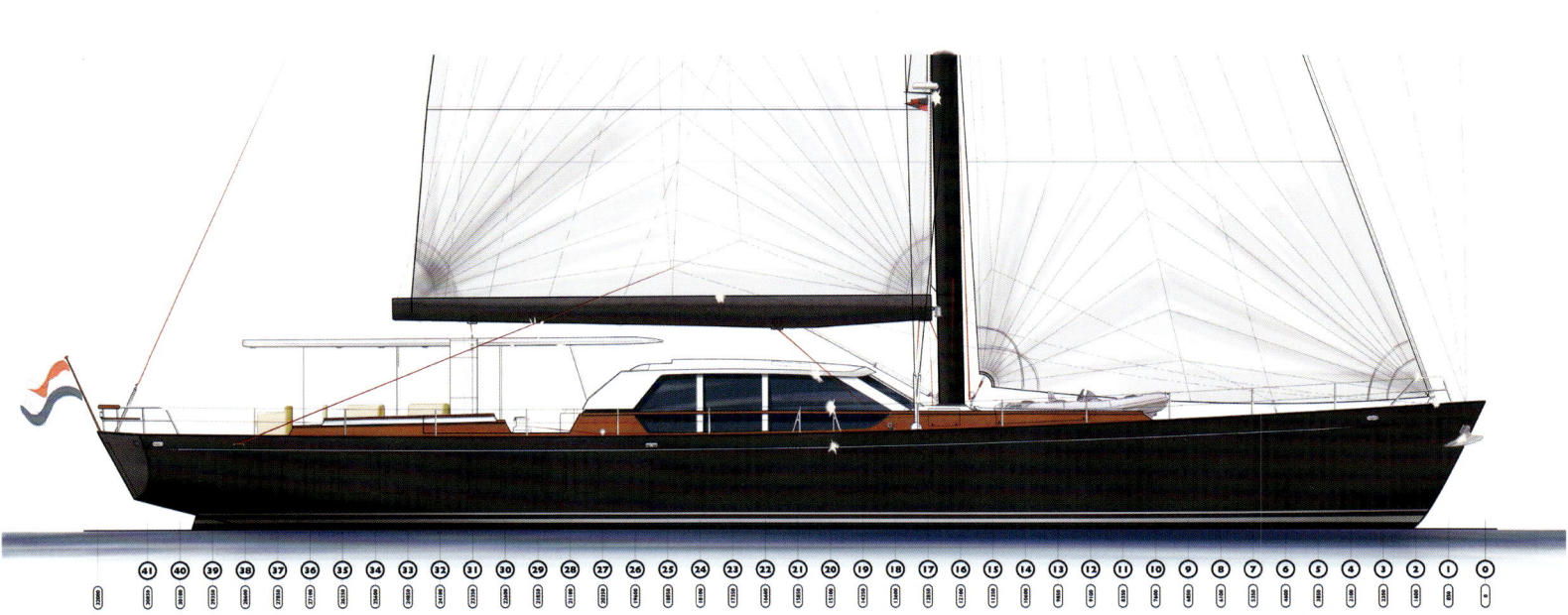

V1
D1
D1
V1
SOFT SIDE
MAST COMPRESSION
CONTINOUS DECK ACCROSS
SOFT SIDE
DWL
RIGID HULL BOTTOM

GENERAL ALARM

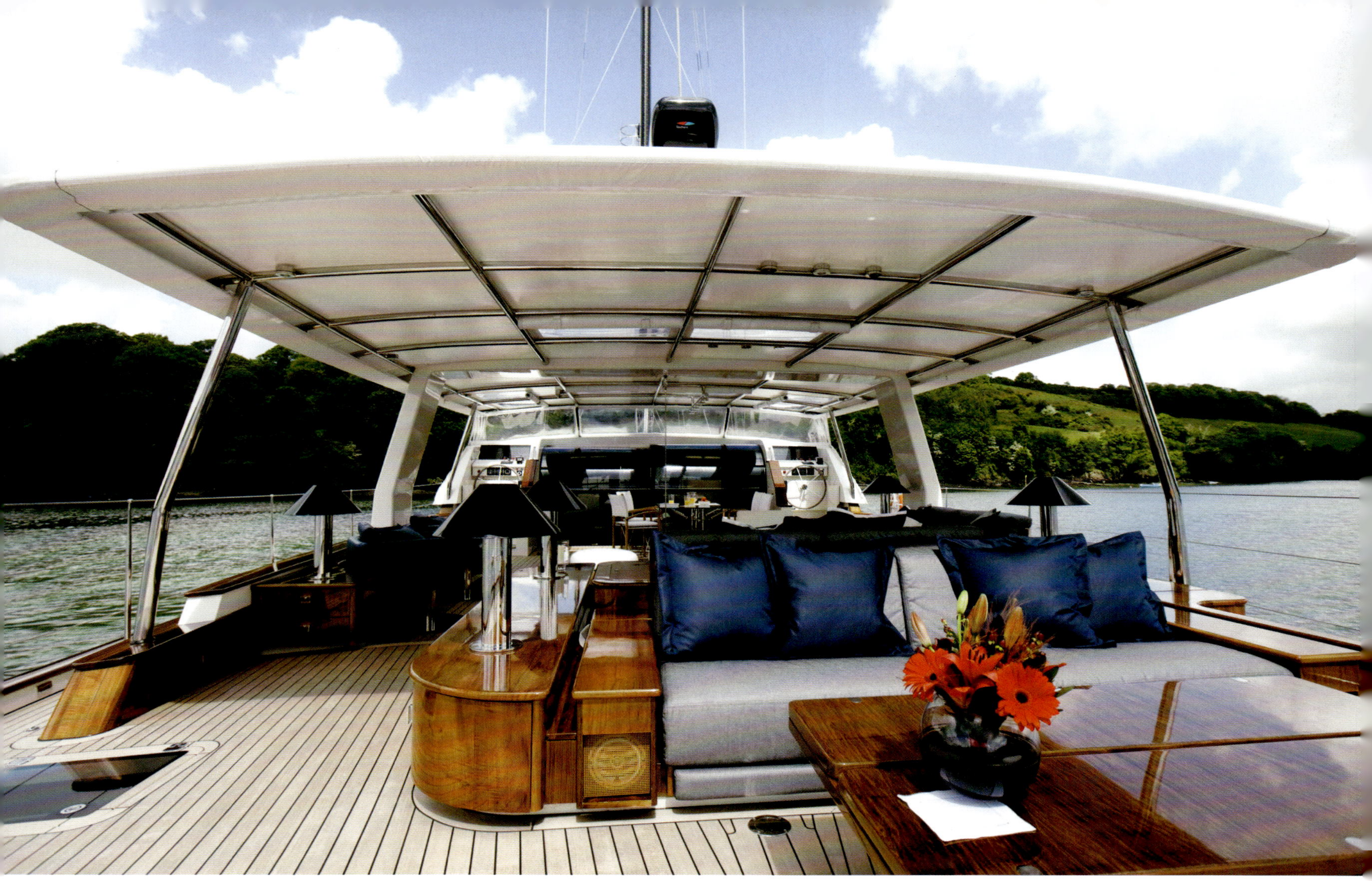

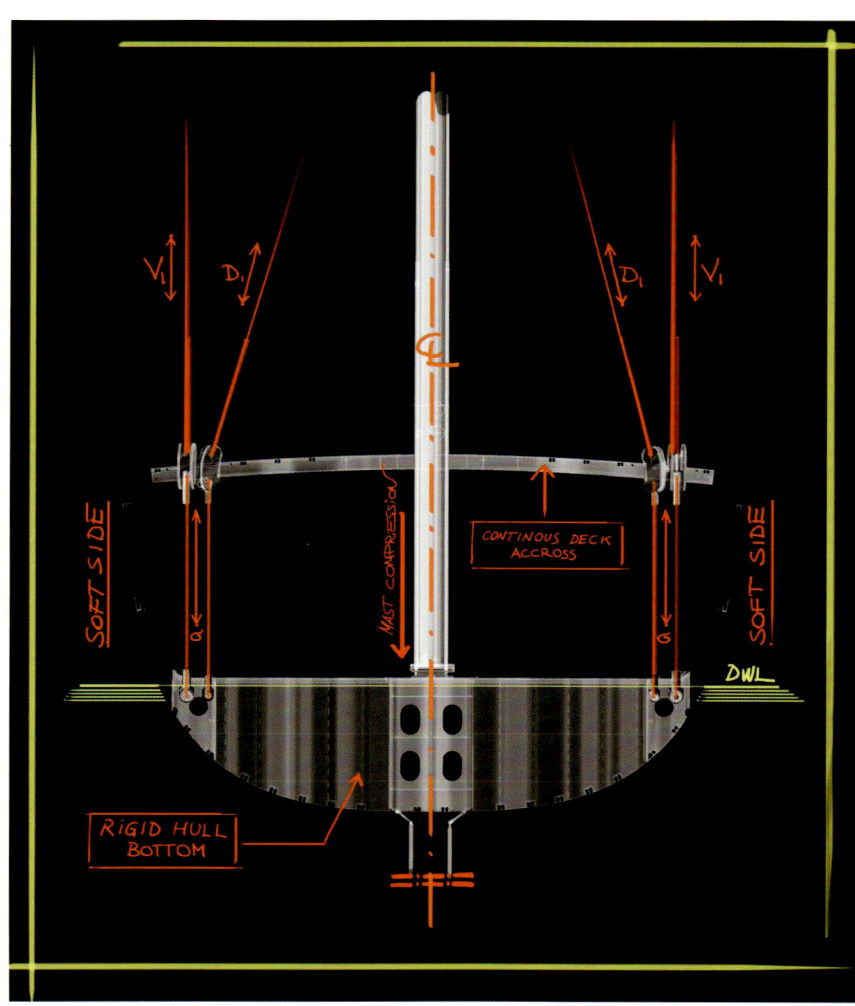

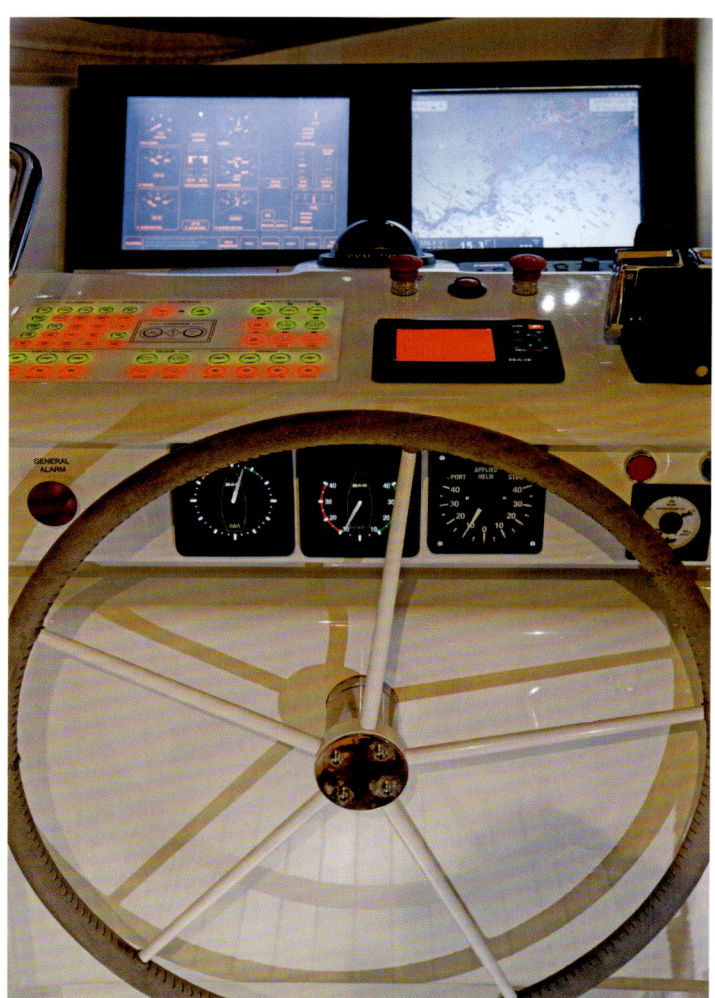

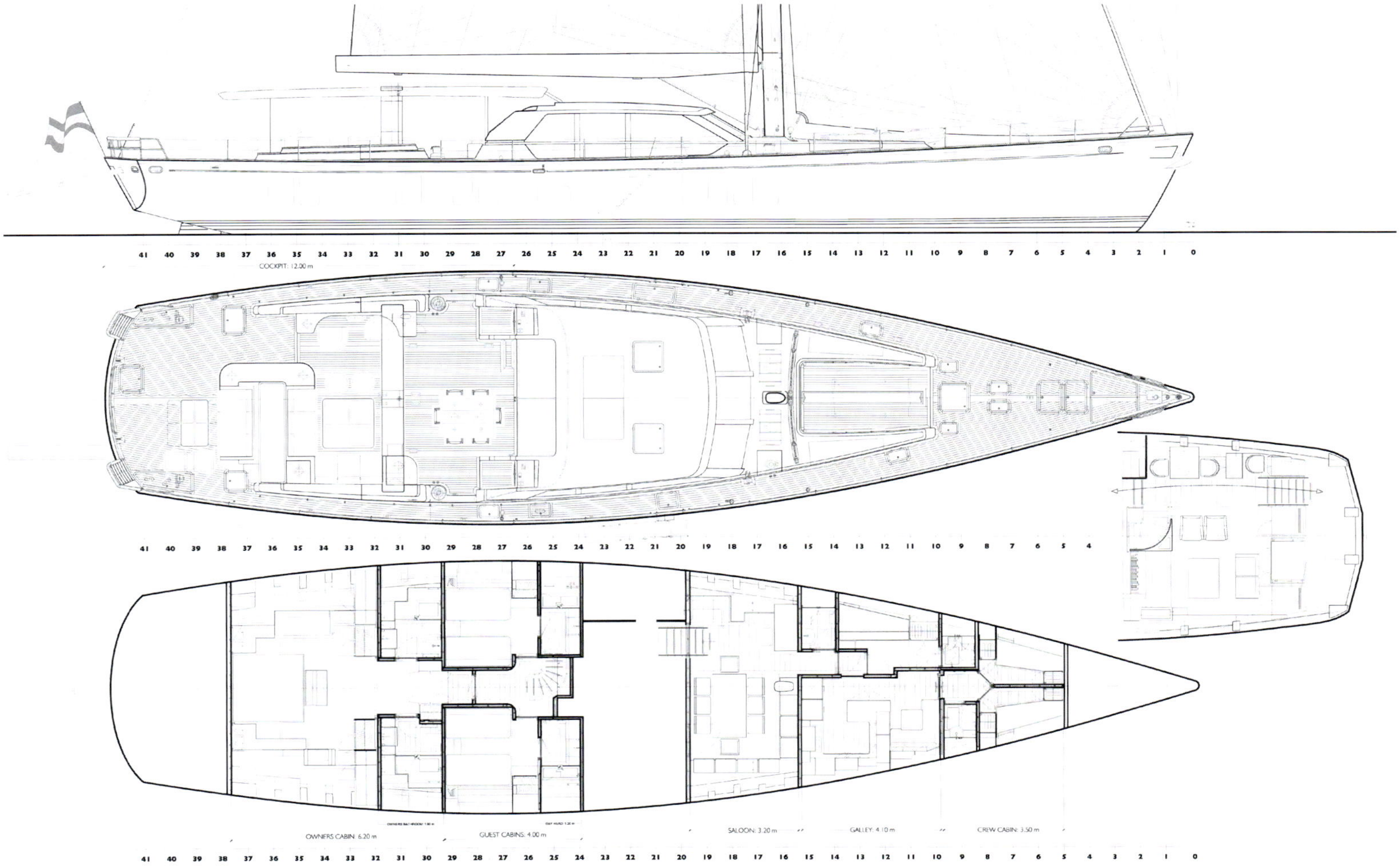

COCKPIT: 12.00 m
OWNERS CABIN: 6.20 m
GUEST CABINS: 4.00 m
SALOON: 3.20 m
GALLEY: 4.10 m
CREW CABIN: 3.50 m

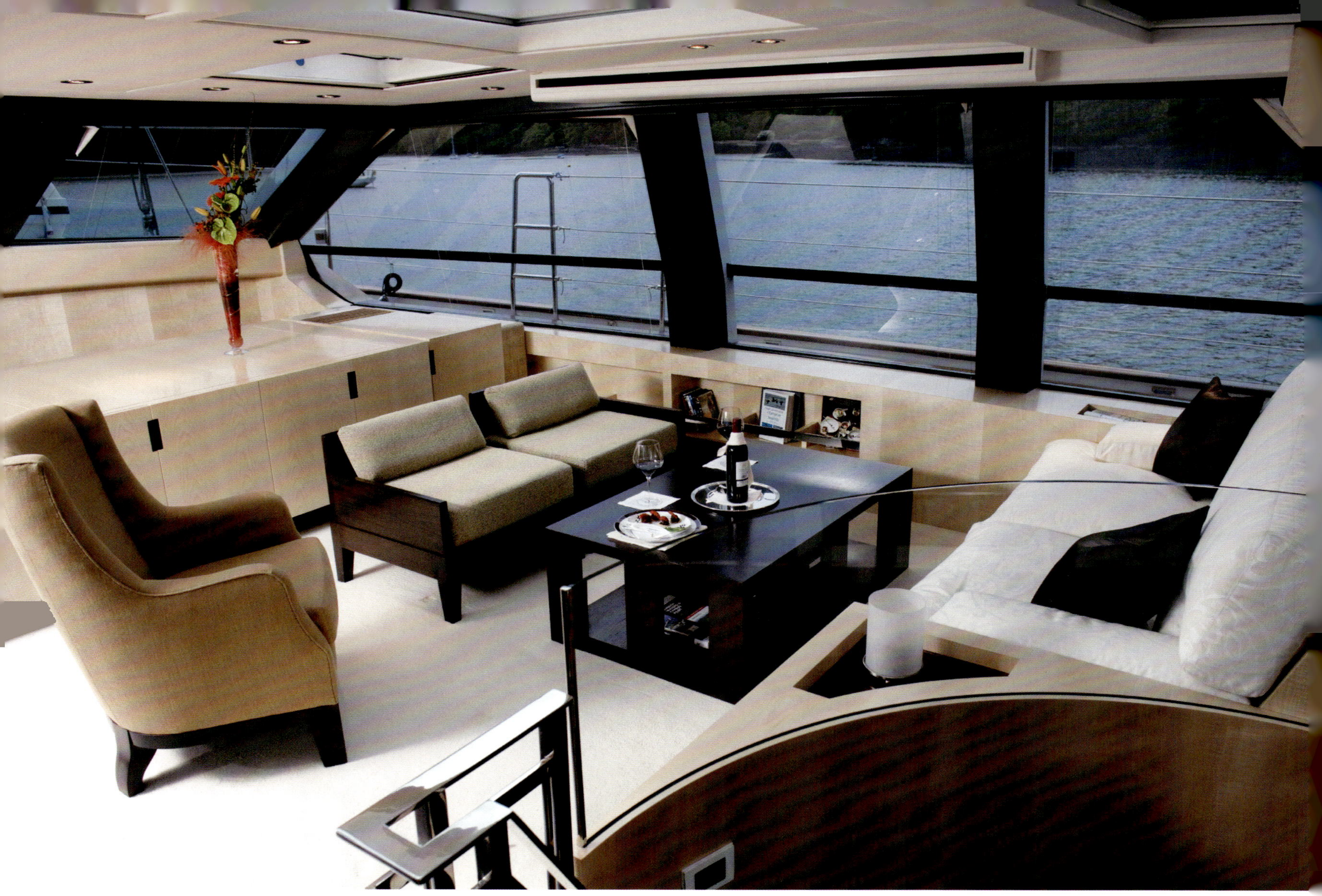

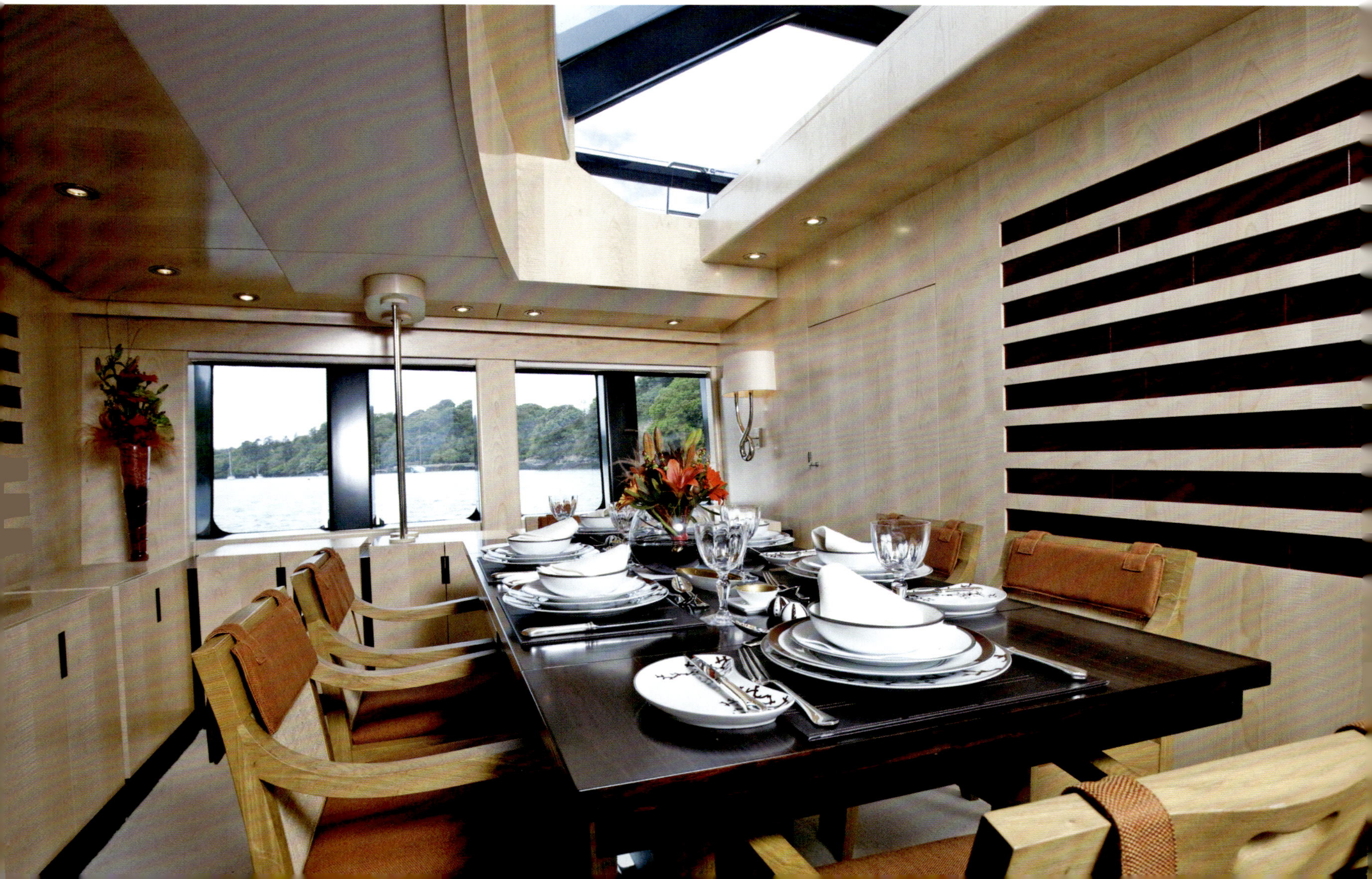

　　这款 32 米长的帆船游艇设计目的是为了提升室外生活质量，创造一种"从家到家"的感觉。采用独特的 24 x 全景式舷窗设计，充分利用了自然采光。

　　游艇的主人要求内部设计简单舒适，不追求过分奢华的装饰。目的在于创造一种"公寓式"外观与风格，事实上，这与常见的船体设计完全不同。

　　最后的外观轮廓清晰、高雅时尚、充满现代感，它融合了典型的西班牙建筑风格。外观使用了鲜艳的西克莫木材，与点缀其间的黑色斑马木形成了鲜明的对比。

　　两个浴室也极具当代风格，使用大理石水池、墙砖和大量的反光不锈钢与铬钢装饰，效果极佳。并且，浴室中的大窗设计独具匠心。

　　设计突出强调了操舵室与尾部甲板间宽敞的通道，以便于船主可以与朋友、亲人舒适地进出其间，欣赏巨大的电视屏幕，或者聆听高保真音响系统传出的音乐。这实际上和一个陆地上的公寓非常相似，几乎一模一样。

　　起居甲板上有一个供船主使用的船舱，其空间之大，远远超过了平常所见的 32 米游艇上的面积。这也意味着，两个休息用的客舱空间宽敞，但不是通常意义上的"大空间"。船长室与船员舱也是如此，足够宽敞，但并不显得空荡。

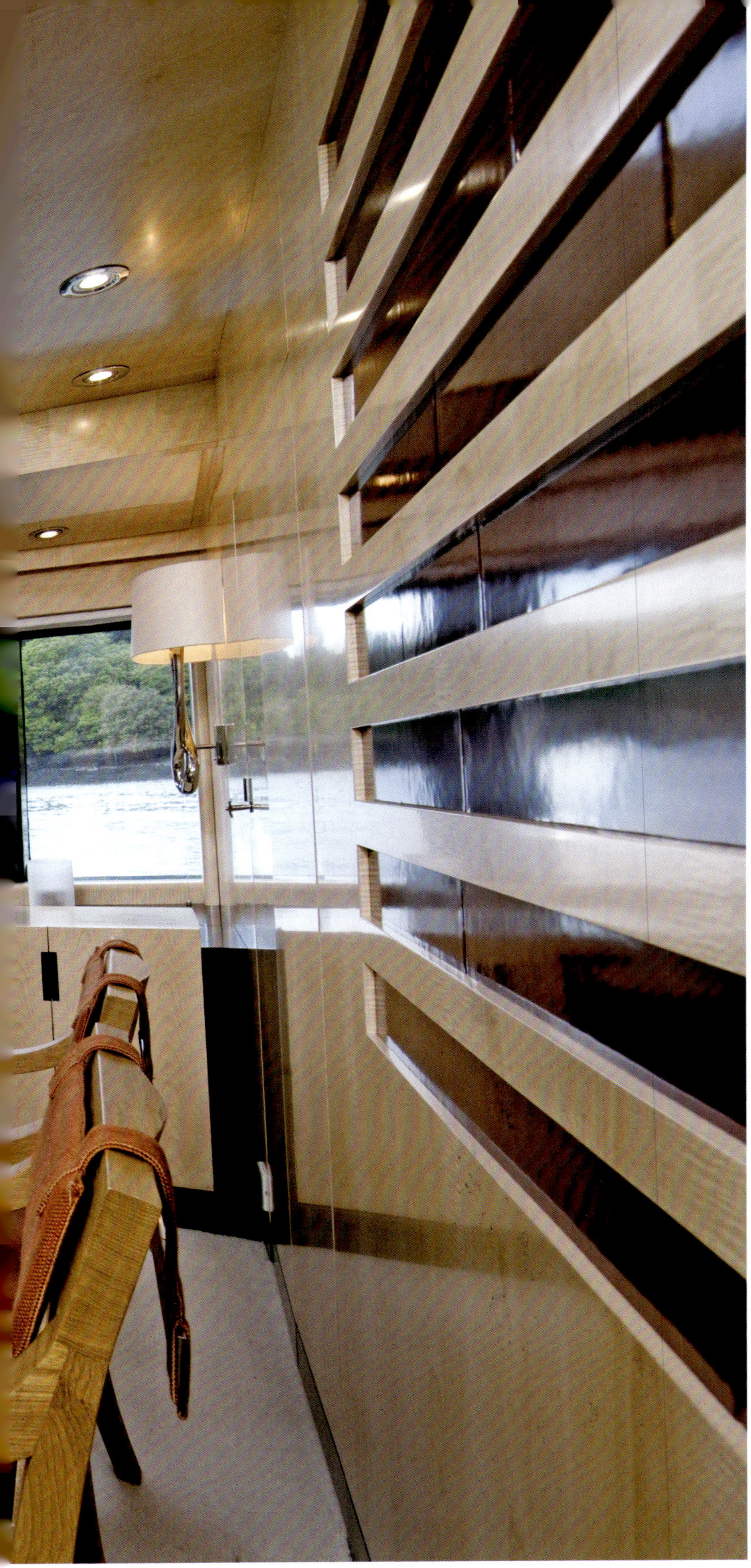

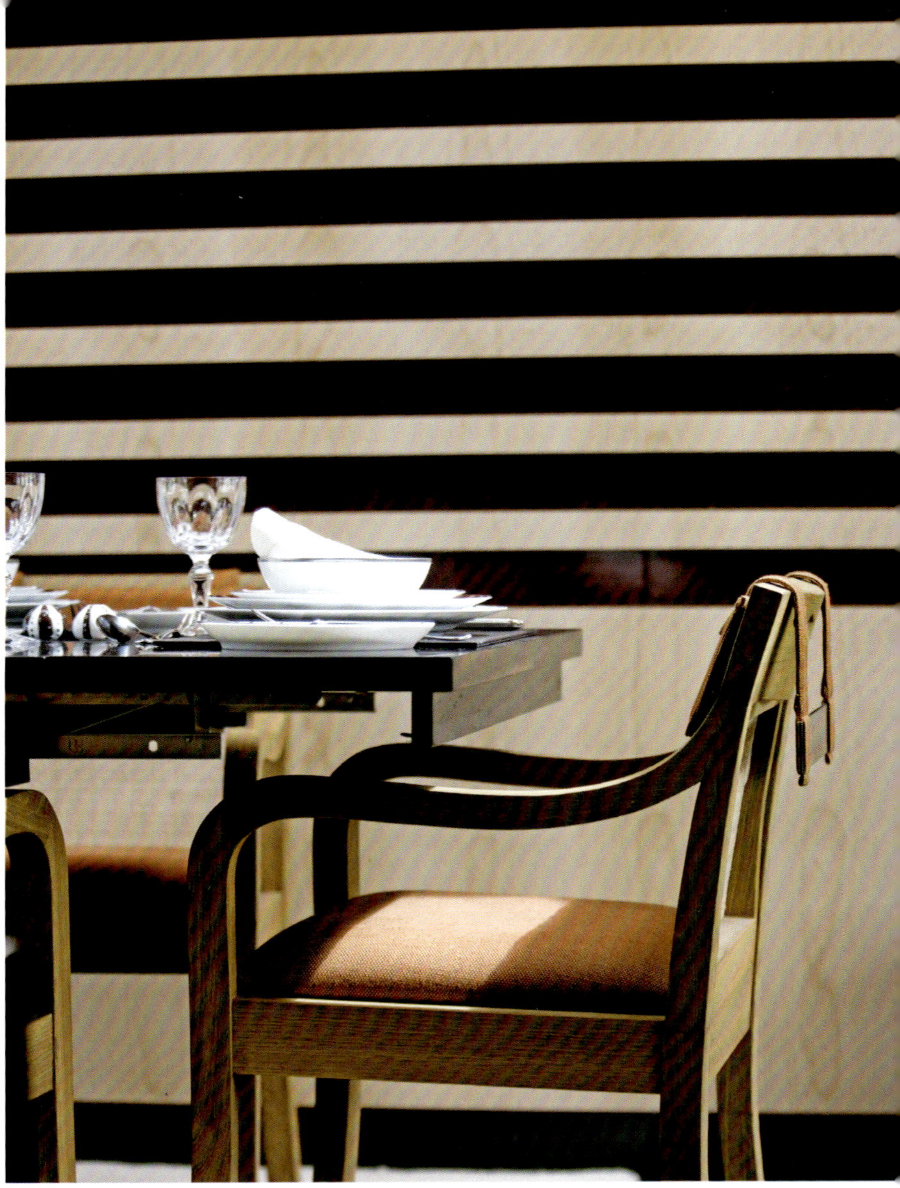

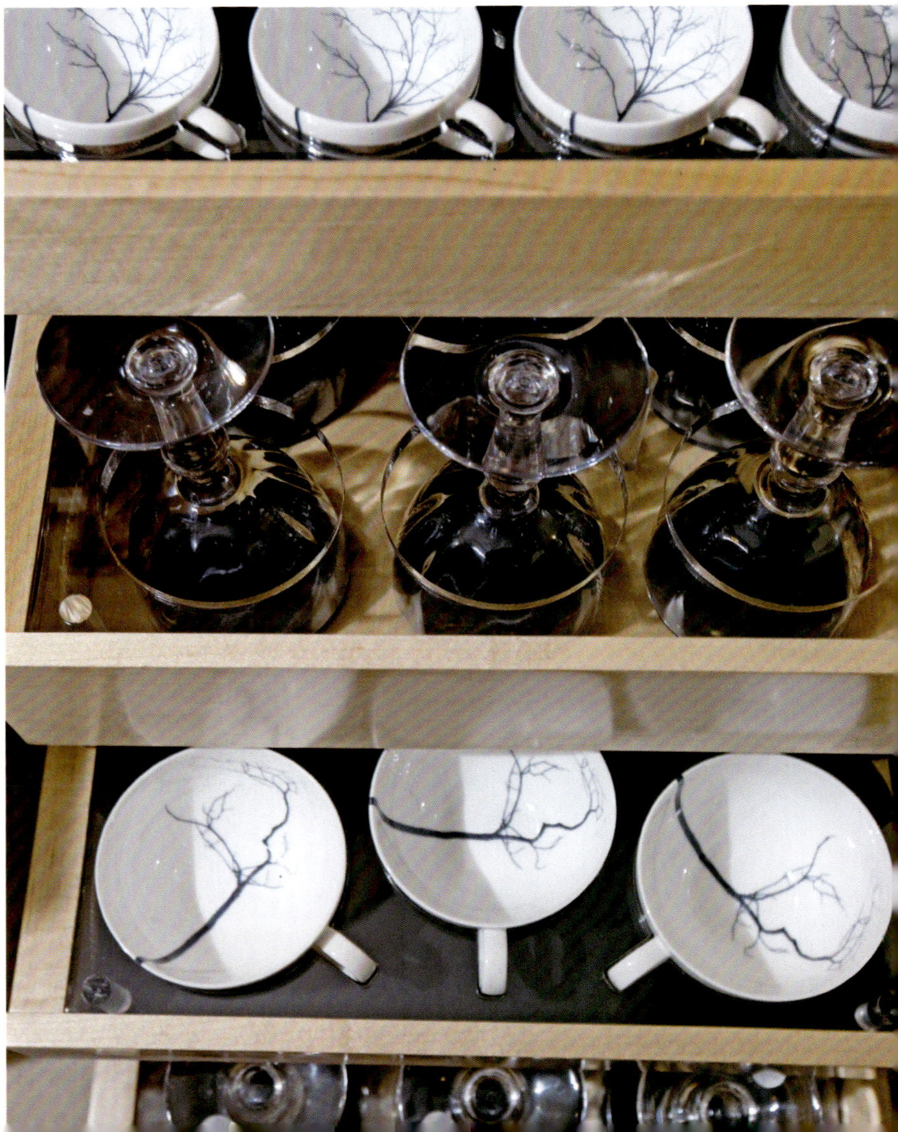

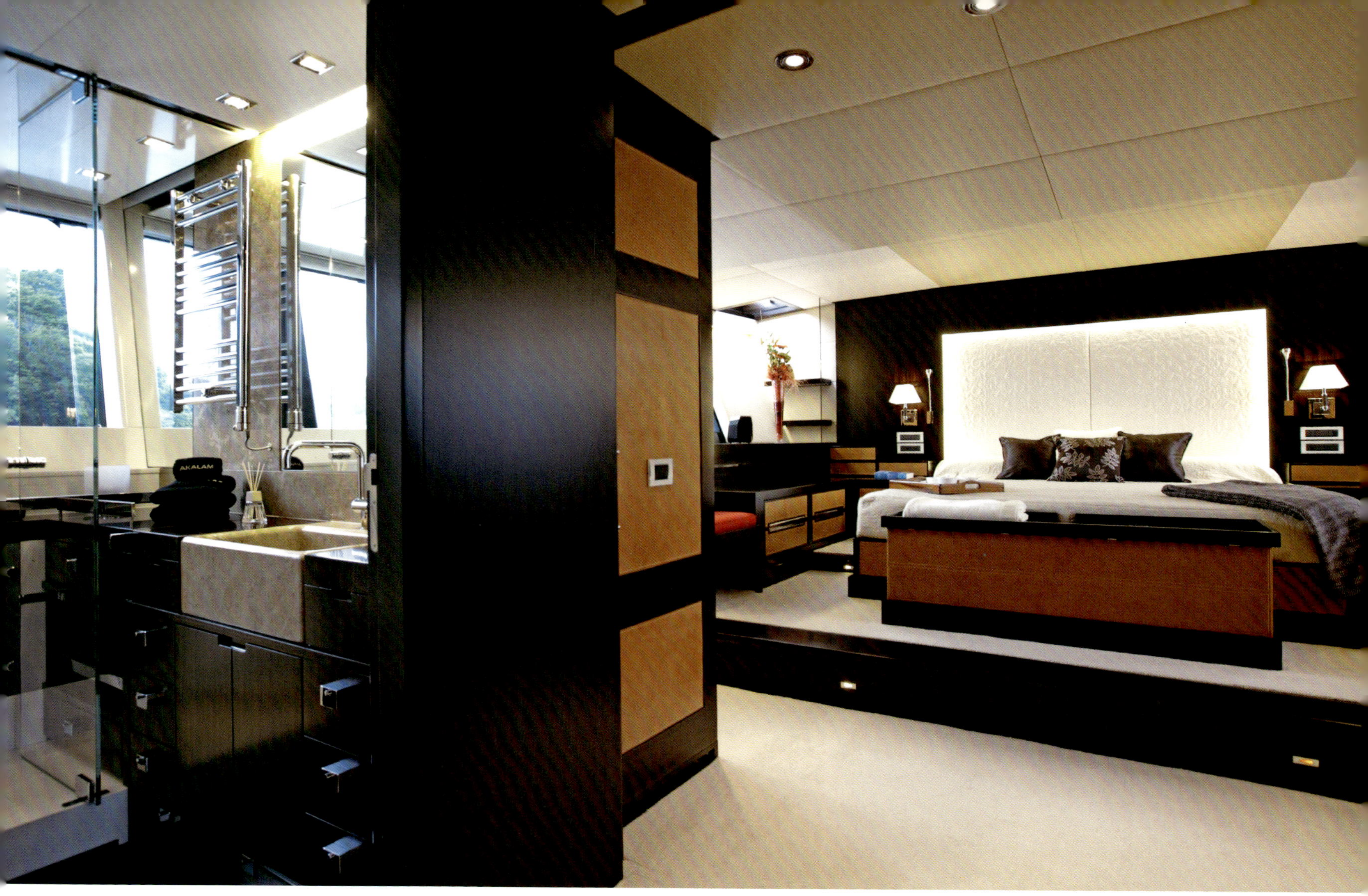

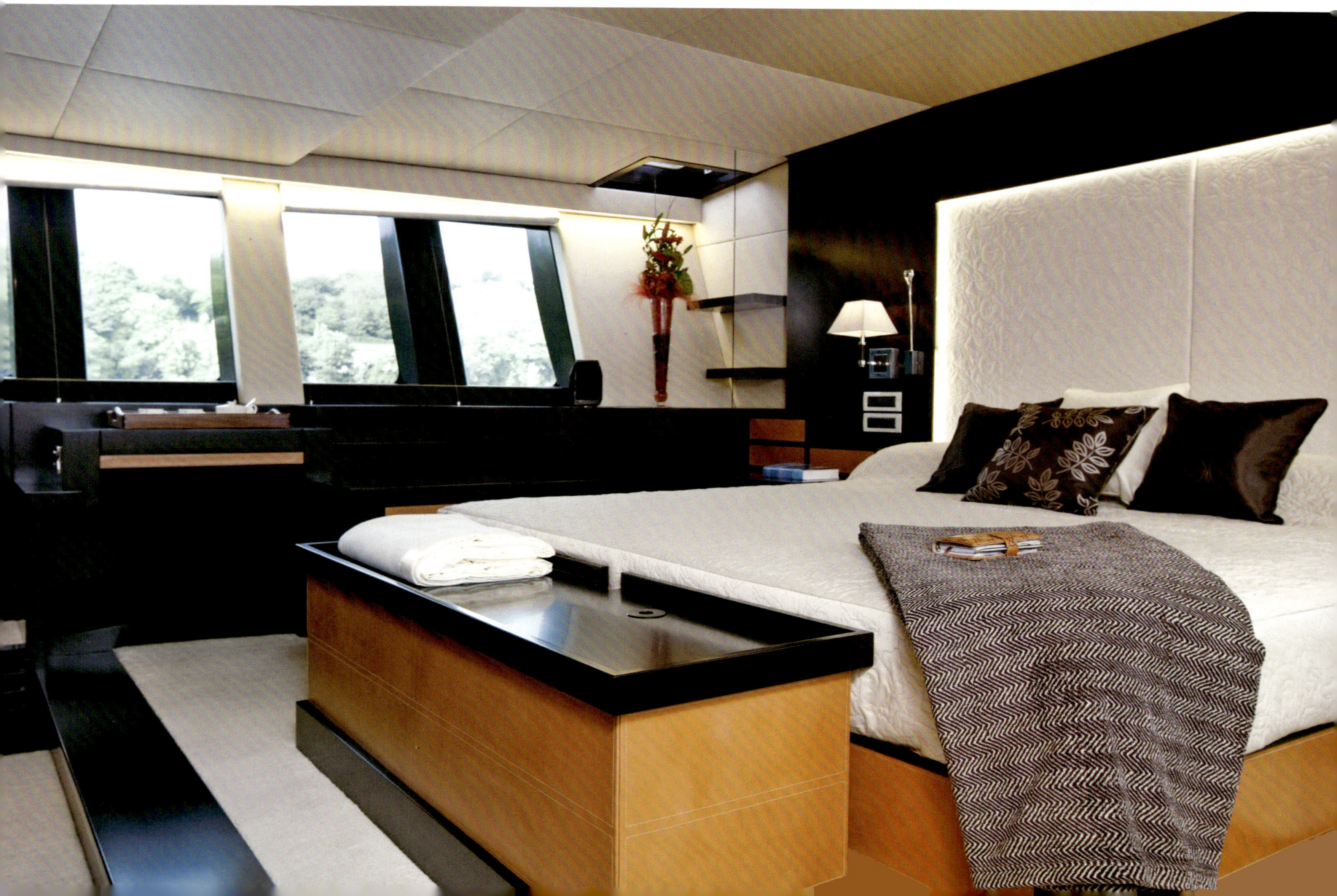

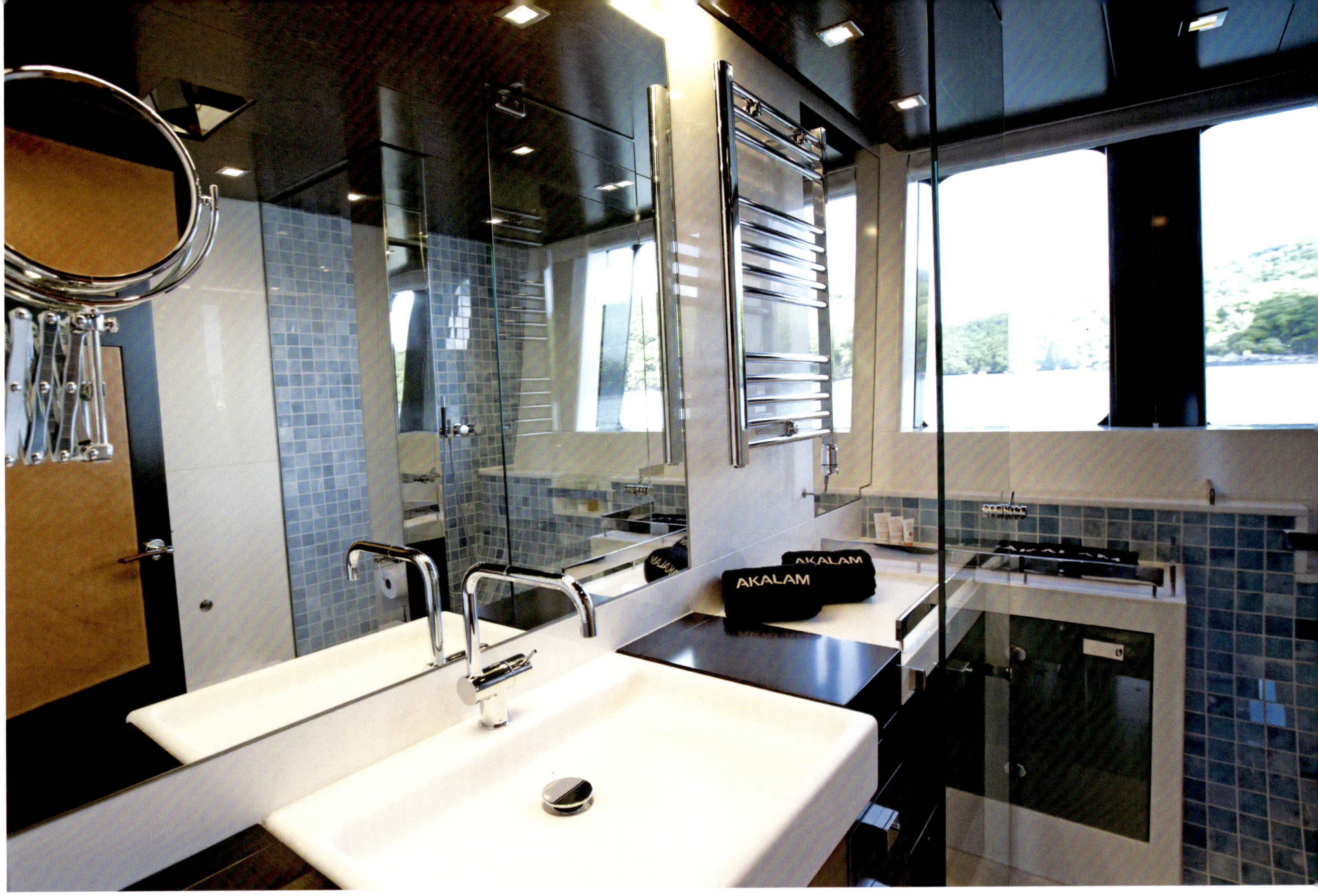
AKALAM
AKALAM

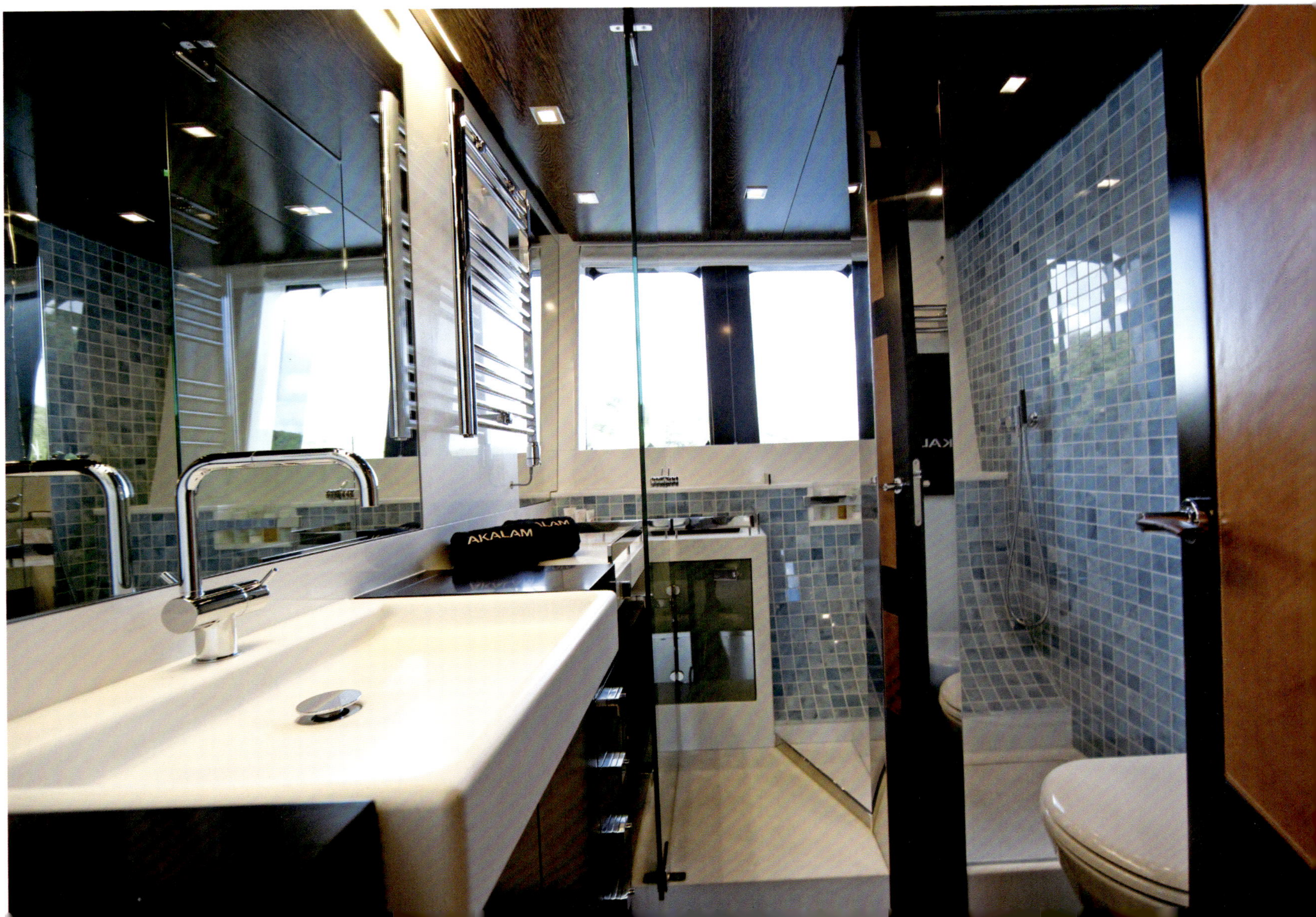
AKALAM

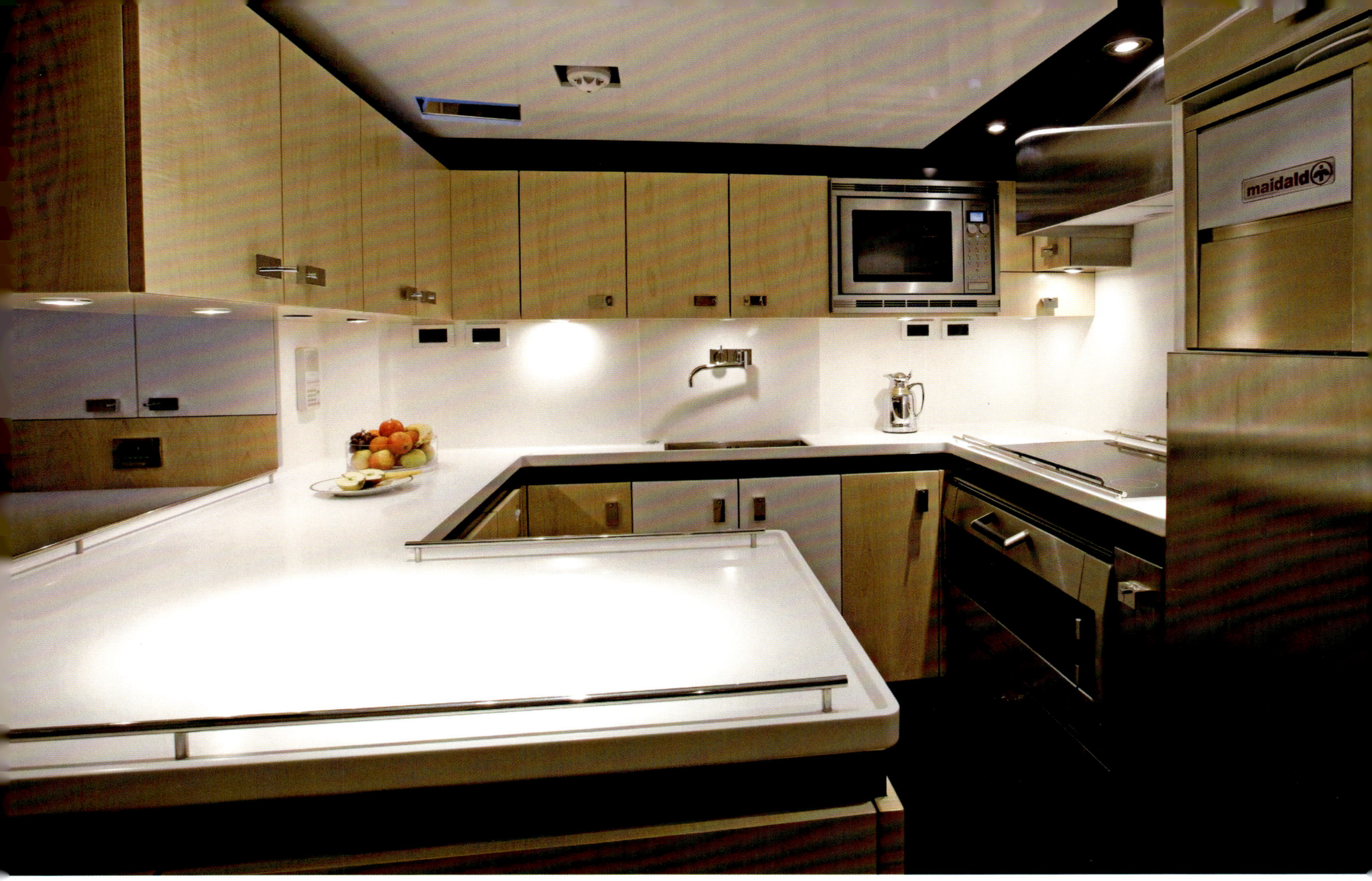
maidaid

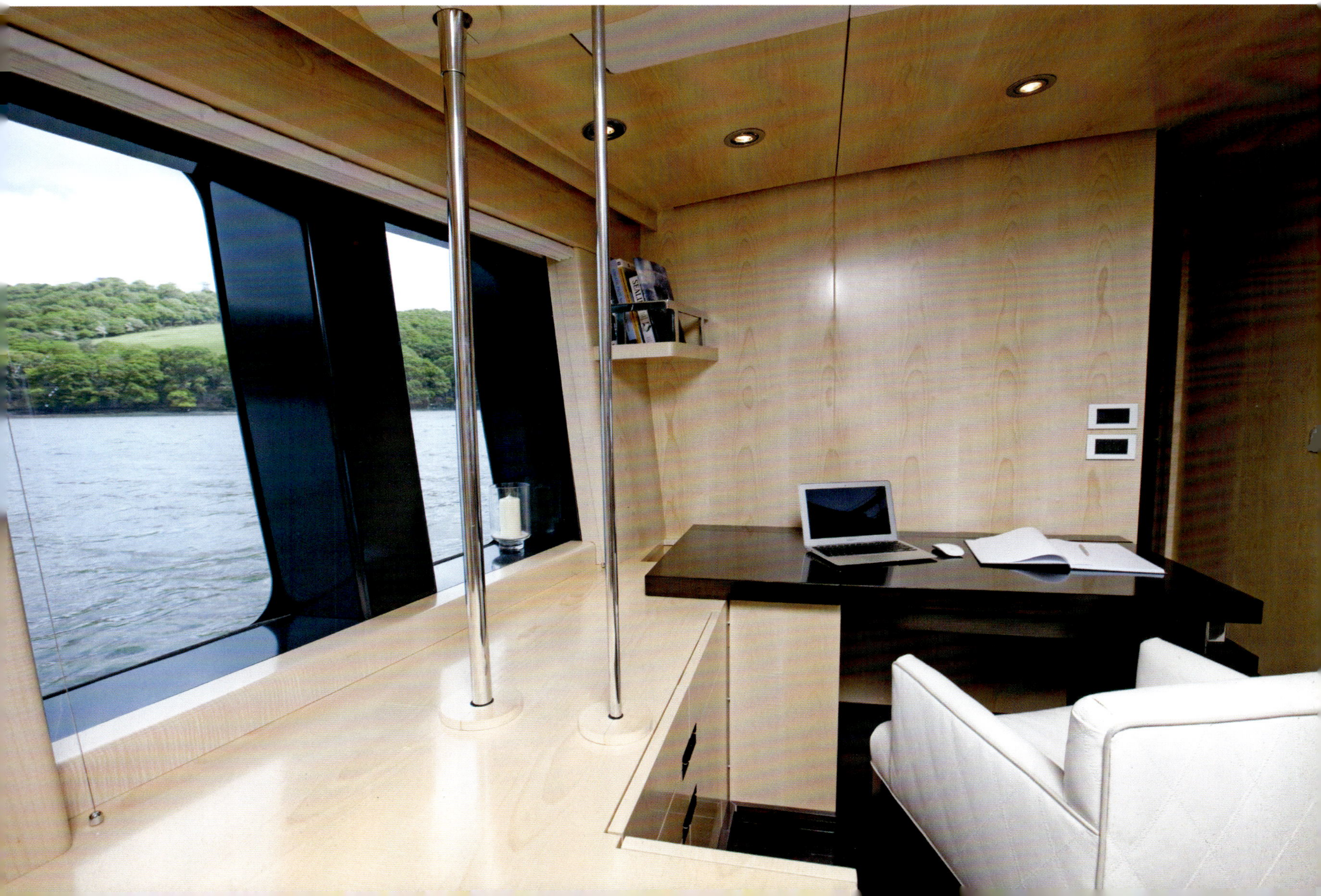

MY MYSTIC

> INTERIOR DESIGN   Schnaase Interior Design
> EXTERIOR DESIGN   Diana Yacht Design
> LENGTH   46m
> BEAM   9m
> MAX SPEED   17kn
> CRUISING SPEED   12kn
> PHOTOGRAPHER   Bruce Thomas

For MY Mystic believe it or not, but it started with nuts. Mr and Mrs Basaran the owners of MY Mystic came to see the designers and told them they were producing and dealing with hazelnuts but now opened a shipyard, CMB yachts in Antalya, Turkey, showing plans of a 45-meter-motoryacht from Dutch office Diana Yacht Design.

As Schnaase Interior Design has some experience with signature styles, the designers thought that the interior design of the vessel for this new born shipyard need to be significant different from the others. And the designers immediately thought it should address to oriental tastes. The designers call it Nouveau Art Deco.

Already their very first sketch of the owners stateroom included lots of golden accents in a very early stage and fully refers to the typical Art Nouveau look with its typical precious Macassar wood. Rich materials and strong designs were recommended. As well as the typical huge glass

chandeliers and wall lamps which stem from the original Art deco phase.

Strong dark trims and profiles for the walls and skirting boards. Impressive glass chandeliers, mother of pearl-inlays and details, fancy loose furniture, crystal, as well as new materials as the shimmering Majilite panels at the walls; modern design language, big handles with golden finish, typical Art Nouveau fabric patterns, together with modern fabric application. Warm golden Onyx on the floors, mixed with real leather tiles and silk.

The layout features some unexpected points of view as well: The most forward part of the main deck provides a full gym with big mirror, treadmill and power plate. Full sauna included. The owners area is on the upper deck and has its own private aft deck in front of it. The area consists of a big stateroom, huge walk-in-wardrobe, bathroom with bathtub and separate shower as well as private office.

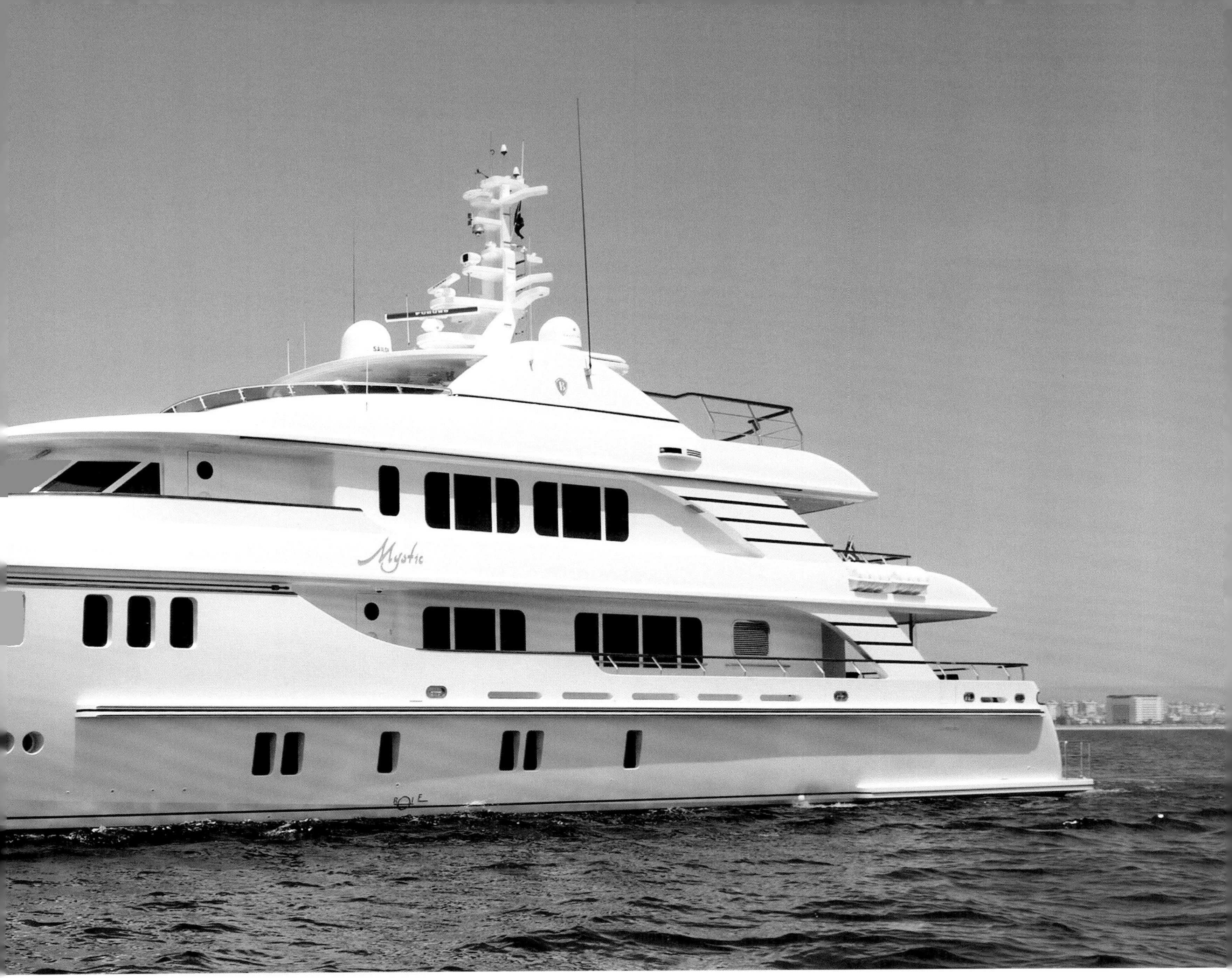

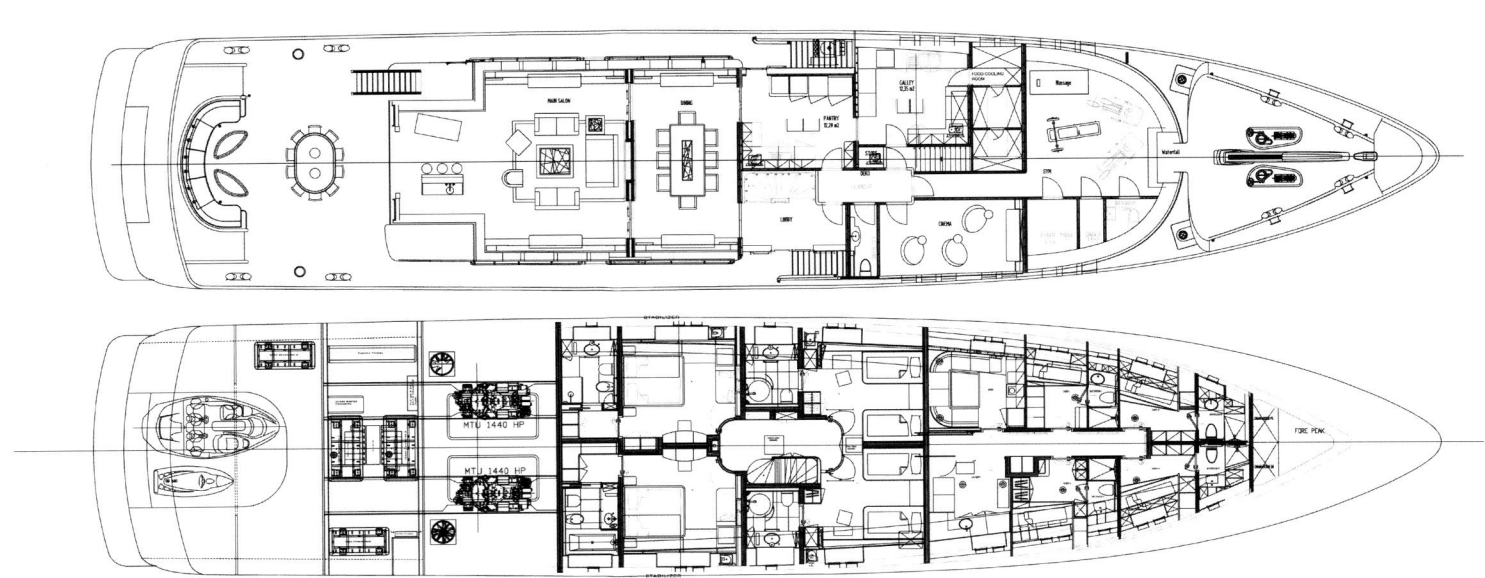

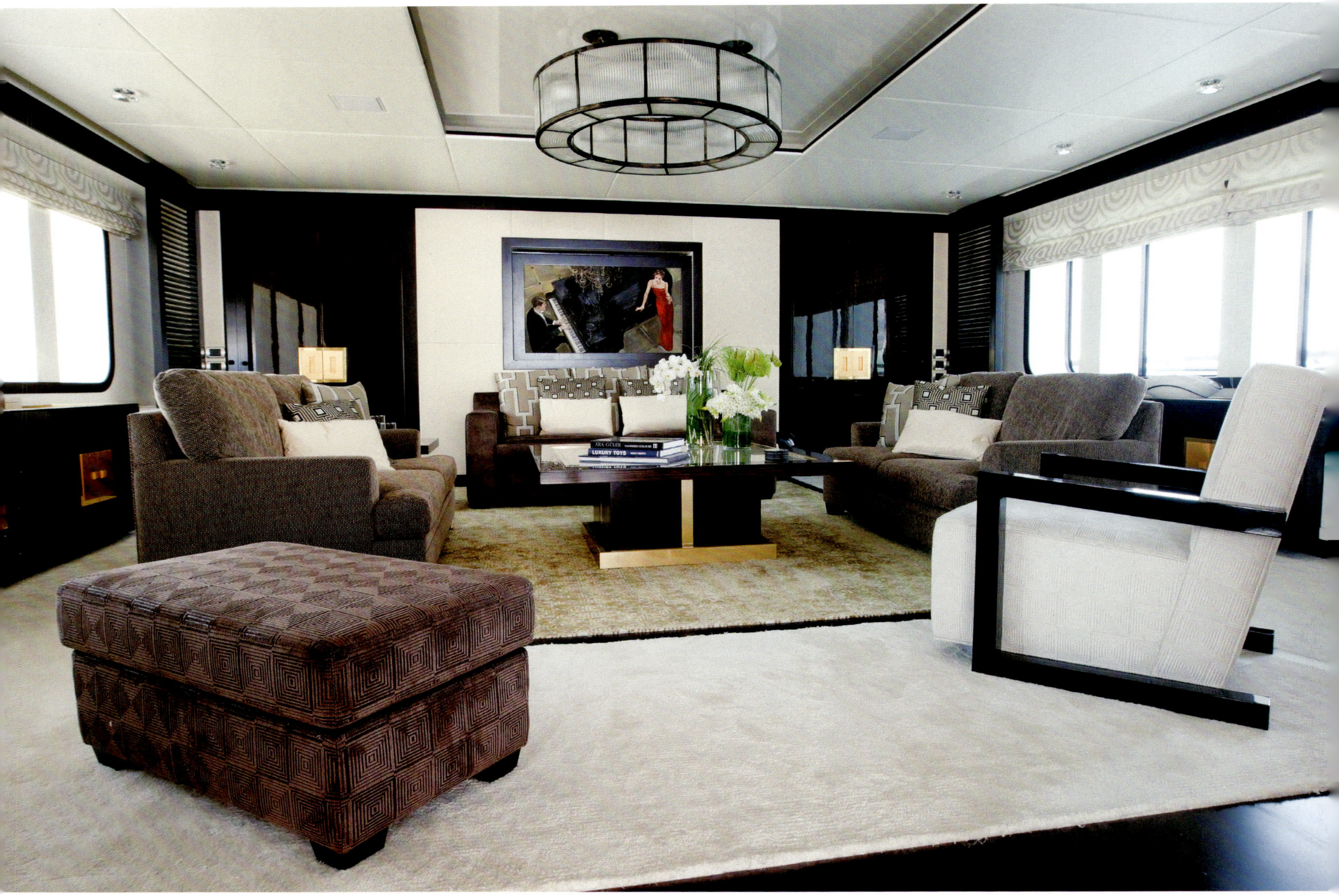

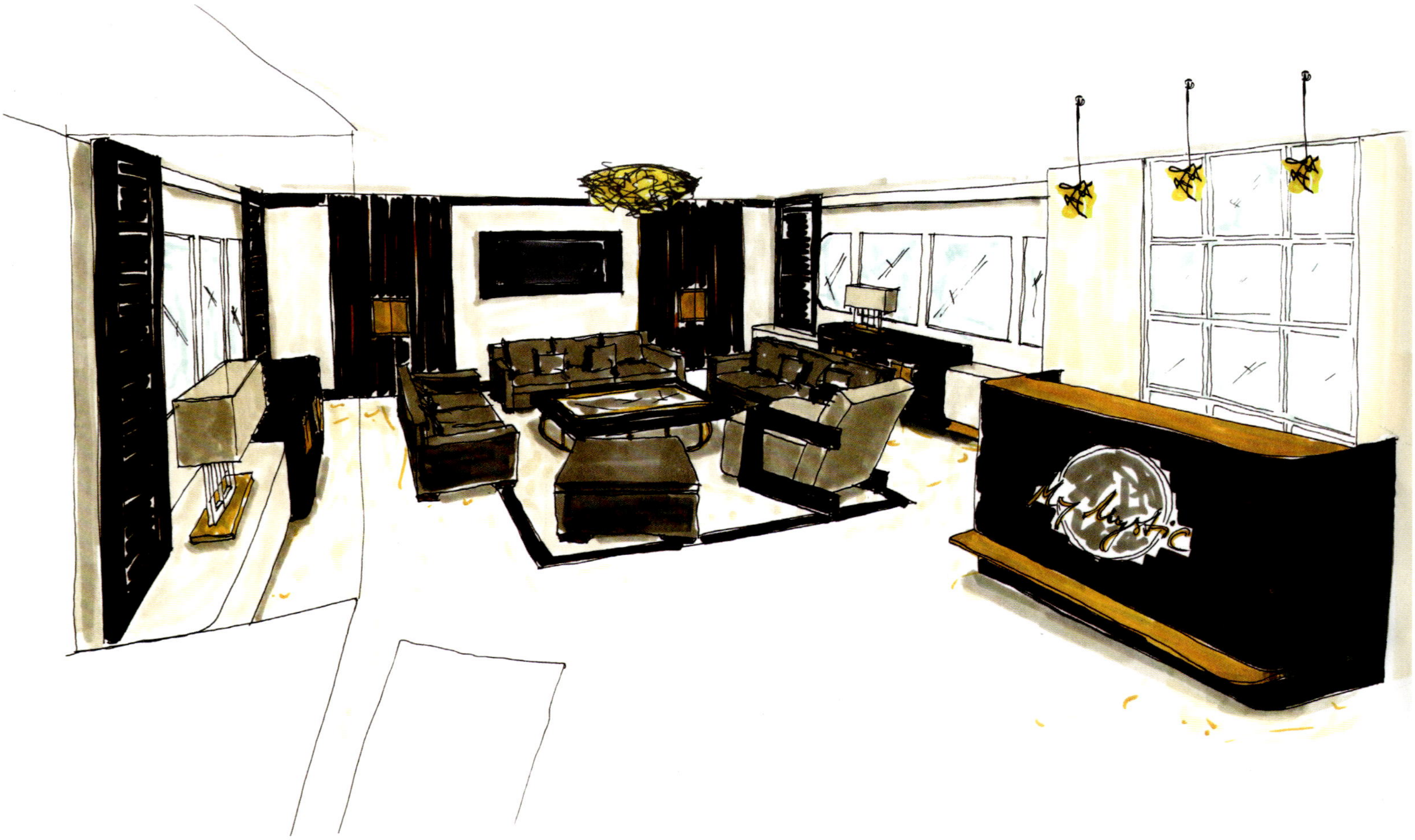
My Mystic

说起"神秘之舟"这艘游艇，还要从榛子说起。巴萨兰夫妇是这艘游艇的主人，他们找到设计师，告诉他们，他们以前一直做生产和加工榛子的生意，现在他们又接管了一家CMB游艇厂，位于土耳其安塔利亚。并给设计师出示了一份由荷兰戴安娜游艇设计公司设计的一艘长45米的机动游艇的设计方案。

因为Schnaase室内设计公司在设计风格上有较好的经验，所以他们想让这个新的造船厂的游艇内部设计与众不同。很快他们就认为，游艇应该具备东方气质，于是将之命名为"新装饰艺术（Nouveau Art Deco）"。

在最初阶段的第一稿设计中，设计师就在船主舱加入了大量的金色元素，使用昂贵的苏拉威西乌木，充分体现出新艺术主义的风格。并采用丰富的材料和浓重的设计。巨大的玻璃吊灯和墙灯也都源于原始的装饰艺术运动时期。

墙体和踢脚线采用了深黑色的装饰，玻璃吊灯令人惊叹，珠宝镶嵌饰品，精致新奇的散装家具，水晶和Majilite墙板等新材料，现代设计风格，金色抛光的大手柄，典型的新艺术主义纺织图案，现代纺织技术。地板上的浅黄色缟玛瑙，辅以真皮贴砖和丝绸。

船体的布局设计也给人意外之喜：主甲板的最前端是一个设施完备的健身房，内有大镜子、跑步机和力量盘，还有一个桑拿浴室。船主区在上层甲板，前方还有一个私人的船尾甲板，整个区域包括高级舱室、大型衣帽间、卫生间（带浴缸和独立淋浴区）以及私人办公室。

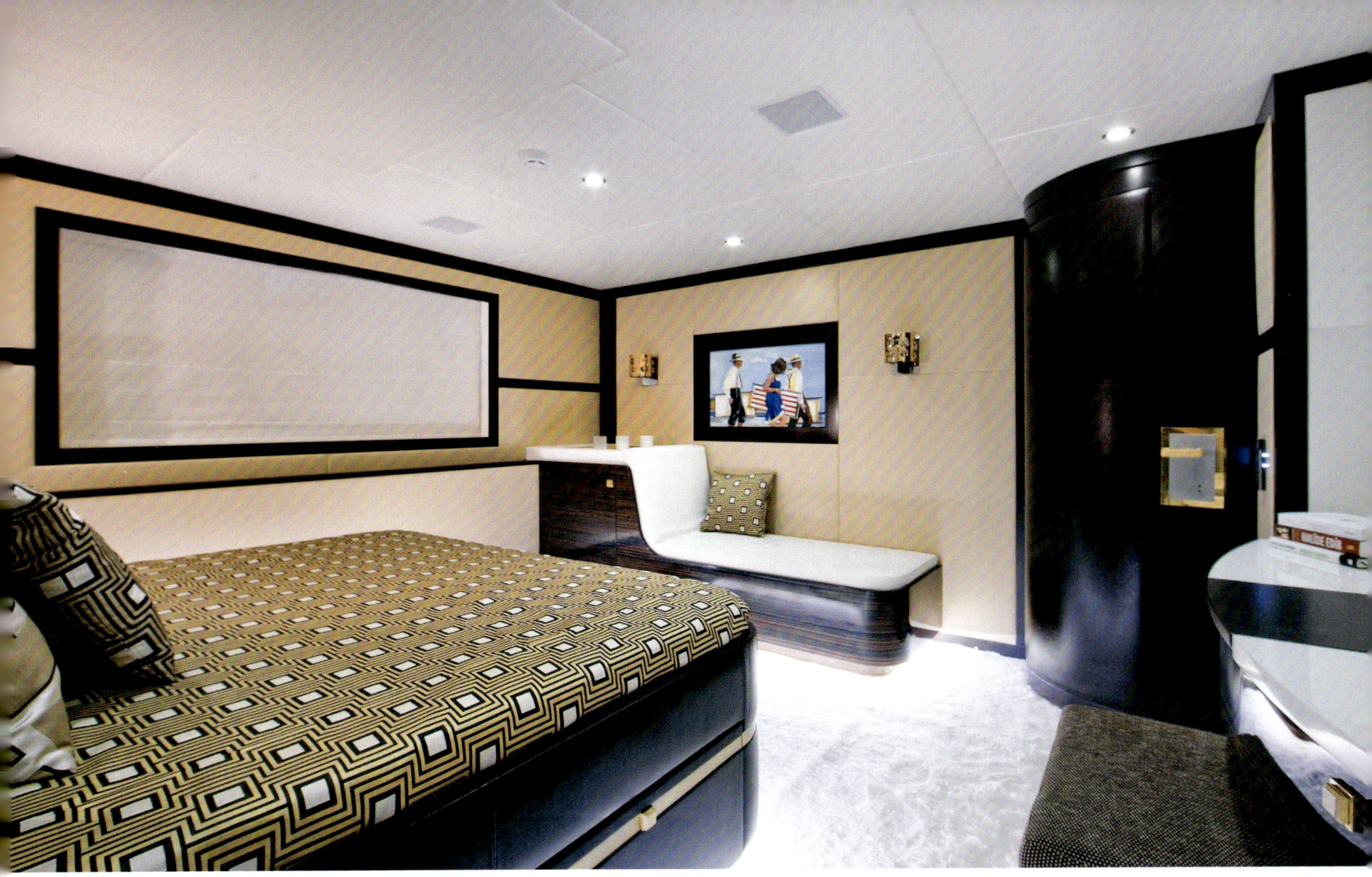

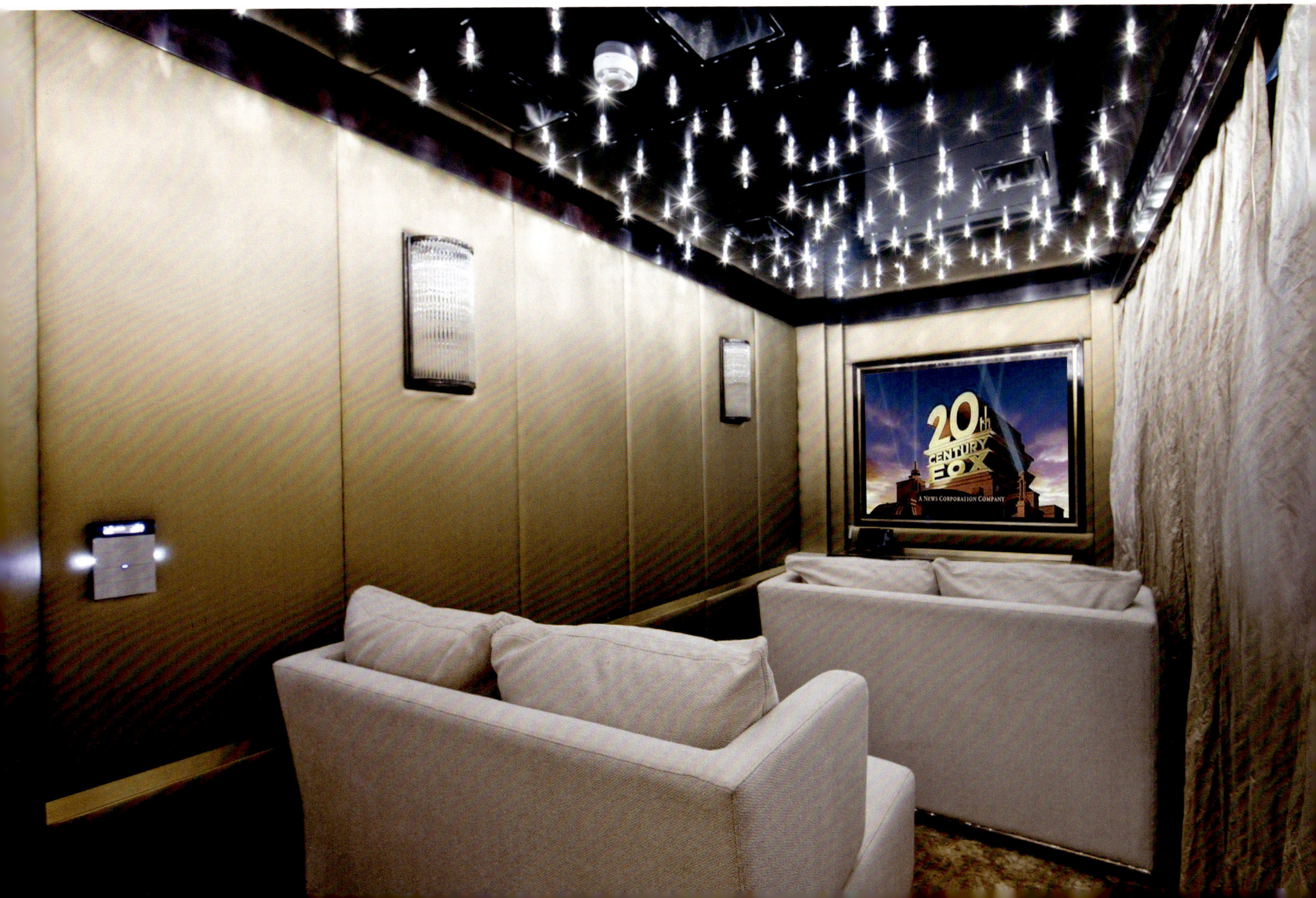
20th
CENTURY
FOX
A NEWS CORPORATION COMPANY

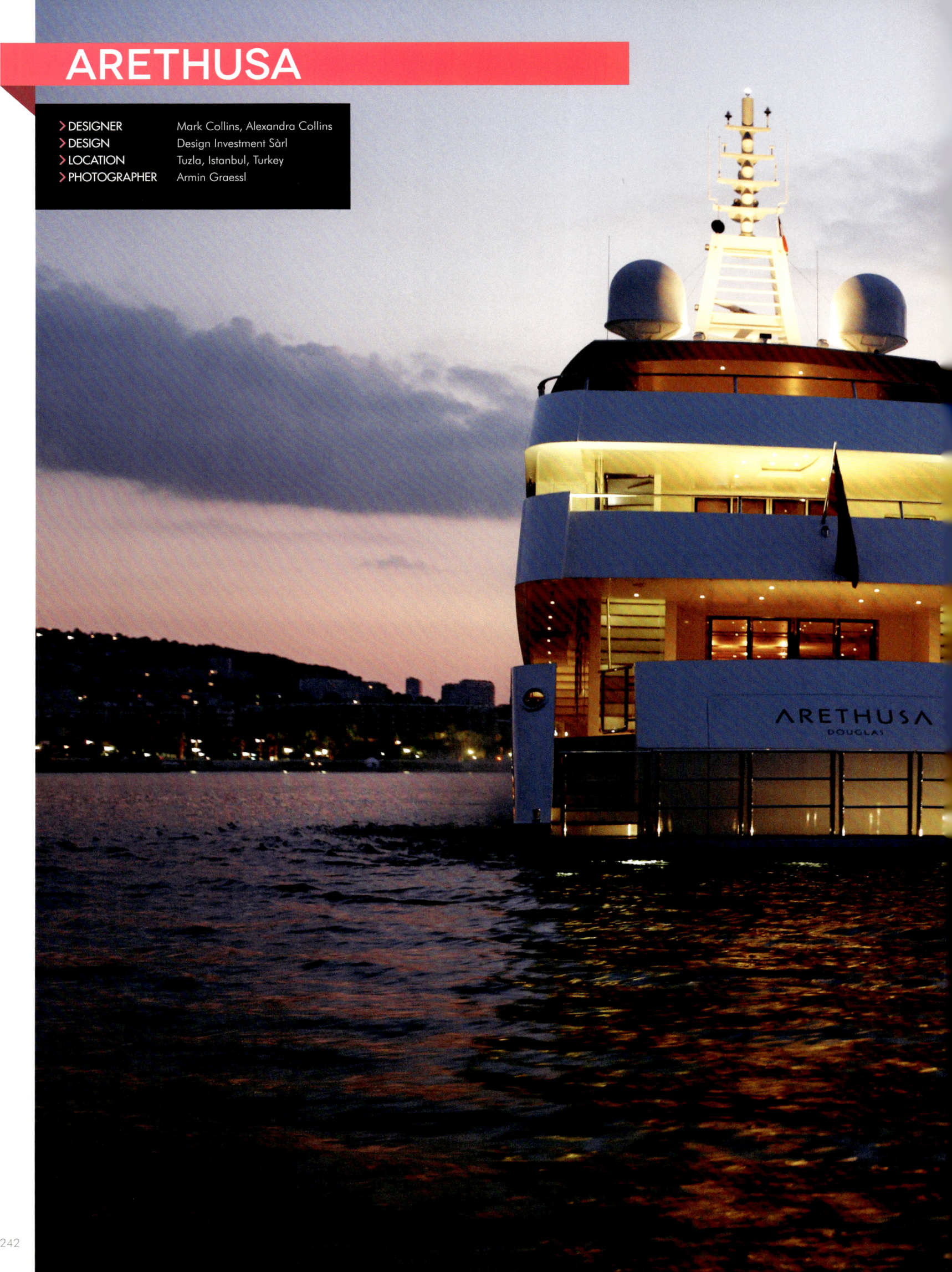

ARETHUSA

> DESIGNER   Mark Collins, Alexandra Collins
> DESIGN   Design Investment Sàrl
> LOCATION   Tuzla, Istanbul, Turkey
> PHOTOGRAPHER   Armin Graessl

ARETHUSA
DOUGLAS

242

The request of the shipyard was to create a modern and yet comfortable yacht where exterior and interior are developed in harmony and create a synergy between the two. As a result the exterior is sculptured out of a block offering ample shaded outdoor spaces and a general feel of space on the decks. This design approach goes all the way to the very top of the yacht and gives it the unique cap above the sundeck that characterizes it. The almost minimalistic interior offers a modern and comfortable environment where the relaxing atmosphere is enhanced by soft color shades and warm lightning.

The outside melts with the inside; Big windows allow the sun light to shine inside and it is reflected on the pieces of art and their gold leaves. The simple shapes are carried outside and reflected also in the overall exterior of the yacht; Deck seating arrangements are the connecting elements from inside to outside they blend into the exterior features and create a harmonious overall picture. The picture of freedom, wideness and seemingly endless horizon that stands for a stay on a motor yacht is brought into the yacht and is reflected in the style and choice of materials.

Throughout the decks weather in the 4 guest cabins or the spacious owner's cabin with lounge area, separated bathroom and dressing as well as a private office this concept has been carried through. The richness of the material choice in combination with gold and oak wood is reflected best in the main deck dining and lounge area. The upper deck salon offers a more informal meeting environment where relaxing is possible in front of an open fire place and where inside and outside melt together represented by a bar that is found inside and outside. The sundeck with Jacuzzi and comfortable seating, lounging furniture rounds up the coherent appearance of the yacht. This yacht represents Design Investments second project in the yacht world. The collaboration with the shipyard started on "Pherousa" that is currently under construction. She is the bigger sister yacht and the exterior design appears even more powerful on this 67m vessel. Mark and Alexandra started working together on yacht projects after having gained experience in automotive design, transportation design in general and more specific on aircraft interior design. In all their work the ability to come up with tailor made solutions for confined spaces is the connecting point. Their passion for innovation and mobility is the base of all their new design concept weather for a new A380 cabin interior for Airbus or a new generation seat for an airline.

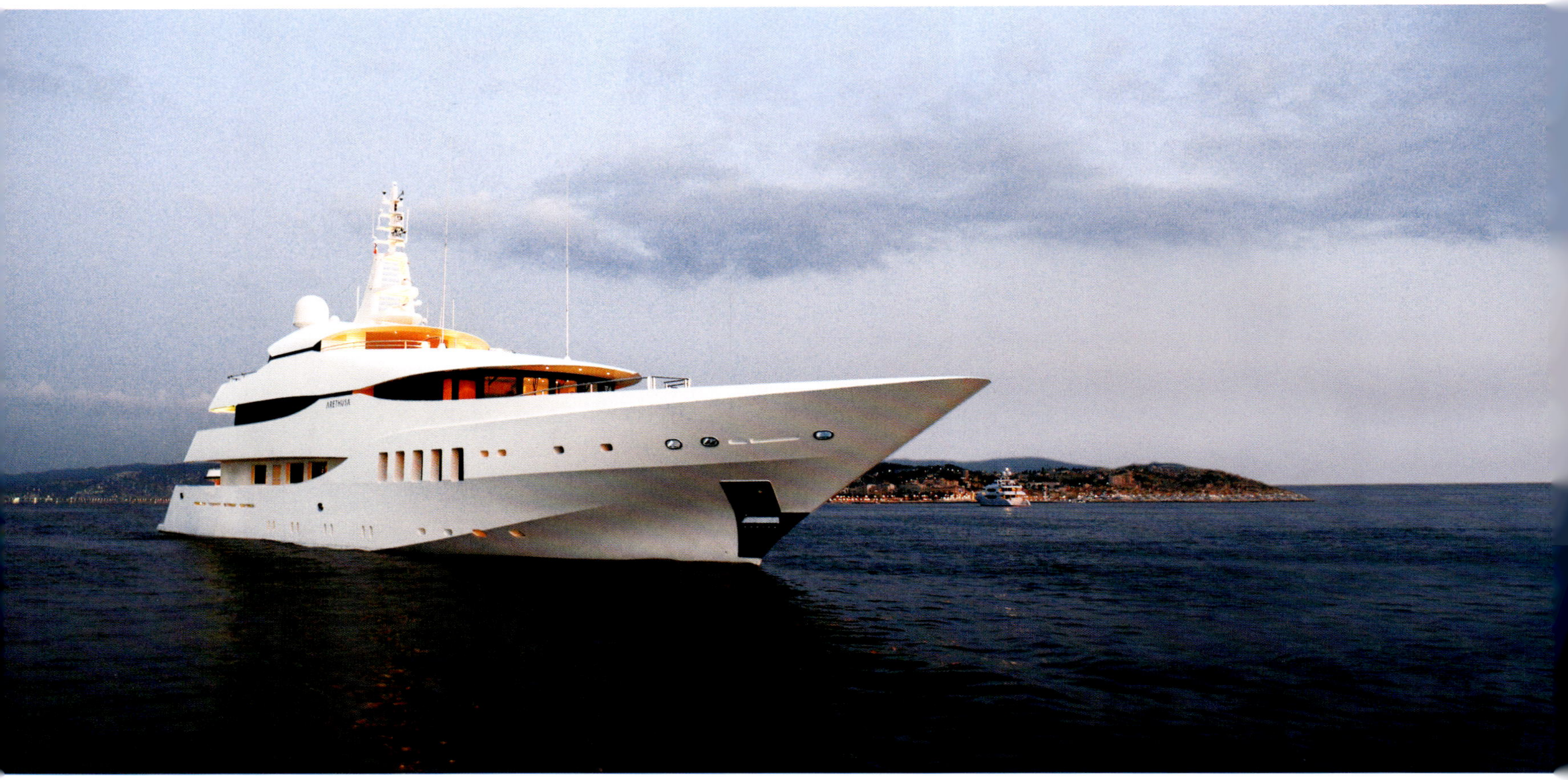
ARETHUSA

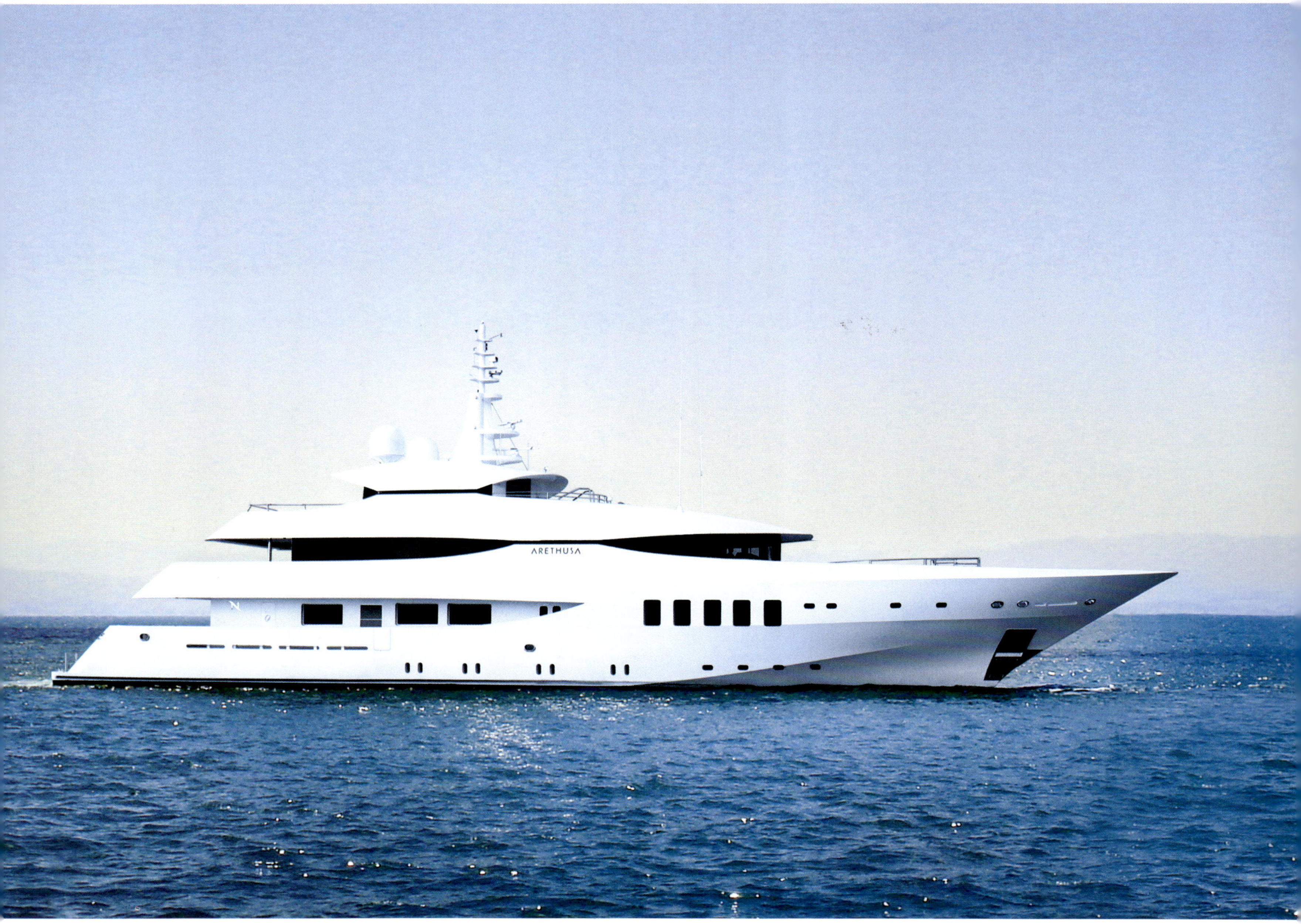
ARETHUSA

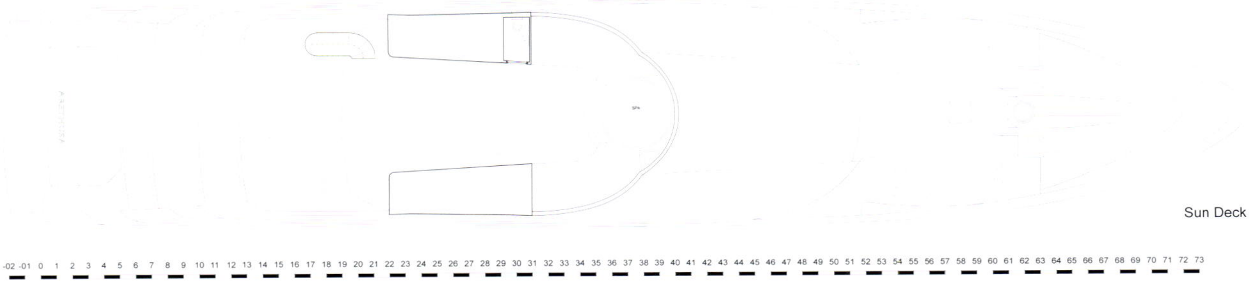

Sun Deck

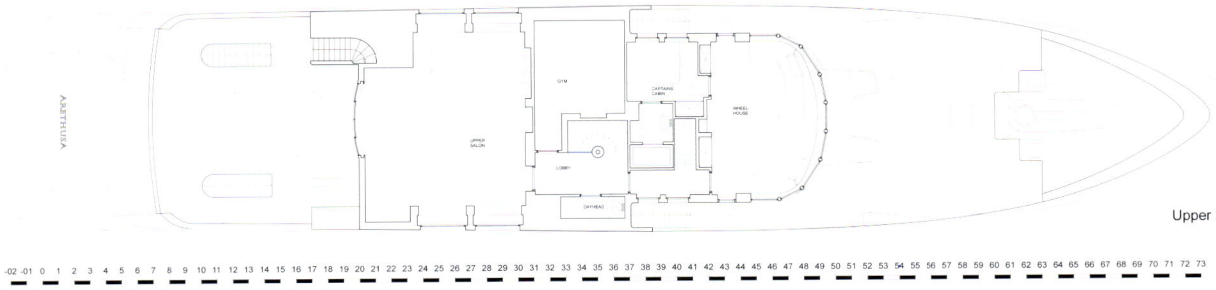

-02 -01 0 1 2 3 4 5 6 7 8 9 10 11 12 13 14 15 16 17 18 19 20 21 22 23 24 25 26 27 28 29 30 31 32 33 34 35 36 37 38 39 40 41 42 43 44 45 46 47 48 49 50 51 52 53 54 55 56 57 58 59 60 61 62 63 64 65 66 67 68 69 70 71 72 73

Upper Deck

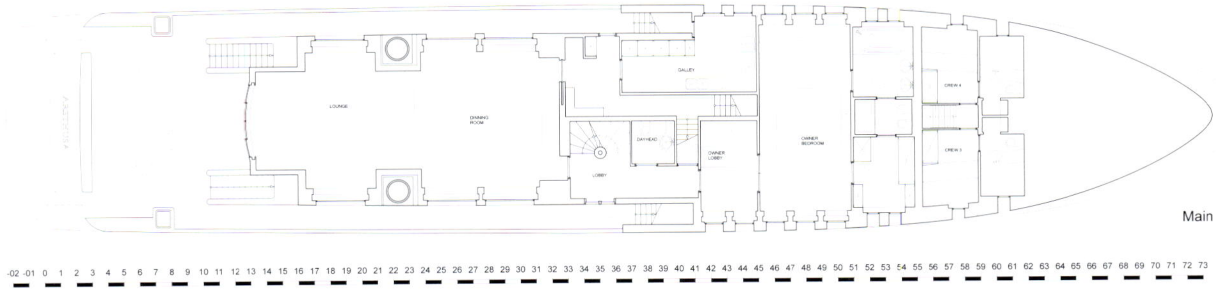

-02 -01 0 1 2 3 4 5 6 7 8 9 10 11 12 13 14 15 16 17 18 19 20 21 22 23 24 25 26 27 28 29 30 31 32 33 34 35 36 37 38 39 40 41 42 43 44 45 46 47 48 49 50 51 52 53 54 55 56 57 58 59 60 61 62 63 64 65 66 67 68 69 70 71 72 73

Main Deck

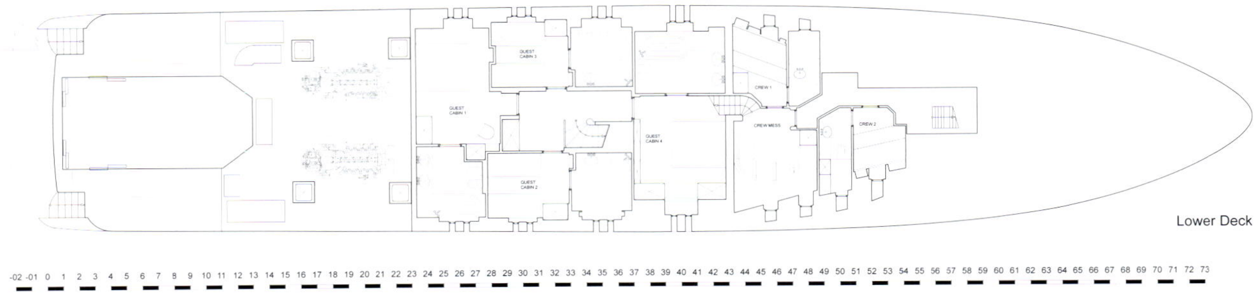

-02 -01 0 1 2 3 4 5 6 7 8 9 10 11 12 13 14 15 16 17 18 19 20 21 22 23 24 25 26 27 28 29 30 31 32 33 34 35 36 37 38 39 40 41 42 43 44 45 46 47 48 49 50 51 52 53 54 55 56 57 58 59 60 61 62 63 64 65 66 67 68 69 70 71 72 73

Lower Deck

-02 -01 0 1 2 3 4 5 6 7 8 9 10 11 12 13 14 15 16 17 18 19 20 21 22 23 24 25 26 27 28 29 30 31 32 33 34 35 36 37 38 39 40 41 42 43 44 45 46 47 48 49 50 51 52 53 54 55 56 57 58 59 60 61 62 63 64 65 66 67 68 69 70 71 72 73

　　造船厂要求建造一艘舒适的现代化游艇，船内外部设计和谐，并在内部设计和外部构建上做到平衡协调。基于以上宗旨，游艇外部结构留出足够的遮棚室外空间，甲板上给人一种空阔感。这一设计方案一直延伸到顶部，从而造就了这艘游艇的出彩之处——上层甲板上独特的顶盖设计。近乎简约的游艇内部给人一种现代化兼舒适之感，柔和的色彩和温暖的照明设计为艇内氛围增添了几分惬意。

　　游艇外部与室内装饰相融合；大窗设计让足够的光线射入室内，又反射到陈设的艺术品和金叶饰品上面；外部整体设计以简洁为主。甲板上的座位安排与室内装饰相接，使整个游艇内外浑然一体，形成一幅和谐融洽的图景。身处机动游艇之上，眼前一望无际的水面，以及船上所选材料的质地和风格，处处给人自由、宽敞的印象。

　　甲板从头至尾，不论在 4 间客舱，还是在带有娱乐区的宽敞的船主套房，甚至包括独立卫生间、梳妆室和私人办公室都沿用了这一设计理念。选材方面丰富而考究，尤其体现在主甲板餐厅和娱乐厅，均采用了金色和橡木组合。上层甲板客舱内设有会客厅，客人可围坐于一个开放的壁炉前，享受轻松舒适的气氛；壁炉由一个栏杆隔开，把室内外两部分巧妙地结合在一起。配备有水流式按摩浴缸，舒适坐卧以及休闲家具装饰的上层甲板集中体现了游艇流畅连贯的外貌。这艘游艇是设计投资公司在游艇建造领域的又一大工程。此设计公司目前正与造船厂合作建造 "Pherousa" 号游艇。船体总长 67 米，这将是一艘继 Arethusa 号之后，规模更大，且在外部设计上更显威力的姊妹游艇，负责设计的马克和亚历山大在机动车设计、交通运输工具设计以及要求更高的航天器内部结构设计方面积累工作经验之后，共同致力于游艇建造工程，诸如以上工作都要求设计者能为限定的空间提出量身定做的解决方案，这种能力至关重要；同时，又要有不断追求创新的激情和灵活的能动性。这些能力无论在为空中客机设计新型的 A380 室内结构，还是为某一条航线设计新一代座椅，都是提出新颖设计理念的基石。

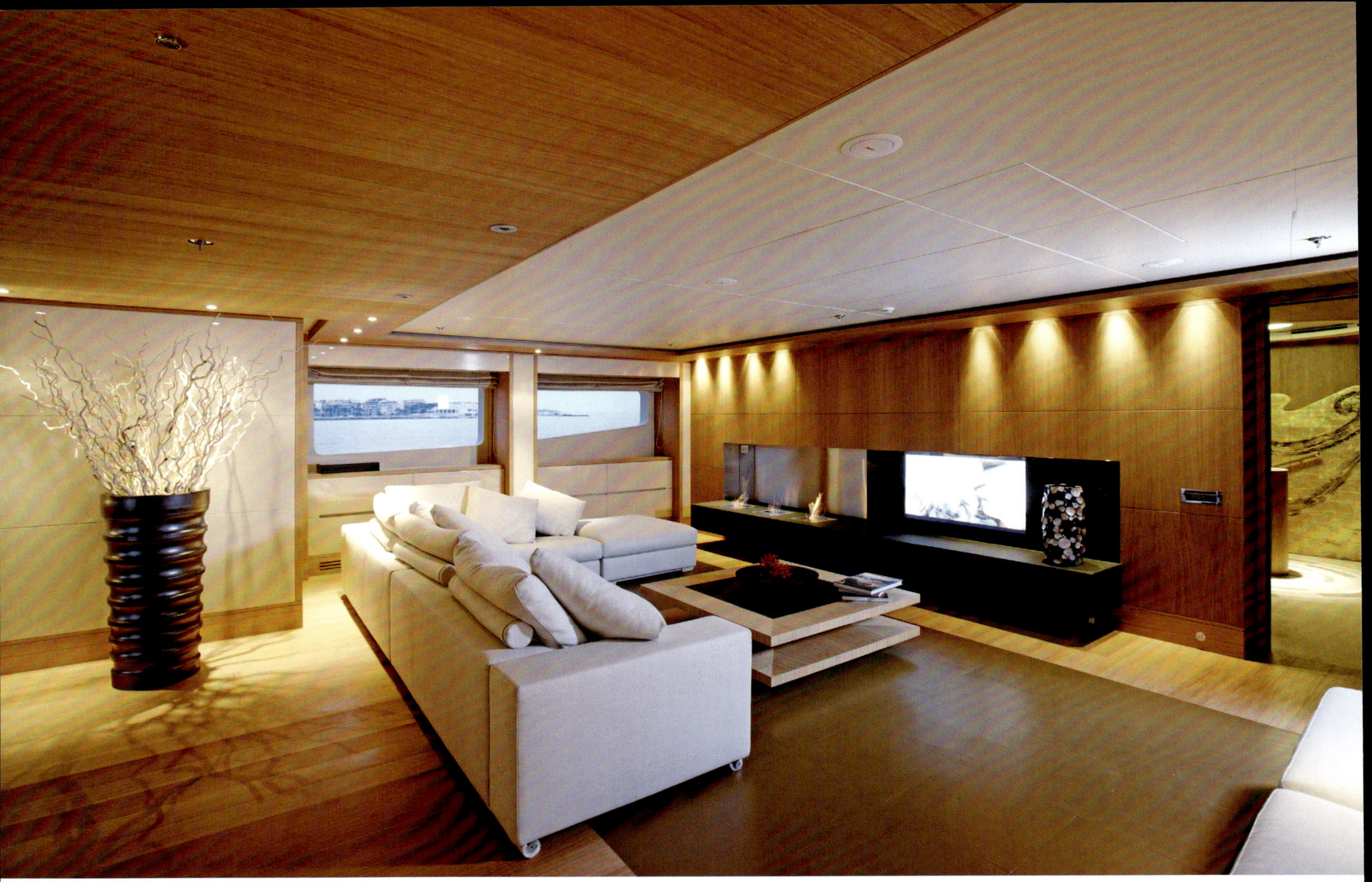

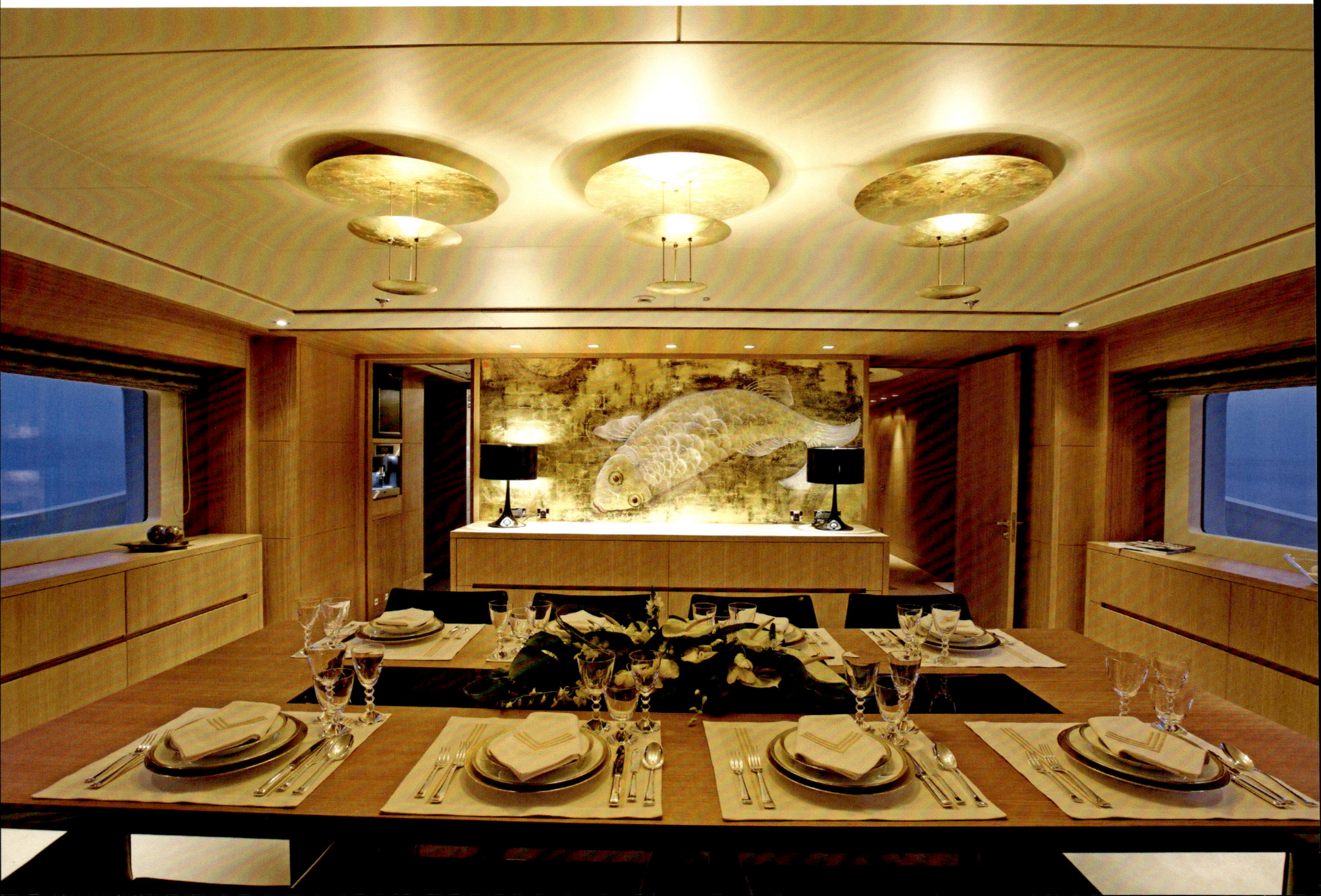

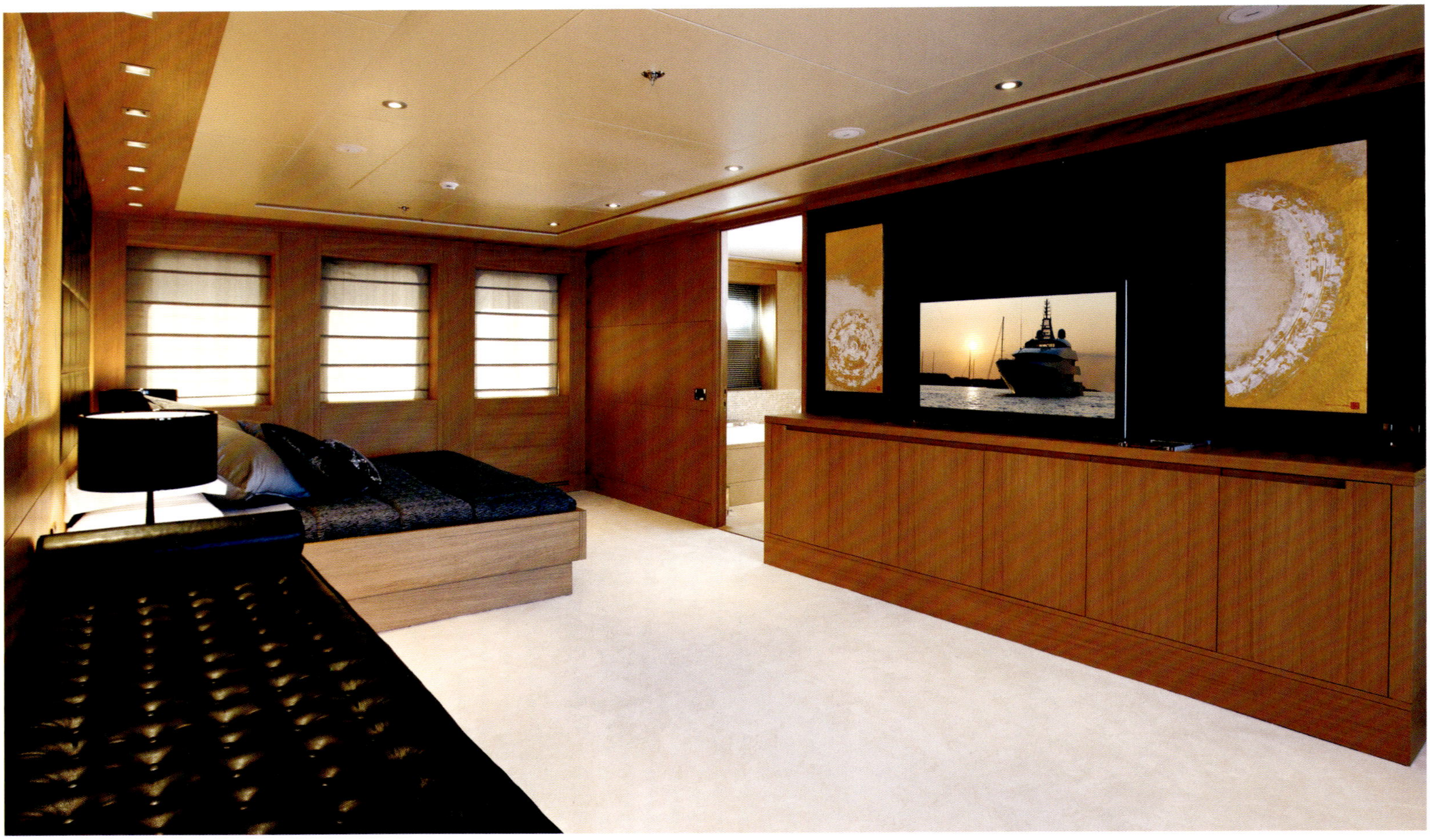

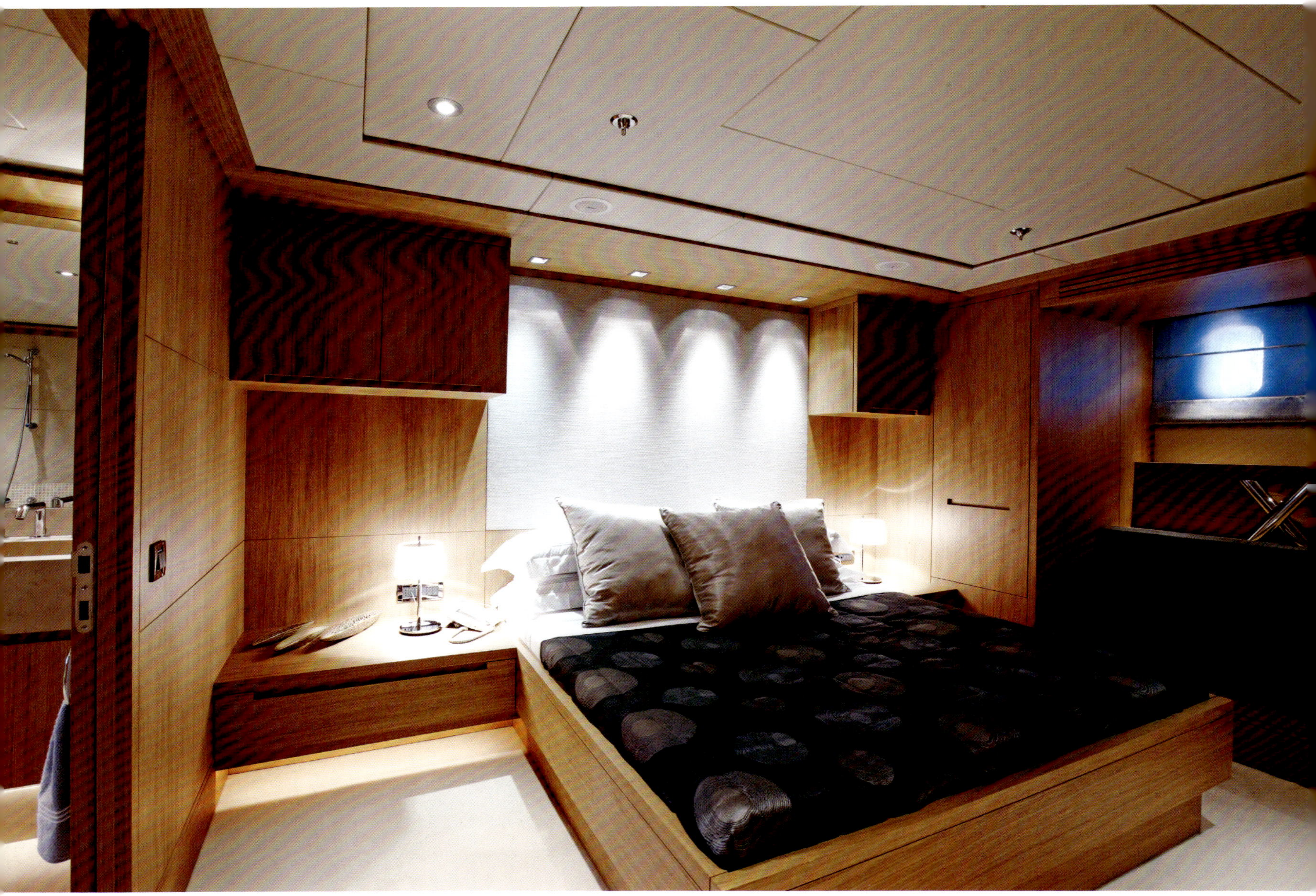

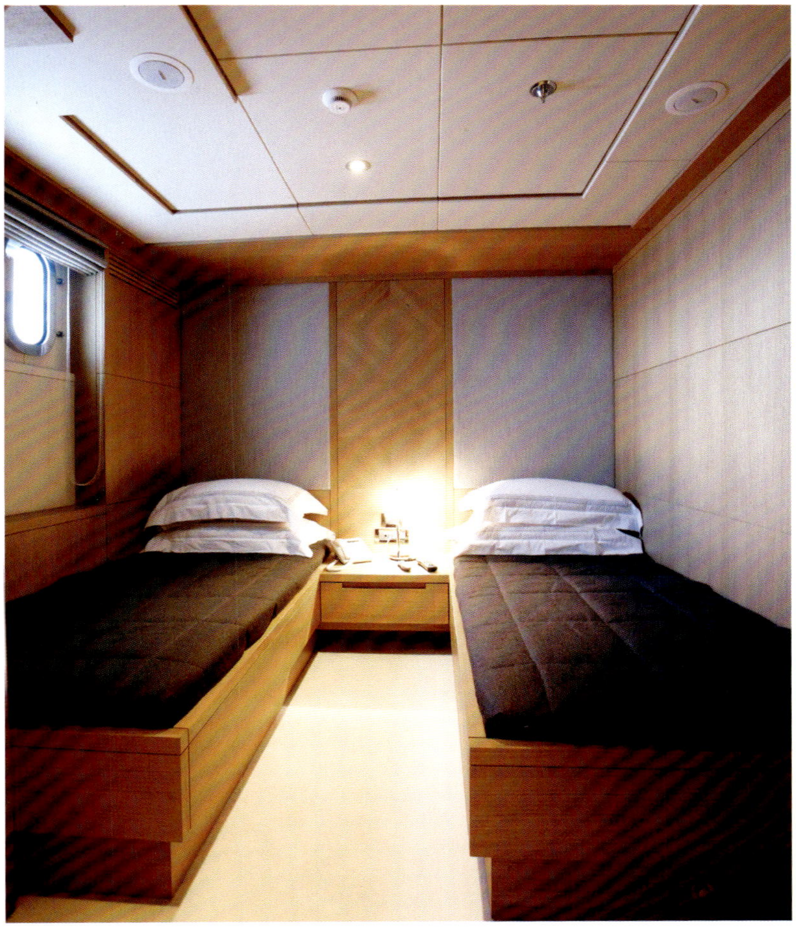

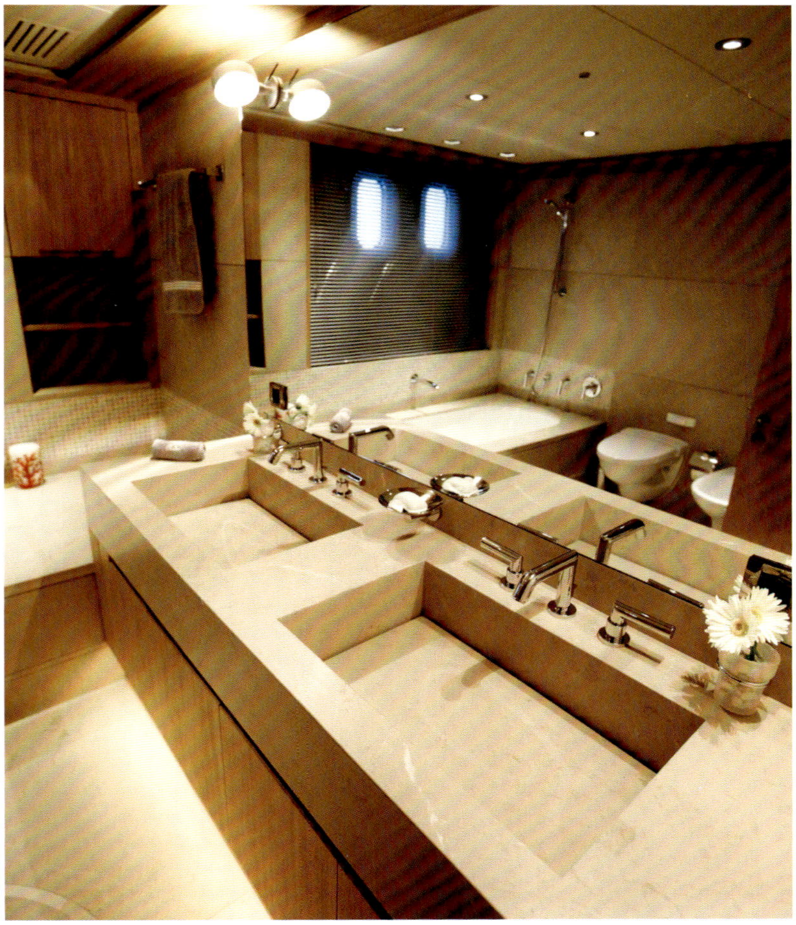

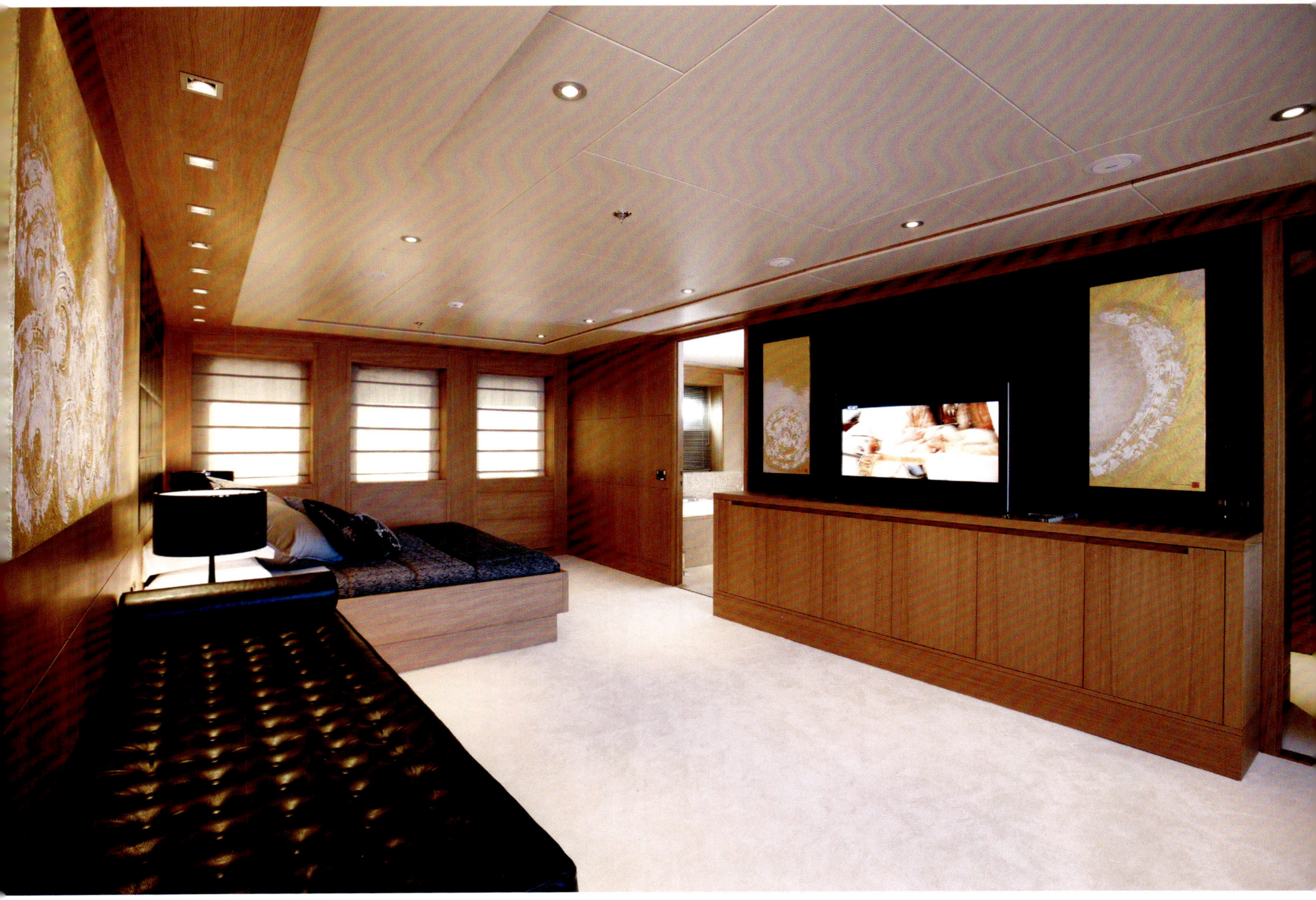

SUNREEF 114

> **DESIGN**   Sunreef Yachts
> **LENGTH**   35m
> **BEAM**   12.8m

> The interior design was very much influenced by the Owner's wife who wanted to have something extraordinary. That is why she chose all the materials and colours herself with the close assistance of the SY design team who arranged the interiors according to yin and yang philosophy (CHE's logo) highlighting harmony and balance on board. She went for caramel bamboo wood applied to all floor/furniture surfaces contrasted by grey upholstery and high-gloss turquoise table tops and decoration elements. The teak deck - both below decks and topside - adds the finishing touch to the whole design. As for space division on the main 60m² deck, the request was to have one huge open space which comprises a big saloon, lounge area, helm station and a professional galley divided from the saloon by a glass wall to keep the impression of one, fluid and uncut space. The owner loves cooking as well as watching his crew prepare food, which is why he requested to have the galley up. Panoramic windows in the saloon and cabins enhance the impression of spaciousness and light.

　　内部设计方面很大程度上受船主夫人影响，她希望达到不拘泥于传统的装饰效果；太阳礁设计团队依据"阴阳哲学"（CHE的标志）设计内部结构，以突出游艇和谐与平衡的理念，在设计团队的倾力协助下，夫人亲自挑选材料和颜色。船上所有地板/家具表面都依她的喜好采用焦糖色竹木材料，与灰色的家具装饰和高光泽度的绿松石桌面和各处装饰元素形成色彩对比。游艇下方和顶部的柚木甲板对整个设计起到了画龙点睛的修饰效果。在60平方米的主甲板上，对空间分隔提出的要求是，将宽敞且开阔的空间分隔成以下部分：一间大客舱、休息区、一间操舵室和一间专业水准的厨房，厨房与客厅之间由一扇玻璃墙相隔，以营造出空间的整体感和流畅完整的感觉。船主爱好烹饪，同时也喜欢欣赏船员备餐的情景，因此要求把厨房建于此处。客舱内的全景窗和隔间增强了游艇内的空间感和亮度。

> **DESIGN** Redman Whiteley Dixon
> **NAVAL ARCHITECT** Dubois Naval Architects
> **SHIPYARD** Royal Huisman Shipyard
> **LENGTH** 57.5m
> **TEXT** Justin Redman, Director, Redman Whiteley Dixon

> "The opportunity to initiate the conceptual design of a large sailing yacht, independently of a naval Architect or yard, is a rare one and to be grasped with both hands. To create an interior arrangement around the owners needs and only when resolved, to then "wrap" a sailing yacht around that requirement is perhaps unique. And so it was with TWIZZLE.

Working again with Todhunter Earle and reforming the successful partnership that created the interiors of the owner's previous yacht, MY TWIZZLE, Redman Whiteley Dixon were part of a highly creative collaboration which challenged preconceptions of how a flybridge ketch should be laid out, how it should function and how it should look and feel and become part of you.

To achieve this, extensive studies developed perfect sightlines from each space, long uninterrupted views through the main deck interior from stem to stern, the blurring of inside and outside spaces in order to enlarge the interior almost without realisation and the science of circulation to provide private entrances for owners, hidden stairs for crew service and effortless and logical circulation for all.

To then create an interior emotion that did not shout, but quietly enveloped you in an atmosphere of calm elegance. It was to exude a simplicity of line and palette, so that the reaction of family and guests as they came aboard would be one almost of relief. The line and the palette were simplified with only two horizontal lines or levels in each space, the palette also by choosing colours that toned together; creams, beiges, greys, duck egg blues, but set against bitter chocolate lacquers, fumed timbers and creamy wide boards.

Designing this interior was a joy, inspired by extraordinary owners and constructed by an interior team at Royal Huisman whose attention to detail is second to none.

This was a rare privilege."

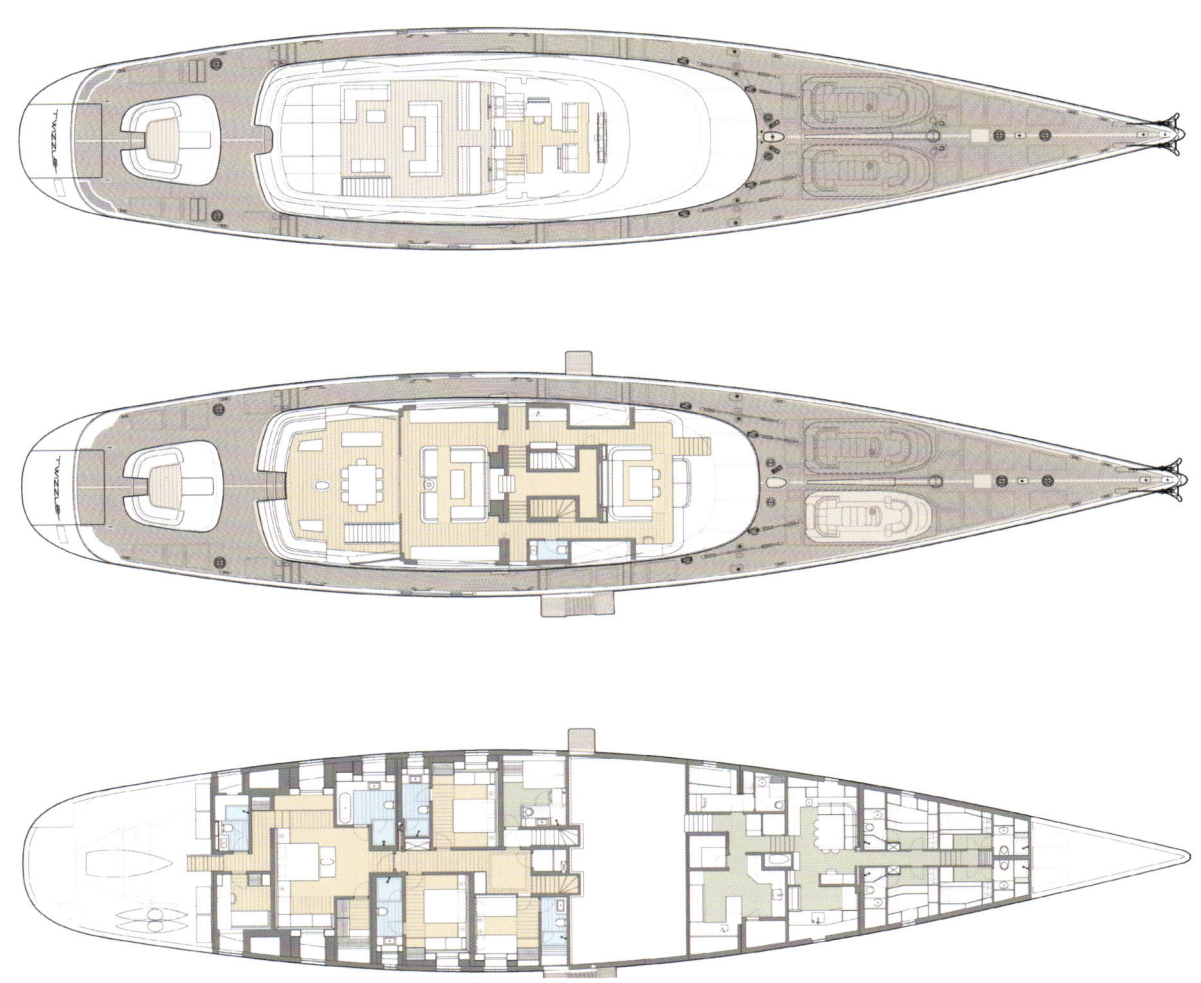

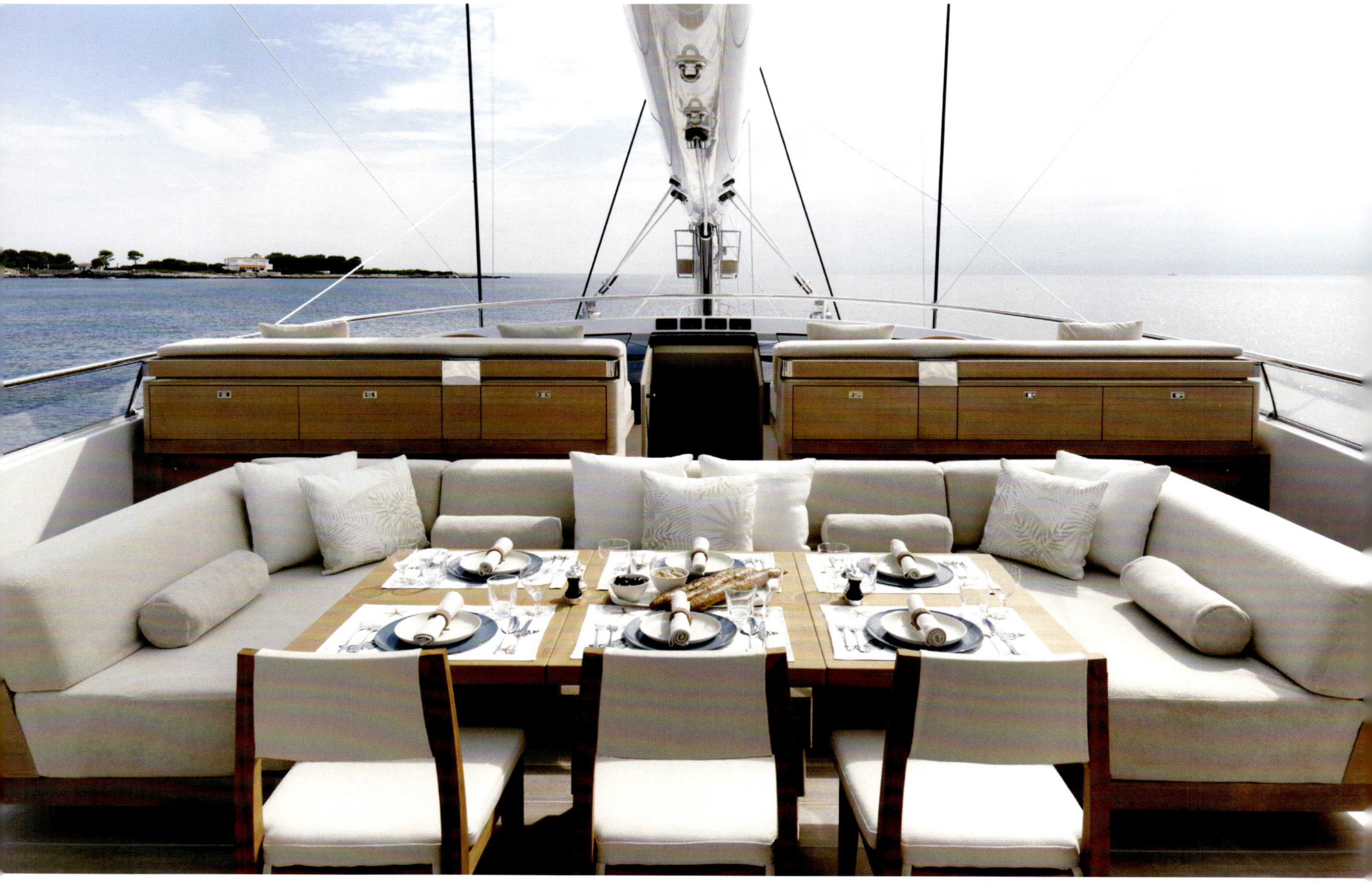

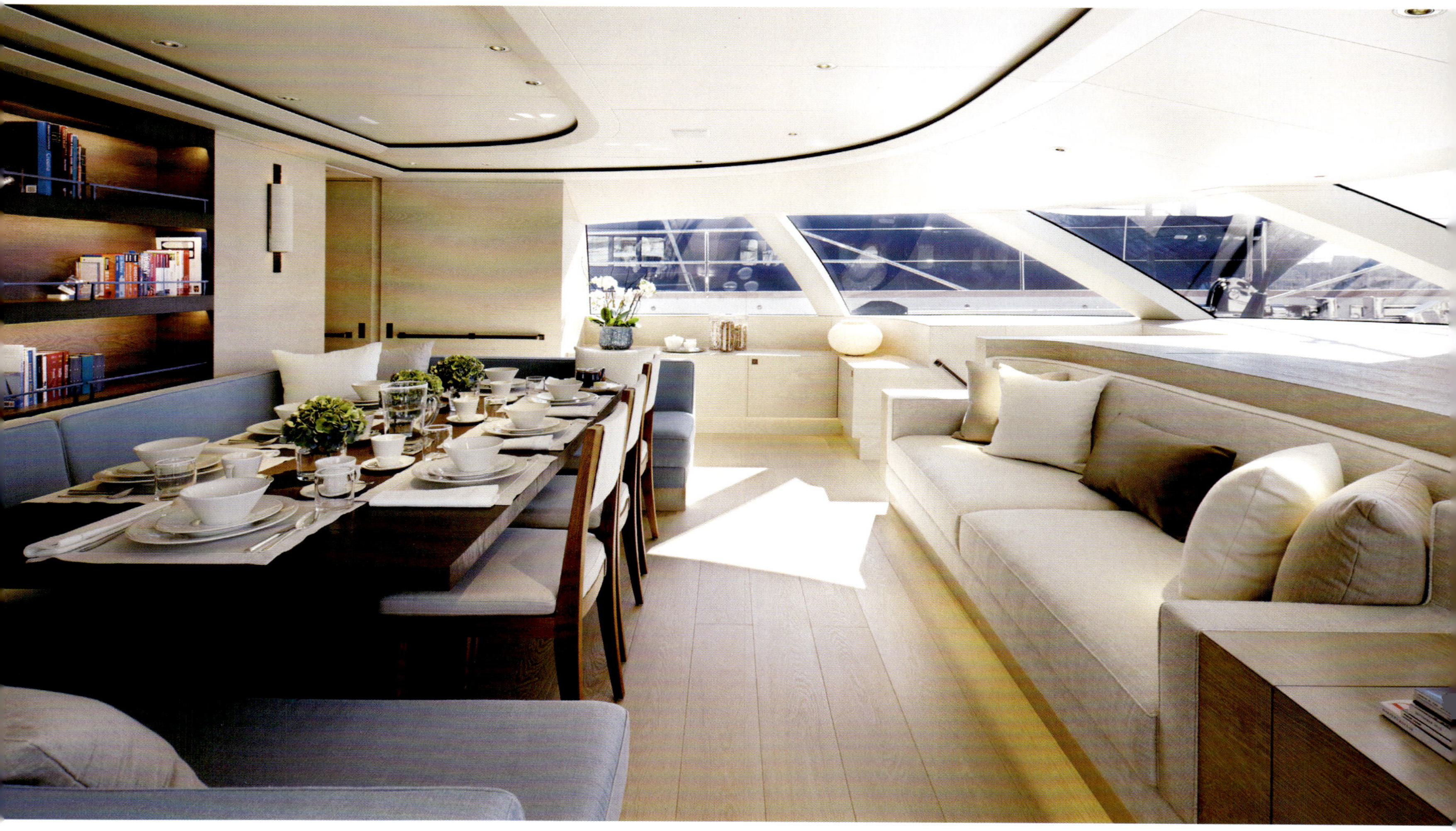

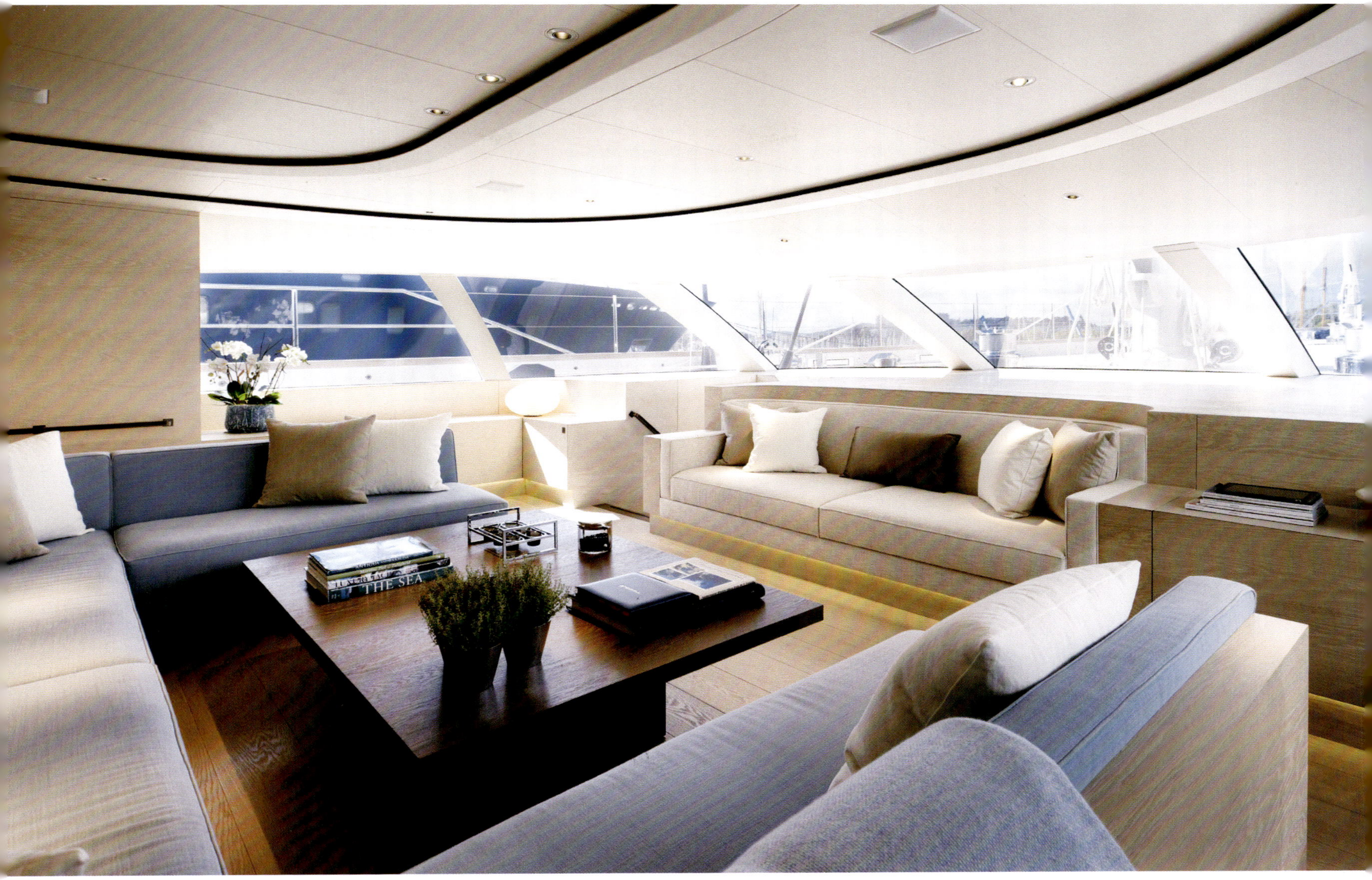
THE SEA

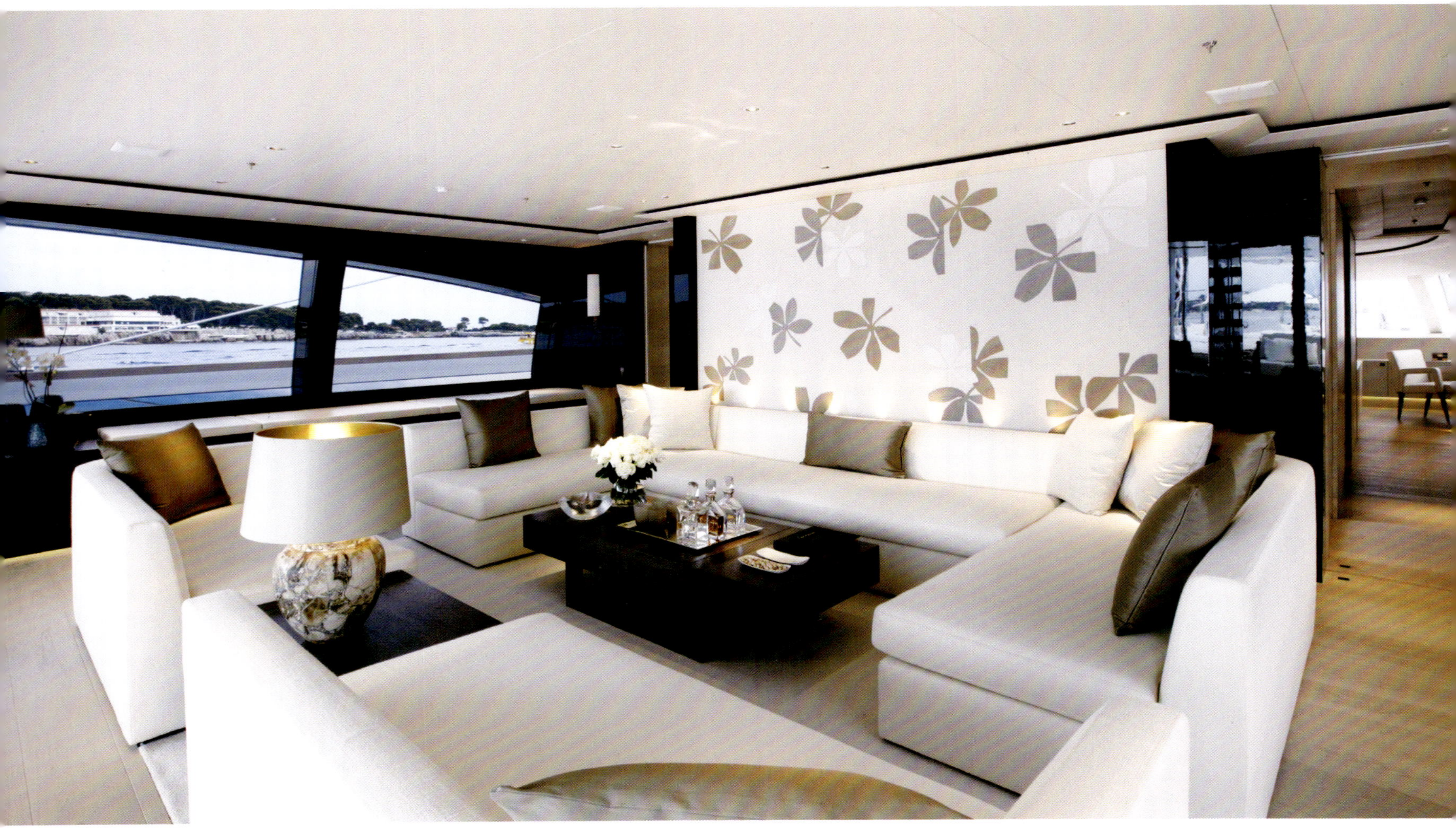

　　"由造船厂独立完成一艘大型游艇的概念设计是一个千载难逢的好机会，值得全力以赴。根据船主的需求进行室内装潢、内部设计完成之后，加上和谐的室外设计，这种要求恐怕是独一无二的。这艘游艇就是这样设计的。

　　英国雷德曼·怀特利·迪克逊设计公司（Redman Whiteley Dixon）的设计师们曾负责船主的另一艘游艇"我的泰舟"（MY TWIZZLE）的内部设计，这次与托德亨特·厄尔（Todhunter Earle）装饰公司再度携手，并对设计团队进行改组。雷德曼·怀特利·迪克逊设计公司是一个具有创新精神的团队，他们曾挑战过怎样设计双桅纵帆船、怎么操作、外观如何、怎样使操舵者与船融为一体。

　　设计师们进行了大量研究，使每个空间都达到了最完美的视觉效果。游览者的视野可以穿越主甲板，船头到船尾的景致一览无余。设计师们对室内外空间交界处进行了模糊处理，无形中增大了室内的视觉空间。通道的科学设计为船主提供了私人入口，为船员设计了出入自如的隐蔽楼梯，使所有人感受到了出入的轻松与便利。

　　室内设计没有张扬，而是静静地给人一种清新雅致的美感。设计上采用了简约的线条和色调，可以让主人和客人在船上感受到一种舒适轻松的氛围。线条和色调都采用简约风格，每个空间仅使用两条水平线，色调的选用也基本一致，包括乳白色、米色、灰色、淡青色，它们与深褐色的漆料、深色的木材以及奶油色的甲板互相映衬。

　　有才华出众的主人提供灵感，有注重细节的皇家豪氏威马团队进行施工，这次的室内装潢是一个愉悦的过程，它是独一无二的。

　　这是一次难得的设计之旅。"

50M MYSTERE SHADOW

> **DESIGN** — Pastrovich Studio
> **NAVAL ARCHITECT** — Robert Mc Farlene
> **SHIPYARD** — Houma Shipyards USA, Monaco Marine

> **LENGTH** — 47.55m
> **BEAM** — 11.58m
> **MAX SPEED** — 10kn

The history. When Exterior and Interior design join together to become one single force; when the owner's briefing is so clear and intense the ideas came out without difficulty and the pencil becomes an uncontaminated power which draw what owner wants. Few concept sketches were done during the first week of intense work to fix on paper all dreams and ideas. We all liked and we started. Nine month later the new Mystere was delivered. This is what happened during the winter-spring 2010-2011 refit process of the 50m Mystere Shadow vessel. The refit time has been so short that ideas were not authorized to rest because drawings needed to be done for the imminent construction. We should probably call this project "Nine Months Adrenaline" or "Nine Months Ecstasy" just to make people understand the high number of hearrt beat held during the entire design and building process. During this short time the shipyard, Monaco Marine, put a great effort to be able to deliver the vessel in time, living to me and my team the possibility of experimenting new ideas which were daily growing up. Till the last minute, till the last call, till the last emotion before hearing the heart beat slowing down at a normal bite rate at the delivery day.

Transformer has been one of the key words during the first meeting with the owner. This word define the design scope: a Yacht capable to change his function and appearance while satisfying different purposes. The yacht mutation has been one of the most relevant subjects which drove all design choices. Mystere wanted to be storage for many tender during navigation and a floating fun island during the day & night while at the anchor. It could be called the beach club, or the resort on the sea, or the disco on the water, or the island…or simply a place where to relax with friends and family.

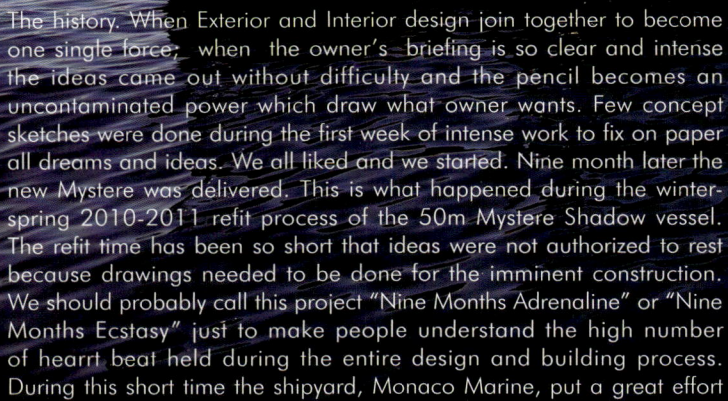

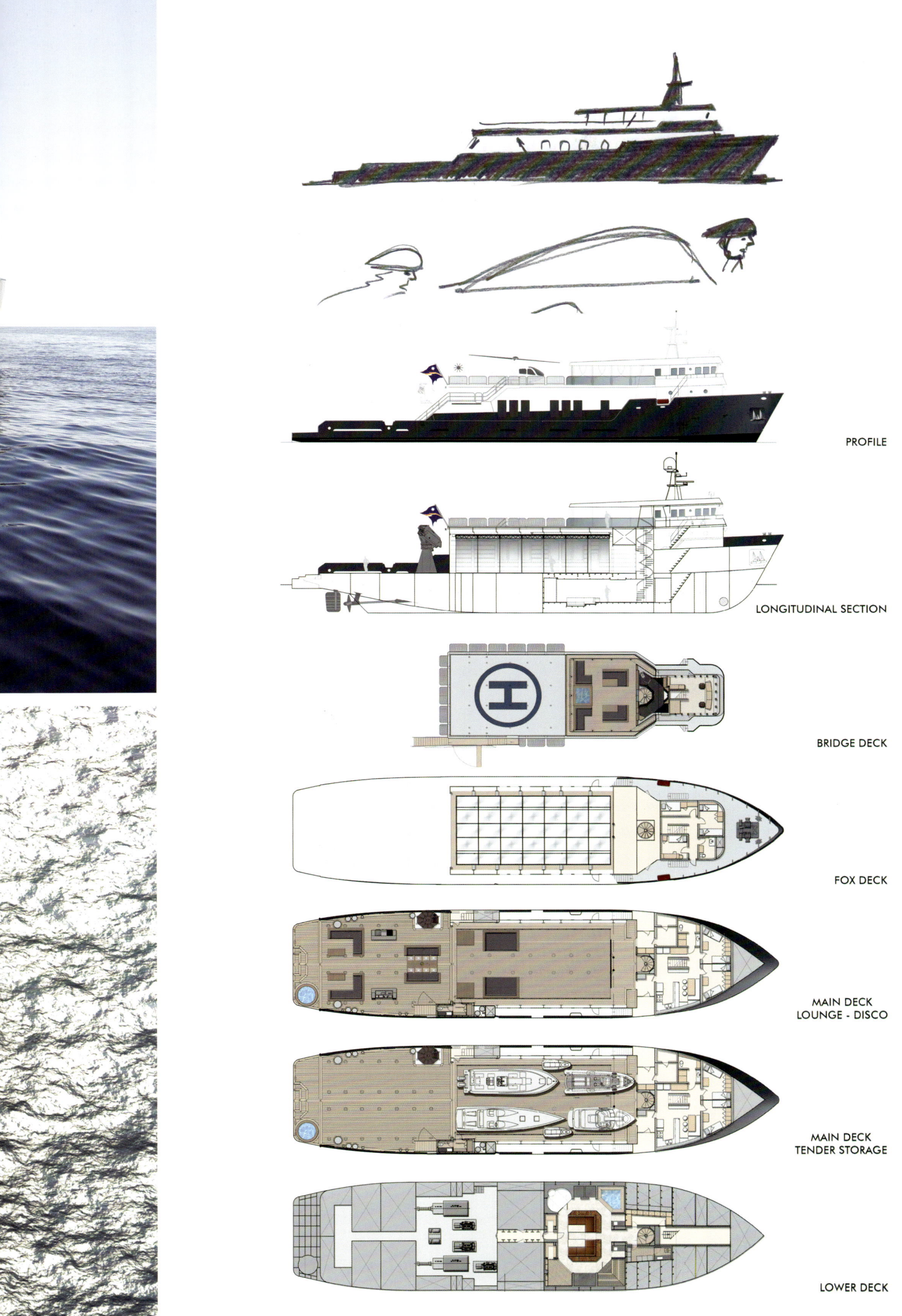

PROFILE

LONGITUDINAL SECTION

BRIDGE DECK

FOX DECK

MAIN DECK
LOUNGE - DISCO

MAIN DECK
TENDER STORAGE

LOWER DECK

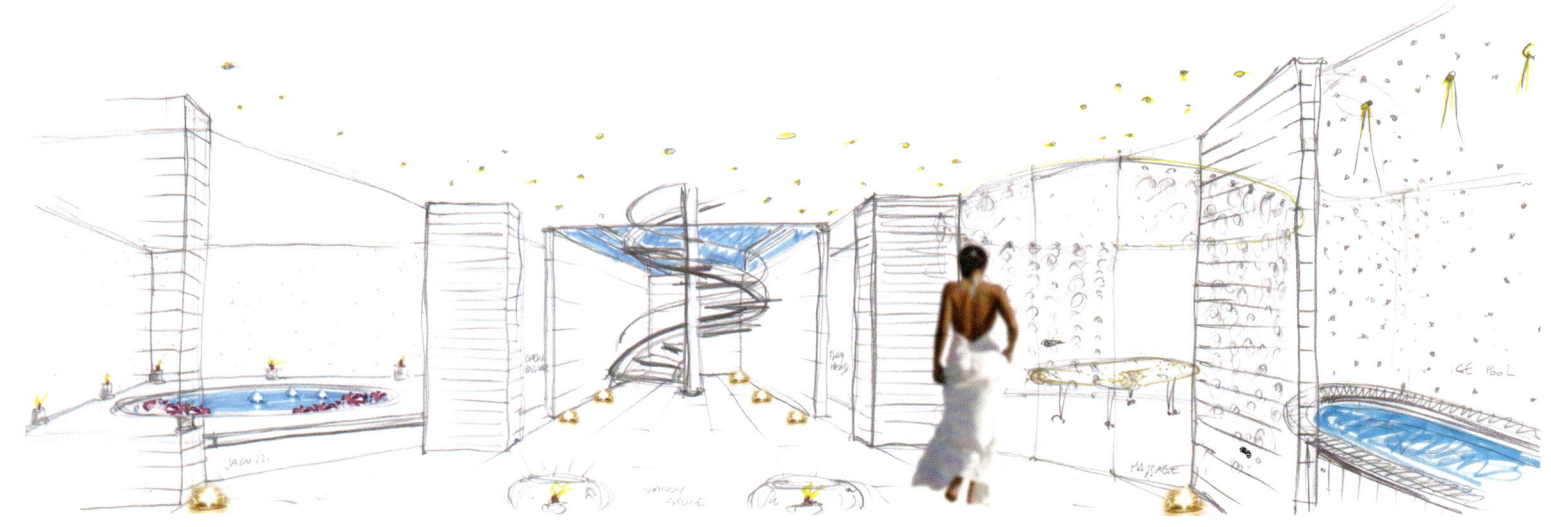

　　背景： 当我们把内部和外部设计方案放在一起考虑，当船主的要求清晰而严格时，游艇的设计思路便顺理成章了，接下来便靠画笔绘出船主的愿景。第一周紧张的工作着重把所有期望和设想落实在纸上，但并未在构图方面有任何概念性的进展；直到我们都一致通过，才正式开始设计。直至九个月之后，才设计完成并交付了崭新的"神秘倒影号"。以上便是 2010 年到 2011 年春季重新装修 50 米长的"神秘倒影号"舰艇期间发生的事。由于约定的装修时间极短，需要立即绘制出图纸，供游艇迅速开工建造，所以，有些想法没来得及反复推敲。也许我们应该把这个工程称作"九月兴奋"或"九月狂喜"，可能这两个词能使人们感受到在游艇的整个设计和建造过程中所经历的紧张和压力。在如此短暂的时间里，摩纳哥舰队造船厂尽力及时交付游艇，才使得我和我的设计团队有可能反复推敲我们的新想法，且每天都有进展；事实上，直到交付游艇那一天，直到最后一刻，最后一个电话，我们所有人的心跳和紧张情绪才趋于缓和。

　　与船主第一次会谈中，其中一个关键词就是"革新"。这个词界定了设计的范围：要设计这样一艘游艇，能在改变其功能和面貌的情况下，满足多种需求。游艇革新已成为设计选择最重大的因素之一。"神秘倒影号"游艇既要成为航海中客货运的交通船，又要成为在停泊时日夜浮于海上的娱乐度假岛。可以称其为海滩俱乐部，或者海上旅游胜地、水上迪斯科舞厅，或者小岛等，亦或简单来说，它就是一个与亲友一起休闲放松的消遣之地。

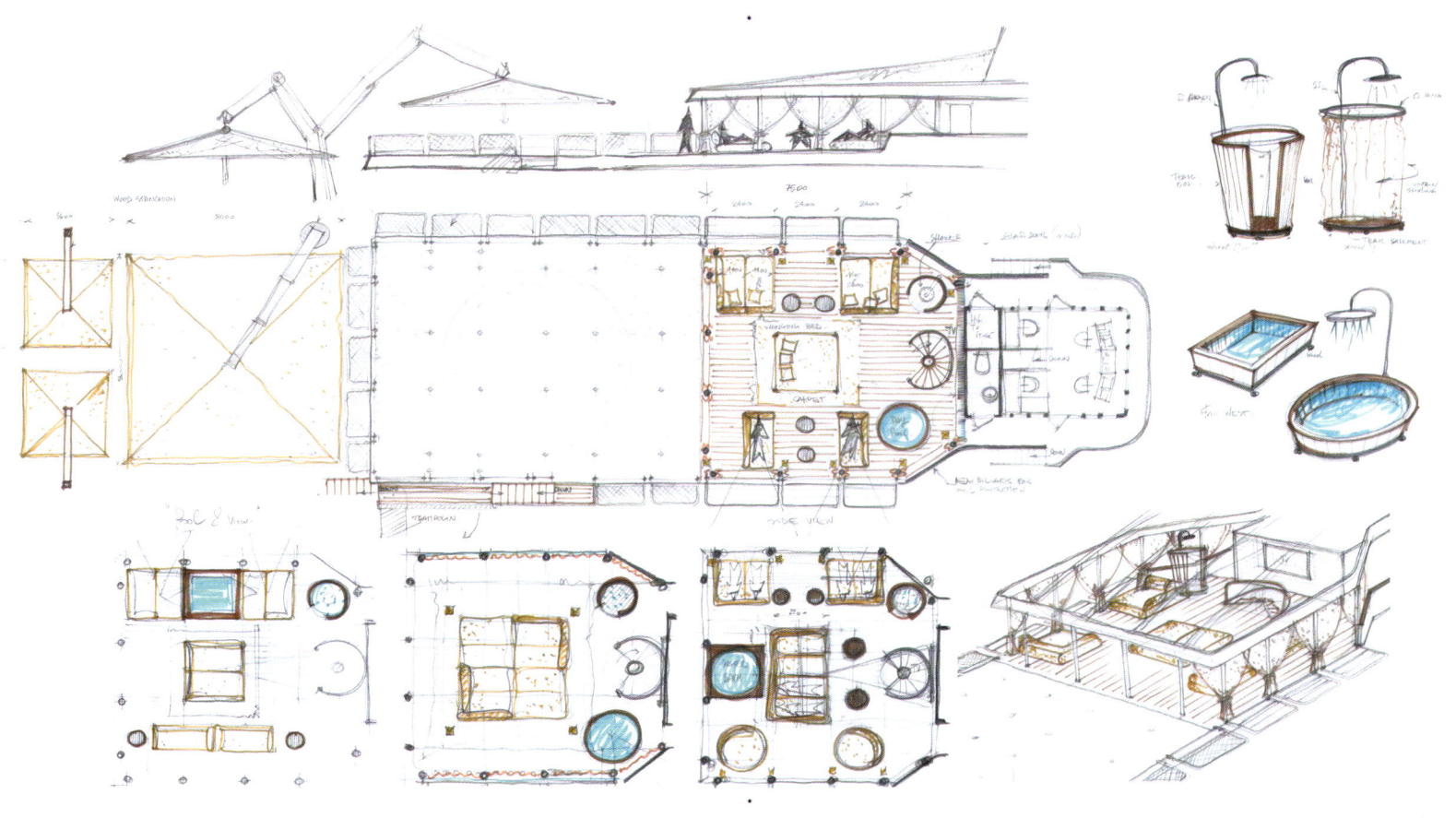

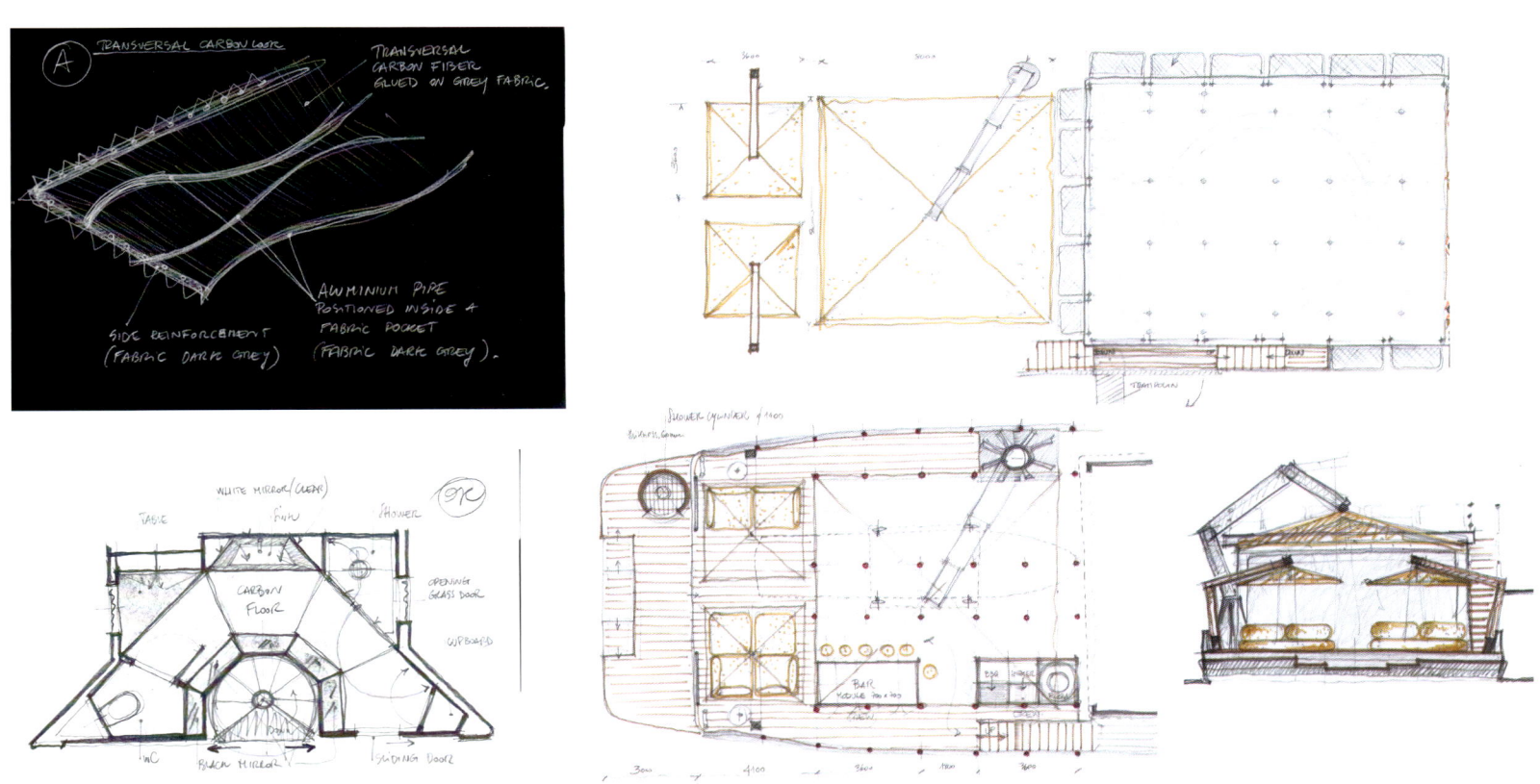

SAUNA
TROPICAL SHOWER
ICE SHOWER FROM BASKET
COLD POOL
FR.25
CREW PASSAGE
FR.23
FR.20
FR.137
FR.27
1400
TV
CREW STAIRCASE
TOILETTE DAY HEAD
FR.20
STEAM
JACUZZI
MASSAGE
2500
3200
2500

STARS
STEAM
SAUNA
TV
ICE POOL
RELAX
MASSAGE
JACUZZI

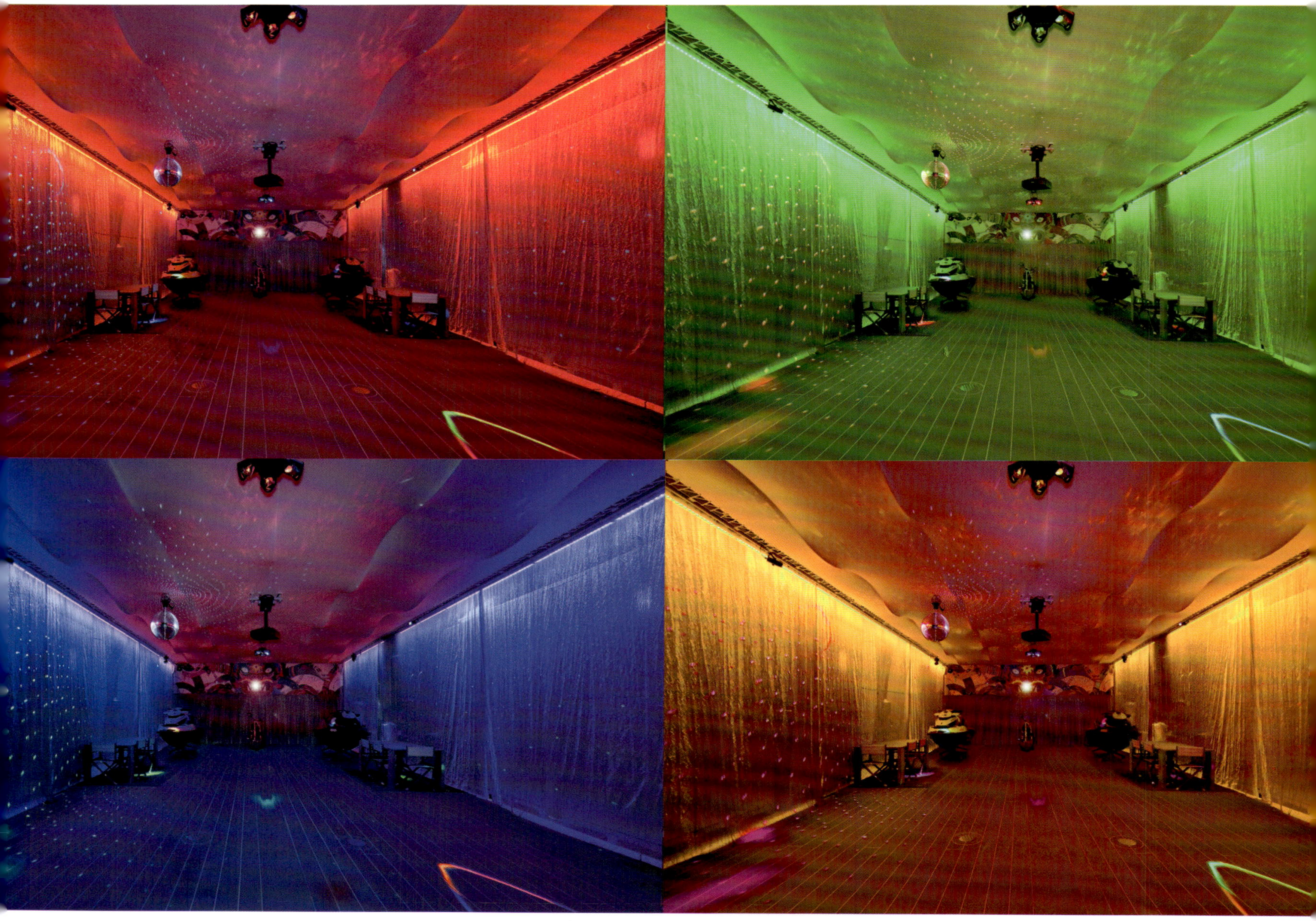

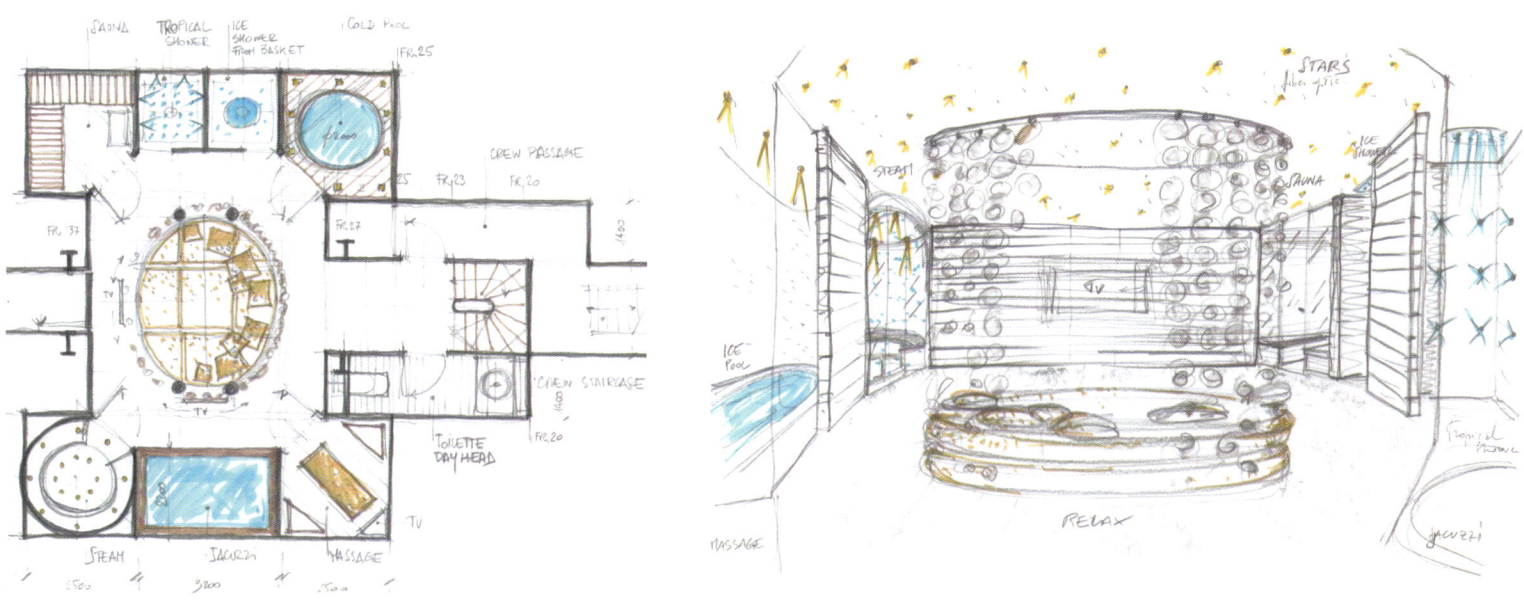

3000
2500
3000
SAUNA
TROPICAL SHOWER
ICE SHOWER
JACUZZI
SIBERIAN LARCH
OIL TANK
STONE WALL
DAY HEAD
STEAM
COLD POOL
MASSAGE

UNDER THE STARS
TROPICAL SHOWER
ICE SHOWER
STEAM
GYM WALL
TV
SAUNA
ICE POOL
JACUZZI
Relax

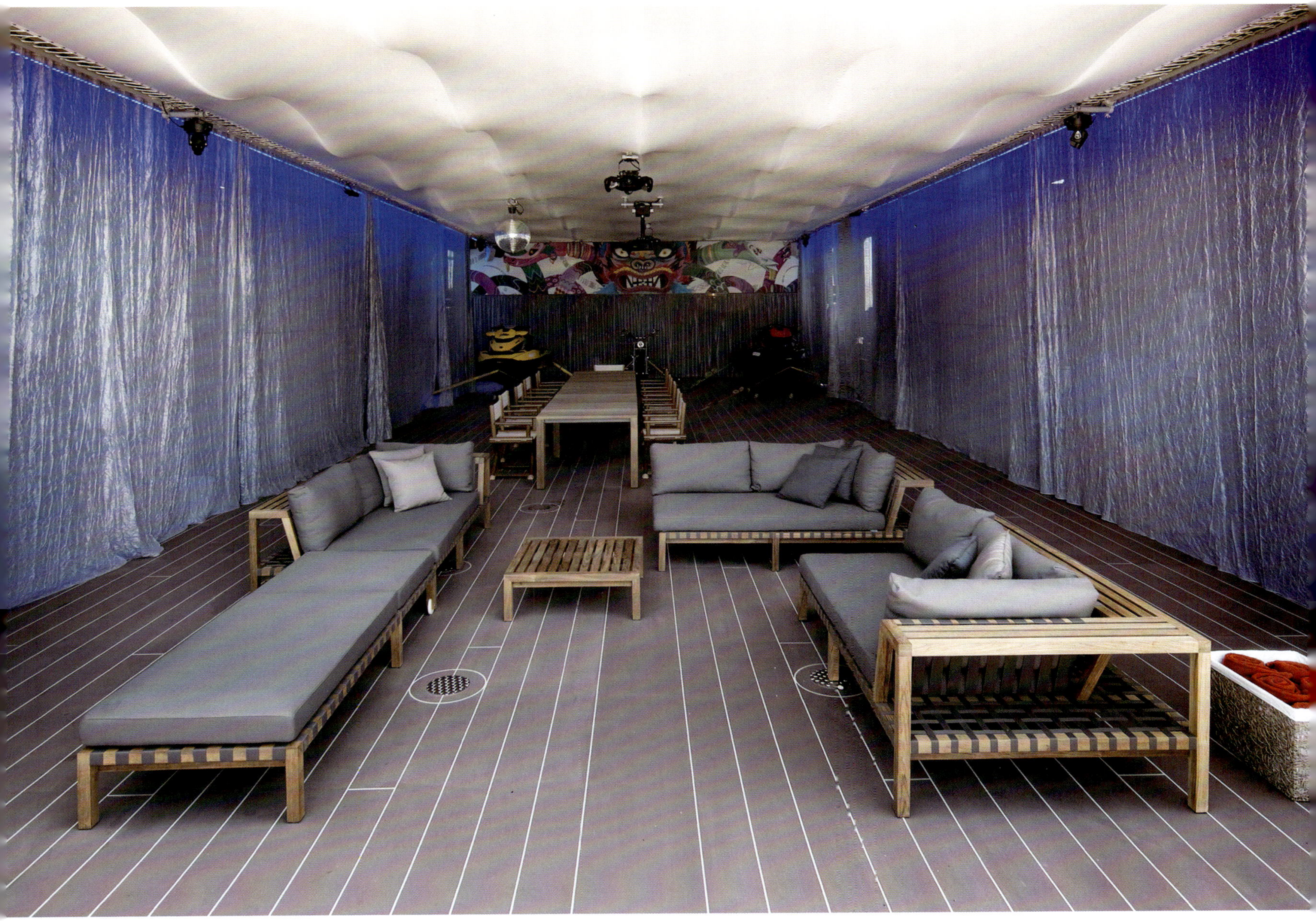

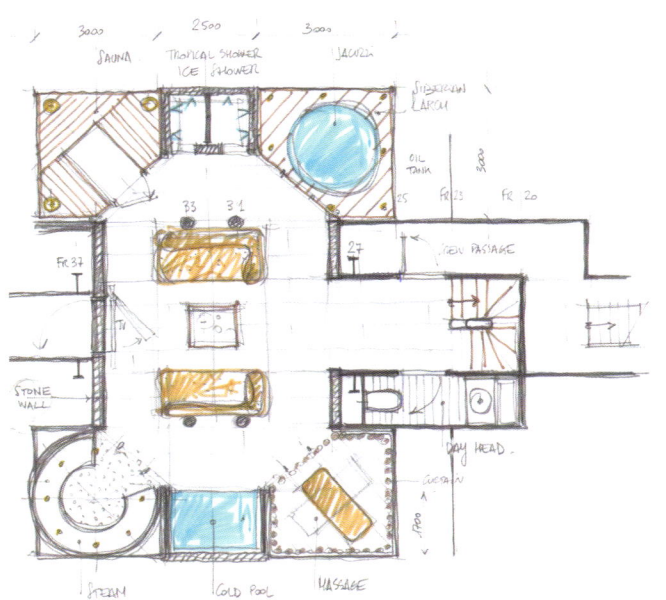

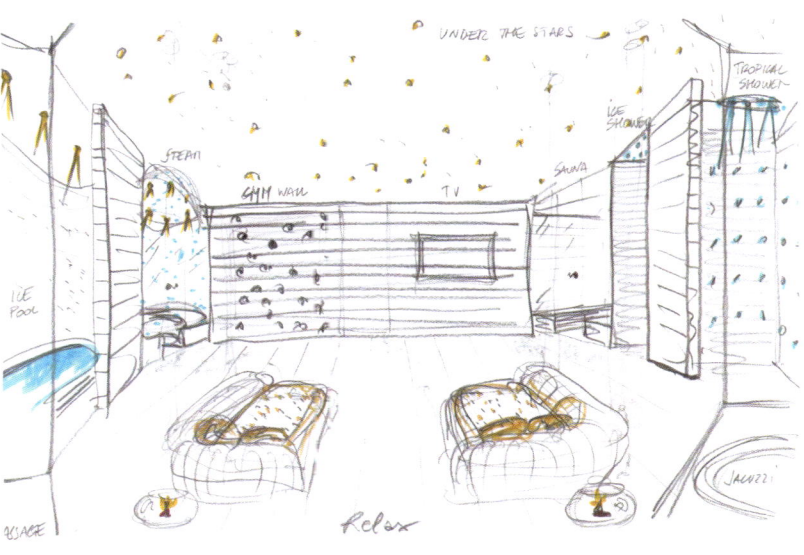

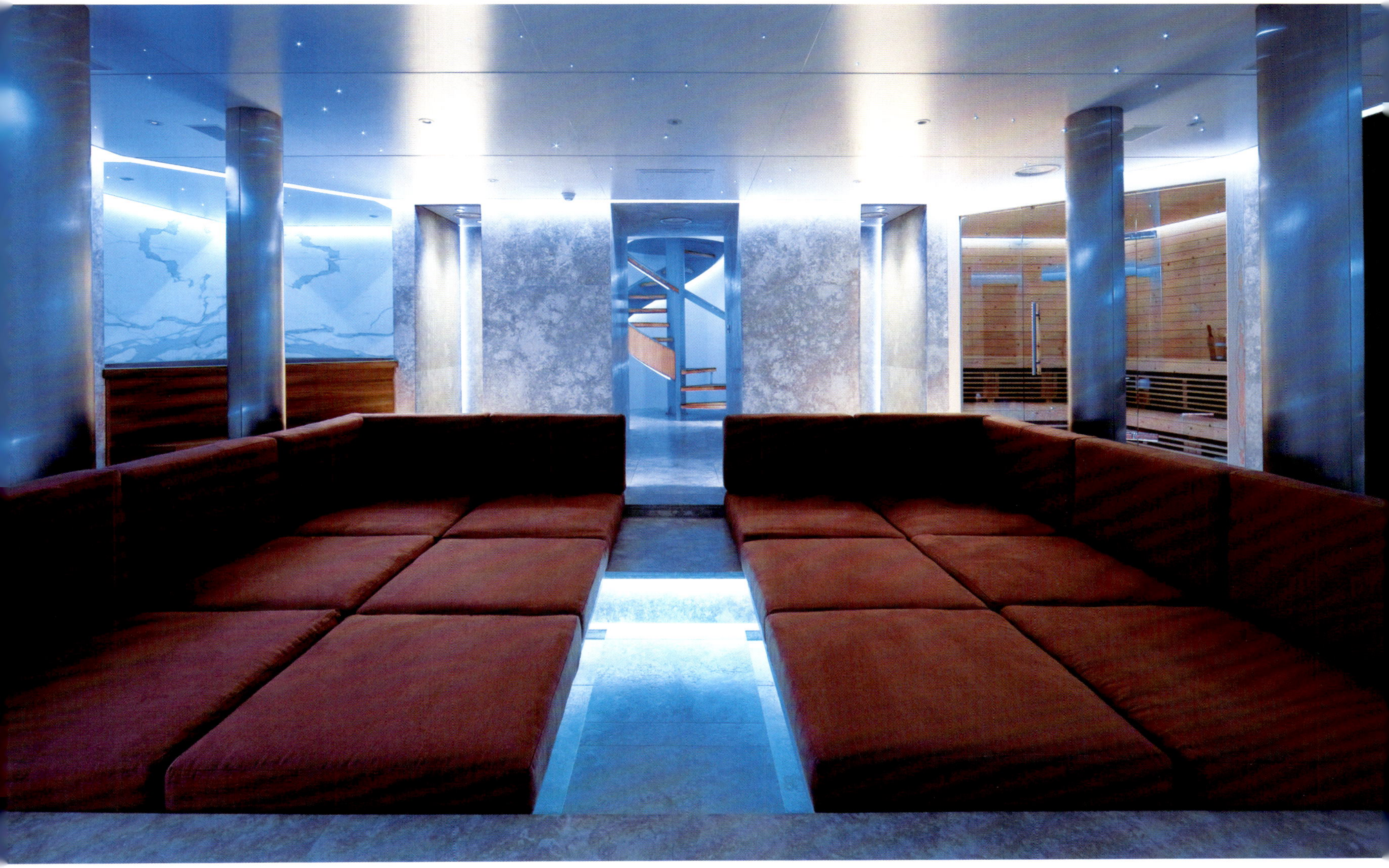

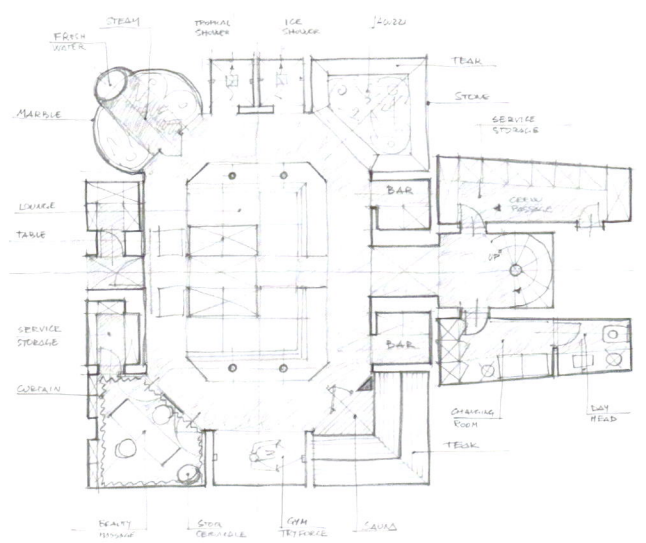

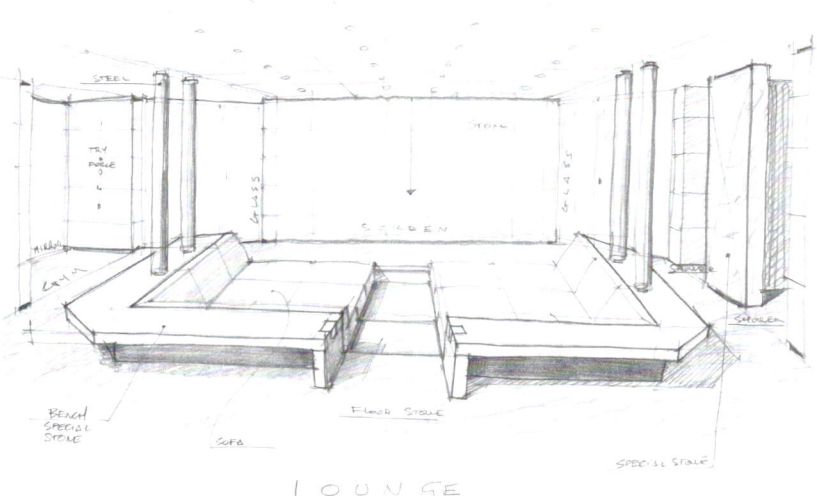

LOUNGE

DAMRAK II

> **DESIGN**   Sunreef Yachts
> **LENGTH**   21.5m
> **BEAM**   9.3m
> **MAX SPEED**   25kn

> Launched in May 2011, DAMRAK II is an upgraded version of DAMRAK launched in 2009 and owned by a French client. The yacht is the sixth unit of the popular 70 Sunreef Power model offered since 2008. This model has been designed by the Sunreef Yachts design studio with the assistance of Laurent Bourgnon, a famous French sailor and owner of the first unit (JAMBO – now in French Polynesia). It was designed as a stylish, fast and stable power vessel with a fine-tuned line of the hull and its underwater section. The streamlined hull helps to take advantage of the wave power and reduce fuel consumption, especially when combined with low draft and light hull structure.

The interior of the yacht is divided into the common living space and private cabins. The spacious living-room is accessible from the cockpit. The living-room is combined with the dining-room and fully equipped kitchen (four-zone induction cooker, microwave oven, two electric ovens, large refrigerator and freezer, dishwasher, wine chiller, ice dispenser, many storage compartments and bar-table). Three double guest cabins with individual bathrooms and one crew cabin are available directly from the living-room. In the mid-ship section, there is a lower helm with complete navigation, communication and control equipment. Another comfortable sofa in this area means the captain need never drive alone. The helm station leads to the owner's cabin located in the foredeck section, along the fly bridge. The owner's cabin is furnished with a king-size bed, desk, sofa, night tables , wardrobes, private wine cellar and a spacious bathroom with separated shower and toilets located in the starboard hull. Panoramic views of the sea can be enjoyed from thebeamwide owner's cabin. From the lower helm station, the sunny flybridge – the Sunreef trademark – is accessible.

The cockpit of DAMRAK II is an ideal place to relax from burning sun or have lunch with friends in refreshing sea breeze. The cockpit is furnished with a large dining table, sofa, chairs, resting mattresses, a wash basin for quick freshening up and small handy refrigerator. Supplies for longer journeys or water toys can be neatly hidden in storage compartments.

More sunbathing mattresses with special drink holders can be found in the bow section. Guest may enjoy beautiful sights and sunbathe comfortably at the same time.

DAMRAK II

　　2011年5月推出的"达麦二号"是2009年推出的"达麦号"游艇的升级版，船主是一位法国客户。这是2008年以来推出广受喜爱的"70太阳礁帆船动力游艇系列"的第六款，由太阳礁帆船设计工作室设计，并得到了法国著名水手劳伦特·伯纳的协助，他也是该系列第一款游艇"珍宝"（目前，"珍宝"在法国波利尼西亚）的拥有者。"达麦二号"设计时尚，行驶高速，动力稳定，船体型线与水下型线设计精良。特别是在低负荷、船体结构很轻的情况下，这种流线型的船体可以充分利用波浪的力量，从而降低耗油量。

　　游艇内部分为普通的生活区与私人舱室。生活区宽敞明亮，可以直通驾驶舱。生活区包括了餐厅和设备齐全的厨房（四头电磁炉、微波炉、两个电烤炉、大型冰箱和冷冻设备、洗碗机、冰酒器、冰水机，大量的储藏隔间和吧台）。此外，还有三个配有独立卫生间的双人客舱以及一个船员舱，都可以直通生活区。在船的中部，安装了低位船舵，并配有全套导航、通讯和控制系统。旁边还有一个舒适的沙发，这就意味着船长掌舵的时候，旁人可以陪伴左右。从船舵出发，沿着驾驶桥楼就可以到达位于船头甲板的船主舱。船主舱内设有特大卧床、弓桌、沙发、床头柜、衣橱、私人酒窖以及位于船身右舷的宽敞的卫浴间，内有独立的淋浴间和马桶。船主舱是船体最宽的地方，可以领略到全景式的海景。从底层的船舱站可以到达阳光明媚的驾驶桥楼——这也是太阳礁的标志。

　　"达麦二号"的驾驶舱是避暑休闲、享受清爽海风、与朋友共进午餐的理想场所。舱内设有一张大餐桌、沙发、椅子、休息坐垫、便捷洗漱盆、小型便携式冰箱。储存隔间里可以整齐地存放着长途旅行用的物品和水上用具。

　　船头有很多日光浴垫，配有独特的酒水架。客人同时可以享受美丽的海景和舒适的日光浴。

SALPERTON IV

> DESIGN COMPANY	Adam Lay Studio
> NAVAL ARCHITECT	Dubois Naval Architects
> LENGTH	45m
> PHOTOGRAPHER	Superyacht Media

Salperton IV is clean, slick, minimal and much more modern than the owner's previous yachts. Adam Lay Studio has worked closely with the owner in applying a simpler style to the joinery. Spaces flow cleanly with the same refreshing openness to the upper and lower saloon making outside light and air a definite feature of these interior spaces. The saloon skylight is enlarged, the ranch slider doors to the cockpit widened and the extra half a metre in the saloon makes the space flow even more comfortably. Specially custom-designed pieces of furniture, built from Wenge, are set-off against the predominant Walnut joinery and add a further dimension to this unique sailing yacht. New sofas, table and bar designs mean the yacht has a very different feel to Salperton III whilst maintaining the best features of the highly successful design. The cabins are clean contemporary spaces with Bronze and leather door hardware set off against the simple clean walnut joinery and hemp wall coverings. Specialist Oyster Oak flooring, combined with luxurious wool and silk carpets leading to the beautifully appointed en-suites, continue the elegant slick style. Clean, minimal sanitary and tapware fittings from Dornbracht, add to the homogenous design throughout the yacht, set against a rare French flamed-and-brushed grey marble.

The extremely versatile cockpit seating area, the most used area on Salperton IV, provides an excellent level of comfort for an outdoor entertaining space in which guests can revel, whilst keeping in close contact with the helmsman, and thereby feeling at one with the sailing experience. A new design for the sofas and cockpit table along with small changes to the sail control console and aft sunpads bring the exterior styling in-line with the more modern interior style.

The crew area is also simple in style but no less elegant. The galley is enviably appointed for the very best in culinary creation and the cabins continue the slick modern style with walnut and painted bulkhead panelling and generous stowage space. Practicality for the wear-and-tear of the crew area was always foremost in Adam Lay's mind when selecting the finishes. The crew area has been rearranged to create two generous crew cabins forward, and a practical captain's cabin aft. Full galley and pantry spaces, laundry and a crew's mess complete the crew area. Dark walnut joinery is balanced with painted upper level surfaces and light oak flooring.

The opportunity to develop on the platform of a previously successful design allows the owner, shipyard and designer to concentrate on specific areas and develop those areas in a new and exciting direction. The owner admits Salperton III is hard to beat so the changes have been more in terms of interior style than arrangement.

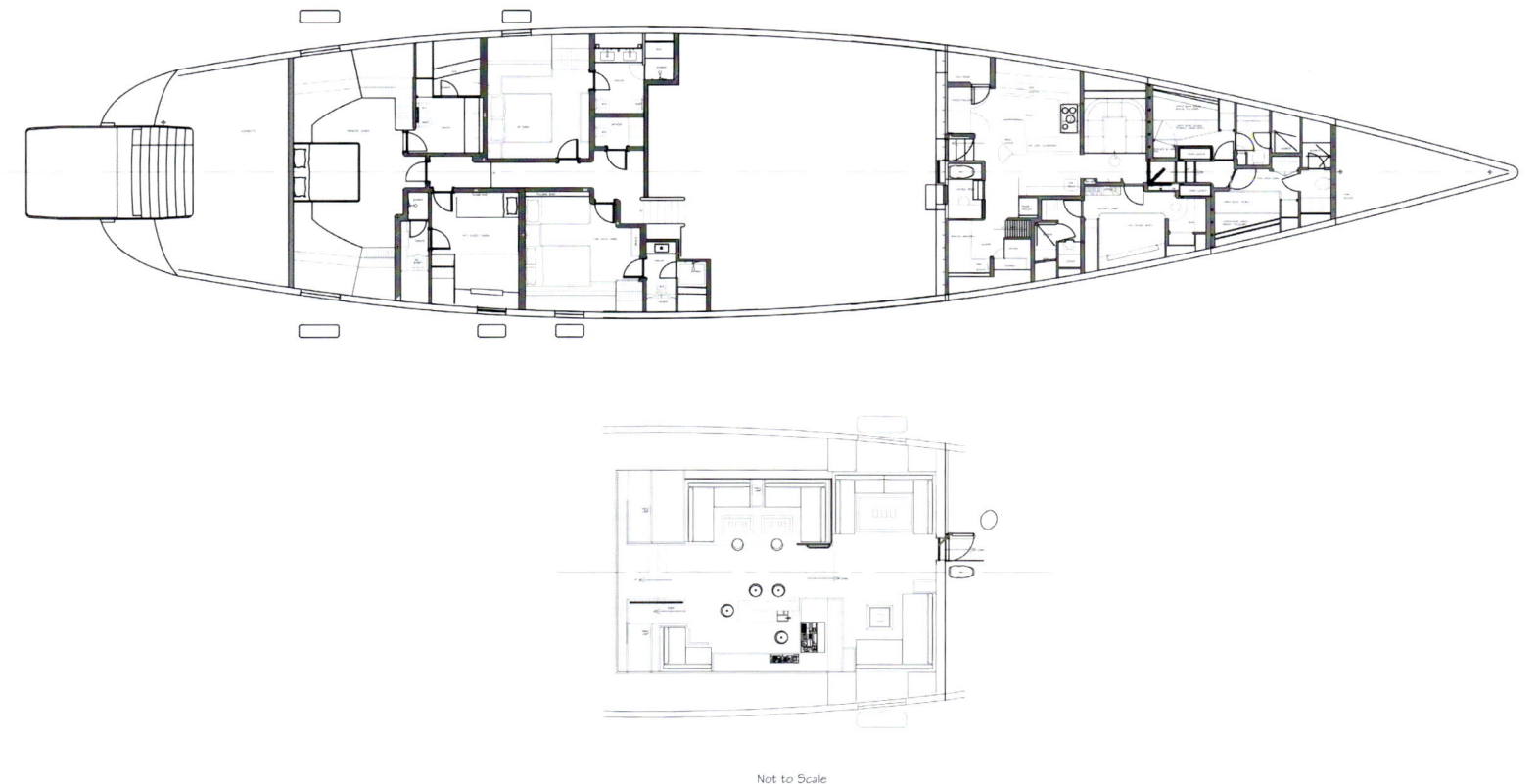

Not to Scale

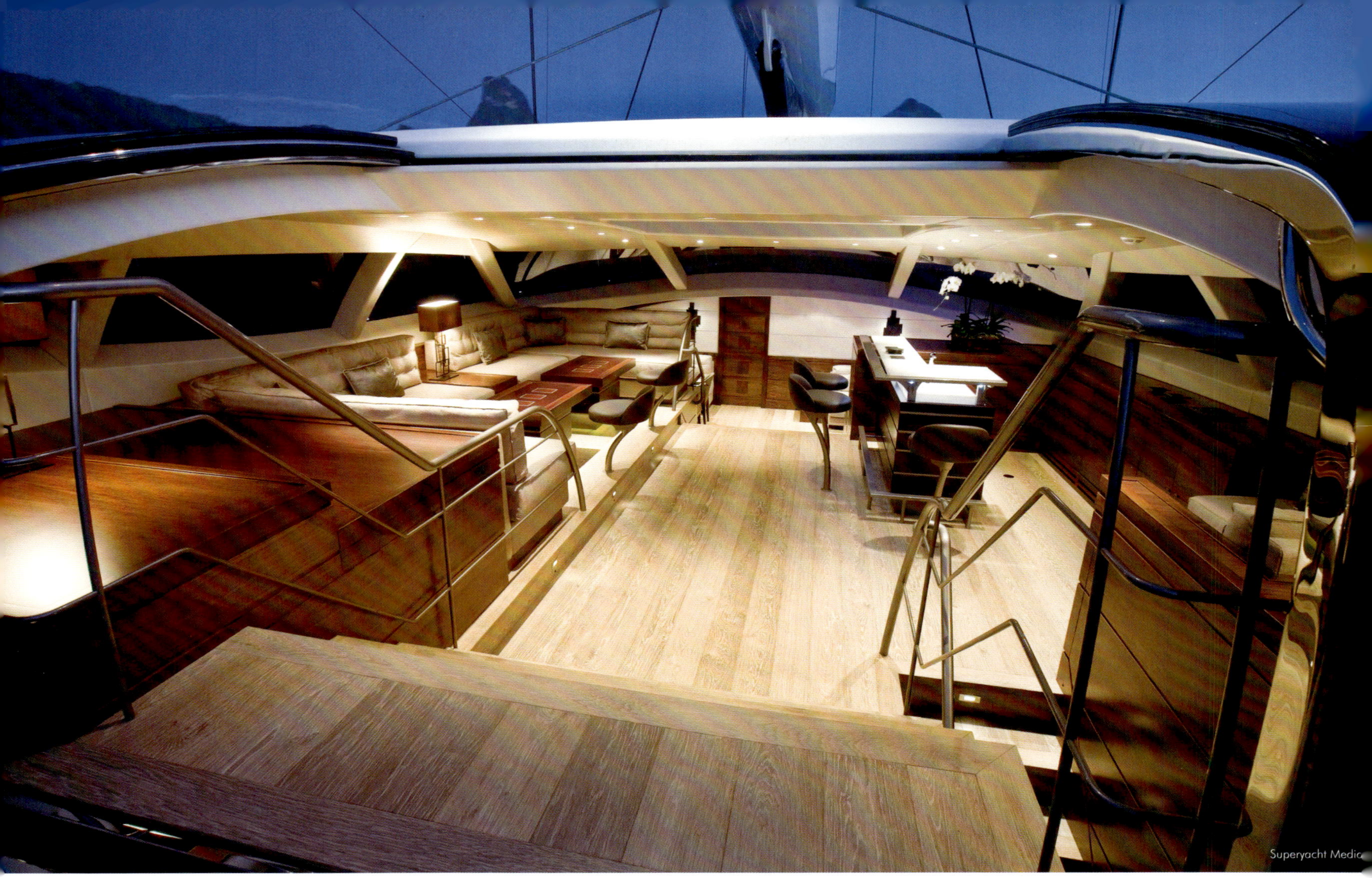

Superyacht Media

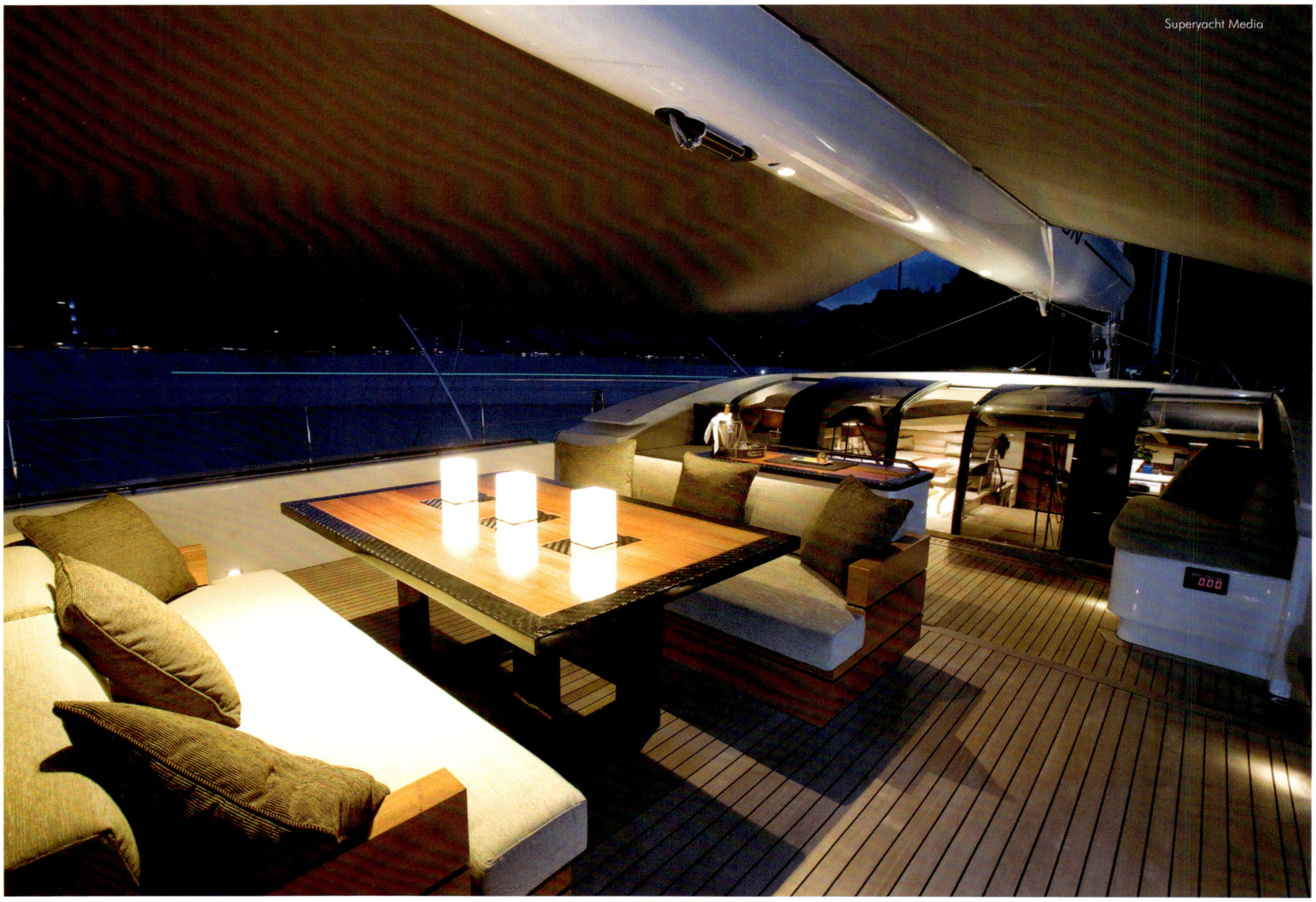

Superyacht Media

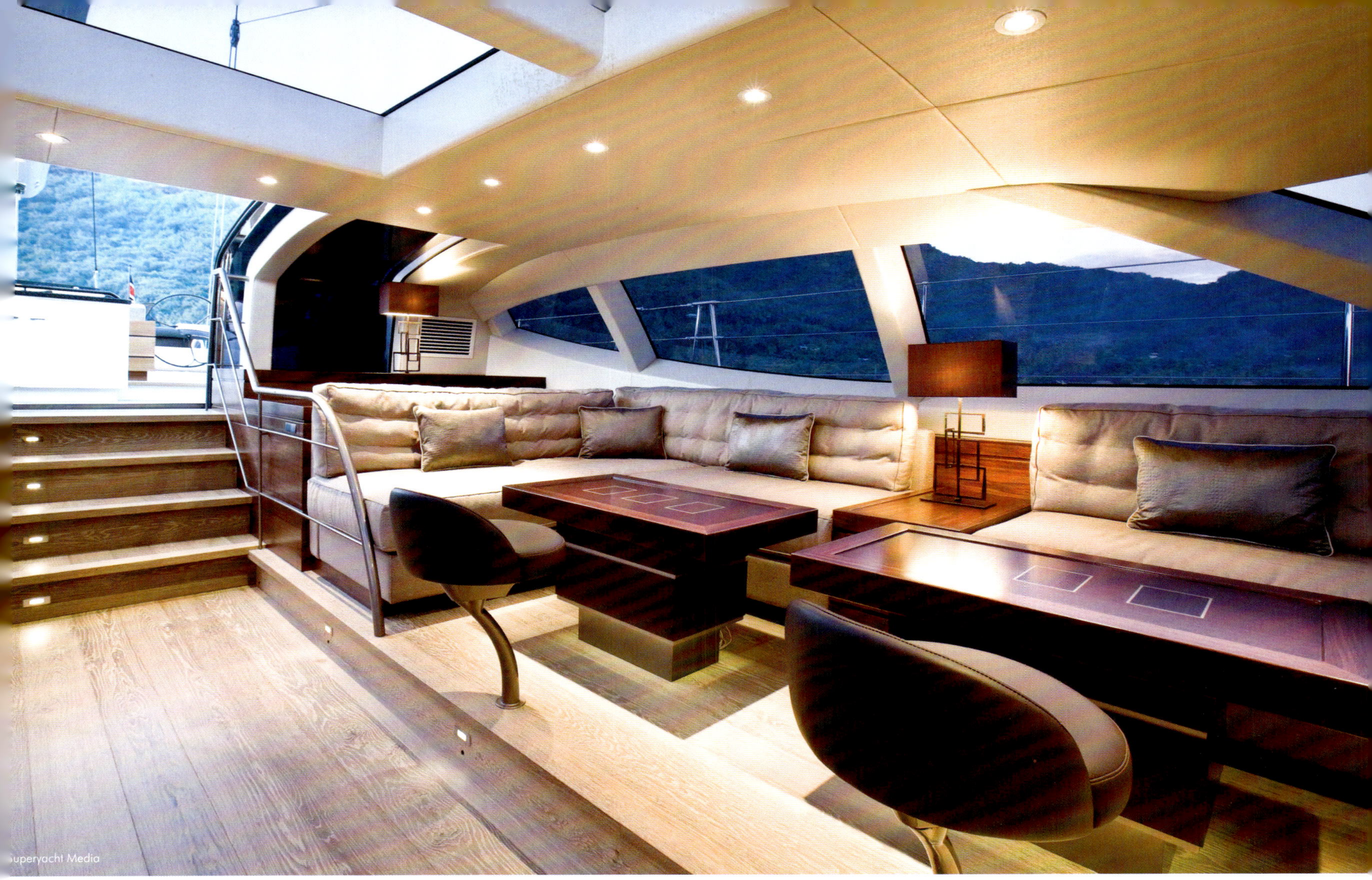
Superyacht Media

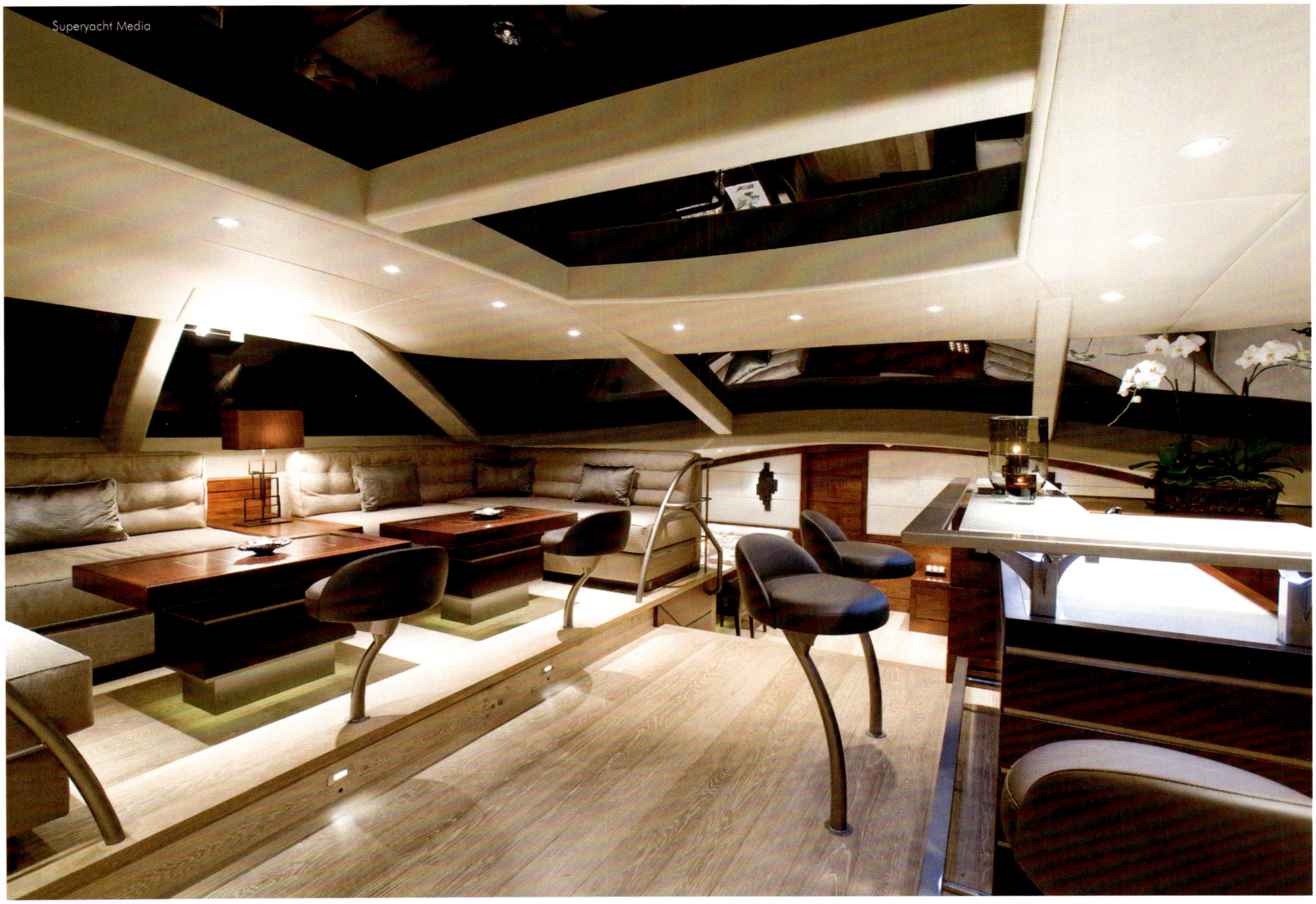
Superyacht Media

　　"Salperton 4"游艇干净、漂亮、体型小、比船主先前所有的游艇都时尚亮丽。Adam Lay设计室与船主密切合作，将简单大方的设计运用到木工设计方面。上层和下层大厅都采用了露天设计，令人耳目一新，也使得室内空间具备了室外光照和空气流通的特性。大厅的天窗被改大，通往驾驶舱的滑动门也得以拓宽0.5米，让整个空间的使用更具舒适感。从刚果的文盖特别定制的家具，与大量使用的胡桃木工艺，形成鲜明对照，拓展了这艘机帆游艇的空间维度。新的沙发、餐桌和吧台设计使这艘游艇有了与"Salperton 3"游艇完全不同的风格，同时也保持了这一系列游艇成功设计的精华。舱室空间采用青铜材料，整洁现代。皮革门饰与简约整洁的胡桃木工艺、棕榈墙板交相呼应。专门定制的硬橡木地板，配以豪华的毛绒丝织地毯，延伸到各个精美的套房，继续着高雅的光亮式风格。德国"当代"牌洁具与水龙头制品不仅干净，而且小巧，贯穿整个游艇设计，与一种罕见的火烧加刷磨工艺的法国灰色大理石形成呼应。

　　驾驶舱极具多功能的座位区，是"Salperton 4"使用频率最高的地方，为室外娱乐提供了完美的舒适空间，游客可以在此尽情狂欢，同时紧挨着舵手，也就能感受到在海上航行的激动。沙发、驾驶舱餐桌采用了新型设计，航海控制台和船尾的阳光浴垫也得以小小改进，这让室外风格与更加现代的室内风格保持统一。

　　船员区风格简约，但丝毫不失高雅。厨房的各种设施都是最好的，舱室也继续延续着一贯的现代美学风格，采用胡桃木与喷漆隔离镶板木料，并留有大量储物空间。在Adam Lay设计室选择抛光剂的时候，就已经考虑到了船员区的实际损耗是最大的。船员区重新进行了规划，在前面设计了两个大的船员舱，在船尾设计了一个实用的船长舱。设施齐备的厨房和储物空间、洗衣间和船员食堂构成了整个船员区。深色胡桃木工艺与表层喷漆、浅色橡木地板互为映衬。

　　在之前成功的设计基础上的再次创新，让船主、造船厂和设计师都能够集中在特定的区域，并将之改进到新的令人赞叹的水平。船主承认："Salperton 3"游艇很难超越，所以多是在室内风格上进行改进，很少在结构上有大的改动。

Superyacht Media

Superyacht Media

ANGELS SHARE

> **DESIGN**   Eidsgaard Design
> **SHIPYARD**   Lurssen Shipyard
> **PHOTOGRAPHER**   Stefan Bravin

> Completed in December 2010, Angels Share was a complete re-build project awarded to Eidsgaard Design and completed at Lurssen Shipyard in Germany. The Owners had been drawn to Eidsgaard Design following the success of their work on both interior and exterior of the award winning 45 meter S/Y Saudade built by Wally Yachts.

The Angels Share, previously launched under the name S/Y Dream was taken to Lurssen shipyard to undergo a complete rebuild. It consists of Main Saloon, Dining area, 3 Guest cabins and Owners cabin (all en-suite). Crew accommodation is for 5/6, with a separate galley, crew mess and nav station. The interior design brief was to create a relaxed "holiday" feel in which to while away the hours reading or relaxing with the maximum connection to the sea. For an interior style the Owners wanted a synthesis of Japanese tea house meets Norwegian summer cottage. In achieving this Eidsgaard Design have employed playful elements such as the wall mounted bunks that when stowed resemble traditional luggage trunks.

Since her delivery Eidsgaard Design has been rewarded for their part in the re-design of this exceptional yacht, picking up awards from the International Superyacht Society and World Superyacht Awards for best re-fit 2011.

　　"Angels Share" 号游艇于 2010 年 12 月完工，是 Eidsgaard 设计公司和德国 Lurssen 造船厂联合打造的一艘翻新船。船主之所以选择这家设计公司，主要是因为该公司成功完成了由 Wally Yachts 游艇公司打造的 45 米长的 S/Y Saudade 游艇的室内外设计。

　　这艘 "Angels Share" 游艇原本的名字是 "S/Y Dream"，后来被送到 Lurssen 造船厂进行全面的翻新。游艇包含大厅、餐区、三个客舱和一个船主舱（均有独立卫生间）。船员舱可容纳 5~6 人，并有独立厨房、食堂和领航站。内部设计的精髓是要创造一种舒适恬淡的 "度假" 之感，在船上可以读书看报，打发时光，与大海充分接触。船主希望这艘游艇的内部风格能融合日本茶室与挪威避暑农舍的精华。为了达到这个目标，Eidsgaard 设计公司采用了一些活泼的元素，例如修建了一些靠墙的床铺，当床铺折叠收起的时候，像极了一个个传统的行李箱。

　　自从游艇问世以来，Eidsgaard 设计公司就成了这艘无与伦比的翻新游艇的最大的功臣，为这艘游艇赢得了国际超级游艇协会的多项荣誉，并获得 2011 世界最佳翻新超级游艇大奖。

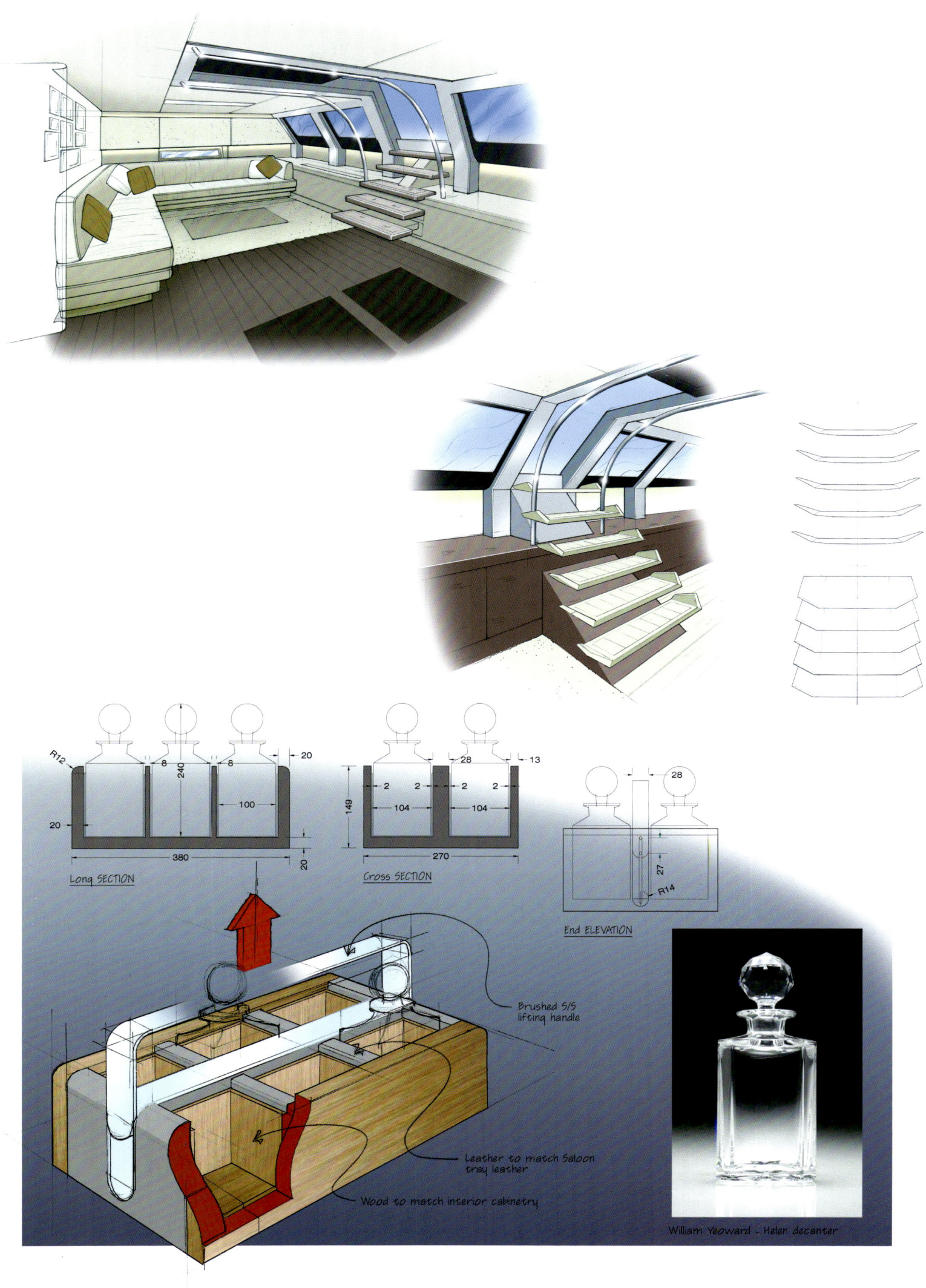

Long SECTION

R12

240

8 8

20

100

20

380

20

Cross SECTION

28

13

2 2 2 2

149

104 104

270

End ELEVATION

28

27

R14

Brushed S/S
lifting handle

Leather to match Saloon
tray leather

Wood to match interior cabinetry

William Yeoward - Helen decanter

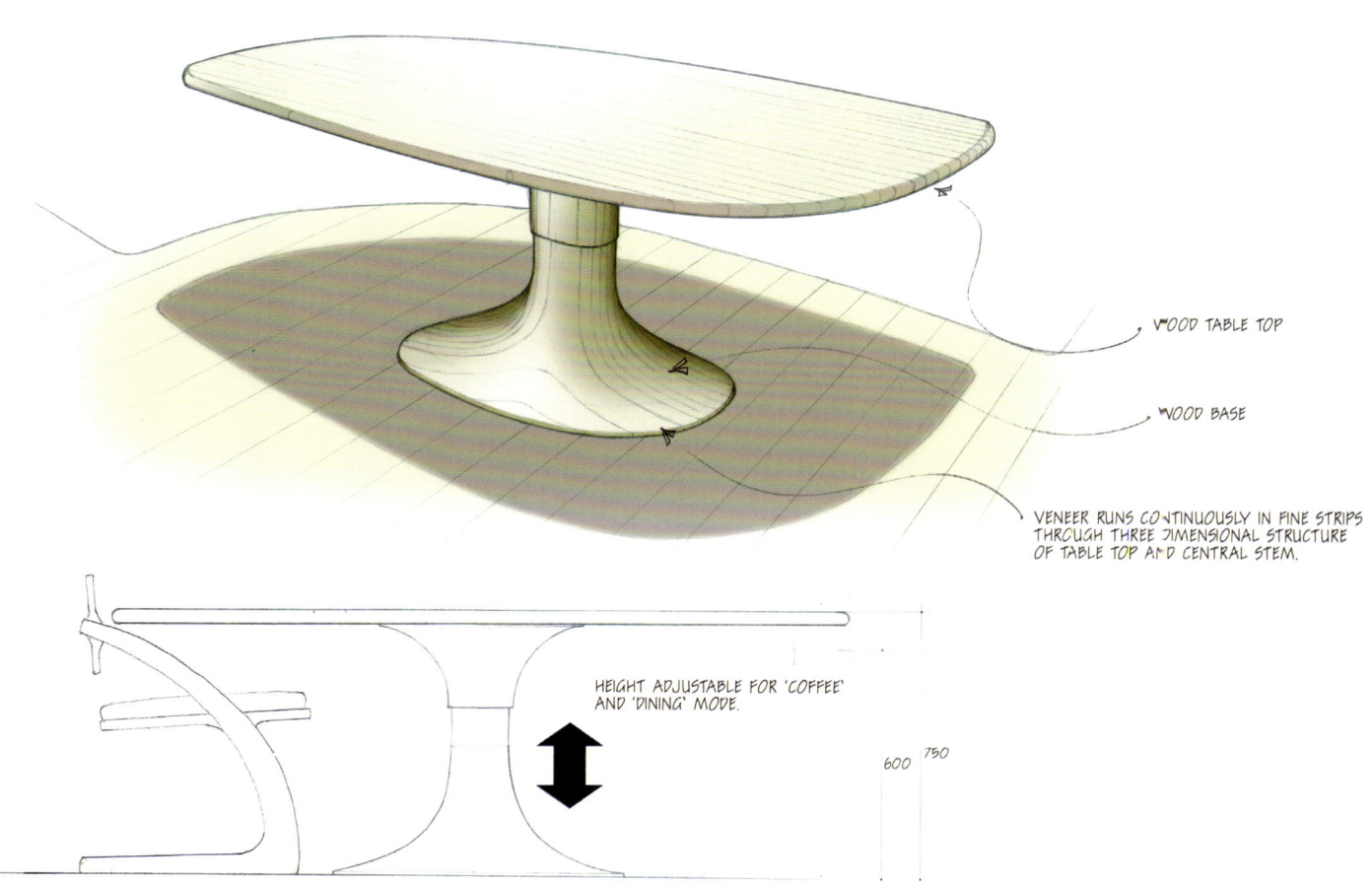

WOOD TABLE TOP

WOOD BASE

VENEER RUNS CONTINUOUSLY IN FINE STRIPS
THROUGH THREE DIMENSIONAL STRUCTURE
OF TABLE TOP AND CENTRAL STEM.

HEIGHT ADJUSTABLE FOR 'COFFEE'
AND 'DINING' MODE.

600 750

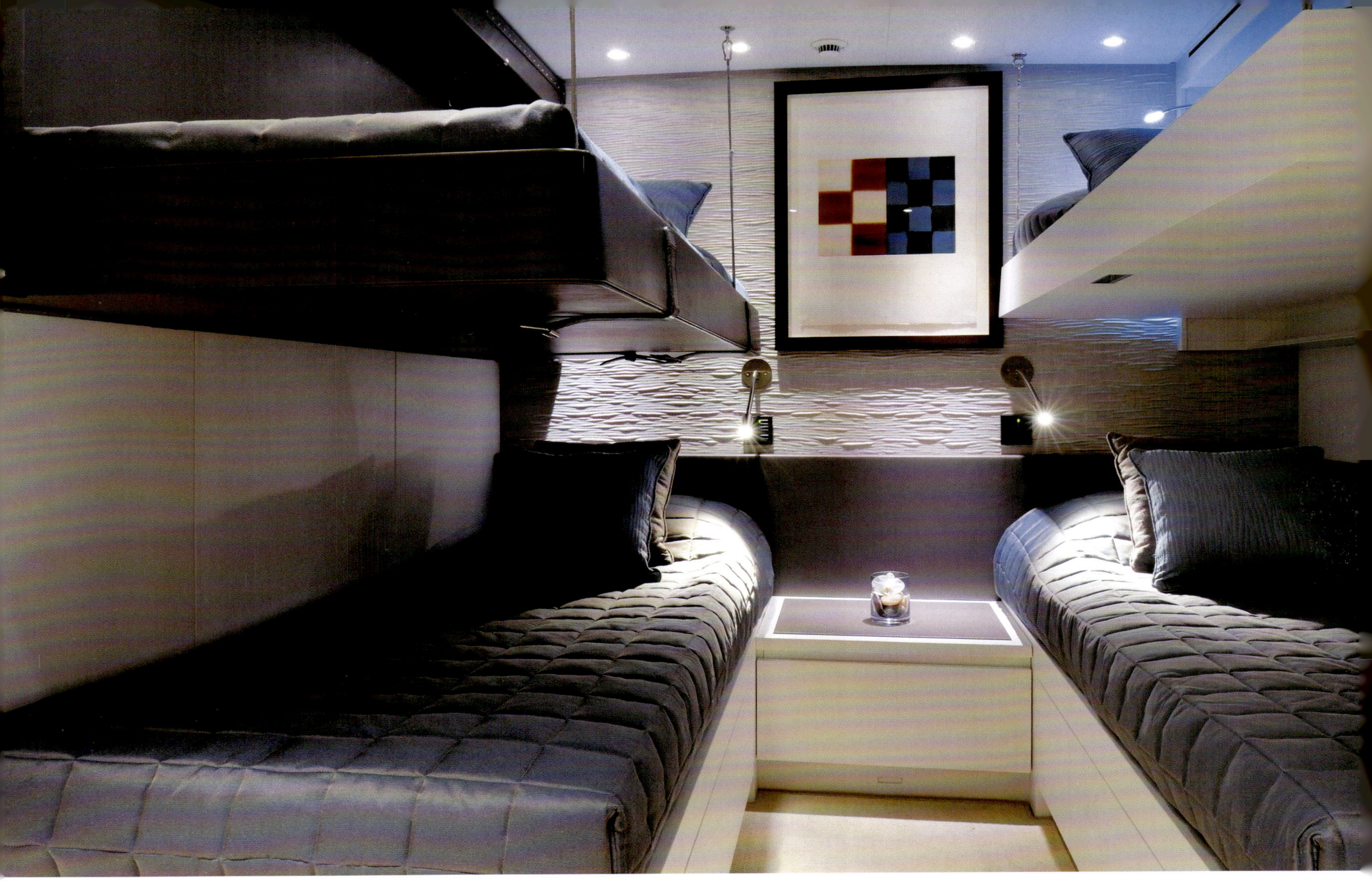

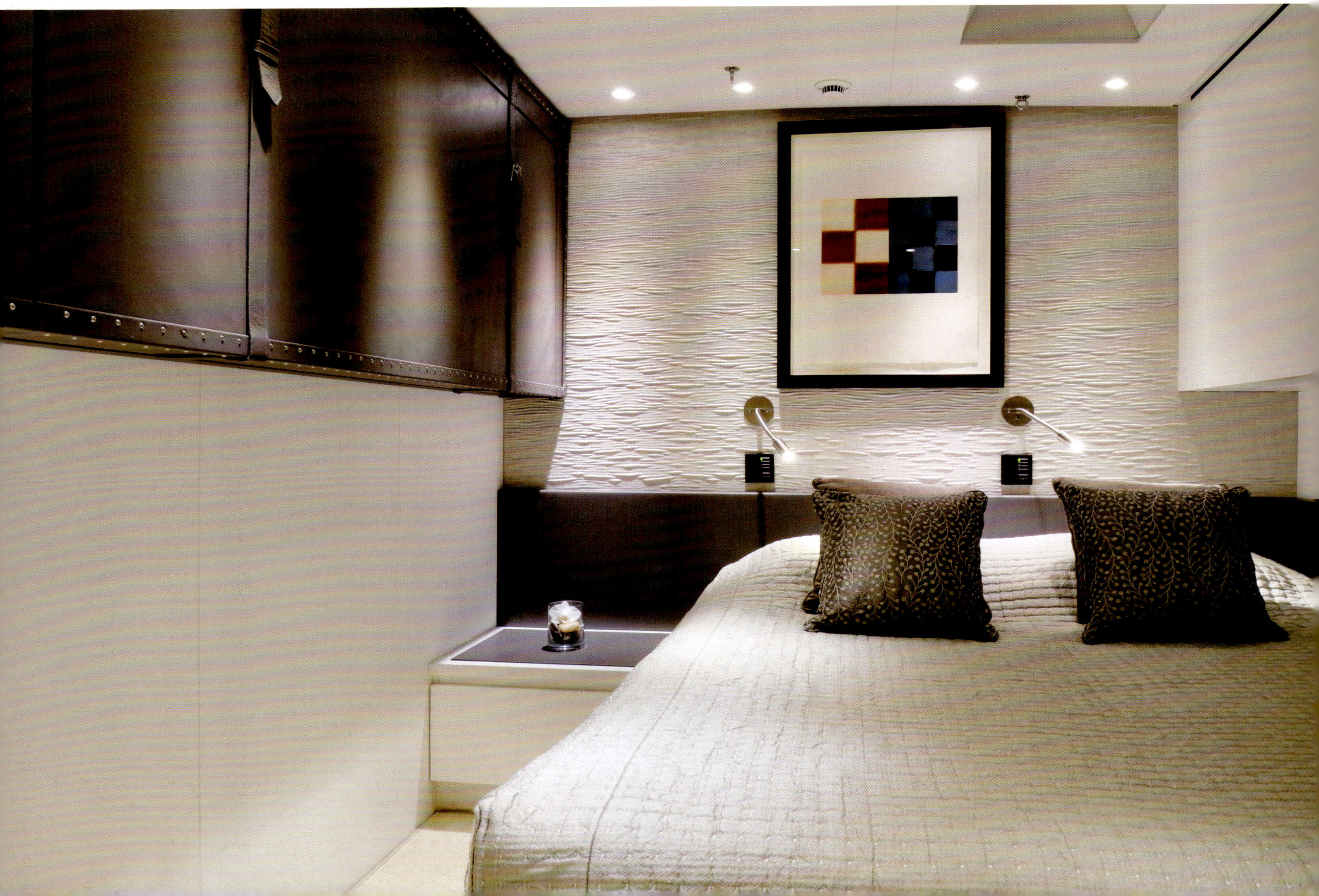

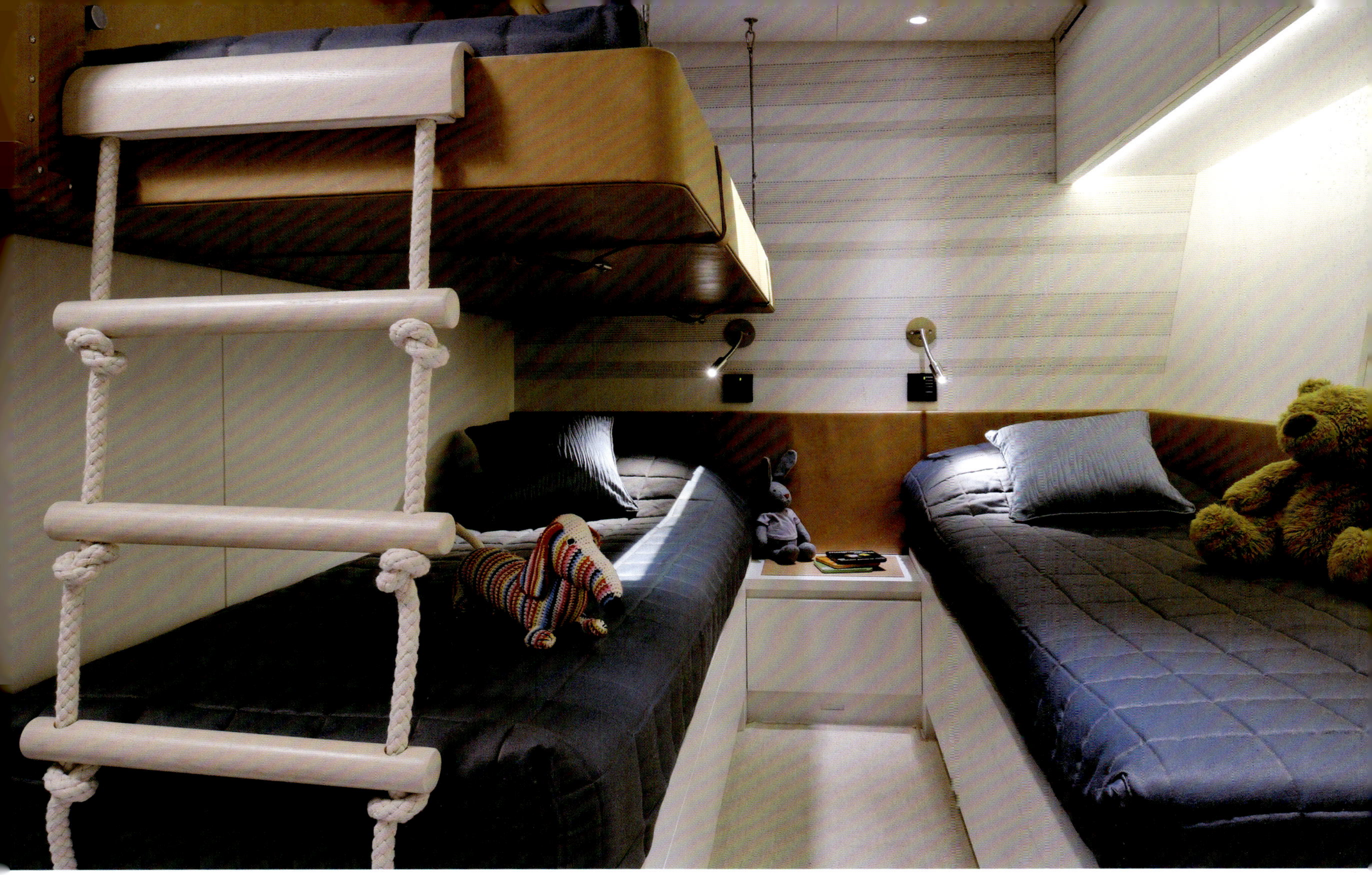
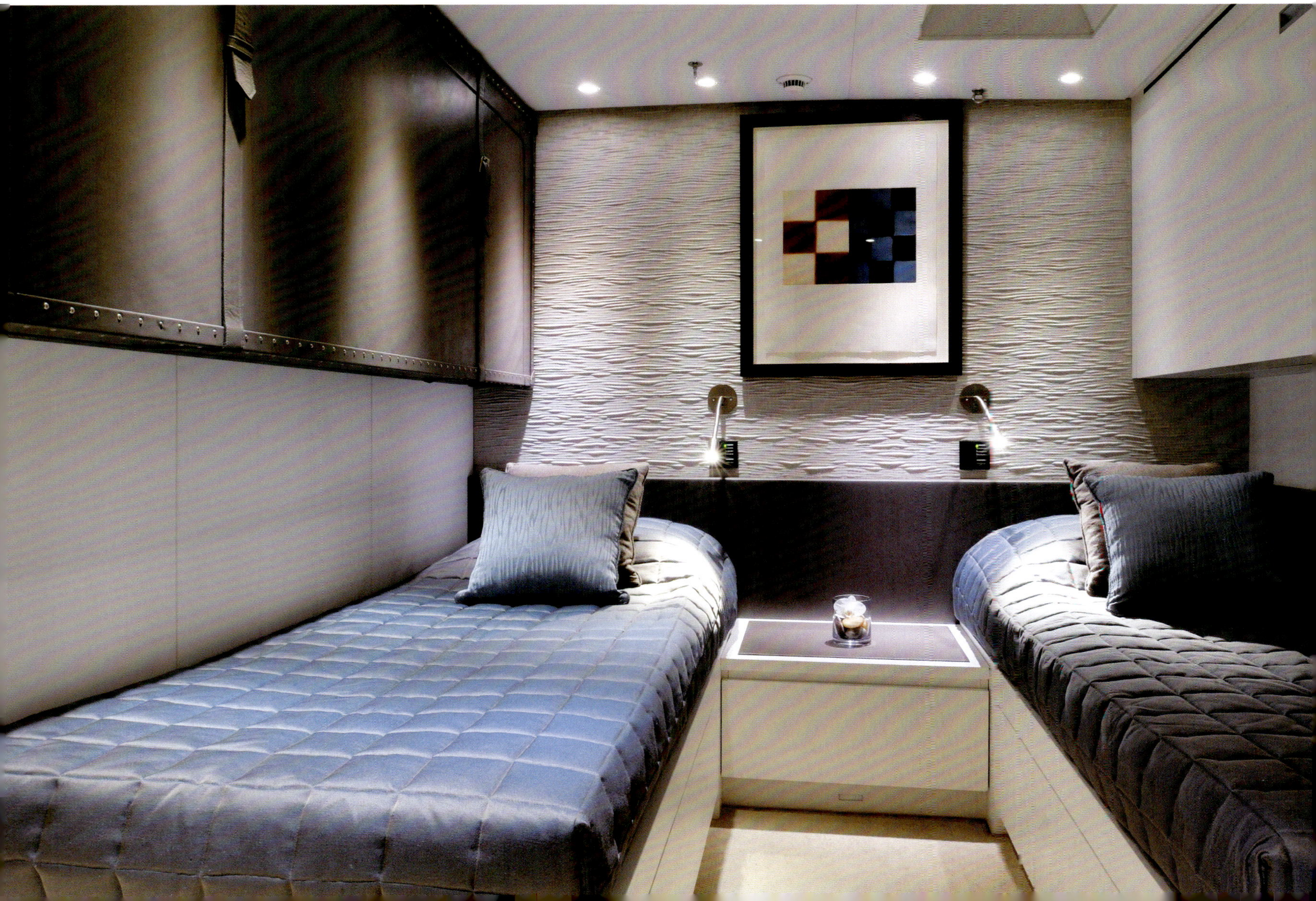

ODYSSEY

> Odyssey's Interior was born following the request of the Owner to have a light modern ambience which could reflect his taste and his life style and where he could relax with his family when far from his worldwide business.

After visiting his houses we thought about a design concept based on perspective where the eyes could never stop and where the lines should be the protagonists. We designed horizontal panels of whitened oak in satin finishing and wengè wood for the horizontal recessed filets and for main frame of walls and ceilings.

Particular attention has been reserved to the symmetries of each room and the materials used: light panels of beige stretched materials and white leather where the oak and the wengè veneers could integrate in a soft way creating games of contrast and lighting effects.

In all the decks we have used a custom whitened oak parquet made by Antico Cadore, the best wood floor producer for the most beautiful chalets of the famous winter season mountain towns like the Italian

Cortina d'Ampezzo or the Swiss Saint Moritz. The final result of all these interior ingredients is a light modern scenery where dark lines cross light panels of wood and fabrics.

Central Yacht is a partnership of experienced professional designers, engineers and operators who bring a complete harmony to a yacht design where form and function combine, where every detail is examined not just for its aesthetic beauty but its functional correctness. The result is a yacht that is not only beautiful to live in but practical to own and operate.

Central Yacht develops the design in close harmony with the owner turning dream into practical reality. During construction Central Yacht supervises the build drawing on their extensive experience to maximize quality and hence reliability in operation. Very close attention is paid to accessibility for service items, equipment easy to service will most likely be well maintained AND enable efficient use of crew time. It does not matter if the yacht is very beautiful if it is unreliable in use and denies the owner full or reliable enjoyment.

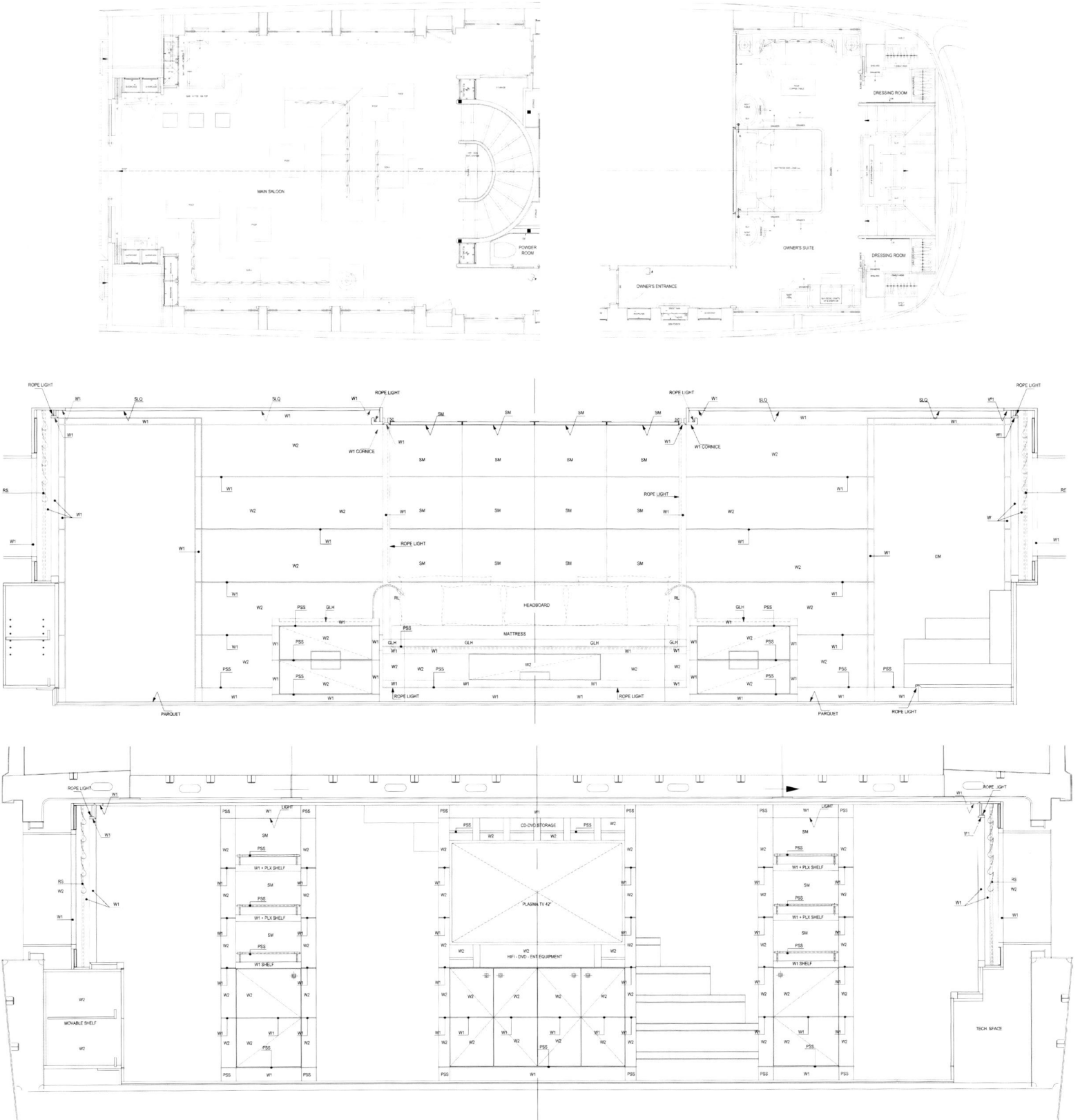

　　"奥德赛"号游艇的内部设计按照船主的要求，创造了一种明亮、现代的环境，反映出船主的品位与生活风格，船主可以在游艇上与家人尽情放松，远离自己在全球的商务活动。

　　在参观了船主的住宅后，设计师考虑采用立体式的设计理念，在船上，视野开阔，不受阻挡，船体的线形尽收眼底。设计采用水平磨光的白橡木板，内嵌水平崖豆木，此外，崖豆木还是墙体和天花板的主结构材料。

　　需要特别注意的是每个房间的对称结构和使用的材料：导光板采用米色拉伸材料和白色皮革。橡木和崖豆木饰板的和谐搭配让整个空间显现出鲜明的反差和照明效果。

　　所有的甲板上都设计了一块白色的橡木拼花地板，由Antico Cadore公司制造，该公司是最好的木地板制造商，曾给一些著名的冬季山城建设过最漂亮的农舍，如意大利的科尔蒂纳·安佩佐和瑞士的圣莫里茨。暗色线条穿过木质或布质的导光板，这样的内部装饰最终给游艇带来了明亮现代的建筑风格。

　　中央游艇公司常年与经验丰富的专业设计师、工程师和技术人员合作，最后完成的游艇设计实现了形式与功能的完美统一，每个细节都反复检查，不仅外部美观，而且功能完善。最终的游艇不仅美观舒适，适宜居住，而且非常实用，便于操作。

　　中央游艇公司全力遵循了船主的要求，在设计中让船主的美梦变成现实。在建造过程中，中央游艇公司监控了整个设计图纸，用丰富的经验将质量第一和信誉至上践行到底。特别要注意的是，检修服务周到细致，一些简单的维修设施将随时得到保障，而且尽可能不影响游艇的正常运转。所以当游艇出现故障时，不会影响游艇的美观，也不会干扰船主在游艇上的尽情享受。

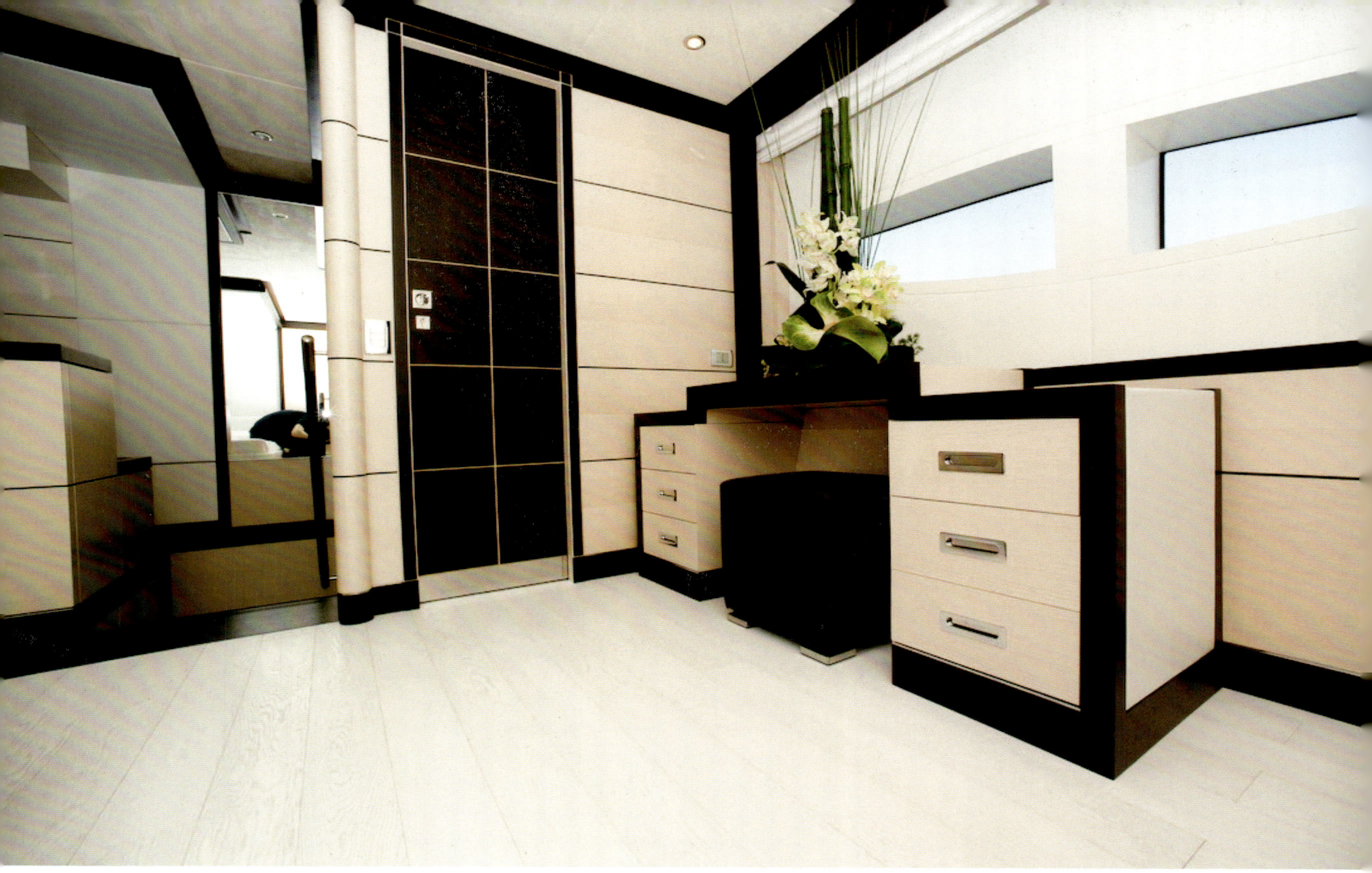

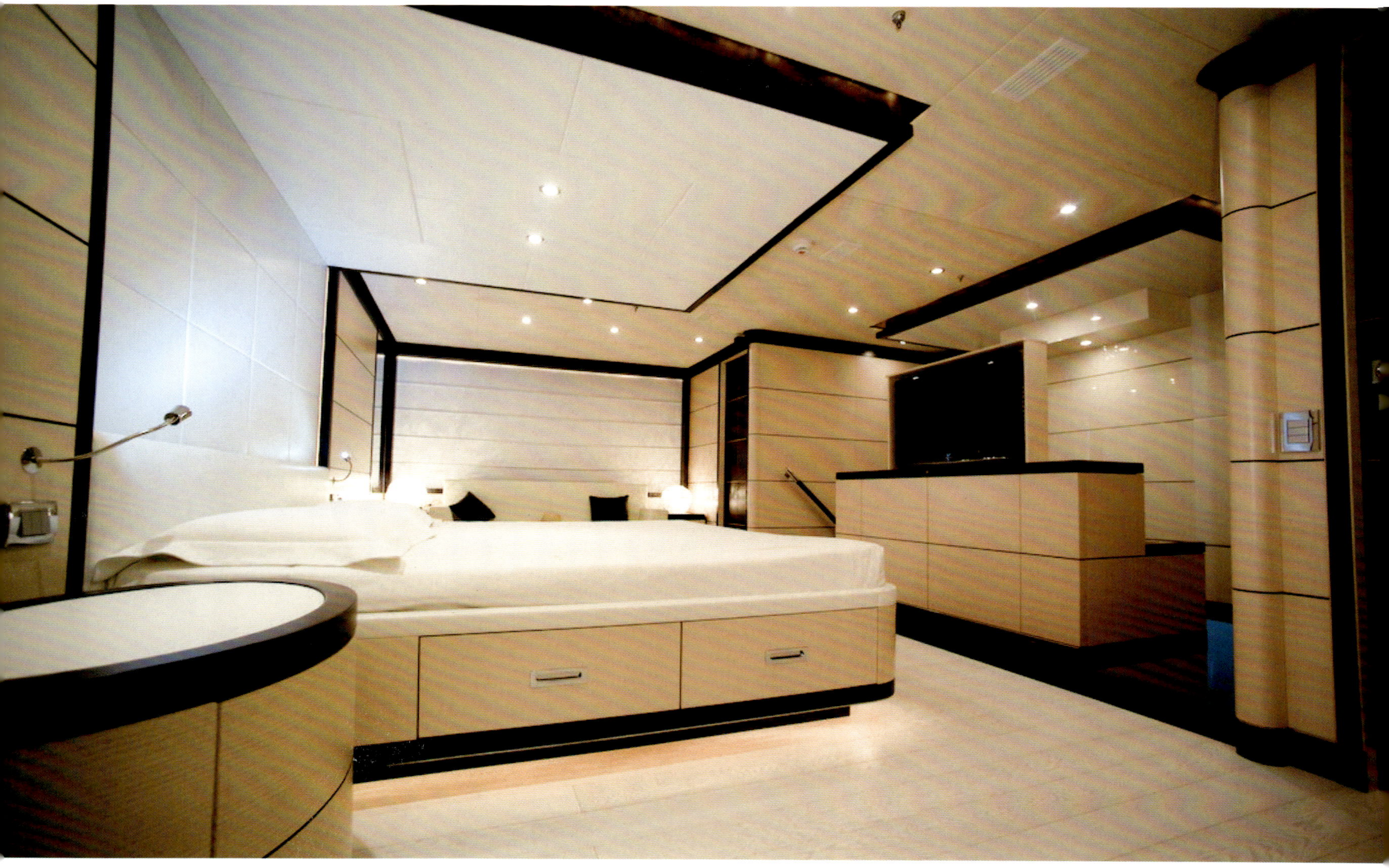

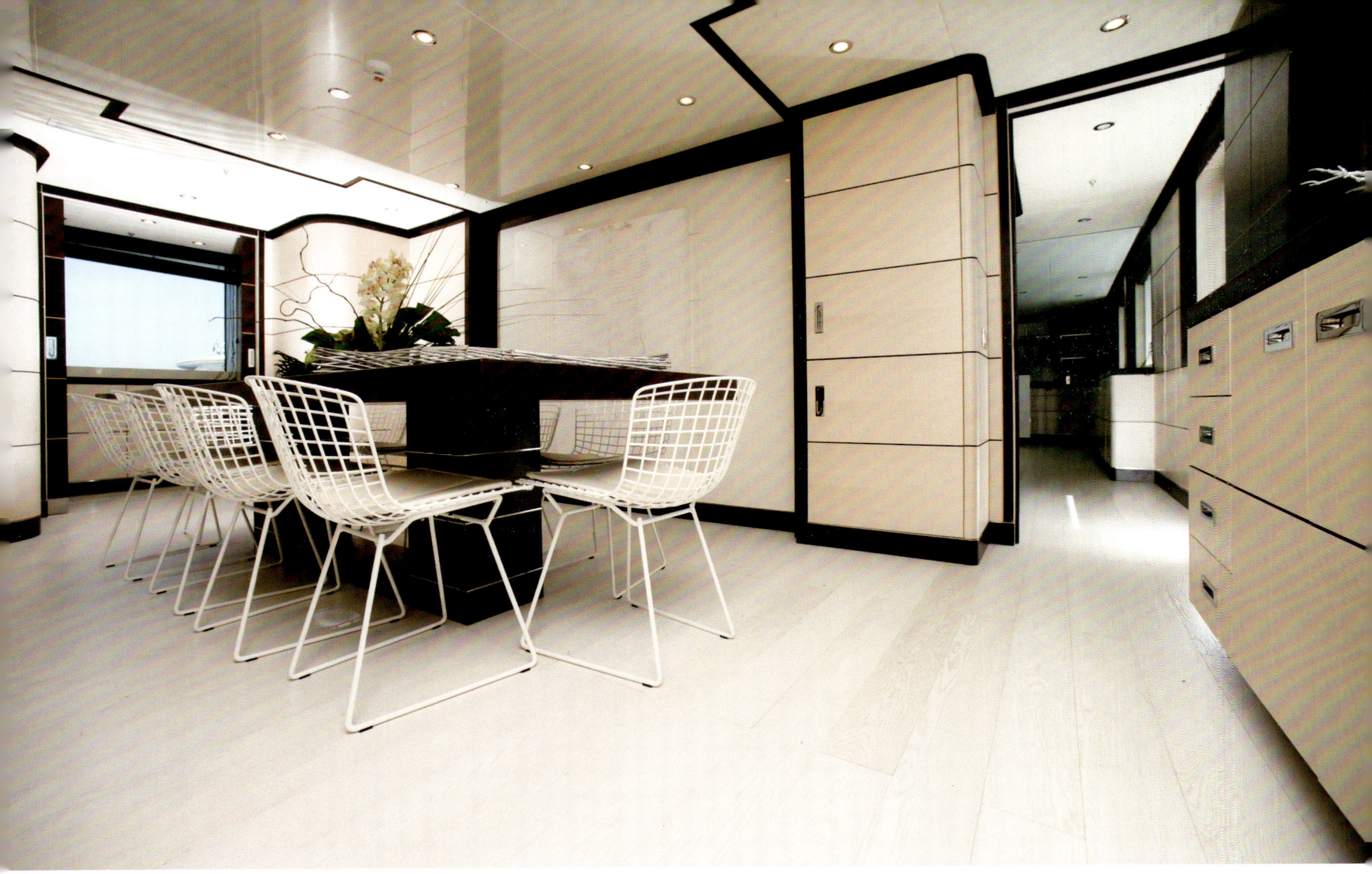

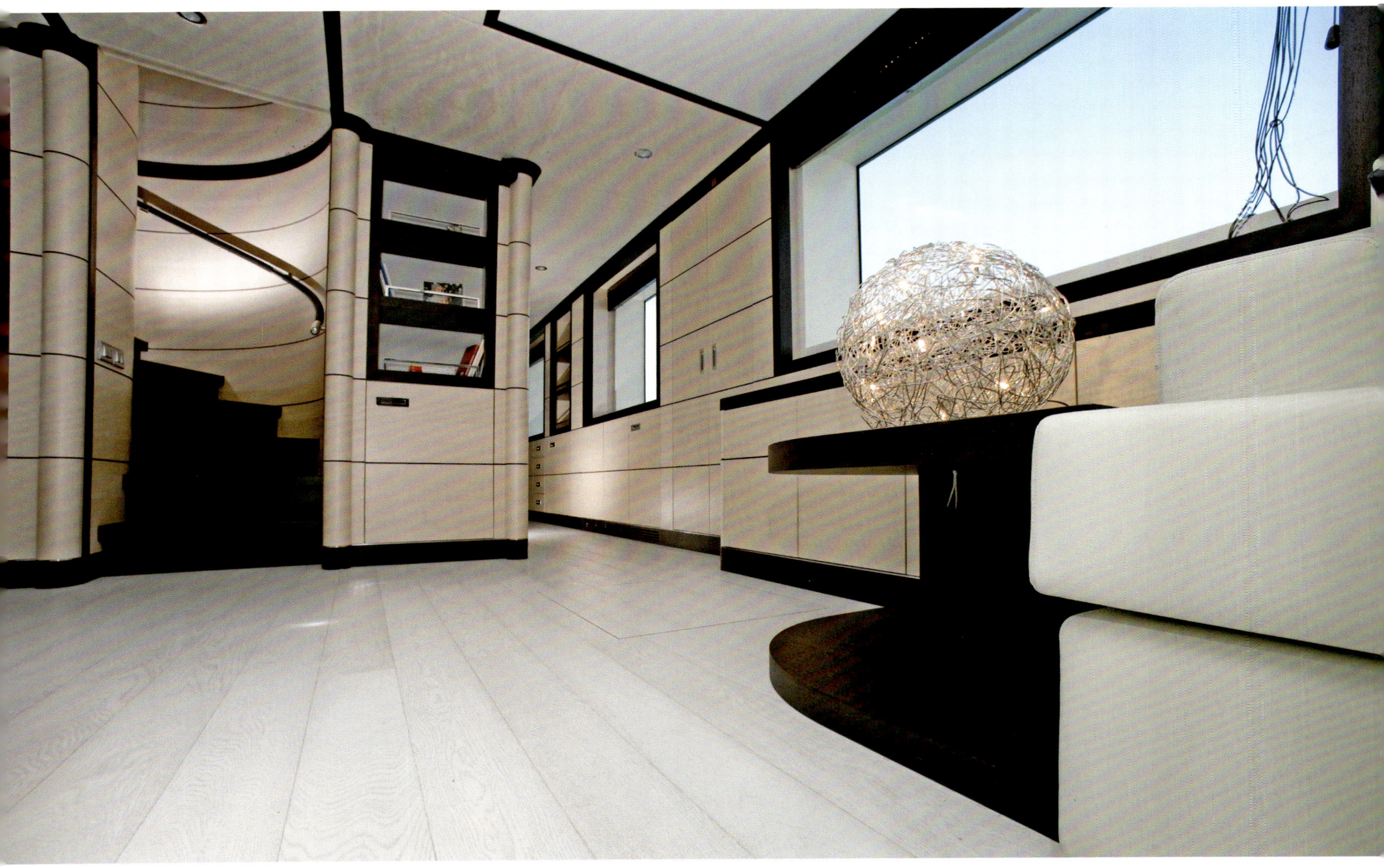

ELEANOR ALLEN

> INTERIOR DESIGN	Kirschstein Designs Ltd
> NAVAL ARCHITECTURE	Diana Yacht Design
> LENGTH	34.5m
> BEAM	7m
> MAX SPEED	12kn

> This 31 year old Feadship had a complete interior refit and external work completed by the well know Italian yard Arredamenti Porto based in Genoa. This yard was commissioned for its accuracy and speed and its enviable reputation particularly in the refit field. The old interior was completely removed down to the bare hull and a complete new layout was installed. All this work was completed in about 6 to 8 months so the American owner and his wife could enjoy the Mediterranean season.

The design of the new interior was entrusted to the well know designer Michael Kirschstein of Kirschstein Designs Ltd as well as a close family friend and interior decorator Julie Neupert who was already very familiar with the owners style of living.

The owner worked closely with these two designers and Arredamenti Porto to create a cozy atmosphere with a combination of subtle fabric colours and mahogany interior joinery inlaid with emperador marble. This created the inviting and new interior desired by the owner and his family.

Externally Arredamenti Porto removed the old garage for a mini moke in the stern and created a far more useful lazzarette space for much needed storage. Other additions like the boat deck awning and more exterior lounging and dining areas have turned this old yacht back into a superb classic yacht with the style befitting her age but with all the modern amenities.

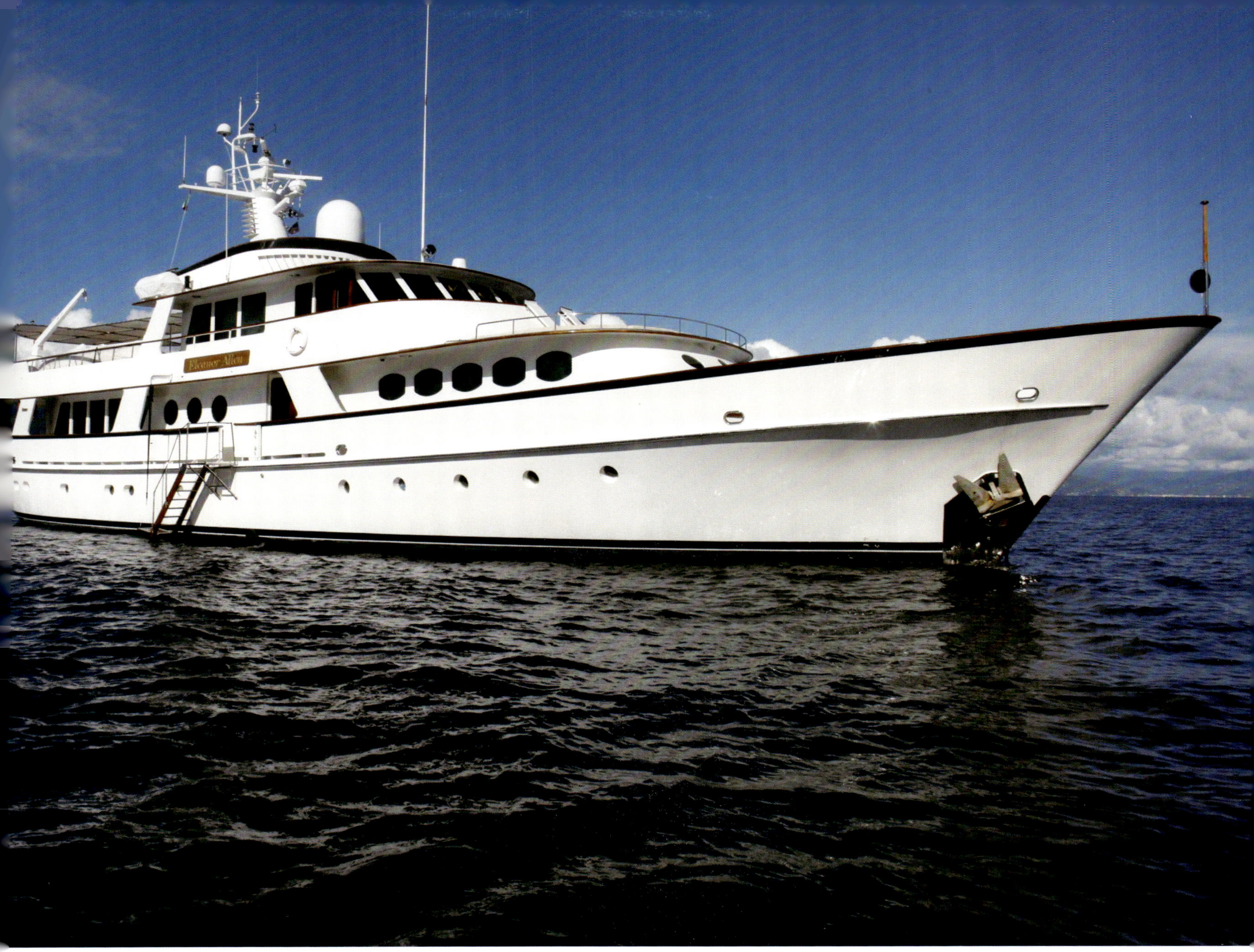

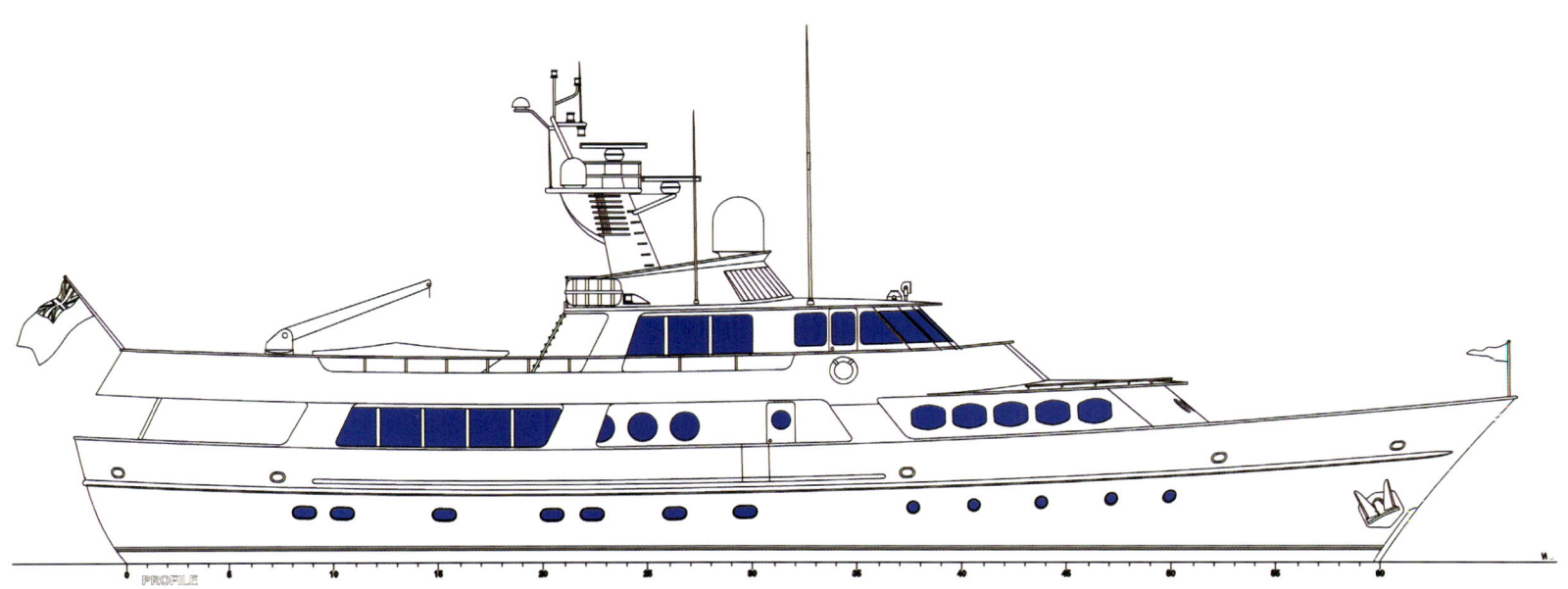

PROFILE

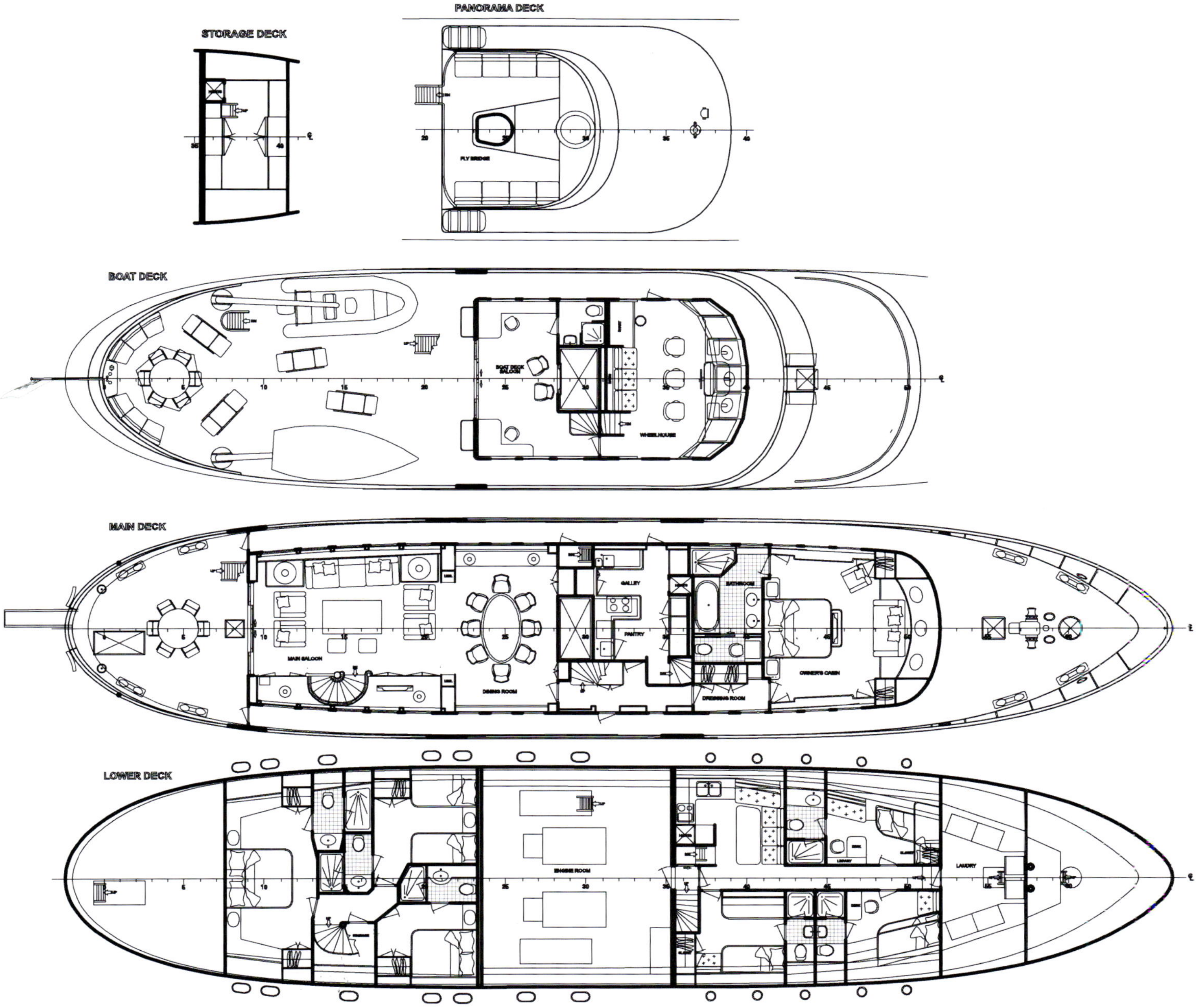

STORAGE DECK

PANORAMA DECK

FLY BRIDGE

BOAT DECK

BOAT DECK
DAY HEAD

WHEEL HOUSE

MAIN DECK

GALLEY

MAIN SALOON

PANTRY

BATHROOM

DINING ROOM

OWNERS CABIN

DRESSING ROOM

LOWER DECK

ENGINE ROOM

LIBRARY

LAUNDRY

这艘 31 年船龄的游艇由位于热内亚的意大利著名造船厂 Arredamenti Porto 对其内部和外部进行了彻底的翻新改造。该船厂一向以工艺精确、高效快速而著称，特别是在船舶的翻新方面。旧船的内部结构被彻底摒弃，只剩下光秃秃的船体，然后重新加载了新的结构。所有的这些改造都是在 6 到 8 个月内完成的，这样这艘游艇的美国主人和他的妻子就可以享受地中海的夏日风光了。

新的游艇内部设计工作交给了 Kirschstein 设计有限公司的著名设计师 Michael Kirschstein，还有一位内部设计师 Julie Neupert 也参与了设计，他是船主一家的好朋友，非常熟悉船主一家的生活习惯。

船主与两位设计师和 Arredamenti Porto 造船厂进行了密切的合作，创造出了舒适惬意的风格，内装采用了精细的各色织物，镶嵌了啡网大理石的红木。焕然一新、极具魅力的内部设计得到了船主一家人的赞叹和青睐。

船厂把游艇外部位于船尾的旧车库改造成一个小型的储藏室，为游艇创造了更加实用的储物空间，满足了更多的储物需求。其他的变化，如救生艇甲板上增加了天篷，设计了更多的休息区和用餐区。这些改变让这艘旧船变成了一艘高级经典游艇，不仅体现出了它的悠久历史，还凸显了它的现代化设施。

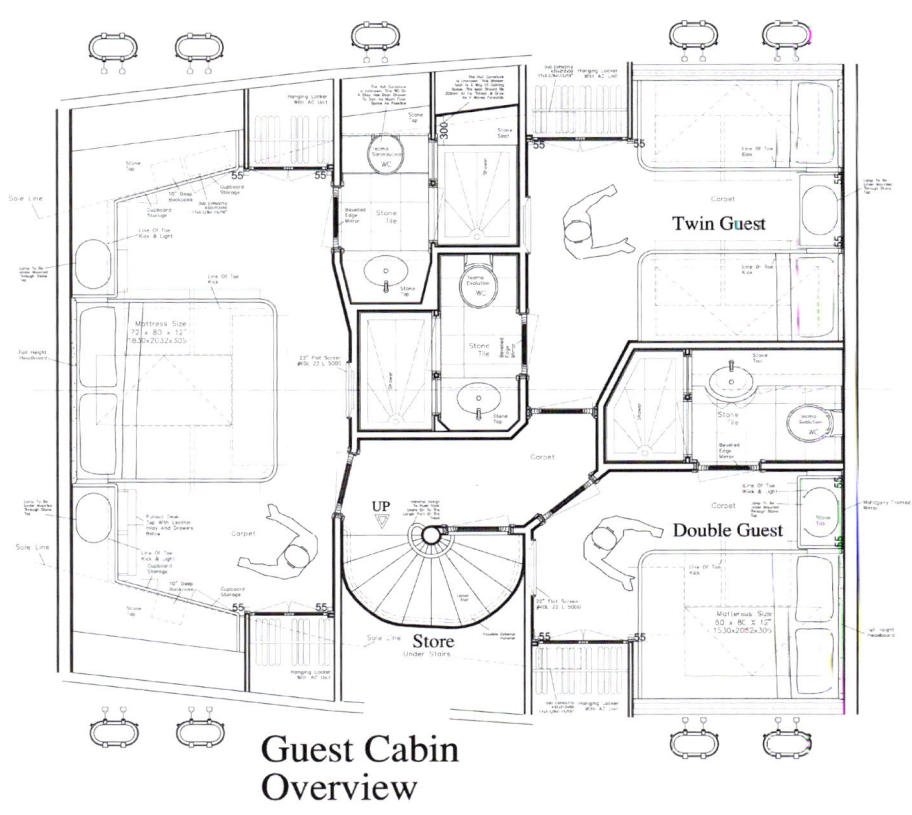

Twin Guest

UP

Double Guest

Store
Under Stairs

**Guest Cabin
Overview**

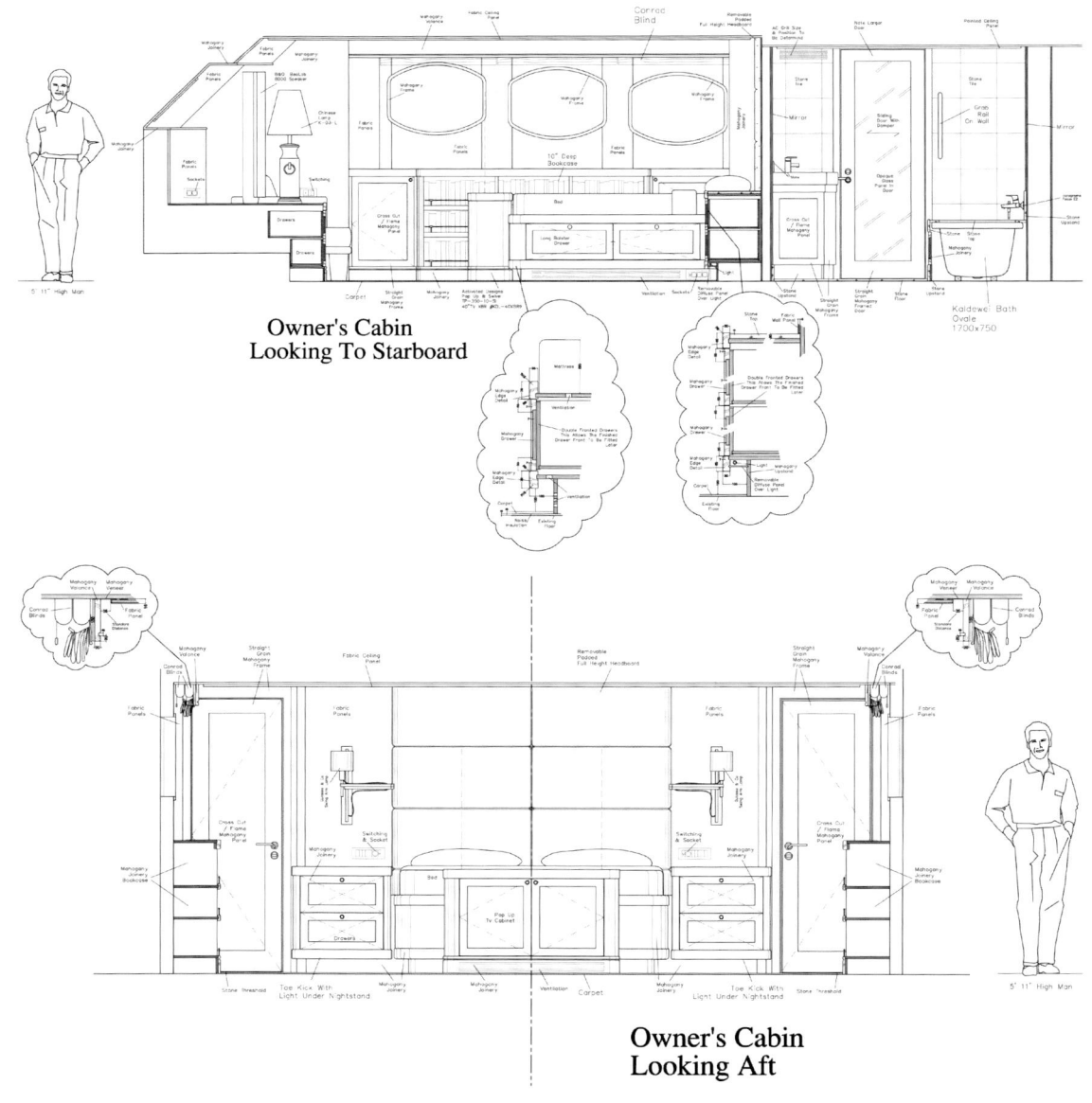

**Owner's Cabin
Looking To Starboard**

**Owner's Cabin
Looking Aft**

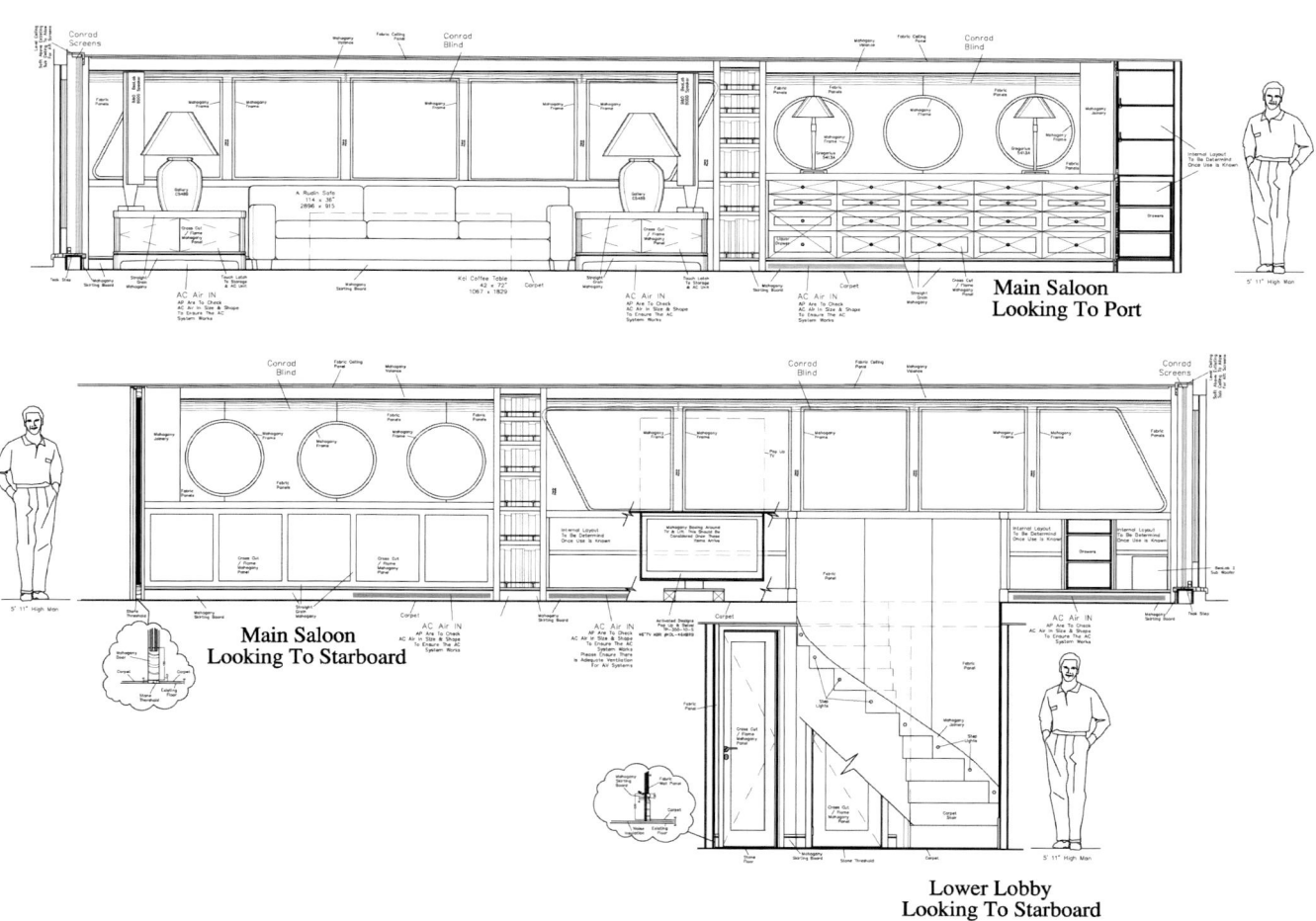

**Main Saloon
Looking To Port**

**Main Saloon
Looking To Starboard**

**Lower Lobby
Looking To Starboard**

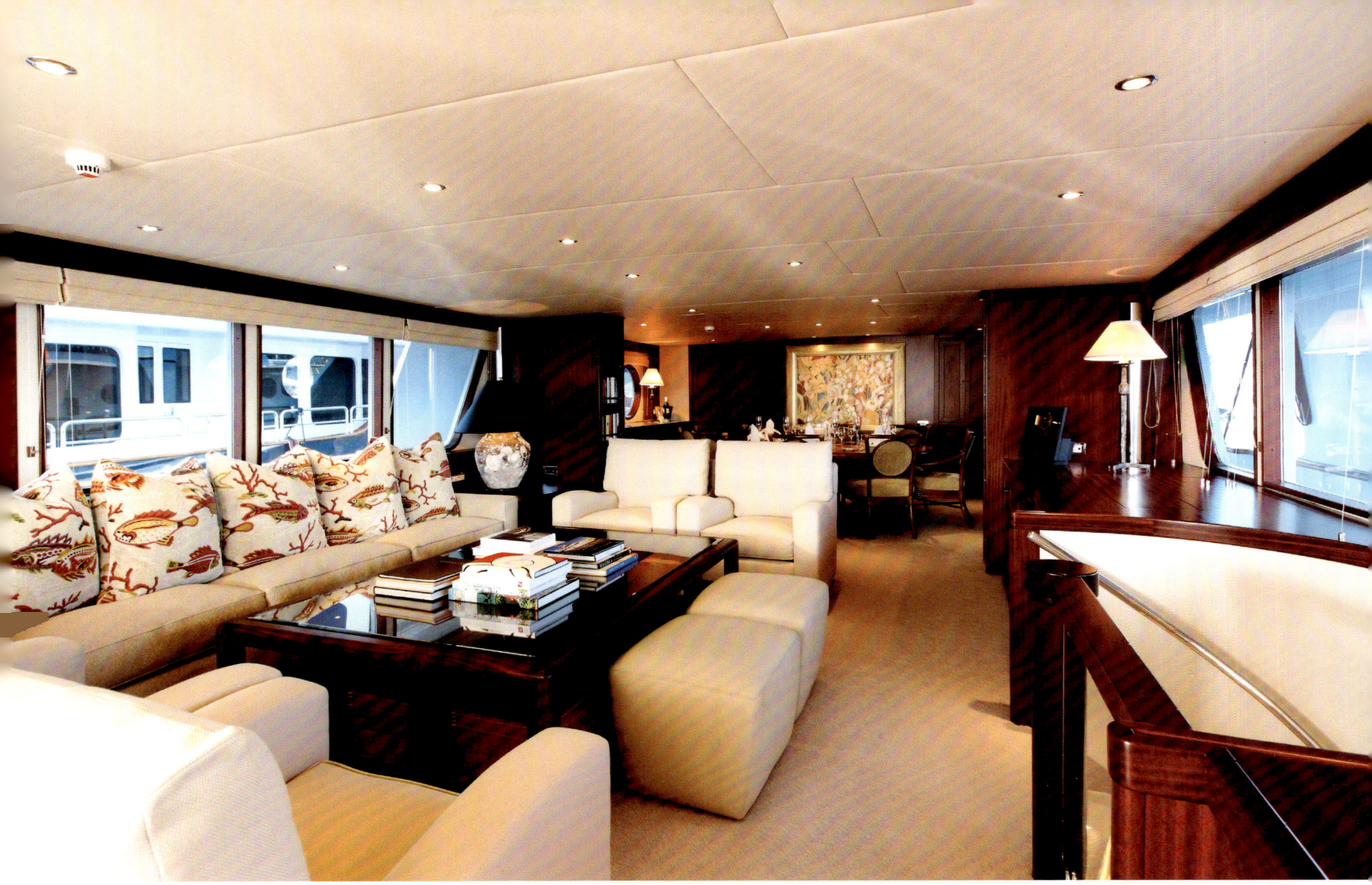

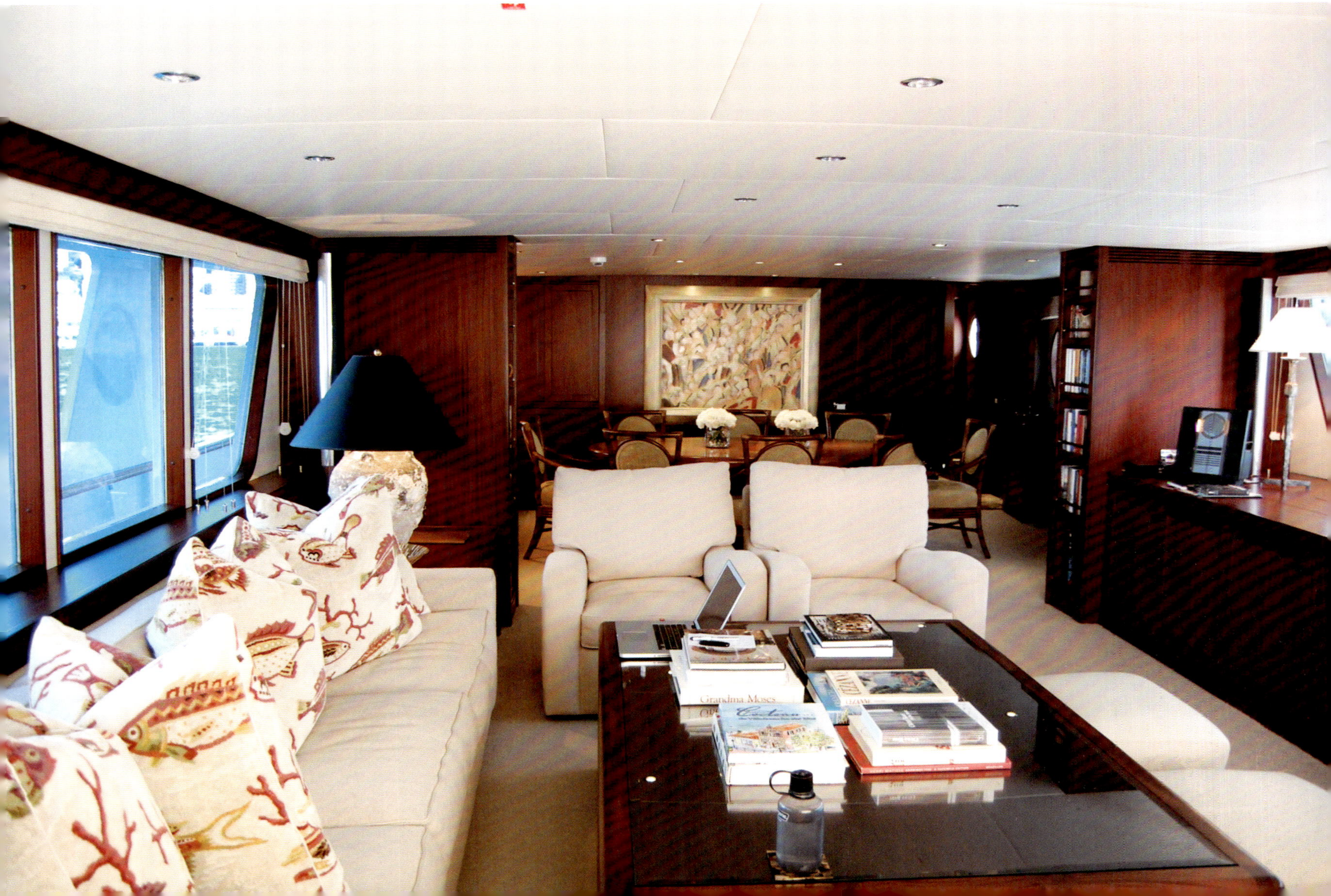
Grandma Moses

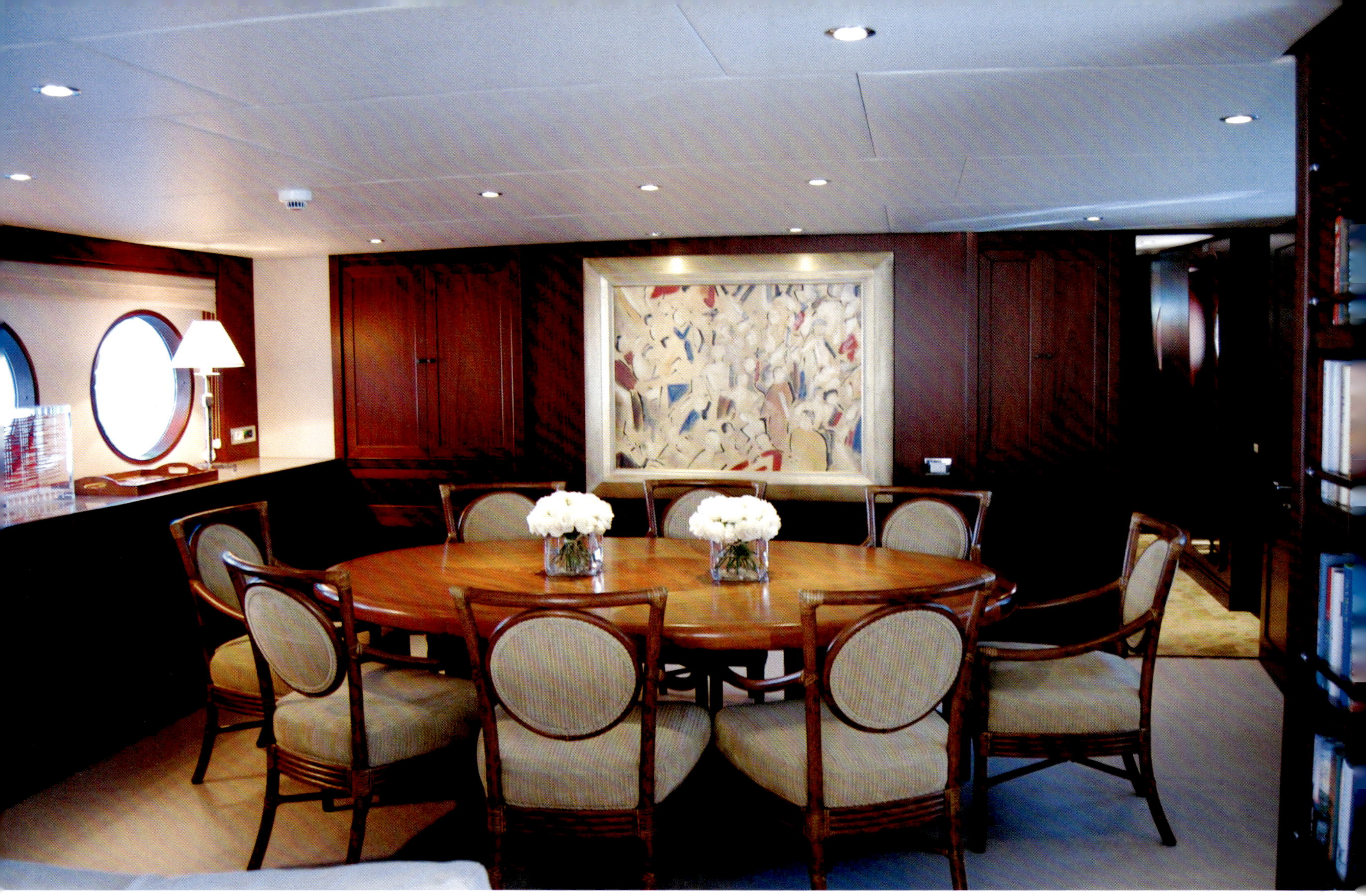

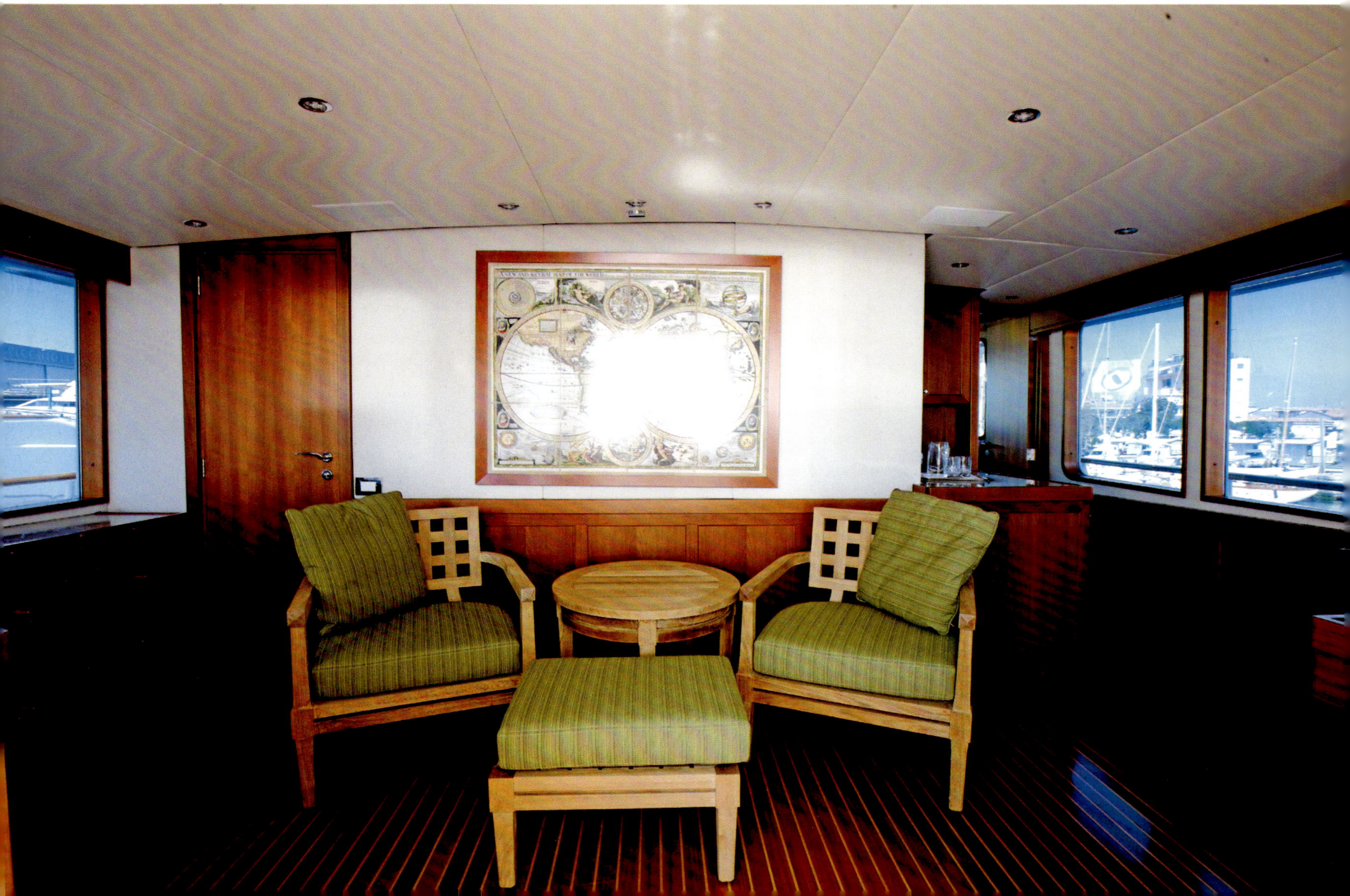

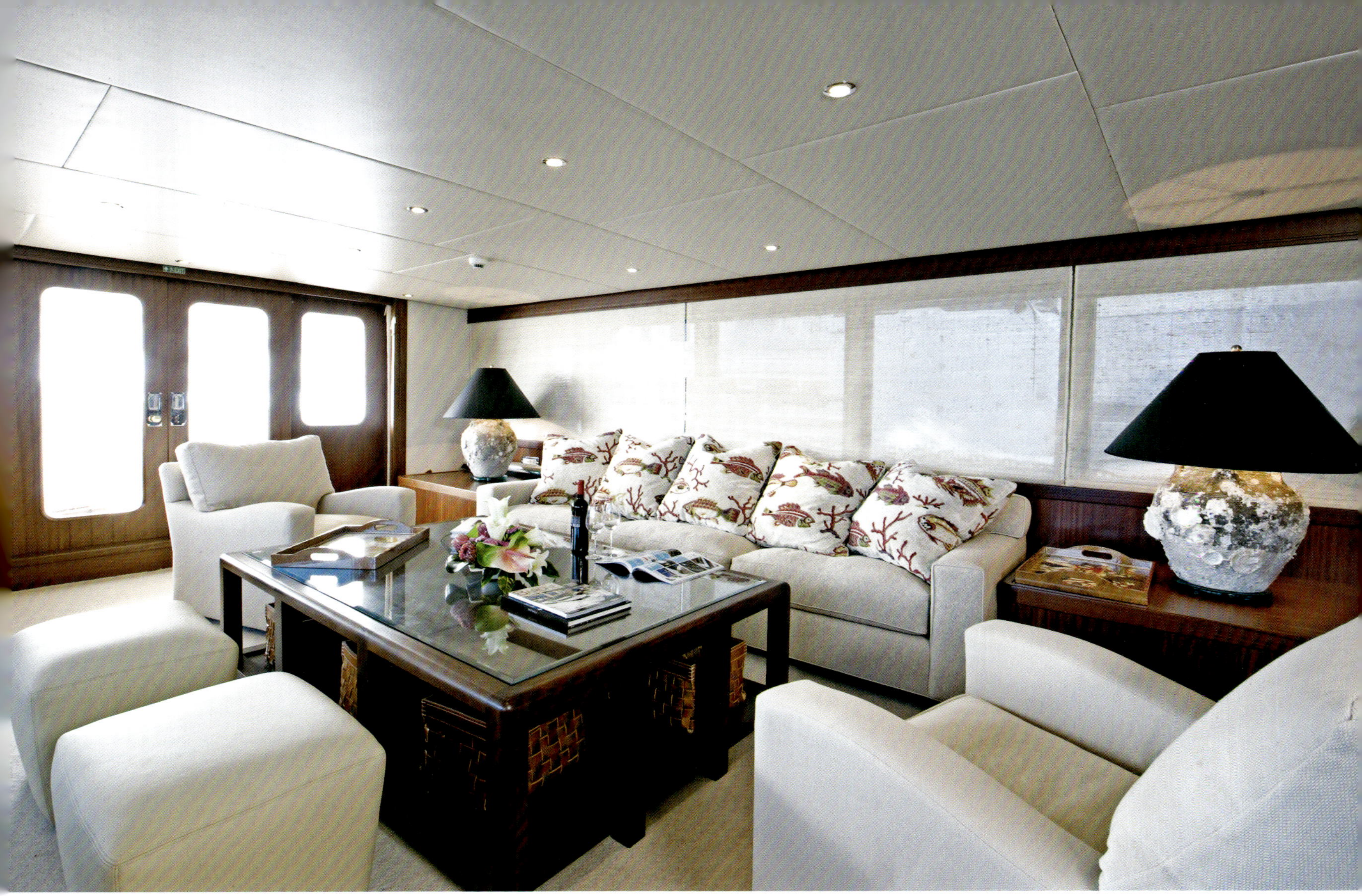
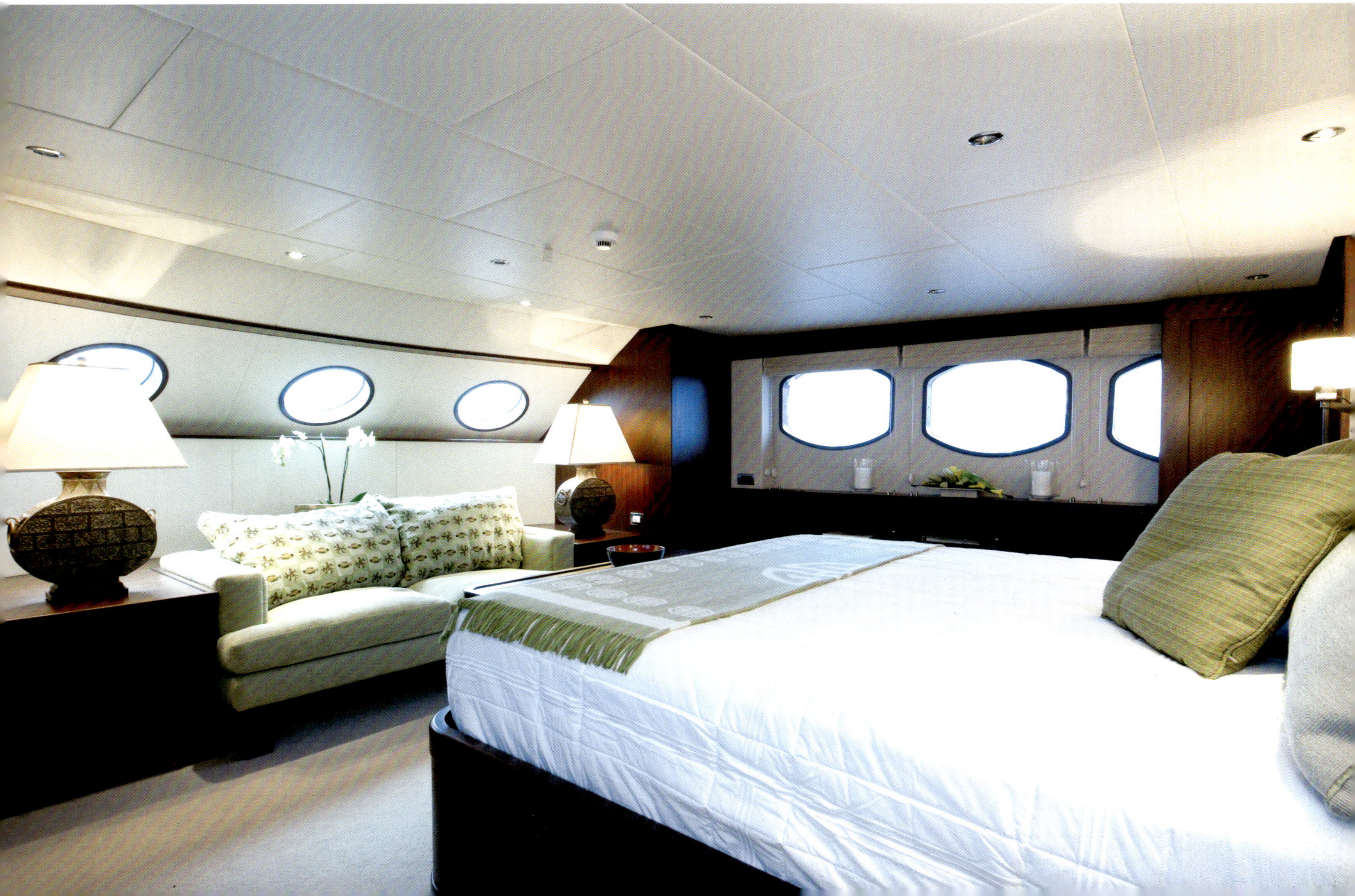

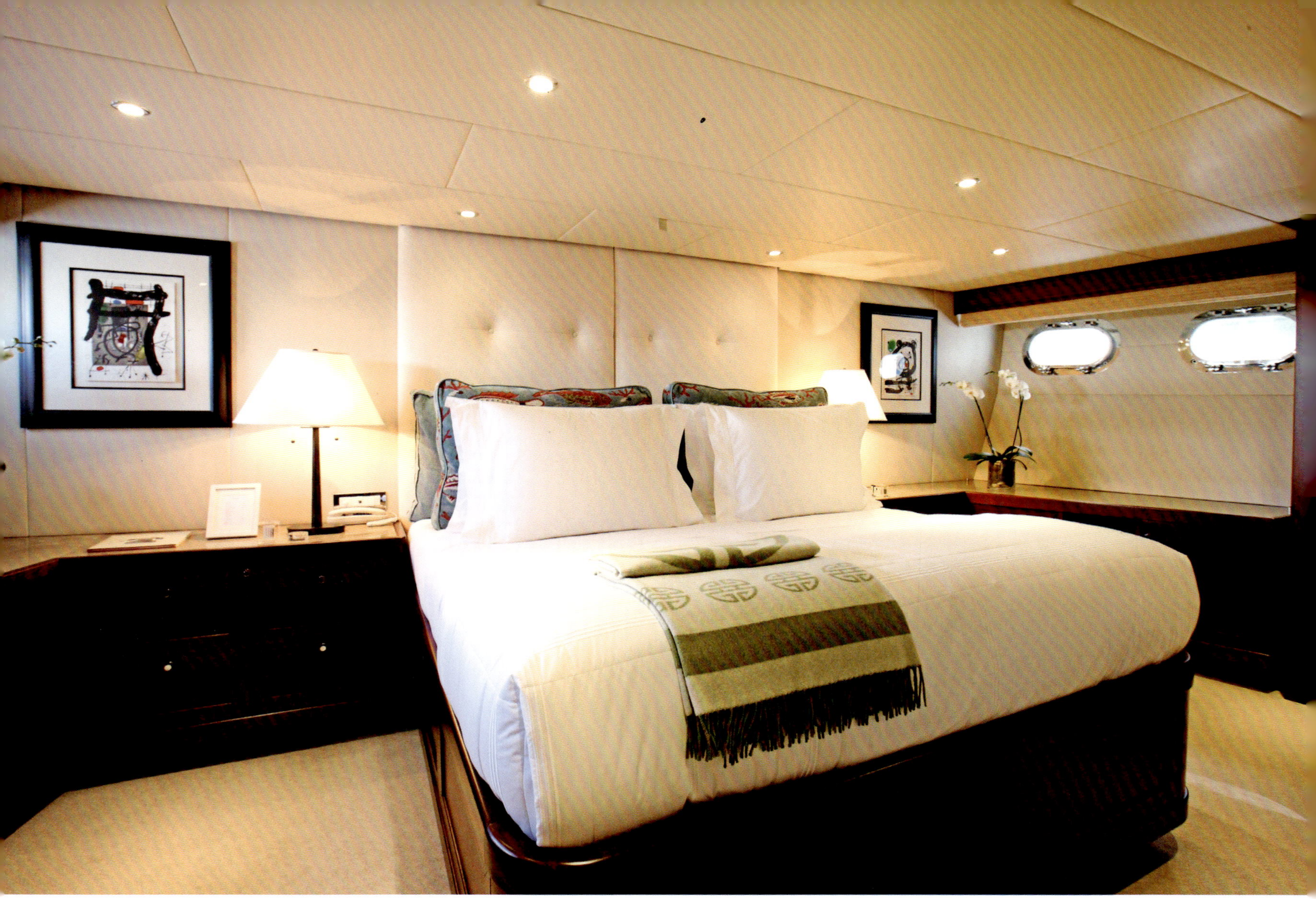

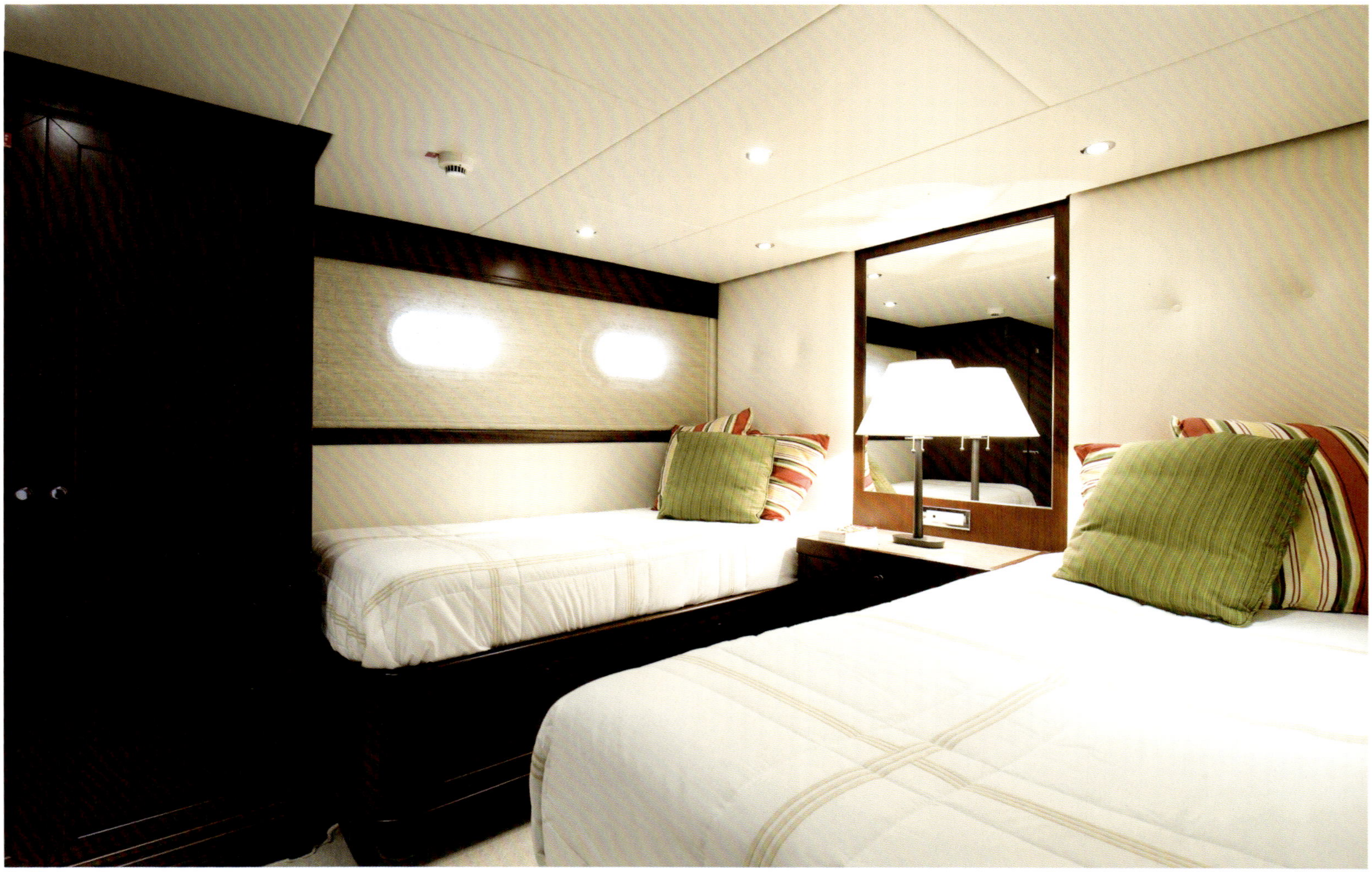

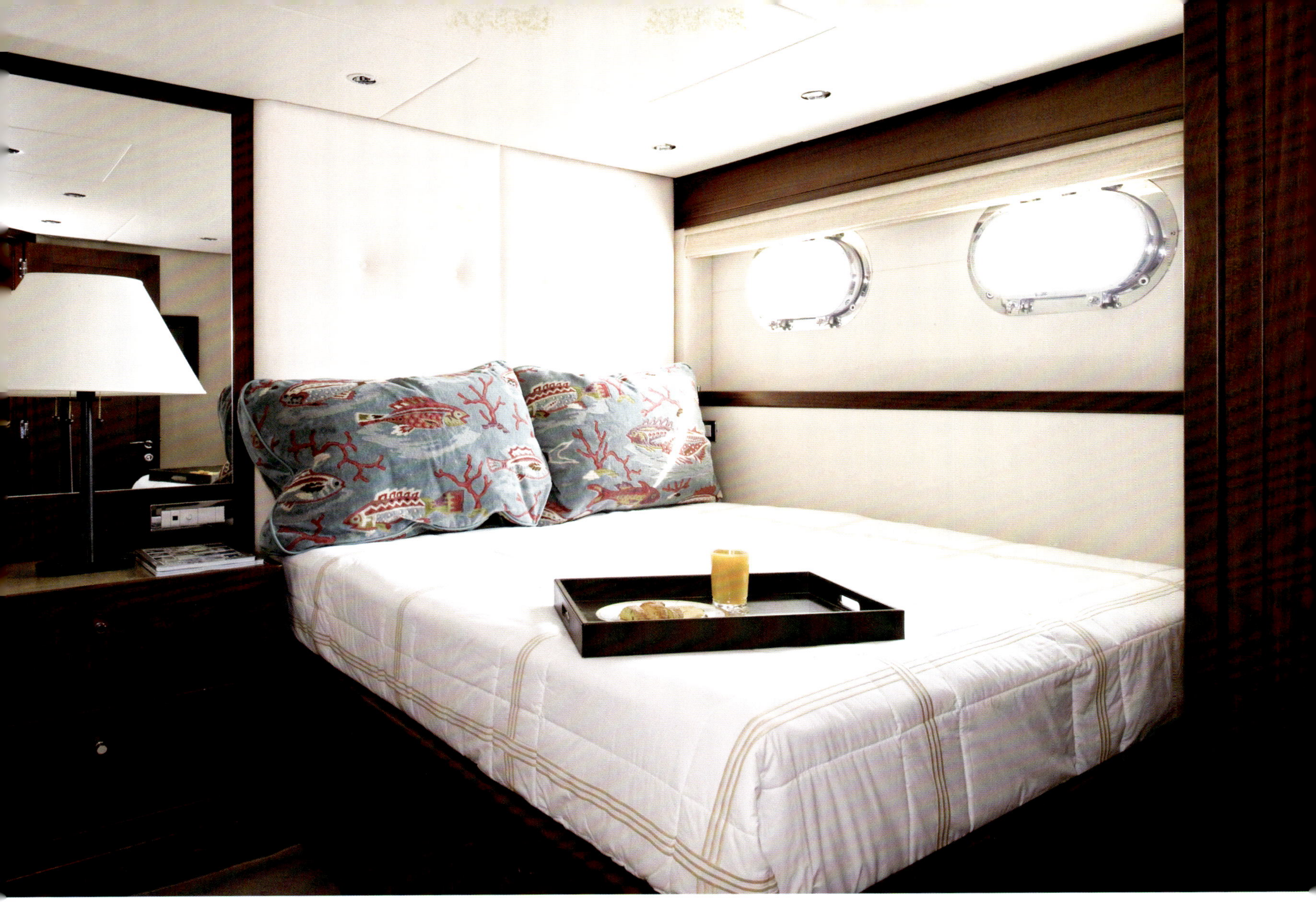

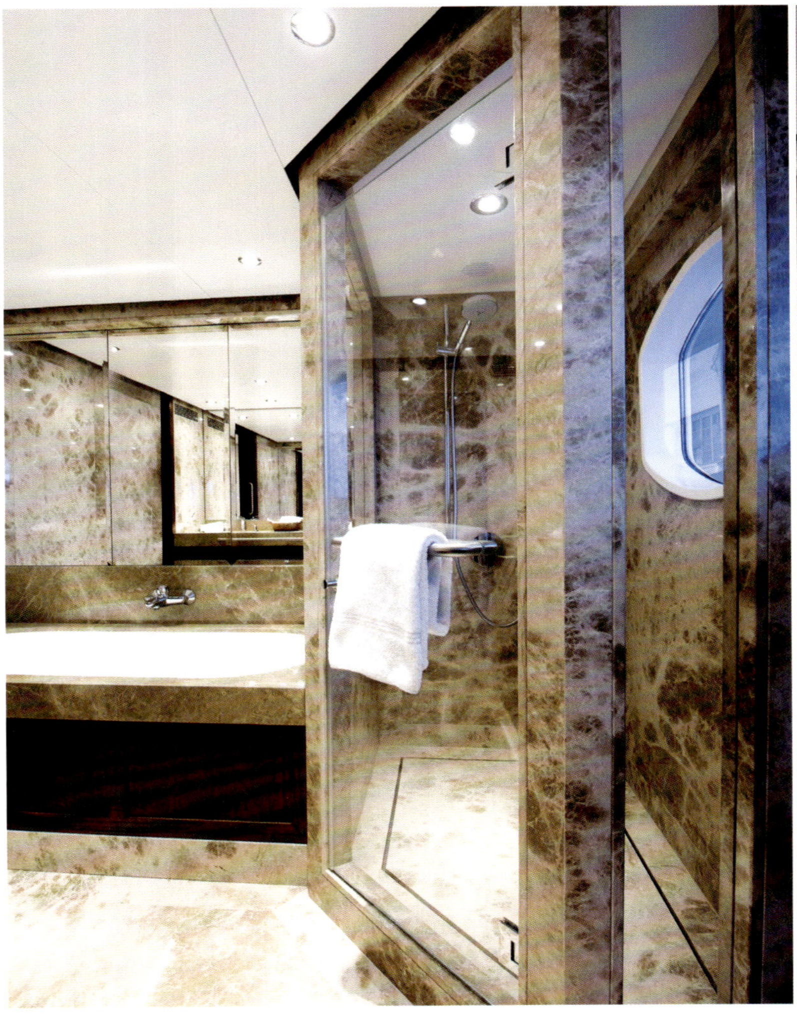

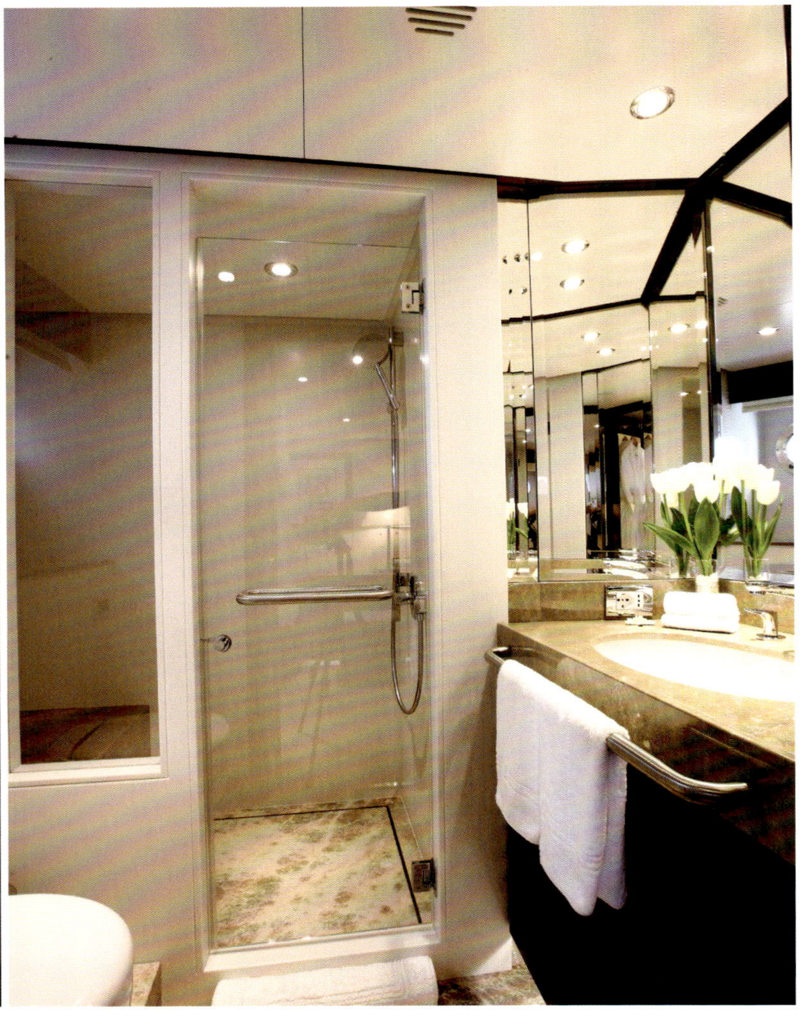

LADY POWER

> DESIGN	Camillo Costantini	
> BEAM	6.80m	
> MAX SPEED	31kn	

> The interiors are laid out very functionally. The saloon (conversation area, play area and bar) extends to starboard after the stairs into a dining area which can also be used as a home cinema thanks to its large plasma screen. To port, on the other hand, is a day toilet followed by the raised bridge, and the galley which leads down to the crew quarters. Amidships on the lower deck we find the full-beam master followed by two two-berth guest cabins with third jury bunk and a lovely VIP stateroom in the bow. The décor is unusual: dark or very dark mahogany and ebony furnishings, gold and black inlaid marble, black sofas and bridge. Lots of crocodile-effect leather trim. The leitmotif is a shell that seems to be unfurling. It's there in the furnishings in the bar, on the dining table and on the head-linings with the occasional daring flourish, such as the child-size golden putto in the dining area. The fly has three circular areas: one with a round dining table, the other with a bar and games table, and the third with an enormous sun pad.

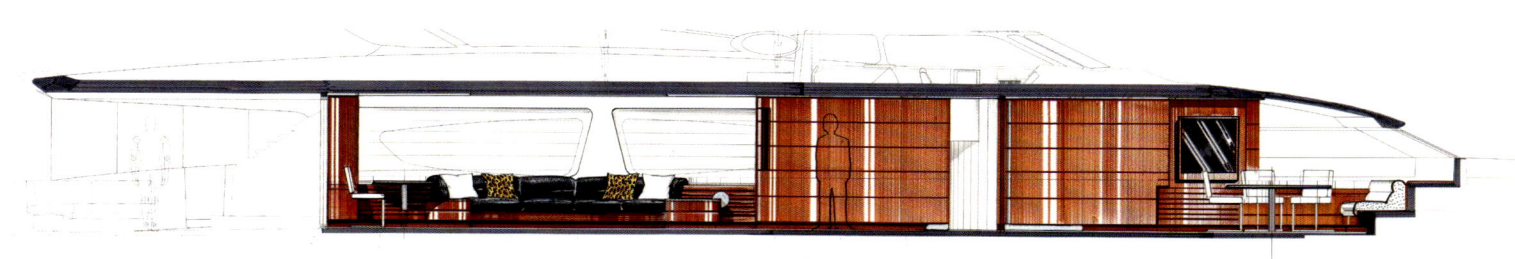

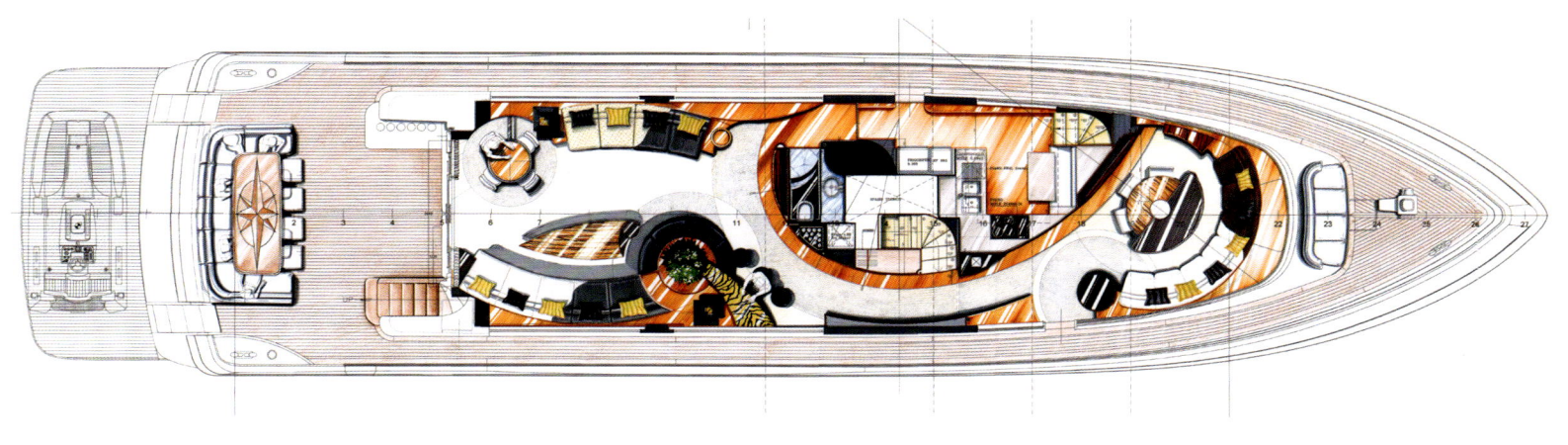

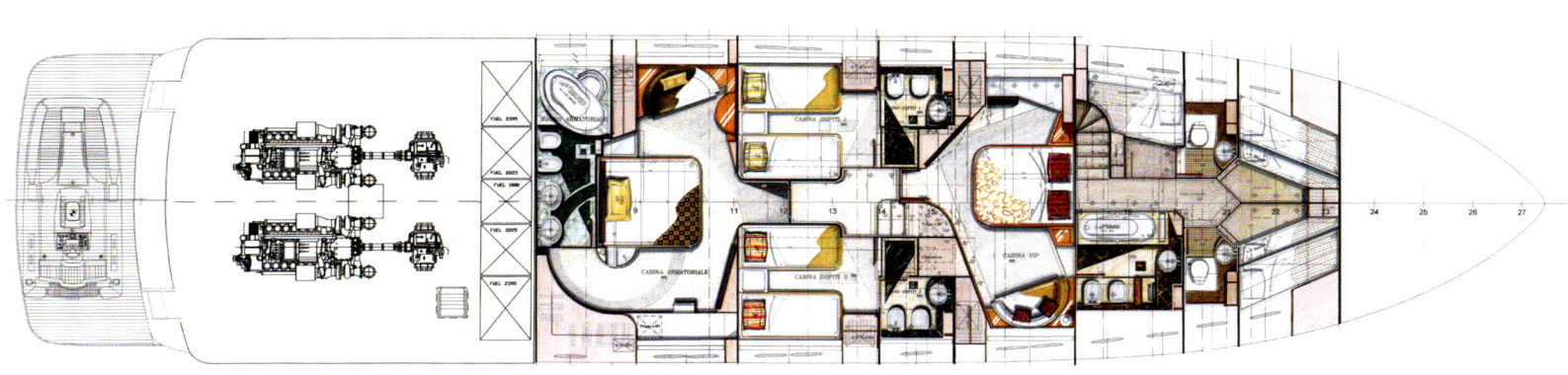

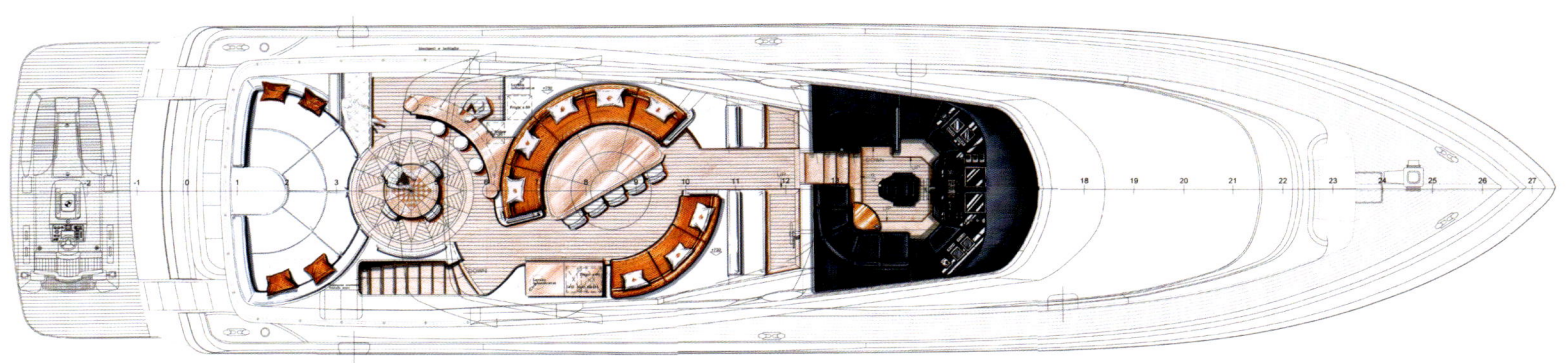

游艇的内部设计注重功能性。大厅（包括交流区、娱乐区、吧台）一直延伸到右舷，右舷的楼梯通向用餐区，那里安装的等离子大屏幕使用餐区也变成了一个家庭影院。在大厅的另外一侧，左舷有一个日用卫生间，旁边是一座桥楼和厨房（通向船员区）。在底层甲板的中部，可以看到最宽敞的船主房间，旁边是两个双人客房，客房内还可以设置第三个临时床铺，此外在船头还有一个贵宾包厢。装饰也与众不同，采用了棕色或黑色的红木和乌木家具，金色与黑色镶嵌的大理石、黑色的座椅和桥楼。大量使用鳄鱼皮效果的真皮配料。装饰的主题是一个像要展开的贝壳。体现在吧台的家具、餐桌及顶沿贴边的奢华装饰上，例如，餐厅里金色的爱神丘比特男童像。游艇有三个圆形区域：一个配有圆形餐桌，一个安置了吧台和棋牌桌，还有一个则有巨大的日光浴垫。

legno ebano
soffitto finito
24
Specchio
Tv
89
Frigo
Ice maker
sportello
12
13

12
specchio
13
54
26
Frigo & Fabbricatore ghiaccio
51
vassoi estraibili portabottiglie
Tubolare acciaio Ø5
76
58
pedane

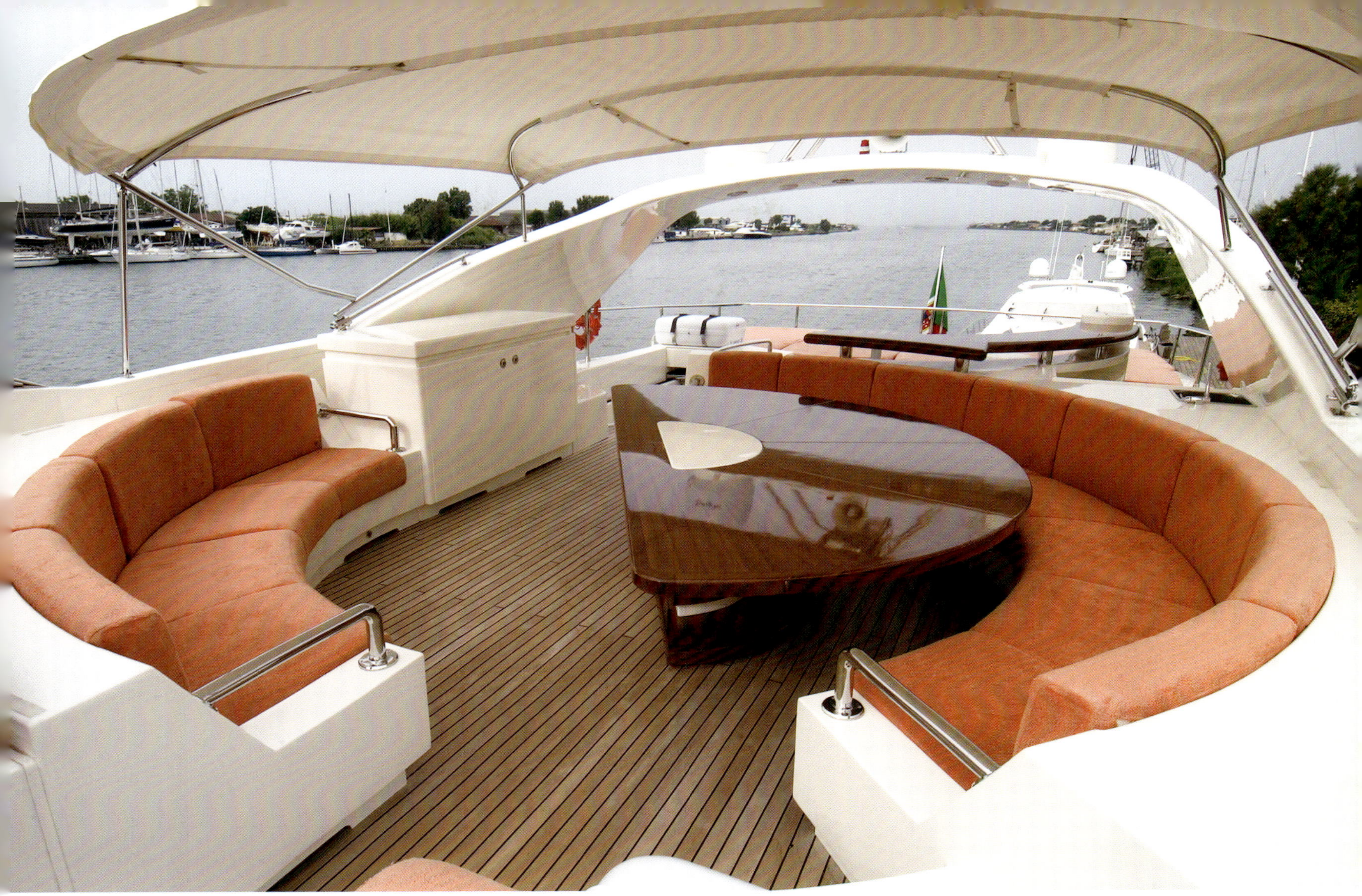

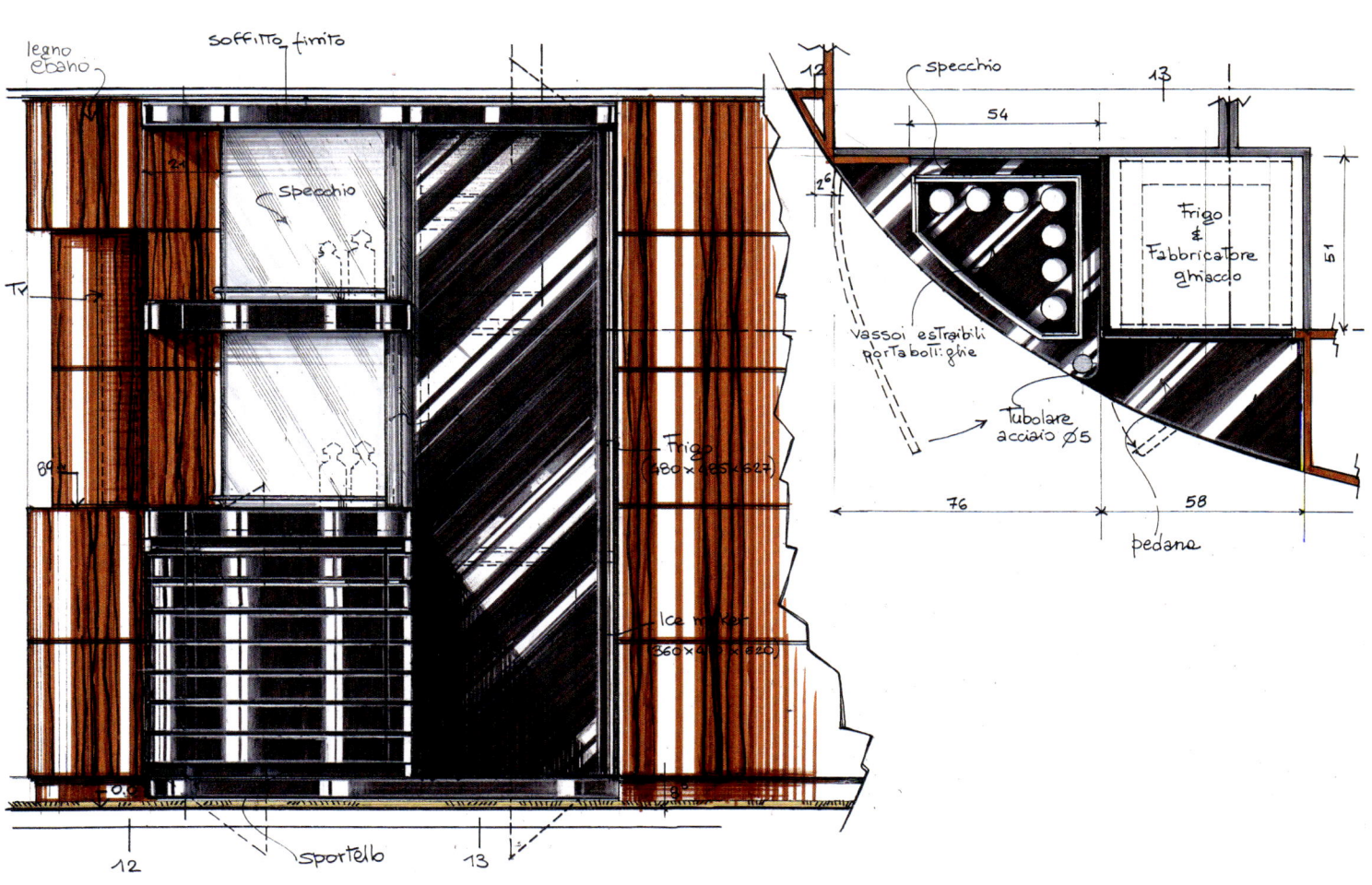

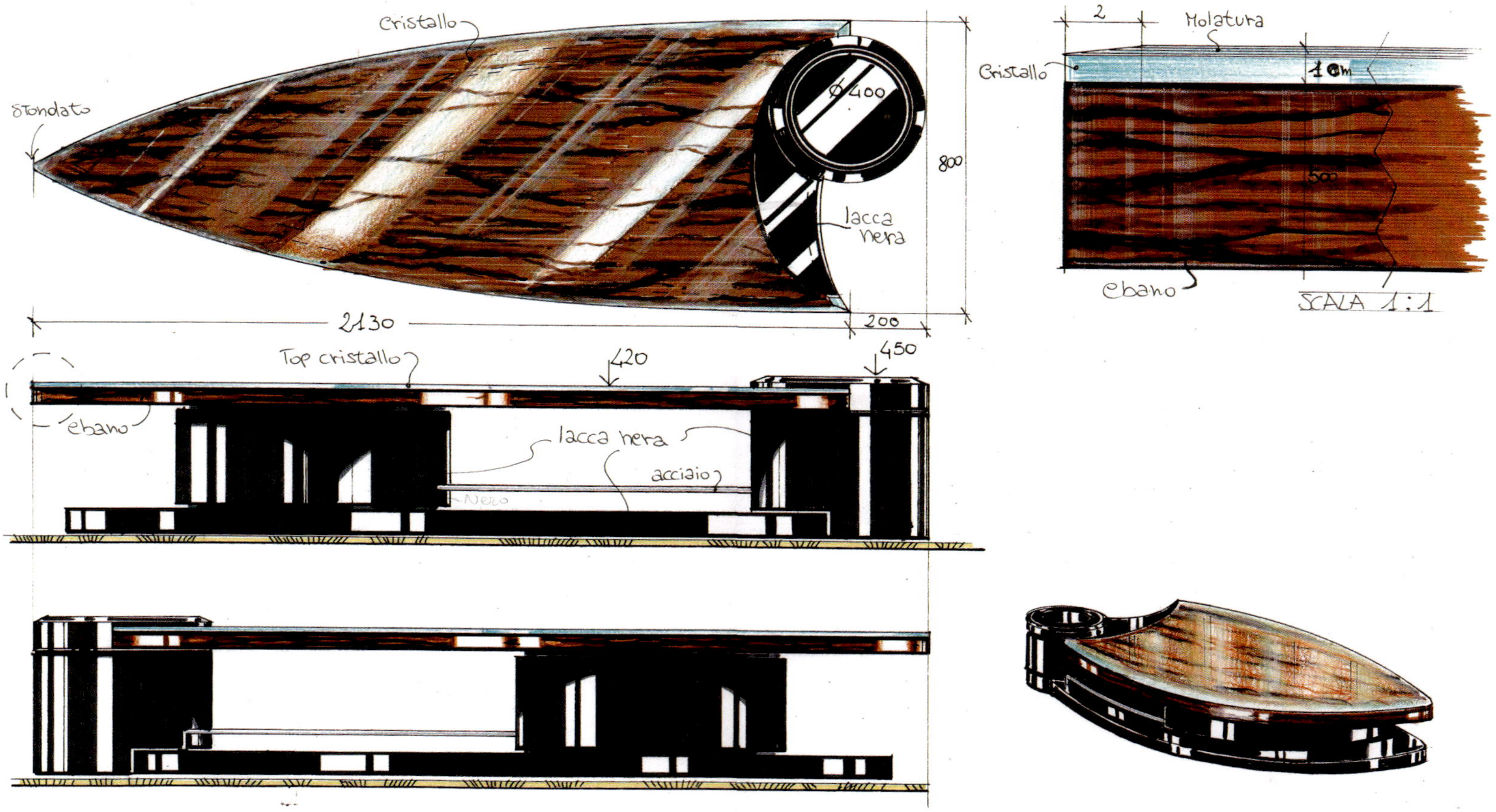

Cristallo

stondato

Ø 400

800

lacca nera

2   Molatura

Cristallo   1 cm

ebano   500   SCALA 1:1

2130   200

Top cristallo   420

450

ebano   lacca nera   acciaio

Nero

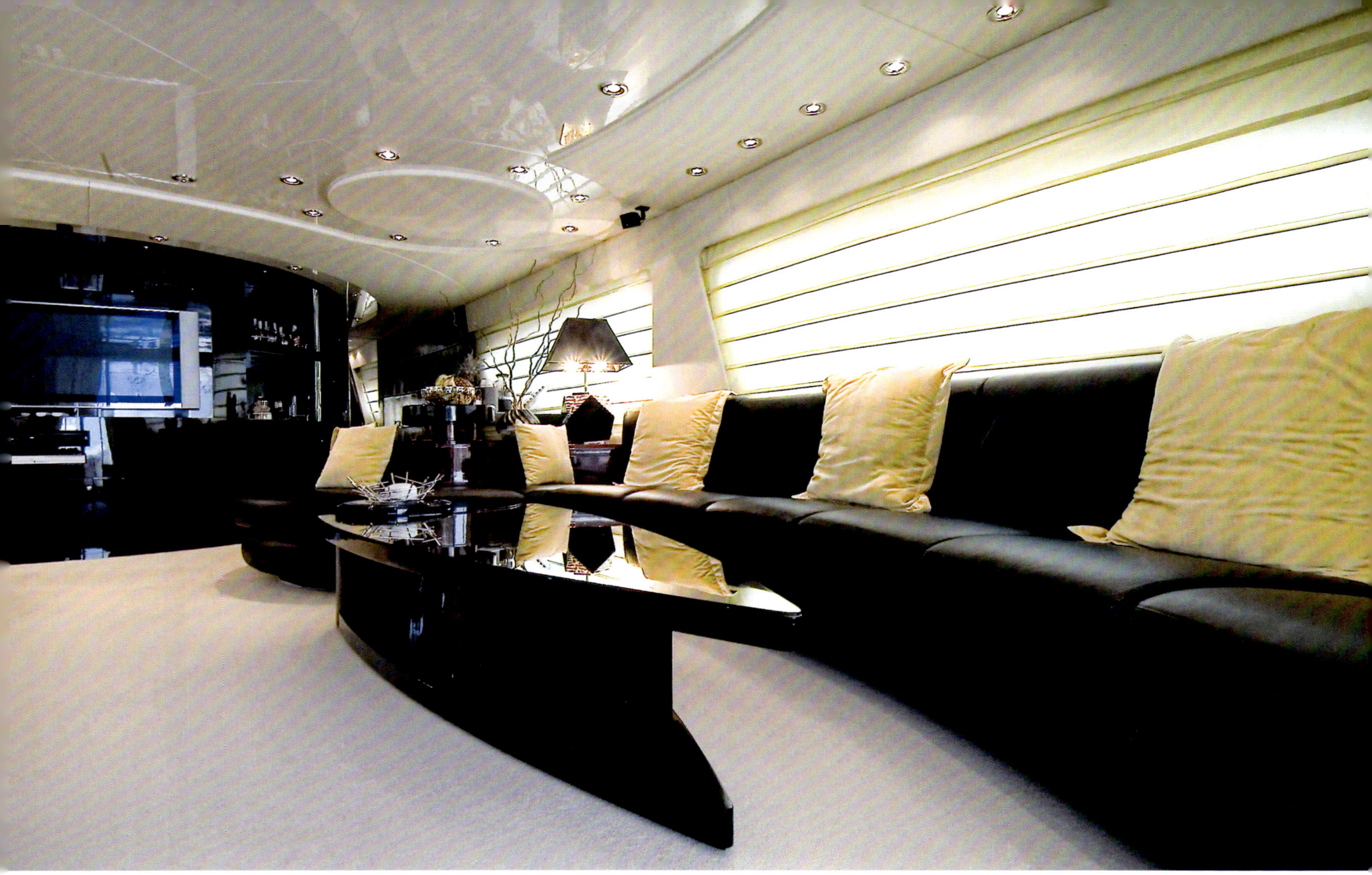

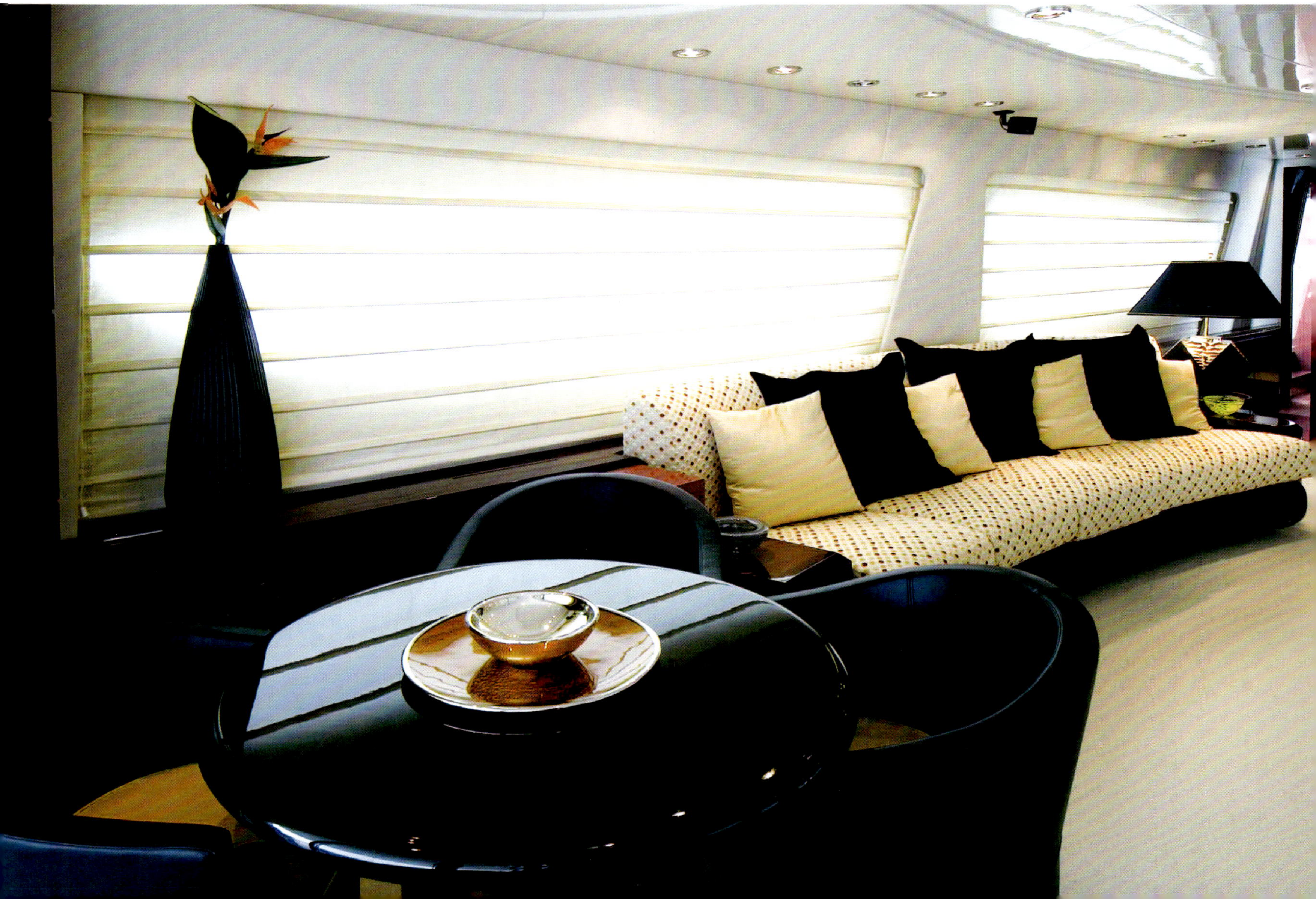

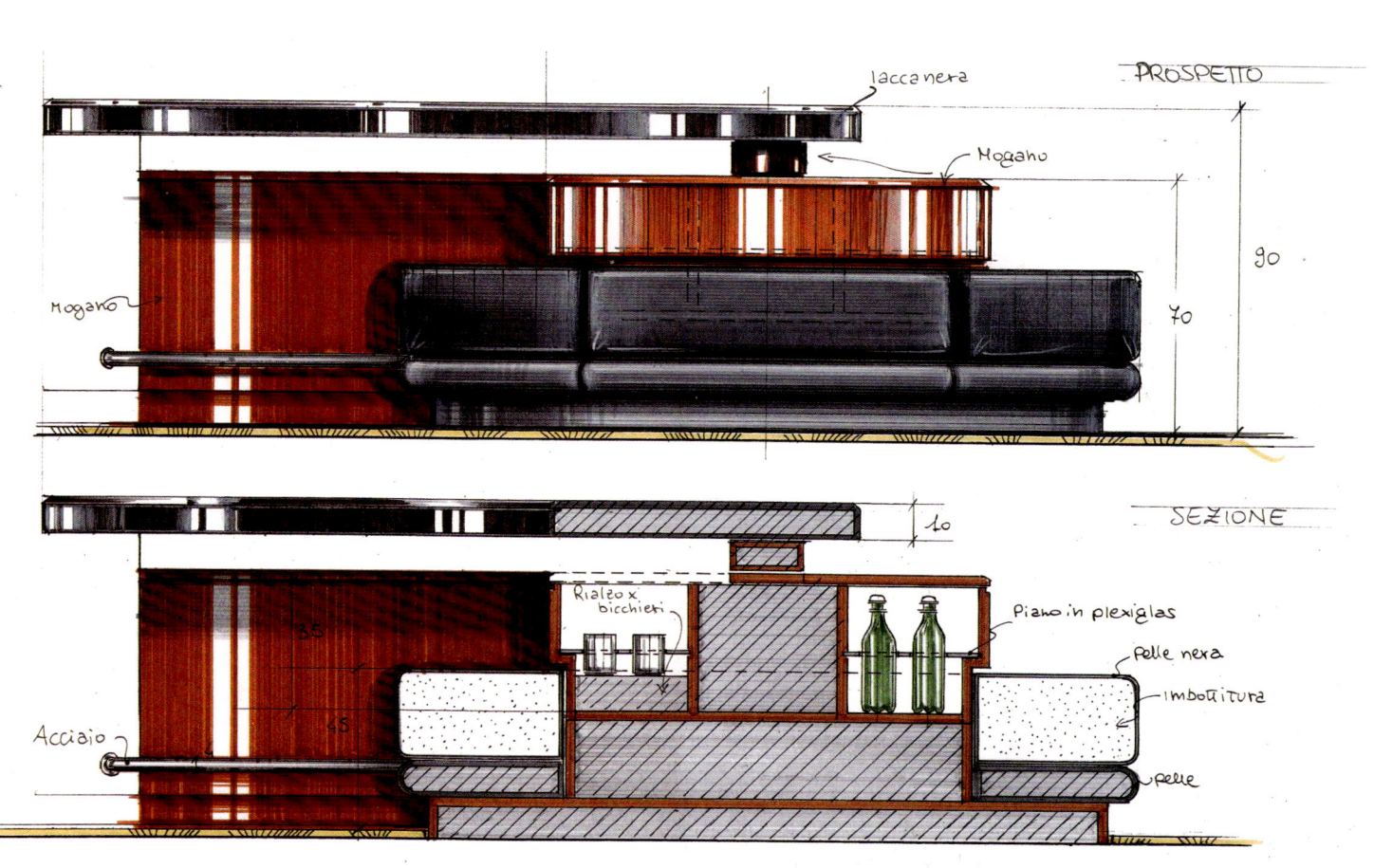

laccanera

PROSPETTO

Mogano

Mogano

90

70

Acciaio

SEZIONE

10

Rialzo x
bicchieri

Piano in plexiglas

Pelle nera

imbottitura

35

45

pelle

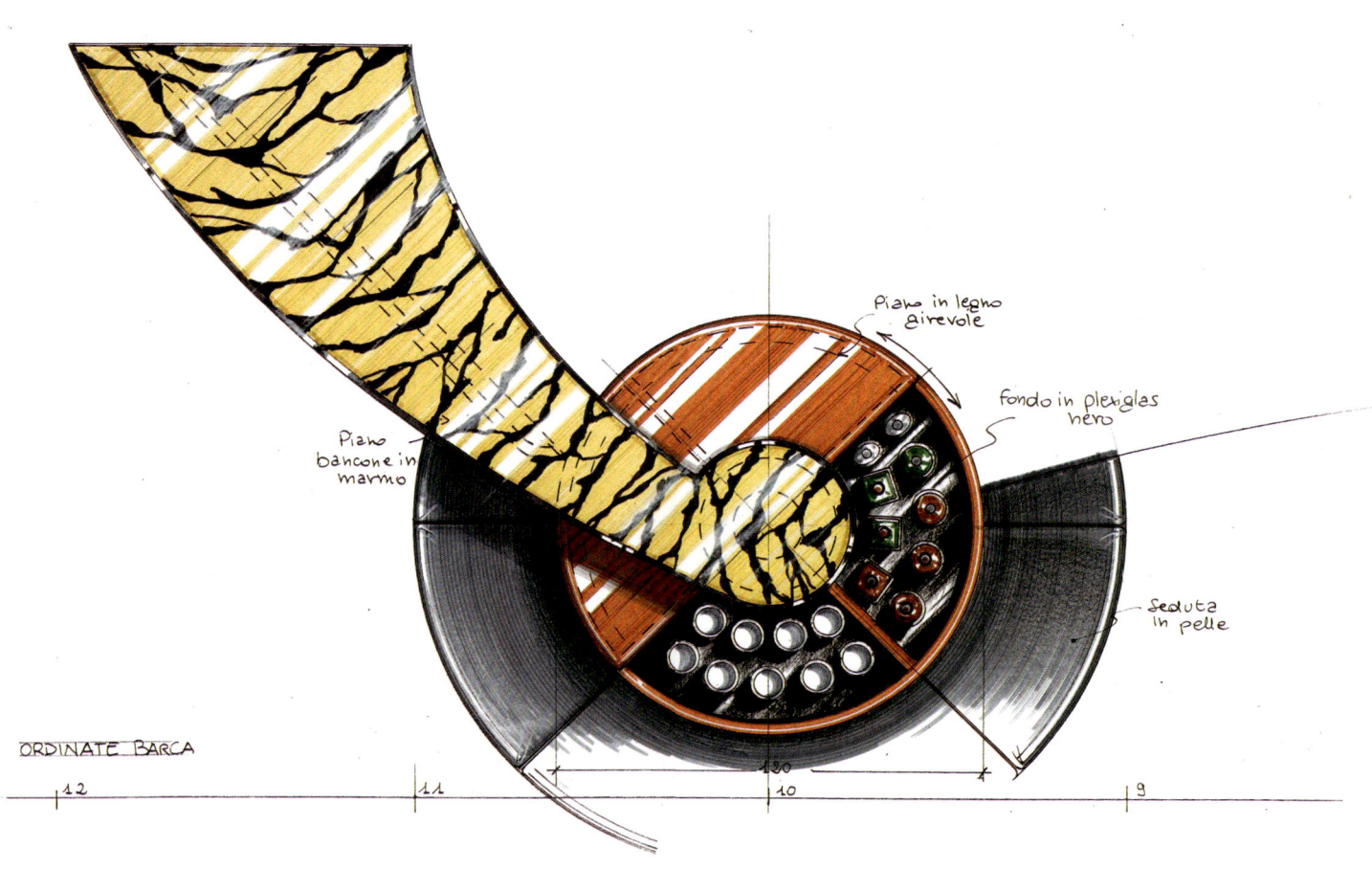

Piano in legno
girevole

Piano
bancone in
marmo

fondo in plexiglas
nero

Seduta
in pelle

ORDINATE BARCA

12   11   130   9
                        10

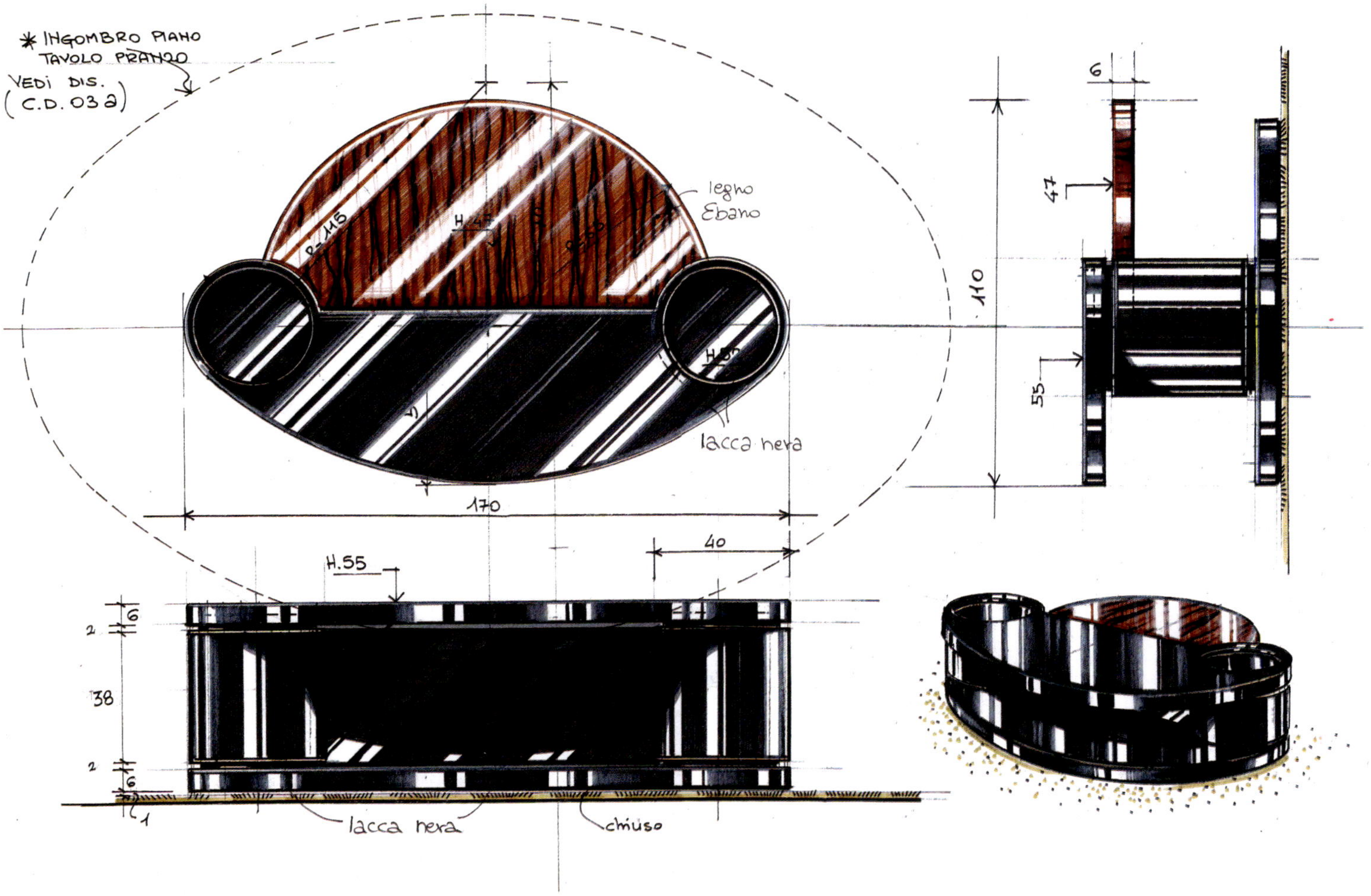

* INGOMBRO PIANO
TAVOLO PRANZO
VEDI DIS.
(C.D. 03a)

legno
Ebano

R.115

H.

lacca nera

6

47

110

55

170

40

H.55

6

2

38

2

6

1

lacca nera

chiuso

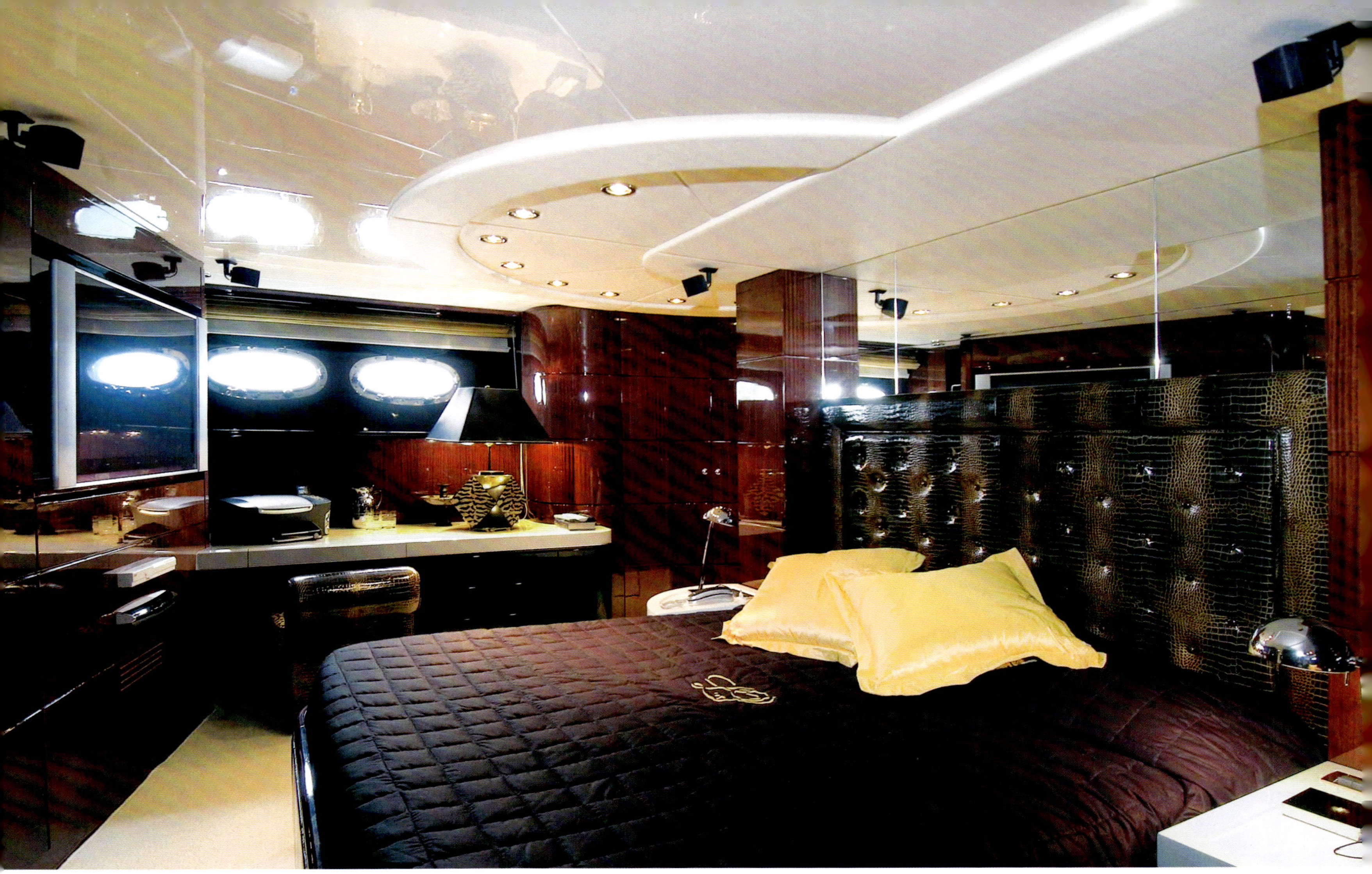

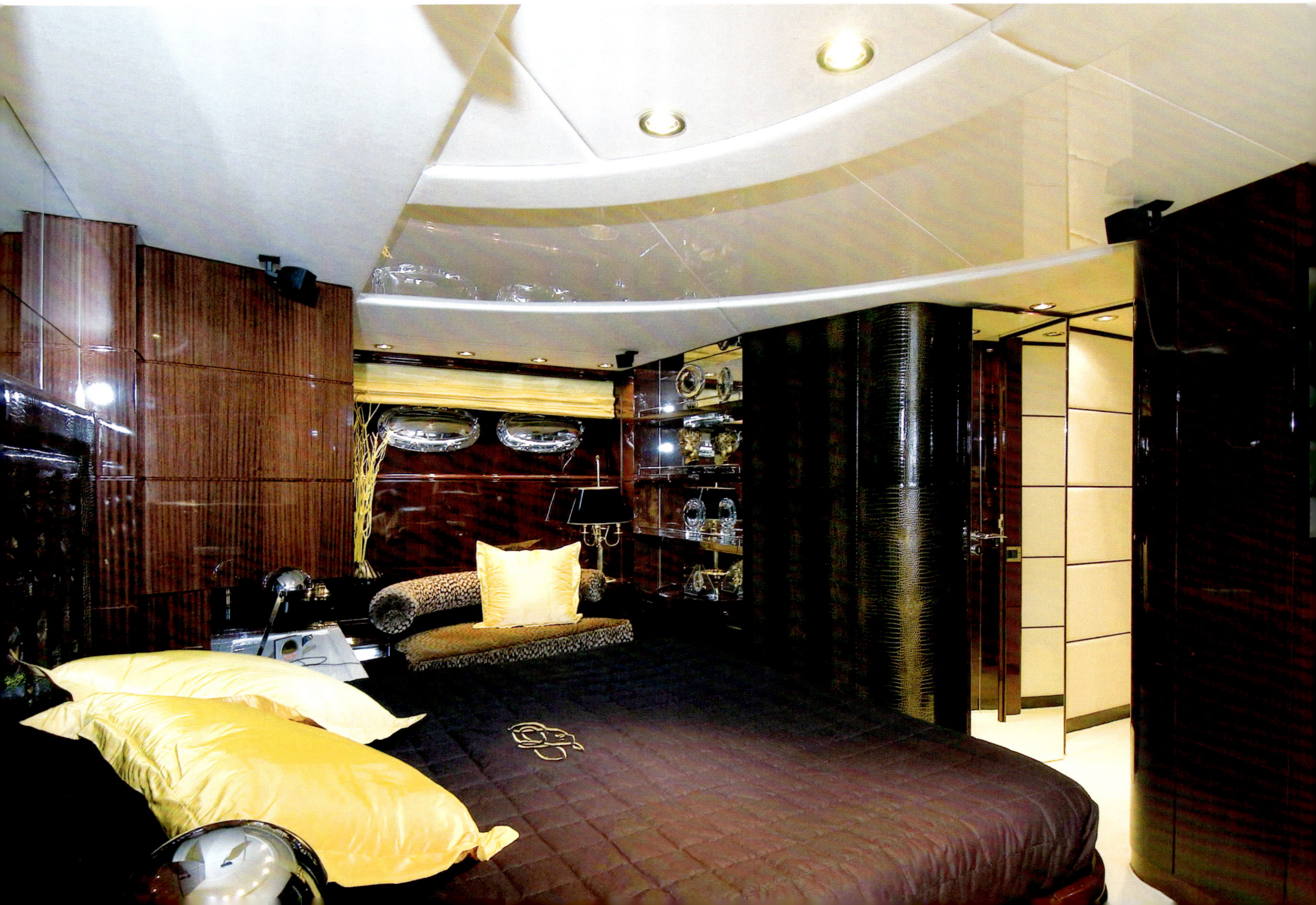

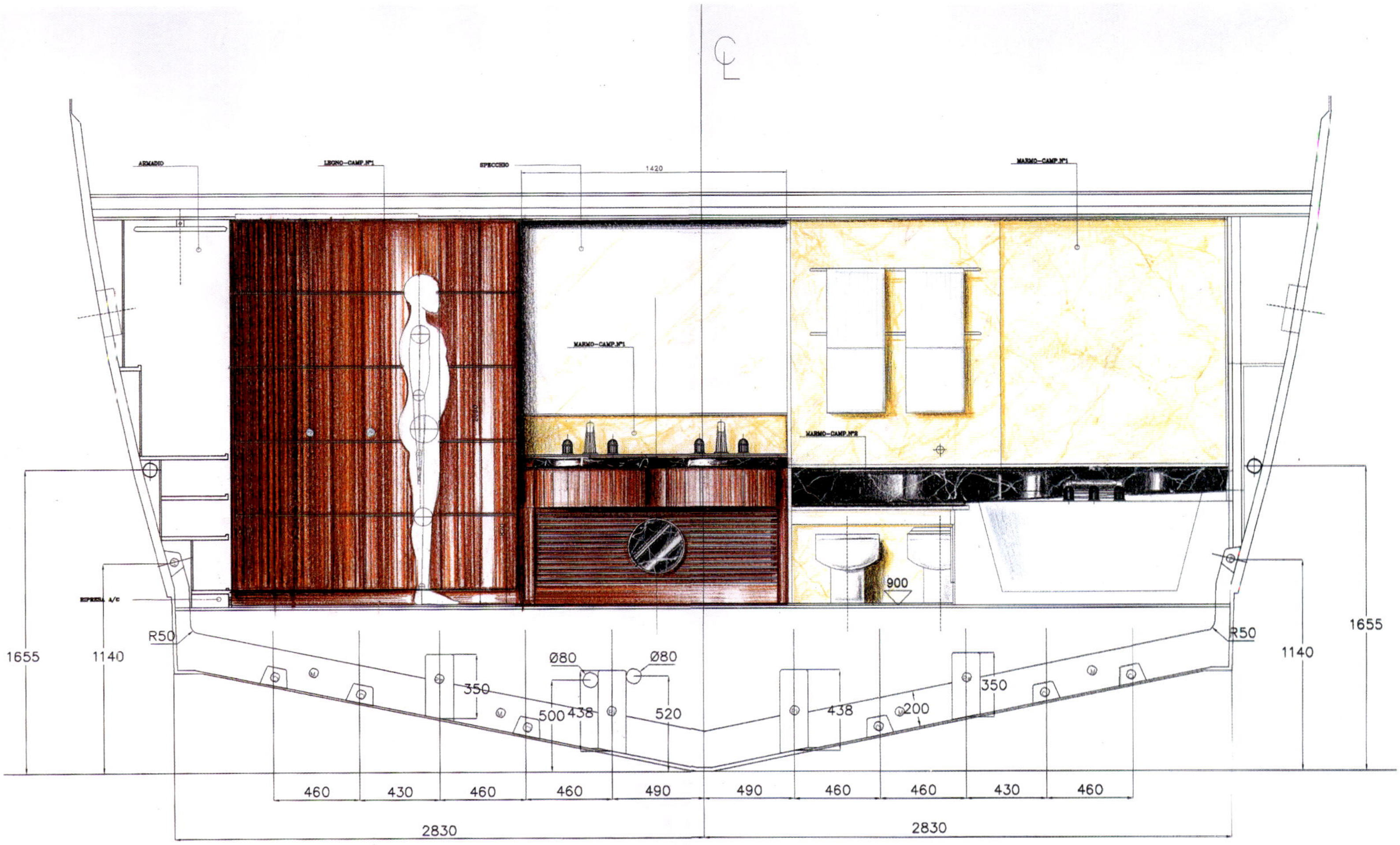

1420
900
R50
R50
1655
1140
1655
1140
Ø80
Ø80
350
350
500
438
520
438
200
460
430
460
460
490
490
460
460
430
460
2830
2830

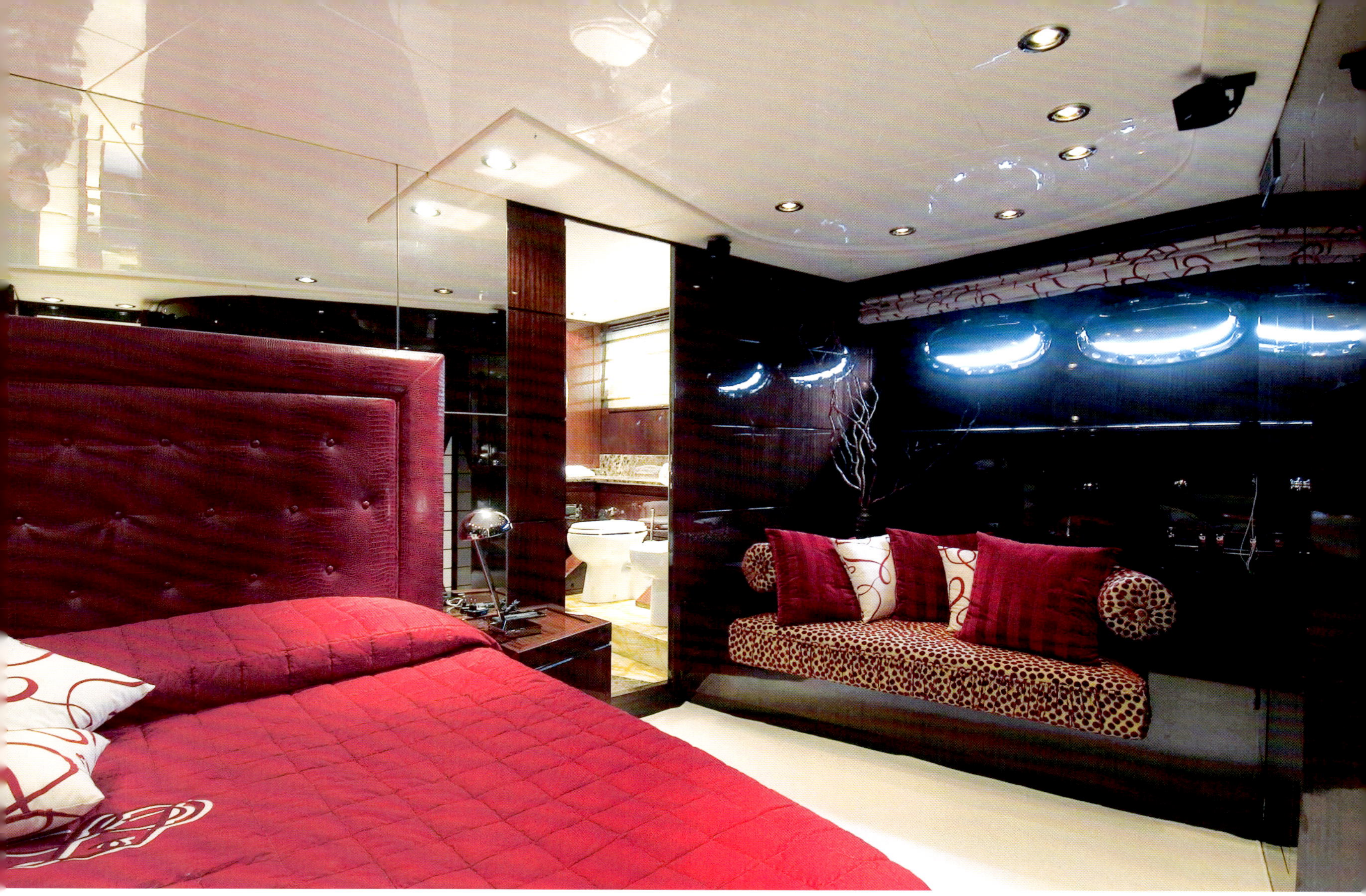

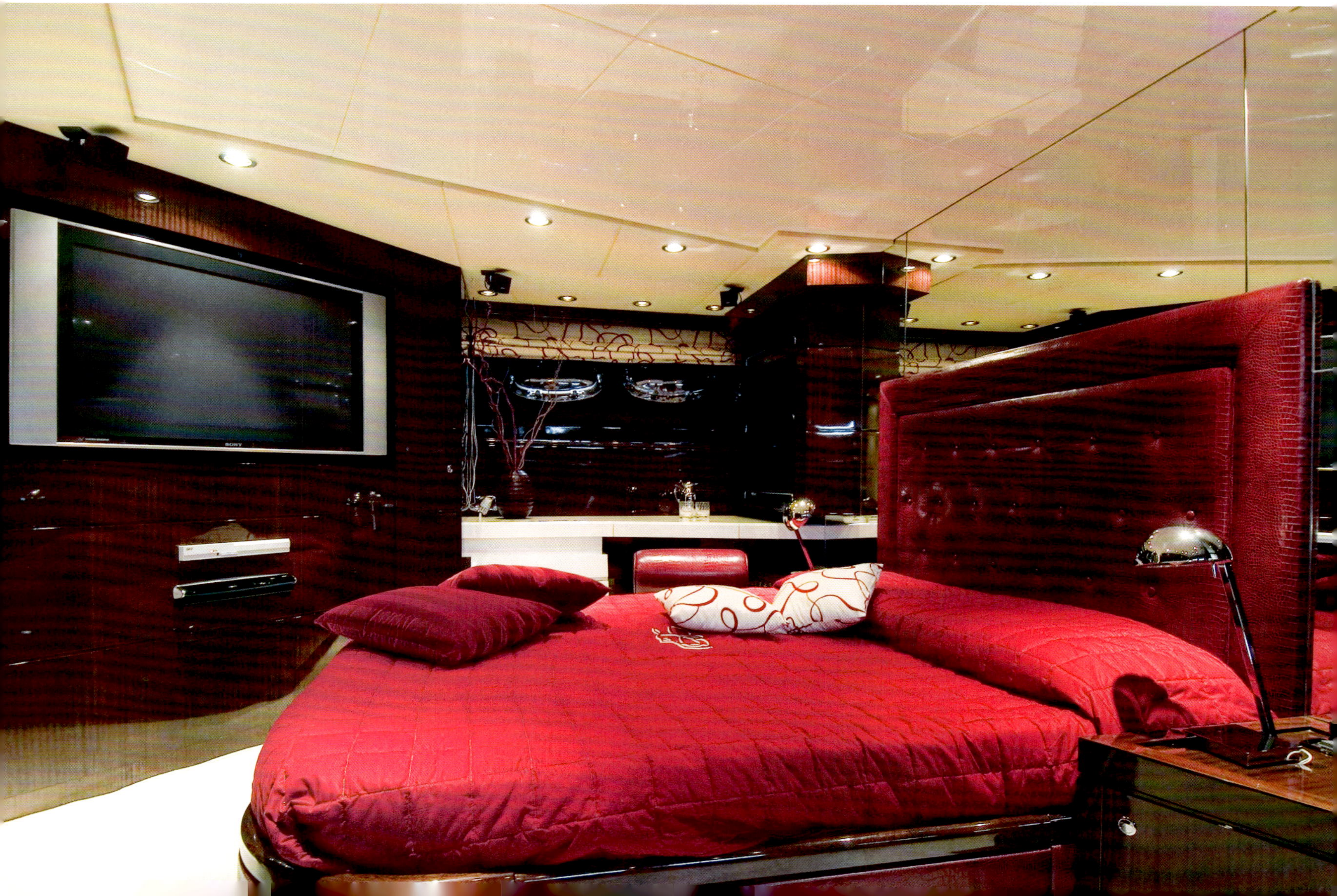

SKY YACHT

> **DESIGNER**   Mark D. Stumer, Peter Johns,
                     Michael Spitaleri, William
                     Minnear, Jessica Licalzi,
                     Sharlene Teitel
> **DESIGN COMPANY** Mojo Stumer Associates
> **PHOTOGRAPHER**   David Churchill

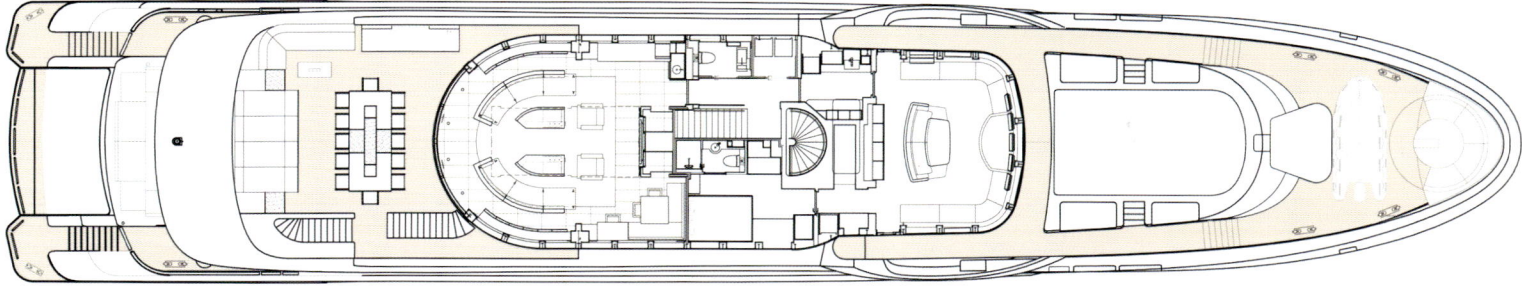

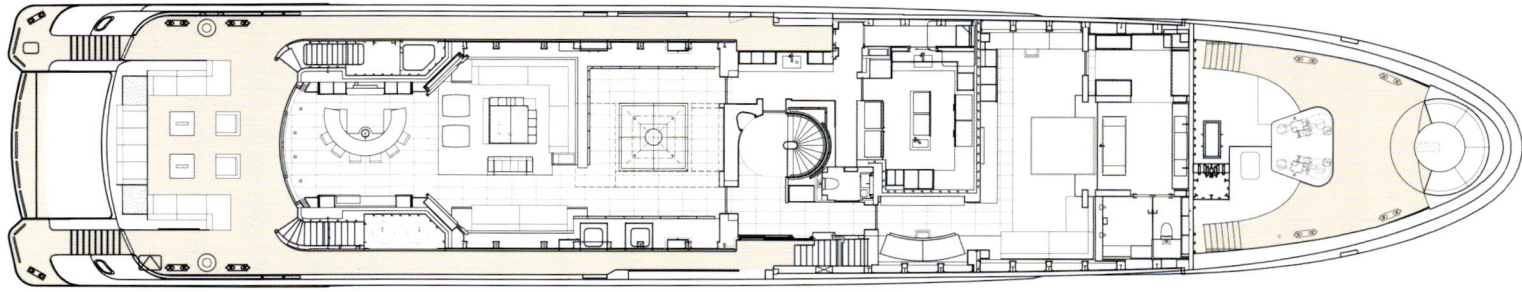

A yacht offers constraints and opportunities to architects and designers alike. An interesting set of challenges arises when it is realized that a vision must not only be structurally sound, innovative, aesthetically beautiful and comfortable, but it must also float. Being afloat in a modernists retreat has been a long sought after dream for these clients.

MSA had the vision of designing a modern space with sleek, linear edges and custom furniture. This all sounds like a goal easy enough to attain until it's brought into the boating world, where codes, regulations and practicality make things more difficult. Typically the interiors of yachts look similar, due to functionality or circulation; the designs tend to have rounded edges. MSA's solution was proportions. If every element, from the custom furniture to the stainless steel trims, were carefully proportioned correctly, the linear design would be successful.

The state of art design of this yacht incorporates the latest technology, utilizing carbon fiber. The finest goods were chosen to adorn the yachts interior. Outdoor textiles were employed in the interior spaces to ensure the client would have the calming, clean white aesthetic that they sought after, without compromising the durability and longevity. Hand selected Macassar Ebony with a high lacquer finish wraps each wall of the main deck and the floors are clad in custom silk carpet. In keeping with the European heritage of the vessel, all the custom designed furnishings and accoutrements were made in the old country.

The client wanted to ensure that their crew would have the most advanced technology to work with. No expense was spared. From the engine room to the toilets to the acoustical system to the shower hinges, every aspect of the workings of the ship was thought through diligently and with care. Throughout their history the European boat manufacturer has credited "passion as the driving force behind the performance and perfection they deliver. They strive for perfection both technically and aesthetically." This project is the crowning glory of yacht designers and architects alike.

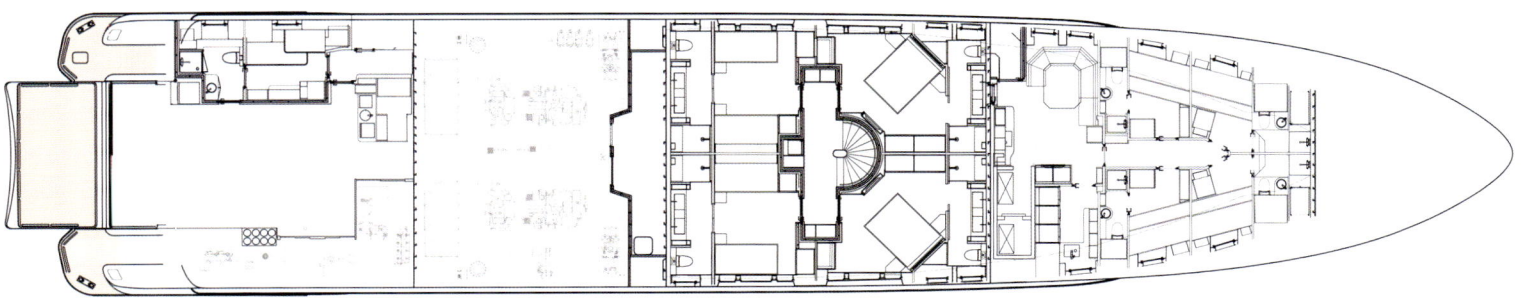

PLANS

10 8 6 4 2 0   10   20

GRAPHIC SCALE (IN FEET)

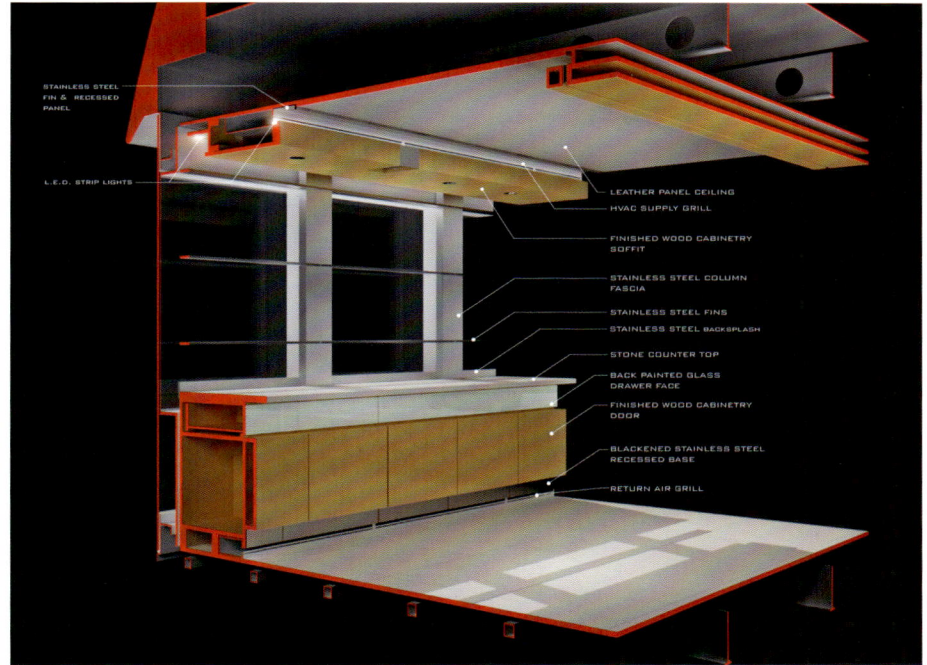

STAINLESS STEEL
FIN & RECESSED
PANEL

L.E.D. STRIP LIGHTS

LEATHER PANEL CEILING
HVAC SUPPLY GRILL
FINISHED WOOD CABINETRY
SOFFIT
STAINLESS STEEL COLUMN
FASCIA
STAINLESS STEEL FINS
STAINLESS STEEL BACKSPLASH
STONE COUNTER TOP
BACK PAINTED GLASS
DRAWER FACE
FINISHED WOOD CABINETRY
DOOR
BLACKENED STAINLESS STEEL
RECESSED BASE
RETURN AIR GRILL

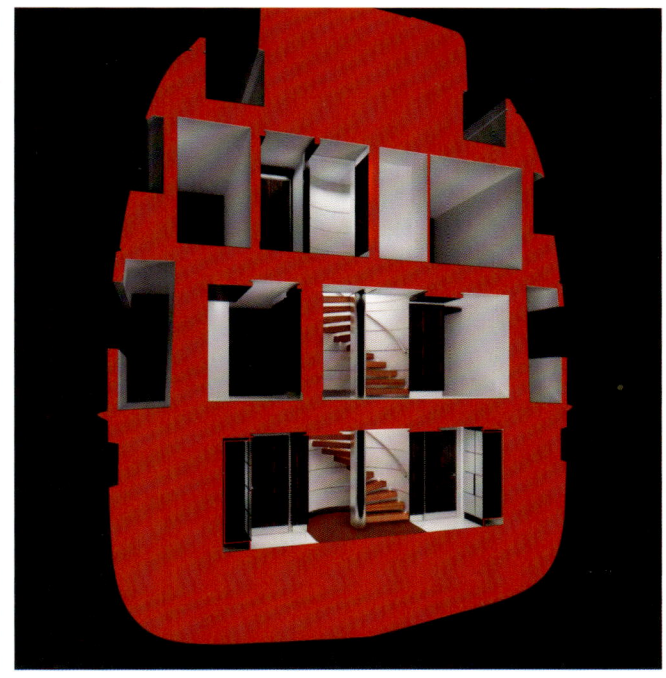

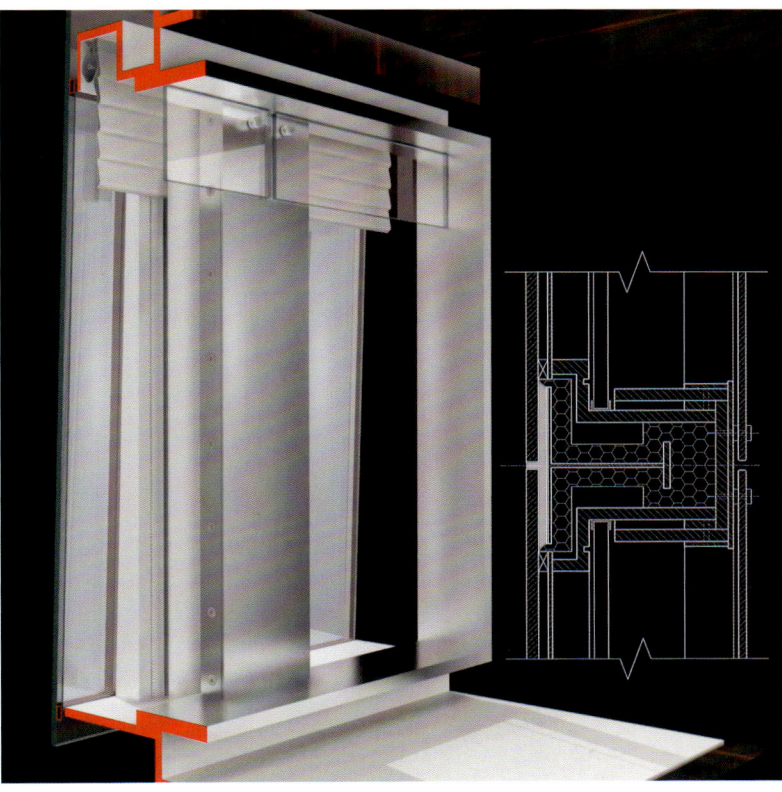

一艘游艇不仅给建筑师和设计师们带来了困扰，也带来了机遇。一系列有趣的挑战在于，要确保实现外观不仅结构合理、富有创新、美观得体、方便舒适，还要意识到这一切都必须满足船在海上行驶的需要。对这些客户来说，在对现代生活的疲惫后，能回到大海生活静养，是他们长久以来的梦想。

MSA设计公司希望设计出这样的一艘游艇：光滑的线型边角、定制的家具使游艇现代气息十足。这样的目标听起来并不费劲，但如果考虑到游船的水上环境，其设计标准、规则和实用功能都与陆地上截然不同，这一切都没那么容易了。典型的列子就是，由于功能和出入口的局限，很多游艇的内部设计都大同小异，设计时大都倾向于使用圆形拐角。MSA提出的解决方案是调整比例，从定制家具到不锈钢装饰，每种元素的比例都要做到准确细致，这样才会达成成功的线型设计。

这艘游艇设计顶尖，采用了最新科技——碳纤维。游艇内部设计采用了最好的装饰材料，同时内部空间还采用了户外用的纺织材料，确保客户能体验到他们所梦想的宁静、纯洁、白色的美感，同时又不失材料的耐用性与持久性。精心挑选的檀木和上好的漆面抛光，覆盖了主甲板的每面墙。地板也铺了一层定制丝织地毯。游艇传承了欧洲舰艇制作的技艺，所有的定制设施与供给都在原产国生产。

客户要求确保船员能使用最先进的技术设备，在花费方面不遗余力。从引擎室到卫生间，从音响系统到浴室门铰，游艇运行的方方面面都做到了精益求精。纵览历史，欧洲造船师一直秉承"热情是勤奋工作和追求卓越的动力，为技术和美学极致奋斗不息"。这艘游艇是这些设计师和建筑师们最高的荣耀。

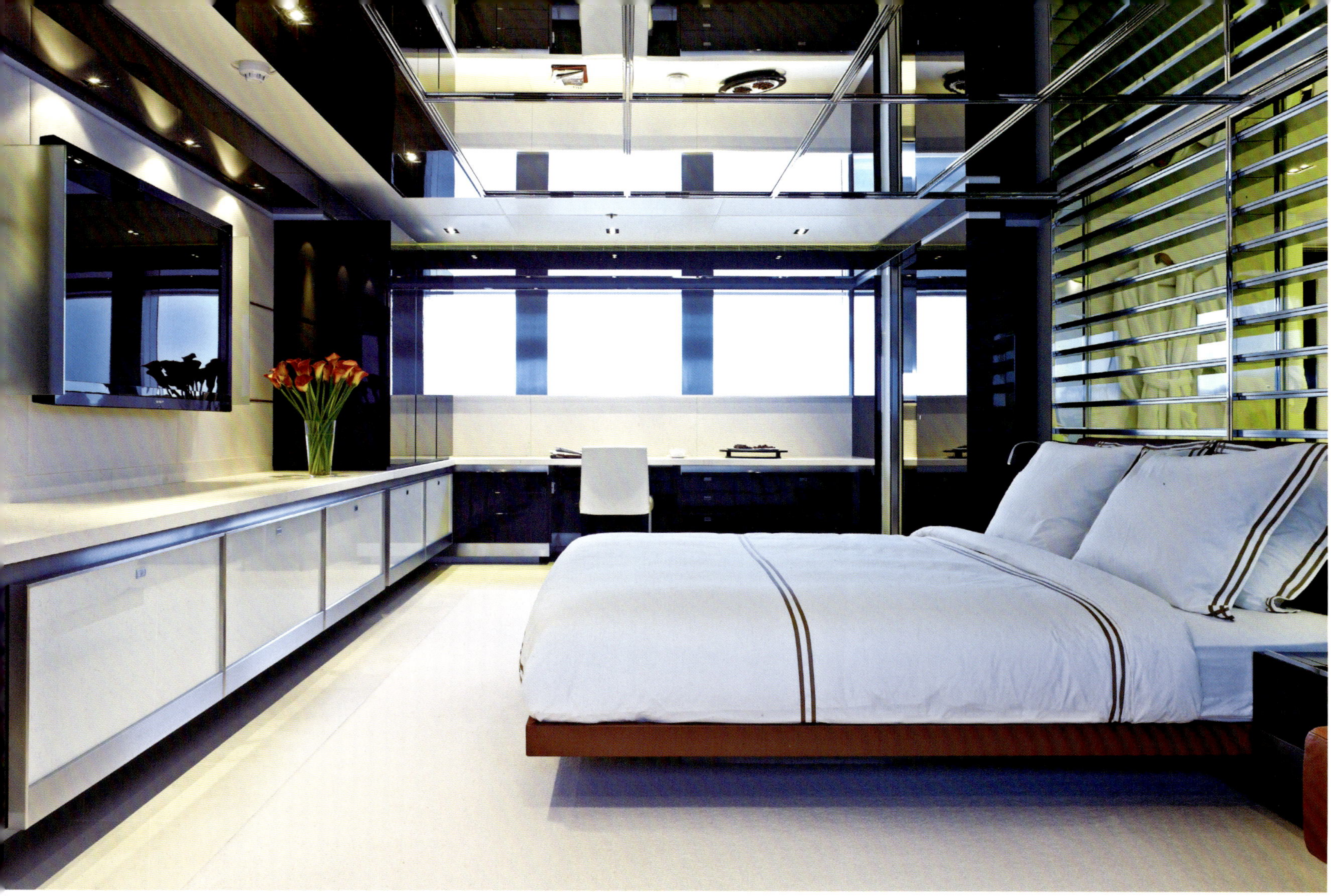
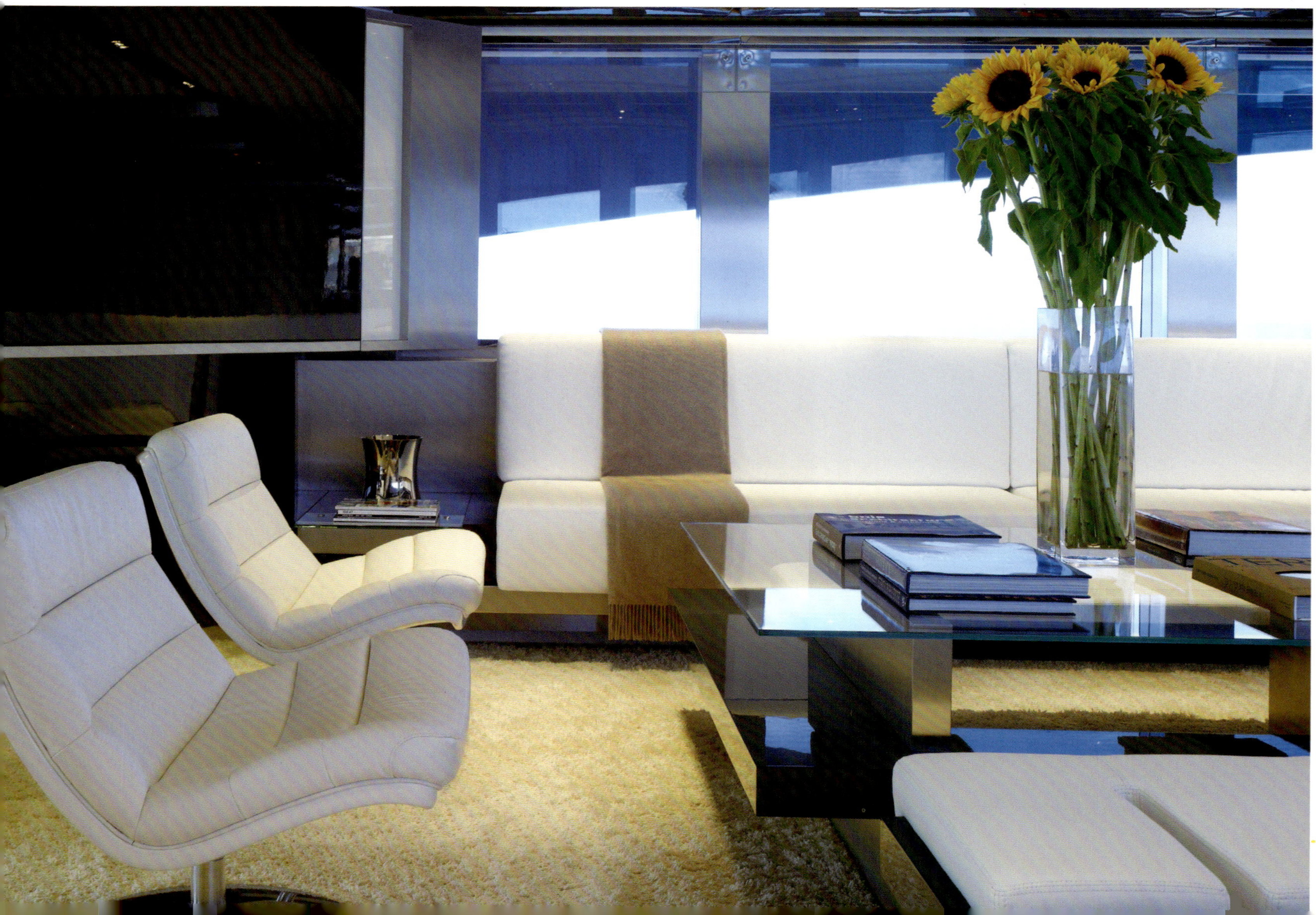

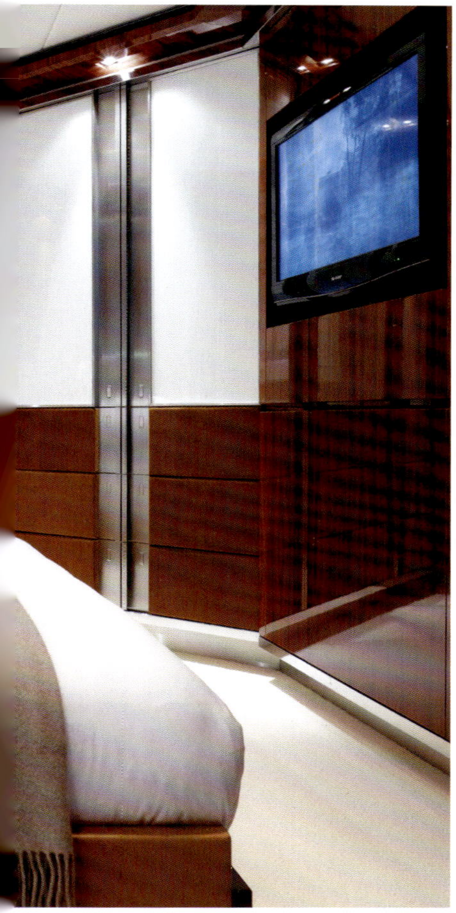
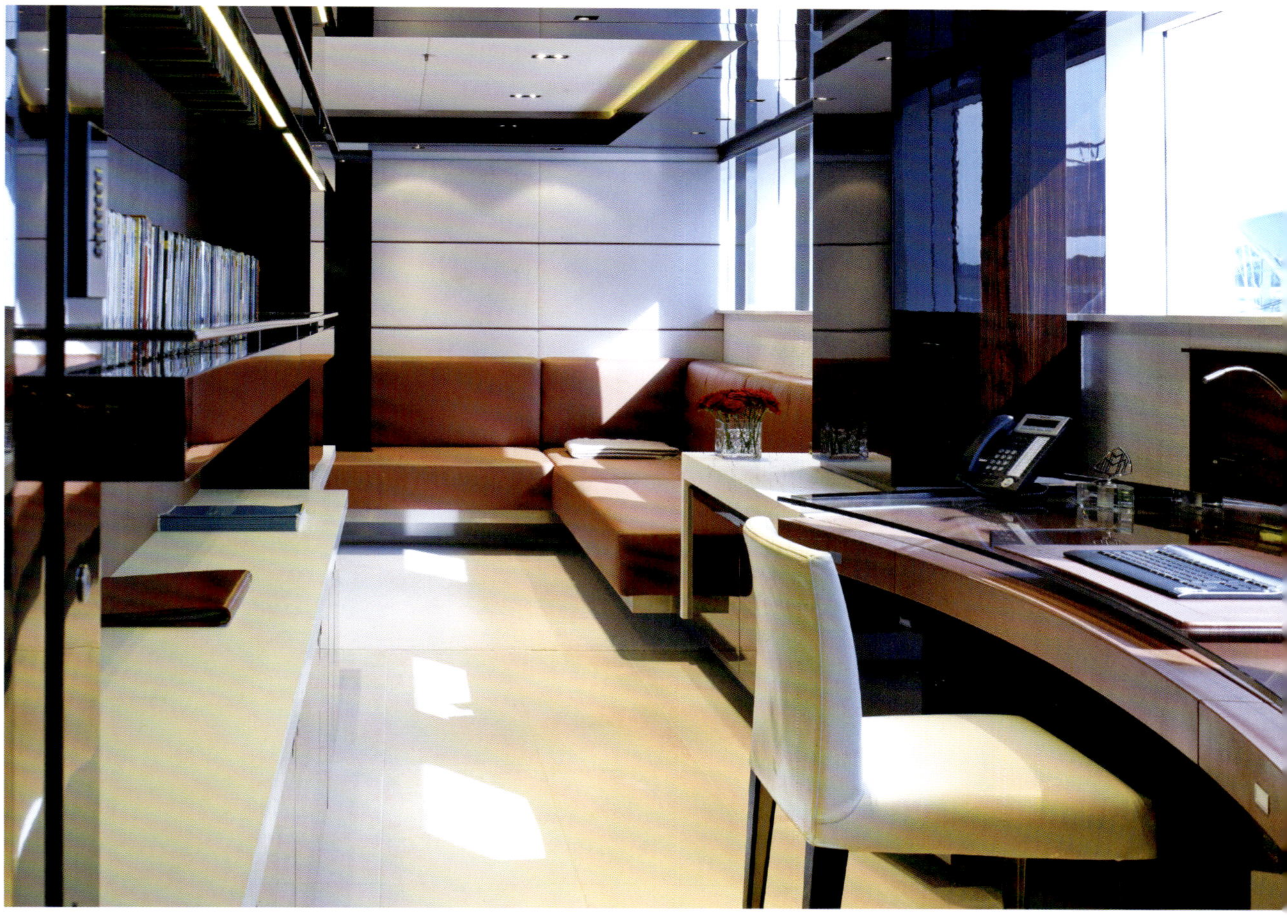
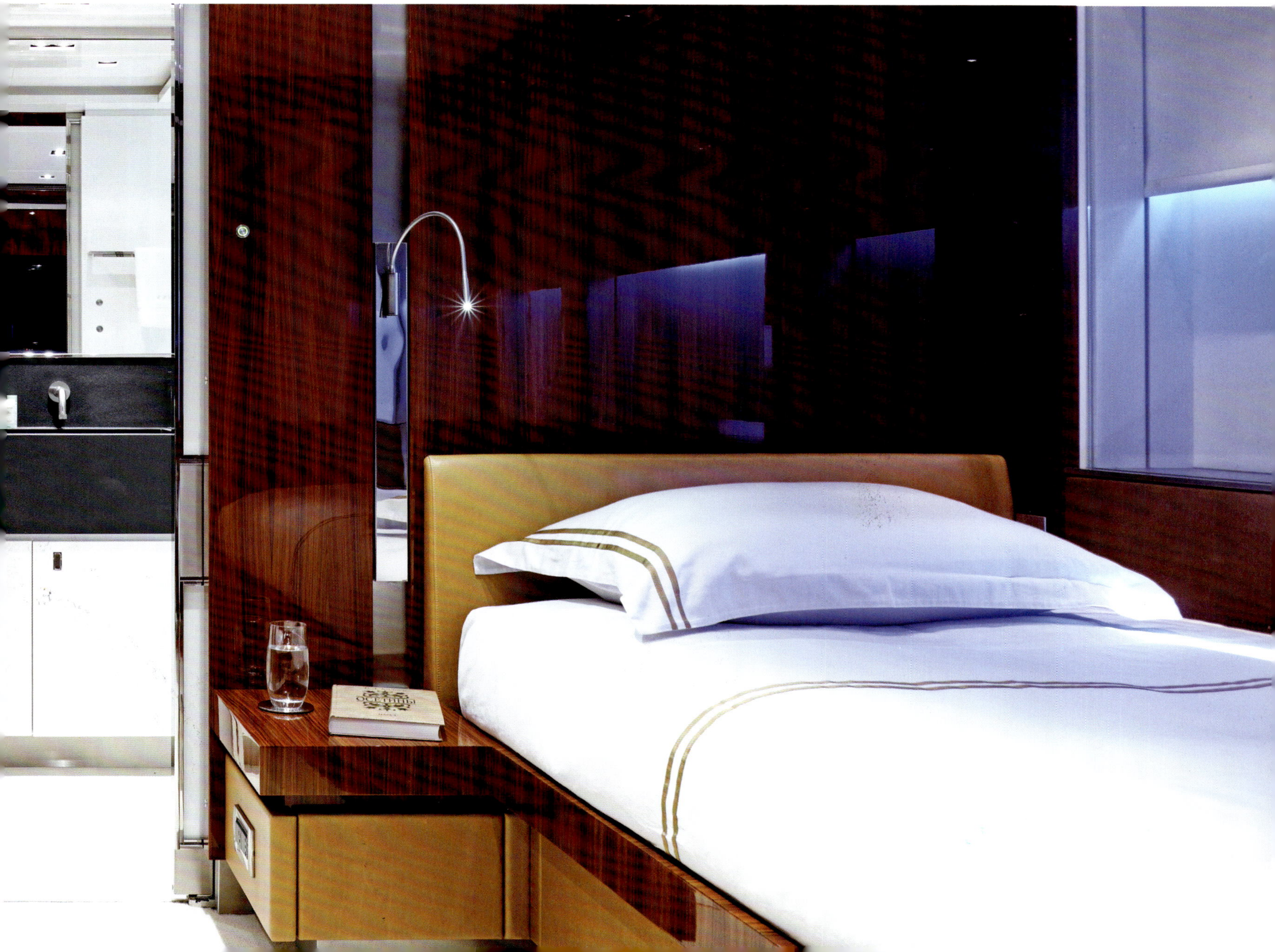

MY MEAMINA

> INTERIOR DESIGN	Studio Massari
> SHIPYARD	Benetti Shipyard
> LENGTH	59.30m
> BEAM	10.4m

> Meamina is a mega yacht built by Benetti Shipyard. Exterior lines are by Stefano Natucci whereas Studio Massari took care of the interior design and decoration.

The owner requested Studio Massari to give a classic interior design but with some modern touches. First of all the yacht should have had a cosy character and be able to give emotions creating astonishment with innovation accents. This is the challenge Studio Massari had to face making the interior design of MEAMINA a new concept through the use of new concept and unique design.

Each Studio Massari's projects has distinctive characters originating from owners' requirements. A good designer is should be like a good tailor who knows how to shape the tailor made suit for his client to make him feeling good wearing it. We have created ambiances that encase a sense of new design but not so far away from the classic styles. The achieved balance with this classic oddness give a distinctive character and a sober cozy elegance to this yacht.

Meamina has a traditional layout with a spacious living area on the main deck where the dining is separated from the seating area in order to distinguish the different areas and their functionality. Precious woods have been used throughout the vessel combined with high level wood inlays that make the door cabinet and tables very precious. Very refined precious leather selections have been combined with the wood selections. White upholstery works balance the dark ambiances and their moldings creating familiar and comfortable ambients. The main foyer is characterized by an inlay onyx marble floor and the lift trunk all wrapped in leather with some wood touch accents.

The master suite has two separated offices, his and her. Several elements such has bed, nightstands and desks make this suite unique. Upper Skylounge is the family area, the perfect place to get relaxed and be among friends with its warming character. The calm atmosphere you can breathe on board makes the whole yacht very hospitable without omit a sophisticated elegance with decorative solutions with no ostentation.

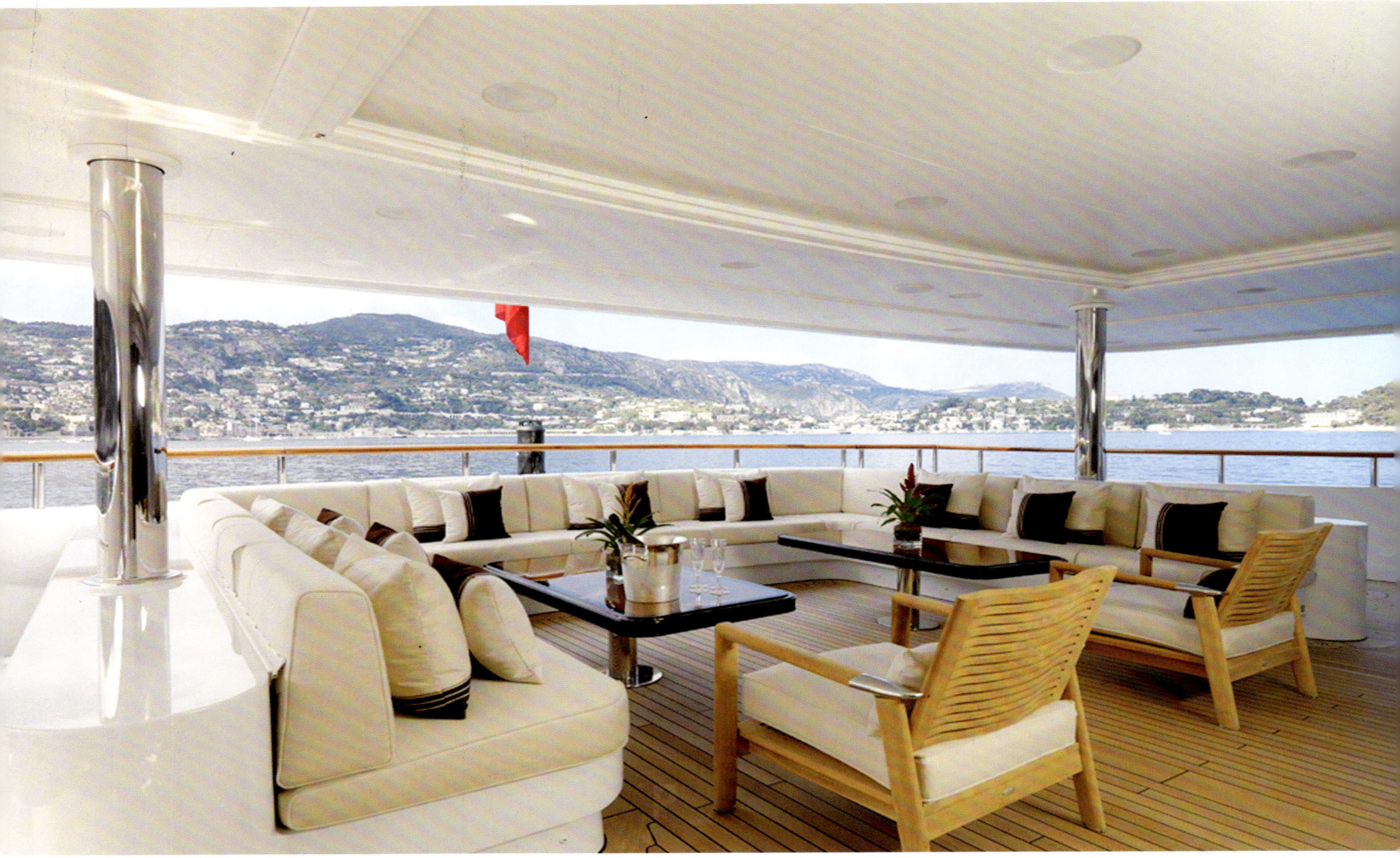

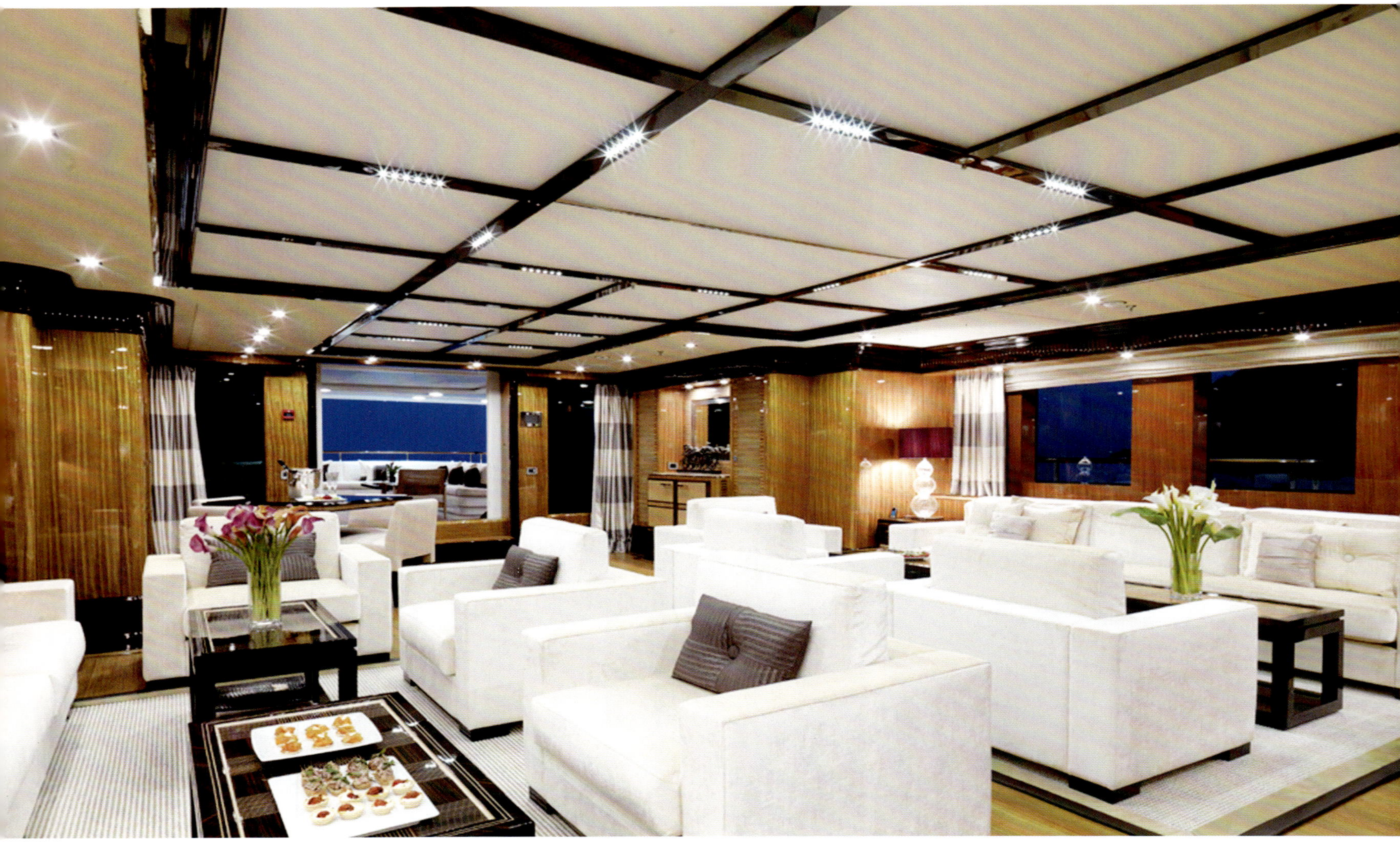

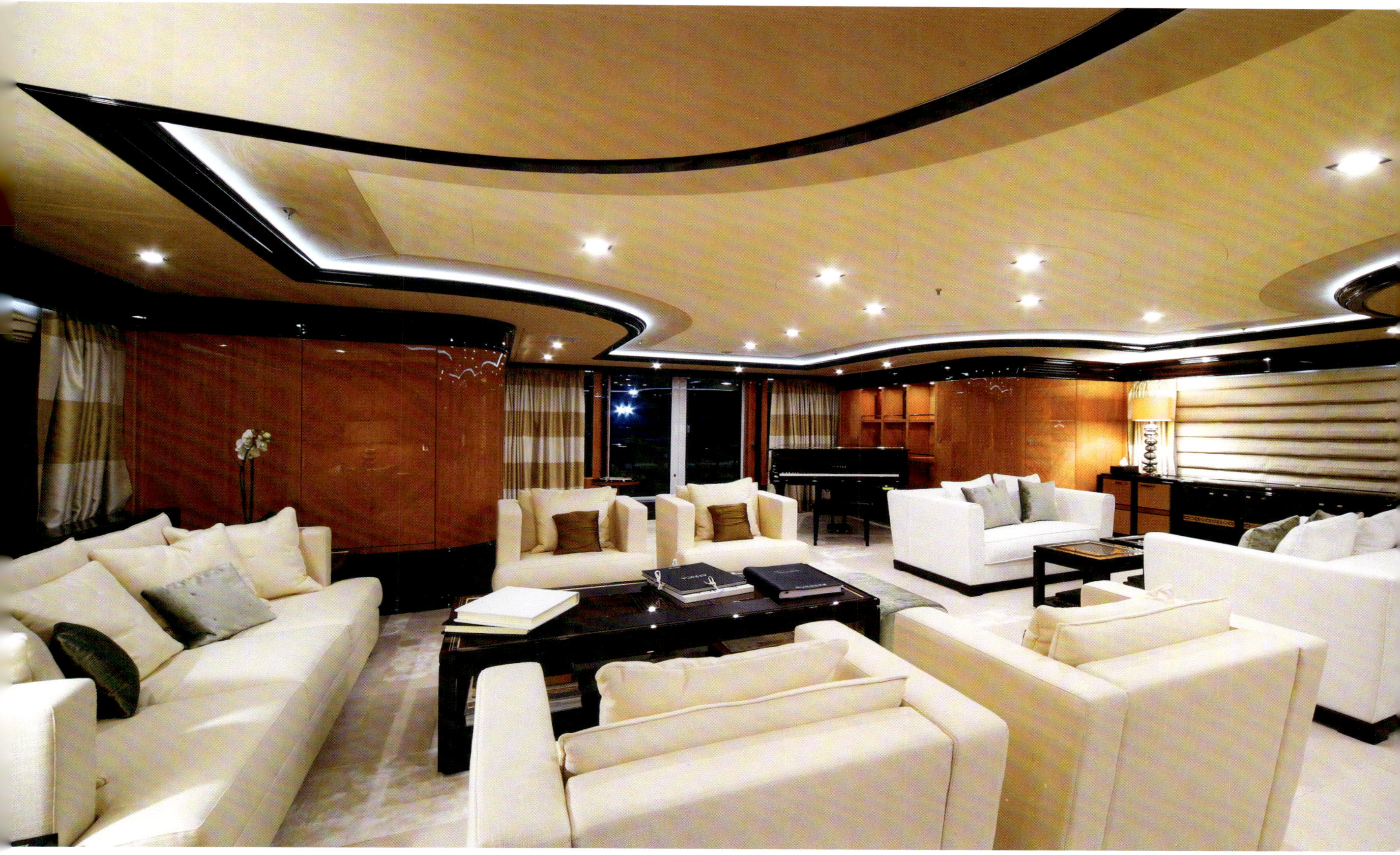

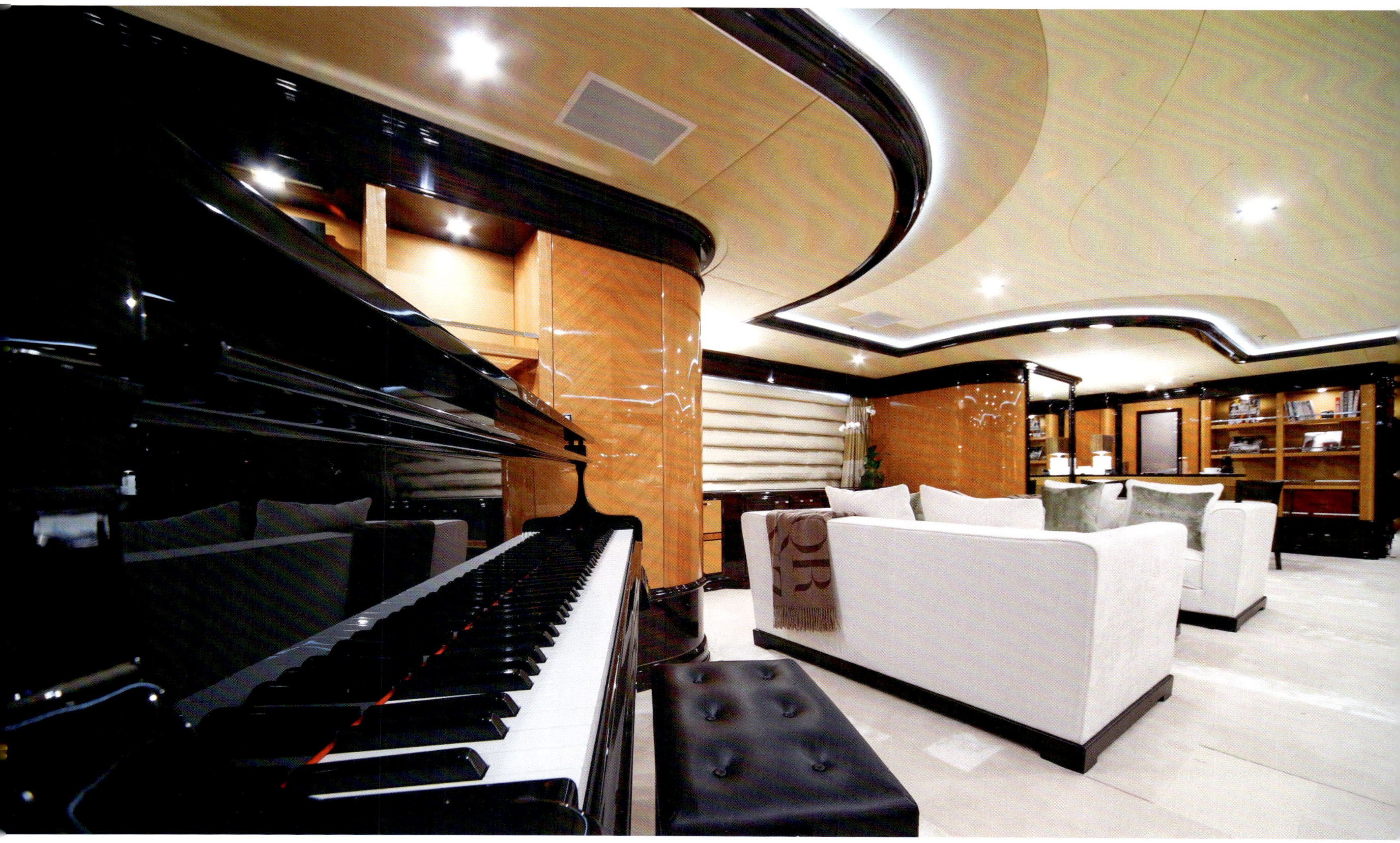

AXEL VERVOORDT
PICASSO
ASSOULINE
L'Art tribal
d'Afrique Noire
ARTS PREMIERS

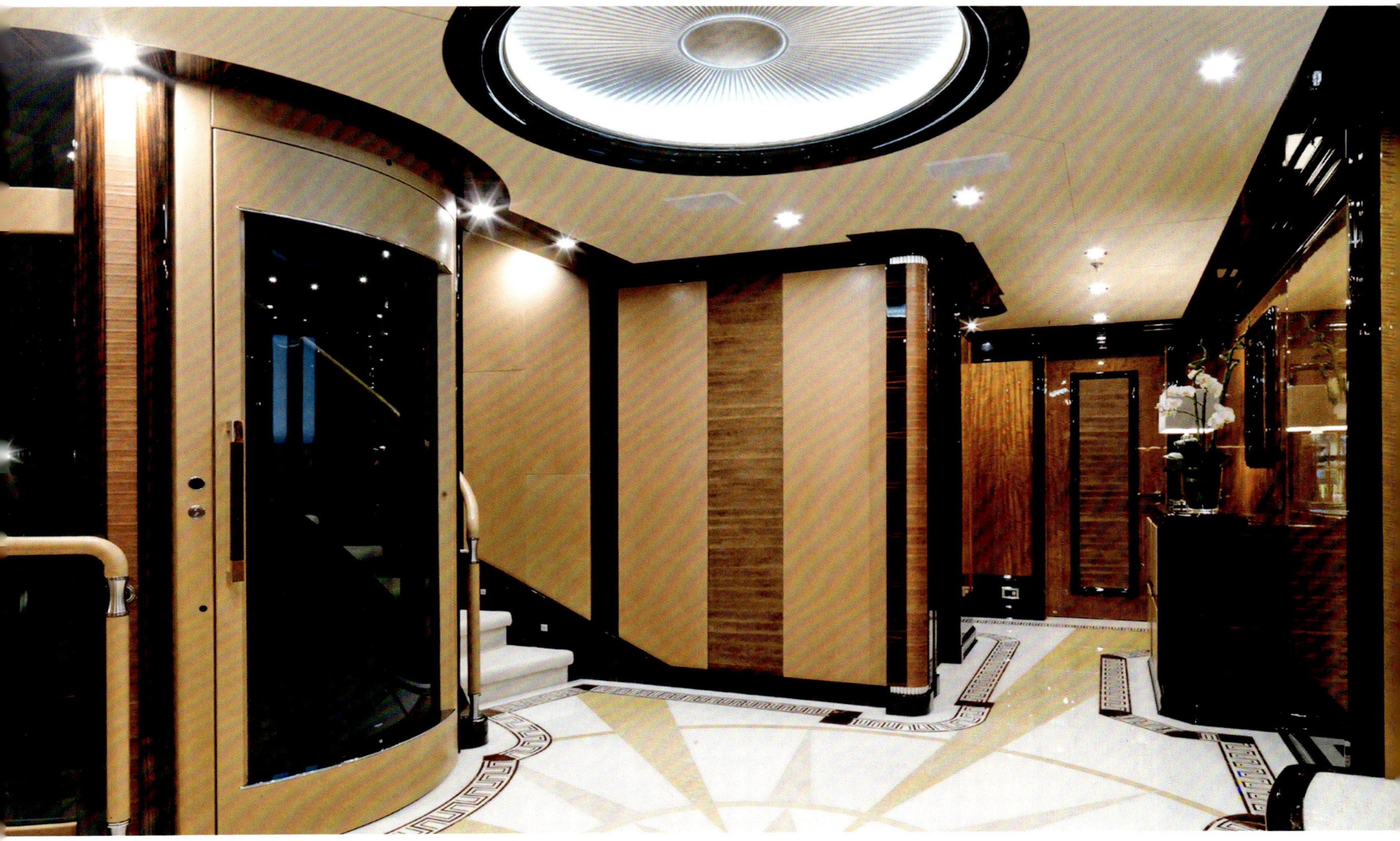

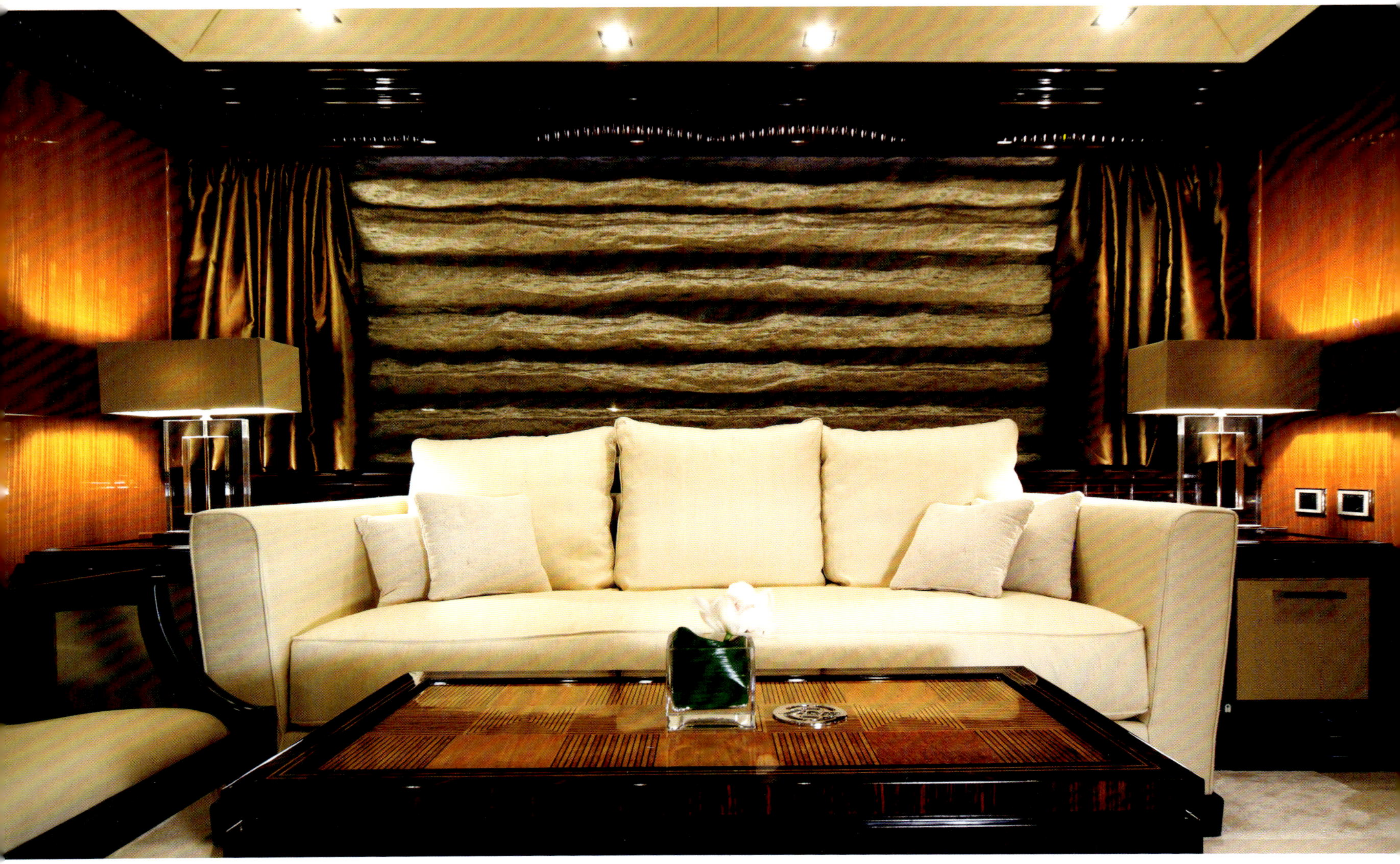

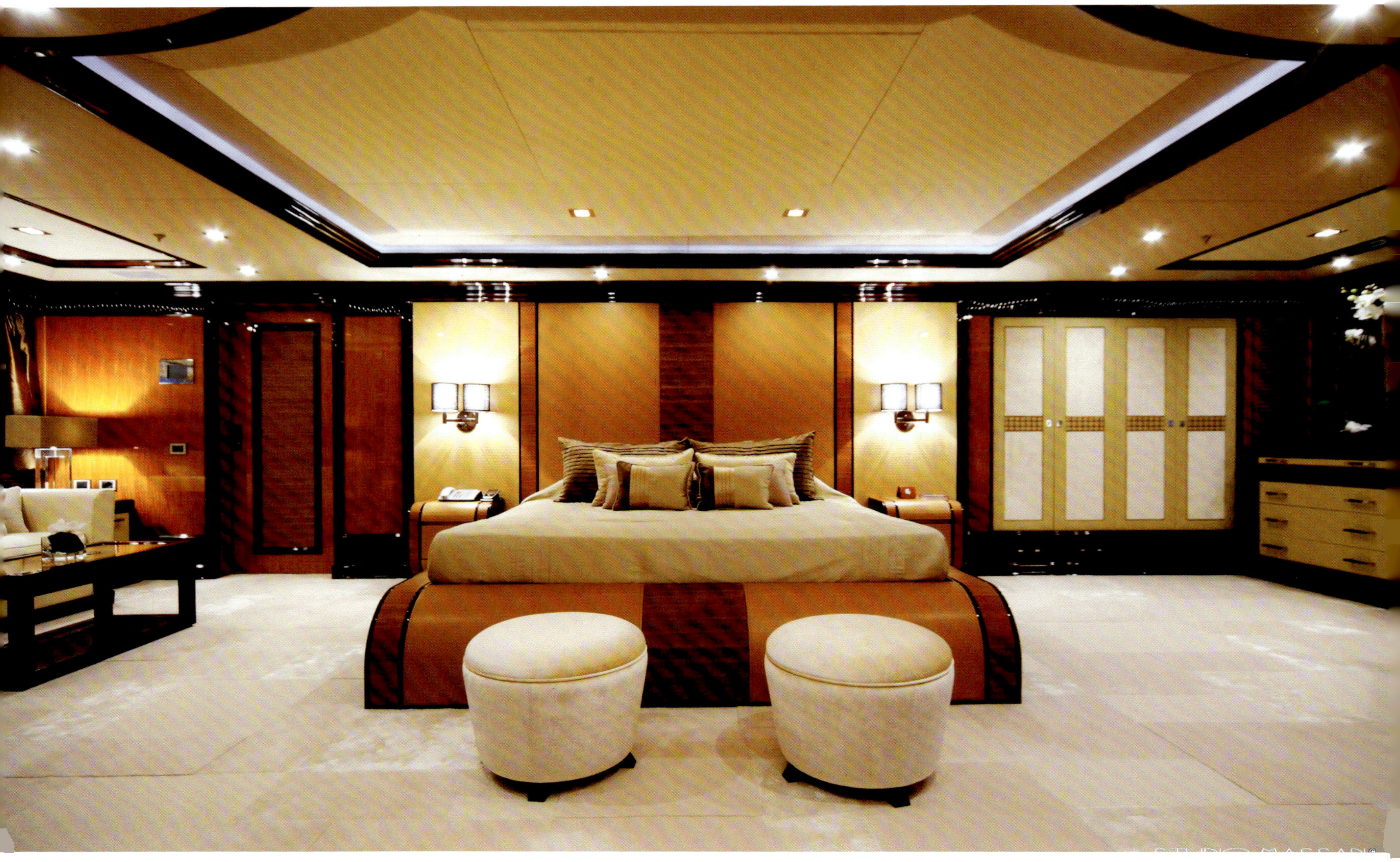

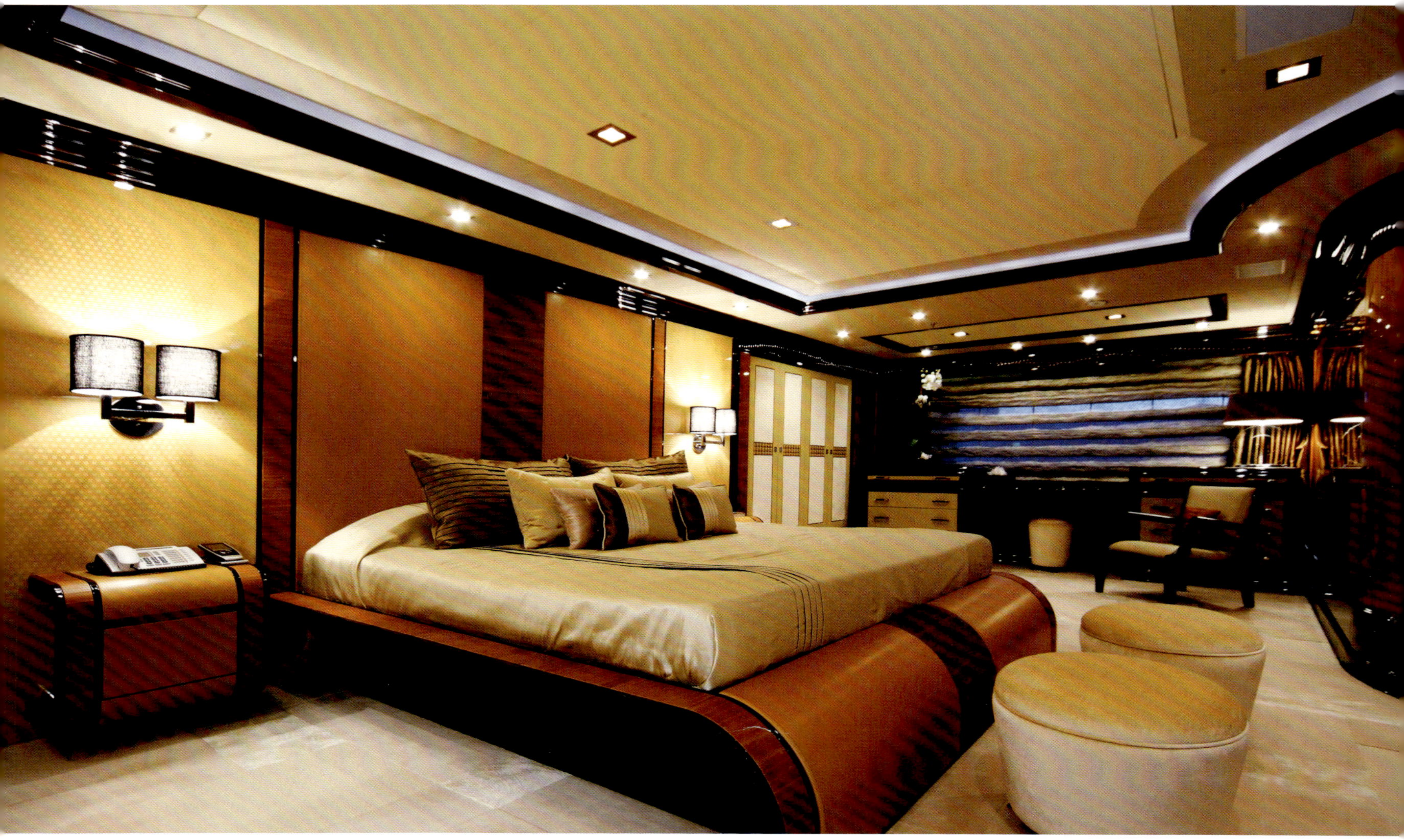

　　"Meamina"是意大利Benetti（贝内蒂）造船厂建造的大型豪华游艇。外部轮廓由设计师Stefano Natucci完成；内部设计和装修由Massari（马萨里）设计工作室负责。

　　船主要求Massari设计工作室设计出古典而又不失现代气息的内部风格；首先，要求游艇一定要舒适优雅，能够给人一种新颖、眼前一亮的惊叹感觉。以上便是负责内部设计的Massari工作室面对的挑战：要完成这项任务，需要有独特、创新的设计方案，进而得出新的设计理念。

　　由于船主的意愿和要求不同，每一个内部设计作品都有与众不同的特点。一名出色的设计师如同是一位好裁缝，二者都懂得为客户量身定做满足客户需求和意愿的产品。设计团队已经得出了新颖独创的设计，同时又不失典雅。在近乎奇特的古典风格与现代气息的平衡协调中创造出了别具一格的特色和优雅舒适的氛围。

　　"Meamina"系列游艇秉承一贯的传统布局，主甲板上留有宽敞的会客厅，在这里，为了细致地区分各个不同的区域及其功能，就餐区和休息区是各自独立的。在选材方面，整个游艇内部装饰均使用昂贵木材，同时配有高档镶嵌装饰，使门柜和座椅家具看起来极为贵重。家具的选材上，均为精致珍贵的皮革和木材，另有，白色的家具平衡了暗淡色调的氛围；同时，装饰用的嵌线创造了熟悉、舒适的环境。主厅最引人注目的特点是镶嵌玛瑙和大理石地板，电梯的升降机外围都包裹有皮革，皮革质地与木制家具装饰巧妙地组合。

　　船主套房有两个独立办公室，分别为船主及其夫人专用。室内装饰如床、床头柜、书桌等使整个套房更显得与众不同。上层的露天阳光平台是专供全家人聚会所用。有亲朋好友围绕身旁，沐浴在温暖的阳光下，这里无疑是休闲娱乐的绝佳场地；船上平静安详的氛围，让人倍感温暖，同时，精致沉稳的内部设计装饰，使整艘游艇不失优雅干练的气息。

IÑIGO TOLEDO

Iñigo is the Managing Director of Barracuda Yacht Design , in charge of running the company on a day to day basis and ensuring all areas of work are up to high standards, whether it's naval architecture, structures, interior design, overall planning or detailed engineering.

Past experience as Technical Coordinator on no less than two Americas Cup campaigns for his country and Project Management for the Spanish Royal Yacht "Fortuna", powered by gas turbine engines are examples of the technical competence and respect that Iñigo has earned within both Spanish and International yachting circles.

PASTROVICH STUDIO

R&D is considered, at Pastrovich Studio, as one of the key point to anticipate the design and the technology of the future. His view to design interiors and exteriors strongly connected has been developed and shown with the concept design for the refit of the Ocean Tug 77m Khozam and 88m Oceanic. The design of the 99m Xvintage in collaboration with Wartsila and Fincantieri is the result of a realistic synergy between design and technology to comply the future IMO Tier III rules imposing a strong reduction of NOx emission.

"my future is to listen the world and people around me". The challenge is just a way to believe.

SUNREEF YACHTS

Sunreef Yachts is the leading designer and builder of luxury sailing and power catamarans and superyachts from 60 to 200 feet in the world. Each custom-made yacht is designed in great detail for the most demanding customers and delivers the best in comfort, style and safety. Every yacht boasts high-performance sailing, luxurious accommodation, expansive living spaces, and extravagant and innovative design features.

STAND BY

STAND BY is an interior design studio based in Milan and founded by designer-architect Marijana Radovic. It specializes in custom interiors for yachts, hotels, other residential and public interiors, urban design, furniture and even private jets. The studio is dedicated to keeping the harmony of space by creating functional and reduced interiors and cleaning them from unnecessary details while opening them to the surrounding environment and light in recognition of the idea that space is the real luxury. This year STAND BY celebrates 5 years of activity: not only still STANDing but also outSTANDing!

CAMILLO COSTANTINI

Italian, almost 30 years experience, in styling and yacht interiors of many of the most important and well-known yacht in the world. Costantini collaborated until 1992 as art director with Luigi STURCHIO & PARTNERS arranging styling and interiors of many yachts, including LADY MOURA. After 1992 Costantini opened his own design office based in Rome, where he still arranging styling and interiors of mega-yachts, but also civil architecture's new designs.

REDMAN WHITELEY DIXON LTD.

Located in the New Forest, a stone's throw from the historic village of Bucklers Hard, where Nelsons Naval fleet was built, is the fitting location for the award winning Studio of Redman Whiteley Dixon.

Former Central School of Art graduates Justin Redman and Mark Whiteley founded the company in 1993; originally designing Sailing Yachts from their Chelsea Wharf Studio, London.

In September 2001 they moved to Beaulieu, Hampshire and joined forces with ex John Munford Designer and Naval Architect Tony Dixon. Trained architect Toby Ecuyer joined the company in 2004 and in 2007 became the company's Creative Director.

Having four individual characters at the helm has enabled Redman Whiteley Dixon to build a repertoire over the past 18 years ranging from 48ft to 155m, interiors and exteriors for Motor Yachts and Sailboats alike.

Privileged to have penned some of the world's most prestigious yachts, they are currently designing several of the industry's most exclusive projects.

LUCA DINI

Born in Florence in 1967, Luca Dini has been involved with the yacht design world for over 20 years. Specialising in styling megayacht interiors and exteriors, he founded Luca Dini Design in 1996. The company has grown steadily and now has various outposts devoted to general architecture, interiors, design objects, and, of late, residential and automobile design (most notably a recent collaboration with Lancia on the Lancia Delta Yacht Design Concept). Dini has even designed private jets. Over the last few years, he has experimented heavily with materials and forms, revisting evocative images and trends from the past, to highly with materials and forms, revisting evocative images and trends from the past, to highly futuristic effect. A fine example of Dini's work is the Admiral 54 Sea Force One for which he created both the exterior and interior designs. Dini has also left his stamp on numerous other projects for high-profile yards of the likes of Cantieri Navali Lavagna-Admiral, Mariotti-Amy, Isa, Mondomarine, CBI Navi, Tecnomar and Kifaru Yachts.

CRN SHIPYARD

CRN Shipyard, based in Ancona (Italy), is developed in an almost 80,000-square-metre area, 25,000 of which are covered, and can accommodate construction of ships up to 90 metres.

It is a "multibrand" area dedicated to the construction of the entire CRN fleet and some of the Ferretti Custom Line range and represents one of the largest production facilities in Europe.

The shipyard is built directly on the Adriatic sea: a unique and extremely valuable area which is like a small private harbour; the CRN marina is 250 metres long and equipped with three docks measuring 100, 100 and 40 metres respectively. Here ships and maxi yachts are fitted and completed.

The shipyard has a 120m slip way used to launch mega yachts measuring from 43 metres. To launch composite maxi yachts up to 40 metres in length and 220 tons in weight, the shipyard uses a travel-lift, also used to haul boats in for tests.

The shipyard also has three modern sheds, 90 metres long, 28 metres wide and 25 metres high, technically advanced facilities equipped with all extract ventilation systems, compressed air, power stations and overhead cranes to handle materials to go on board. The covered area has 6 facilities dedicated to steel and aluminium vessels and 2 facilities for the construction of maxi and mega yachts in composite.

HOT LAB : YACHT & DESIGN

Hot Lab Studio began its story in Milan in 2004, based on the collective imagination, talent and creative spirit of three young Italian designers, namely Michele Dragoni, Enrico Lumini and Antonio Romano, each with previous experience in industrial, automotive and interior design, materials and processes.

From day one, Hot Lab Studio began delivering outstanding projects and styling, characterised by supreme elegance, subtly and warmth, accompanied by meticulous attention to detail, quality and innovation. The prominent projects realised worldwide, accolades received and prestigious awards achieved testify Hot Lab works, alongside private customers and the industry's leading boatyards, to deliver the ultimate. Each yacht design is conceived, using a combination of carefully hand-drawn sketches and detailed computer renderings, ensuring, down to the very last detail, that the client's requirements are matched and their dreams fulfilled. Hot Lab accompanies clients through every stage of the design and development process, including frequent design meetings, visits to the boatyard and liaison with suppliers and subcontractors. Hot Lab has received numerous reviews in renowned yachting, lifestyle and architectural magazines, often being praised for its dedication and work in collaboration with some of the most prestigious Italian and British Universities and its participation at various Events, Exhibitions and Brainstorming sessions. Recently Hot Lab has also won the prestigious ShowBoats Design Awards 2011 with the M/Y Noor as best Interior Design for Semi-Displacement yachts.

JESSICA LICALZI

Jessica Licalzi graduated from New York Technical Institute in 2007 with a degree in Fine Arts. Upon joining Mojo Stumer Associates, p.c. she has expanded her resume to include high end corporate interiors and residential work. She works closely with project managers to formulate and resolve practical resolutions for the corporate environment. She is on the forefront of ever-changing needs of the commercial client and successfully creates comfort in spaces in which we live.

NEWCRUISE – YACHT PROJECTS & DESIGN

The success of NEWCRUISE relies on innovation, enthusiasm, expertise and exceptional design. For 20 years the Hamburg yacht project and design house with its enthusiastic, 15-strong team under designer and partner trio Frank E. H. Neubelt, Roland Krueger and Katharina Raczek has been active internationally in the design, development and realisation of spectacular superyachts.

Every NEWCRUISE yacht is unmistakeably unique. The individuality and personality of the customer are always reflected in the design and naval architecture and in the creation of the interior style and layout.

For more information visit

www.newcruise.de

KIRSCHSTEIN DESIGNS LTD

Michael Kirschstein obtained a BA (Hons) degree in design and then spent a year on Sea Cloud, a 107M luxury soil yacht as Chief Carpenter. He has worked for Terrance Disdale and Donald Starkey before setting up his well respected design house in 1994. He has used his expensive knowledge of yacht design combined with his partial carpentry skills to great effect on numerous yacht projects around the world.

THOMAS J. MOJO

As principal in charge of the Human Resources of Mojo Stumer Associates Architects, Mr. Mojo believes that the strength of the firm is in the quality of the people who work at the firm; therein lies the strength of an excellent office dedicated to the advancement of architecture.

MICHAEL SPITALERI

Michael has had the opportunity at Mojo Stumer Associates, p.c. to work on a variety of key residential and commercial projects as well as expand the office's digital development. He developed his design experience with projects and competitions of both large and small scale with focus on commercial and residential high rise as well as hospitality design. Having the ability to work on projects both nationally and internationally, gave him the tools to meet the demands of today's progressing built environment.

SHARLENE TEITEL

Working as an interior designer for Mojo Stumer Associates, p.c. and bringing with her over 20 years of experience in the field of interior design, Sharlene is breaking boundaries in contemporary design. Sharlene went on to work at Windham House and then Ralph Lauren Home, designing for celebrity clients, as well as a strong following of regular clientele. Her strengths include space planning, layout and utilization of furnishings and color coordination. Focusing on residential design, Sharlene has created her own style, the likes of which can be seen through all her Mojo Stumer projects.

ART–LINE INTERIORS

Marilyn Bos-de Vaal and Frank Pieterse, graduates of the Art Academy of Utrecht, founded Art-Line in 1983. They first intended to do architectural design. But after being asked to style their first motoryacht, they were awarded the design of the ultra light interior for the record-breaking Octopussy, and the even faster Moonraker. The success of these super yachts proved that they could create an attractive space within a very complex technical structure. The publicity about these two yachts spread quickly through the yachting community, and they began receiving more opportunities to design yacht interiors for semi-custom and custom super yachts over a wide range of sizes. Their work is inspired by their training in, and commitment to, contemporary art and architecture applied to designing floating, moving shelters. They try to make each Art-Line interior represent an ideal balance between function and emotion, the basic ingredients clients want in a luxury yacht. Art-Line's use of colour, form, and texture allows them to offer clients wide choices in styling each individualised space. But to them, design is not just a matter of assembling components: it requires applying insight into clients' personalities and desires to complete each project to their satisfaction.

ADAM LAY

Adam Lay, together with his wife Kelda, established Adam Lay Studio in 2003 following 8 years working for one of the top 5 custom superyacht design companies in the world, John Munford Design. Adam has an honours degree in Industrial Design specialising in yacht design from Coventry University. As part of his degree Adam worked for a famous English Naval Architect which is where his passion for yacht design really took hold. Adam comes from a long line of ship builders from the North East of England and he continues a family profession which dates back to the 1800s.

Adam Lay Studio continues to build on the reputation it already has through its considerable experience. Since 2003, the studio has been building a reputation for award-winning creative design coupled with a discreet, honest and conscientious approach.

FIPA ITALIANA YACHTS

Fipa Italiana Yachts was founded in 1980 by Francesco Guidetti and his wife Mirna Santucci.
• 1985: purchase of the Maiora brand, founded at the start of the 70s
• '90s: Fipa acquired the historic shipyard Intermare
• 2001: purchase of the AB Yachts brand, founded in 1992
• 2005: purchase of the Cbi Navi → this allowed the Group to satisfy any request: from the elegant flying bridge motor yacht in fiberglass (Maiora) to the fast open cruiser with waterjets propulsion (AB Yachts), to the displacement vessel in steel and aluminum suitable for long cruiser (Cbi Navi).

SCHNAASE INTERIOR DESIGN

Based in Hamburg, Birgit Schnaase and her team have been designing interiors for yachts and ships of every size for the past 16 years. Recently, she has also taken on projects for private jets and homes.
She has also completed design tasks with the most prestigious shipyards and architects in the world – from refitting a 25-year-old Swan sailing yacht for a keen regatta yachtsman to designing the interiors of a 60m motor yacht for an Arab sultan´s family.
Birgit Schnaase always tailors her work to the individual preferences of her clients:From initial sketches through advice on shipyard selection or a full bid invitation to the completion of turnkey projects.

CENTRAL YACHT LTD

Central Yacht is a partnership of experienced professional seafarers and architects with unparalleled experience of designing, building and operating yachts of the highest calibre.
By thoroughly analysing and understanding the practical operation of luxury yachts they are able to create the most efficient vessels where form truly follows function and beauty is not just skin deep.

www.centralyacht.com

PAULINE NUNNS

Pauline Nunns (RIBA), a Chartered Architect and Interior Designer, formed P.M.Nunns Associates in 1978, initially to work on the creation and design of new buildings and the alteration and restoration of great historic houses and interiors, subsequently extending her services to design superyacht and luxury yacht interiors.

EIDSGAARD DESIGN

Founded in 2005 Eidsgaard Design has quickly risen to become one of the most sought after names in the superyacht design industry. Its Directors Peder Eidsgaard, Ewa Eidsgaad and Ben Harrison have varied backgrounds, which have been brought together to form this dynamic trio.
Peder ("peter") was born in Great Britain and grew up in Oslo, Norway. He gained a Bachelor of Science degree in design in Switzerland before joining Andrew Winch Designs in 1996 for nine years. He decided on his chosen career after reading about London's superyacht designers in a magazine when he was 12 years old.
Ewa ("eva") was born in Poland and studied finance in Paris before joining Goldman Sachs in 1996, where she worked for 9 years as a Vice President. She has always had a keen interest in design and photography which she now incorporates into her interior decorating role.
Ben was born in Great Britain and grew up on the river Dart in Devon. He studied architecture at Newcastle University before joining Andrew Winch Designs in 2000, where he worked for seven years. Having sailed since the age of 5 and coming from an architectural family background, Ben has combined these two passions in yacht design.

ALEXANDRA COLLINS

Alexandra is managing partner and responsible for business development and project management. She has consulted for over 15 years to clients worldwide in the aircraft interior, yacht interior and interior design area.

MARK COLLINS

Mark is managing partner and director and responsible for the development of new mobility projects and in charge of technical coordination and supervision. He has over 15 years of experience in the automotive, aircraft and yacht industries.

FEADSHIP

FEADSHIP
ROYAL DUTCH SHIPYARDS

Based in the Netherlands and with roots dating back to 1849, Feadship is recognised as the world leader in the field of custom superyachts. Each Feadship is defined by its superb craftsmanship and sets the standard in every aspect of design, engineering and construction. These bespoke motoryachts are created in partnership with owners who are prepared to invest in a wonderful building experience and reap the rewards for many years to come in terms of both pleasure and re-sale value. Feadship also operates dedicated charter and refit services exclusively for Feadships.

FRANCK DARNET DESIGN

They design bright and attractive interiors to live in, which provides pleasure and a sense of space. Interior volumes must be wide and uncluttered to optimize the visual perspective and site-lines.
A few inches, a slight curve, a recess joint can change the perception of volume.
They fulfill their clients' desires: some dream about a classical interior, others about an ultra-contemporary atmosphere. Such extremes make their job tremendously exciting and gratifying.
In both cases, the conceptual approach and the attention to detail remain the same.
Their obsession: draw the perfect line, pay attention to the slightest details, and also adapt the functionality of the interior layouts to the rhythm and life style of the owners and their crew.

WILLIAM MINNEAR

William Minnear's project experience with Mojo Stumer Associates, p.c. includes commercial and high-end residential work. He works closely with principal Mark Stumer in the design development and project management of several of the office's key projects. Mr. Minnear graduated from The New York Institute of Technology School of Architecture in 1996 with a Bachelor of Architecture Degree.

STUDIO MASSARI

The name of Studio Massari is often associated with illustrious Italian and foreign yards that enjoy a worldwide reputation for quality and style. The Studio works with a range of motor and sail yachts from 20 to over 100 meters in length. The Studio Massari has also risen to meet the challenge of other stimulating experience, designing home collections for Radice © presented at recent editions of the Milan Furniture Fair. The Studio Massari expresses a typically Italian style, where an emphasis on the fusion of tradition and innovative energy is combined with an eclectic approach to decoration and a desire for perfection in the use of cutting-edge technology and materials. "By satisfying our client's desires, passion and dreams we hope to sail together, like a seasoned crew, towards the destination of totally original design" Alessandro Massari concludes. A destination where exclusivity is the order of the day.

MARK D. STUMER

Mark D. Stumer is one of the founding principals at Mojo Stumer Associates Architects. He has practiced architecture as a principal for over 30 years. Before the formation of Mojo Stumer Associates Architects, he worked for a New York City architectural firm where he was lead designer on many award-winning projects.

LÜRSSEN YACHTS

LÜRSSEN

Based in Germany, Lürssen is the leading shipyard for large luxury yacht building. The combination of constant innovation over the last 135 years, the high quality of the work, the dedicated work force, its discretion, and especially the close interaction with the client are highly valued by its customers. Lürssen is a total facility shipbuilder, complete with sales, engineering, design, construction and logistical teams plus a full training service.

后记

　　本书的编写离不开各位设计师和摄影师的帮助，正是有了他们专业而负责的工作态度，才有了本书的顺利出版。参与本书的编写人员有：

AB Yachts – Fipa Group, Adam Lay Studio, Admiral Techhnical Department, Alexandra Collins, Armin Graessl, Baglietto Shipyards, Barracuda Yacht Design, Benetti Shipyard, Bruce Thomas, Camillo Costantini,Cbi Navi – FIPA GROUP, Central Yacht Ltd, Cor D. Rover, CRN Engineering, David Churchill, De Voogt, De Vries Shipyardt, Design Investment Sàrl, Diana Yacht Design, Dick Holthuis, Director, Dubois Naval Architects, Eidsgaard Design, Espen Øino Naval Architects, Feadship, Filippetti Yacht, Franck Darnet Design, Frank L. Pieterse, Hot Lab: yacht & design, Houma Shipyards USA, Iñigo Toledo, Ivan Bura, Javier Munoz, Jessica Licalzi, Justin Redman, Kirschstein Designs Ltd, Klaus Jordan, Lloyd Images, Luca Dini Design, Lürssen Yachts, Marilyn Bos- de Vaal, Mark Collins , Mark D. Stumer, Maurizio Paradisi, Michael Spitaleri, Monaco Marine, Mondo Marine Engineering, NEWCRUISE - Yacht Projects & Design, Nobiskrug, Pastrovich Studio, Pauline Nunns, Pendennis Shipyard, Peter Johns, Philip Zepter Yachts, Redman Whiteley Dixon, Robert Mc Farlene, Royal Huisman Shipyard, Schnaase Interior Design, Sharlene Teitel, Sinot Yacht Design, Stand By, Studio Massari, Studio Scanu, Sunreef Yachts, Sunrise Yachting Ltd, Superyacht Media, Toby, Ecuyer, William Minnear, Zuccon International Project + Centro Stile CRN, Elaine Chou, Shirley Qu, Nancy Wong, Kara Zheng, Alisa Hui, Anna Law

ACKNOWLEDGEMENTS

We would like to thank everyone involved in the production of this book, especially all the artists, designers, architects and photographers for their kind permission to publish their works. We are also very grateful to many other people whose names do not appear on the credits but who provided assistance and support. We highly appreciate the contribution of images, ideas, and concepts and thank them for allowing their creativity to be shared with readers around the world.